MOON
BEST OF
CALIFORNIA
STATE PARKS
Jenna Blough & Kayla Anderson

CONTENTS

350

368

412

Half Moon Bay

WELCOME TO CALIFORNIA'S STATE PARKS

California's state parks are vignettes, each a pocket evoking wildly different landscapes, elevations, and history. The spectacular wild coastline harbors stretches of golden sand, rocky coves, rolling dunes, and wave-carved bluffs. Inland, stark desert and alpine green collide, and mountain peaks offer views over the blue of the Pacific Ocean. Spring brings migrating whales and wildflowers that blanket the hills. California's history is also on display, telling the story of both Native Californians and seekers to the golden state.

Although California is the most populated state, you can still find solitude among the ancient redwoods, eroded badlands, rugged canyons, and shimmering lakes, each place offering a chance to delve into the state's unique character and landscape.

Whether you're on a day trip, a weekend getaway, or the adventure of a lifetime, these parks are the best of what the Golden State has to offer.

Emerald Bay

TOP 10 EXPERIENCES

1 Staring up at the redwoods at **Jedediah Smith Redwoods State Park,** home to some of the oldest trees in the world (page 48).

2 Kayaking the sparkling blue waters of Lake Tahoe at **Emerald Bay State Park** (page 191).

3 Exploring the trails in the heart of Big Sur at **Pfeiffer Big Sur State Park** (page 287).

4 Hiking **Mount San Jacinto State Park's** scenic trails to explore subalpine forests, granite peaks, and mountain meadows (page 479).

5 Spending a beach day exploring the scenic coves of **Montaña de Oro State Park** (page 322).

6 Taking in the sandy shoreline and ocean waves dotted with surfers at **Huntington State Park** (page 428).

7 Wandering through the forest to see the vistas of the Pacific Ocean at **Sue-meg State Park** (page 69).

8 Admiring the striking tufa towers, calcium carbonate spires that rise above the lake's surface, at **Mono Lake Tufa State Natural Reserve** (page 235).

9 Learning more about California's past, from forts built by early gold-seekers to Native Californian culture, at **historical state parks** (page 30; pictured, Hearst Castle).

10 Visiting **Anza-Borrego Desert State Park's** vast landscape to stargaze, hike, and camp (page 500).

WHERE TO GO

NORTHERN CALIFORNIA

From the ancient redwoods to the jagged headlands of the North Coast, the entire region of Northern California from the Bay Area and Sacramento up to the Oregon border is a hidden gem for outdoor adventurers. With picturesque alpine lakes and mountains in between, the remote wildness of Northern California makes it ideal for mountain biking, hiking, camping, swimming, and more.

CENTRAL CALIFORNIA

Central California is known for its scenic coastline running south of the Bay Area down to Santa Barbara. It's where the Pacific Coast Highway gives access to beaches with sand dunes, rugged cliffs, wildflower-filled hikes, and sea caves, as well as charming coastal towns with opportunities for camping, kayaking, and whale watching. A series of historic parks preserves California's past from European outposts to gold mining.

SOUTHERN CALIFORNIA

Across six desert parks visitors can experience deep canyons, Joshua tree habitat, colorful cliffs, volcanic landscapes, and a stretch of the Colorado River with opportunity for hiking, camping, boating, four-wheel drives, and stargazing. From south of Santa Barbara down to San Diego, Southern California's beaches offer famous surf spots, developed areas with bike trails and amusement piers, and bluff-top campgrounds, as well as wilder coastlines with rocky coves and tide pools. Mountain parks feature granite peaks, subalpine forest, and meadows for hiking and camping.

SEASONS OF CALIFORNIA

High season for state parks travel is summer from **Memorial Day to Labor Day.** This is when the kids start their summer breaks and families travel—which means the campgrounds fill up fast. Summer is also when desert parks can have extreme temperature highs. In general, the best times to visit are the **spring and fall,** when the parks are not as crowded and the weather is more mild.

Whale watching is possible for most of the year, extending from February through November; however, the best times for whale watching depend on the species. Gray whales migrate south from December to February and return north from March to May, making December through May the most popular times for gray whale watching. Humpback whales are most commonly seen from April through November, as they are drawn to the food supply along the coast. Blue whales are typically spotted in the summer months, from June to

September. Orcas may occasionally be seen during peak migration seasons. Whales can be spotted from the shore or on chartered boat tours. California's Central Coast is a popular whale-watching location.

NORTHERN CALIFORNIA

Many of the North Coast parks are foggy and damp year-round, getting lots of rain in the wintertime between October and April. Temperatures tend to stay in the moderate 45-65°F (7-18°C) range year-round. The San Francisco Bay Area is known for its not-too-hot, not-too-cold weather and consistent fog, ranging from 50-60°F (10-16°C) year-round. Inland, there's a wider variety of climates. The mountainous parks usually have sunny and temperate summers (75-85°F/24-29°C) and colder winters (20-32°F/-7-0°C), with snowfall starting in November and lasting through March or April. This is especially worth noting for the Tahoe parks, which can experience road closures in winter. The Sacramento area is hotter, with summers over 100°F (38°C).

CENTRAL CALIFORNIA

Central California's climate varies depending on elevation and proximity to the coast. Summer tends to be hot inland, where temperatures average between 90-105°F (32-40°C). Winters are cooler and wetter, with average highs between 50-60°F (10-16°C) and lows from 35-45°F (1-7°C). The coast tends to be more moderate, with temperatures rarely getting above 75°F (24°C) even in the summer. However, there is a high chance of fog all year long.

SOUTHERN CALIFORNIA

Southern California's climate varies depending on elevation, proximity to the coast, and desert areas. Desert areas are known for extremely hot summers and mild winters with cool nights. Summer daytime temperatures can reach 100-115°F (38-46°C) with nighttime lows between 70-85°F (21-29°C); winters have average daytime highs between 65-75°F (18-24°C) and chilly nights with temperatures between 40-50°F (4-10°C). The coast is more moderate year-round, with temperatures rarely getting above 80°F (27°C) even in summer. Mornings can be overcast with a marine layer in May and June.

WILDFIRE WARNING

As the environment continues to change, wildfires are becoming more devastating in California, affecting its state parks. Wildfires tend to be most prevalent in the **June-September** months, but earthquakes, floods, and power outages can affect state park operations as well. Before you visit, check out the California State Parks Significant Incidents Updates page to make sure the park(s) you want to go to aren't affected.

hiking in Humboldt Redwoods State Park

AVOID THE CROWDS

The best way to avoid the crowds is to **travel at off-peak times** as much as possible. Consider traveling outside of high season (summer), arriving early in the day or visiting in the evening, and choosing weekdays over weekends. California's coast has moderate temperatures year-round, making it a great destination in fall, winter, and spring for less crowded beaches and a much easier time reserving a campsite. Fall is an excellent time to visit desert parks when temperatures are mild and there are fewer visitors than in spring.

It's also a good idea to **find the more remote parks.** The Central Coast beaches, located far from California's largest metropolitan areas, tend to offer more breathing room than Southern California's beaches, particularly during the off-season. Desert parks overall tend to be the least crowded, making them good for solitude.

KNOW BEFORE YOU GO

PARK PASSES

Day use passes are used for vehicle entry and can be purchased in person at state parks. Parking fee receipts can be used for entrance to any other local California State Park charging the same or lower rates if they are used on the same day. If you are camping at a California State Park, your camping pass can be used as the entrance pass. There are no fees for walking or biking into a state park.

Annual Passes

Several annual passes that are good for vehicle day use entry can be purchased online through the California State Parks store (www.store.parks.ca.gov).

- The **California Explorer Vehicle Day Use Annual Pass** ($195) is valid for entry to 134 state parks, including Southern California beaches.
- The **Golden Poppy Vehicle Day Use Annual Pass** ($125) is valid for entry to 112 state parks, including reservoirs, destination parks, and Northern California beaches.
- The **Historian Passport Day Use Admission Annual Pass** ($50) allows admission for up to four people to state historic parks with a per-person admission fee.

Add-on passes sold by California State Parks include the **Boat Use Annual Pass** ($100) and the **Oversized Vehicle Pass** ($75) for big RVs or motor homes 25-plus ft long or at least 9 ft wide (8 m long or 3 m wide) to drive on park roads.

Discount Passes

There are also several discounted passes available online through the California State Parks store (www.store.parks.ca.gov).

- The **Golden Bear Pass** (free) is valid for vehicle day use to many state parks for CalWORKs, SSI, and Tribal TANF recipients and individuals 62 and older with income under a certain threshold.
- A **Senior Golden Bear Pass** ($20) provides free entry for individuals 62 and older and a spouse/domestic partner to many state parks in non-peak season.
- The **Adventure Pass** (free) is good for fourth graders and their families to 54 select state parks.
- The **Disabled Discount Pass** ($3.50) is a lifetime pass providing individuals with permanent disabilities a 50 percent discount on vehicle day use, camping, and boat use fees.
- The **Distinguished Veteran Pass** (free) is a lifetime pass providing use of all basic facilities including day use, camping, and boating for free.

RESERVATIONS

Campgrounds and Lodging

Many of the state's campgrounds are wildly popular and fill up fast; the demand during the **high season** (Memorial Day-Labor Day) and holiday weekends can far exceed supply. That's why most campsites at state parks during the high season must be reserved in advance through **Reserve California** (800/444-7575; www.reservecalifornia.com) from two days up to six months out from your vacation. Outside of the high season, many campgrounds that are open year-round take campers on a first-come, first-served basis.

Day Use Areas and Activities

Some popular state parks with limited space have **advance parking reservations,** such as Big Basin Redwoods (though it is recommended, not required). Reservations are required for some **day use areas** in Northern California's redwoods parks, including the Fern Canyon Day Use Area in Prairie Creek Redwoods State Park. Reservations are also required for **tours.** Tours of Hearst Castle in the Hearst San Simeon State Historical Monument and Mitchell Caverns in the Providence Mountains State Recreation Area require reservations. As with campsites, reservations are available through **Reserve California** (800/444-7575; www.reservecalifornia.com). Be sure to check online prior to visiting to see if reservations are needed for any part of your visit.

GETTING AROUND

People who aren't from California are often surprised at how big the state is—it can take up to 12 hours to drive its entire length from the Oregon border down to Mexico. The Amtrak train and its Greyhound bus partner have routes all over the US and on California's major corridors, but direct access to the state parks via public transportation is virtually nonexistent. The vast majority of parks require a car to reach; car rentals are available at California's major airport hubs.

Overall, California state parks are very safe to travel around, but there is spotty to nonexistent cell service and potentially incorrect GPS mapping directions in remote areas.

Goat Rock on the Sonoma Coast

BEST OF THE BEST

CALIFORNIA STATE PARKS

BEST HIKING

FERN CANYON LOOP

Prairie Creek Redwoods State Park
EASY

Walk through a lush living green canyon along the Fern Canyon Loop Trail, which also connects to the gold-flecked Gold Bluff Beach and Elk Meadow (page 63).

DIPSEA TRAIL

Mount Tamalpais State Park
STRENUOUS

Run or hike the famous 9.7-mi (15.6-km) Dipsea Trail, which puts on the oldest trail race in America, from Mill Valley to Stinson Beach (page 148).

FALL CREEK TRAIL TO LIME KILNS

Henry Cowell Redwoods State Park
EASY

Trails through towering trees meander all through the park, but head over to the Fall Creek Unit and find remnants of the stone lime kilns buried beneath a blanket of emerald redwood sorrel (page 272).

MUGU PEAK

Point Mugu State Park
STRENUOUS

The Chumash Trail follows an ancient route to Mugu Peak, where you can spot the Channel Islands out in the Pacific Ocean (page 409).

SAN JACINTO PEAK

Mount San Jacinto State Park
STRENUOUS

A trek from idyllic Round Valley through pine forest and granite outcroppings goes to snowcapped San

Dipsea Trail on Mount Tamalpais

Jacinto Peak for panoramic views (page 485).

STONEWALL PEAK

Cuyamaca Rancho State Park
MODERATE

Walk through red manzanita and white boulders to Stonewall Peak's sheer summit with views of meadows, peaks, and Lake Cuyamaca (page 496).

BORREGO PALM CANYON TRAIL

Anza-Borrego Desert State Park
MODERATE

Explore rocky Borrego Palm Canyon to find a hidden oasis with deep pools and fan palms (page 509).

Fern Canyon, Prairie Creek Redwoods State Park (top); Desert View Trail at Mount San Jacinto State Park (middle); Borrego Palm Canyon Trail, Anza-Borrego Desert State Park (bottom)

BEST BEACHES

SONOMA COAST STATE PARK

From beachcombing at South Salmon Creek Beach to tide-pooling at Shell Beach, Sonoma Coast's 17 mi (27 km) of shoreline has something for everyone (page 133).

HALF MOON BAY STATE BEACH

The 4 mi (6 km) of beaches connected by the California Coastal Trail stretch from the southern point of Half Moon Bay to Pillar Point, offering plentiful picnicking, beachcombing, surfing, and sea-fishing opportunities (page 243).

POINT LOBOS STATE NATURAL RESERVE

Aptly called "the crown jewel of the State Park System," Point Lobos has eight different beaches, some ideal for tide-pooling, some ideal for sightseeing, and some great access points for scuba diving (page 276).

CAYUCOS STATE BEACH

The long arc of sand that is Cayucos State Beach is framed by low coastal hills and the charming, historic town of Cayucos, making it a classic beach destination (page 304).

MONTAÑA DE ORO STATE PARK

A walk down to bluff-backed Spooner's Cove reveals tidal pools, sea caves, and pebbly Islay Creek spilling into the Pacific Ocean (page 322).

Santa Monica State Beach

LEO CARRILLO STATE PARK

North Beach's wide stretch of sand gives way to tide pools, sea caves, and rock arches for exploring on the south end of the beach (page 412).

SANTA MONICA STATE BEACH

This stretch of coastline blends natural beauty with seaside fun, including its iconic Santa Monica Pier, which is home to an amusement park, restaurants, and a solar-powered Ferris wheel (page 420).

CRYSTAL COVE STATE PARK

Coast-carved cliffs, rocky tide pools, and sandy coves make the 3 mi (5 km) of beach a standout amid Southern California's miles of spectacular coastline (page 436).

SAN CLEMENTE STATE BEACH

Cut down through eroded sandstone bluffs to the sandy beach, its combination of balmy climate and mellow waves making it a great spot for swimming and surfing (page 447).

beach at Sonoma Coast State Park (top); Half Moon Bay State Beach (middle); tidepools at Crystal Cove State Park (bottom)

San Clemente State Beach

BEST HISTORIC SITES

SUE-MEG STATE PARK

Walk through the reconstructed village where the native Yurok people originally built homes and structures out of redwood planks, stone, and willow ties (page 69).

FORT HUMBOLDT STATE HISTORIC PARK

Walk the easy interactive trail through an outdoor logging display and over to the Surgeon's Quarters and Corral to learn about the North Coast's contentious history between early gold rush settlers and Indigenous peoples (page 80).

ANGEL ISLAND STATE PARK

Visit the US Immigration Museum and artillery batteries to learn more about the role Angel Island played as an arrival and departure spot for immigrants and as a military stronghold (page 153).

INDIAN GRINDING ROCK STATE HISTORIC PARK

Visit the rare chaw'se (grinding rock) where the Miwok people gathered and mashed acorns into the 1,000-bedrock-mortar platform (page 201).

BODIE STATE HISTORIC PARK

Stroll the remains of the isolated former mining town, where over 200 buildings are kept in a state of arrested decay (page 228).

Bodie State Historic Park

HEARST SAN SIMEON STATE HISTORICAL MONUMENT

The Grand Rooms Tour allows visitors to peek into the opulent social rooms, tiled swimming pools, and extensive antiquities collection of the Hearst Castle estate (page 296).

EL PRESIDIO DE SANTA BARBARA STATE HISTORIC PARK

Begin your self-guided tour of the historic fort at the Northwest Corner to explore soldiers' residences, the padre's quarters, and a hand-painted chapel (page 350).

OLD TOWN SAN DIEGO STATE HISTORIC PARK

Explore the core of restored and original historic buildings surrounding Plaza de Almas/Washington Square for a snapshot of San Diego's early days from 1821 to 1872 (page 470).

Indian Grinding Rock State Historic Park (top); Old Town San Diego State Historic Park (middle); Grand Rooms Tour at Hearst Castle (bottom)

INDIGENOUS PEOPLES OF CALIFORNIA

Miwok Village at Indian Grinding Rock State Historic Park

Our state parks preserve California's natural resources as well as California's layered cultural history. As visitors to state parks, we travel lands that have seen thousands of years of human experience. We cross the ancient trails, village sites, and trade routes of California's first peoples who adapted to California's wildly diverse landscape. Today there are 109 federally recognized Indian tribes in California and others still seeking federal recognition. California State Parks has launched the **Reexamining our Past Initiative,** an effort designed to critically examine geographic place names, develop strategies for historical interpretation, and support the creation of artwork that offers perspective on the past and present.

State parks covered in this book that feature Indigenous sites include:

- Sue-meg State Park (page 69)
- Indian Grinding Rock State Historic Park (page 201)
- Point Mugu State Park (page 403)
- Old Town San Diego State Historic Park (page 470)
- Anza-Borrego Desert State Park (page 500)

UNIQUE EXPERIENCES

KAYAKING THROUGH SEA CAVES

Van Damme State Park

Kayak along the Mendocino coast through sea caves, keeping an eye out for anemones, sea stars, fish, different algae, and other colorful creatures (page 122).

CROSS-COUNTRY SKIING ON AN OLYMPIC BIATHLON RANGE

Ed Z'berg Sugar Pine Point State Park

On the mountain side of the state park is a nice 12-mi (20-km) system of cross-country ski trails that was once part of the 1960 Olympics (page 180).

STAYING THE NIGHT AT A LIGHTHOUSE

Pigeon Point Light Station State Historic Park

Watch out for migrating whales behind the Fog Signal Building . . . or, if you're staying the night, watch out for them while soaking in the hostel's hot tub overlooking the Pacific (page 255).

SEEING THE MIGRATING MONARCH BUTTERFLIES

Pismo State Beach

Each year between November and February, thousands of migrating western monarch butterflies converge on the eucalyptus groves of

touring Mitchell Caverns in Providence Mountains State Recreation Area

riding beach buggies at Oceano Dunes SVRA (left); poppies in Antelope Valley California Poppy Reserve (right)

the Monarch Butterfly Grove (page 337).

RIDING BEACH BUGGIES

Oceano Dunes State Vehicular Recreation Area

Rent or bring your own all-terrain vehicle (ATV) and take a spin through the extensive dune fields at Oceano Dunes SVRA (page 340).

SEEING THE WILDFLOWERS

Antelope Valley California Poppy Reserve

For a few glorious weeks in spring, wildflowers blanket the hills, turning the desert grasslands into a mosaic of color highlighted by the delicate orange of the state flower (page 382).

TOURING LIMESTONE CAVES

Providence Mountains State Recreation Area

Guided tours take visitors into Mitchell Caverns, a set of deep limestone caves draped with stalactites and stalagmites (page 397).

STARGAZING AT AN INTERNATIONAL DARK SKY PARK

Anza-Borrego Desert State Park

The park and the town of Borrego Springs have taken measures to preserve their dark skies, earning an International Dark Sky Park designation and making the region prime for viewing the dazzling night skies (page 511).

monarch butterflies in the Monarch Butterfly Grove, Pismo State Beach

BEST CAMPING

AGATE BEACH CAMPGROUND

Sue-meg State Park

Camp nestled in the pines and enjoy the best of wildlife and hiking trails amid the sound of waves crashing against the rocky headlands (page 78).

WRIGHT'S BEACH CAMPGROUND

Sonoma Coast State Park

Camp close enough to smell the salty air and hear the crashing waves from Wright's Beach, the perfect place to take a family (page 140).

MORRO BAY CAMPGROUND

Morro Bay State Park

Nestled in mixed forest between the park's marina, golf course, and hiking trails, this campground offers an adventure-filled weekend walking distance from your campsite (page 320).

EL CAPITÁN STATE BEACH CAMPGROUND

El Capitán State Beach

This campground is pitched on bluffs above the Pacific, with campsites under a canopy of sycamores and oaks that grow along El Capitán Creek (page 348).

RICARDO CAMPGROUND

Red Rock Canyon State Park

Dramatic cliffs form the backdrop at Ricardo Campground, where campsites are established in the cove-like

Ricardo Campground at Red Rock Canyon State Park

spaces at the base of the sandstone formations (page 376).

PROVIDENCE MOUNTAINS STATE RECREATION AREA CAMPGROUND

Providence Mountains State Recreation Area

The campground is situated on an isolated ridge with sweeping views of the wide desert valleys, jagged mountain ranges, and volcanic mesas below (page 401).

PICACHO CAMPGROUND

Picacho State Recreation Area

The developed sites at remote Picacho Campground are well-spaced amid striking volcanic rock formations a stone's throw from the Colorado River (page 524).

Picacho Campground at Picacho State Recreation Area

Prairie Creek Redwoods State Park

NORTHERN CALIFORNIA

In a place where the thick swaths of trees and impressive mountains are the first thing you notice, Northern California is known for its natural beauty and slower pace of life.

It's the place to wiggle your toes in the sand in front of the chilly Pacific Ocean or where you can wander slowly through a fairy-tale-esque sea of redwood sorrel, looking for mushrooms and bright yellow banana slugs (and Bigfoot). The rain and the regular coastal fog keep everything lush and green, and it's easy to find solace on the dense forest floor.

Step back in time and learn about the rich history of the area. Parks like Sue-meg and Indian Grinding Rock highlight Indigenous culture while Fort Humboldt and Angel Island bring military history to life.

Northern California is also a great base for adventure, with dramatic waterfalls, breathtaking hikes, and fresh alpine lakes right at your fingertips. Take to the water and explore sea caves by kayak, drive scenic roadways, or enjoy the break from the crowds and spend your nights stargazing.

However you choose to explore, breathe in the fresh air and make memories.

BEST NORTHERN CALIFORNIA STATE PARKS

PARK NAME	LANDSCAPE	DAY USE ENTRANCE FEE
Jedediah Smith Redwoods State Park	Forest	$8
Prairie Creek Redwoods State Park	Forest	$8
Sue-meg State Park	Coast	$8
Fort Humboldt State Historic Park	Historic site	free
Humboldt Redwoods State Park	Forest	free
McArthur-Burney Falls Memorial State Park	Waterfall	$10
Russian Gulch State Park	Coast/forest	$8
Van Damme and Mendocino Headlands State Parks	Coast/forest	$8/free
Armstrong Redwoods State Natural Reserve	Forest	$10
Sonoma Coast State Park	Coast	$10
Mount Tamalpais State Park	Mountain	$8
Angel Island State Park	Island	$3 (not including ferry ticket or mooring fee)
Folsom Lake State Recreation Area	Lake	$10-12
Ed Z'berg Sugar Pine Point State Park	Lake	$10
D.L. Bliss State Park	Lake	$10
Emerald Bay State Park	Lake	$10
Indian Grinding Rock State Historic Park	Historic site	$8
Calaveras Big Trees State Park	Forest	$10-12

CAMPING OPTIONS	SUGGESTED VISIT LENGTH	PAGE
1 campground	1 day	page 48
2 campgrounds, cabins	2 days	page 58
3 campgrounds, cabins	2 days	page 69
none	half day	page 80
3 campgrounds, dispersed sites	1 day	page 86
2 campgrounds, cabins	1 day	page 96
1 campground	1 day	page 105
1 campground	2 days	page 114
none	half day	page 126
4 campgrounds	1 day	page 133
2 campgrounds, cabins, dispersed sites	2 days	page 142
4 campgrounds	1 day	page 153
2 campgrounds, dispersed sites	1 day	page 163
1 campground	2 days	page 173
3 campgrounds	half day	page 183
2 campgrounds	1 day	page 191
1 campground	half day	page 201
2 campgrounds	half day	page 208

BEST NORTHERN CALIFORNIA STATE PARKS
Jedediah Smith Redwoods SP
Prairie Creek Redwoods SP
Sue-meg SP
Fort Humboldt SHP
Humboldt Redwoods SP
McArthur-Burney Falls Memorial SP
Russian Gulch SP
Van Damme and Mendocino Headlands SP
Armstrong Redwoods SNR
Sonoma Coast SP
Mount Tamalpais SP
Angel Island SP
Folsom Lake SRA
Ed Z'berg Sugar Pine Point SP
D.L. Bliss SP
Emerald Bay SP
Indian Grinding Rock SHP
Calaveras Big Trees SP
Oregon Caves NM
Lava Beds NM
Redwood National Park
Whiskeytown-Shasta-Trinity NRA
Lassan Volcanic NP
Point Reyes NS
Goose Lake
Shasta Lake
Eagle Lake
Lake Almanor
Honey Lake
Lake Oroville
Clear Lake
Lake Berryessa
Lake Tahoe
PACIFIC OCEAN
Crescent City
Arcata
Eureka
Scotia
Leggett
Mendocino
Ukiah
Healdsburg
Jenner
Santa Rosa
Petaluma
Napa
Vallejo
San Rafael
Berkeley
Oakland
San Francisco
San Mateo
San Jose
Weed
Redding
Red Bluff
Chico
Oroville
Williams
Canby
Alturas
Susanville
Blairsden
Downieville
Sierraville
Truckee
Roseville
SACRAMENTO
Placerville
South Lake Tahoe
Stockton
Modesto
Merced
0 25 mi
0 25 km

NORTHERN CALIFORNIA STATE PARKS 3 WAYS

THE REDWOODS GETAWAY

In the uppermost coastal corner of California next to the Oregon border, the Redwood National and State Parks have some of the most immaculately preserved old-growth redwood forests in the world. This route starts at the northernmost park and works its way south down US-101.

Day 1

Depending on where you're coming from, the majority of this day might be spent making your way to **Jedediah Smith Redwoods State Park.** Once there, set up camp at Jedediah Smith Campground before hiking through the redwoods on trails like the Grove of Titans or Boy Scout Tree Trail.

Day 2

Spend the morning driving Howland Hill Road. Afterward, break down the campsite and make your way 40 minutes (30 mi/48 km) south on US-101 to **Prairie Creek Redwoods State Park.**

Set up camp at either Gold Bluffs Beach Campground or Elk Prairie Campground before heading to Fern Canyon. (Note: Day use permits are required and can be reserved online.) Walk the famous loop to take in the *Jurassic Park*-like atmosphere.

Day 3

Get an early start and head to the visitor center to see the Roosevelt elk; the Red Schoolhouse herd can often be seen grazing in the meadows near the center. Afterward, grab a map from the visitor center and drive the Newton B. Drury Scenic Parkway. In the afternoon, spend time relaxing on Gold Bluffs Beach or exploring one of the park's many trails.

Day 4

After breakfast, break down camp and make your way 30 minutes (21 mi/34 km) south to **Sue-meg State Park.** Get a good overview of the park by hiking the Rim Trail, taking some time to explore the short spur trails like the one that leads to Ceremonial Rock. In the afternoon, visit Sumêg Village and learn about the history and culture of the Yurok people. If you want to take a short half-day trip to another park, consider driving 45 minutes (32 mi/52 km) south to Eureka for a walk around **Fort Humboldt State Historic Park.**

THE BAY AREA GETAWAY

This itinerary includes everything the San Francisco Bay Area has to offer, from redwoods and coastal tide pools, from the top of Mount Tamalpais back down to the famous Angel Island. Hiking and biking trails in these parks will give you incredible views from all perspectives, though Karl the Fog may creep in and obscure them.

Day 1

Start your day off at **Armstrong Redwoods State Natural Reserve** hiking through the Armstrong Redwoods Grove Loop, where you can spot Icicle Tree, the Parson Jones Tree, and the giant 1,400-year-old Colonel Armstrong Tree. If you want a longer jaunt, take the East Ridge Trail to get better views of vistas and meadows. On your way out, be sure to visit the Nature Store to pick up a fun souvenir.

In the afternoon, drive 30 minutes (15 mi/24 km) west on CA-116 to reach the Pacific Ocean and CA-1 to find yourself at the northern end of **Sonoma Coast State Park**'s boundaries. Continue south on CA-1, making your way down the coast and stopping at the many beaches and overlooks such as Goat Rock, Shell Beach, and South Salmon Creek Beach. Take a quick walk around the Bodega Head Trail before staying the night at Bodega Dunes Campground.

Day 2

Wake up to the sound of the crashing waves, pack up camp, and head to **Mount Tamalpais State Park,** 1.5 hours (60 mi/97 km) south of the Sonoma Coast along CA-1. Once you get to Stinson Beach, catch the Panoramic Highway and follow it 4 mi (6 km) into the park. Drive up to East Peak Summit and hike to the fire lookout (hopefully it's a clear day so you can see views of the entire Bay Area). Set up camp at either Bootjack Campground or Pantoll Campground, and hike to the historic 3,750-seat Mountain Lookout Theater.

Day 3

Get up early, pack up camp, and drive 20 minutes (8 mi/13km) east on CA-131 to Tiburon, where you'll catch the ferry to **Angel Island State Park.** Spend the day at one of the Bay Area's most famous military outposts, taking a tram tour or biking around the entire island along Perimeter Road to hit all the stops. Visit the US Immigration Station Museum, hike up to Mount Livermore, and have lunch in Ayala Cove. Stay the night either on the island or in San Francisco.

Day 3

THE TAHOE GETAWAY

In the most inland region of Northern California, Lake Tahoe's surrounding mountains feed snowmelt into the big, beautiful freshwater gem. The three Tahoe state parks covered in this summertime itinerary are an easy way to sample all this area has to offer. The parks are all close enough that you can easily set up a home base at one of the parks and make excursions to the others. This itinerary assumes you'll be camping both nights at Emerald Bay State Park.

Day 1

On the southwest corner of the biggest freshwater lake in North America, **Emerald Bay State Park** is one of the most photographed places in the world. After snapping a pic from the Emerald Bay Overlook, walk down to the Tahoe shoreline and Vikingsholm mansion where you can take a guided tour. Hike the Rubicon Trail in either direction around the cove. Stay the night under the stars at Eagle Point Campground.

Day 2

Start your day with a morning kayak to Fannette Island to see the Tea House. In the afternoon, take the Rubicon Trail to the adjacent **D.L. Bliss State Park** and visit Balancing Rock. Watch for the traditional galis dungal (bark house) at the base of the trail leading up to the stone formation. End your visit with a picnic at Calawee Cove before making your way back to camp.

Day 3

Drive CA-89 north 15 minutes (9 mi/14 km) to **Ed Z'berg Sugar Pine Point State Park.** Hike the Dolder Nature Trail, and then take a tour through the Hellman-Ehrman Mansion. If you're looking for a little more trail time and a little more solitude, take the General Creek Trail to Lily Pond. Head back to Emerald Bay for a picnic dinner along the shoreline.

sunset at Emerald Bay State Park

Ed Z'berg Sugar Pine Point State Park

Rubicon Trail

TOP EXPERIENCE

JEDEDIAH SMITH REDWOODS STATE PARK

A few miles away from the rugged coastline, Jedediah Smith Redwoods State Park has more than 10,000 acres (4,000 ha) of ancient redwood groves, approximately 7 percent of all old-growth redwoods left in the world. The oldest redwoods here are around 2,000 years old and still growing. Ferns, azaleas, and rhododendrons bask in their shade and nutrient-rich soil.

ADDRESS: 1561 US-199, Crescent City

PHONE: 707/464-6101

WEBSITE: www.nps.gov

DAY USE HOURS: Sunrise-sunset

AREA: 10,430 acres (4,221 ha)

The land was originally home to the Tolowa people, who built cavernous houses of redwood planks, fished for salmon, and hunted elk. The gold rush in the 1850s brought miners but also violence toward the Tolowa people, resulting in one of the biggest massacres in US history. Despite their traumatic history, the Tolowa have rebounded their population to more than 1,800 people today.

Established in 1929, Jedediah Smith Redwoods State Park was named for the fur trapper who, in 1821, was the first non-native person to have ventured over the Mississippi River and through the Sierra Nevada to the Pacific Coast. The Frank D. Stout Memorial Grove became its first landmark. In 1994, the National Park Service and California State Parks came together to comanage Jedediah Smith and other nearby redwoods parks to give greater protection to the entire 105,000 acres (42,500 ha) of redwood forest, creating Redwood National and State Parks.

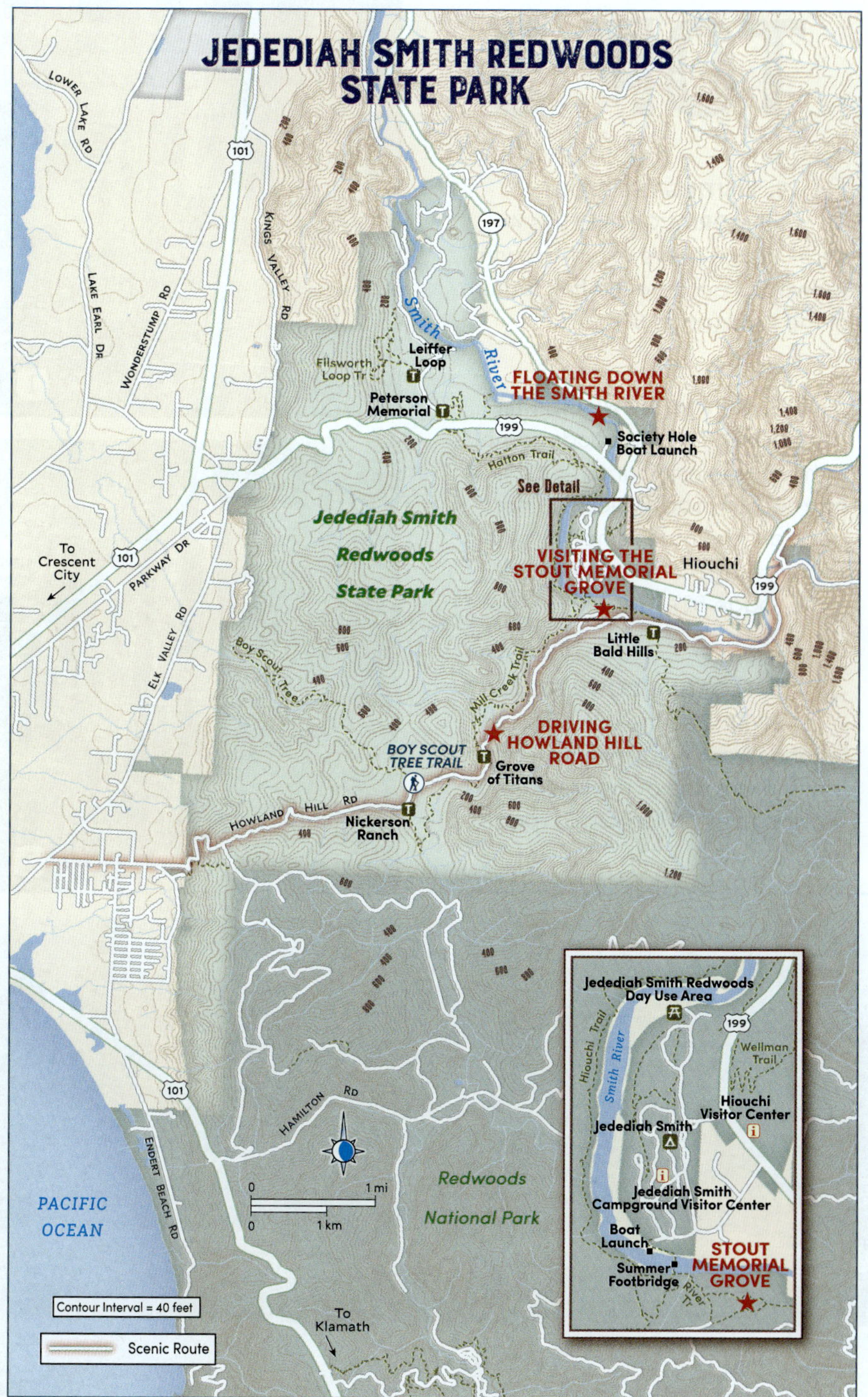

JEDEDIAH SMITH REDWOODS STATE PARK
Lower Lake Rd
Lake Earl Dr
Wonderstump Rd
Kings Valley Rd
Smith River
Leiffer Loop
Ellsworth Loop Tr
Peterson Memorial
FLOATING DOWN THE SMITH RIVER
Society Hole Boat Launch
Hatton Trail
See Detail
Jedediah Smith
Redwoods
State Park
VISITING THE STOUT MEMORIAL GROVE
Hiouchi
Little Bald Hills
To Crescent City
Parkway Dr
Elk Valley Rd
Boy Scout Tree
Mill Creek Trail
DRIVING HOWLAND HILL ROAD
BOY SCOUT TREE TRAIL
Grove of Titans
Howland Hill Rd
Nickerson Ranch
Hamilton Rd
Redwoods
National Park
PACIFIC OCEAN
Endert Beach Rd
To Klamath
Contour Interval = 40 feet
Scenic Route
0 1 mi
0 1 km
Jedediah Smith Redwoods Day Use Area
Hiouchi Trail
Smith River
Wellman Trail
Hiouchi Visitor Center
Jedediah Smith
Jedediah Smith Campground Visitor Center
Boat Launch
Summer Footbridge
River Tr
STOUT MEMORIAL GROVE

TOP 3

★ **1. VISITING THE STOUT MEMORIAL GROVE:** This 44-acre (18-ha) grove of old-growth redwoods became the first feature of the park (page 51).

★ **2. DRIVING HOWLAND HILL ROAD:** The redwoods come right up against your car on this narrow dirt road, which has not been altered much since 19th-century stagecoaches used the route (page 52).

★ **3. FLOATING DOWN THE SMITH RIVER:** See the tall living legends from a kayak or raft on the Smith River, one of the last free-flowing rivers in California (page 54).

1

2

3

PLANNING YOUR TIME

Those looking to camp or to establish a base for exploring the rest of Redwood National Park may want to stay a few nights. This park is close to Crescent City and the Oregon border, so if you're coming in from the north or headed to the coast via US-199, it's a good place to start your multiday redwoods exploring. However, for most people a single day is sufficient to see all the major sights.

Nearby state parks include Prairie Creek Redwoods State Park (25 mi/40 km).

ENTRANCE AND FEES

Jedediah Smith Redwoods has **one main park entrance** off US-199 across the street from the Hiouchi Visitor Center. A self-registration kiosk collects the $8 fee near the parking lots in the day use area; another kiosk is in front of the campground entrance.

VISITOR CENTERS

Jedediah Smith Redwoods has two visitor centers, both on the eastern side of the park.

Hiouchi Visitor Center

1600 US-199, Hiouchi; 707/464-6101; 9am-5pm daily mid-May-Oct., 10am-4pm Thurs.-Mon. Nov.-mid-May

Hiouchi Visitor Center issues backcountry permits, shows a park movie, and has a picnic area.

Jedediah Smith Campground Visitor Center

1440 US-199, Hiouchi; 707/464-6101; 9am-5pm daily Memorial Day-Labor Day

The Jedediah Smith Campground Visitor Center has brochures; it's between the campfire arena and restrooms near the park's entrance.

WEATHER

In the summer temperatures average around 60°F (16°C), while the winter months can drop to 40°F (4°C) and can bring up to 100 in (254 cm) of rain. Though this park is farther inland from the Pacific coastline than others, the fog still rolls in during the summer months. The best time to visit is either in the spring or the fall, when it's not as crowded and the forest is lush but not too wet.

SIGHTS

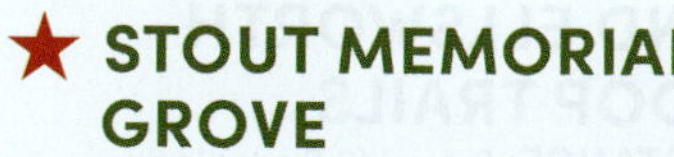

★ STOUT MEMORIAL GROVE

This 44-acre (18-ha) pocket of old-growth redwoods has some that are 300 ft (91 m) tall, and the sword ferns all along the forest floor look equally thriving and healthy. The Stout Grove, also known as Frank D. Stout Memorial Grove, became the first feature of the Jedediah Smith Redwoods, saved from destructive logging when Clara W. Stout donated this tract of forest to the Save the Redwoods League. The easiest way to get there is to drive Howland Hill Road and park in the lot next to the grove. (Note that Howland Hill Road may be closed; check at the visitor center first.) There is also a footbridge crossing the Smith River from the bottom of the campground, but it's only open in the summer and dependent on water levels.

SCENIC DRIVES

★ HOWLAND HILL ROAD

DISTANCE: 10 mi (16 km)
DURATION: 1 hour
START: Elk Valley Rd. off US-101, Crescent City
END: South Fork Rd. off US-199, Hiouchi

The redwoods come right up against your car on this narrow dirt road, which has not been altered much since the 19th-century stagecoaches used the route. It takes about an hour to drive the full length of the road, which cuts through the heart of the park and links to popular hiking trails such as Boy Scout Tree Trail and the famous Stout Grove. Given how close the trees are to the road, RVs, trailers, and other large vehicles are not allowed on it.

The road sometimes closes in winter due to storm damage, and once a year, usually in early summer, the road will close for resurfacing. Before embarking, check in with the visitor center to make sure it's open.

HIKING

This park offers an excellent introduction to the redwoods with its 20 mi (32 km) of hiking trails, providing a nice mix of easy and moderate hikes that meander through a vibrant natural atmosphere teeming with thriving plant life and impressively tall trees. For hikes that leave from Howland Hill Road, check in with the visitor center first to make sure the road is open; depending on the season, it may be closed due to storm damage or for resurfacing.

GROVE OF TITANS

DISTANCE: 1.5 mi (2 km) loop
DURATION: 45 minutes
EFFORT: Easy
TRAILHEAD: Howland Hill Rd.

The trail to Grove of Titans was rebuilt in the summer of 2022 to pay homage to a group of impressive trees. To protect the natural forest floor, 1,500 ft (457 m) of wooden boardwalks as well as stairs and single-track dirt paths were constructed. This short loop starts and ends off Howland Hill Road and joins up with the 6-mi (10-km) moderate Mill Creek Trail, if you want to make a longer hike out of it.

LEIFFER LOOP AND ELLSWORTH LOOP TRAILS

DISTANCE: 2.4 mi (3.8 km) loop
DURATION: 1 hour
EFFORT: Moderate
TRAILHEAD: Walker Rd.

The Leiffer Loop starts and ends on Walker Road, and the Ellsworth Loop

TOP HIKE

BOY SCOUT TREE TRAIL

DISTANCE: 5.5 mi (8.9 km) round-trip
DURATION: 3 hours
EFFORT: Moderate
TRAILHEAD: Howland Hill Rd.

Thought to be one of the tallest trees in the park, the 238-ft-tall (72-m-tall) Boy Scout Tree is named after the Crescent City Boy Scout chapter who built this trail back in the 1930s. The tree is actually made up of two coast redwoods that joined together. Starting at Howland Hill Road, this trail meanders through the forest past the Boy Scout Tree to Fern Falls, rising in elevation 951 ft (290 m) over the 5 mi (8 km).

Trail is a small offshoot of the Leiffer Loop. Most people start at one point on **Walker Road,** hike the **Leiffer Loop,** veer off onto the **Ellsworth Loop Trail,** follow that back to the Leiffer Loop, and pick it up to lead back to Walker Road. Maples, coast redwoods, California hazel, and western hemlock trees grow along this route, along with wildflowers including trillium, glossy Clintonia, and wild ginger popping up in spring. There is a parking lot at the base of Walker Road off US-199, where the easy, 0.8-mi (1.3-km) Simpson-Reed Grove Trail also starts.

RECREATION

BIKING

Little Bald Hills Trail

DISTANCE: 19.6 mi (31.5 km) round-trip
DURATION: 1.5 hours
TRAILHEAD: Howland Hill Rd.

The Little Bald Hills Trail is popular with mountain bikers. The single-track trail is rated for those of intermediate ability and has a 1,958-ft (597-m) elevation climb. The trail starts from the parking pullout on Howland Hill Road (check road status before visiting) and climbs through the redwoods to a primitive campground, crosses the Smith River national area boundary line, and descends Paradise Flat Trail to South Fork Road.

★ KAYAKING AND RAFTING

If you're not afraid of getting wet, consider spending the day in or around the **Smith River.** Park rangers may give **kayak tours** (www.nps.gov/redw/planyourvisit/kayaktours.htm; $15 pp) as river conditions and

kayaking the Smith River

staffing allow, but you're also welcome to drop your own kayak in at **Society Hole boat launch,** or at the launch near the **summer footbridge** at the campground, which is only open in the summer. A kayak rental shop is in nearby Hiouchi.

Redwood Rides (www.redwoodrides.com; $89-134 pp) offers fun "Redwood Float" kayak and rafting adventures. All abilities are welcome, and you get a unique perspective of the redwoods from one of the clearest tributaries in the US.

FISHING

Anglers like to catch king salmon, cutthroat trout, and steelhead in the Smith River. The park has two boat launch ramps—one called Society Hole and another near the summer footbridge at the campground that's only open during summer. People ages 16 and older must carry a valid California fishing license, available to buy online through the California Department of Fish and Wildlife (https://wildlife.ca.gov).

CAMPING

Jedediah Smith Redwoods has **one campground** with 89 sites, each equipped with a table, fire ring, and cupboard, with restrooms nearby. There are no hookups for motor homes or trailers, but a few of the sites are spacious enough to fit an RV up to 36 ft (11 m) long. Most of the other campsites can accommodate RVs up to 25 ft (8 m) long and trailers up to 21 ft (6 m). Restrooms, coin-operated showers, water spigots, and a dump station are available.

Jedediah Smith Campground is open year-round. Book your campsite online through **Reserve California** (800/444-7575; www.reservecalifornia.com; $35/night)

fly-fishing

from two days up to six months out from your trip.

BEST CAMPGROUND

Jedediah Smith Campground

The main campground at this park has 89 sites, which include a few smaller hike-in/bike-in sites interspersed with a few bigger sites that can fit trailers and motor homes. There are also some wheelchair-accessible sites. The most popular sites are numbers 51 through 60 because they are along the Smith River and quieter.

CABINS

The park also has four ADA-accessible, hard-roofed cabins ($100/night) in the middle of the campground, complete with heaters, lights, and electricity. There's no kitchen or bathroom, and guests need to bring their own bedding. Each cabin has two bunk beds, a double bed under a twin. Each cabin also has its own outdoor barbecue, fire pit, picnic table, and bear box; maximum occupancy per cabin is six people. Reserve a cabin online through the Reserve California website up to six months in advance.

FOOD AND LODGING

Crescent City is a short 10-minute drive west from the park and has grocery stores, gas stations, restaurants, hotels, and motels. Named after its crescent moon-shaped stretch of sandy beach, Crescent City is the only incorporated town in Del Norte County, with a population of around 7,000 people. Follow the Redwood Highway east of the park and you'll come upon **Hiouchi** a half mile (0.8 km) away. It is a small drive-through town with just an RV park, motel, and diner.

BEST PICNIC SPOT

Jedediah Smith Redwoods Day Use Area

Considered the jumping-off point for all recreational activities, this day use area is right on the banks of the Smith River. A multitude of picnic tables and accompanying barbecues dot the shores and under the redwoods.

summer footbridge (left); day use area (right)

BEST NEARBY

REDWOOD NATIONAL PARK

The 139,000-acre (56,250-ha), 50-mi-long (80-km-long) Redwood National Park (www.nps.gov/redw; free) exists to protect 45 percent of the world's remaining old-growth coast redwoods. Redwood National Park stretches from Orick to the Oregon border and comprises many different areas, including several state parks. Jedediah Smith Redwoods State Park and Prairie Creek Redwoods are part of both the California State and National Park systems, and either annual pass works to get in. Its five visitor centers—Hiouchi Visitor Center, Jedediah Smith Campground Visitor Center, Crescent City Information Center, Prairie Creek Visitor Center, and Thomas H. Kuchel Visitor Center—have information about all the redwood parks and are stocked with fun souvenirs, maps, and friendly rangers.

It's also close to the campground and summer footbridge leading to the Stout Memorial Grove. Parking costs $8.

GETTING THERE

CAR

Jedediah Smith Redwoods State Park is approximately 5 mi (8 km) northeast of **Crescent City.** From US-101 north, take exit 794 to get on US-199 toward I-5/Grants Pass. Continue on US-199 for a half mile (0.8 km) to the entrance of the park.

The park is 73 mi (117 km) southwest of **Grants Pass, Oregon,** the next major city where US-199 connects with I-5.

PUBLIC TRANSPORTATION

Amtrak (www.amtrak.com) maintains bus stops in Hiouchi and Crescent City. The Hiouchi bus stop has no shelter, but it drops you right next to the Hiouchi Café a half mile (0.8 km) away from Jedediah Smith Redwoods. The **Redwood Coast Transit** (707/308-7433; https://redwoodcoasttransit.org) has a bus traveling US-199 from Crescent City to Gasquet that goes directly through the park, called Route 199.

PRAIRIE CREEK REDWOODS STATE PARK

ADDRESS: 127011 Newton B. Drury Scenic Pkwy., Orick

PHONE: 707/464-6101

WEBSITE: www.nps.gov/redw

DAY USE HOURS: Sunrise-sunset

AREA: 14,000 acres (5,666 ha)

Prairie Creek Redwoods is where movies are made, the natural remoteness creating a perfect backdrop for films like *Jurassic Park* and *Return of the Jedi*. Vibrant green plant life and old-growth redwoods thrive here as five-finger, lady, sword, chain, and deer ferns flow down abrupt 50-ft (15-m) stone canyon walls.

Its tranquility extends to Gold Bluffs Beach. In 1850, miners crossing the North Coast noticed bits of gold on its sandy base, but filtering the small specks out of the sand seemed like too much work, so they carried on.

Long before the Europeans and miners came, the Yurok people were the original inhabitants of the park and surrounding areas. Here and at Sue-meg, Yuroks traveled by canoes, fished for salmon, hunted for deer, elk, and small mammals, and foraged for food. But when gold was found near Fern Canyon by the settlers, the Yurok were overwhelmed and their population diminished. Fortunately, in recent years the tribe has regenerated, and close to 5,500 natives now live in the Humboldt and Del Norte areas.

From ancient trees and majestic elk to thriving ferns and gold-dusted beaches, Prairie Creek holds centuries-old secrets and generations of time passed through untouched nature.

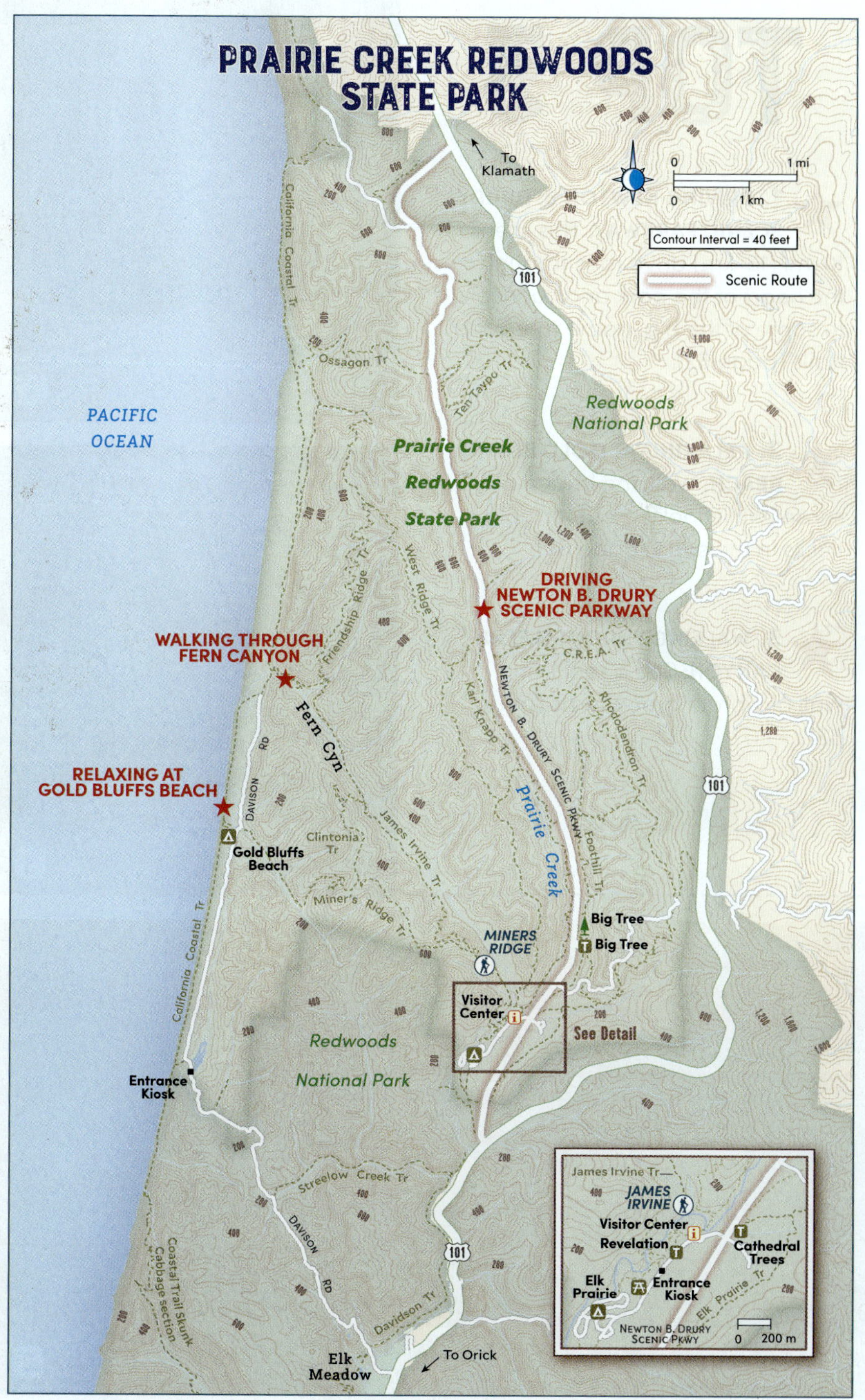
PRAIRIE CREEK REDWOODS STATE PARK
To Klamath
0 1 mi
0 1 km
Contour Interval = 40 feet
Scenic Route
PACIFIC OCEAN
California Coastal Tr
Ossagon Tr
Ten Taypo Tr
Redwoods National Park
Prairie Creek Redwoods State Park
West Ridge Tr
Friendship Ridge Tr
DRIVING NEWTON B. DRURY SCENIC PARKWAY
WALKING THROUGH FERN CANYON
C.R.E.A. Tr
Fern Cyn
Karl Knapp Tr
NEWTON B. DRURY SCENIC PKWY
Rhododendron Tr
RELAXING AT GOLD BLUFFS BEACH
DAVISON RD
Gold Bluffs Beach
Clintonia Tr
James Irvine Tr
Prairie Creek
Foothill Tr
Miner's Ridge Tr
Big Tree
Big Tree
MINERS RIDGE
Visitor Center
See Detail
Redwoods National Park
Entrance Kiosk
Streelow Creek Tr
DAVISON RD
Coastal Trail Skunk Cabbage section
Davidson Tr
Elk Meadow
To Orick
James Irvine Tr
JAMES IRVINE
Visitor Center
Revelation
Cathedral Trees
Elk Prairie
Entrance Kiosk
Elk Prairie Tr
NEWTON B. DRURY SCENIC PKWY
0 200 m

TOP 3

★ **1. DRIVING NEWTON B. DRURY SCENIC PARKWAY:** This scenic 10-mi (16-km) drive runs through the heart of the park and connects to some of the big-name trees and trails (page 62).

★ **2. RELAXING AT GOLD BLUFFS BEACH:** Walk the beach at sunset while looking out for gold flecks in the sand (page 63).

★ **3. WALKING THROUGH FERN CANYON:** See a real living wall of vibrant green ferns (page 63).

1

3

2

PLANNING YOUR TIME

It's worth spending at least one night in one of the park's campgrounds, which will also give you more of a chance to spot an elk and his harem or fall asleep to the crashing waves at Gold Bluffs Beach. Just be sure to get supplies (snacks and water) before you venture into the park, as there are no food and beverage amenities within the grounds. The park is open daily, but you'll need a reservation to get to Fern Canyon and Gold Bluffs Beach via Davison Road in the summer since parking is so limited.

Nearby state parks include Sue-meg State Park (21 mi/34 km).

ENTRANCES AND FEES

There is **one main entrance** into the park where the Elk Prairie Campground is on the south end of the Newton B. Drury Scenic Parkway, as well as a **second entrance station** on the south end of Davison Road to access Gold Bluffs Beach and the Fern Canyon Day Use Area. Prairie Creek Redwoods ($8/vehicle) is 25 mi (40 km) south of Crescent City and 50 mi (80 km) north of Eureka on US-101. Since this park is part of the Redwood National Park system, a national park pass works here as well.

VISITOR CENTER

Prairie Creek Visitor Center

Newton B. Drury Scenic Pkwy.; 707/488-2039; 9am-5pm daily summer, 9am-4pm daily winter

The Prairie Creek Visitor Center is one of the five National Park Service information outlets that operate in conjunction with the Redwood Parks Conservancy nonprofit. Inside there are a bookstore, souvenirs, maps, park information, and exhibits about the redwoods and Civilian Conservation Corps.

RESERVATIONS

A permit is required to visit the **Fern Canyon Day Use Area** and **Gold Bluffs Beach Campground** May 15-September 15 because parking off Davison Road is so limited. The easiest way to obtain one is through the Redwood Parks Conservancy (https://redwoodparksconservancy.org). The permit is free, but there's a $12 entrance fee unless you're camping at Prairie Creek—showing your camping reservation will give you access to the Fern Canyon Day Use Area. Online reservations open on December 15 and can be made up to six months to the day before your trip (you cannot make reservations day-of). However, you don't have to get a permit if you don't drive up Davison Road; Fern Canyon can be accessed from the James Irvine Trail (10 mi/16 km, 4-8 hours) that starts near the Elk Prairie Campground/main entrance station.

WEATHER

Prairie Creek is foggy and damp year-round, getting lots of rain in the wintertime between October and April. The park gets around 63 in (160 cm) of precipitation per year, but temperatures tend to stay in the moderate 45-65°F (7-18°C) range. Fortunately, the morning fog usually dissipates midday, bringing a clear cool canopy landscape ideal for hiking. The best time to visit is in the spring and autumn months when it's less crowded.

ONE DAY IN PRAIRIE CREEK REDWOODS STATE PARK

MORNING

Wake up to the sound of the ocean at Gold Bluffs Beach and then hike through Fern Canyon.

AFTERNOON

Drive to Elk Prairie and have a picnic lunch by the visitor center. Keep your eye out for grazing elk. Drive or bike the Newton B. Drury Scenic Parkway to visit Big Tree and access other trailheads.

SIGHTS

BIG TREE

The very literally named Big Tree in Prairie Creek is 304 ft (104 m) high and thought to be around 1,500 years old. Homesteaders wanted to cut it down and use the stump as a dance floor, but fortunately didn't go through with chopping the giant because they didn't think the wood was good enough to hold their tapping feet. To see Big Tree, pull over on the Newton B. Drury Scenic Parkway from the Big Tree lot less than a mile north of the visitor center. Follow **Big Tree Trail** 0.3 mi (0.5 km) to reach the giant arbor. Other ancient redwoods can also be seen within this five-minute walk.

SCENIC DRIVES

★ NEWTON B. DRURY SCENIC PARKWAY

DISTANCE: 10 mi (16 km)
DURATION: 20-30 minutes
START: Off US-101, 6 mi (10 km) north of Orick
END: Off US-101, 4 mi (6 km) south of Klamath

The Newton B. Drury Scenic Parkway route through the redwoods parallels US-101; this peaceful drive is the epitome of "car hiking," which equates to a 20-30-minute jaunt down a paved single-lane roadway.

Known as "the man who saved the redwoods," Drury (1889-1978) dedicated 40 years of his life to securing an instrumental amount of acreage to the parklands. He served as the director of the National Park Service, Save the Redwoods League, and California State Parks for many years. This parkway connects to the **Ossagon Trail** (which is great for bikers wanting to do the 19-mi/31-km loop) as well as Davison Road, the Coastal Trail, and Streelow Creek.

BEACHES

★ GOLD BLUFFS BEACH

Gold Bluffs Beach is one of the best places to spend the day or camp overnight at Prairie Creek Redwoods, as its long sandy beaches are great for bird-watching, beachcombing, and just sitting on a piece of big driftwood and watching the waves. The orange-tinted bluffs along the shoreline caught the gold miners' eyes back in the 1800s; the bluffs were formed by sediment that came from the Klamath River and solidified.

A part of the **California Coastal Trail** goes along Gold Bluffs Beach, and if you're lucky you might spot seals or the rare snowy plover near or on the sands.

Gold Bluffs Beach Campground is off Davison Road 1.3 mi (2 km) ahead of the Fern Canyon Day Use Area. There's limited parking at Gold Bluffs Beach, therefore an entry permit is needed if you visit in the summertime. One can be reserved online through the Redwood Parks Conservancy (https://redwoodparksconservancy.org).

HIKING

While a lot of the park's most profound features are viewable right from the Newton B. Drury Scenic Parkway, Prairie Creek Redwoods also features 75 mi (121 km) of hiking trails. From the short ADA-accessible Revelation Trail near the visitor center to Big Tree and the famous Fern Canyon, there are plenty of photo opportunities within this unique landscape.

★ FERN CANYON LOOP

DISTANCE: 1 mi (1.6 km) round-trip
DURATION: 30 minutes
EFFORT: Easy
TRAILHEAD: End of Davison Rd.

Fern Canyon is one of the highlights of the entire North Coast redwoods parks system just because it looks so surreal. To check out this 50-ft (15-m) wall of ferns, drive the gravelly Davison Road to the Fern Canyon parking lot (you'll need a permit to access it May 15-September 15, and no trailers or RVs over 24 ft/7 m are allowed on the road). Walk the stem of the "lollipop" loop with a surface area of tree stumps, gravel, fallen tree trunks, and water. At the end of the half-mile (0.8-km) dirt path and over a trickling creek with primitive wooden board bridges, visitors can get up close and personal with this green waterfall filled with all kinds of happy ferns. Expect to hear songbirds, the nearby sea, and trickling water that provides a peaceful habitat for wildlife residents and human visitors alike. You may need to cross parts of Home Creek with ankle-deep water in it, so consider wearing quick-dry hiking shoes.

ELK PRAIRIE TRAIL

DISTANCE: 3.2 mi (5.1 km) round-trip
DURATION: 1 hour
EFFORT: Easy

TOP HIKE

MINERS RIDGE AND JAMES IRVINE LOOP

DISTANCE: 12.4 mi (20 km) round-trip
DURATION: 7 hours
EFFORT: Moderate
TRAILHEAD: Prairie Creek Visitor Center

This loop offers a good breadth of what the park has to offer, showing off old-growth trees, Fern Canyon, a beach walk, and everything in between. From the visitor center, walk 0.6 mi (1 km) to the James Irvine Trail and veer right. Follow it another 3.5 mi (5.6 km) to the Fern Canyon Trail. Go through Fern Canyon to Gold Bluffs Beach and follow the shoreline another 1.2 mi (1.9 km). Cut through the Gold Bluffs Beach Campground to join up with the Miners Ridge Trail and follow it another 3.5 mi (5.6 km) back toward the visitor center. For a shorter hike that doesn't include Fern Canyon, take the James Irvine Trail and veer left instead of right after 0.6 mi (1 km) to jump on the Clintonia Trail. That connects with Miners Ridge, which leads back to the visitor center. That loop is 6.9 mi (11.1 km) total and takes about three hours to hike.

TRAILHEAD: Prairie Creek Visitor Center

Babbling creeks, lace lichen, the elk-viewing meadow, and redwoods hug the pine needle-covered dirt path on this easy forest loop, which also goes around the Elk Prairie Campground. Sturdy wooden bridges help hikers cross over creeks safely, and sword ferns beckon the way.

CATHEDRAL TREES TRAIL

DISTANCE: 3 mi (5 km) round-trip
DURATION: 1 hour
EFFORT: Moderate
TRAILHEAD: Big Tree Wayside/Big Tree parking lot

The Cathedral Trees Trail, accessed via Big Tree Wayside on the Newton B. Drury Scenic Parkway, highlights the "fairy rings," aka a cluster of cathedral trees between that lot and the Prairie Creek Visitor Center. Like the Elk Prairie Trail, an abundance of ferns, patches of redwood sorrel, rushing water, downed trees, and redwood fungi are also found along the trail.

RECREATION

BIKING

Ossagon Trail

DISTANCE: 3.6 mi (5.8 km) round-trip
DURATION: 1 hour
EFFORT: Moderate
TRAILHEAD: Newton B. Drury Scenic Parkway

The out-and-back Ossagon Trail starts at the parkway on the north end of Gold Bluffs Beach and climbs about 700 ft (213 m) through old-growth redwoods, then descends through alder and Sitka spruce groves to the sand.

If you want a longer ride, keep going down the California Coastal Trail to Fern Canyon to bring your total mileage up to 9.7 mi (15.6 km) for an out-and-back ride. To make a day out of it, do the entire 19-mi (31-km) bicycle loop, starting on the Ossagon Trail, going down the hard-packed dirt and gravel Davison Road past Gold Bluffs Beach, and cutting inland on the Streelow Creek Trail. That leads back up to the Elk Prairie Campground, then the paved Drury Parkway (past Big Tree) to close the loop. It takes about 6.5 hours to bike this loop.

Keep in mind that portions of the California Coastal Trail can be flooded and muddy. Fallen branches and tree limbs also often block the path. Pets and e-bikes are not allowed on this trail.

WILDLIFE WATCHING

Roosevelt Elk

On the southern end of the Newton B. Drury Scenic Parkway, the Red Schoolhouse elk herd can often be seen grazing in these meadows near the visitor center. There are places along the meadows to stop and take pictures of them; just be sure to drive slowly and respect the elks' habitat. At one time teetering on becoming extinct, they now are thriving in certain parts of the redwoods. During their August-October mating season, the bulls get very vocal as they try to find partners and fight off the other males. Both the bulls and the cows watching over their calves can be

elk (left); trail at Prairie Creek Redwoods State Park (right)

extremely aggressive if humans get too close. Going up to an elk is not only dangerous, it's against state law. The park encourages people who are taking pictures to use a telephoto lens. Boyes Prairie, a big span of meadow that hugs Prairie Creek Redwoods, is closed to visitors.

The best time to see Roosevelt elk is early in the morning and/or at sunset. Drive slowly when on the Drury Parkway or other unpaved roadways, and when hiking or biking, don't veer off the trails for your safety and the elks'.

CAMPING

Prairie Creek Redwoods has **two main campgrounds,** Elk Prairie Campground and Gold Bluffs Beach Campground. It also has a few hike-in/bike-in sites, cabins, and three non-reservable environmental sites. Reservations can be made online through Reserve California (800/444-7275; www.reservecalifornia.com; $35/night) from two days up to six months in advance January-September. Campsites are first-come, first-served October-December.

The maximum size for trailers to access the park is 24 ft (7 m) long; for RVs it's 27 ft (8 m) long. No hookups or dump stations are available.

BEST CAMPGROUNDS

Elk Prairie Campground

127011 Newton B. Drury Scenic Pkwy., Orick; 707/488-2039

The Elk Prairie Campground has 75 family campsites for tents and RVs. It is open year-round, and several sites are wheelchair-accessible. Sites 25-29 are closest to the trail that leads to the visitor center, Revelation Loop, and amphitheater. Sites 70-76 are closest to the Davison Trail. There are two restrooms with hot showers, and firewood is available to buy on-site. It is highly recommended to make reservations as far as you can in advance between Memorial Day and Labor Day.

Gold Bluffs Beach Campground

Davison Rd., 3 mi/4.8 km north of Orick; reservation-only May-Sept.

Gold Bluffs Beach Campground, close to Fern Canyon, is highly sought after, so make sure to book your site(s) as soon as you know your vacation dates. There are 26 campsites for tents and RVs up to 24 ft (7 m) long; any vehicle bigger than that won't make it down Davison Road. Trailers are not allowed for this reason. Amenities include flush toilets, water, solar showers, and ocean views, but don't expect to find any power outlets anywhere in the campground. Wi-Fi is available, but spotty. Sites 7, 9, and 12-17 are closest to the beach.

CABINS

Meadow Cabins

800/444-7275; www.reservecalifornia.com; $80/night

The first four sites past the Elk Prairie Campground entrance station are basic cabins right next to a big meadow. All cabins are ADA-accessible and have electricity, heaters, and lights. A cabin has two bunk beds, each with a twin plank over a double, fitting up to six people. There are no mattress pads, and visitors need to bring their own bedding. The cabin sites each have an outdoor barbecue, fire pit, bearproof box, picnic bench, and space for a small tent if there's a couple in your group that wants to sleep outside. Smoking, pets, or cooking inside the cabin is not allowed.

FOOD AND LODGING

For peace of mind, you'll want to make sure you have a full tank of gas, food, and camping supplies before venturing down Davison Road into the Gold Bluffs Beach/Fern Canyon area. **Orick** is a tiny town with one or two small motels, a restaurant, and a market with a couple of gas pumps and camping supplies. It's 8.5 mi (14 km, a 30-minute drive) from Gold Bluffs Beach Campground and 5 mi (8 km, an 8-minute drive) from the main Prairie Creek Redwoods entrance station on the Drury Parkway. **Klamath** is 5 mi (8 km) north of the top of the Drury Parkway; it has an RV park and a Holiday Inn Express but is also pretty sparse.

BEST PICNIC SPOTS

Elk Prairie Campground

One of the best places to have lunch at Prairie Creek Redwoods is underneath the redwoods, of course. A plethora of picnic tables are between the Elk Prairie Campground and Visitor Center, underneath the shaded canopy of a few of Humboldt's giants. Short hikes such as the Nature Trail, Revelation Trail, and Cathedral Trees Trail are close by.

BEST NEARBY

California Coastal Trail

CALIFORNIA COASTAL TRAIL

Called "The Longest Hike" in California, the California Coastal Trail (https://californiacoastaltrail.org) spans 1,200 mi (1,931 km) from the Oregon border all the way down to Mexico. Sections of it are paved, and some are rugged single-track wilderness paths. Humboldt Section 2 of the trail, going from Gold Bluffs Beach Campground to Orick, is the first longest section from the Oregon border. It's an almost 12-mi (19-km) stretch of verdant topography open mainly to hikers, but mountain bikers can access parts of this trail, too.

The California Coastal Trail passes through other top-notch state parks including Sue-meg, Fort Humboldt, Mendocino Headlands, Russian Gulch, Van Damme, Sonoma Coast, Half Moon Bay, Point Lobos, and beyond.

GETTING THERE

CAR

The 14,000-acre (5,666-ha) Prairie Creek Redwoods State Park is close to the town of **Orick** and 50 mi (80 km) north of **Eureka,** along US-101. Heading northbound, the Prairie Creek Redwoods Visitor Center is about 1.2 mi (1.9 km) off US-101. It's off exit 753 onto the Newton B. Drury Scenic Parkway. The Parkway is 10 mi (16 km) long, and the visitor center is on the south end of it. Just remember that trailers or RVs bigger than 24 ft (7 m) cannot drive on Davison Road to Fern Canyon.

SUE-MEG STATE PARK

Up in the northwest corner of California, Sue-meg sits on a prominent bluff jutting out into the Pacific Ocean. Intense waves smash up against the rocky bluffs below, adding to the visual drama. Beyond the sandy beaches and tide pools, the park encompasses grassy meadows and a thriving dense forest, making Sue-meg one of the most peaceful and resplendent parks in the state parks system.

ADDRESS: 4150 Patrick's Point Dr., Trinidad

PHONE: 707/677-3570

DAY USE HOURS: Sunrise-sunset

AREA: 640 acres (259 ha)

Formerly known as Patrick's Point, Sue-meg became the park's new name in 2021 when the California State Parks and Recreation Committee voted it in to further reflect the heritage and culture of the Indigenous Yurok people, who are the area's original inhabitants. The term ***sumêg*** means "forever" in Yurok language.

In a place where the ferns and trees outnumber the people, the park's thriving flora and fauna are accessible through its decent network of hiking trails. The Rim Trail, which traces the coast and connects beach trails at the north and south ends of the park (Palmer's Point and Agate Beach), can't be missed.

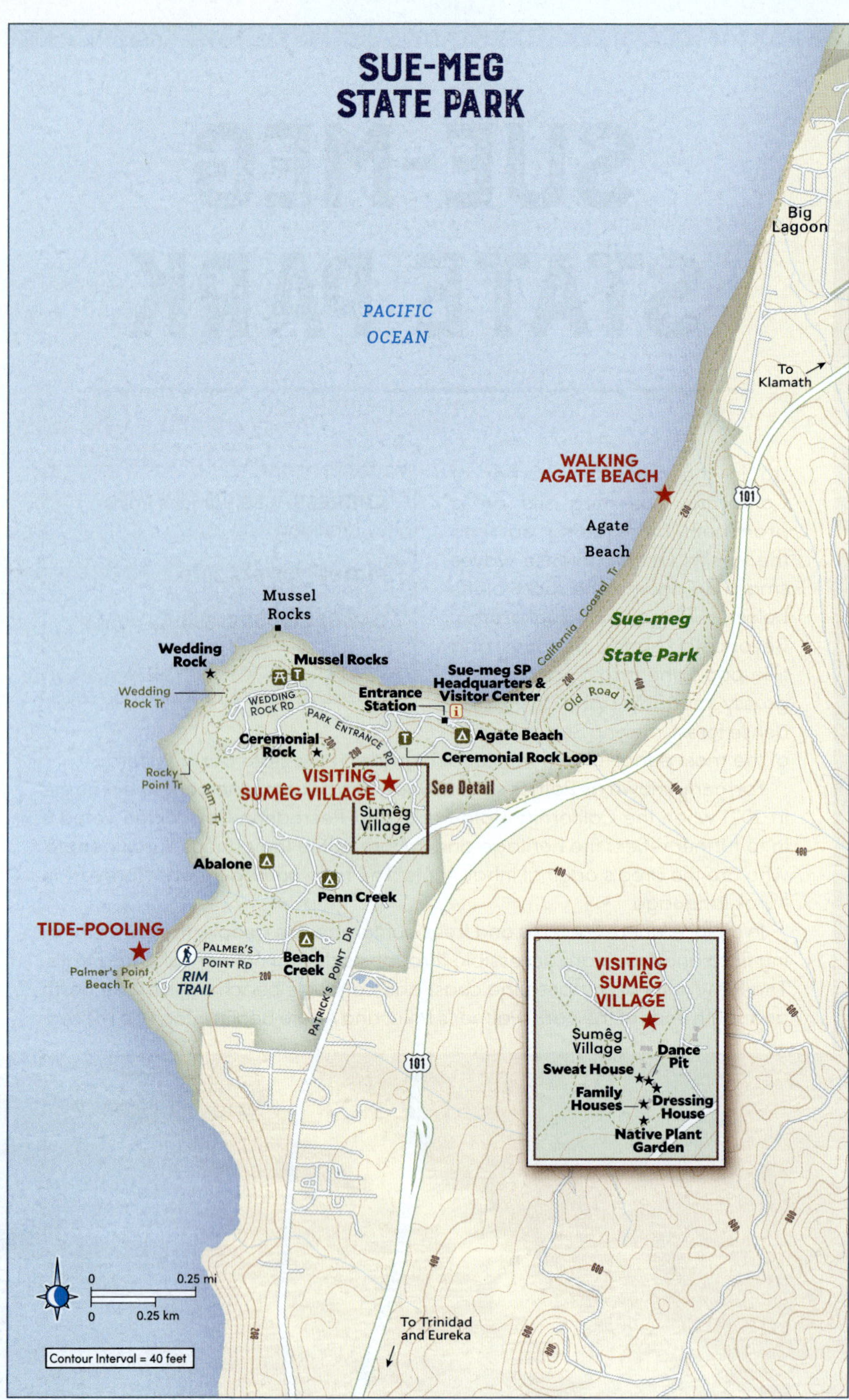
SUE-MEG
STATE PARK
PACIFIC
OCEAN
Big
Lagoon
To
Klamath
WALKING
AGATE BEACH
101
Agate
Beach
California Coastal Tr
Sue-meg
State Park
Mussel
Rocks
Wedding
Rock
Mussel Rocks
Sue-meg SP
Headquarters &
Visitor Center
Wedding
Rock Tr
Wedding
Rock Rd
Park Entrance Rd
Entrance
Station
Old Road Tr
Ceremonial
Rock
Agate Beach
Ceremonial Rock Loop
Rocky
Point Tr
Rim Tr
VISITING
SUMÊG VILLAGE
See Detail
Sumêg
Village
Abalone
Penn Creek
TIDE-POOLING
Palmer's
Point Rd
Beach
Creek
Palmer's Point
Beach Tr
RIM
TRAIL
Patrick's Point Dr
101
VISITING
SUMÊG
VILLAGE
Sumêg
Village
Dance
Pit
Sweat House
Family
Houses
Dressing
House
Native Plant
Garden
0
0.25 mi
0
0.25 km
Contour Interval = 40 feet
To Trinidad
and Eureka

TOP 3

★ **1. VISITING SUMÊG VILLAGE:** Constructed in the 1990s, Sumêg Village has traditional houses made of redwood, showcasing the history and culture of the Yurok people (page 73).

★ **2. WALKING AGATE BEACH:** Jasper, quartz, and flecks of fool's gold interspersed with driftwood are found all along the water's edge on this pebbly beach (page 73).

★ **3. TIDE-POOLING:** When the ocean's tide recedes, all kinds of bright and interesting sea animals can be spotted in the tide pools near Palmer's Point (page 76).

ONE DAY IN SUE-MEG STATE PARK

MORNING

After loading up on supplies in Trinidad, head to the park and begin by checking out the visitor center. Afterward, park at the lot at the Agate Beach Campground or Wedding Rock Road and hit the Rim Trail.

AFTERNOON

Have a picnic at Agate Beach, then walk over to **Sumêg Village.** After paying homage to Sue-meg's original inhabitants, get back in your car and head to the southern part of the park, being sure to stop by Palmer's Point on your way out.

PLANNING YOUR TIME

It's possible to see the whole park in a day, but with Sue-meg's plethora of campsites and hiking trails you can easily fill at least two days. There are no food or beverage outlets within Sue-meg's boundaries, so come with your own snacks.

Nearby state parks include Prairie Creek Redwoods State Park (21 mi/34 km).

ENTRANCE AND FEES

Sue-meg State Park is a few miles north of Trinidad and 58 mi (93 km) south of Crescent City. The **one entrance** into the park is off Patrick's Point Drive, which is accessible from US-101 or from Trinidad. The park is open daily, but its hours change often in the off-season. The daily access fee is $8 per vehicle.

VISITOR CENTER

Sue-meg State Park Headquarters and Visitor Center

4150 Patrick's Point Dr.; 707/677-1945; 10am-4pm daily May-Sept., 10am-4pm Wed.-Sun. Oct.-Apr.

The Sue-meg State Park Headquarters and Visitor Center are directly across from the park's entrance. There are restrooms and picnic tables available. Inside, displays show the Yurok's history and traditions, types of California redwoods, and a map of all the Indigenous tribes in the state. Souvenirs and novelty gifts are for sale, too.

WEATHER

It's usually foggy and it rains a bit more in the fall and winter months, but the air temperatures stay a pleasant 38-62°F (3-17°C) all year long. The best time to go is in the spring and the fall when it's less crowded.

SIGHTS

★ SUMÊG VILLAGE

Constructed in the 1990s, Sumêg Village showcases the history and culture of the Yurok people and neighboring Karuk and Hoopa tribes. The various structures within the village include **family homes** that peek up from the ground made of naturally fallen redwood and stone, as well as a sunken **dance pit.** The **native garden** next to the village grows plants that the tribe used in basket-weaving, medicine, and more. The original village was used as a seasonal encampment that covered a larger area north and south of the park; the reconstruction is meant to reflect the traditional architecture. Park at Red Alder Campground for the quickest access to the village. In the summertime, the park hosts free guided tours daily through the village as well as on the weekends in the off-season. Head to the visitor center to get more information.

PALMER'S POINT

At the very south side of the park at the end of Palmer's Point Road, you can park and look out over the ocean and see spectacular marine life. It's common to see and hear sea lions from Palmer's Point, or you might catch a glimpse of migrating whales in the autumn months. A steep staircase and sandy trail lead down to what's called **Cannonball Beach** for its big boulders, which is ripe for tide-pooling.

WEDDING ROCK

Wedding Rock is worth a stop as it has some of the most dramatic scenes of waves crashing against the boulders and long views of the foamy Pacific shoreline. Park in the lot off Wedding Rock Road, which is a bit inland, and has access to the Rim Trail and Overlook Trail as well as Wedding Rock Trail.

BEACHES

AGATE BEACH

Before heading to the beach, take in the sea breeze and the views of Agate Beach from the parking lot above the Agate Beach Trail, then take the short yet steep walk (0.5 mi/0.8 km round-trip, 15 minutes, moderate) down to the water. After descending the wooden staircase, you'll see miles of small rocks, pebbles, and grainy sand lining the tumultuous ocean. Jasper, quartz, and flecks of fool's gold interspersed with driftwood are found all along the water's edge. You may come across a neat gem, but keep in mind rockhounding is highly discouraged as too many people taking agates home can disrupt what makes this place so special.

While Agate Beach is a popular surf spot for the locals, who come dressed head to toe in thickly lined wetsuits to help withstand the cold sea, this isn't the best place for beginners due to its forceful undertows, sleeper waves, and rocky coastline.

The Agate Beach Campground is

on the northern end of the park. To get there via car, drive down Park Entrance Road around the meadow and stay to the right heading toward the Agate Beach Campground. This drive also provides 270-degree views of Ceremonial Rock as well as the wildflowers and grasses that surround it.

HIKING

The Rim Trail intersects with all trails in the park; it is not only the primary access point for all the ocean overlooks, but the trail is cut to lead to the more inland forested Ceremonial Rock and Lookout Rock Trails. The Rim Trail is the best/only way to get to Rocky Point, Patrick's Point, and the Rim Trail Overlook, and it connects them all.

WEDDING ROCK TRAIL

DISTANCE: 1 mi (1.6 km) round-trip
DURATION: 15 minutes
EFFORT: Easy
TRAILHEAD: End of Wedding Rock Rd.

Heading north around the main part of the park's outcropping, Wedding Rock Trail has panoramic views of the Pacific Ocean. It takes about 8 minutes to get to the built-in stony ledge, with sandy sea-blown wooden stairs leading to the main scene.

CEREMONIAL ROCK LOOP TRAIL

DISTANCE: 1 mi (1.6 km) round-trip
DURATION: 30 minutes
EFFORT: Moderate
TRAILHEAD: Rim Trail at Park Entrance Rd.

Consider taking the Rim Trail to the middle of the park in a hike toward Ceremonial Rock. The Rim Trail intersects with Park Entrance Road, becoming the Ceremonial Rock Trail and continuing to the Agate Beach Campground amenities. There's also the Ceremonial Rock Meadow Trail and Ceremonial Rock Loop Trail, but all lead to the same place: the top of a rock that has expansive ocean and grasslands views.

Wedding Rock (left); view of Agate Beach (right)

TOP HIKE
RIM TRAIL

DISTANCE: 4 mi (6.4 km) round-trip
DURATION: 2 hours
EFFORT: Easy
TRAILHEAD: Palmer's Point Rd.

The 2-mi (3.2-km) Rim Trail (one-way from Palmer's Point Road to the Agate Beach Campground) follows the shoreline, therefore most of it has great ocean views. It is right next to the Abalone Campground, Wedding Rock parking lot, and Agate Beach Campground, making it easy to pitch a tent and jump on the trail right from your campsite. The Rim Trail itself is a flat dirt path with boughs of red alder, Sitka spruce, ferns, fir trees, and other dense foliage that line the way. Chirping songbirds, bunnies, and chipmunks may cross your path too.

CALIFORNIA COASTAL TRAIL

DISTANCE: 12.8 mi (20.6 km) round-trip
DURATION: 5 hours
EFFORT: Strenuous
TRAILHEAD: Agate Beach

This segment of the California Coastal Trail (https://californiacoastaltrail.org) is good way to get a taste of the trail that traces California's coastline. Walk along the gravelly shoreline from Agate Beach and you'll be on the CCT, which leads to Humboldt Lagoons State Park 1.6 mi (2.5 km) away. There's no definitive line of where Sue-meg ends and Big Lagoon Beach begins, but you can turn back anywhere on Agate Beach to stay within Sue-meg's park boundaries. The entire CCT within Sue-meg consists of sand/dirt (the Rim Trail), the beach (Agate), and road shoulder (from Palmer's Point); its uneven surface—especially along Agate Beach, which may be next to impossible to cross even during low tide—is what makes this section of the CCT difficult. Note the tide schedule before embarking and make sure you leave plenty of time to complete the trip before the tide comes in if leaving the park from Agate Beach.

RECREATION

WILDLIFE WATCHING

A bounty of flora and fauna live within this diverse ecological landscape, where the ocean meets the forest.

★ Tide Pools

When the ocean's tide recedes, all kinds of bright and interesting sea animals can be spotted in the tide pools at **Cannonball Beach** near Palmer's Point. The best time to go is when the tides are low, as rising tides cut off access down to the beach. The visitor center posts tide schedules. The rocks can be slippery, so wear good hiking shoes with non-slip soles and expect your feet to get wet. Rangers lead free two-hour tide pool walks in certain months on which you can see purple shore crabs, ochre stars, and orange cup coral. Note: Swimming is discouraged because of the chilly water and strong currents. At the southernmost end of the park where Palmer's Point Road meets the end of the bluff, take Palmer's Point Beach Trail (0.5 mi/0.8 km round-trip, 15 minutes, strenuous) to reach the tide pools.

Marine Mammals

If you're lucky you may be able to catch a glimpse of a gray whale pod migrating to or from Alaska and Baja California, Mexico, in the spring and the fall. California gray whales spend their summers in the Bering Sea and winters in Mexico; they start heading south from Alaska in October, which is when they are closest to the shoreline, and then return north to their feeding grounds in February and March. The majestic behemoths travel up to 10,000 mi (16,000 km) along the Pacific Coast in any given year, and the best place to spot them is at **Palmer's Point** or from **Wedding Rock.**

Harbor seals and Steller sea lions also spend their time at Sue-meg State Park, often all year long

CONDOR CONSERVATION

Park officials have continued to collaborate with the Yurok people in recent years to bring back the population of condors, the incredible land bird known to consume roadkill and carrion. Aggressive hunting during the westward expansion in the 19th century was the main cause of wiping out the condor population, and they were completely extinct in the wild by 1987. A couple of dozen condors remained in the entire world, all living in zoos.

Now there is an effort to restore the wild population through a captive breeding program. Condors do not actively hunt for prey despite their impressive 9.5-ft (3-m) wingspan. Yurok people believe they help restore balance in the world and are working with conservationists to bring condor numbers back up. Eight condors were released within Sue-meg in 2022, and another four per year will be released for the next 20 years.

The proper storage of trash and food is more important than ever to keep the Prey-go-neesh (the Yurok word for California condor) thriving and other wildlife safe. For more information about the Condor Reintroduction Program, visit the National Park Service Redwoods website at www.nps.gov/redw.

basking on the rocks. The best place to see them is also at Palmer's Point. Sea lions have earflaps, short claws on their front flippers, and the ability to use their hind flippers to "walk" on land, while harbor seals have long front claws and point their back flippers away from them, scooting on their belly on any land.

Birds

Between the ocean and the forest, Sue-meg is also a popular place for our avian friends. Birds including winter wrens, red crossbills, common murres, and different varieties of migrating geese hang out near the sea, while squawky blue Steller's jays and hawks have been spotted inland.

CAMPING

Sue-meg has 124 campsites split up between **three main campgrounds** as well as a group camping area and cabins. Campsites must be reserved online in advance May-September through Reserve California (800/444-7275; www.reservecalifornia.com; $35/night) and are available on a first-come, first-served basis October-April. Reservations can be made up to six months ahead of the current date. Each reservation includes parking for one vehicle; trailers up to 30 ft (9 m) can fit comfortably in any site, but there are no hookups.

Coin-operated showers are available in each of the campgrounds for overnight guests, and the bathrooms have power outlets. Every campsite has a fire pit, picnic table, fire grill, food storage box, and water spigots close by. Be sure to always store food properly as there are black bears and condors in the area, and leaving food out can carry a hefty fine. Since Sue-meg is so lush and moist, burn bans don't occur here too often, but you must bring your own firewood.

BEST CAMPGROUNDS

Penn Creek Campground

The 15 sites within the Penn Creek Campground (sites 1-15) are closest to the park entrance and visitor center, located on Palmer's Point Road. It's the most "inland" campground of the park aside from Beach Creek, the group camping area.

Abalone Campground

Across from Penn Creek Campground, Abalone Campground (sites 16-85) has a lot more spaces and is closer to the ocean. Sites 50, 52, 53, 55, and 57 are closest to the Rim Trail, and you can watch the sunset within a five-minute walk of your site.

Agate Beach Campground

Agate Beach Campground (sites 86-124) is the other sought-out campground because of its proximity to the ocean and California Coastal Trail. It is the northernmost campground of Sue-meg, and you can hear the waves crashing from just about any site. Campsites 86-88 are close to the Rim Trail.

CABINS

Agate Cabins

800/444-7275; www.reservecalifornia.com; $80-100/night

If you don't feel like pitching your own tent, four Agate Cabins near Sumêg Village are also available. Each cabin can sleep up to six people and is only available to reserve online six months from the current date. The cabins are bare bones, though, so you'll still want to BYOB (Bring Your Own Bedding). Each one has two full bunk beds, two electrical outlets, heating, and countertop but no bathroom or running water. Bathrooms are located behind the cabins near the Agate Beach trailhead. The cabins book out fast in the summer; you have the best chance of snagging one midweek in the off-season winter months.

FOOD AND LODGING

The closest place to find food, gas, and hotels is **Trinidad,** a few miles south of the park via US-101. A few oceanfront bed-and-breakfasts are on Patrick's Point Drive as well, but that road can sometimes be inaccessible due to rockslides. Trinidad has a few diners, a coffee shop near the ocean, and a grocery store with everything you need for your camping trip.

BEST PICNIC SPOT

Wedding Rock Road

A nice picnic area, parking lot, and restrooms are off Wedding Rock Road at the base of Mussel Rocks Trail. It also links to the Rim Trail and is a short walk away from other trailheads, so the tables provide a nice respite throughout the day of looking at Sue-meg's sights.

GETTING THERE

CAR

The 1-sq-mi (2.6-sq-km) Sue-meg Park is approximately 30 mi (48 km, 30 minutes) north of Eureka, and 58 mi (93 km, 1 hour) south of Crescent City along US-101. Patrick's Point Drive is off exit 734 from US-101 northbound, and then a half mile (0.8 km) away from the entrance station and visitor center. The roads are paved, and signs are clearly marked directing you into and around the park. Patrick's Point Drive between Trinidad and the park sometimes closes due to rockslides; the closure will be noted on Google Maps and on signs at the entrances detouring you over to US-101—the more common and direct route.

FORT HUMBOLDT STATE HISTORIC PARK

Up on an often-foggy bluff at the southern end of Eureka across from Humboldt Bay is a historic settlement that gives visitors a glimpse into early pioneer military life and logging past. Its open grassy parade grounds are dotted with historic logging equipment, clapboard white buildings, and evidence regarding Fort Humboldt's dark past in its treatment of Indigenous peoples.

ADDRESS: 3431 Fort Ave., Eureka

PHONE: 707/445-6547

WEBSITE: https://redwoodparksconservancy.org

DAY USE HOURS: 8am-5pm

AREA: 17 acres (7 ha)

In the mid-1800s, clashes between Native Californians and settlers seeking gold escalated. Vigilantes were attacking Indigenous people, and newcomers were desperate for support from the government. Eventually the 4th Infantry US Army intervened, establishing Fort Humboldt in 1853 to help keep the peace. In the late 1800s the property was sold to W.S. Cooper, whose family later donated it to the City of Eureka. It became a state historic park in 1955.

One of the park's most famous residents was former president Ulysses S. Grant, who was temporarily stationed at Fort Humboldt when he was a lieutenant. Meandering through the grounds will give you a good idea of Eureka's history, and it's a nice place to stop for a picnic and to stretch your legs.

FORT HUMBOLDT STATE HISTORIC PARK
Bayshore Mall
To Eureka
101
Interpretive Tr
Train Shed
Outdoor Logging Display
District Office
WALKING THE INTERPRETIVE TRAIL
FORT AVE
Fort Humboldt
State Historic Park
Interpretive Tr
Interpretive Tr
BROADWAY ST
Hospital/ Museum
Fort Parade Grounds
TAKING A MOMENT OF SILENCE AT THE CORRAL
GOING INSIDE THE SURGEON'S QUARTERS
FORT AVE
Park Entrance
HIGHLAND AVE
HIGHLAND AVE
101
MCCULLENS AVE
0 50 yds
0 50 m
Contour Interval = 20 feet
0 0.5 mi
Tuluwat Island
Samoa
Samoa Channel
4TH ST
101
I ST
Eureka
BROADWAY ST
101
HENDERSON ST
Map Area
Fort Humboldt SHP

TOP 3

1. GOING INSIDE THE SURGEON'S QUARTERS: A rendition of a settler home with modest furnishings gives visitors a glimpse into how a fort surgeon lived (page 83).

2. TAKING A MOMENT OF SILENCE AT THE CORRAL: Hundreds of Indigenous people died at the fort after being relocated here for their "protection" from aggressive settlers (page 84).

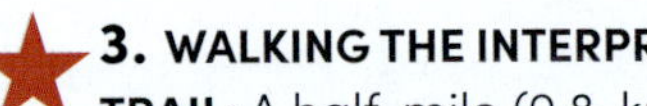

3. WALKING THE INTERPRETIVE TRAIL: A half-mile (0.8-km) easy interpretive trail loops around the Outdoor Logging Display and the perimeter of the park, leading you to all of Fort Humboldt's main features (page 84).

PLANNING YOUR TIME

It takes no more than an hour to see everything here, and the picnic tables on the parade grounds are a lovely place to have lunch. Get there early on a weekday to have the park to yourself and then take the rest of the day to explore nearby Eureka. A district office is at the end of the decent-size parking lot, and a restroom is adjacent to it.

Nearby state parks include Humboldt Redwoods State Park (30 mi/48 km) and Sue-meg State Park (32 mi/51 km).

ENTRANCE AND FEES

There is **one main entrance** to the park. The main parking lot has a decent number of spaces, although it can fill up fast due to park employees working at the district office headquarters. There's room to park bigger vehicles (buses or RVs) on the side of the road before entering the park.

No fees or reservations are needed to enter Fort Humboldt.

VISITOR CENTER

District Office

3431 Fort Ave., Eureka; 707/445-6547; 8am-4pm Mon.-Fri.

While Fort Humboldt doesn't have a proper visitor center, the district office in front of the Outdoor Logging Display and next to the parking lot has brochures and usually someone inside.

WEATHER

Being close to the bay, fog rolls into the park like clockwork in the mornings and evenings. It rains a lot November-May, and temperatures are around 40-50°F (4-10°C), about 10 degrees cooler than in the summer months. The best time to go is in July or August, when it's warmest and driest.

SIGHTS

The park envelops a large dried-grassy area known as the **parade grounds** between the Surgeon's Quarters and the hospital. This was historically an empty, open space used for gatherings, living quarters, and auctions, and was also the site of the Corral.

TOURS

Volunteer docents give free **guided tours** year-round for visitors by request, which is a wonderful way to learn more about the fort's complicated history. Email forthumboldtfieldtrip@gmail.com for more information.

★ SURGEON'S QUARTERS

A modest clapboard house at the edge of the meadow gives visitors a glimpse into how a fort surgeon lived in the 1850s. One room shows a fireplace, a rocking chair, and a chest of clothes, while another shows a desk, a small table, and an extremely uncomfortable-looking bed. The Surgeon's Quarters were reconstructed in the 1980s (it is not

hospital and picnic area (left); train shed (right)

an original building) based off Lady of the Fort Harriet St. John Simpson's letters that she sent to her family chronicling life in Eureka.

★ CORRAL

On the parade grounds in front of the commissary, an 80-ft (24-m) circle of rope represents the size of the corral, an open-air containment area in the grassy parade grounds. It was intended to hold captive Indigenous prisoners and also those who needed protection from vigilante settlers who were taking over their villages, and conditions were abysmal for the hundreds of people who ended up within it. At least 200 Wiyot people died during that time from dysentery and violence before the corral was shut down.

TRAIN SHED

The train tracks lead you to the train shed, where you can view locomotive memorabilia as well as the park's permit to operate a steam boiler. Eureka's own John Dolbeer invented the "steam donkey" in 1881—a locomotive that helped move Humboldt's massive redwood logs.

OUTDOOR LOGGING DISPLAY

On the other side of the train shed, check out the intricacies of the Dolbeer and Willamette "steam donkeys" and equipment such as the Washington Slackline Yarder. Huge chunks of trees are on display on a railcar bed to give a sense of the massive size of the logs and what it took to move them. Other famous old-school locomotives are also on display here.

HOSPITAL/MUSEUM

Of the 16-18 original buildings at Fort Humboldt, only the hospital/museum remains. Located a few hundred yards down from the Surgeon's Quarters on the edge of the parade grounds, the hospital/museum is hardly ever open except to those who join a guided tour. Inside the hospital, there is some medical equipment, Indigenous pottery, and the story of the Indigenous people's relationship to the fort.

★ INTERPRETIVE TRAIL

DISTANCE: 0.5 mi (0.8 km) round-trip
DURATION: 10-15 minutes

EFFORT: Easy
TRAILHEAD: Parking lot

An easy interpretive trail loops around the Outdoor Logging Display and the perimeter of the park, leading you to all of Fort Humboldt's main features. After parking your vehicle, start your walk down the self-guided interpretive trail counterclockwise to see the Outdoor Logging Display and follow the train tracks to the train shed, where you can view locomotive memorabilia.

FOOD AND LODGING

Fort Humboldt is in the spread-out town of Eureka, which has several hotels, stores, restaurants, and other tourist attractions intertwined. Everything is mostly accessible from Broadway Street/US-101. There is **no camping** at the state historic park.

BEST PICNIC SPOT

Parade Grounds Picnic Area

A good place to eat lunch is at one of the picnic tables on the parade grounds behind the hospital/museum. Be sure to wear mosquito repellent.

GETTING THERE

CAR

Fort Humboldt is located along US-101/Broadway Street in Eureka, off Highland Avenue. If you're not on the coast already, then there are several routes to take coming from inland Northern California. If you're traveling on I-5, take CA-299 west from Redding. In about 3 hours, depending on traffic, you'll meet the ocean at Arcata. Eureka is 8 mi (13 km) south of Arcata on US-101.

HUMBOLDT REDWOODS STATE PARK

ADDRESS: 17119 Avenue of the Giants, Weott

PHONE: 707/946-2263

WEBSITE: www.humboldtredwoods.org

DAY USE HOURS: Open 24 hours

AREA: 53,000 acres (21,448 ha)

Up on the northwest corner of California, redwoods far outnumber the people; their towering presence can hardly be ignored. The coastal redwoods, Douglas firs, and other lush greenery take over the land as this park plays host to the largest old-growth redwood stands in the world. Some of the trees are up to 350 ft (107 m) tall, and at least one (the Dyerville Giant) is thought to be 2,000 years old.

Before the settlers came, the Sinkyone people lived among the redwoods for thousands of years. Their land stretched from the Eel River's stem to its South Fork, south to the town of Leggett and to the ocean. The tribal groups in the North Coast today have been instrumental in the conservation and preservation of the redwoods, using centuries-old methods to heal the land.

More than 17,000 acres (6,880 ha) of the 53,000-acre (21,448-ha) Humboldt Redwoods State Park are redwoods, and the famed Avenue of the Giants runs along the eastern side of the park. This park also features 37 hiking trails and several campgrounds.

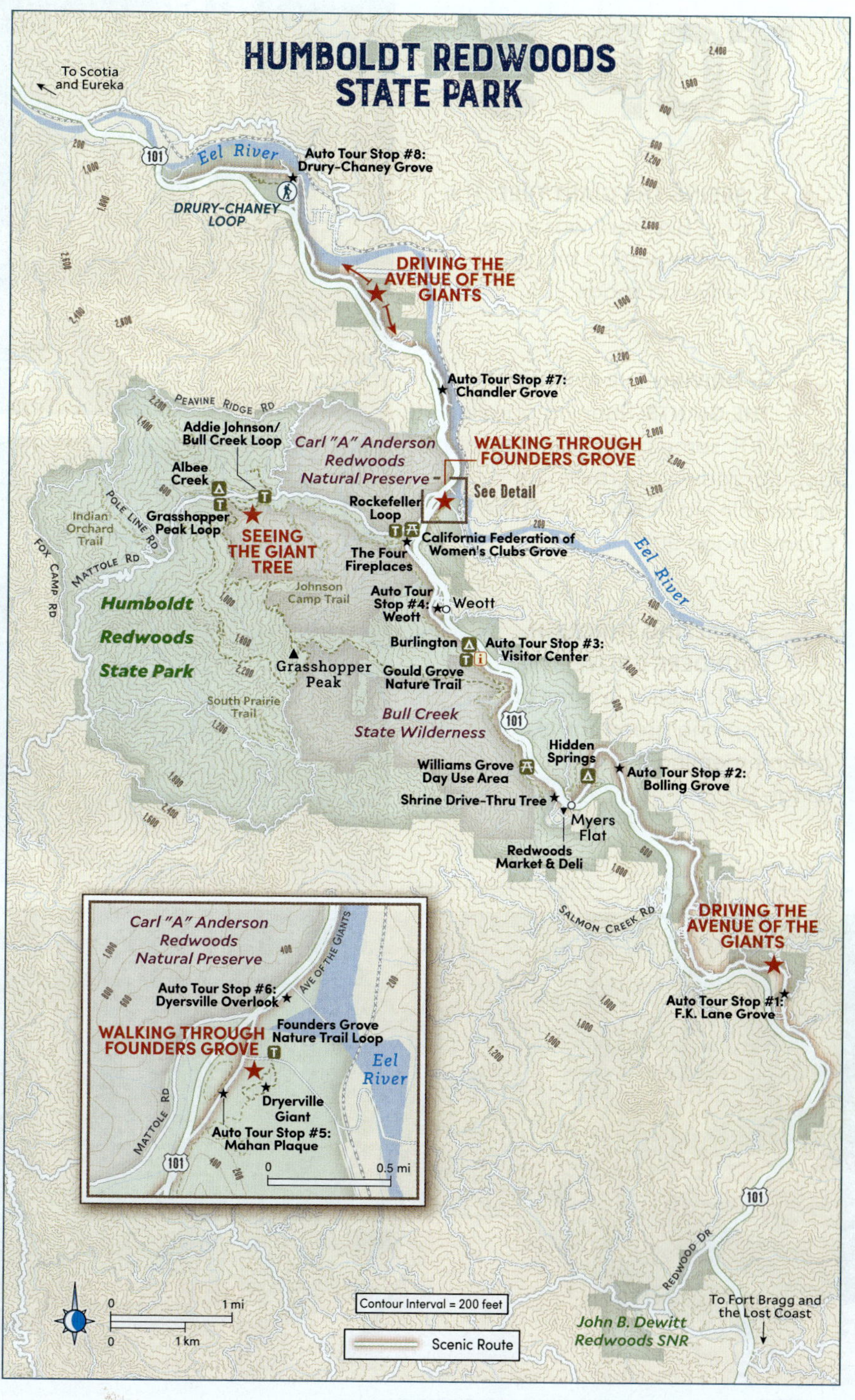
HUMBOLDT REDWOODS STATE PARK
To Scotia and Eureka
Eel River
Auto Tour Stop #8: Drury-Chaney Grove
DRURY-CHANEY LOOP
DRIVING THE AVENUE OF THE GIANTS
Auto Tour Stop #7: Chandler Grove
PEAVINE RIDGE RD
Addie Johnson/ Bull Creek Loop
Carl "A" Anderson Redwoods Natural Preserve
WALKING THROUGH FOUNDERS GROVE
See Detail
Albee Creek
Indian Orchard Trail
POLE LINE RD
Grasshopper Peak Loop
SEEING THE GIANT TREE
Rockefeller Loop
California Federation of Women's Clubs Grove
The Four Fireplaces
FOX CAMP RD
MATTOLE RD
Johnson Camp Trail
Auto Tour Stop #4: Weott
Weott
Humboldt Redwoods State Park
Burlington
Auto Tour Stop #3: Visitor Center
Grasshopper Peak
Gould Grove Nature Trail
South Prairie Trail
Bull Creek State Wilderness
101
Hidden Springs
Williams Grove Day Use Area
Auto Tour Stop #2: Bolling Grove
Shrine Drive-Thru Tree
Myers Flat
Redwoods Market & Deli
SALMON CREEK RD
DRIVING THE AVENUE OF THE GIANTS
Auto Tour Stop #1: F.K. Lane Grove
Carl "A" Anderson Redwoods Natural Preserve
AVE OF THE GIANTS
Auto Tour Stop #6: Dyersville Overlook
WALKING THROUGH FOUNDERS GROVE
Founders Grove Nature Trail Loop
Eel River
Dryerville Giant
MATTOLE RD
Auto Tour Stop #5: Mahan Plaque
0 0.5 mi
REDWOOD DR
0 1 mi
0 1 km
Contour Interval = 200 feet
Scenic Route
John B. Dewitt Redwoods SNR
To Fort Bragg and the Lost Coast

TOP 3

★ **1. SEEING THE GIANT TREE:** The park's "Big Tree" was once considered the world's biggest coastal redwood (page 90).

★ **2. DRIVING THE AVENUE OF THE GIANTS:** Running parallel to US-101, some of the park's most popular redwood groves are accessible via the Avenue of the Giants (page 90).

★ **3. WALKING THROUGH FOUNDERS GROVE:** The grove is blanketed in ferns and awe-inspiring green sorrel, complementing the redwoods (page 91).

ONE DAY IN HUMBOLDT REDWOODS STATE PARK

MORNING

Start your day at the visitor center on the Avenue of the Giants and walk through the 0.6-mi (1-km) Gould Grove Nature Trail, then hop back in your car and drive 5 mi (8 km) to Founders Grove.

AFTERNOON

Have a picnic at the California Federation of Women's Clubs Grove Day Use Area next to the hearthstone and consider going for a swim in the Eel River. End your day with a short walk through Rockefeller Forest.

PLANNING YOUR TIME

You can get a good taste of what the North Coast redwoods have to offer in this park in a day. There are plenty of campsites and over 100 mi (161 km) of trails if you want to make a weekend out of it.

Nearby state parks include Fort Humboldt State Historic Park (30 mi/48 km) and Sue-meg State Park (62 mi/100 km).

ENTRANCES AND FEES

Humboldt Redwoods is one of California's only state parks that doesn't charge an entrance fee. The only part of Humboldt Redwoods that costs money is the Williams Grove Day Use Area ($8/vehicle) on the lower eastern side of the park. The **two entrances** into Humboldt Redwoods are at the north end and south end of Avenue of the Giants.

VISITOR CENTER

Humboldt Redwoods Visitor Center

Avenue of the Giants, Myers Flat; 707/946-2263; 9am-5pm daily May-Sept., 10am-4pm daily Oct.-Apr.

The visitor center is about 18 mi (29 km) north of the Avenue of the Giants south entrance, exit 645 off US-101. It's also the third stop on the Avenue of the Giants Auto Tour, and has educational interactive exhibits, a gift shop, a library, and a theater that's open daily.

WEATHER

While the weather changes quickly up in the North Coast, it never gets too hot or too cold. The redwoods receive anywhere from 63-80 in (160-203 cm) of rain a year, which mostly falls December-February, and temperatures typically stay between 45-65°F (7-18°C). The coastal fog tends to roll in early in the morning year-round, keeping everything moist, but tends to burn off by noon. Autumn is the best time to visit because there are fewer people around.

SIGHTS

★ GIANT TREE

About one third, or 17,000 acres (6,880 ha), of the park is old-growth redwood forest, which is the largest expanse of ancient redwoods left on Earth. In the 1990s, the park's "Big Tree" was considered the world's biggest coast redwood (until Hyperion Tree, discovered in 2006, beat it out), and you can see it right from the parking lot in Upper Bull Creek Flat off Mattole Road. A lot of people just snap a pic of the Giant Tree and leave, but many other impressive redwoods are there to admire within a 10-minute walk out into the quieter forest away from the road.

THE FOUR FIREPLACES

Over at the California Federation of Women's Clubs Grove Day Use Area—Federation Grove for short—is a four-chimneyed-cornered hearthstone deemed the Four Fireplaces. It was designed by Julia Morgan, who was an architect for Hearst Castle in 1933, to commemorate the Federation's success in saving the old-growth redwoods around it. Picnic tables are there, and the Eel River is close enough to swim in. The Federation Grove Day Use Area is off exit 663 from US-101.

SCENIC DRIVES

AVENUE OF THE GIANTS

DISTANCE: 31 mi (50 km)
DURATION: 1-2.5 hours
START: US-101 exit 674
END: US-101 exit 645

The aptly named 31-mi-long (50-km-long) stretch of CA-254 hugs the eastern portion of the park and Eel River South Fork, running through some of the park's most popular redwood groves as well as old mining towns and connecting to Shelter Cove's beautiful beaches. It takes about an hour to drive the Avenue without stops, but with them, designate around 2.5 hours to check it all out. The Avenue of the Giants Auto Tour has eight stops on the drive; from south to north these include: #1: F.K. Lane Grove; #2: Bolling Grove; #3: Visitor Center; #4: Weott; #5: Mahan Plaque; #6: Dyersville Overlook; #7: Chandler Grove; and #8: Drury-Chaney Grove.

Technically outside the park but well worth a stop, the **Shrine Drive-Thru Tree** is arguably the Avenue of the Giants' most famous attraction. It's located 4 mi (6 km) south of the visitor center in Myers Flat and costs $15 to take a vehicle through.

HIKING

More than 100 mi (161 km) of hiking trails are available in Humboldt Redwoods State Park, and many of them are flat and easily navigable. The trees and plant life stay green and moist all year long, with some areas covered in redwood sorrel that is hard to find anywhere else.

★ FOUNDERS GROVE NATURE TRAIL LOOP

DISTANCE: 0.5 mi (0.8 km) round-trip
DURATION: 10 minutes
EFFORT: Easy
TRAILHEAD: Dyerville Rd.

This short and fairly flat loop starts at Founders Tree, and its midpoint is through the thriving greenery at the fallen Dyerville Giant—a redwood that once dwarfed the Statue of Liberty. The compacted dirt path is about 6 ft (2 m) wide with wooden boardwalks crossing over some of the thick plant sections. Since this trail is so close to US-101 and Avenue of the Giants, it's one of the most visited in the park. It's wheelchair- and stroller-friendly with less than a 3 percent grade, so pretty much everyone can enjoy it.

GOULD GROVE NATURE TRAIL

DISTANCE: 0.9 mi (1.4 km) round-trip
DURATION: 20 minutes
EFFORT: Easy
TRAILHEAD: Humboldt Redwoods Visitor Center

Enjoy the scenery of old-growth trees, blankets of lush redwood sorrel, and vibrant green ferns while walking this short loop close to the visitor center. Trees get up to 300 ft (91 m) tall in this grove, and you'll pass through the remains of early logging camps. This trail also leads to the Eel River

Founders Grove Nature Trail Loop

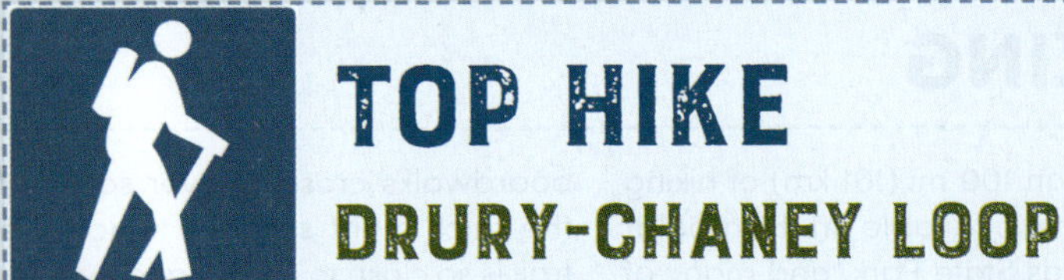

TOP HIKE

DRURY-CHANEY LOOP

DISTANCE: 2.3 mi (3.7 km) round-trip
DURATION: 45 minutes
EFFORT: Easy
TRAILHEAD: Avenue of the Giants, 13 mi (21 km) north of the Humboldt Redwoods Visitor Center

This flat trail through the redwoods is perfect for hikers who want a bit more than the Founders Grove Loop and don't want to deal with the crowds. Except for the lush brown pine needle-sprinkled path, the entire forest floor is flush with bright green redwood sorrel, with a few ferns and moss-covered logs scattered among the redwoods and bay laurels. This trail is in the northern end of the park.

and is close to the Burlington and hike/bike campgrounds.

BULL CREEK FLATS LOOP

DISTANCE: 7.8 mi (12.6 km) round-trip
DURATION: 3 hours
EFFORT: Moderate
TRAILHEAD: Lower Bull Creek Flats at Mattole Rd.

If you're visiting the park between April-October, when Bull Creek is generally low enough to be crossed by a seasonal footbridge, consider hiking the Bull Creek Loop. This loop joins the Bull Creek Flats Trail on the southern side of Bull Creek and the Big Tree Trail on the north side. A hardpacked dirt path winds through tall shady canopies. Walk through a tree trunk archway or atop a fallen tree trunk over the creek, perhaps spotting a banana slug or redwood forest wildflower. The south side of the loop is the best place to start—it's quieter and better for an out-and-back trek. Note that if the park has received a lot of rain, the creek may not be crossable and you may need to do an out-and-back at that point.

ADDIE JOHNSON TRAIL

DISTANCE: 2.4 mi (3.9 km) round-trip
DURATION: 1 hour 15 minutes
EFFORT: Moderate
TRAILHEAD: Unmarked turnout off Mattole Rd., 500 ft (160 m) west of Big Trees Day Use Area

This out-and-back trail starts past Upper Bull Creek and ascends 561 ft (171 m) fast through the redwoods before you reach a clearing that marks Addie Johnson's gravesite. It's considered a moderately challenging trail because of the quick elevation gain, so you're not likely to see very many other people on this trail.

RECREATION

BIKING

Some of the best expert mountain biking trails are here in the redwoods, including the 17-mi (27-km) **Grasshopper Peak Loop** off Mattole Road. However, this trail is steep—with a 3,923-ft (1,196-m) elevation gain, you need to be ready to pedal. **Peavine Ridge Road** on the other side of Mattole Road is equally as difficult. To protect the environment, mountain bikes are only allowed on multiuse trails.

FISHING

Fishing for steelhead trout is popular in the South Fork of the Eel River, which tends to be more stocked in the spring and fall as the fish migrate from the sea to freshwater realms. Chinook, coho salmon, and rainbow trout swim around these waters as well. It's best to come with your own fishing gear as the closest sport shops are in Eureka, a half hour away. A fishing license is required; purchase one through the California Department of Fish and Wildlife (https://wildlife.ca.gov).

SWIMMING

While there are quite a few trails leading to swimming spots along the Eel River, the water rarely gets warmer than 64°F (18°C). For those feeling brave, try the swimming hole near the California Federation of Women's Clubs Grove Day Use Area; you can towel off next to the hearthstone and have lunch at one of its many picnic tables.

CAMPING

Humboldt Redwoods has 250 campsites between its **three family campgrounds:** Burlington, Albee Creek, and Hidden Springs. All are kept impeccably clean and have a picnic table, fire ring, and fresh-water spigots close by. Restrooms with hot coin-operated showers are also at each of the campgrounds. Some of these sites can fit trailers and motor homes up to 24 ft (7 m); however, there are no hookups or a dump station. Reservations for these three campgrounds are site-specific and must be made through Reserve California (800/444-7275; www.reservecalifornia.com; $35/night). The park also has environmental, horse, trail, and group camps ($5/night). Except for the trail camps, all reservations are site-specific and must be made through Reserve California.

BEST CAMPGROUNDS

Albee Creek Campground

Open mid-May through mid-October, Albee Creek is a 40-site campground located off Mattole Road, 5 mi (8 km) west of Avenue of the Giants. It connects to the Rockefeller Forest, swimming holes, and hiking and mountain biking trails. Reservations must be made online.

Burlington Campground

The Burlington Campground is open year-round and has 57 campsites along with 3 hike-in/bike-in sites. It's next to the visitor center, about 2 mi (3 km) south of Weott on Avenue of the Giants. A few easy short trails shoot off from the campground, including a nature trail that leads to the Eel River. Sites that have not been reserved online in advance are available on a first-come, first-served basis for one night at a time.

Hidden Springs Campground

About 5 mi (8 km) south of the visitor center and close to Myers Flat, the Hidden Springs Campground has 137 sites in the coniferous forest. It's only open Memorial Day-Labor Day, and the entrance station only returns calls in-season. This campground has the Hidden Springs Beach Trail that leads to the south fork of the Eel River and is also close to the Williams Grove Trail.

BEST NEARBY

LOST COAST

The famed Lost Coast of California is a rugged and untamed stretch of land that runs from Shelter Cove to Mattole River in Humboldt and Mendocino Counties, with 4,000-ft-high (1,219-km-high) rough terrain cuddling the Pacific Ocean. It takes about an hour to get there from Humboldt Redwoods by taking US-101 up to Fern Ridge, then cutting west through Ferndale and driving another 18 mi (29 km) to reach the ocean. It's a beautiful drive through undeveloped coastal California land popular for its rugged hiking trails in a true wilderness landscape.

FOOD AND LODGING

The closest places to find food, gas, and real beds are in **Myers Flat** and **Scotia.** Myers Flat is a tiny town 10 mi (16 km) south of the visitor center with a population of just over 100 people, but there's a café, market, and post office. Scotia, 20 mi (32 km) north of the visitor center on US-101, has a few hundred more residents, as well as a shopping center, movie theater, museum, hotel, gas station, and one bar/restaurant.

BEST PICNIC SPOT

California Federation of Women's Clubs Grove Day Use Area

Just 3 mi (5 km) north of the visitor center, this area has barbecue grills, restrooms, a trail to a great swimming hole, access to hiking trails right on the edge of Rockefeller Forest, and the famous Four Fireplaces structure.

GETTING THERE

CAR

Humboldt Redwoods State Park is right off US-101 on the 31-mi (50-km) Avenue of the Giants (CA-254) scenic route. The two roads run parallel and sometimes intersect each other. Eureka is 45 mi (72 km) north of the park; you can hop on US-101 from Avenue of the Giants and it takes you right to the center of town.

MCARTHUR-BURNEY FALLS MEMORIAL STATE PARK

In the pine tree-filled Lassen National Forest on the quiet two-lane Volcanic Legacy Scenic Byway is a massively wide and powerful 129-ft (39-m) cascade. This picturesque Northern California gem that Theodore Roosevelt called one of the great wonders of world became McArthur-Burney Falls Memorial State Park in 1926, making it one of the oldest official designated areas in the California State Parks system.

ADDRESS: 24898 Hwy. 89, Burney

PHONE: 530/335-2777

WEBSITE: https://burneyfallspark.org

DAY USE HOURS: 8am-sunset

AREA: 910 acres (368 ha)

Long before Samuel Burney and the McArthurs settled near the Pit River, the band of Ilmawi people pulled salmon and trout out of the creeks and nearby Britton Lake. They gathered and hunted food by building pits and driving larger game into them, hence the name Pit River.

Over 100 million gal (379 million li) of water flow into the pool below the falls every day, making this an ideal park to swim, fish, camp, hike, and escape from urban life (and the heat). McArthur-Burney Falls Memorial State Park has been thrilling visitors for generations.

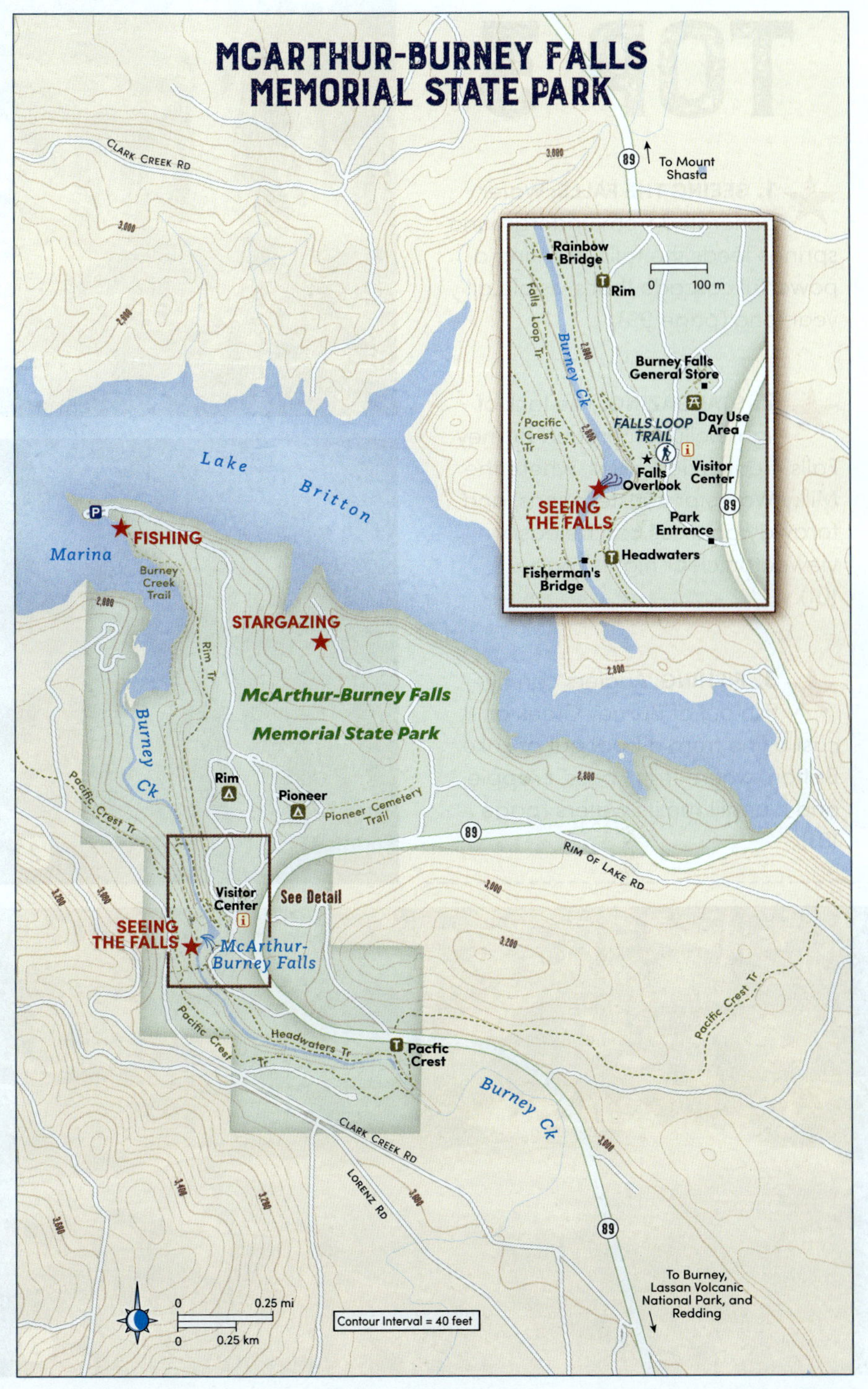
MCARTHUR-BURNEY FALLS MEMORIAL STATE PARK
Clark Creek Rd
89
To Mount Shasta
Rainbow Bridge
Rim
0
100 m
Falls Loop Tr
Burney Ck
Burney Falls General Store
Day Use Area
Pacific Crest Tr
FALLS LOOP TRAIL
Visitor Center
Falls Overlook
SEEING THE FALLS
Park Entrance
Headwaters
Fisherman's Bridge
Lake Britton
Marina
FISHING
Burney Creek Trail
STARGAZING
Rim Tr
McArthur-Burney Falls Memorial State Park
Burney Ck
Pacific Crest Tr
Rim
Pioneer
Pioneer Cemetery Trail
Rim of Lake Rd
Visitor Center
See Detail
SEEING THE FALLS
McArthur-Burney Falls
Pacific Crest Tr
Headwaters Tr
Pacfic Crest
Burney Ck
Pacific Crest Tr
Clark Creek Rd
Lorenz Rd
To Burney, Lassan Volcanic National Park, and Redding
0
0.25 mi
0
0.25 km
Contour Interval = 40 feet

TOP 3

★ **1. SEEING THE FALLS:** Water generated from underground springs feeds the falls, creating a powerful cascade that's visible all year long (page 99).

★ **2. STARGAZING:** The lack of light pollution around Burney Falls creates dark skies, where the Milky Way, star constellations, and faraway galaxies can be easily viewed on clear nights (page 101).

★ **3. FISHING:** Anglers can fly-fish out of Burney Creek or cast a line from a boat out of Lake Britton, where trout, bass, crappie, and bluegill run its waters (page 101).

1

2

3

PLANNING YOUR TIME

Burney Falls has an abundant flow year-round, making this a nice park to visit in any season, and you only need about a half day here to see the falls and hike the loop. However, the park can get packed with people starting as early as April and lasting into October, especially on the weekends. CA-89 gets congested with traffic, and there can be an hour wait to get into the park. Due to its limited capacity, the park is subject to close when it gets too busy, so be sure to arrive early.

ENTRANCE AND FEES

There's **one main entrance** into McArthur-Burney Falls Memorial State Park, off CA-89. It costs $10 to park for the day or $35 to stay overnight at the campground. The entrance station is closed in the off-season (winter months), so be sure to bring exact change or a credit/debit card to pay at the automatic payment machine found in front of the visitor center.

VISITOR CENTER

Burney Falls Visitor Center

24898 Hwy. 89, Burney; 530/335-2777; 11am-4pm Wed.-Sun.

The visitor center is just past the entrance station across from the Falls Overlook. Renovated in 2015, it's chock-full of interesting indoor and outdoor exhibits, books, artifacts, maps, souvenirs, and more. It even has microscopes and a 17-minute movie about the park.

WEATHER

Perched on the eastern edge of the Cascade Range at a 3,100-ft (945-m) elevation, the park's temperatures can range from 20°F (-7°C) and possibly snowing in the winter to 85°F (29°C) and hot in the summer. Rain is more prominent than snow between November and March; the area receives an average of 28 in (71 cm) of precipitation. CA-89 never really closes due to snow, but the roads can get icy, so it's best to carry chains and check the road conditions if traveling in the winter. The spring and autumn months are the best time to visit.

SIGHTS

★ MCARTHUR-BURNEY FALLS

Fed by underground springs, the 129-ft (39-m) waterfall is a powerful cascade that's visible all year long. The falls originally formed from a single lava flow 200,000 years ago that hardened into a 43-sq-mi (111-sq-km) rocky ledge. The basalt is between 10-120 ft (3-37 m) thick, which reinforced into straight cliffs and scarps from which the cascade descends.

For the best views, head to the **Falls Overlook** directly facing the falls, conveniently located right next to the parking lot. From here, you can walk the **Falls Loop Trail,** taking paved switchbacks to the base of the cascades. In the hot summer months, many people swim in the pool at the bottom of the waterfalls.

DISTANCE: 1.1 mi (1.7 km) round-trip
DURATION: 30 minutes
EFFORT: Easy
TRAILHEAD: Falls Overlook

This 1.1-mi (1.7-km) trail starts at the parking lot, where you get the best view of the energetic cascades. Doing this paved loop counterclockwise will take you to the base of the falls, and you'll feel the misty air after navigating the few switchbacks. At the bottom, follow along Burney Creek until the wooden Rainbow Bridge crosses over it. Many people stop and swim here in the chilly waters if they feel so inclined. At this point, you're on the side with the falls and will climb around 160 ft (49 m) to the hidden overlook (you won't see the falls because you'll be standing over them, but you'll hear them). Keep walking and you'll come upon the Pacific Crest Trail junction and another bridge where anglers cast their lines.

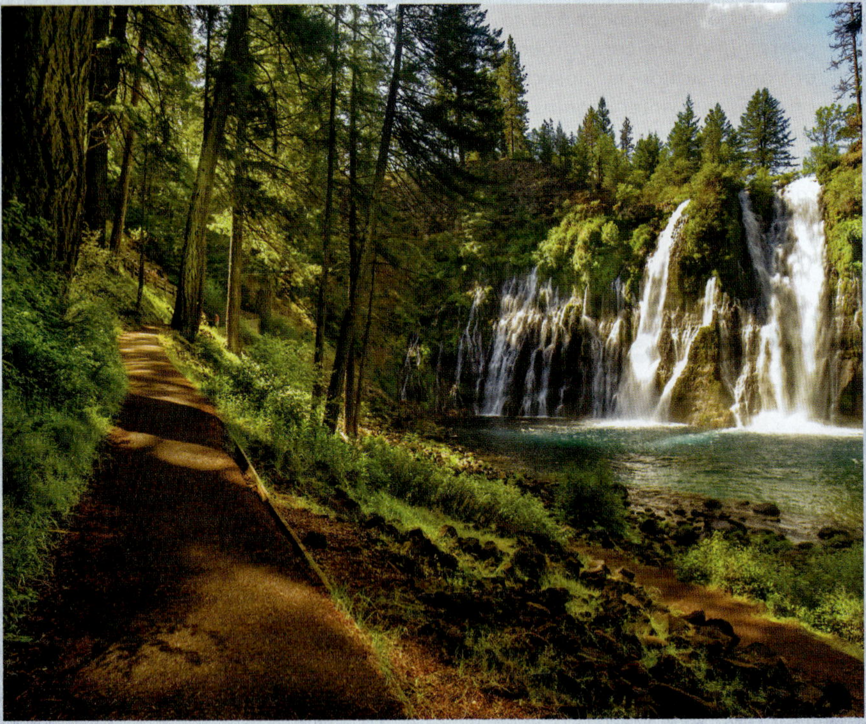

HIKING

The 910-acre (368-ha) McArthur-Burney Falls Memorial State Park has 5 mi (8 km) of trails within Lassen National Forest. The focal point is the falls, but trails wind along coniferous forests, a freshwater creek, and Lake Britton as well. A part of the Pacific Crest Trail also passes through the southwestern part of the park.

PIONEER CEMETERY TRAIL

DISTANCE: 2.5 mi (4 km) round-trip
DURATION: 1 hour
EFFORT: Easy
TRAILHEAD: Burney Falls General Store next to the visitor center

This pleasant, relatively flat out-and-back hike leads from the campground to Lake Britton, passing a historic cemetery on the way. The small final resting place is carved out in a wooded grove with two stone markers paying respect to the residents below. This trail is bikeable, too.

RIM TRAIL

DISTANCE: 2.6 mi (4.2 km) round-trip
DURATION: 1 hour
EFFORT: Easy
TRAILHEAD: Burney Falls Visitor Center parking lot

The out-and-back Rim Trail heads toward Lake Britton and eventually connects with Burney Creek to end at the marina. Starting at the parking lot next to the Falls Overlook, take the dirt path on the left side of the Rim campsites before heading into the remote shade tree-filled area.

HEADWATERS TRAIL

DISTANCE: 1.8 mi (2.9 km) round-trip
DURATION: 40 minutes
EFFORT: Easy
TRAILHEAD: Falls Overlook

This trail starts at the Falls Overlook, but instead of heading north toward the Burney Creek Trail, go south to meet up with the Headwaters Trail. It follows the creek down the eastern edge of Burney to some good fishing spots. You'll know you're going the right direction if you see the Fisherman's Bridge and end up at the Pacific Crest Trail footbridge. There are great views of Burney Falls from this side, but keep in mind that parts of the trail can be closed due to flooding in the winter months.

RECREATION

 STARGAZING

The dark skies in this remote part of California make for ideal stargazing as planets, galaxies, constellations, and the Milky Way shine above the trees on clear evenings. The best way to see the stars is to stay in the park, in either the campground or one of the cabins, in the springtime when it's less crowded. Walking the Pioneer Cemetery Trail on a calm, dark night is a good way to see the stars—if you're not too superstitious about what else can come out at night.

 FISHING

Trout, crappie, bass (largemouth and smallmouth), and bluegill all love

Burney's clear waters, which bring anglers from all over to try to catch them. It's common to see people fishing on the banks of Burney Creek near the falls, especially in the fall months, or casting their lines in the nearby Lake Britton to hook some catfish or carp. Lake Britton has a marina, pier, parking lot, restrooms, and picnic tables at Burney Creek Cove. A few bait-and-tackle shops are in and around Burney. Be sure to get your fishing license through the California Department of Fish and Wildlife (https://wildlife.ca.gov; $20.52 for a one-day license) before your visit.

CAMPING

The McArthur-Burney Falls Memorial State Park campground has 102 standard reservable campsites ($35/night) and 24 primitive cabins ($105/night) within **two campground loops**—the Rim Camp and the Pioneer Camp. There's also a hike-in/bike-in site closest to the Pioneer Cemetery Trail. Since the park gets so crowded in the summer, campsites and cabins must be booked in advance through Reserve California (800/444-7275; www.reservecalifornia.com) mid-May–September. If you come during a busy time and the park is full, you should still have a parking spot waiting for you at your campsite.

The campground is open year-round, but a large portion of it is closed in the wintertime. After the first major snow, only around 30 campsites are available for snow camping ($35/night, pay on-site). Restrooms and showers are available in both the Pioneer and Rim Camps.

The park can accommodate RVs up to 32 ft (10 m) long, and a

cabin at Burney Falls

sanitation station is located at the north end of the campground close to sites 25 and 93. Firewood is sold at the entrance station and the camp host by site 25. All campsites are a short hike from both the lake and the falls.

BEST CAMPGROUNDS

Rim Camp

The Rim Camp loop has 62 sites, two of them being accessible cabins (59 and 62) closest to the Rim Trail. All sites have a fire ring, picnic table, and food locker; restrooms with flush toilets and showers are near sites 10, 51, and 25-30 at the northern end of the loop. Sites 1 and 3 have electricity hookups; sites 23, 27, 30, 47, and 51 are also ADA-accessible.

Pioneer Camp

Sites 63-128 are in the Pioneer loop. All 22 rustic cabins are in the first quadrant driving in before arriving at the standard tent/RV sites. All campsites have a picnic table, fire ring, and food locker, but no hookups. Showers are near sites 113-120, and more restrooms are close to sites 95 and 107. A hike-in/bike-in site is next to site 75 on the start of the Pioneer Cemetery Trail.

CABINS

530/335-5713

Most of the one-room and two-room cabins (starting at $105/night) at Burney Falls are at the southernmost part of the Pioneer Camp loop. Each cabin is equipped with propane heaters, wood floors, padded platform bunk beds, and wide 6-ft (2-m) covered decks. There's also a campfire ring, picnic table, and space for one tent outside. The cabins do not have electricity or running water, and you must bring your own sleeping bags, linens, and battery- or solar-powered lights for when it gets dark. Reservations for cabins can be made online through Reserve California (800/444-7275; www.reservecalifornia.com) for the April-October months; the cabins are unavailable in the off-season.

FOOD AND LODGING

McArthur-Burney Falls Memorial State Park is about 10 mi (16 km) north of Burney, a town of about 3,000 people on CA-299. Burney is the closest town to get gas, food, and supplies, and/or try your hand at the slots at the Pit River Casino. It also has a few motels, but overall, it's more of a quiet, sleepy, remote town. There are a few privately run campgrounds and RV parks close to Burney Falls.

GENERAL STORE

Main Road past the Burney Falls Visitor Center; 530/529-1747; 9am-5pm Fri.-Tues. mid-Apr.-mid-Oct.

The state park does have its own general store with supplies, small snacks, ice cream, and souvenirs. It's pricey but worth it if you don't want to leave the park. The camp store also rents kayaks, canoes, and boats out of the marina. It is open mid-April through mid-October, closed in the winter.

BEST NEARBY

LASSEN VOLCANIC NATIONAL PARK

Just 41 mi (66 km) south of Burney Falls is Lassen Volcanic National Park (21820 Lassen National Park Hwy., Mineral; 530/595-4480; www.nps.gov/lavo; open 24 hours; $10-30), featuring the largest plug dome volcano in the world. Boiling mud pots, steaming fumaroles, lakes, hiking trails, and campgrounds can be found within this 106,000-acre (42,900-ha) outdoor playground. To get there from Burney Falls, turn right on CA-89, go through Hat Creek, and arrive in Old Station. Stay on CA-89 heading south to get to the western entrance of the park at Manzanita Lake. CA-89 goes directly through the park, but closes often in the winter due to snow.

BEST PICNIC SPOT

McArthur-Burney Falls Memorial State Park Day Use Area

Many people come to Burney Falls for the day, or to stop off and see the impressive cascades on their Northern California road trip. The Falls Overlook is also the launching point for many of the park's best hikes; across from it is this big group picnic area next to the visitor center and general store. It costs $10 to park for the day and gets quite busy in the summer months.

GETTING THERE

CAR

McArthur-Burney Falls Memorial State Park is on CA-89 about 10 mi (16 km) northeast of Burney; its entrance sign is right on the two-lane highway. The cities closest to Burney Falls are Redding and Mount Shasta, both about an hour away. From Redding, take CA-299 east to Burney and head north on CA-89 for 6 mi (10 km). To get there from Mount Shasta, take CA-89 south, aka the Volcanic Legacy Scenic Byway.

RUSSIAN GULCH STATE PARK

ADDRESS: 45051 Brest Rd., Mendocino

PHONE: 707/937-5804

WEBSITE: www.mendoparks.org

DAY USE HOURS: 6am–sunset

AREA: 1,162 acres (470 ha)

At the very western edge of Highway 1 where the Pacific Ocean waves crash against the jagged bluffs, Russian Gulch State Park is the farthest north of the three best Mendocino parks, just above Mendocino Headlands and Van Damme State Parks. This park is centered around where the Russian Gulch tributary meets the ocean, marked by the famous Frederick W. Panhorst Bridge. The bridge is part of CA-1 and looks similar to Big Sur's Bixby Bridge but is less crowded.

The Pomo people first inhabited Mendocino about 3,000 years ago, living in redwood bark houses; gathering and hunting food including seaweed, shellfish, game, and acorns; and collecting other natural materials to use and trade. Around 5,000 Pomo descendants still live in the area and uphold woven basketry tradition.

With its mile and a half (2.5 km) of sea frontage and 3 mi (5 km) of walkable lush canyon, the park's most popular activities are hiking and exploring sea caves. The Devil's Punchbowl is a must-visit, formed by crashing waves that left a 100-ft-wide, 60-ft-deep (30-m-wide, 18-m-deep) hole.

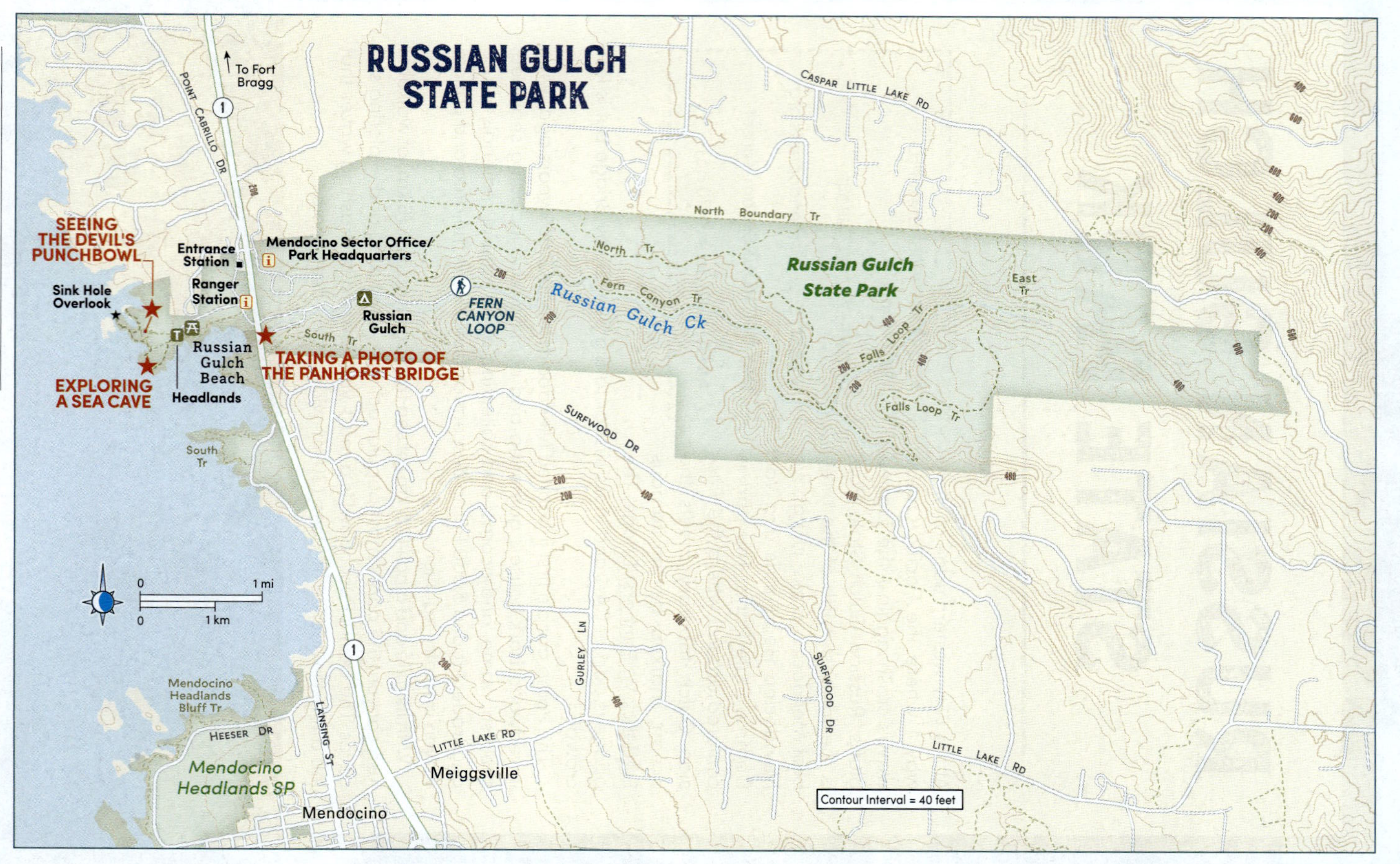
RUSSIAN GULCH STATE PARK
To Fort Bragg
POINT CABRILLO DR
CASPAR LITTLE LAKE RD
North Boundary Tr
North Tr
Russian Gulch State Park
East Tr
SEEING THE DEVIL'S PUNCHBOWL
Entrance Station
Mendocino Sector Office/ Park Headquarters
Ranger Station
Sink Hole Overlook
Russian Gulch
FERN CANYON LOOP
Fern Canyon Tr
Russian Gulch Ck
Falls Loop Tr
South Tr
Russian Gulch Beach
Headlands
TAKING A PHOTO OF THE PANHORST BRIDGE
EXPLORING A SEA CAVE
SURFWOOD DR
0
1 mi
0
1 km
GURLEY LN
Mendocino Headlands Bluff Tr
HEESER DR
LANSING ST
LITTLE LAKE RD
Meiggsville
Mendocino Headlands SP
Mendocino
Contour Interval = 40 feet

TOP 3

★ **1. TAKING A PHOTO OF THE PANHORST BRIDGE:** The striking 527-ft (160-m) bridge was named after photographer Frederick W. Panhorst (page 108).

★ **2. SEEING THE DEVIL'S PUNCHBOWL:** Russian Gulch is best known for its collapsed sea cave about 200 ft (61 m) away from the bluffs called Devil's Punchbowl (page 109).

★ **3. EXPLORING A SEA CAVE:** The best view of these seaside rock indentions is on the water from a kayak, but you can also get a nice view from the Headlands Trail (page 110).

PLANNING YOUR TIME

It's possible to see most of what Russian Gulch has to offer in a day. Walk the easy Headlands Trail in an hour to get the best views of Panhorst Bridge and Devil's Punchbowl, but if you have longer then hike up its Fern Canyon Trail as well to see its waterfall. Or if it's sunny, just lie on the sandy beach near the bridge all day.

Nearby state parks include Mendocino Headlands (3 mi/5 km) and Van Damme (5 mi/8 km).

ENTRANCE AND FEES

It costs $8 per car to visit Russian Gulch for the day, and the **one entrance** station is off CA-1 just north of the Panhorst Bridge.

Entrance Station

707/937-0497; 8am-6pm daily summer, 8am-4pm daily winter

The Russian Gulch State Park's entrance station kiosk is open year-round, but hours change depending on staffing. They try to stay open later on weekends in the summer.

VISITOR CENTER

Mendocino Sector Office/ Park Headquarters

707/937-5804; 8am-5pm Mon.-Fri.

The Mendocino Sector Office/Park Headquarters are at Russian Gulch just past the entrance station, but this is more for park workers and not a true visitor center. They do sell California State Parks passes, though.

WEATHER

Winter rain and summer fog keep Russian Gulch cool and temperate year-round, but when the fog burns off mid-morning in the summertime air temperatures can get up to 72°F (22°C). In the winter, temperatures average in the 40-56°F (4-13°C) range. The Pacific Ocean usually stays between 50-58°F (10-14°C), so abalone divers tend to wear a wetsuit or drysuit in the winter. Wear layers and waterproof clothing to be ready for anything. The best time to visit is in the summer (May-October) when the air temperature is the warmest.

SIGHTS

★ FREDERICK W. PANHORST BRIDGE

Also called the Panhorst Bridge and Russian Gulch Bridge, this open-spandrel deck arch bridge stretches 100 ft (30 m) over Russian Gulch Creek where the tributary meets the sea. It was named after Frederick W. Panhorst, who worked for the California Division of Highways from 1931-1960; it replaced the original wooden trestle bridge due to the advent of vehicles that weighed much more than a six-horse team. The best views of the bridge are from the Headlands Trail or looking up at it from the beach. A Russian Gulch Bridge Viewpoint Area is past the entrance station on Russian Gulch State Park Road before the Headlands trailhead.

★ DEVIL'S PUNCHBOWL

A must-see on your Russian Gulch trip is the Devil's Punchbowl, the product of a sea cave that collapsed a couple hundred feet away from the Pacific Ocean shoreline. The hammering waves created a tunnel and left a hole 100 ft (30 m) in diameter and 60 ft (18 m) deep. You can view it from the top of the rock accessible from the Headlands Trail; wooden fences around the sinkhole ensure you don't get too close to the edge. To get there, park at the lot on the end of Russian Gulch State Park Road and take the Headlands Trail.

BEACHES

RUSSIAN GULCH BEACH

Russian Gulch has a sandy beach right under the Panhorst Bridge where Russian Gulch Creek flows into a small bay. Scuba divers and paddlers explore the waters around here, and you can swim, but the water is cold. The rocks next to the shoreline can make for some good tide-pool exploring. To get to the beach, head southwest on Russian Gulch State Park Road from the entrance for 0.6 mi (1 km) and park in the paved lot near the base of the bridge.

view of the Panhorst Bridge from the beach at Russian Gulch

HIKING

About 15 mi (24 km) of trails run through Russian Gulch, which include easy coastal headlands hikes, beach walks, and waterfall-spotting through shady forest. The North Trail (hike-only) starts at the campground and connects to the Falls Loop Trail; the South Trail is a shorter route that runs south of Russian Gulch Creek and connects to the South Headlands Trail.

HEADLANDS TRAIL

DISTANCE: 0.75 mi (1.2 km) round-trip
DURATION: 10 minutes
EFFORT: Easy
TRAILHEAD: Parking lot at the end of Russian Gulch State Park Rd.

The mostly flat Headlands Trail runs along the craggy bluffs pretty much the entire coastal length of the park. There are parking areas at South Headlands Trail, near the ranger station at Panhorst Bridge, and in the northern peninsula part of the Headlands Trail. Thick green shrubbery and tall pines provide a nice contrast to the bright blue ocean. Views of sea caves and Devil's Punchbowl are along this trail as well.

FALLS LOOP TRAIL

DISTANCE: 3.8 mi (6.1 km) round-trip
DURATION: 2 hours
EFFORT: Moderate
TRAILHEAD: Horse Camp, Caspar-Little Lake Rd. (County Road 409)

Located in the eastern part of the park among dense forest, the sounds of trickling water, and chirping birds, the fastest way to get on the Falls Loop is via Russian Gulch's north boundary near the horse camp. From there you hike down to the North Trail and get on the Falls Loop Trail at the 36-ft (11-m) photo-worthy waterfall. This route takes about two hours to complete; you'll encounter lichen-covered trees, slick rocks, downed trees, fast-moving water, and slow-moving banana slugs.

To get to the trailhead from the main day use area, head northbound on CA-1 for 1.7 mi (2.7 km), then turn left at the first cross street, which is Caspar-Little Lake Road, following it 3.3 mi (5.3 km) to the park's northeastern boundary parking lot.

RECREATION

KAYAKING

People are welcome to launch their kayaks in the calm Russian Gulch cove by the beach and paddle along the coastline to peek in and around sea caves. More advanced kayakers who don't mind bigger swells tend to venture farther out of the protected cove to see additional arches and rock gardens. There are no kayak rentals at the park, but there's an outfitter in nearby Mendocino.

★ Sea Caves

Paddling along the Pacific Ocean coastline gives you the best vantage point of the sea caves. A few of them are right below the Headlands Trail. On the south side, you can even

DISTANCE: 5.1 mi (8.2 km) round-trip
DURATION: 2.5 hours
EFFORT: Moderate
TRAILHEAD: Russian Gulch Campground

The North Trail basically runs parallel to the multiuse (hiking and biking) Fern Canyon Trail, so you can make a loop by starting at the campground and walking east along the Fern Canyon Trail until it joins up with the **North Trail,** then taking that back. The Fern Canyon Trail runs right along Russian Gulch Creek until you reach the Falls Loop/North Trails intersection; you can combine this with the Falls Loop to make for a longer hike. Along with the incredible fern-filled forest, downed trees, babbling creek, and lush atmosphere, pink rhododendrons pop up in the springtime.

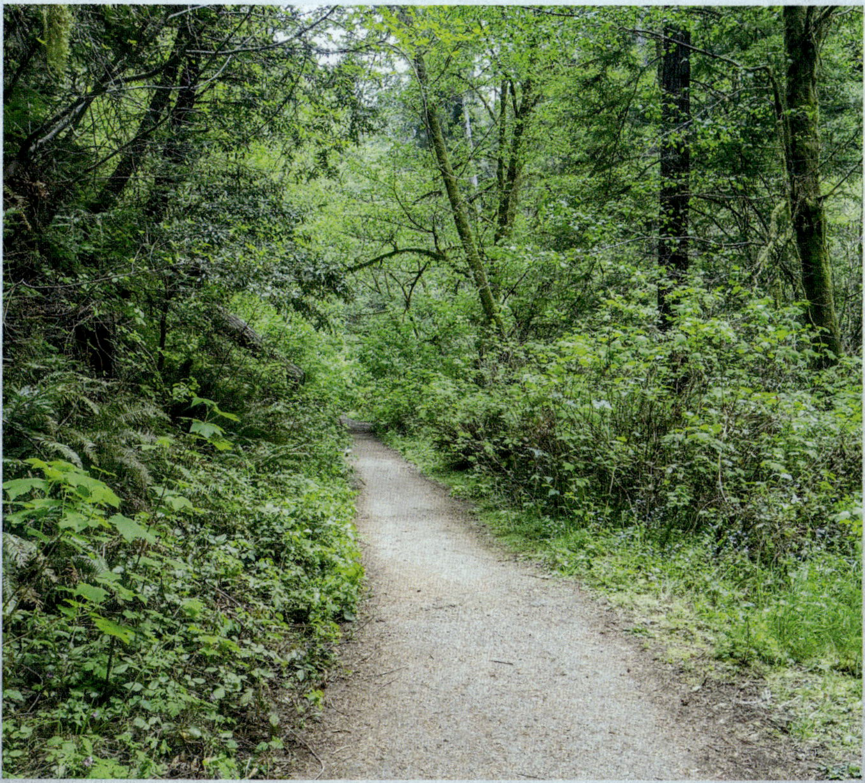

paddle through a grotto to get to Mendocino Bay.

DIVING

Russian Gulch is great for scuba diving due to its easy entry into a protected cove and the variety of sea anemones, nudibranchs, sea stars, and fish that hang out in the rocky reefs. Abalone fishing is also a popular activity along the Mendocino coast, but it must be done without scuba gear and following California Ocean Sport Fishing Regulations (https://wildlife.ca.gov). Abalone season is usually open April-June and August-November, but always check the California Fish and Wildlife website for current information.

CAMPING

Russian Gulch has **one campground** only open during summer, May-September. Reservations can be made up to six months in advance through Reserve California (800/444-7275; www.reservecalifornia.com; $40-45/night). Russian Gulch also has four horse camps (reservations 707/937-5804; $35/night) with corrals, fire rings, and a well in the northeastern part of the park off Caspar-Little Lake Road (County Road 409), and one group tent campsite ($140/night) with space for 9-40 people and up to 10 cars.

BEST CAMPGROUND

Russian Gulch Campground

The campground's 26 campsites are within a short walk of the beach, nicely spread out between the pines providing distance from your neighbors. Each site has a picnic table, fire ring, grill, and food locker; restrooms with flush toilets, tap water, and coin-operated showers are close by.

Russian Gulch Campground

FOOD AND LODGING

The town of **Mendocino** is the closest charming little coastal town, 3 mi (5 km) south of Russian Gulch. There is a market, café, and art center in the main downtown area; cottages and inns are within walking distance of Mendocino Headlands State Park. Wineries, distilleries, and cannabis dispensaries are also within its vicinity.

BEST PICNIC SPOT

North Headlands Trail Picnic Area

There are several places within the park to stop and have some snacks, but the most scenic, relaxing spot is in the picnic area off the North Headlands Trail. Picnic tables dot the wide-open grassland, with lichen-laden pines and magnificent views of the Panhorst Bridge and crashing ocean waves against the cliffs. Fire grills and a restroom are in this area, and the Devil's Punchbowl is a short walk away on a well-defined dirt path.

GETTING THERE

CAR

Russian Gulch is three hours away from the two major cities closest to it, Eureka and San Francisco. The closest town to Russian Gulch is Mendocino, 3 mi (5 km) south of the park. From Mendocino, take CA-1 northbound for 1.7 mi (2.7 km) and turn off north of the Panhorst Bridge onto Brest Road. It's another mile (1.6 km) to the entrance station.

VAN DAMME AND MENDOCINO HEADLANDS STATE PARKS

Jutting out over the Pacific Ocean, Mendocino Headlands State Park hugs the town of Mendocino. Just south, Van Damme State Park is made up of wetlands, beaches, coastal bluffs, redwoods, and even a pygmy forest.

At 347 acres (140 ha), Mendocino Headlands is the smaller of the two, best known for its interesting rock arches and historic Ford House, which is now a museum sharing the history of Mendocino and the Pomo people who lived here thousands of years before gold rush miners. It's also home to Portuguese Beach. Rectangular Van Damme and its trails follow the Little River to where it meets the ocean at Van Damme Beach.

The close proximity makes it easy to combine both parks into one visit. The fresh tributaries feeding into the ocean, abundance of plant life, sea cave exploring, headlands hikes, and camping opportunities make visiting these parks bucket list-worthy.

VAN DAMME STATE PARK

ADDRESS: 8001 N. CA-1, Mendocino

PHONE: 707/937-5804

WEBSITE: www.mendoparks.org

DAY USE HOURS: 6am-sunset

AREA: 1,831 acres (741 ha)

MENDOCINO HEADLANDS STATE PARK

ADDRESS: Lansing St., Mendocino

PHONE: 707/937-5804

WEBSITE: www.mendoparks.org

DAY USE HOURS: 6am-sunset

AREA: 347 acres (140 ha)

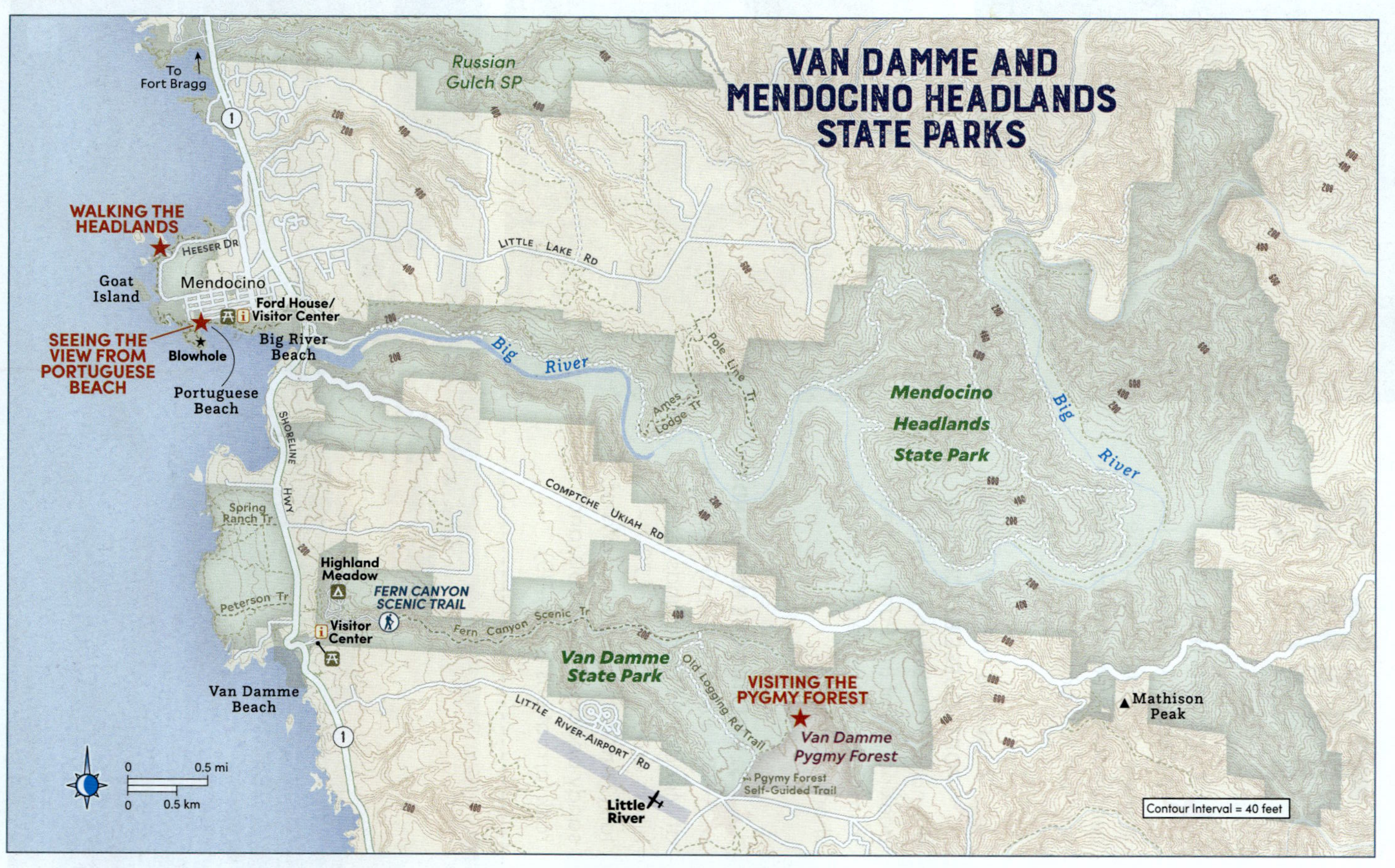
VAN DAMME AND MENDOCINO HEADLANDS STATE PARKS
To Fort Bragg
Russian Gulch SP
WALKING THE HEADLANDS
Heeser Dr
Goat Island
Mendocino
Ford House/ Visitor Center
SEEING THE VIEW FROM PORTUGUESE BEACH
Blowhole
Big River Beach
Portuguese Beach
Little Lake Rd
Big River
Pole Line Tr
Ames Lodge Tr
Mendocino Headlands State Park
Shoreline Hwy
Comptche Ukiah Rd
Spring Ranch Tr
Peterson Tr
Highland Meadow
FERN CANYON SCENIC TRAIL
Fern Canyon Scenic Tr
Visitor Center
Van Damme State Park
Old Logging Rd Trail
VISITING THE PYGMY FOREST
Van Damme Pygmy Forest
Pygmy Forest Self-Guided Trail
Van Damme Beach
Little River-Airport Rd
Little River
Mathison Peak
0.5 mi
0.5 km
Contour Interval = 40 feet

TOP 3

★ **1. VISITING THE PYGMY FOREST:** Walk the wooden boardwalk and marvel at the centenarian trees that are only a few feet tall (page 118).

★ **2. SEEING THE VIEW FROM PORTUGUESE BEACH:** View the natural rock arch formation peeking out of the Pacific Ocean from Portuguese Beach's sandy shores (page 119).

★ **3. WALKING THE HEADLANDS:** The 4.8-mi (7.7-km) Bluff Trail at Mendocino Headlands leads hikers around the top of 70-ft-tall (21-m-tall) cliffs with views of sandy beaches, tide pools, and rock formations (page 119).

1

2

3

PLANNING YOUR TIME

With so many activities to choose from, plan to spend at least two days exploring these parks.

Nearby state parks include Russian Gulch State Park (3 mi/5 km).

ENTRANCES AND FEES

Mendocino Headlands is free to enter, encompassing the unincorporated town of Mendocino along the headlands. The Van Damme State Park entrance station is right along CA-1 close to Van Damme Beach. The cost is $8 to visit that park for the day.

VISITOR CENTERS

Van Damme State Park Visitor Center

707/937-4016; www.mendoparks.org; 11am-2pm Thurs.-Sat. Memorial Day-Labor Day

Van Damme State Park has a log cabin-like visitor center originally built by the Civilian Conservation Corps in the 1930s to use as a recreation hall. Located between the Van Damme entrance station and its campground, the visitor center—complete with a stone chimney—has an underwater surge channel model, a mural of the original Pomo people, souvenirs, brochures, and more. A big grassy area with lots of picnic tables surrounds the visitor center.

Ford House/Visitor Center

45035 Main St., Mendocino; 707/937-5397; www.mendoparks.org; 11am-4pm daily

Sitting on the rugged Mendocino shoreline where Big River meets the ocean, the Ford House is both a museum and a visitor center containing brochures, travel information, souvenirs, seasonal displays, and permanent exhibits showing what Mendocino looked like in the 1800s. There are also china dishes used by Martha Ford, the first woman to live in this house from 1854-1872.

WEATHER

Since the parks are right next to each other, Van Damme and the Mendocino Headlands experience similar weather. Temperatures range from 40-50°F (4-10°C) in the winter months, getting up to 80-85°F (27-29°C) in July and August. Mendocino tends to get rain 11 months out of the year, with most of it falling December-February.

EVENTS

Mendocino Music Festival

45100 Main St., Mendocino; 707/937-2044; https://mendocinomusic.org

Every year, more than two dozen live concerts—featuring everything from bluegrass and jazz to symphonies, opera, and every kind of music in between—are held for two weeks in July right in the Mendocino Headlands. Tickets usually go on sale in early May, and the concerts are held in tents set up 100 ft (30 m) away from the Ford House.

SIGHTS

 PYGMY FOREST

The main draw of Van Damme State Park is hands-down the Pygmy Forest. This interesting patch of dwarfed trees was once part of the Pacific Ocean, but as the earth changed and evolved over time, the sea level receded and created a family of terraces. The five verandas there currently range from 100,000-500,000 years old, and a new one is being formed. However, the mixture of beach deposits, sand dunes, and greywacke sandstone isn't an ideal base for trees to grow, which is why the pygmies don't get very tall even though they can be 100 years old. An easy, well-built 0.2-mi (0.3-km) wooden boardwalk goes through the Pygmy Forest, making this an ideal hike for families.

MENDOCINO ARCH

Less than a mile (a 17-minute walk) away from the Ford House around the cliffs on the Mendocino Headlands Bluff Trail, a hole peeks through a cave-like rock formation, patiently excavated by the Pacific. This is one of the few naturally made grottos seen on the trail.

POINT MENDOCINO BLOWHOLE

Less than a half mile (0.8 km) away from the Ford House, there's a big blowhole on the south side of Point Mendocino. It's more accurately labeled a sinkhole, where the ocean caused a bit of the landmass to cave in. The resulting hole is marked by a fence going around it to keep people from falling in.

Van Damme Beach (left); Big River Beach (right)

BEACHES

Several beaches near and within Mendocino Headlands State Park are more accessible than others depending on the tides, and Van Damme has a beach near its campground. Since there can be big waves, sudden drop-offs, and riptides in these freezing cold waters, swimming is not advised.

VAN DAMME BEACH

The small sand and pebbly beach at the base of a quiet cove protected by rock outcroppings on either end makes for an ideal spot for kayakers and scuba divers to launch. Little River also joins up with the ocean at this beach, which provides an extended verdant plant community and home for certain fish species. Beachcombing and abalone diving are also popular here, when it's allowed.

BIG RIVER BEACH

Where the mouth of Big River meets the Pacific Ocean just south of the town of Mendocino, a big sandy beach within Mendocino Headlands State Park boundaries shares space with the estuary. This is a popular spot for kayakers, canoers, and stand-up paddleboarders due to its easy access.

★ PORTUGUESE BEACH

On the south side of Mendocino Headlands State Park near the Ford House, a trail with wooden steps down to this beach is accessible from the west side of Main Street. At high tide there isn't much room to lay out a towel, but you can see the Portuguese rock arch from here, and the town of Mendocino looks cool from below.

HIKING

SPRING RANCH TRAIL

DISTANCE: 2.6 mi (4.2 km) round-trip
DURATION: 1 hour
EFFORT: Easy
TRAILHEAD: Gordon Lane

According to the Mendocino Land Trust, the actual Spring Ranch Trail that follows the rugged coastal bluff on the northwestern end of the park is only 1.25 mi (2 km) long, but there are a couple of different ways to get to there from access points off CA-1. The out-and-back route from Gordon Lane suggests you park and walk 0.2 mi (0.3 km) to Spring Ranch where the bluff meets the ocean, walk along the south edge of the cliff to a point in about a half mile (0.8 km), then turn around and go back. During low tide, you may be able to spot sunbathing seals and interesting rock algae.

★ MENDOCINO HEADLANDS BLUFF TRAIL

DISTANCE: 4.8 mi (7.7 km) round-trip
DURATION: 1.5 hours
EFFORT: Easy
TRAILHEAD: Ford House/Visitor Center

Starting at the Ford House, this trail

view from Mendocino Headlands Bluff Trail

hugs the coastline from the top of the bluffs, going around the entire headland and town of Mendocino. On this easy, flat, hard-packed sand path, pass Portuguese Beach and the Point Mendocino blowhole; keep going to see various arches and rock formations off in the distance. The Mendocino Headlands Bluff Trail is about 2.5 mi (4 km) one-way from one side of the headlands to the other. Pretty wildflowers and the wooden staircase to Portuguese Beach are also off this trail.

RECREATION

KAYAKING

While abrupt jagged cliffs make up most of the Mendocino shoreline, **Van Damme Beach** has a nice, protected cove to launch a kayak and get a seaside perspective of the park. All the Mendocino state parks have sea caves, and some of these coastal rock enclaves are big enough to fit a kayak in. Paddling into the sea caves can make you feel like a character in *The Goonies* looking for a treasure of bright green algae and sea stars. There are a few kayak shops in Mendocino that give guided tours, and all ability levels are generally welcomed since the coves are protected.

Big River in Mendocino Headlands State Park is also a big enough estuary to kayak and canoe in. Launch your boat from the end of South Big River Road and paddle through the lazy river; perhaps a sea otter or seal will join you, too.

DIVING

Along with scuba diving within the nice mellow cove on the beach, a popular activity at Van Damme is abalone fishing, for which it is a point of entry. However, you have to free-dive for it (no scuba gear), are limited on the number you can catch, and can only get abalone in certain seasons (usually April-June and August-November). Always check the California Fish and Wildlife website for current updates and regulations.

WILDLIFE WATCHING

Marine Mammals

Scout for spouts at Mendocino state parks every March when the Mendocino coast celebrates the great gray whale migration with guided walks, live music, a gray whale exhibit at the Ford House/Visitor Center, and more. Docents lead guided walks to the best whale-watching outposts along the Mendocino Headlands Bluff Trail and Van Damme's Spring Ranch Trail, and give campfire talks spotlighting the magnificent marine mammals. Visit www.mendoparks.org for more information.

TOP HIKE

FERN CANYON SCENIC TRAIL

DISTANCE: 7.9 mi (12.7 km) round-trip
DURATION: 3 hours
EFFORT: Moderate
TRAILHEAD: Fern Canyon trailhead parking lot

Thick dense greenery including sword ferns, licorice ferns, and five-finger ferns soak up the rich moist soil under Douglas fir trees, redwoods, and myriad other pines and conifers along Little River. The Fern Canyon Scenic Trail follows the gurgling tributary where coho salmon run, meeting up with the Old Logging Road (created by oxen pulling timber) loop close to 3 mi (5 km) in. This trail was first cut to haul wood to the mouth of the river where early settler William H. Kent had his lumber mill. The lush atmosphere is punctuated by birdsong and babbling water flows. Most of this trail is accessible to wheelchair-users, but there are parts that can get muddy in the rainy months; 10 wooden bridges help hikers cross the forest floor. This loop also provides a connection to the Pygmy Forest.

CAMPING

There is **no camping** at Mendocino Headlands as it's just a day-use area, but Van Damme has **one campground** with 74 sites. It has mostly standard sites ($45/night), a hike-in/bike-in site ($10/night), and a group campsite ($160/night). The campground has drinking water, restrooms, and hot showers, and each site has a picnic table, food locker, and firepit.

Booking a reservation ahead of time is a must when traveling in the summer season and can be done through Reserve California (800/444-7575; www.reservecalifornia.com) two days up to six months in advance. Sites 1-13 can be reserved year-round, but others are available on a first-come, first-served basis in the off-season. A couple of the campsites accommodate trailers up to 35 ft (11 m) long, but there are no hookups available.

BEST CAMPGROUND

Highland Meadow Campground

The first 13 campsites (Little Loop) make up the sites closest to the entrance station and visitor center, and these sites can be reserved year-round. Sites 14-30 (Little River Spur) weave around Little River and provide the best access to the Fern Canyon Trail. The Upper Loop is known more for its sunshine and grassy meadow, and has most of the sites within the park—43 of them. Be careful choosing a site that goes up to the meadow; some of them are not level.

FOOD AND LODGING

If the campground is full or if you don't feel like pitching a tent, then there are a few inns and cottages to choose from close to Van Damme State Park and within Mendocino. There is a market and gas station in Little River to stock up on supplies and fuel, but Fort Bragg is 12 mi (19 km) north and much more populated with gas stations, grocers, and people.

BEST PICNIC SPOTS

Van Damme State Park Visitor Center

After grabbing some snacks at the Mendocino or Little River Market and driving to the park, you'll find a slew of picnic tables near the visitor center in Van Damme State Park. It's on the campground side, so you can get to the Fern Canyon Trail from here, or cross CA-1 and go to the beach. This is a good starting point for your Van Damme State Park adventure, and it costs $8 to park there for the day.

Ford House/Visitor Center

The picnic tables in the lush lawns around the Ford House at Mendocino Headlands State Park provide a nice spot to post up close to the ocean after walking the Headlands Bluff Trail or exploring other parts of Mendocino.

GETTING THERE

Mendocino Headlands State Park is right in the town of Mendocino, which is 10 mi (16 km) south of Fort Bragg and 36 mi (58 km) north of Point Arena on CA-1. Van Damme State Park is 3 mi (5 km) south of Mendocino Highlands in Little River, California.

CAR

To get to the Mendocino Headlands from San Francisco, take US-101 north for 83 mi (134 km, 1 hour 15 minutes) into Sonoma County, then take exit 522 onto CA-128. Drive northwest on CA-128 for 58 mi (93 km, 1 hour 15 minutes) where it connects with CA-1 at Navarro River. Mendocino Headlands State Park is 10 mi (16 km, 15 minutes) north of Albion on CA-1. In Mendocino, the park is a little over a mile (1.6 km) away to get to the north side of the Headlands. Turn left on Little Lake Road, right on Lansing Street, and left onto Heeser Drive to find parking.

To get to Van Damme State Park from the Mendocino Headlands, head northeast on Heeser Drive toward the Ford House for a half mile (0.8 km) and turn right onto Lansing Street. In another half mile (0.8 km), turn left onto Little Lake Road. Turn right onto CA-1 heading south, and Van Damme State Park is 2.5 mi (4 km) away.

TRAIN AND BUS

The **Mendocino Transit Authority** (https://mendocinotransit.org) runs buses from Fort Bragg all the way over to Willits, down to Santa Rosa, and up the coast along CA-1. Line 60/the purple route (also called "The Coaster") serves the Mendocino area from Fort Bragg to the Navarro River Junction on CA-1. There's a bus stop at Little River Market, about a mile (1.6 km) away from Van Damme State Park, and you can catch that to Main Street and Lansing, close to the Ford House in Mendocino Headlands State Park. It's about a 10-minute ride and costs $1.50-2.25 one-way.

The **Amtrak** (www.amtrak.com) railway system stops in Willits, and from there you can catch the Line 65/red route to Fort Bragg, then connect with Line 60/purple route down to Mendocino. It takes about 2 hours to get from Willits to Fort Bragg and then another 40 minutes to an hour to get to the town of Mendocino.

ARMSTRONG REDWOODS STATE NATURAL RESERVE

ADDRESS: 17000 Armstrong Woods Rd., Guerneville

PHONE: 707/869-2015

WEBSITE: https://stewardscr.org

DAY USE HOURS: 8am-one hour after sunset

AREA: 805 acres (326 ha)

An impressive grove of ancient redwoods resides in the 805-acre (326-ha) Armstrong Redwoods State Natural Reserve. More than 9 mi (14 km) of hiking and horseback trails are available for visitors, along with an outdoor theater space and nature store.

The Kashaya Pomo people were the original inhabitants of this area, who lived along the coast and the major tributary now called the Russian River. When Russian fur trappers came, the Kashaya Pomo worked for them doing agricultural labor. Descendants of the Kashaya Pomo are still around today and have a reservation in Sonoma County.

The reserve is named after Colonel James B. Armstrong, who was ironically a lumber baron. He appreciated both the commercial uses and beauty of redwoods. After he died, the redwood forest changed hands in his family a few times before coming under California State Parks management in 1934. The Colonel Armstrong Tree in the grove less than a mile away from the visitor center is named after him.

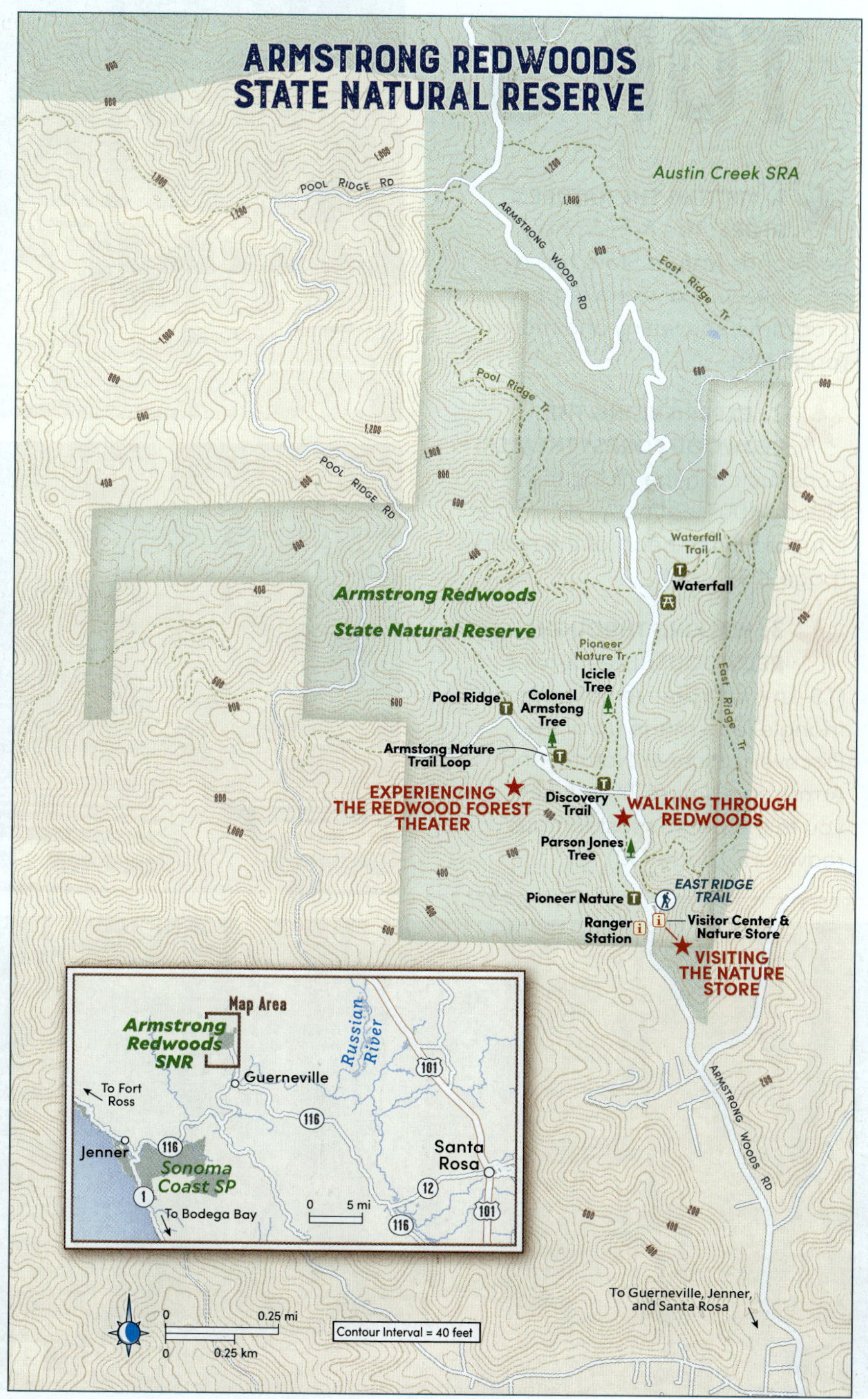
ARMSTRONG REDWOODS STATE NATURAL RESERVE
Austin Creek SRA
POOL RIDGE RD
ARMSTRONG WOODS RD
East Ridge Tr
Pool Ridge Tr
Armstrong Redwoods State Natural Reserve
Waterfall Trail
Waterfall
Pioneer Nature Tr
Icicle Tree
Pool Ridge
Colonel Armstong Tree
Armstong Nature Trail Loop
EXPERIENCING THE REDWOOD FOREST THEATER
Discovery Trail
WALKING THROUGH REDWOODS
Parson Jones Tree
Pioneer Nature
EAST RIDGE TRAIL
Ranger Station
Visitor Center & Nature Store
VISITING THE NATURE STORE
Map Area
Armstrong Redwoods SNR
Russian River
Guerneville
To Fort Ross
Jenner
Sonoma Coast SP
To Bodega Bay
Santa Rosa
0 5 mi
To Guerneville, Jenner, and Santa Rosa
0 0.25 mi
0 0.25 km
Contour Interval = 40 feet

TOP 3

1. VISITING THE NATURE STORE: The Armstrong Redwoods Nature Store has a nice collection of exhibits, park programs, souvenirs, and more (page 129).

2. EXPERIENCING THE REDWOOD FOREST THEATER: Constructed in the 1930s, the historic 400-seat open-air theater is tucked in the heart of the reserve (page 129).

3. WALKING THROUGH REDWOODS: The 1.2-mi (1.9-km) interpretive nature trail triangle loop made up of the Discovery, Pioneer Nature, and Armstrong Nature Trails takes you to the park's most famous redwoods (page 130).

PLANNING YOUR TIME

The main highlights of this reserve are focused within a mile (1.6 km) from the visitor center, making it easy to see it all in a half-day visit.

Nearby state parks include Sonoma Coast State Park (14 mi/23 km).

ENTRANCE AND FEES

There's **one entrance** on Armstrong Woods Road, 2 mi (3 km) up from CA-116 in Guerneville. Past the entrance, there's the visitor center, parking lot, and kiosk where you pay your daily parking fee of $10. Pedestrians and bicyclists can enter for free.

VISITOR CENTER

★ Armstrong Redwoods Visitor Center and Nature Store

707/869-2958; 11am-3pm daily

The Armstrong Redwoods Visitor Center and Nature Store is close to the entrance station and renowned redwood grove. The Nature Store includes historical and cultural interpretive displays, apparel, souvenirs, maps, information, and friendly docents. Find games, puzzles, and redwood forest "fog" globes. This is a must-visit before embarking on the redwood loop trail.

WEATHER

Being a mere half hour away from the ocean, Armstrong Redwoods gets that California coastal fog year-round that'll make you thankful you brought layers of clothing. In the summer, the fog usually burns off in the afternoon, and it warms up quite a bit. From May to October, the air temperatures can reach up to 85°F (29°C) in the dead of summer, but rarely drop below 50°F (10°C). The park gets an average of 7 in (18 cm) of rain in the winter months between December and February. The spring and autumn months are the best time to visit, when the temperatures are mild and there aren't as many people around.

SIGHTS

REDWOOD FOREST THEATER

Constructed in the 1930s, the historic Redwood Forest Theater is an open-air venue surrounded by the tall trees in the heart of the reserve. It is occasionally used for concerts, poetry slams, performances, and other events put on by the **Stewards of the Coast and Redwoods** (https://stewardscr.org) to raise funds to continue the park's stewardship, education, and conservation efforts.

HIKING

Armstrong Redwoods has 9.2 mi (14.8 km) of trails, two of which (the East Ridge and Pool Ridge Trails) flow into nearby Austin Creek State Recreation Area. Since temperatures fluctuate between the recreation area and natural reserve, bring lots of water and layered clothing.

★ ARMSTRONG REDWOODS GROVE LOOP

DISTANCE: 1.2 mi (2 km) round-trip
DURATION: 30 minutes
EFFORT: Easy
TRAILHEAD: Armstrong Redwoods Visitor Center

The ADA-accessible interpretive loop is the heart of Armstrong. Starting at the visitor center, the **Pioneer Nature Trail** brings you first to the **Parson Jones Tree,** 0.1 mi (0.2 km) away. Standing at 310 ft (94 m) tall, it's the tallest redwood in the park. If you continue up Pioneer Nature Trail, you'll eventually encounter **Icicle Tree,** which features a massive amount of redwood burls. Walk down the **Armstrong Nature Trail** to the next junction, where the 1,400-year-old namesake **Colonel Armstrong Tree** lives. There's also a tree-hugging platform on this loop. Continue on the **Discovery Trail** to complete the loop. This trail has interpretive signs in braille.

EAST RIDGE, WATERFALL, AND PIONEER TRAIL LOOP

DISTANCE: 2.3 mi (4.3 km) round-trip
DURATION: 1 hour 15 minutes
EFFORT: Moderate
TRAILHEAD: Armstrong Redwoods Visitor Center

As an alternative to hiking the full **East Ridge Trail,** you can start on the East Ridge Trail and turn off on the **Waterfall Trail** before reaching the Austin Creek State Recreation Area boundary line. In this loop, you'll pass Fife Creek, go through a picnic area, and pick up the **Pioneer Nature Trail** on the eastern side of the Armstrong Grove. Keep your eyes out for owls, and be sure to stop at Icicle Tree and look at its uncommonly big burls. As the "waterfall" in the name suggests, the trail meets Fife Creek Falls, where water flows over green-blanketed rocks into the main tributary.

Colonel Armstrong Tree (left); Icicle Tree (right)

TOP HIKE

EAST RIDGE TRAIL

DISTANCE: 3.1 mi (5 km) round-trip
DURATION: 2 hours
EFFORT: Strenuous
TRAILHEAD: Armstrong Redwoods Visitor Center

The out-and-back East Ridge Trail hugs the eastern side of the reserve. It starts at the visitor center and climbs 0.7 mi (1.1 km) up to the MacMahon Fire Road/Austin Creek State Recreational Area boundary, continuing another 1.6 mi (2.6 km) to the McCray Ridge Fire Road near the Bullfrog Pond Campground. Tall trees, gorgeous mountain vistas, grassy meadows, and moss green-covered stumps mark the trail.

FOOD AND LODGING

While Armstrong Redwoods is only a day use area and therefore has **no camping,** the natural reserve is right next to the Austin Creek State Recreation Area with a 23-site campground. Just 2 mi (3 km) south of the park, the town of Guerneville has hotels, inns, and other campgrounds to accommodate those staying overnight. Founded in the 1850s by the Guerne family, its cute little main street has a smattering of shops set against a forest background. The Russian River is also nearby.

BEST PICNIC SPOT

Near Fife Creek

Nine picnic tables, a large barbecue pit, and three grills are available to post up at 0.75 mi (1.2 km) north of the entrance station on Armstrong Woods Road. Restrooms and a parking lot ($10/vehicle) make picnicking here most convenient.

GETTING THERE

CAR

The nearby town of Guerneville is 2 mi (3 km) south of Armstrong Redwoods, intersecting with CA-116 crossing east to west in the heart of Guerneville.

The quickest way to reach the reserve from Santa Rosa, 22 mi (35 km) southeast, is to take US-101 north/River Road up through Fulton to Guerneville, and then follow Rio Nido Road to Armstrong Woods Road for the remaining 2 mi (3 km). Alternatively, travel west on Occidental Road to CA-116 and then north through Graton to Guerneville.

SONOMA COAST STATE PARK

Sweeping cliffs, thriving tide pools, vibrant wildflowers, sandy beaches, and the steady rise and fall of the ocean are just a few of the splendors this California seaside landscape holds. Making up 17 mi (27 km) of shoreline spanning from Jenner to Bodega Bay, the Sonoma Coast highlights the best of California's craggy headlands, distinct beaches, and coves.

ADDRESS: 10439 CA-1, Jenner

PHONE: 707/875-3483

WEBSITE: https://stewardscr.org

DAY USE HOURS: 8am-sunset generally

AREA: 9,619 acres (3,893 ha)

Long ago, the Coast Miwok and Pomo people inhabited the area, fishing, hunting, and gathering on the California coast's fertile lands. This became an official state park in 1938, and descendants of the Indigenous people from all over the Northern California area still come here to keep their traditions alive today.

Succulent- and flower-filled grassy headlands trails go along the cliff line to treat hikers and sightseers to the maximum number of vantage points for gray whale and bird-watching, especially at Bodega Head. From spying sunbathing harbor seals at Goat Rock Beach to playing in the sand at Wright's Beach, there's so much to see and do here, it's hard to figure out where to start.

SONOMA COAST STATE PARK
Guerneville
RIVER RD
116
1
Sonoma Coast State Park
COAST HWY
WATCHING FOR HARBOR SEALS AT GOAT ROCK
Jenner
Jenner Visitor Center
Goat Rock Beach
116
Willow Creek Environmental
RIVER RD
Blind Beach
Kortum Tr
Sonoma Coast State Park
1
Red Hill Tr
TIDE-POOLING AT SHELL BEACH
Pomo Canyon
Pomo Canyon Environmental
Shell Beach
Kortum Trail
Wright's Beach
Wright's Beach
Duncan's Landing
Duncan's Landing
Gleason Beach
Portuguese Beach
COAST HWY
Schoolhouse Beach
Carmet Beach
Arched Rock Beach
Marshall Gulch
Coleman Beach
Miwok Beach
North Salmon Creek Beach
Salmon Creek Ranger Office
BEACHCOMBING AT SOUTH SALMON CREEK BEACH
Bodega Dunes
Bodega Dunes
Bodega Bay
1
Sonoma Coast State Park
Bodega Harbor
PACIFIC OCEAN
BODEGA HEAD TRAIL
0
2 mi
0
2 km
Contour Interval = 200 feet

TOP 3

★ **1. BEACHCOMBING AT SOUTH SALMON CREEK BEACH:** Sonoma has miles of sandy coastline and dramatic bluffs to explore, but the wide stretch of sand at South Salmon Creek Beach behind the Bodega Dunes Campground is ideal for surfing and finding cool pieces of driftwood (page 137).

★ **2. WATCHING FOR HARBOR SEALS AT GOAT ROCK:** Hundreds of these big blubbery mammals can be seen sunbathing on the shore, especially during birthing season (page 139).

★ **3. TIDE-POOLING AT SHELL BEACH:** When the tide is up, find crabs, sea anemones, and small fish hanging out in the crevices (page 140).

2

PLANNING YOUR TIME

CA-1 runs the length of the park, from Jenner to Bodega Bay, and from there you can pick up all the viewpoint access roads. Plan on spending a full day at minimum to hop between Sonoma Coast's premier spots. From south to north, you can hike Bodega Head, drive to Duncan's Landing, go tide-pooling at Shell Beach, stop at the Jenner Visitor Center, and watch seals bask on Goat Rock Beach all in one day. Two main campgrounds close to the water are near the south end—Wright's Beach and Bodega Dunes.

Nearby state parks include Armstrong Redwoods State Natural Reserve (14 mi/23 mi).

ENTRANCES AND FEES

Sonoma Coast State Park has four campgrounds and **eight day use areas** that are mostly accessible off CA-1. The day use fee is $10 per vehicle per day. The **two entrance stations** are at Bodega Dunes and Wright's Beach Campgrounds.

VISITOR CENTER

Jenner Visitor Center

10439 CA-1, Jenner; 707/865-9757; 11am-3pm daily

The Jenner Visitor Center is right in the heart of the town of Jenner on the Russian River inlet, along CA-1. Staffed by **Stewards of the Coast and Redwoods** (https://stewardscr.org) volunteers, the center is open every day year-round from 11am-3pm. The shop/info center has interpretive displays, fun souvenirs (like the world's smallest crayon set, ideal for nature journaling), maps, and brochures of other things to do in the area.

WEATHER

It's common to experience a cold wind stream coming off the Pacific Ocean onto the headlands, and that combined with the rolling fog will make you want to pack plenty of layers. In the summer when the sun comes out, the fog tends to burn off midday, creating a clear and temperate environment, but even then, you'll want to be prepared for rain,

Shell Beach (left); South Salmon Creek Beach (right)

wind, or fog. Temperatures usually range from 45-60°F (7-16°C) in the winter and never get up past 72°F (22°C) in the summer. Springtime is the best for bird-watching, vibrant plant blooms, whale watching, and harbor seal birthing season.

BEACHES

So many beaches and cliffside overlooks are encapsulated in this state park. From south to north, these are some of the best.

★ SOUTH SALMON CREEK BEACH

South Salmon Creek Beach has 2 mi (3 km) of sandy shores ripe for beachcombing, surf-fishing, and sunbathing. Dogs, fires, and horses aren't allowed on the beach to help protect the endangered snowy plover. Sometimes seals and birds hang out where Salmon Creek meets the ocean. Salmon Creek Beach is right off CA-1, 1.5 mi (2.5 km) north of the Bodega Dunes Campground.

PORTUGUESE BEACH

About 2 mi (3 km) north of Salmon Creek Beach on CA-1, Portuguese Beach is another wide crescent-shaped stretch of sand splitting the ocean from the succulent-covered bluffs. Fishing, picnicking, and kite-flying are popular activities, but be careful of the water—while it looks inviting to swim in, it's cold, and the shelf drops about 5 ft (1.5 m) out where the sea can then capture you in an undertow. It's best to always stay on shore.

DUNCAN'S LANDING OVERLOOK

Another 1.5 mi (2.5 km) north of Portuguese Beach is Duncan's Landing. While it is more an overlook than a beach, it is a nice place to stop, stretch your legs, and watch the ocean below. On the road to the peninsula (Duncan's Landing Overlook Road off CA-1), the ocean waves occasionally crash against a big rock right on the edge of the bluff, creating a dramatic picturesque spray that comes close to the roadway.

HIKING

While many people come for the beaches, Sonoma Coast State Park also has 19 mi (31 km) of trails, mostly along the rugged cliffs overlooking the water. From Russian Gulch to Bodega Head, hiking trails connect to picnic areas, campgrounds, vista points, and more. There are also 5 mi (8 mi) of trails available to horseback riders in the Bodega Dunes area.

KORTUM TRAIL

DISTANCE: 8.8 mi (14.1 km) round-trip
DURATION: 3.5 hours
EFFORT: Moderate
TRAILHEAD: Goat Rock

The Kortum Trail is a single-track hard-packed sandy path carved out through thickly carpeted plant life, meandering along bluffs and oceanside meadows. It runs a good

TOP HIKE

BODEGA HEAD TRAIL

DISTANCE: 1.6 mi (2.6 km) round-trip
DURATION: 40 minutes
EFFORT: Easy
TRAILHEAD: End of Westshore Rd.

Bodega Head is a 4-mi-long (6-km-long) peninsula at the very bottom of Sonoma Coast State Park, famous for protecting the rest of Bodega Bay from the open sea while also providing ideal habitat for thousands of seabirds. An easy 1.6-mi (2.6-km) looped trail goes around the Head, giving visitors 360-degree views of the Pacific Ocean, the town of Bodega Bay, and more. It's a great place to view the sunset, watch for gray whales, or have a picnic. Parking here is free, but it can get crowded in the summer.

chunk of the park's coastline, from Goat Rock to Wright's Beach. You can extend your trek to include Goat Rock Beach (at the south end of the Russian River) on the north end of the park and go past Wright's Beach, walking another 0.3 mi (0.5 km) to Duncan's Landing. You can also park at Shell Beach to jump on the Kortum Trail.

RED HILL-POMO CANYON TRAIL LOOP

DISTANCE: 5 mi (8 km) round-trip
DURATION: 2.5 hours
EFFORT: Moderate
TRAILHEAD: Pomo Canyon Campground, Willow Creek Rd.

This trail loop gives the most sweeping bird's-eye views of the Sonoma coastline, guiding hikers from the Pomo Canyon environmental campground through Red Hill down to where CA-1 meets Shell Beach. Grasslands, meandering rivers, coastal fog, and bushy shrubbery can be found along the Red Hill ancient Indigenous trade loop, which makes up a good portion of the hike. The Red Hill loop is a little over 2 mi (3 km) long, which is about a half mile (0.8 km) away from the Pomo Canyon Trail on either end. It goes along grassy hills, through redwood groves, and past the 1,040-ft (317-m) Red Hill before ending at the rocky ridge overlooking the Pacific Ocean.

To drive to the Pomo Canyon trailhead from Shell Beach, go north on CA-1 for 1.5 mi (2.5 km) and then turn right onto Willow Creek Road in Bridgehaven. Follow that road for another 1.5 mi (2.5 km) to reach the Pomo Canyon environmental campground.

RECREATION

WILDLIFE WATCHING

★ Marine Mammals

Near the northern end of the park across from the Russian River estuary and Jenner Visitor Center, **Goat Rock Beach** is where harbor seals tend to hang out. Harbor seals always go back to the same beaches where they were born to start families of their own, and it seems a lot of harbor seals hailed from Goat Rock Beach. You can see hundreds of them from Jenner during pupping season March-May. For everyone's safety, stay at least 50 yards (45 m) away. While harbor seals look cute and innocent, they will attack you if you threaten them, especially when they have little ones nearby. Newborn seal pups can't swim for up to three months, and so these blubbery sea mammals hang out and sunbathe while their moms feed within eyesight.

The southern part of Sonoma Coast State Park at **Bodega Head** is the best place to see migrating whales. Gray and blue whales will cross this section of waters mostly between January and May. The gigantic gray whales are easier to spot because they stir up the ocean floor close to the continental shelf to eat shrimp and other bottom dwellers, while blue whales like colder, deeper waters.

★ Tide Pools

South of Goat Rock is **Shell Beach,** a popular spot for tide-pooling. Find mussel-covered rocks and interesting invertebrates such as sea anemones, starfish, and hermit crabs hanging out in their saltwater abodes. In recent years, *Velella velellas* (also known as fly-by-the-sea sailors) have been washing up on shore. Only climb around the rocks when the tide is low, watch out for sneaker waves, wear good anti-slip shoes, and look at—don't touch—the sea animals. To get to Shell Beach, take CA-1 to Pacific View Drive and go to the end.

CAMPING

There are **four campgrounds** within state park boundaries, two that are open year-round: Wright's Beach and Bodega Dunes ($45/night). They can be reserved ahead of time through Reserve California (800/444-7575; www.reservecalifornia.com) two days to six months in advance; any open spots will be available on a first-come, first-served basis to campers who are on-site within that 48-hour window. Reservations are highly recommended for the summer season, weekends, and holidays.

Pomo Canyon and Willow Creek ($25/night) environmental campgrounds are available on a first-come, first-served basis and are subject to weather-related closures. Neither of them is on the reservation system, but you can call 707/875-3483 to gauge availability.

BEST CAMPGROUNDS

Wright's Beach Campground

Above Duncan's Landing in the middle of the park, Wright's Beach Campground ($45/night) has 27 developed sites near its sandy shoreline. Trailers up to 27 ft (8 m) long can camp here, but hookups are not available. Showers or potable water aren't available either—the closest refill stations and coin-operated hot showers are at Bodega Dunes Campground south of Wright's Beach. Every site has a fire ring,

Bodega Head (left); Bodega Dunes Campground (right)

picnic table, and paved parking pad. Any vehicles that don't fit in the campsite parking spurs can use the overflow parking area nearby. Sonoma Coast State Park charges $10 more for "premium" sites 1-10 closest to Wright's Beach.

Bodega Dunes Campground

About 5 mi (8 km) south and eight beaches later, Bodega Dunes Campground has 100 campsites on its grounds. Bodega Dunes has the most amenities and is north of Bodega Harbor, about a 20-minute walk to South Salmon Beach. This campground has restrooms, hot showers, a campfire center, potable water, and an RV sanitation station available among its sandy hills. All sites have picnic tables and fire rings.

There's also a **hike-in/bike-in** camping area between sites 82 and 83 in Bodega Dunes. The communal site has a fire ring, picnic table, and food locker for all no-vehicle-attached campers to use. It costs $10 per night to stay here, for a maximum of two nights.

FOOD AND LODGING

The closest town to Sonoma Coast State Park is **Jenner,** which has a few inns, a café, a wine bar, a gas station, and a smattering of homes right there next to the state park's northern boundary. However, most people couple their Sonoma Coast State Park trip with a visit to **Bodega Bay,** which is right across from Bodega Head in the southernmost part of the park. Several upscale lodges, grocery stores, vineyards, and shops are in Bodega Bay, along with another gas station.

BEST PICNIC SPOT

Duncan's Landing

In the middle of the park close to Wright's Beach, Duncan's Landing is down a lollipop-shaped paved road off CA-1. It circles around a small, rugged peninsula, featuring a parking lot, picnic tables, natural green carpet coverings, and ample bird-, whale-, and sunset-watching opportunities. The only downside is there are no restrooms here.

GETTING THERE

CAR

Sonoma Coast State Park is about 2 hours (68 mi/109 km) north of San Francisco on US-101 or CA-1, both of which follow the Pacific Ocean coastline closely. There are many entrances into the park from Jenner to Bodega Bay. Santa Rosa is the closest city to the park; it's 24 mi (39 km) east of it via CA-12.

MOUNT TAMALPAIS STATE PARK

Mount Tamalpais State Park, named after the Coast Miwok language *támal pájis,* meaning "west hill," is rich in hiking, amazing views, wildlife, wildflowers, and picnic spots. Flanked by Golden Gate National Recreation Area and Stinson Beach, this state park surrounds the Muir Woods National Monument. As one of the oldest parks in the state park system, Mount Tamalpais (or "Mount Tam," as locals call it) has 6,300 acres (2,550 ha) of hiking trails, redwoods, and 750 kinds of plants.

ADDRESS: 3801 Panoramic Hwy., Mill Valley

PHONE: 415/388-2070

WEBSITE: www.friendsofmttam.org

DAY USE HOURS: 7am-sunset

AREA: 6,300 acres (2,550 ha)

Before Mount Tamalpais officially became a state park in 1928, native Coast Miwok communities lived here, using redwood bark to make cone-shaped shelters. The Tamalpais name was first recorded in 1845 and the name stuck. . . along with the legend of "The Sleeping Lady."

Visitors—many of them avid hikers and birders—come to Mount Tamalpais from all over the world to enjoy the sweeping vistas, flora, and fauna of the Bay Area.

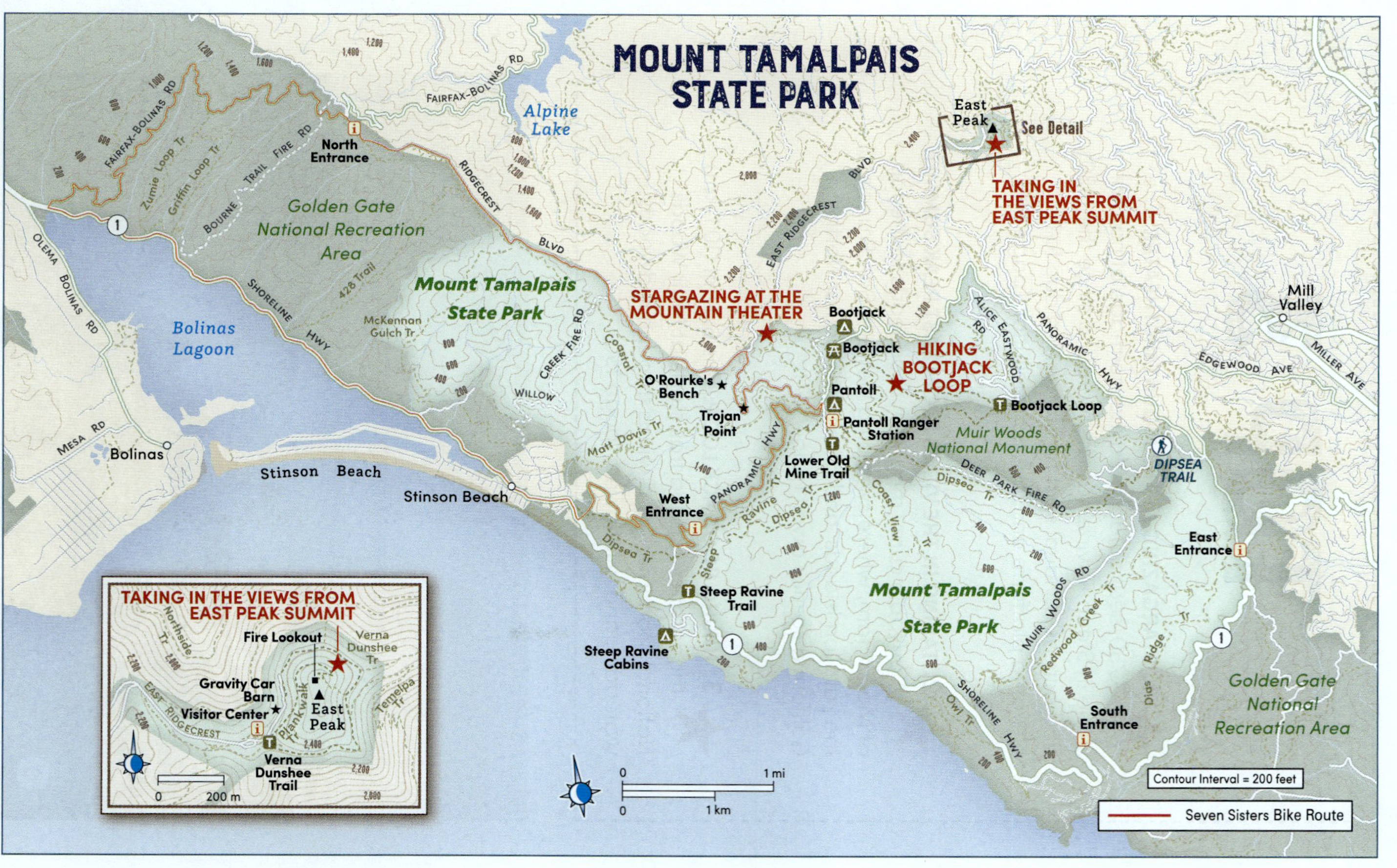

MOUNT TAMALPAIS STATE PARK
East Peak
See Detail
TAKING IN THE VIEWS FROM EAST PEAK SUMMIT
Alpine Lake
FAIRFAX-BOLINAS RD
RIDGECREST BLVD
EAST RIDGECREST BLVD
North Entrance
Zumie Loop Tr
Griffin Loop Tr
BOURNE TRAIL FIRE RD
Golden Gate National Recreation Area
428 Trail
OLEMA BOLINAS RD
SHORELINE HWY
Bolinas Lagoon
Mount Tamalpais State Park
McKennan Gulch Tr
WILLOW CREEK FIRE RD
Coastal Tr
STARGAZING AT THE MOUNTAIN THEATER
Bootjack
HIKING BOOTJACK LOOP
O'Rourke's Bench
Trojan Point
Pantoll
Pantoll Ranger Station
Bootjack Loop
Muir Woods National Monument
ALICE EASTWOOD RD
PANORAMIC HWY
Mill Valley
EDGEWOOD AVE
MILLER AVE
Matt Davis Tr
Lower Old Mine Trail
DIPSEA TRAIL
DEER PARK FIRE RD
Dipsea Tr
Coast View Tr
Ravine Tr
Steep Ravine Trail
West Entrance
East Entrance
MESA RD
Bolinas
Stinson Beach
Steep Ravine Cabins
MUIR WOODS RD
Redwood Creek Tr
Dias Ridge Tr
Owl Tr
South Entrance
TAKING IN THE VIEWS FROM EAST PEAK SUMMIT
Northside Tr
Fire Lookout
Verna Dunshee Tr
Gravity Car Barn
Visitor Center
Plankwalk
East Peak
Temelpa Tr
EAST RIDGECREST
Verna Dunshee Trail
0 200 m
0 1 mi
0 1 km
Contour Interval = 200 feet
Seven Sisters Bike Route

TOP 3

★ **1. STARGAZING AT THE MOUNTAIN THEATER:** The 3,750-seat outdoor playhouse made of natural stone in Steep Ravine has been around since the 1930s and acts as an ideal spot for stargazing due to its elevated platform and low light pollution (page 146).

★ **2. TAKING IN THE VIEWS FROM EAST PEAK SUMMIT:** A drivable curvy mountain road leads to the top of Mount Tam, where sweeping views of San Francisco, the Farallon Islands, and other spectacular Northern California scenes await (page 147).

★ **3. HIKING BOOTJACK LOOP:** This 6.3-mi (10.1-km) moderately graded trail starts at Muir Woods National Monument and winds through redwoods, waterfalls, and wildflowers (page 150).

PLANNING YOUR TIME

Mount Tamalpais is open year-round, appealing to birders, sightseers, and outdoorspeople. If you're really into hiking, it's best to try to spend a couple of days at the park and pitch a tent at either Bootjack or Pantoll Campgrounds to be the closest you can to the trails. Due to its proximity to San Francisco, it's a popular spot for a day trip to escape the city and take in the serene above-the-fog views from Mount Tam's East Peak or find solitude on one of its redwoods hikes. You'll get a good sense of what the park has to offer in one solid day.

Nearby state parks include Angel Island State Park (9 mi/14 km), Half Moon Bay State Beach (36 mi/58 km), and Sonoma Coast State Park (60 mi/97 km).

ENTRANCES AND FEES

Mount Tamalpais has **five entrances.** The northern entrance is by Audubon Canyon Ranch on West Ridgecrest Boulevard; the south entrance is next to Golden Gate National Park on Muir Woods Road; the east entrance is off CA-1; the west entrance is next to Stinson Beach on the Panoramic Highway; and there's an entrance on the Panoramic Highway close to Pantoll going up to East Peak (Pantoll Road to East Ridgecrest Boulevard). This state park doesn't charge an entrance fee, but the Pantoll, Bootjack, and East Peak parking areas do cost $8/vehicle. Bootjack and East Peak day use areas have picnic tables, firepits, and restrooms.

VISITOR CENTERS

Mount Tamalpais Visitor Center

Top of East Ridgecrest Blvd./Old Railroad Grade Trail; 415/258-2410; noon-4pm Sat.-Sun.

The visitor center at the top of Mount Tam's East Peak has books, maps, souvenirs, and more, along with free panoramic views of the Bay Area. The old Gravity Car Barn is up there, too. Sitting at a 2,571-ft (4,138-m) elevation, this visitor center is only staffed on the weekends.

Pantoll Ranger Station

801 Panoramic Hwy., Mill Valley; 415/388-2070; call for hours

The Pantoll Ranger Station in the middle of the park is next to the campground and has maps of hiking trails and information for visitors.

WEATHER

San Francisco's climate has been called "Mediterranean with cool summers," making Mount Tamalpais State Park comfortable year-round. Temperatures in the summer may top 75°F (50°C), while spring and fall temperatures stay around 50-70°F (10-21°C). The Bay Area fog rolls in often, keeping the area moist and chilly (especially in summer during the month of "Fogust") and possibly obscuring your views. The winter and springtime months are the best time to see Mount Tam's cascading waterfalls.

ONE DAY IN MOUNT TAMALPAIS STATE PARK

MORNING

Coming in from the East Entrance, drive up the Panoramic Highway to East Peak; it should take about 45 minutes to get to the Mount Tamalpais Visitor Center. Stop by the Mountain Theater on the way.

AFTERNOON

After hiking around East Peak, stop and have a picnic at Rock Spring, where Ridgecrest Boulevard intersects with Pantoll Road. Then take Pantoll Road down to the ranger station, where many of the park's most famous trails converge. Drive west on the Panoramic Highway to end your day at Stinson Beach.

SIGHTS

★ MOUNTAIN THEATER

The 3,750-seat outdoor playhouse made of natural stone in Steep Ravine has been around since the 1930s and acts as an ideal spot for stargazing due to its elevated platform and low light pollution. The Mt. Tam Astronomy Program (www.mttamastronomy.org) hosts free astronomy nights at the Mountain Theater—also called the Cushing Memorial Amphitheatre—where guides help attendees interpret the night sky and provide telescopes for viewing. The Mountain Play Association (www.mountainplay.org) also hosts live theater events there.

view from East Peak Summit (left); Mountain Theater (right)

★ EAST PEAK SUMMIT

Many people go to Mount Tam to see the incredible sights from its peak, and the easy, short Verna Dunshee Trail is at the tip-top of Mount Tamalpais, offering 360-degree views from Mount Diablo to Mount Saint Helena on a clear day. Sitting at a 2,571-ft (4,138-m) elevation, East Peak tends to be above the fog line, making you feel like you're floating above the clouds. The 1.3-mi (2-km) Verna Dunshee Trail, starting at the visitor center, circles the peak.

Gravity Car Barn

In the early 1920s, Marinites built the Mount Tamalpais Scenic Railway, deemed the "Crookedest Railroad in the World." The 2,200-ft (670-m) climb took an hour to get from Mill Valley to the top of Mount Tamalpais, going 10 mph (16 kph). The railway shut down after a fire in 1929, and the advent of automobiles made the Mount Tamalpais Scenic Railway obsolete. The Gravity Car Barn still stands today at East Peak behind the visitor center, open on weekends.

O'ROURKE'S BENCH

Called the "Vista of San Francisco," O'Rourke's Bench is accessible off a trail that starts close to where West Ridgecrest Boulevard meets Pantoll Road. It's a short walk from the Rock Spring parking lot, leading 0.3 mi (0.5 km) and climbing a mild 70 ft (21 m) to a stone sitting spot. Once you're there, you'll find its 2,040-ft (622-m) altitude stretches over the sparkling Pacific Ocean.

TROJAN POINT

A short walk from a parking pull-out on Pantoll Road, Trojan Point is another vista point making you feel like you're on top of the world. This grassy hill is on the western side of the park, and likely one of the most photographed places at Mount Tam. To get there, take the Panoramic Highway to Pantoll Road; the 0.3-mi (0.5-km) walk with a 30-ft (9-m) elevation gain leads to grassy meadows—bright green in the winter and golden yellow in the summer—overlooking the expansive ocean and bay.

HIKING

Mount Tamalpais has more than 60 mi (97 km) of trails within the park, many that intersect with the 200-mi (322-km) single-track trail system spanning the land also managed by the Marin Municipal Water District, National Park System, and Golden Gate National Recreation Area. Conservationists and avid trail-seekers have spent nearly a century building out these trails to show off the best of the area's views, features, flora, and fauna.

STEEP RAVINE TRAIL

DISTANCE: 4 mi (6.4 km) round-trip
DURATION: 2-3 hours
EFFORT: Moderate
TRAILHEAD: Pantoll Campground or CA-1 near Stinson Beach

As one of Mount Tam's most visited trails, Steep Ravine is exactly how it sounds—a moderately challenging ravine filled with ferns, fallen trees, tall stands of redwoods, and waterfalls running into Webb Creek. The out-and-back trail has lots of stairs and a steep wooden ladder that

TOP HIKE
DIPSEA TRAIL

DISTANCE: 9.7 mi (15.6 km) round-trip
DURATION: 6-7 hours
EFFORT: Strenuous
TRAILHEAD: Stinson Beach or Muir Woods Visitor Center

The famous Dipsea Trail isn't for the faint of heart, but it is perfect for those who want a challenging workout with lots of different terrain to hike or run through. This out-and-back trail starts at Stinson Beach, climbs over Mount Tamalpais, and ends at Muir Woods. You can do it in reverse, but then you'd have to pay parking fees at Muir Woods. This famous trail has redwoods, wooden bridge stream crossings, moss-covered rocks, views of the Pacific Ocean, luscious ferns, and a 680-stone-step staircase. The Dipsea Race is held the second Sunday in June and is the oldest trail race in America—the first one was held in 1905.

connects the trail along a waterfall, so wear good slip-resistant shoes. For more of a workout, start at Stinson Beach and ascend up the mountain several thousand feet—doing it in reverse means you'll be going mostly downhill.

VERNA DUNSHEE AND PLANKWALK TRAILS

DISTANCE: 1.3 mi (2 km) round-trip
DURATION: 40 minutes
EFFORT: Moderate
TRAILHEAD: East Ridgecrest Blvd. parking lot

This double-looped route is up on Mount Tam's East Peak, where the best panoramic views of the Bay Area await. This two-trail combination starts at the East Peak parking lot/visitor center at the Verna Dunshee Trail outer loop. The paved path (along with gravel, dirt, and leaf-covered sections) has a viewing platform, wooden boardwalks, and metal railings going around the mountain. The inner-loop Plankwalk Trail starts out with a moderately steep ascent atop nicely laid wooden planks, but then turns into a rocky, narrow dirt path leading up to the fire lookout station. The East Peak area and its trails are open year-round, all the time, but it can be spooky when the area is socked in fog, so take it slow and steady.

LOWER OLD MINE TRAIL

DISTANCE: 2.2 mi (3.5 km) round-trip
DURATION: 1 hour 15 minutes
EFFORT: Moderate
TRAILHEAD: Pantoll Ranger Station

Grassy meadows, rolling hills, forested areas, and a commanding ocean view make this a good place to watch the sunset. A 0.4-mi (0.6-km) part of this trail is wheelchair-accessible from the Pantoll Ranger Station. If you want a longer hike, make a loop out of it with Steep Ravine and Dipsea, or Bolinas Ridge

Steep Ravine Trail

and Cataract Trails heading toward Stinson Beach.

★ BOOTJACK LOOP

DISTANCE: 6.3 mi (10.1 km) round-trip
DURATION: 3 hours
EFFORT: Moderate
TRAILHEAD: Muir Woods parking lot

Tall redwood tree canopies, creeks, dense plant life, and cascading waterfalls line this loop going through the forest on the eastern side of the park. Lots of steps contributing to its 1,158-ft (353-m) elevation gain make this a moderately graded trail. There is a parking fee at Muir Woods ($9-13) where the cluster of trails, including Bootjack, begin.

RECREATION

BIKING

Even though Mount Tamalpais is rumored to be the birthplace of mountain biking, it hasn't really been allowed on the state park's trails since 1984. However, the park launched a pilot program in fall 2024 allowing mountain bikes and Class 1 e-bikes on 6.6 mi (10.6 km) of 10 Mount Tam trails.

However, the 17.7-mi (28.5-km) **Seven Sisters** cycling loop is popular with road bikers—starting at Stinson Beach, ride north on CA-1 to Fairfax Bolinas Road and climb 2,257 ft (688 m) up to Ridgecrest Boulevard. Traverse across the ridgeline to the Rock Spring intersection, and fortunately it's all downhill from there. Take Pantoll Road to the Panoramic Highway and ride on the road west to Stinson Beach.

WILDLIFE WATCHING

Birds

This cool, coastal area filled with grassy meadows, lush forests, ocean, and estuarine settings plays home to bobcats, foxes, and at least 150 species of birds. Everything from great horned owls to northern harriers can be seen; the best bird-watching is from the **Dipsea Trail** and **Rock Spring area.**

CAMPING

Mount Tamalpais State Park (415/388-2070) maintains **two standard campgrounds** open year-round as well as a group campground. Bootjack and Pantoll Campgrounds ($25/night) each have 15 campsites off the Panoramic Highway and are available on a first-come, first-served basis. There is an $8 parking fee. The campsites at these two campgrounds each have a picnic table, food locker, fire ring, and drinking water and restrooms nearby (but no showers). There's no trailer or RV camping.

BEST CAMPGROUNDS

Pantoll Campground

This 15-site campground is off the Panoramic Highway at a 1,400-ft (427-m) elevation and is close to many of the park's premier hiking trails. This campground is open

BEST NEARBY

Muir Woods

MUIR WOODS NATIONAL MONUMENT

Near the eastern side of Mount Tamalpais State Park in Mill Valley is the Muir Woods National Monument (1 Muir Woods Rd., Mill Valley; 415/561-2850; www.nps.gov/muwo; 8am-sunset daily; $15), managed by the National Park Service. These old-growth coast redwoods have been federally protected since 1908 thanks to President Theodore Roosevelt.

A paved trail up to 2 mi (3 km) long called the Redwood Creek or Main Trail guides people to the Founders Grove, Bohemian Grove, and Cathedral Grove. Four wooden bridges cross Redwood Creek; the very last one (Bridge 4) is the starting or ending point for Mount Tamalpais's Bootjack Trail and the state park's Camp Alice Eastwood Trail.

Parking and/or shuttle reservations are needed for going into Muir Woods, and these are different from the National Park System's entrance fees. Visit https://gomuirwoods.com to make your reservations.

year-round, and reservations are on a first-come, first-served basis; get more information at the Pantoll Ranger Station next to the campground. Restrooms with flush toilets and potable water are available.

Bootjack Campground

Bootjack is Pantoll's sister campground also off the Panoramic Highway at a 1,400-ft (427-m) elevation. It is also open year-round, with reservations on a first-come, first-served basis; it's close to great hiking trails, and offers the same amenities as Mount Tam's other 15-site campground.

CABINS

Mount Tam's **Steep Ravine Cabins** ($100/night) are some of the most highly sought-out accommodations in the park. It was so hard to get a reservation there that the California

State Parks system is currently testing out a drawing pilot program where visitors apply for a reservation for free online through Reserve California for their preferred dates and are notified if they are selected. Steep Ravine also has seven **environmental campsites** ($25/night) near the cabins that must be reserved ahead of time but are not part of the cabin lottery system.

FOOD AND LODGING

Stinson Beach is near the west entrance, and Mill Valley is closest to the east entrance of Mount Tam. Stinson Beach is quiet and spread out, popular for surfing, swimming, and picnicking. Amenities such as restaurants, cafés, and a couple of hotels make Stinson Beach a popular destination in itself. Mill Valley is heavily populated and has a gas station, restaurants, bakeries, and more.

BEST PICNIC SPOT

Bootjack Picnic Area

This tranquil, peaceful area found off the Panoramic Highway of Mount Tam (in the same general area of the Pantoll Campground, Matt Davis Trail, and Old Mine Trail) is surrounded by stands of gentle giants. It has picnic tables, restrooms, and barbecue grills, complemented by the meditative sounds of the babbling Redwood Creek close by.

GETTING THERE

CAR

The major highways that go into Mount Tamalpais from the Bay Area include US-101 and the coastal scenic CA-1. CA-1 runs along Stinson Beach on the western side of the park. US-101 is a straight shot north from San Francisco up over the Golden Gate Bridge, which has a toll fee. The Panoramic Highway goes through the park.

If visiting Muir Woods National Monument, be sure to book your parking reservation ahead of time through the Muir Woods Shuttle (www.gomuirwoods.com). Along with parking reservations, it also provides transportation to Muir Woods that links into Mount Tamalpais.

BUS

The Marin Transit's West Marin Stagecoach (https://marintransit.org) runs a daily route to destinations in west Marin, including Mount Tamalpais and the Golden Gate National Recreation Area. All buses have a couple of bike racks and are wheelchair-accessible.

ANGEL ISLAND STATE PARK

Angel Island is the largest naturally made atoll in the heart of the bustling Bay Area, and the only way to get there is by boat or ferry. Many people go to Angel Island for the day to hike Mount Livermore, bike the Perimeter Road, or see historic sites.

PHONE: 415/435-1915

WEBSITES: www.angelisland.com; https://angelisland.org

DAY USE HOURS: 8am-sunset

AREA: 740 acres (299 ha)

This island used to be part of the mainland 10,000 years ago before it broke off into the ocean during an ice age. The Coast Miwok people used the island to fish, hunt, and camp on the oak woodland and grass-covered terrain. In 1775, Spanish navigator Lt. Juan Manuel de Ayala sailed his ship into the bay, and a century later, the US Army built Camp Reynolds on the island to defend the San Francisco Bay during the Civil War in 1863. Angel Island also played a part in the 1898 Spanish-American War, World War I, World War II, and the Cold War. The base was decommissioned in 1962, and most of the island went into the hands of California State Parks.

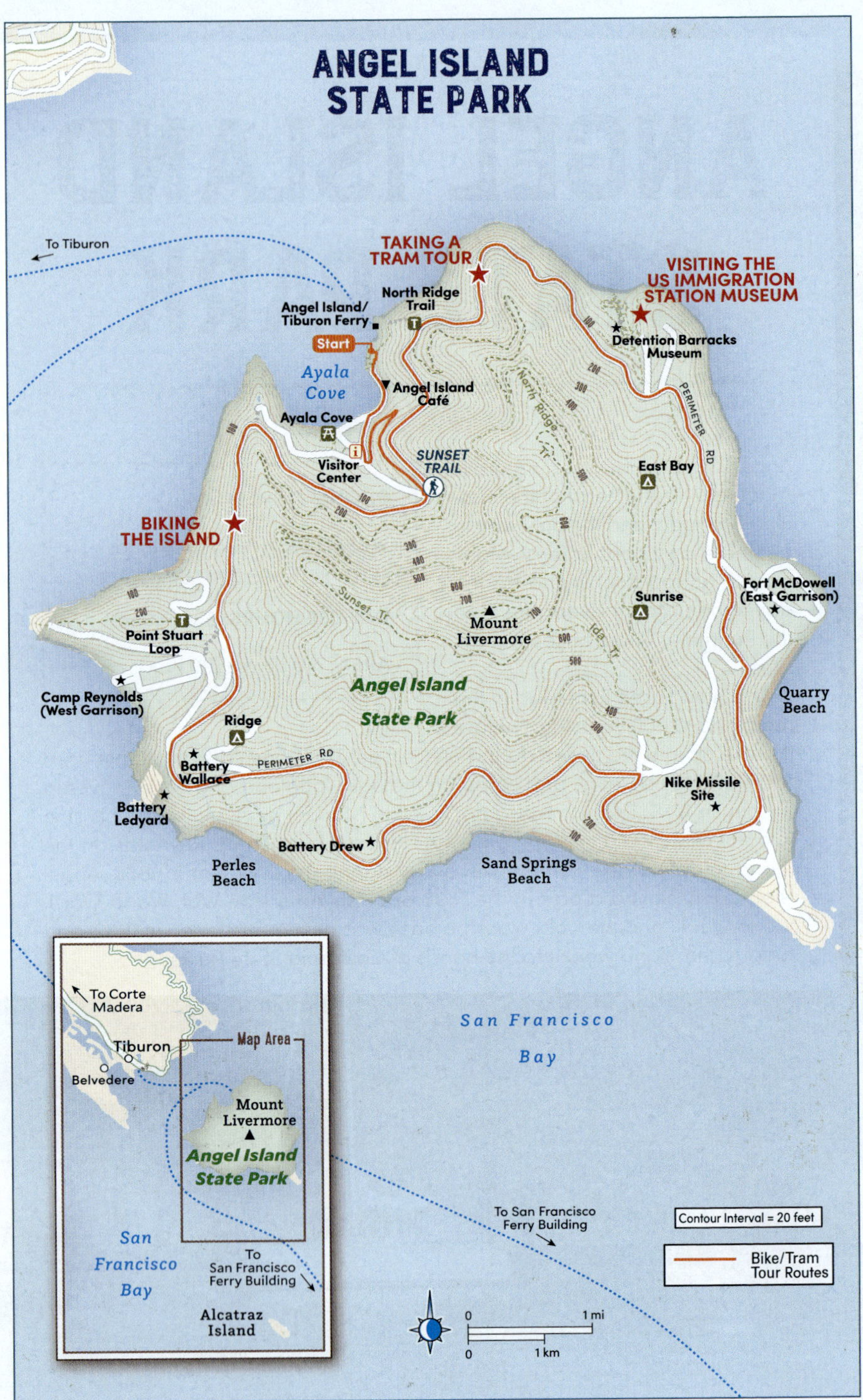
ANGEL ISLAND STATE PARK
To Tiburon
TAKING A TRAM TOUR
VISITING THE US IMMIGRATION STATION MUSEUM
North Ridge Trail
Angel Island/ Tiburon Ferry
Start
Ayala Cove
Angel Island Café
Detention Barracks Museum
Ayala Cove
Visitor Center
SUNSET TRAIL
North Ridge Tr
PERIMETER RD
East Bay
BIKING THE ISLAND
Sunset Tr
Mount Livermore
Ida Tr
Sunrise
Fort McDowell (East Garrison)
Point Stuart Loop
Camp Reynolds (West Garrison)
Angel Island State Park
Quarry Beach
Ridge
Battery Wallace
PERIMETER RD
Nike Missile Site
Battery Ledyard
Battery Drew
Perles Beach
Sand Springs Beach
To Corte Madera
Tiburon
Belvedere
Map Area
Mount Livermore
Angel Island State Park
San Francisco Bay
To San Francisco Ferry Building
Alcatraz Island
San Francisco Bay
To San Francisco Ferry Building
Contour Interval = 20 feet
Bike/Tram Tour Routes
0 1 mi
0 1 km

TOP 3

★ **1. TAKING A TRAM TOUR:** Angel Island Company operates a tram around the island, pointing out and narrating the history, culture, and key features of the place (page 157).

★ **2. VISITING THE US IMMIGRATION STATION MUSEUM:** The island's former immigration center processed hundreds of thousands of people looking for new opportunities in America (page 157).

★ **3. BIKING THE ISLAND:** Ride along Perimeter Road past Camp Reynolds and sandy Quarry Beach, and take in the view of Golden Gate Bridge from Battery Ledyard (page 159).

PLANNING YOUR TIME

The island is open year-round, but many services are limited or unavailable in the winter months. The **Angel Island Company** (415/435-5537; www.angelisland.com) runs the amenities in the park; visit their website for more details on the café, trams, and bike rentals. Plan to spend a full day here to experience everything the island has to offer.

Nearby state parks include Mount Tamalpais State Park (9 mi/14 km from Tiburon, 15 mi/24 km from San Francisco) and Half Moon Bay State Beach (39 mi/63 km from Tiburon, 27 mi/43 km from San Francisco).

ENTRANCE AND FEES

The **one entry point** into Angel Island is at **Ayala Cove.** The daily park entrance fee ($3) is covered through the ferry ticket price, camping reservation, or boat mooring price.

VISITOR CENTER

Angel Island Visitor Center

Ayala Cove, entry kiosk; 415/435-5390; 11am-2:30pm daily high season Apr.-Nov., limited winter hours

In Ayala Cove, an expansive two-story mansion welcomes visitors. The ground floor offers displays and interesting historical information, while lovely picnic grounds and lawns surround the center.

RESERVATIONS

Ferry tickets from Tiburon to the island through **Angel Island/Tiburon Ferry** are available in person and can also be booked online in advance. Ferry tickets for the **Golden Gate Bridge Angel Island Service** can only be bought on-site at the San Francisco Ferry Terminal Gate C, and they are likely to sell out during high season.

Angel Island tram tickets can be bought up to 48 hours in advance through the **Angel Island Company** (415/435-5537; www.angelisland.com), and they also sell out during the high season. If they have any free seats the day you visit, you can buy same-day tickets in Ayala Cove at the Angel Island Café.

WEATHER

The San Francisco Bay Area is known for its not-too-hot, not-too-cold weather and a consistent fog that comes in without warning that residents seem to be opinionated about (they even named it Karl). The Bay Area has sunny, clear days with temperatures around 70-75°F (21-24°C) in the late summer months; winter tends to be gray and rainy, with average temperatures around 55-65°F (13-18°C). The ferries may adjust their operating schedules if the waves are too big in the bay. The best time to visit is during the summer months (March-October) when the café is open and all the tours are running.

SIGHTS

TOURS

★ Tram Tour

415/435-5537; www.angelisland.com; $12-18

A 50-person tram goes around Perimeter Road, complemented by an audio recording spouting interesting and historical facts about this landmass in the San Francisco Bay. These hour-long tours leave from Ayala Cove and run counterclockwise around the island. The last stop is the Immigration Station, where you can hop off and explore before either walking or taking another tram back. Times and days of the tours change depending on the season—in winter the trams will likely only run on the weekends, one going out in the morning and one in the afternoon, but in summer they run every day and more frequently.

★ US IMMIGRATION STATION MUSEUM

www.aiisf.org; 11am-2:30pm Wed.-Sun.; free

From 1910 to 1940, Angel Island had an immigration processing center that took in hundreds of thousands of foreigners from all around the world looking for new opportunities in America. However, due to the Chinese Exclusion Act in 1882, many Asian immigrants had to wait days, weeks, and sometimes years for their entry applications to be accepted. This West Coast version of Ellis Island now serves as a museum sharing the stories and names of those who made it here.

DETENTION BARRACKS MUSEUM

www.aiisf.org; 11am-2:30pm Wed.-Sun.; $5-7

In a separate building next to the Immigration Station, the Detention Barracks Museum held newly arrived foreigners after coming through the immigration processing center. Here people were locked in a crowded dorm until they passed an entry hearing and medical screening. The detention center held close to 300,000 immigrants before it closed in 1940. Visitors can walk through the re-created barracks either on their

deer on Angel Island (left); Fort McDowell (right)

own ($5) or on a self-guided tour ($7).

CAMP REYNOLDS (WEST GARRISON)

Established in 1863 by the US Army, Camp Reynolds was created to help ward off Confederate sympathizers and naval force threats. A series of artillery batteries, including Battery Ledyard's two rapid-fire 5-inch guns and Battery Wallace's single 8-inch rifle, are viewable from Perimeter Road. The buildings, including a historic bakehouse and officers' buildings, aren't open to the public, but there are informational signs where you can learn more. The camp is located on the west side of the island.

FORT MCDOWELL (EAST GARRISON)

Activity on the island grew as soldiers reporting for overseas duty came here en route to their battles. A detention camp was built next to the quarry on the eastern side to house troops exposed to or suffering from contagious diseases. Wander around the historic buildings and read signs to learn about those who lived there; the buildings themselves are not open to the public. Campsites, a group picnic area, restrooms, and a baseball diamond are there today.

BEACHES

There are a few beaches on the island for those willing to brave the wind. Swimming is technically allowed, but the water is cold, the currents are strong, and there's no lifeguard on duty.

QUARRY BEACH

Located on the east side of the island, Quarry Beach is narrow and sandy and, most importantly, the best protected from the wind.

PERLES BEACH

Perles Beach is on the southwest side of the island at the end of a more difficult downhill climb. But the views are beautiful from the island's biggest stretch of sand.

view from Sunset Trail (left); view from North Ridge Trail (right)

TOP HIKE
SUNSET TRAIL

DISTANCE: 4.9 mi (7.9 km) round-trip
DURATION: 2 hours
EFFORT: Moderate
TRAILHEAD: Perimeter Rd. behind Ayala Cove

Walk to Mount Livermore at 788 ft (240 m) above sea level via the Sunset Trail. Leaving from Ayala Cove, Sunset Trail offers 3 mi (5 km) of around a 672-ft (205-m) altitude gain from Perimeter Road up to Mount Livermore. The trail intersects with the North Ridge Trail about 1,760 ft (536 m) down from the mountain, allowing you to choose your own adventure for how you want to get back. The elevation gain means this trek can be challenging, but the views at the top make it all worth it. This trek is off-limits to bicyclists.

HIKING

Angel Island has 13 mi (21 km) of hiking trails; 5.5 of those miles (8.9 km) make up the paved Perimeter Road, acceptable for biking or walking.

NORTH RIDGE TRAIL

DISTANCE: 4.2 mi (6.8 km) round-trip
DURATION: 2 hours
EFFORT: Moderate
TRAILHEAD: Ayala Caove near Angel Island Café

The other way to get to the highest point of Angel Island is to hike up there via the North Ridge Trail. This trail starts on the east side of Ayala Cove with a 144-stair climb leading up to Perimeter Road. It crosses the paved path, and the single-track dirt path follows the ridge, displaying beautiful views of cities across the bay before heading inland toward the mountain. The total elevation gain from sea level to the top is 797 ft (243 m).

RECREATION

 BIKING

Bicyclists can cruise down 9 mi (14 km) of trails, more than 5 mi (8 km) of those being on the paved Perimeter Road. Top-of-the-line mountain bikes and Specialized e-bikes are rented by the hour or by the day through the **Angel Island Company** (415/435-5537; www.angelisland.com; $16-64 mountain bike, $26-99 e-bike) out of Ayala Cove. With your own wheels, roll along Perimeter Road past Camp Reynolds and sandy Quarry Beach, and take in the view of Golden Gate Bridge from Battery Ledyard.

Perimeter Road

DISTANCE: 5.5 mi (8.9 km) round-trip
DURATION: 2.5 hours
TRAILHEAD: Ayala Cove

This paved roadway goes around the entire island, which is walkable, bikeable, or drivable, and passes by all major landmarks including the US Immigration Station Museum, Fort McDowell, Battery Drew, Battery Ledyard, and Camp Reynolds. While the road is accessible for different modes of transportation, there is a 350-ft (107-m) elevation change with the most drastic altitude gains being the climb from Ayala Cove toward the Immigration Station. A powered-up e-bike can get you there easily. There is a 15 mph (24 kph) speed limit on this road.

CAMPING

Angel Island has **a few primitive camping areas.** Picnic tables, potable water, food-storage lockers, and pit toilets are nearby. Camping is open year-round, and sites must be booked from two days up to six months in advance of arrival through Reserve California (800/444-7575; www.reservecalifornia.com; $30/night).

Be prepared to carry your camping equipment up to 2 mi (3 km) to the site. Bring charcoal or camp stoves to cook food on; wood fires aren't allowed. Winds can gust up to 30 mph (48 kph) on the island, and some of the sites are quite exposed to the elements. In other words, stake that tent firmly into the ground. Bring bug repellent and prepare for frosty mornings.

Angel Island has four environmental camping areas with sites you can kayak to, which also must be booked in advance through Reserve California.

BEST CAMPGROUNDS

East Bay Campsites

The three campsites (numbers 1-3) facing the East Bay on the same side of the island as the US Immigration Station are mostly protected from the

East Bay Campsite (left); on the ferry leaving San Francisco (right)

wind, although site 3 is in more open-air hillside, so it gets quite gusty.

Ridge Campsites

The Ridge sites (numbers 4-6) are on the other side of the island, between Battery Wallace and Battery Drew. They face the Peninsula, giving views of the San Francisco skyline and Golden Gate Bridge.

Sunrise Campsites

Next to the East Bay sites, the Sunrise sites (numbers 7-9) can be reserved as a group camp accommodating up to 24 people or booked individually for single campers. Each site has a picnic table, views of the East Bay, and little to no shade.

FOOD AND LODGING

Angel Island Company (https://angelisland.com), the state park's concessionaire partner, operates a café in Ayala Cove. Beyond that, you'll have to bring in your own snacks before boarding the ferry. Water stations are all over the island to refill your water bottle.

On the mainland, there are a lot of restaurants, markets, and hotels near the ferry docks in Tiburon and at the San Francisco piers. Tiburon is a coastal town packed with lots of amenities—there's even a café, hotel, and farm restaurant all within the vicinity of the ferry station.

ANGEL ISLAND CAFÉ

Ayala Cove; 415/435-3392; https://angelisland.com; 10am-3pm daily summer; $28-32 for boxed lunch

Angel Island Café sells sandwiches, salads, snacks, and beverages. Check its website to make sure they're open before you go to the island.

BEST PICNIC SPOT

Ayala Cove

Picnic tables for smaller groups are scattered on the grass in front of the visitor center as well as a short jaunt away from the ferry dock. There are four reservable group picnic areas in Ayala Cove as well, with bathrooms, the visitor center, docks, water, and paved roads around the site.

GETTING THERE

Most people get to the park by public ferry out of Tiburon or San Francisco, but some visitors take their private boats or charters. If bringing your own boat, Angel Island State Park charges a mooring fee of $28-30 for docking the first boat for up to 24 hours.

FERRY

Angel Island/ Tiburon Ferry

21 Main St., Tiburon; 415/435-2131; https://angelislandferry.com; $18 round-trip, park entrance fee included

The ferry from Tiburon runs seven days a week from Memorial Day to

Labor Day (four trips per day midweek and hourly on the weekends except at noon). Its operations are reduced in the shoulder seasons (closed Mon.-Tues.) and are sporadic in the winter (weekends only). It's a 12-minute ride to the island. During summer, the earliest ferry departs from Tiburon at 10am and the last ferry leaves the island between 3:20pm and 5:20pm depending on the day you go. Bikes are welcome to board for a dollar extra per bike. Book your tickets online to ensure you get a seat on the boat.

Angel Island/San Francisco Ferry

1 Ferry Building Gate B, San Francisco; 415/455-2000; www.goldengate.org; $19-31 round-trip, park entrance fee included

The **Golden Gate Bridge Highway and Transportation District** ferries people to Angel Island seven days a week year-round all day long. Tickets can be purchased on-site at the ferry terminal; the ticket machines are open 24 hours a day and you must be at the dock at least 15 minutes before departure. The 30-minute ferry goes to Angel Island four times a day Monday-Friday (9:25am, 10:55am, 1:55pm, and 3:55pm) and departs from Angel Island at 10:10am, 11:35am, 2:40pm, and 5pm. On the weekends and holidays, the ferry does three runs to and from the island. Bikes can be brought onto the ferry free of charge.

CAR

Tiburon is 17 mi (27 km, 40 minutes) north of San Francisco via US-101 and CA-131 west. There are no tolls northbound across the Golden Gate, but the return trip to San Francisco will cost between $9.25 and $10.25 (www.goldengate.org).

PUBLIC TRANSPORTATION

The Bay Area Rapid Transit, aka **BART** (www.bart.gov), runs a subway connecting the cities between Oakland, the East Bay, San Francisco, San Jose, and Peninsula areas. The closest BART stop to where you can catch the Golden Gate ferry to the island is Embarcadero, 0.4 mi (0.6 km) away from 1 Ferry Building, a seven-minute walk. BART connects to the San Francisco International Airport and Oakland International Airport as well. This is one of the only parks you can get to directly from the airport without having to rent a car.

FOLSOM LAKE STATE RECREATION AREA

A half hour away from the California State Capitol, Folsom Lake Recreation Area provides outdoor enthusiasts a reprieve from the sweltering summer heat with a plethora of boating, fishing, and swimming activities on its two manmade reservoirs, Folsom Lake and Lake Natoma. Within its 19,564 acres (7,917 ha), this state park boasts 95 mi (153 km) of hiking and biking trails, mostly along the 75 mi (121 km) of shoreline, not to mention interesting historic landmarks as well. Its 32-mi-long (51-km-long) bike path connects the park to Old Sacramento, and it also encompasses the American River Trail.

ADDRESS: 7806 Folsom-Auburn Rd., Folsom

PHONE: 916/988-0205

WEBSITE: www.folsomlakemarina.com

DAY USE HOURS: 6am or 7am-9pm summer, 7am-6pm or 7pm winter (varies by location)

AREA: 19,564 acres (7,917 ha)

The Southern Maidu and Nisenan tribes called the Sacramento/Folsom area home, and they spent the winters in permanent shelters along the American River.

Today fishing and wakeboarding are the most popular activities at Folsom Lake, while smaller, wake-free Lake Natoma is ideal for sailing and kayaking. However, these manmade reservoirs fluctuate quite a bit depending on drought conditions, so be sure to check the water levels if you plan to do some water sports.

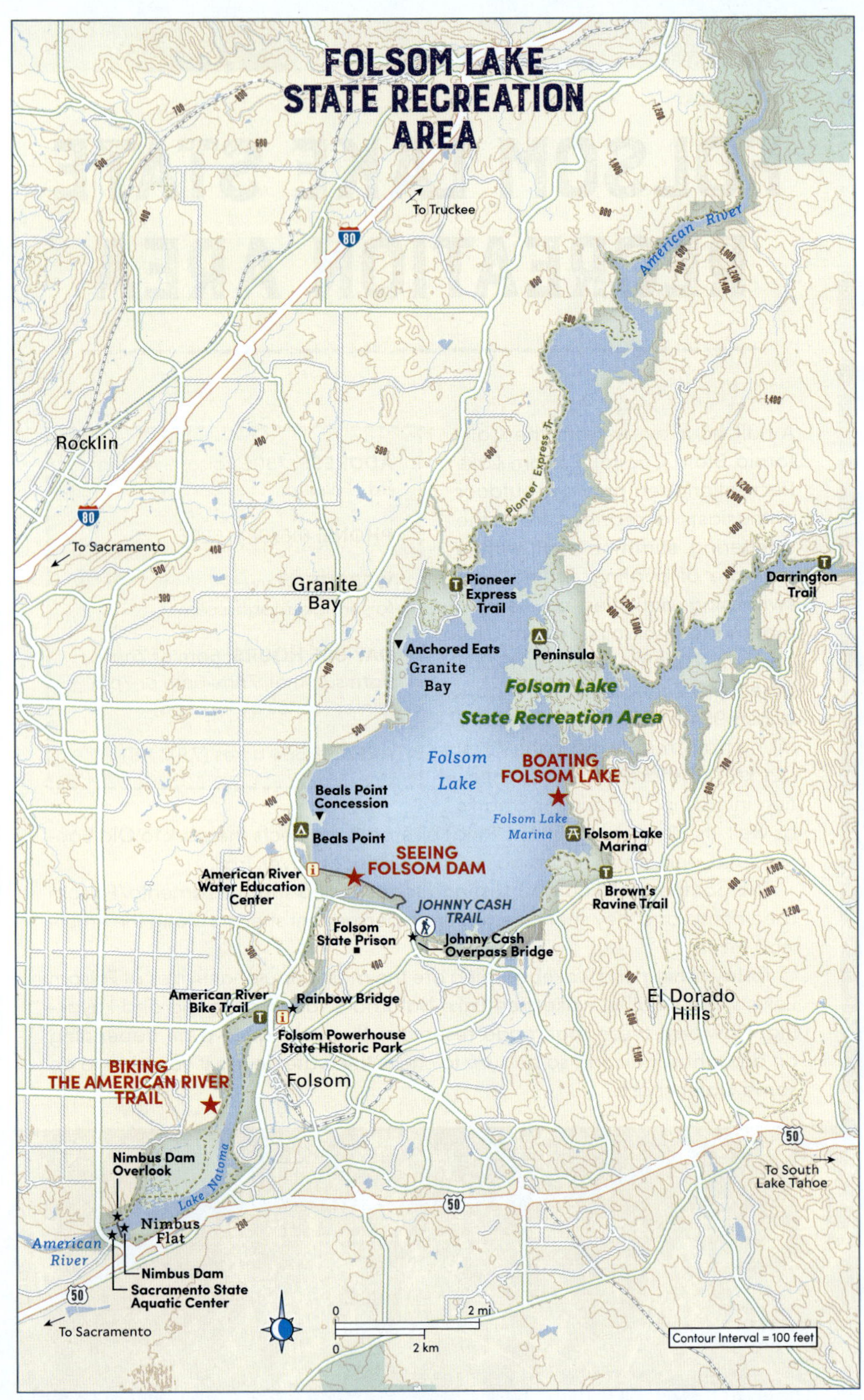
FOLSOM LAKE
STATE RECREATION
AREA
To Truckee
80
American River
Rocklin
80
To Sacramento
Pioneer Express Tr
Granite
Bay
Pioneer
Express
Trail
Darrington
Trail
Anchored Eats
Granite
Bay
Peninsula
Folsom Lake
State Recreation Area
Folsom
Lake
BOATING
FOLSOM LAKE
Beals Point
Concession
Beals Point
Folsom Lake
Marina
Folsom Lake
Marina
SEEING
FOLSOM DAM
American River
Water Education
Center
JOHNNY CASH
TRAIL
Brown's
Ravine Trail
Folsom
State Prison
Johnny Cash
Overpass Bridge
American River
Bike Trail
Rainbow Bridge
Folsom Powerhouse
State Historic Park
El Dorado
Hills
BIKING
THE AMERICAN RIVER
TRAIL
Folsom
50
Nimbus Dam
Overlook
Lake Natoma
To South
Lake Tahoe
50
Nimbus
Flat
American
River
Nimbus Dam
Sacramento State
Aquatic Center
50
To Sacramento
0
2 mi
0
2 km
Contour Interval = 100 feet

TOP 3

★ **1. SEEING FOLSOM DAM:** The 9-mi-long (14-km-long) concrete structure can hold close to 12,000 acres (4,856 ha) of water and is most impressive when water is flowing out of it (page 167).

★ **2. BIKING THE AMERICAN RIVER TRAIL:** To see most of the rec area and get in a good workout, cycle a part of the 32-mi (51-km) trail (page 170).

★ **3. BOATING FOLSOM LAKE:** Getting on the water is a must at this 11,500-acre (4,654-ha) freshwater lake, especially when water levels are high (page 170).

PLANNING YOUR TIME

Most people who visit Folsom Lake State Recreation Area are locals taking a few hours of their day to walk or bike around the Folsom area. Visitors wanting to take in the whole park should plan on spending at least a day to have time for hitting the trails, seeing the sights, and most importantly, getting on the water.

The recreation area is open year-round, but its hours vary by the season.

Nearby state parks include Indian Grinding Rock State Historic Park (48 mi/77 km) and Emerald Bay State Park (84 mi/135 km).

ENTRANCES AND FEES

Folsom Lake State Recreation Area has at least **six entrances.** The most popular place to spend the day is in **Granite Bay,** accessed off Douglas Boulevard on the upper west side of Folsom Lake; the second most popular is the **Beals Point Day Use Area** and campground off Folsom-Auburn Road. Day use fees range from $10-12 depending on the season; it costs $10 to launch a boat at its two motorized boat launch areas (at Granite Bay and Brown's Ravine).

VISITOR CENTER

While Folsom Lake State Recreation Area doesn't have a specific visitor center, its sister park, the **Folsom Powerhouse State Historic Park** on Lake Natoma, does.

American River Water Education Center

7785 Folsom-Auburn Rd., Folsom; 916/537-7053 or 916/537-7300; www.usbr.gov/mp/arwec; 10am-4pm Tues.-Fri.

The American River Water Education Center is managed by the Bureau of Reclamation within the recreation area's boundaries, next to the Folsom Dam. You can view exhibits regarding the American River watershed and learn about California's water supply.

WEATHER

The weather in the area is marked by dry hot summers and mild rainy winters. Highs are usually around 94-105°F (34-41°C) in summer and 55-60°F (13-16°C) in winter. The best (and busiest) time to go to Folsom Lake State Recreation Area is in summer when the water levels tend to be the highest. The Folsom Lake water levels dictate what kind of recreation you can enjoy there; in a normal rain year the water levels are the highest May-September, then it drops considerably. At lower lake levels (426 ft/130 m or lower), most if not all of the boat ramps go out of service.

EVENTS

This recreation area holds a variety of special events throughout the year, from bass-fishing competitions, sailboat regattas, and rowing challenges to turkey trots and horseback endurance races. The best way to find out what's going on at Folsom Lake is to visit its website.

ONE DAY IN FOLSOM LAKE RECREATION AREA

MORNING

If you only have a day, the best place to spend it is at Granite Bay because it has the most amenities. Pick up some food at the snack bar and launch your boat from one of the concrete ramps, or if the water's too low, rent a kayak or paddleboard and head to the beach.

AFTERNOON

Spend the afternoon swimming, picnicking, and/or biking, and find the Anchored Eats floatin' food boat if you want a more substantial meal without having to drive out of the rec area.

SIGHTS

★ FOLSOM DAM

Folsom Lake exists because of the dam that was built in 1955. When there's a high demand for electricity in the Sacramento area, its turbines can be automatically turned on, which results in a huge increase of water flow. You can no longer drive or walk over the dam, but the paved Folsom Lake Crossing Road, below Beals Point, offers the best views of Folsom Dam. A paved path was built next to the two-lane roadway to give pedestrians and bikers some distance from the cars.

JOHNNY CASH OVERPASS BRIDGE

Between Folsom Lake and Lake Natoma is the famous Folsom State Prison, put on the map by country singer Johnny Cash's song "Folsom Prison Blues." The prison is well hidden among the recreation area and still operational, so you wouldn't want to go there unless you have a planned visit with an inmate. In 2014, a pedestrian/cycling bridge along the Johnny Cash Trail was built over Folsom Lake Crossing Road; its architecture is modeled after the prison's East Gate.

NIMBUS DAM OVERLOOK

About 7 mi (11 km) downstream from the Folsom Dam is the Nimbus Dam, which creates Lake Natoma. The Nimbus Dam is a fellow hydroelectric dam that regulates the water released from Folsom, and its concrete gravity construction is 87 ft (27 m) high and 1,093 ft (333 m) long. Eighteen radial gates control the flow. The best place to see the dam is from the overlook on the Natoma Lake American River Trail Loop.

RAINBOW BRIDGE

https://folsomrainbowbridge.com

This beautifully designed arched two-lane crossing going over the

Folsom Dam (left); Rainbow Bridge (right)

American River was the largest concrete bridge in Sacramento County when it was built in 1917. Its arc reached 209 ft (64 m) and connected Folsom to surrounding cities to address the needs of the area's growing population. In the mid-2000s, it was knocked down and a replica put in its place. The new version was rebuilt as a walking/biking path next to Greenback Lane. The easiest way to get there is to park near the Folsom Powerhouse State Historic Park and walk about 500 ft (152 m) to it.

BEACHES

GRANITE BAY

There's a reason why Granite Bay is the most popular part of the recreation area: With boat ramps, a snack bar, picnic areas, sandy beach, buoyed-off swimming, and lifeguards, this place has it all. People flock here in the summertime when temperatures reach 100°F (38°C), and the snack bar rents out beach equipment such as volleyball sets, kayaks, paddleboards, and badminton sets.

HIKING

Folsom Lake State Recreation Area has 95 mi (153 km) of trails ideal for bikers, hikers, and horseback riders, and most of them—paved and unpaved—loop around major landmarks and waterways such as Folsom Lake, Lake Natoma, and the American River.

PIONEER EXPRESS TRAIL

DISTANCE: 14.5 mi (23.3 km) round-trip
DURATION: 5.5 hours
EFFORT: Strenuous
TRAILHEAD: Granite Bay Beach

This strenuous out-and-back route

TOP HIKE
JOHNNY CASH TRAIL

DISTANCE: 6.5 mi (10.4 km) round-trip
DURATION: 2.5 hours
EFFORT: Moderate
TRAILHEAD: 50 E. Natoma St., Dan Russell Rodeo Arena

The best way to access the Johnny Cash Trail is by parking at the Dan Russell Rodeo Arena and getting on the trail from there. Public art pieces paying homage to Johnny Cash are installed along the trail, and the Robbers' Ravine Bridge is a cool arched wooden walkway that's one of the most Instagrammed spots in Folsom. The bridge is 1.2 mi (1.9 km) north of the rodeo arena parking lot on the Johnny Cash Trail, following the American River and just before the prison. From there you can turn around and go back to Natoma Street or up to Folsom Lake Crossing. Its gradual elevation gains make this a moderately graded trail. It's open year-round, and there's no bad time to ride or walk this trail.

starts on the western end of Folsom Lake from Granite Bay, and the single-track trail runs all the way up the North Fork of the American River in Auburn. Its 1,512-ft (461-m) elevation gain is great for trail running, but on a mountain bike it gets quite technical in some places. This trail was established in 1849 during the gold rush to get to the mining camps along the American River. Watch out for thistles and foxtails hiding in the grasses.

BROWN'S RAVINE TRAIL

DISTANCE: 4.2 mi (6.8 km) round-trip
DURATION: 1.5-2.5 hours
EFFORT: Moderate
TRAILHEAD: Parking lot off Green Valley Rd.

Kitty-corner across Folsom Lake from Granite Bay, the out-and-back Brown's Ravine Trail is a moderately challenging but not too long hike that hugs a peninsula in the Lakeridge Oaks area. It tends to get more crowded in the summer when bike riders, birders, and horseback riders use the trail. Grassy meadows, gorgeous lake views, sandy beaches, and wildlife (egrets, deer, and bald eagles) can be spotted on this trail along with wildflowers, big shade trees, and driftwood forts. The parking fee is $12.

RECREATION

 BIKING

Folsom Lake State Recreation Area trails—paved and unpaved—are mixed-use for hiking, biking, and equestrian activities. It's common to see equal parts hikers and bikers on the Johnny Cash Trail and Lake Natoma Trail, but only advanced and expert riders go on the dirt single-track Pioneer Express Trail. There aren't any bike rental places within the recreation area, but there are several outfitters in Folsom.

American River Trail

DISTANCE: 32 mi (51 km)
DURATION: 10 hours
TRAILHEAD: Beal's Point, Folsom Lake

The American River Trail (also called the American River Parkway and Jedediah Smith Memorial Trail) draws all kinds of cyclists. The entire 32-mi (51-km) path goes from Beals Point at Folsom Lake all the way down to Discovery Park in downtown Sacramento outside of the state recreation area; only 14 mi (23 km) of the route are within the rec area boundaries. The American River Trail follows the American River on the opposite side of Folsom Prison and Johnny Cash Trail, crossing the Rainbow Bridge and Folsom Boulevard, going through Black Miners Bar, and following the length of Lake Natoma. It crosses Nimbus Dam and intersects with Hazel Avenue, continuing out of rec area boundaries. If attempting the entire trail, park at Beals Point at the top and consider parking a chase car at Discovery Park at the bottom.

Darrington Trail

DISTANCE: 16 mi (26 km) round-trip
DURATION: 6-7 hours
TRAILHEAD: Darrington bike lot

This lovely single-track dirt path is popular for hikers and bikers, but everyone seems to share the trail well. Starting at the bottom of Folsom Lake, this trail goes up into Brush Creek Ranch and Salmon Falls, climbing 1,400 ft (427 m) before then turning back.

 BOATING AND FISHING

Water sports are the main draw for the recreation area. Folsom Lake has about 12 boat ramps, but which ones are open or closed depends on the water levels.

Anglers flock here to try to catch trophy-size bass, but king salmon and rainbow trout have been hooked within Folsom Lake's waters, too. The **Nimbus Flat Day Use Area** has a fishing pier on Lake Natoma as well, where fishers can catch trout, bass, and catfish. A valid fishing license is required (available online at https://wildlife.ca.gov), and there are specific regulations as to how many and what size and type of fish you can catch.

Folsom Lake Marina at Brown's Ravine

661 Green Valley Rd., El Dorado Hills; 916/933-1300; www.folsomlakemarina.com; 9am-5pm daily

As one of the largest marinas open year-round, the Folsom Lake Marina has launch ramps, boat slips, and a Chevron gas dock selling 87 octane fuel. It also has a snack bar/bait shop/marine supply store that sells candy, chips, ski ropes, worms, nightcrawlers, and other fishing supplies. However, it does not sell fishing licenses.

Sacramento State Aquatic Center

1901 Hazel Ave., Gold River; 916/278-2842; www.sacstateaquaticcenter.com; 8am-8pm daily mid-Apr.-mid-Aug.; $15/hour single kayak, $20/hour canoe/tandem kayak, $18/hour stand-up paddleboard

The Sacramento State Aquatic Center rents human-powered vessels such as SUPs, canoes, and kayaks, as well as offering lessons and teaching water safety classes. The Aquatic Center is found on Lake Natoma in Gold River; its hours of operation change based on the season. Since equipment is rented by the hour, most people just paddle around nearby Nimbus Flat.

CAMPING

Folsom Lake State Recreation Area has plenty of primitive places to pitch a tent and **two developed campgrounds:** Beals Point and Peninsula Campgrounds. Campsites can be reserved online through Reserve California (800/444-7275; www.reservecalifornia.com) from two days up to six months in advance. Sites for tent camping range from $28-33 depending on whether you are going in peak season or in winter; RVs pay from $48-58. There are a few wheelchair-accessible sites available.

There are two group campsites at Black Miners Bar: Granite Bay has 10 primitive **boat-in sites** ($20/night), and Avery's Pond has environmental sites that can be reserved by mail or in person at the Folsom Lake Sector Office (7755 Folsom-Auburn Rd., Folsom; 9am-4pm Mon.-Fri.).

BEST CAMPGROUNDS

Beals Point Campground

Just above Folsom Dam, Beals Point has 69 campsites that accommodate tents, trailers, and RVs up to 31 ft (9 m) long. Full hookups are near sites 50-69 in the motor home part of the campground, as well as a sanitation dump station. Potable water, showers, and ADA-accessible restrooms are here, too.

Peninsula Campground

This remote, year-round campground has 85 family campsites that fit trailers up to 18 ft (5 m) long and RVs up to 24 ft (7 m) long. Hookups aren't available, but a dump station is, along with flush toilets and piped drinking water. You can get there by driving 10 mi (16 km) in from Pilot Hill (off CA-49) or by boat, but the nearby launch ramps may be a bit sketchy (or outright closed) if the lake drops below 431 ft (131 m). Camping is available here on a first-come, first-served basis in the winter months.

FOOD AND LODGING

Folsom, specifically the Folsom Historic District, is within walking distance of Rainbow Bridge and offers plenty of restaurants, stores, and lodging options in the area.

Folsom Lake State Recreation Area's own **food concessions** at **Granite Bay** and Folsom Lake Marina at **Brown's Ravine** are open Memorial Day–Labor Day.

GRANITE BAY BEACH

Anchored Eats

www.anchoredeats.com; 6am–9pm daily summer

The famous floating food boat that was docked at Granite Bay Beach took over the Snack Shack on the shore, so now it has two locations: brick-and-mortar on the shore and an on-the-water concessionaire. Along with selling slushies, Folsom Blues burgers, and beach merchandise, it rents kayaks, paddleboards, and giant floaties.

Folsom Lake Marina

folsomlakemarina.com; 7am–7pm daily summer

The snack bar at the marina sells chips, nonalcoholic beverages, ice cream, and heat-and-eat sandwiches.

BEST PICNIC SPOT

Folsom Lake Marina

While many sites within the recreation area have parking, tables, barbecues, and restrooms, the Folsom Lake Marina has that and more, including a snack bar, launch ramp, tackle shop, and boat slips.

GETTING THERE

CAR

Folsom Lake State Recreation Area is about 25 mi (40 km) away from downtown Sacramento, which can take anywhere from 30–45 minutes to get to depending on traffic. The fastest way is usually via US-50 east to the Beals Point/Granite Bay entrance, but taking I-80 east and cutting over onto Douglas Boulevard in Roseville will get you there as well.

BUS

The **El Dorado Transit 50 Express** (https://eldoradotransit.com) follows a route along US-50 from Placerville to Folsom, while the **Sacramento Regional Transit District** (https://sacrt.com) manages the Folsom Stage Line. Its Route 10 to Historic Folsom stops at the Lake Natoma Crossing.

ED Z'BERG SUGAR PINE POINT STATE PARK

Nestled in the middle of Tahoe's quiet West Shore under acres of towering namesake pines, the Ed Z'berg Sugar Pine Point State Park, like Emerald Bay, is one of Big Blue's hidden gems. The sprawling grounds are home to the Hellman-Ehrman Mansion, a 11,000-sq-ft (1,022-sq-m) home built in 1903 used as a summer retreat by wealthy families.

ADDRESS: 7360 Westlake Blvd., Tahoma

PHONE: 530/525-9528

WEBSITE: www.sierrastateparks.org

DAY USE HOURS: Sunrise-sunset

AREA: 2,000 acres (809 ha)

Across CA-89 from the Hellman-Ehrman Mansion is the year-round General Creek Campground. The original 1960 cross-country ski trail system on this side of the park was rediscovered and restored in 2010; its nice flat terrain is ideal for beginners. Skiing and snowshoeing extend to the Dolder Nature Trail as well, making it one of the best year-round trails in Tahoe.

The Washoe tribe used Sugar Pine as a summer retreat long before settlers came, drawn to the lake's incredible bounty of fish, game, and edible plants. The State of California bought the Hellman-Ehrman Mansion and property around it in 1965, named it Sugar Pine Point, and then renamed it to Ed Z'berg Sugar Pine Point State Park in 2004.

ED Z'BERG SUGAR PINE POINT STATE PARK
To Tahoma and Tahoe City
Edwin L. Z'berg Natural Preserve
Sugar Pine Point Navigational Light
10TH AVE
9TH AVE
FIR ST
ALDER AVE
4TH AVE
3RD AVE
Yellow Trail
Dolder Nature Trail
WALKING THE DOLDER NATURE TRAIL
Campground Entrance
89
General Creek
North Boathouse
West Shore Sports
TOURING THE HELLMAN-EHRMAN MANSION
Pier
GENERAL CREEK TRAIL
Blue Trail
Nature Center/ Gift Shop
Lakefront Interpretive Trail
Park Office
General Creek Trail
Red Trail
Green Trail
South Boathouse
Entrance Station
SKIING THE GENERAL CREEK TRAIL SYSTEM
Lake Tahoe Basin Management Unit
West Shore Bike Trail
Orange Trail
Red Trail
McKinney Lake
Ed Z'berg Sugar Pine Point State Park
Site of the 1960 Olympic Biathlon Range
LAKE TAHOE
Meeks Bay
Lily Pond Trail
Meeks Bay
Lily Pond
Lake Tahoe Basin Management Unit
General Creek Trail
General Creek
0 0.5 mi
0 0.5 km
Contour Interval = 40 feet

1

2

TOP 3

1. TOURING THE HELLMAN-EHRMAN MANSION: A short walk away from Big Blue, this historic mansion is available to tour in the summertime (page 177).

2. WALKING THE DOLDER NATURE TRAIL: Meander through the sugar pines on this easy walk to the historic light beacon (page 178).

3. SKIING THE GENERAL CREEK TRAIL SYSTEM: On the mountain side of this state park is a nice system of cross-country ski trails that are fun for all ability levels (page 180).

3

PLANNING YOUR TIME

One day is sufficient for seeing all this park has to offer whether you are going in the summer or the winter. In the winter, you can easily do a daytime snowshoe hike or cross-country ski jaunt. In the summer, going on a Hellman-Ehrman Mansion tour and doing the lake side hikes in one day is possible; however, it can get congested with cars trying to get into the park, so arrive early. In the summer, consider staying a night or two in the General Creek Campground in case you get delayed.

Nearby state parks include D.L. Bliss and Emerald Bay State Parks (7 mi/11 km).

ENTRANCE AND FEES

There is **one main entrance** to the park (on the lake side) off CA-89 and one entrance into the General Creek Campground off CA-89 across the street on the mountain side. The park is open daily year-round, but the Hellman-Ehrman Mansion tours only operate in the summertime. The parking fee is $10 in the summer, $10 in the winter, or free if you're camping at General Creek Campground.

VISITOR CENTER

Ed Z'berg Sugar Pine Point State Park Nature Center/Gift Shop

7360 Westlake Blvd., Tahoma; 530/525-9528; 10am-4pm daily end of May-Sept.

The main visitor center is in front of the Hellman-Ehrman Mansion amid the cluster of historic structures. On the right side, there's an Indigenous galis dungal hut, and the left side provides access to the Dolder Nature Trail. It's open during the summer and acts as a one-stop shop for maps, gifts, books, water, and ice cream along with exhibits on birds, wildflowers, trees, and biology.

WEATHER

The weather in Tahoe is quite pleasant; most of the year it's sunny and temperate, with summer temperatures upward of 75-80°F (24-27°C), dipping into the lower 40s (4-7°C) at night. Since snow makes the Tahoe basin significantly colder December-April, winter temperatures range from 15 to 40°F (-10 to 5°C). CA-89 around Emerald Bay can close in the winter if there's a big snowstorm, making it impossible to get here from the South Shore unless you drive all the way around the lake, but storms usually don't affect those coming from the North Shore. The summer and autumn months are the best times to visit when the climate is most ideal.

ONE DAY IN ED Z'BERG SUGAR PINE POINT STATE PARK

MORNING

If visiting in the summer, get here early to secure a parking spot and hike the Dolder Nature Trail. If you want to get more mileage, go across the street to the General Creek Campground and hike some of the ski trails.

AFTERNOON

Have a picnic under the sugar pines along the Lakefront Interpretive Trail and tour the Hellman-Ehrman Mansion. Spend the rest of the day swimming, paddleboarding, or hanging out at the beach.

SIGHTS

★ HELLMAN-EHRMAN MANSION

Built in 1903, this 11,000-sq-ft (1,022-sq-m) mansion, located on the lakeside past the entrance station, was used as an informal summer home for many years by Sydney and Florence Hellman-Ehrman. Designed by Walter Danforth Bliss (where the name of the nearby D.L. Bliss came from), the estate was the first of its kind in the Tahoe area to have advanced indoor plumbing. The Hellman-Ehrmans also utilized steam-powered generators until commercial electricity became available in 1927. The interior of the eight-bedroom/seven-bath estate (also referred to as The Pine Lodge) features original redwood beam structures, Spanish hand-hammered metal light fixtures, and a birdcage elevator no longer in operation.

Daily 30-minute **tours** (530/583-9911; $10) of the mansion run from Memorial Day weekend through the end of September; tickets can be purchased day-of in person at the visitor center in front of the estate. When tours aren't available, you can still walk the grounds around the home, you just can't go inside.

Surrounding the Hellman-Ehrman Mansion are the caretaker's cottage by the lake, tennis courts, butler's cabin, maids' quarters, icehouse, powerhouse, pump house, and more, but one structure in particular is a favorite of kids' field trips: the historic wooden commode. The wooden remnants of the **Caretaker's Outhouse** are located on the north side of the 0.8-mi (1.3-km) Lakefront Interpretive Trail, north of the mansion.

SUGAR PINE POINT NAVIGATIONAL LIGHT

On the beach side of the park once stood an operating maritime light tower that was the highest in the US, at 6,200 ft (1,890 m) above sea level. While the tower is no longer there, a diamond-shaped light post marks the spot. Find it via the Dolder Nature Trail.

SITE OF THE 1960 OLYMPIC BIATHLON RANGE

At the end of the 3.3-mi (5.4-km) intermediate Red Trail in the General Creek Campground, find the biathlon range used in the 1960 Olympics based at Palisades Tahoe. The biathlon is a sport involving a combination of cross-country skiing and rifle target shooting. In the late 1990s the state park restored the ski trails that were used in the biathlon event; the site is marked by a tall sign with the Olympic rings paying homage to its history.

BEACHES

Under the Hellman-Ehrman Mansion's grassy knoll, an inviting and unnamed sandy beach gives visitors ample space to swim, picnic, or hang out on the pier. People often come here to kayak or stand-up paddleboard in Lake Tahoe as well.

HIKING

Sugar Pine Point State Park is one of the only public places in North Lake Tahoe with highly accessible miles of sandy beachfront, but its trail system is impressive, too, as it appeals to both summer and wintertime hikers.

★ DOLDER NATURE TRAIL

DISTANCE: 2.1 mi (3.4 km) round-trip
DURATION: 45 minutes
EFFORT: Easy
TRAILHEAD: Sugar Pine Point Visitor Center

After touring the park's main grounds, go down the paved path and over the bridge to connect with the Dolder Nature Trail and into the Dolder Nature Reserve. Keep an eye out for tree squirrels, birds, and the huge sugar pine cones. This trail leads to the site of an old lighthouse, now marked by a diamond-shaped post. It also acts as the Yellow Trail for cross-country skiers and snowshoers in the winter. Access the trailhead from the visitor center, following the short paved 0.3-mi (0.5-km) path (called the Rod Beaudry Trail) down to General Creek and crossing over the wooden bridge. Here it becomes the Dolder Nature Trail, a dirt and leaf-/pine-needle-covered path that becomes sandy as you get closer to the beach and diamond-shaped post that used to be a lighthouse. It's likely you'll encounter a few chattering chickarees up in the trees if you cross too far into their territory, but they're harmless. Another cross-country trail system also glides through here.

TOP HIKE

GENERAL CREEK TRAIL TO LILY POND

DISTANCE: 5.5 mi (8.9 km) round-trip
DURATION: 2 hours
EFFORT: Easy
TRAILHEAD: General Creek Campground

This is one of the favorite hikes for West Shore locals because it's usually not crowded and is in dense forest, providing solitude and a link to Desolation Wilderness (a popular hiking area through the western crest of the Sierra Nevada), the Tahoe Rim Trail, and the Pacific Crest Trail. Meadows, clear pools, some granite rock slabs, and lots of green trees and shrubbery line the single-track dirt path. To access this trail, go to the end of the General Creek Campground and follow the historic 1960 Olympics cross-country ski trail (the Red Trail on the park's Cross-Country Ski Map)—which served as the first site to the biathlon range—to Lily Pond. This trail is open year-round and provides solace in the pines; the fragrant mule's ears pop up in the springtime, and Tahoe's small animals, birds, bears, coyotes, and even porcupines utilize the trail.

RECREATION

★ CROSS-COUNTRY SKIING AND SNOWSHOEING

More than 12 mi (20 km) of cross-country ski trails are available on the General Creek Campground area, 6 mi (10 km) of which are groomed. The parking fee is $10 in the snowy months. The trail system is clearly marked, mostly flat, and winds through quiet pines, open meadows, and babbling stream paths. The trails are named after the colors of the rainbow, but do not denote ability level. For instance, the Green and Blue Trails are the flattest beginner ones, and the Red Trail is the longest, intermediate one. If you forgot your skis but really want to check out these trails, rent a pair in Tahoe City.

Visitors are welcome to snowshoe along the cross-country ski trails, too, as long as you don't walk directly on the ski tracks. State Park Interpreters take groups snowshoeing on a moderately graded trail once a month in winter when the natural light is the brightest. **Full moon snowshoe hikes** ($45 pp) are held January-April and last an hour and a half. The cost includes snowshoe rentals, parking, and a tour guide.

KAYAKING

Sugar Pine Point's gentle shoreline and easy access make it a good spot to launch a human-powered vessel in the summer. Sugar Pine Point will sometimes partner with West Shore Sports in Tahoe City to hold **full moon kayak tours,** taking guests on an alpenglow adventure paddling from the historic light post to the park's southern boundary looking out to Meeks Bay. Visit the Sierra State Parks Foundation website (www.sierrastateparks.org) for more information.

BIKING

West Shore Bike Trail

DISTANCE: 3.5 mi (5.6 km) round-trip to Meeks Bay
DURATION: 1 hour 15 minutes
EFFORT: Moderate

Ed Z'berg Sugar Pine Point State Park in winter (left); kayaking (right)

THE SUGAR PINES

There are at least three dozen species of trees in the Tahoe National Forest, but people seem most impressed with the massive size of the pine cones that the sugar pine trees produce. The trees themselves get tall, too, capable of extending up to 250 ft (76 m) into the sky and having a trunk diameter of up to 8 ft (2 m). Their pine cones are generally between 10-20 in (25-50 cm) long but can grow up to 24 in (60 cm) in length. No wonder the chickarees go crazy for these things.

Sugar pine trees are only found in the western United States, mostly in California. They also grow in Oregon, parts of Nevada, and areas in Baja, Mexico. However, excessive logging from the Comstock Lode era and introduction of the white pine blister rust has threatened the sugar pines in Tahoe. The **Sugar Pine Foundation** (https://sugarpinefoundation.org) exists to help keep the species healthy and thriving (while also mitigating its risks), and they offer lots of community events, inviting people to plant sugar pine seedlings and learn more about them.

Sugar pines have a reddish-brown wrinkled bark, and their branches are long and stick straight out (except when their gigantic cones weigh them down). Their long, sharp green needles are bundled in groups of five.

While sugar pines grow all around the lake, most of them are found on the West Shore and in abundance in the 2,000-acre (809-ha) Sugar Pine Point State Park.

TRAILHEAD: Sugar Pine Point State Park entrance

As part of the ongoing effort to connect all of Lake Tahoe with a paved bike path, this portion of the West Shore Trail is popular for hiking, biking, and skateboarding. Head south on the trail from Sugar Pine Point and you'll eventually end at Meeks Bay Resort; or go north and follow it through Homewood all the way to Tahoe City for a farther trip (10 mi/16 km one-way).

CAMPING

Sugar Pine Point State Park has **one campground** with 175 sites, which is on the inland mountain side of CA-89. Reservations can be made through Reserve California (800/444-7275; www.reservecalifornia.com; $35/night) from two days to up to six months in advance from mid-May through mid-October. Ten group campsites are available, too. In the off-season winter months, a few sites are available on a first-come, first-served basis.

Every space in this densely wooded park has a picnic table, a bearproof box for food storage, and ample space for parking—up to eight people can fit in one campsite. Each reservation includes a spot for one car (and a trailer up to 26 ft/8 m long) or an RV up to 32 ft (10 m) long. Some sites are wheelchair-friendly, and hot coin-operated showers are available in the summer (but not the winter). There are no hookups. Restrooms have flush toilets and tap water, and there is a campfire center near the entrance station. Be sure to always store your food properly and use the bear box—bears know how to break into coolers and vehicles, which can be quite damaging to your property and to the bear.

BEST CAMPGROUND

General Creek Campground

General Creek Campground (renamed dukMéʔem wáťa in 2025) has a variety of tent sites, 10 group sites, 11 ADA-accessible sites, and RV/trailer-accommodating ones (which make up most of the sites). They are set up in six loops.

FOOD AND LODGING

The closest gas stations can be found in Tahoe City, 9 mi (14 km) north of the park, and South Lake Tahoe, 20 mi (32 km) south of it. Tahoe City has a bunch of shops, restaurants, and small hotels along its main street. It is less populated than the city of South Lake Tahoe, which is close to casinos, more beaches, and attractions, along with lots of restaurants and hotels. CA-89 leads to both cities.

BEST PICNIC SPOTS

Lakefront Interpretive Trail

There are several picnic tables along the shoreline in the main area of the park, below the Hellman-Ehrman Mansion along the Lakefront Interpretive Trail. The tables offer a place to put swimming equipment, snacks, towels, and whatever else you have close to the beach, and are within a short distance to the Hellman-Ehrman Mansion, pier, and historic buildings.

GETTING THERE

CAR

Sugar Pine Point State Park sits in the middle of Tahoe's West Shore on CA-89, 9 mi (14 km) south of Tahoe City, 20 mi (32 km) north of South Lake Tahoe, 30 minutes south of Truckee (23 mi/37 km), and 1 hour southwest of Reno (60 mi/97 km). Sacramento is 118 mi (190 km) away via CA-50 to CA-89 (2 hours 15 minutes). However, note that CA-89 around Emerald Bay closes in the winter if there's too much snow, so sometimes the only way to access Sugar Pine Point is from the northern side of the lake. Check the Caltrans website (https://roads.dot.ca.gov) for roadway status.

D.L. BLISS STATE PARK

Connecting to Emerald Bay State Park and sharing the Maritime Heritage Underwater Trail, D.L. Bliss is named after the prominent industrialist/mining magnate/lumberman Duane Leroy Bliss, who lived from 1833 to 1907 and owned a lot of land on Lake Tahoe's West Shore. After he passed away, his family donated much of it to California State Parks.

ADDRESS: 9881 CA-89, South Lake Tahoe

PHONE: 530/525-9528

WEBSITE: https://sierrastateparks.org

DAY USE HOURS: Sunrise-sunset

AREA: 1,830 acres (741 ha)

Much like its sister park, D.L. Bliss has a multitude of sugar pines, Douglas firs, Jeffrey pines, ponderosas, and other coniferous trees known to exist in the Tahoe National Forest. Chipmunks, birds of prey, and black bears also call this place home.

The Washoe people were the original inhabitants of D.L. Bliss, which they called "da-ow-a-ga," meaning "edge of the lake." In the mid-1800s, around 10,000 sq mi (25,900 sq km) of Tahoe land was taken away from the Washoe. Today, reconstructed traditional bark winter homes referred to as galis dungals are available to view at this park and in surrounding areas.

Many people come to D.L. Bliss to camp, swim in Calawee Cove, and hike the Rubicon Trail into Emerald Bay.

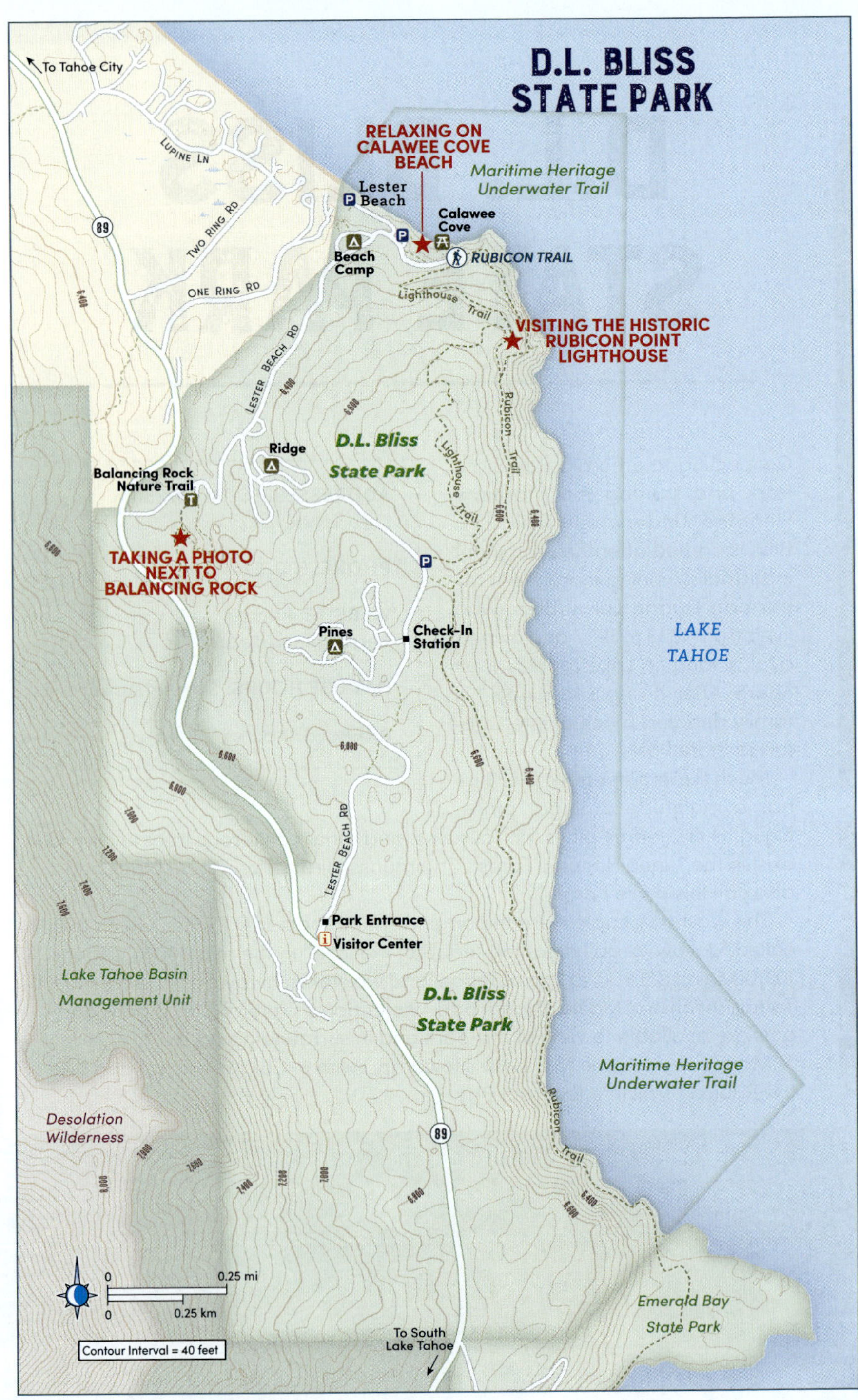
D.L. BLISS STATE PARK
To Tahoe City
LUPINE LN
TWO RING RD
ONE RING RD
89
RELAXING ON CALAWEE COVE BEACH
Maritime Heritage Underwater Trail
Lester Beach
Calawee Cove
Beach Camp
RUBICON TRAIL
Lighthouse Trail
VISITING THE HISTORIC RUBICON POINT LIGHTHOUSE
LESTER BEACH RD
Rubicon Trail
D.L. Bliss State Park
Ridge
Lighthouse Trail
Balancing Rock Nature Trail
TAKING A PHOTO NEXT TO BALANCING ROCK
Pines
Check-In Station
LAKE TAHOE
LESTER BEACH RD
Park Entrance
Visitor Center
Lake Tahoe Basin Management Unit
D.L. Bliss State Park
Maritime Heritage Underwater Trail
Rubicon Trail
Desolation Wilderness
89
0
0.25 mi
0
0.25 km
Emerald Bay State Park
To South Lake Tahoe
Contour Interval = 40 feet

TOP 3

★ **1. TAKING A PHOTO NEXT TO BALANCING ROCK:** This peculiar sight is made up of one exceptionally large 130-ton (118-tonne) granite stone precariously placed on top of the other (page 186).

★ **2. VISITING THE HISTORIC RUBICON POINT LIGHTHOUSE:** This reconstructed wooden structure was one of the four original beacons that helped direct the S.S. *Tahoe* steamship safely from shore (page 187).

★ **3. RELAXING ON CALAWEE COVE BEACH:** The aquamarine waters produced by snowmelt are rejuvenating, to say the least (page 187).

2

PLANNING YOUR TIME

D.L. Bliss is the busiest in the summertime when the kids are out of school and boating season is well underway. You won't find parking after 10am in the summer, so plan accordingly. The campground and its proximity to Emerald Bay is the big draw to this park, so plan on staying at least two days.

Nearby state parks include its adjacent sister park, Emerald Bay State Park, and Ed Z'berg Sugar Pine Point State Park (7 mi/11 km).

ENTRANCE AND FEES

D.L. Bliss State Park is on the southwestern end of Lake Tahoe, north of Emerald Bay on CA-89. There is **one official entrance** into D.L. Bliss across from the park headquarters and visitor center where you pay your parking fee ($10) and then drive farther into the park. Your parking fee at either Emerald Bay or D.L. Bliss (and even Ed Z'berg Sugar Pine Point) gives you access to all parks for the day.

VISITOR CENTER

D.L. Bliss Visitor Center

9881 CA-89, South Lake Tahoe; 530/525-7277; call for hours, daily Memorial Day-Labor Day

The visitor center is right at the park entrance and has a few parking spaces before the road dips down into the campground and hiking trails where other parking lots/pullouts are available (by Calawee Cove Beach, the Pines Campground, and Balancing Rock trailhead). Inside the center there are exhibits, maps, and cold beverages.

WEATHER

Weather in the Sierra Nevada can turn on a dime, so it's always best to wear layered clothing. Summer temperatures tend to be in the 75-80°F (24-27°C) range, dropping to around 40°F (4°C) when the sun dips below the mountains. That 40°F (4°C) becomes the high in the winter months. When visiting in December-March especially, check the weather forecast because sometimes 4WD or chains are necessary to drive into the area. Big blizzards and mass snow accumulations causing avalanche danger can shut down the highway around Emerald Bay. Call **Caltrans** (800/427-7623; https://roads.dot.ca.gov) for current road conditions. The best time to visit is in the summer when the park is fully open and the sunny weather is most consistent.

SIGHTS

 BALANCING ROCK

What sets D.L. Bliss apart from any other Tahoe state park is the peculiar Balancing Rock, made up of one exceptionally large and heavy granite stone that looks precariously placed on top of the other. The top rock weighs an estimated 130 tons (118 tonnes) and may erode over time, but for now people love to take photos next to this natural wonder. To reach the rock, follow the easy

jumping into the water at D.L. Bliss (left); Balancing Rock (right)

0.5-mi (0.8-km) Balancing Rock Nature Trail marked at the northwestern end of the park, close to the Ridge Campground. Whatever you do, don't push on it.

★ HISTORIC RUBICON POINT LIGHTHOUSE

This structure looks more like an outhouse than a lighthouse, but it's situated at one of the best vantage points of Lake Tahoe from the West Shore. Built in 1919, the Rubicon Point Lighthouse was one of the original four beacons that helped direct the S.S. *Tahoe* (a steamship that Duane Leroy bought) safely to or away from shore. This lighthouse was abandoned and a new one constructed at Sugar Pine Point a few years later. In its heyday, the Rubicon Point Lighthouse was the highest lighthouse in the United States, sitting at a 7,000-ft (2,134-m) elevation, but it is now nonfunctional. It is just a 1.5-mi (2.4-km) walk from Calawee Cove Beach and Rubicon Point.

BEACHES

★ BLISS BEACH

This beach is split into two sections—the northern part known as **Lester Beach** and the south end referred to as **Calawee Cove.** Calawee Cove is next to an abrupt rock wall against one of the deepest parts of the lake, so it's common to see locals jumping off the cliffs here in the summer. Bliss Beach has a gentle shoreline with a sandy bottom, but there's no cordoned-off swimming area, so you have to be careful of boat traffic.

TOP HIKE

RUBICON TRAIL

DISTANCE: 8.2 mi (13.2 km) one-way
DURATION: 6-9 hours
EFFORT: Moderate
TRAILHEAD: D.L. Bliss or Eagle Point Campground

The entire length of the Rubicon Trail from D.L. Bliss to the Emerald Bay Eagle Point Campground is around 8 mi (13 km) one-way, so it can take the good part of the day to hike. From D.L. Bliss, the Rubicon starts at Calawee Cove and hugs the shoreline, passing the old Rubicon Point Lighthouse and dropping down into Emerald Bay. It's best to stay the night at one of the D.L. Bliss or Emerald Bay campgrounds, or park a car at each point if trying to hike this trail in one swoop.

RECREATION

DIVING

While all the sunken features of the **Maritime Heritage Underwater Trail** are in Emerald Bay, the underwater park extends into D.L. Bliss. The original diving/underwater hiking trail follows the on-land Rubicon Trail, where interesting rock features are best seen from below the surface. Be sure to swim through Emerald Bay on your diving trip; more information about the Maritime Heritage Underwater Trail is available there.

CAMPING

D.L. Bliss has 165 campsites across **three campgrounds** that are only open in the summer after most of the snow has melted, May-September. Reservations can be made up to six months in advance through Reserve California (800/444-7275; www.reservecalifornia.com; $35-45/night). Each campsite has a picnic table, bearproof food locker, and fire ring. Restrooms with flush toilets, tap water, and showers are in each campground. D.L. Bliss can fit motor homes up to 18 ft (5 m) long or trailers up to 15 ft (4 m) long.

This state park has one group campsite ($165/night) that can only accommodate tents between the Ridge and Beach campgrounds.

BEST CAMPGROUNDS

Pines Campground

The Pines Campground (sites 1-90) is closest to the campground entrance station, about a half mile (0.8 km) down from the main entrance.

Ridge Campground

The Ridge Campground (sites 91-112) is closest to the group campsite and Balancing Rock Nature Trail.

Beach Camp

Beach Camp (sites 141-165) is closest to Calawee Cove and the Lake Tahoe shoreline, in the northernmost part of the park. The premier "beach" lakefront campsites are $10 more per night.

FOOD AND LODGING

The two closest towns to D.L. Bliss with gas stations, hotels, and shopping areas are Tahoe City, 17 mi (27 km) north of the park, and South Lake Tahoe, 13 mi (21 km) east of the park on CA-89. Tahoe City has a quaint downtown with a main street full of shops, restaurants, and cafés, whereas South Lake Tahoe is a spread-out, more populated city.

BEST PICNIC SPOT

Calawee Cove

Since picnic tables are only available at the campsites at D.L. Bliss, consider taking your towels, water toys, and basket of snacks to post up at

Calawee Cove. This is the best place to swim and create a day use base camp for those in your party who want to further explore the sights and trails.

GETTING THERE

CAR

D.L. Bliss State Park is on CA-89, about 1.5 mi (2.5 km) north of Emerald Bay State Park on the southwest shore of Lake Tahoe. It takes two hours to drive to D.L. Bliss from Sacramento via CA-50. You must bring your own vehicle as there's no public transportation nearby, and finding a parking spot can be hard during the high season. Emerald Bay is right next to D.L. Bliss, so you can walk between the parks via the Rubicon Trail.

EMERALD BAY STATE PARK

In the southwest corner of beautiful blue Lake Tahoe, Emerald Bay is one of the most photographed places in the world thanks to its stunning natural landscape. The pine tree-studded environment surrounds the crystal clear lake. In the southwest corner of the alpine basin, a painting-worthy cove marks Emerald Bay.

ADDRESS: 138 Emerald Bay Rd., South Lake Tahoe

PHONE: 530/541-3030

WEBSITE: https://sierrastateparks.org

DAY USE HOURS: Sunrise-sunset

AREA: 1,533 acres (620 ha)

In the middle of the cove, you'll find a rock- and pine-covered island, which is the only island in Lake Tahoe. On top of Fannette Island is a tea house, built by millionaire Lora Josephine Knight.

The Washoe people lived here first, and the tribe is still actively engaged in keeping their culture alive. California State Parks bought Emerald Bay in 1953, and since it's easily viewable from CA-89 driving around the lake, it is a popular place to stop and take pictures any time of the year.

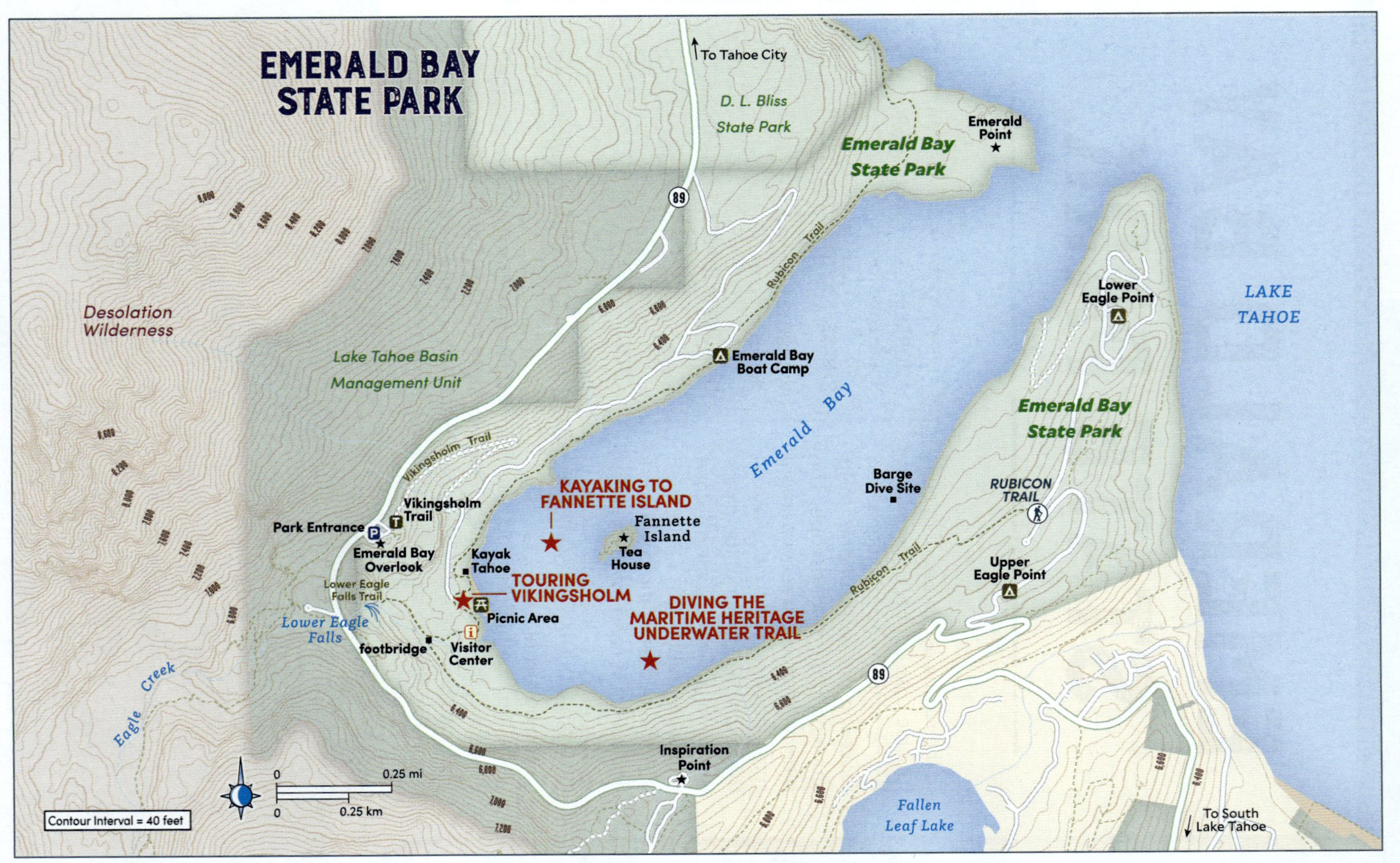
EMERALD BAY STATE PARK
To Tahoe City
D. L. Bliss State Park
Emerald Bay State Park
Emerald Point
89
Rubicon Trail
Desolation Wilderness
Lake Tahoe Basin Management Unit
Emerald Bay Boat Camp
Lower Eagle Point
LAKE TAHOE
Emerald Bay
Emerald Bay State Park
Vikingsholm Trail
Barge Dive Site
RUBICON TRAIL
KAYAKING TO FANNETTE ISLAND
Fannette Island
Tea House
Park Entrance
Emerald Bay Overlook
Kayak Tahoe
TOURING VIKINGSHOLM
Lower Eagle Falls Trail
Picnic Area
Lower Eagle Falls
footbridge
Visitor Center
DIVING THE MARITIME HERITAGE UNDERWATER TRAIL
Upper Eagle Point
Eagle Creek
Inspiration Point
0.25 mi
0.25 km
Contour Interval = 40 feet
Fallen Leaf Lake
To South Lake Tahoe

TOP 3

★ **1. TOURING VIKINGSHOLM:** Built in the late 1920s, Vikingsholm is one of the finest examples of Scandinavian architecture (page 195).

★ **2. KAYAKING TO FANNETTE ISLAND:** For a unique Tahoe experience, paddle over to the Tea House on Fannette Island (page 198).

★ **3. DIVING THE MARITIME HERITAGE UNDERWATER TRAIL:** A series of underwater exhibits comprises the largest and most diverse diving museum in the nation (page 198).

ONE DAY IN EMERALD BAY STATE PARK

MORNING

Be sure to park at the Emerald Bay Overlook parking lot as early as you can to guarantee a spot. Take in the views from the overlook before walking down to Vikingsholm and taking the 30-minute tour of the famed mansion.

AFTERNOON

Kayak over to the Tea House on Fannette Island for a different perception of Emerald Bay. Or, if you don't feel like getting in the water, hike the Rubicon Trail to Emerald Point.

PLANNING YOUR TIME

You can quickly stop, get out, stretch your legs, and take in the incredible view of Lake Tahoe from CA-89, but it's worth spending a whole day to see Fannette Island, visit Vikingsholm, and go on a hike.

Nearby state parks include its adjacent sister park D.L. Bliss State Park and Ed Z'berg Sugar Pine Point State Park (9 mi/14 km).

ENTRANCE AND FEES

Emerald Bay State Park is in the southwest region of Lake Tahoe on CA-89. There is **one main entrance** and parking lot at the Emerald Bay Overlook, easily noticeable from the main road. You can also hike into the park on the Rubicon Trail, accessed from D.L. Bliss or Eagle Point Campground. The fee to park is $3/hour or $10/day.

VISITOR CENTER

Vikingsholm Visitor Center

530/541-6498; 10am-4:30pm daily Memorial Day-Labor Day

The visitor center is next to Vikingsholm castle, a mile-long (1.6-km) hike down from the parking lot via the Vikingsholm Trail. It has a gift shop and artifacts on exhibit; tickets for the Vikingsholm castle tour can also be purchased here.

WEATHER

Temperatures are quite comfortable in the summer, averaging around 75-80°F (24-27°C). Snow starts to fall in November and can persist through March-April, which can shut down the highway going around Emerald Bay. For updated road conditions, visit the Caltrans website (https://roads.dot.ca.gov). While the water temperature of Lake Tahoe is shockingly cold (anywhere from 40-62°F/4-17°C degrees), it never freezes. Summer is the best time to visit as Vikingsholm tours are only available seasonally, and the highway around Emerald Bay may be closed in the winter months due to avalanche danger. However, make sure you get there before 10am to find a parking spot.

SIGHTS

★ VIKINGSHOLM

Known as an environmentally conscious savvy businesswoman, Lora Josephine Knight and her architect traveled to Scandinavia before building Vikingsholm in the late 1920s. Her mansion was known as one of the finest examples of Scandinavian architecture of its time in North America.

Thirty-minute **guided tours** ($18) of the mansion leave on the hour daily from the end of May through September; tickets can be bought day-of at the visitor center next to the castle. If you go in the off-season, the grounds around Vikingsholm are open all year long to walk around on your own.

To get to here, follow the 0.85-mi (1.37-km) Vikingsholm Trail as it descends from the parking lot at the main entrance down to the mansion.

TEA HOUSE

Lora Josephine Knight, the original owner of Vikingsholm, built a small stone structure on **Fannette Island** known as the Tea House. Today only the stone ruins remain. The island is a short 10-15-minute paddle away. You can get there by boat, canoe, kayak, or stand-up paddleboard, but swimming there is not allowed due to the very cold waters and boat traffic.

EMERALD BAY OVERLOOK

On the northern side of the horseshoe-shaped cove, you can park in the main state park lot and walk a hundred yards or so (90 m) to get a direct view of Fannette Island. This also serves as an access point for the Vikingsholm Trail.

Vikingsholm

INSPIRATION POINT

Right off CA-89, this overlook offers a full side view of Fannette Island. The paved path to the point is wheelchair-accessible.

LOWER EAGLE FALLS

Depending on what time of the year you go, the 40-ft (12-m) falls may be raging with fresh snowmelt flowing into the bay, usually in the March-May months. From Vikingsholm, follow the signs to the Lower Eagle Falls Bridge; it's a 0.2-mi (0.3-km) walk.

HIKING

Most of the hikes within Emerald Bay State Park are accessible via the 8.2-mi (13.2-km) Rubicon Trail. Not only does the Rubicon lend the best views to Fannette Island, it also connects to D.L. Bliss State Park, offering a more expansive sight of Big Blue. Tall cedars, ponderosas, sugar pines, quaking aspens, and Douglas firs are just a few of the species that line the trails.

VIKINGSHOLM TRAIL TO LOWER EAGLE FALLS

DISTANCE: 2.5 mi (4 km)
DURATION: 1 hour 15 minutes round-trip
EFFORT: Moderate
TRAILHEAD: Emerald Bay Overlook parking lot

The Vikingsholm Trail starts at the parking lot by the main entrance and descends to the mansion. Follow the signs past the mansion and head up the Rubicon Trail. At the wooden footbridge, take a right (don't cross the bridge) to access the Lower Eagle Falls Trail. This is the best place to see the snowmelt cascading down over granite rocks into Emerald Bay in the spring months. This section of the falls is about 40 ft (12 m) high; Upper Eagle Falls, accessed across the highway out of the park via another trailhead, is about 170 ft (52 m) high.

EMERALD POINT TRAIL

DISTANCE: 5.1 mi (8.2 km) round-trip

view of Fannette Island (left); Lower Eagle Falls (right)

TOP HIKE

RUBICON TRAIL

DISTANCE: 8.2 mi (13.2 km) one-way
DURATION: 6-9 hours
EFFORT: Moderate
TRAILHEAD: D.L. Bliss or Eagle Point Campground

The Rubicon Trail wraps around Emerald Bay, from Eagle Point Campground to the south to D.L. Bliss State Park to the north. The trail gains 2,339 ft (713 m) across 8 mi (13 km), making it a moderately difficult hike, though you can easily choose to hike a portion of it, creating your own out-and-back. It's best to park a car at each point if you're trying to hike this trail in one go.

Highlights along the Rubicon include hiking through the Boat Camp, going past Emerald Point, and following the trail to Calawee Cove Beach in D.L. Bliss.

DURATION: 2 hours
EFFORT: Moderate
TRAILHEAD: Emerald Bay Overlook parking lot

This out-and-back hike to Emerald Point offers great views close to the shoreline of Emerald Bay without having to commit to the full-day Rubicon hike. Starting at the Vikingsholm trailhead, hike down 1 mi (1.6 km) to the mansion, then head left on the Rubicon Trail toward the Boat Camp. Pass through the campground and pier to the end of the peninsula; if you keep going past that point you'll end up in D.L. Bliss.

RECREATION

 KAYAKING

Fannette Island is a 10-minute paddle away. You can beach your boat and scramble up the rocks to the historic stone Tea House, giving a totally new perspective of Emerald Bay.

Kayak Tahoe

Vikingsholm, Emerald Bay; 530/544-2011; https://kayaktahoe.com; single kayak or SUP $38/hour, $100/day, double kayak $50/hour, $120/day

In the summer, Kayak Tahoe rents out stand-up paddleboards and sit-on-top kayaks from the shoreline next to Vikingsholm. There are no reservations; boats are available on a first-come, first-served basis. Kayak Tahoe also gives **guided tours** in two-person kayaks ($80-105/person) during the summer; these must be reserved online at least 48 hours in advance.

★ DIVING

Maritime Heritage Underwater Trail

Lake Tahoe has a rich recreational boating history, and Emerald Bay became the final resting place for some of these sunken barges and vessels. They were purposely scuttled to become a recreational attraction for divers.

California State Parks first established a **Historic Barge Dive Site** consisting of two wooden boat bones on the southeastern end of the bay closest to Eagle Point Campground. It has since expanded to include three other exhibits, allowing scuba divers and snorkelers to follow a full-on underwater trail. Interpretive panels are placed at the dive sites within Emerald Bay.

To learn more about this collection of underwater artifacts—known as the largest and most diverse underwater park in the nation—scuba divers and underwater aficionados can pick up waterproof interpretive cards at the visitor center and local dive shops, or find more information on the Emerald Bay State Park and Sierra State Parks Foundation websites (www.sierrastateparks.org).

BEAR SAFETY

Most people come to Lake Tahoe wanting to see a bear. And while seeing a lumbering bear in the wild is special, human-bear interactions can end badly if not handled with care.

Unsecured food or trash is a big problem in Tahoe, and as the saying goes, "a fed bear is a dead bear," so it's important to be mindful of how you're storing your food. Failure to do this can result in a fine up to $1,000 and/or being kicked out of the park.

bear near Lake Tahoe

Never get close to a bear, block its escape route, run away from the bear, or make aggressive movements toward it. Back away from it slowly, stand tall, and make a lot of noise (like shouting or banging pots and pans) if you need to. Bears only really charge when they feel threatened, so it's best to always keep a respectful distance.

Bears tend to be more prevalent around the Northern California wooded areas. Other state parks in this guide with bear populations include:

- D.L. Bliss State Park
- Ed Z'berg Sugar Pine Point State Park
- Calaveras Big Trees State Park
- Jedediah Smith Redwoods State Park
- Prairie Creek Redwoods State Park
- Humboldt Redwoods State Park
- Mono Lake Tufa State Natural Reserve

CAMPING

Emerald Bay State Park has **two main campgrounds** along the bay: the Eagle Point Campground on the south side of the bay, with 97 spots, and the **Boat Camp** on the north side, with 22 sites available to watercraft campers. All types of campsites must be reserved through Reserve California from two days up to six months in advance mid-May-early September (reservations 800/444-7275, Eagle Point Campground kiosk 530/541-3030; www.reservecalifornia.com; $25-45/night). The campgrounds close for the winter.

A reservation includes parking for one vehicle, along with an additional $8 reservation fee. All the sites have a picnic table, firepit, and bearproof box; the state park charges more for a few "premium" sites in Eagle Point.

At Eagle Point, trailers up to 18-21 ft (5-6 m) are welcome in 52 of the campsites, but there are no hookups. Coin-operated showers are available at Eagle Point Campground. Pets are allowed, but they must be leashed and always attended.

BEST CAMPGROUND

Eagle Point Campground

Sites 1-33 in Upper Eagle Point are closest to the main highway, making it more accessible, as well as to the amphitheater and south Rubicon trailhead. Sites 34-94 in Lower Eagle Point are more popular as they are closer to the lake views and beach walk. Sites 63-72 are next to the 0.25-mi (0.4-km) fire road leading to the beach; the more sprawling sites are down in this campground as well. Site 77 has the best lake views, which is why it's considered "premium."

FOOD AND LODGING

Emerald Bay State Park is 20 mi (32 km) south of Tahoe City and 12 mi (19 km) north of South Lake Tahoe, on CA-89. Tahoe City is a smaller town with a few shops, restaurants, hotels, and gas stations, while South Lake Tahoe has more of an abundance of all those amenities.

BEST PICNIC SPOT

Vikingsholm

Hands-down the best place to enjoy lunch is at Vikingsholm, where a scatter of picnic tables on the shoreline face out onto the bay and Fannette Island.

GETTING THERE

CAR

Emerald Bay State Park is on CA-89, 20 mi (32 km) south of Tahoe City and 12 mi (19 km) north of South Lake Tahoe. It's 110 mi (177 km, 2 hours) northeast of Sacramento via US-50. Unfortunately, there isn't a consistent public transportation service, which can make parking very difficult during the high season. If you find parking at D.L. Bliss State Park, you can hike over to Emerald Bay via the Rubicon Trail.

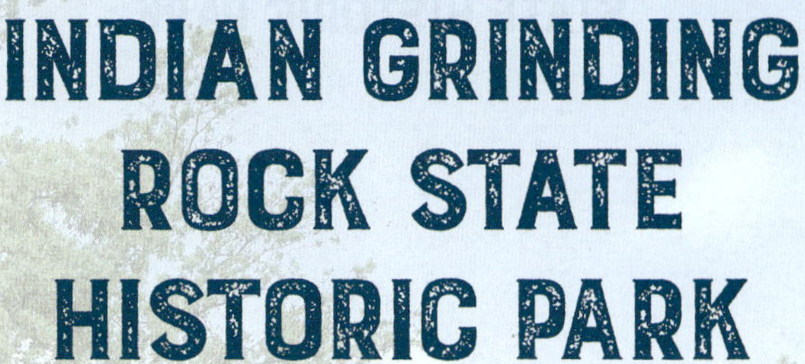

INDIAN GRINDING ROCK STATE HISTORIC PARK

ADDRESS: 14881 Pine Grove Rd., Pine Grove

PHONE: 209/296-7488

WEBSITE: https://chawse.org

DAY USE HOURS: Sunrise-sunset

AREA: 135 acres (55 ha)

In the Sierra Nevada foothills, Indian Grinding Rock State Historic Park transports visitors back to the time when the Northern Sierra Miwok people called this place home. The park has a museum, a campground, a Reconstructed Miwok Village, bark houses, and a roundhouse, but it is best known for (and named after) the marbleized limestone slab with close to 1,185 bedrock mortar holes that were used to grind acorns, grains, and other food. This historic park has the largest collection of these circular depressions in North America.

California State Parks created Indian Grinding Rock State Historic Park in 1968 to emphasize the Indigenous importance of the site and protect a piece of the state's heritage.

This park is all about preserving the environment and paying homage to those who were here before us, so the focus is on the historic bedrock mortars (called chaw'se) and the pleasant atmosphere of oak woodlands, meadows, pine trees, and outdoor exhibits that surround it.

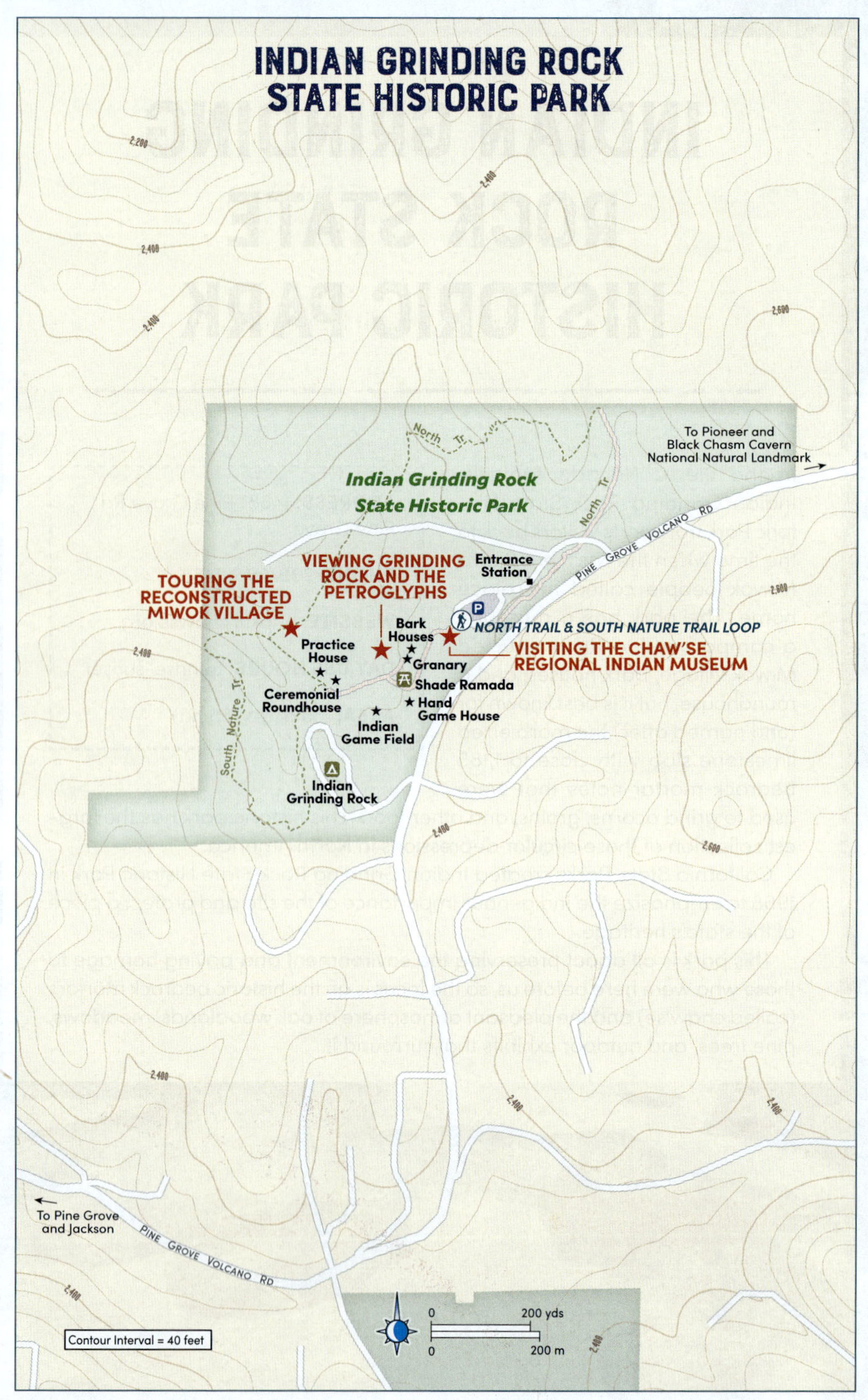
INDIAN GRINDING ROCK
STATE HISTORIC PARK
2,200
2,400
2,400
2,400
2,600
To Pioneer and
Black Chasm Cavern
National Natural Landmark
North Tr.
Indian Grinding Rock
State Historic Park
North Tr.
PINE GROVE VOLCANO RD
VIEWING GRINDING
ROCK AND THE
PETROGLYPHS
Entrance
Station
TOURING THE
RECONSTRUCTED
MIWOK VILLAGE
2,600
Bark
Houses
NORTH TRAIL & SOUTH NATURE TRAIL LOOP
Practice
House
VISITING THE CHAW'SE
REGIONAL INDIAN MUSEUM
2,400
Granary
Shade Ramada
Ceremonial
Roundhouse
Hand
Game House
South Nature Tr.
Indian
Game Field
Indian
Grinding Rock
2,400
2,600
2,400
2,400
2,400
To Pine Grove
and Jackson
PINE GROVE VOLCANO RD
2,400
0
200 yds
0
200 m
Contour Interval = 40 feet
2,400

TOP 3

1. VISITING THE CHAW'SE REGIONAL INDIAN MUSEUM: The museum's exhibits make it a great starting place to learn more about the region's history (page 205).

2. VIEWING GRINDING ROCK AND THE PETROGLYPHS: The main draw of this park is the chaw'se, a giant slab of limestone with more than 1,100 mortar holes (page 205).

3. TOURING THE RECONSTRUCTED MIWOK VILLAGE: This collection of buildings allows current Miwok descendants the opportunity and space to honor their heritage (page 205).

PLANNING YOUR TIME

Most of what Indian Grinding Rock has to offer can be seen in a couple of hours.

ENTRANCE AND FEES

Indian Grinding Rock has **one main entrance** on Indian Rock Road. It's $8 per vehicle (including motorcycles) to park there for the day. The 22-site campground is open year-round and has a separate entrance.

VISITOR CENTER

Chaw'se Regional Indian Museum

209/296-7488; 10am-4pm daily

The Chaw'se Regional Indian Museum doubles as the park's visitor center and ranger station. Admission is free with your paid parking ticket. The museum has a gift shop along with its exhibits, as well as drinking water and restrooms.

WEATHER

Perched 2,400 ft (732 m) above sea level, Indian Grinding Rock State Historic Park has a dry climate with temperature highs around 90°F (32°C) during the summer months and 50°F (10°C) in the winter months. It's mostly sunny in the summer and it rains in the wintertime, with the occasional snow. The best time to visit is in the spring and fall, when you see more flora and fauna, and it's not as busy.

EVENTS

Big Time

Every year on the fourth Friday in September, the Miwok hold a fall festival called Big Time. The campground closes that weekend as local Indigenous people hold ceremonies in the hun'ge (the roundhouse) and surrounding areas with hand games, dancing, storytelling, food, and crafts. Big Time is open to the public and free to attend with the entrance fee, but there is not a fixed events schedule. For more information, go to https://chawse.org.

Indian Grinding Rock (left); Chaw'se Regional Indian Museum (right)

SIGHTS

★ CHAW'SE REGIONAL INDIAN MUSEUM

209/296-7488; 10am-4pm daily

Just past the entrance station is the Chaw'se Regional Indian Museum and a spacious parking lot. The museum's architecture is that of an eco-friendly energy-efficient roundhouse, and inside are a multitude of exhibits displaying the technology, tools, and artisanship of Miwok and other tribes.

★ GRINDING ROCK AND THE PETROGLYPHS

The chaw'se, the Miwok term for mortar cups, is the main draw of this park, which includes a giant slab of limestone with more than 1,100 mortar holes that you can see from a designated viewing platform. The mortars range from shallow dish-size to a couple of inches deep, and were created by smashing acorns and other materials into the stone, which wore it down. These chaw'se areas have also been referred to as "gossip stones" due to the social nature of grinding food together. Petroglyphs were also carved in this area but have eroded with time.

★ RECONSTRUCTED MIWOK VILLAGE

Past Grinding Rock, head toward the South Nature Trail to the Reconstructed Miwok Village. This collection of functional bark houses, granary, Indian game field, shade ramada, and ceremonial roundhouse allows current Miwok descendants the opportunity and space to honor their heritage. Every September when the acorns fall from the trees, Indian families celebrate Big Time at the park—a festival that includes dancing, singing, hand games, storytelling, and acorn-gathering ceremonies.

CAMPING

On the southern end of the park, Indian Grinding Rock State Historic Park Campground has **one campground** with 22 campsites available for overnight stays all year long; they can be booked through Reserve California (800/444-7275; www.reservecalifornia.com; $30-35/night). The sites each have a fire ring and a picnic table; a restroom and showers are in the middle of the campground loop. They can fit vehicles up to 27 ft (8 m) long, and each one has room for two cars—or a car and a vehicle/towed-trailer combo—plus two tents.

Two environmental group sites located in a secluded area in the northern end of the park contain seven bark houses, each of which can sleep up to six people. The unique camping accommodations can be reserved for up to 44 people.

DISTANCE: 3 mi (4.8 km) round-trip
DURATION: 1.5 hours
EFFORT: Easy
TRAILHEAD: Chaw'se Regional Indian Museum

There are two easy built-out trails in this park, the North Trail and the South Trail, that can be walked in two loops, joining up at the Reconstructed Miwok Village.

The North Trail starts near the museum and heads north around the meadow. The first hundred yards or so are wheelchair-accessible before the trail splits off. It passes an old farm site before crossing a creek and coming up on the Reconstructed Miwok Village/bark houses. From here it connects to the South Trail and goes through the forest and edge of the campground, looping back to the roundhouse and the path leading to the Grinding Rock viewing platform and museum on a paved route.

BEST CAMPGROUND

Indian Grinding Rock Campground

Located off the southern end of the park, this well-kept campground is quiet, clean, and open year-round. Tucked within the oak trees and the pines, the best sites are the ones closest to the South Nature Trail (sites 15-16). Site 7 is ADA-accessible.

FOOD AND LODGING

Pine Grove off CA-88 is a small town closest to the park, 2 mi (3 km) away. It has a couple of food options including a café and a burger joint. If you're not camping at the park, consider staying in **Jackson,** 11 mi (18 km) west of Indian Grinding Rock on CA-88. Jackson has grocery stores, gas stations, and a historic main street with shops, restaurants, and a possibly haunted Victorian-era hotel built in 1852 called The National.

BEST PICNIC SPOT

Shade Ramada

Picnic places are aplenty at Indian Grinding Rock State Historic Park, with the best ones being right around Grinding Rock. There are some tables next to the museum, but the shade ramada across from the Grinding Rock viewing platform has tables that can hold up to 150 people. This place is especially buzzing in September during Big Time.

BEST NEARBY

BLACK CHASM CAVERN NATIONAL NATURAL LANDMARK

Gold Country Adventures (15701 Pioneer Volcano Rd., Volcano; https://cavetouring.com; 10am-5pm daily; $22) will take you into the underground world of stalagmites, stalactites, and helictite crystals in 50-minute guided walking tours. The moderately strenuous route drops 100 ft (30 m) below the ground, going through three naturally air-conditioned chambers.

To get to Black Chasm Cavern from Indian Grinding Rock, follow Indian Rock Road until you reach Pine Grove Volcano Road and turn left. Take it for a mile (1.6 km) and make a sharp right turn onto Pioneer Volcano Road. The landmark is 0.2 mi (0.3 km) to the right.

GETTING THERE

CAR

Indian Grinding Rock State Historic Park is one hour (56 mi/90 km) east of Sacramento, 1.5 hours (80 mi/129 km) southwest of South Lake Tahoe, and 1 hour (56 mi/90 km) northeast of Stockton. It's on CA-88 off Pine Grove Volcano Road, 11 mi (18 km) east of Jackson in the heart of Amador County.

From downtown Jackson, take CA-88 east for 9 mi (14 km), then turn left on Pine Grove Volcano Road. If coming from the west, then the campground is the first left off Pine Grove Volcano Road (on Bryson Lane). The main entrance to Indian Grinding Rock is a half mile (0.8 km) past the campground. To get there, make a left on Indian Rock Road.

Caltrans does its best to keep Carson Pass (CA-88) open year-round; crews may close it temporarily in the wintertime if there's avalanche danger and they need to clear out heavy snow.

CALAVERAS BIG TREES STATE PARK

ADDRESS: 1170 E. CA-4, Arnold

PHONE: 209/795-2334

DAY USE HOURS: 6am–6pm

AREA: 6,498 acres (2,630 ha)

In the mountainous heartland between the Tuolumne State Game Refuge and Stanislaus National Forest, Calaveras Big Trees State Park is part of a montane ecosystem that includes volcanic formations, creeks, meadows, and—most famously—stands of giant sequoias. These strong, resilient living legacies can reach up to 325 ft (99 m) tall and 33 ft (10 m) wide, sharing the nutrient-filled soil with other trees in the mixed conifer groves.

Long before this became an official state park, the Miwok people fished, trapped, and hunted in and around their villages in the California yellow pine belt.

The big trees were first noticed by settler Augustus Dowd in 1852, and the next few decades brought about struggles between conservationists and lumbermen. The Calaveras Grove Association formed, helping to create the California State Parks system in conjunction with the Save the Redwoods League and Sierra Club. Calaveras Big Trees became an official California State Park in 1931.

Some of the sequoias that still stand today are believed to be around 2,000 years old. They share the park with other pine trees including ponderosas, incense cedars, white firs, sugar pines, and Pacific dogwoods, along with a variety of wildflowers best seen in the spring after the snow melts and the Walter W. Smith Memorial Parkway reopens.

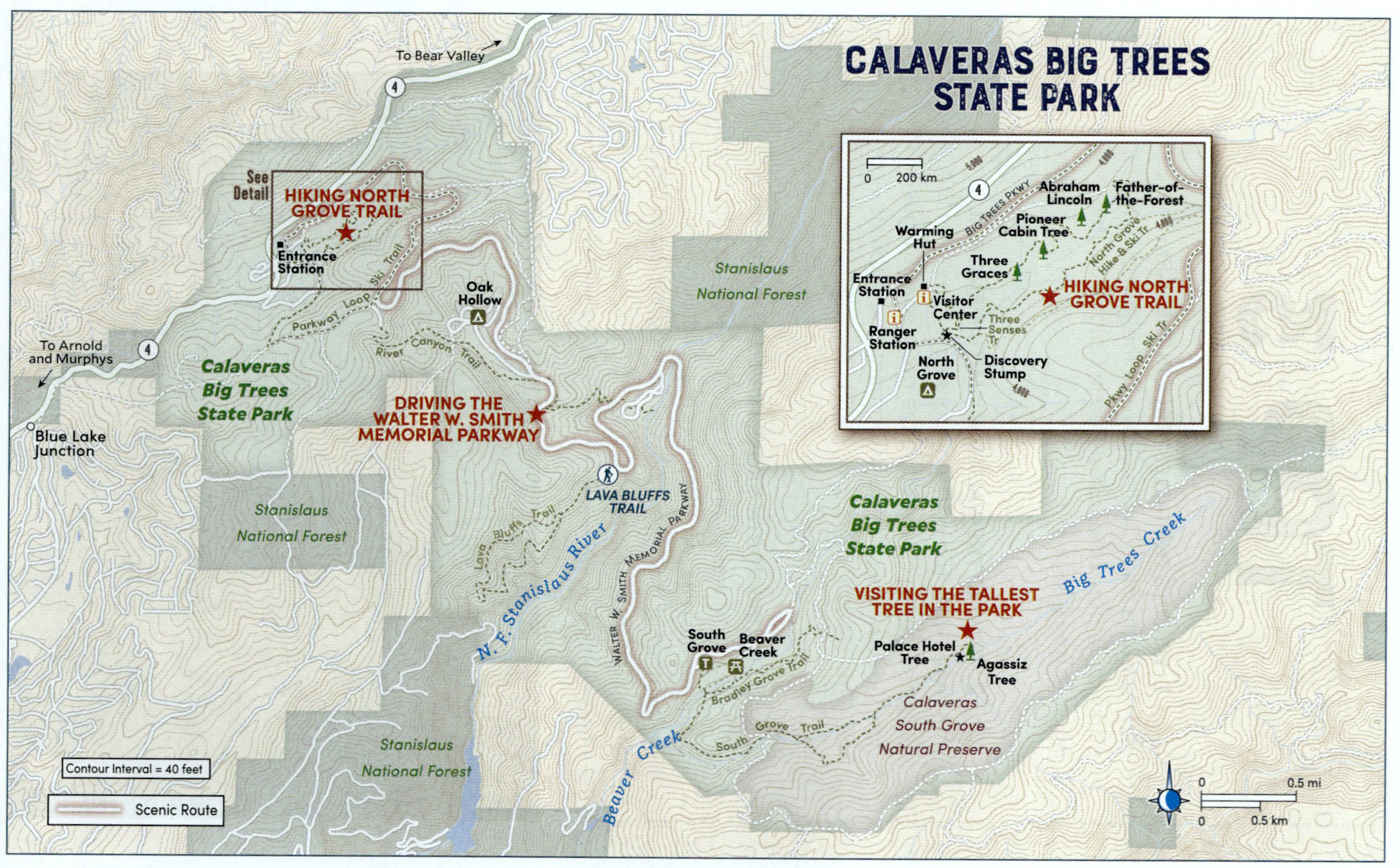

CALAVERAS BIG TREES STATE PARK
0
200 km
4
Big Trees Pkwy
Abraham Lincoln
Father-of-the-Forest
Pioneer Cabin Tree
Warming Hut
Three Graces
North Grove Hike & Ski Tr
Entrance Station
Visitor Center
HIKING NORTH GROVE TRAIL
Ranger Station
Three Senses Tr
North Grove
Discovery Stump
Pkwy Loop Ski Tr
To Bear Valley
4
See Detail
HIKING NORTH GROVE TRAIL
Entrance Station
Parkway Loop Ski Trail
Oak Hollow
River Canyon Trail
To Arnold and Murphys
4
Calaveras Big Trees State Park
Blue Lake Junction
DRIVING THE WALTER W. SMITH MEMORIAL PARKWAY
Stanislaus National Forest
LAVA BLUFFS TRAIL
Lava Bluffs Trail
N. F. Stanislaus River
WALTER W. SMITH MEMORIAL PARKWAY
Stanislaus National Forest
Calaveras Big Trees State Park
Big Trees Creek
VISITING THE TALLEST TREE IN THE PARK
South Grove
Beaver Creek
Palace Hotel Tree
Agassiz Tree
Bradley Grove Trail
Calaveras South Grove Natural Preserve
South Grove Trail
Beaver Creek
Stanislaus National Forest
Contour Interval = 40 feet
Scenic Route
0
0.5 mi
0
0.5 km

TOP 3

★ **1. VISITING THE TALLEST TREE IN THE PARK:** The sequoia-filled South Grove at the end of the parkway features the tallest tree in Calaveras, the Agassiz Tree (page 211).

★ **2. DRIVING THE WALTER W. SMITH MEMORIAL PARKWAY:** The parkway connects to most of the trails and best picnic spots in the area, so you'll get a good idea of the park's environment and habitats via this 9-mi (14-km) drive (page 212).

★ **3. HIKING NORTH GROVE TRAIL:** On this 1.5-mi (2.5-km) well-marked loop you'll see beautiful big trees such as the Three Graces, Old Bachelor, and Father of the Forest, as well as walk on top of Big Stump (page 212).

PLANNING YOUR TIME

While there's much to see in Calaveras Big Trees, you can visit the highlights in half a day. To experience everything, you'll want to spend the night.

Nearby state parks include Indian Grinding Rock State Historic Park (47 mi/76 km).

ENTRANCE AND FEES

The Calaveras Big Trees State Park's **entrance station** (209/795-2334) is at the northern end of the park, close to the visitor center and North Grove campground at the start of the Walter W. Smith Memorial Parkway (also referred to as the Big Trees Parkway on Google Maps). The entrance is clearly marked off CA-4. Parking costs $10-12 for the day.

VISITOR CENTER

Calaveras Big Trees Visitor Center

Walter W. Smith Memorial Parkway off CA-4; 209/795-3840; www.bigtrees.org; 10am-4pm daily

Calaveras Big Trees has one of the more robust welcoming centers of the state park system, offering a visitor center, museum, and bookstore all in one. All kinds of goodies can be found here, including park information, maps, clothing, souvenirs, and trail bars.

WEATHER

At its 4,701-ft (1,433-m) elevation, Calaveras Big Trees is subject to snow in the wintertime, which is great if you are into sledding, snowshoeing, or cross-country skiing, but unfortunately closes much of the park. The Walter W. Smith Memorial Parkway reopens May 1 or later, depending on how much snow is on the ground. Temperatures are usually pleasantly warm at that time (May-August), hovering between 50-80°F (10-27°C). Spring and autumn are the best times to visit, but temperatures can change drastically, so wear layers.

SIGHTS

 AGASSIZ TREE

At the eastern end of the 5-mi (8-km) South Grove loop, the park's biggest tree—the Agassiz Tree—stands at 250 ft (76 m) tall and more than 25 ft (8 m) in diameter. You'll have to crane your neck to try to see the top.

DISCOVERY STUMP

At the first stop on the North Grove Trail, the remnants of Discovery Tree, the first tree cut down by settlers, still stand. In the early 1800s when the symmetrical tree stood tall, it was more than 280 ft (85 m) tall and at least 25 ft (8 m) in diameter. In 1853, it took five men 22 days to cut down Discovery Tree, and the stump was smoothed over to serve as a dance floor.

FATHER-OF-THE-FOREST

Lying on the forest floor (at number

13 of the *North Grove Trail Guide* provided by the Calaveras Big Trees Association), this tree fell centuries ago and has slowly decomposed, releasing vitamins back into the earth. Feel the rush of oxygen as you walk through the fallen trunk of the tree, the holes providing light where branches once grew.

SCENIC DRIVES

★ WALTER W. SMITH MEMORIAL PARKWAY

DISTANCE: 8.4 mi (13.5 km)
DURATION: 20 minutes
START: Calaveras Big Trees Visitor Center
END: South Grove trailhead

The Walter W. Smith Memorial Parkway connects to most of the trails and best picnic spots in the area, so you'll get a good idea of the park's environment and habitats by taking this lovely drive. Starting at the visitor center, this paved road heads south and accesses its three tributaries—Big Trees Creek at the top, the North Fork Stanislaus River, and Beaver Creek. The road stops at Beaver Creek, where there are restrooms, a picnic area, and the trailhead to South Grove.

HIKING

There are eight hiking trails at Calaveras Big Trees State Park, ranging from easy to strenuous. Most of them are moderately easy.

★ NORTH GROVE TRAIL

DISTANCE: 1.5 mi (2.5 km) round-trip
DURATION: 1 hour
EFFORT: Easy
TRAILHEAD: Calaveras Big Trees Visitor Center

Walter W. Smith Memorial Parkway (left); Discovery Stump on the North Grove Trail (right)

TOP HIKE
LAVA BLUFFS TRAIL

DISTANCE: 2.5 mi (4 km) round-trip
DURATION: 4-6 hours
EFFORT: Moderate
TRAILHEAD: Walter W. Smith Memorial Parkway

Known as one of the more scenic trails at Calaveras Big Trees State Park, the Lava Bluffs loop is right in the middle of the park above the North Fork Stanislaus River. Starting at 4,000 ft (1,219 m) elevation, this trail takes hikers on an adventure sometimes dropping down to 3,700 ft (1,128 m) and climbing to 4,200 ft (1,280 m) through a variety of forest environments, along a centuries-old water ditch, and over volcanic formations. In the springtime, bright purple lupine, leopard lilies, and crimson columbine pop up underneath and around the thick greenery that intensified after the volcanic ridges formed.

Located near the entrance station at the northern end of the park, the North Grove Trail is one of the first and most popular trails at Calaveras Big Trees. Walking counterclockwise from the visitor center, hikers will follow the gentle dirt path to the Big Stump, continue through the forest passing trees including Empire State and Old Bachelor, and walk through the cave-like trunk of Father of the Forest. On the eastern side of the loop, the Abraham Lincoln Tree, Three Graces, and other giant sequoias can be admired. The short, 20-minute Three Senses loop within this North Grove loop near Big Stump offers trail markers in English and braille.

SOUTH GROVE TRAIL

DISTANCE: 5 mi (8 km) round-trip
DURATION: 2 hours 15 minutes
EFFORT: Moderate
TRAILHEAD: End of Walter W. Smith Memorial Parkway/Beaver Creek parking lot

At the southern end of the park, which tends to close in the wintertime, the South Grove offers another stand of sequoias that joined the state park in 1954. The out-and-back trail starts by crossing Beaver Creek with a steady climb up into the lower part of the grove. If you stay along the north side of Big Trees Creek going in a clockwise direction, eventually you'll come to a side trail that takes you to the upper grove and the two largest trees in the park: Palace Hotel Tree and Agassiz Tree.

RECREATION

WINTER SPORTS

The winter trails at Calaveras Big Trees are open to cross-country skiing and snowshoeing, allowing one to quietly take in nature while seeing the giant sequoias covered in a blanket of white. There aren't any equipment rentals within the park, but the nearby towns of Arnold and Murphys have rental options. A **warming hut** for Nordic skiers stocked with hot drinks is open during the weekends in the colder months if staffing allows. These trails are generally open December-April.

Parkway Loop Ski Trail

This 3.5-mi (5.6-km) scenic trail goes through trees both big and small on moderately graded slopes. Orange ski signs mark the route, but it's best to start at Gate 23 of the fire road on the eastern side of North Grove campground and follow the trail in a counterclockwise direction.

North Grove Ski Trail

The North Grove is a relatively flat 1.7-mi (2.7-km) loop perfect for skate-skiing through the sequoias.

Abraham Lincoln Tree

CAMPING

Calaveras Big Trees State Park has 120 campsites between **two campgrounds,** North Grove and Oak Hollow, as well as a couple of primitive environmental sites scattered at the northern and southern ends. Two group camps and cabins are in an area across CA-4/Ebbetts Pass from the entrance station.

All campgrounds are open May-October, and sites can be booked from two days to up to six months in advance through Reserve California (800/444-7575; www.reservecalifornia.com; $35/night). Sites fill up fast in the summertime. A few sites are available in the North Grove in the off-season on a first-come, first-served basis. All sites in the North Grove and Oak Hollow have a fire ring with a grill, bear-proof food locker, and picnic table. Flush toilets, showers, and water spigots are nearby. Calaveras Big Trees State Park can accommodate RVs up to 30 ft (9 m) long and allows eight people per site. The camping fee includes parking for one vehicle; each additional one is $10/night.

BEST CAMPGROUNDS

North Grove Campground

Located at the top of the state park in the heart of all the historical and cultural action, this 74-site campground consists of a loop going around a wide open meadow with Big Tree Creek flowing through it. A mix of conifers provides shade and privacy around the meadow. A dump station near the first sites is free to use for park campers, or $20 for day visitors.

Oak Hollow Campground

Oak Hollow is about 4 mi (6 km) south of the entrance station off the Walter W. Smith Memorial Parkway. There are three loops nestled in a pine and oak forest with 51 sites. This campground is close to the Stanislaus River Trail.

FOOD AND LODGING

Arnold is the closest town, 3 mi (5 km) west of the park on CA-4, aka the Ebbetts Pass Scenic Byway. It's a small town with few amenities—there's a market to pick up camping supplies and a gas station. The next closest town is **Murphys** on CA-4, which has gas, supplies, and a well-stocked farm stand 15 mi (24 km) away from the park.

BEST PICNIC SPOT

Beaver Creek Picnic Area

Beaver Creek has restrooms and is close to the South Grove and Bradley Grove Trails. The spacious picnic tables, grills, and freshwater creek provide plenty to do at this southern end of the park.

BEST NEARBY

road to Bear Valley in the winter

BEAR VALLEY

Bear Valley Mountain Resort (2280 California 207, Bear Valley; 209/753-2301; www.bearvalley.com; daily tickets $69-169) is a popular place to go skiing and snowboarding. Its 1,680 acres (680 ha) has terrain for all ages and abilities accessed via nine chairlifts. The mountain is 30 minutes east of Calaveras Big Trees off CA-4.

GETTING THERE

CAR

Calaveras Big Trees is 77 mi (124 km) east of Stockton on the Walter W. Smith Memorial Parkway off CA-4.

South Lake Tahoe is 115 mi (185 km) north of Calaveras Big Trees. If coming from that direction, take CA-88 west for 74 mi (119 km) into Pioneer. Follow CA-26 west then Railroad Flat Road, Sheep Ranch Road, and Avery Sheep Ranch Road for 34 mi (55 km) and turn left on CA-4. Continue for 7 mi (11 km), passing through Arnold before reaching the park. The Calaveras Connect public bus system also goes to Arnold on its Red Line route.

Point Lobos State Natural Reserve

CENTRAL CALIFORNIA

Driftwood-scattered beaches and rocky coves punctuated by enticing coastal towns make the Central Coast of California a gem.

Find interesting sea creatures while exploring coastal tide pools in the morning and complement it with a hike through the woodlands in the afternoon. Look for migrating whales, birds, and monarch butterflies, or visit the sunbathing harbor seals. Pitch a tent next to the crashing waves or listen to the gentle wind sweep through the Monterey pines and cypress trees in a quiet campsite.

See firsthand the resilience of the forests affected by wildfires and how some of California's oldest state parks have bounced back, ushering in a new era of restoration and land management practices.

There is also spectacular opportunity for road trips along the famous Pacific Coast Highway as it hugs the coast and provides sweeping views of the crashing waves below. Hiking the bluffs, kayaking the bays, and exploring the beaches are other ways to immerse yourself in the landscape here.

Across the state, on the other side of the majestic Sierra Nevada mountain range, you'll find high desert where gold fever drew thousands and ancient limestone spires rising eerily from a saltwater lake.

Pick a theme or embrace the wild shifts in landscape across Central California for a family road trip, a weekend getaway, or a rugged adventure.

BEST CENTRAL CALIFORNIA STATE PARKS

PARK NAME	LANDSCAPE	DAY-USE ENTRANCE FEE
Bodie State Historic Park	Historic site	$8
Mono Lake Tufa State Natural Reserve	Lake	$3
Half Moon Bay State Beach	Coast	$10
Pigeon Point Light Station State Historic Park	Historic site	free
Big Basin Redwoods State Park	Forest	$6
Henry Cowell Redwoods State Park	Forest	$10
Point Lobos State Natural Reserve	Coast	$10
Pfeiffer Big Sur State Park	Mountain/forest	$10
Hearst San Simeon State Historical Monument and State Park	Historic site/coast	$35
Cayucos State Beach and Estero Bluffs State Park	Coast	free
Morro Bay State Park	Coast	free
Montaña de Oro State Park	Coast	free
Pismo State Beach and Oceano Dunes State Vehicular Recreation Area	Coast	free/$5
El Capitán State Beach	Coast	$10
El Presidio de Santa Barbara State Historic Park	Historic site	$5

CAMPING OPTIONS	SUGGESTED VISIT LENGTH	PAGE
none	half day	page 228
dispersed sites	half day	page 235
1 campground	half day	page 243
none	half day	page 250
none	half day	page 256
1 campground	2 days	page 265
none	half day	page 276
1 campground, dispersed sites, cabin	2 days	page 287
none/2 campgrounds	half day	page 296
none	half day	page 304
1 campground	1 day	page 312
1 campground/ dispersed sites	half day	page 322
2 campgrounds	1 day	page 333
1 campground	1 day	page 343
none	half day	page 350

BEST CENTRAL CALIFORNIA STATE PARKS
Sacramento
Santa Rosa
80
5
101
San Rafael
Berkeley
Oakland
Stockton
San Francisco
Half Moon Bay SB
Half Moon Bay
Pigeon Point Light Station SHP
Big Basin Redwoods SP
1
Santa Cruz
Henry Cowell Redwoods SP
Salinas
Point Lobos SNR
Soledad
Big Sur
101
Pfeiffer Big Sur SP
San Lucas
Hearst San Simeon SHM and SP
Paso Robles
Cayucos SB and Estero Bluffs SP
Atascadero
Morro Bay
Morro Bay SP
Montaña de Oro SP
Pismo SB and Oceano Dunes SVRA
Santa Maria
El Capitán SB
Santa Ynez
Santa Barbara
El Presidio de Santa Barbara SHP
PACIFIC OCEAN
Channel Islands National Park
NEVADA
Bodie SHP
Mono Lake
Lee Vining
Mono Lake Tufa SNR
Yosemite NP
99
Fresno
Bakersfield
0
30 mi
30 km

CENTRAL CALIFORNIA STATE PARKS 3 WAYS

THE DREAMY PACIFIC COAST HIGHWAY TOUR

The scenic Pacific Coast Highway (CA-1) leads to many of California's best natural features, marrying the sea to the mountains and providing travelers with many awe-inspiring hikes, sights, and coastal adventures. Within this 155-mi (249-km) stretch of California coastline, there are several state park must-visits.

Day 1

Get an early start at **Pfeiffer Big Sur State Park.** Hike to the mesmerizing Pfeiffer Falls, combining it with the Valley View Overlook Trail. Have a sit-down breakfast or coffee at the Homestead Restaurant, then pick up provisions at the Big Sur Lodge grocer to sustain yourself for your afternoon adventure at **Point Lobos State Natural Reserve.**

Point Lobos is 22 mi (35 km), about a 30-minute drive, north of Pfeiffer Big Sur, right on CA-1. Hike through the cypress grove and then walk the South Shore Trail, keeping an eye out for birds at the Bird Island Overlook. Then hop in the car and drive 1 hour (50 mi/80 km) around the Monterey Bay to Santa Cruz. Stay the night there.

Day 2

Drive the 15 minutes (7 mi/11 km) to **Henry Cowell Redwoods State Park** and start your day off with a walk through the Redwood Grove Loop. If you want to keep going, hike up to the Observation Deck. Stop at the visitor center and the Mountain Parks Foundation Store to learn more about the area and pick up a cool memento.

From there, take CA-9 north for 30 minutes (15 mi/24 km) to **Big Basin Redwoods State Park.** Keep track of how many banana slugs you find as you hike Skyline to the Sea and Meteor Trail Loop. From Big Basin Highway, aka CA-236, take the Empire Grade 22 mi (35 mi) to Davenport and continue 17 mi (27 km) north on CA-1 to **Pigeon Point Light Station State Historic Park** (40 mi/64 km total, 1 hour) where you can stay the night at the hostel.

Day 3

After waking up in a warm bed at Pigeon Point, walk the grounds around the lighthouse and try to spot migrating whales from the deck of the Fog Signal Building. Take a stroll down the half-mile (0.8-km) Mel's Lane to catch the best view of Prisoner Rock. Then, get in the car and drive 30 minutes (22 mi/35 km) north on CA-1 to **Half Moon Bay State Beach.** Post up on the sand and have a picnic or stroll along the Coastside Trail.

EXPLORING THE SAN LUIS OBISPO COASTLINE

Spend a few days exploring a section of California's Central Coast with inviting towns, rocky bluffs, and a slow pace. The Pacific Coast Highway follows 34 mi (55 km) of scenic coastline to connect Montaña de Oro in the southern end to San Simeon in the northern end.

Day 1

The first day of your Central Coast road trip will be dedicated to travel and setting up camp at **Morro Bay State Park.** Iconic Morro Rock, the remnant of an extinct volcano, rises up out of Morro Bay. The campground is set in mixed coastal forest with tent and RV sites. Enjoy a stroll on the boardwalk through the park's natural bay habitat, then have dinner around the campfire at your site.

Day 2

Begin your day with a kayak across the bay, or opt for an excursion to Morro Rock. Kayaks are available for rent at the Kayak Shack at the marina. End your outing with lunch at the park's waterfront café.

In the afternoon, drive the 9 mi (14 km, 20 minutes) south via South Bay Boulevard and Pecho Valley Road to **Montaña de Oro State Park,** known for its secluded beaches and rocky cliffs. Spend an afternoon on the tucked-away shores of Spooner's Cove. For dinner, head back to your campsite or venture into the harbor town of Morro Bay.

Day 3

Break down camp and head north via CA-1 to the historic coastal town of Cayucos, an easy 15-minute (10-mi/16-km) jaunt. This will give you the full day to enjoy the beautiful beaches and scenic fishing pier. While the morning marine layer keeps the coastline shrouded in fog and chill, walk the coastal bluffs of **Estero Bluffs State Park** just north of town. Spend the afternoon at **Cayucos State Beach** swimming or tide-pooling. Stay the night at one of Cayucos's classic beach motels and have dinner in town.

Day 4

After breakfast, make the short drive (16 mi/26 km, 20 minutes) north along CA-1 to **Hearst San Simeon State Historical Monument.** Check in for your tour of Hearst Castle. Walk the rugged driftwood-strewn beaches of **Hearst San Simeon State Park** and appreciate the wildness of the coast before heading 9 mi (15 km) north of the San Simeon Creek Campground to see the elephant seals.

Return to the park and check in to your reserved site at the San Simeon Creek Campground. For dinner, dine at one of the restaurants in Cambria, 2 mi (3 km) south of the campground.

Day 1

Day 2

Day 3

SOUTHERN CENTRAL COAST BEACH TRIP

Enjoy two of the Southern Central Coast's classic beaches on a three-day trip covering 74 mi (119 km). This itinerary gives you plenty of time planted firmly in the sand. Visit Pismo Beach's sand dunes, enjoy the surf at El Capitán, and camp, swim, and hike at these oceanfront destinations.

Day 1

Set up camp at **El Capitán State Beach** Campground where sites are situated in sycamore and oak woodland. Spend time on the beach and hike along the Bluff-Top Trail, which takes in views of the coastline and the distant Channel Islands.

Day 2

Spend the morning on El Capitán's beach looking for the perfect wave, relaxing on the sand, or exploring tide pools before packing up camp to head up the coast. Your destination is **Pismo State Beach,** 1 hour 15 minutes away (74 mi/119 km). The route travels scenic CA-101 through inland hills and the charming rustic towns of the Central Coast wine region. Check into North Beach Campground, your base camp for the next two days. Stroll along the Monarch Butterfly Grove and Meadow Creek Trail to take in the low coastal dunes stretching south of the campground.

Day 3

Spend a full day enjoying Pismo Beach's coast. Begin the morning with an easy hike through the wetlands at Oso Flaco Lake. From here, you will be well positioned to drive your car onto the sand at the **Oceano Dunes State Vehicular Recreation Area** for a picnic. Spend the afternoon renting an ATV and taking a spin through the dune fields. In the evening, explore the classic beach town of Pismo Beach, taking in dinner and sunset from the pier.

Pismo State Beach in the evening fog

Oceano Dunes SVRA

trail through the oak woodland at El Capitán State Beach Campground

BODIE STATE HISTORIC PARK

Before Bodie became the den of iniquity known for daily murders, stagecoach robberies, and saloons, it started as a humble mining camp after gold was discovered by William S. Bodey in 1859. By 1879 the town had a population of nearly 10,000 residents and 2,000 structures. There were 30 active mines, with newspapers and a baseball team alongside brothels and opium dens.

ADDRESS: CA-270, Bridgeport

PHONE: 760/616-5040

WEBSITE: www.bodiefoundation.org

DAY USE HOURS: 9am-6pm May-Sept., 9am-4pm Oct.-May

AREA: 1,016 acres (411 ha)

The boom lasted until 1881 when mines went bankrupt and the population dropped. Still, the two biggest mines produced ore until 1892. That year a fire tore through the business district, and the townspeople and structures further dwindled. The town survived until 1932 when another fire destroyed 95 percent of the structures. A few residents hung on until the late 1940s, when the last mine shut down.

Bodie became a State Historic Park in 1962. Today Bodie is one of the best-preserved ghost towns in the west. The historic zone is kept in a state of arrested decay, a time capsule to the echoes of this once-bustling place.

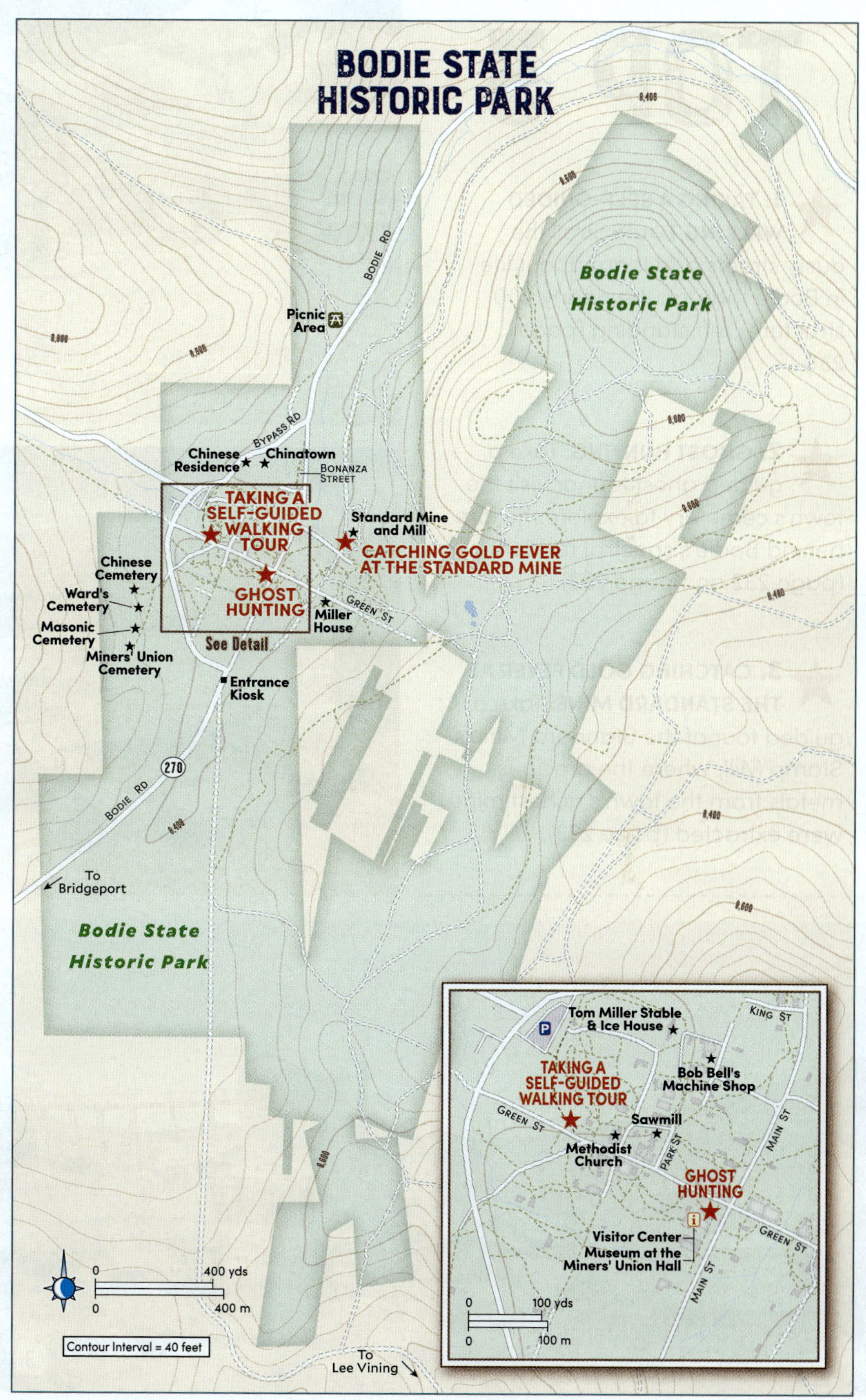

BODIE STATE HISTORIC PARK
Bodie State Historic Park
BODIE RD
Picnic Area
BYPASS RD
Chinese Residence
Chinatown
BONANZA STREET
TAKING A SELF-GUIDED WALKING TOUR
Standard Mine and Mill
CATCHING GOLD FEVER AT THE STANDARD MINE
Chinese Cemetery
Ward's Cemetery
Masonic Cemetery
Miners' Union Cemetery
GHOST HUNTING
GREEN ST
Miller House
See Detail
Entrance Kiosk
270
BODIE RD
To Bridgeport
Bodie State Historic Park
0 400 yds
0 400 m
Contour Interval = 40 feet
To Lee Vining
Tom Miller Stable & Ice House
KING ST
Bob Bell's Machine Shop
TAKING A SELF-GUIDED WALKING TOUR
GREEN ST
Sawmill
Methodist Church
PARK ST
MAIN ST
GHOST HUNTING
Visitor Center
Museum at the Miners' Union Hall
GREEN ST
MAIN ST
0 100 yds
0 100 m

TOP 3

★ **1. TAKING A SELF-GUIDED WALKING TOUR:** Stroll the dusty streets and learn about life in Bodie through the nearly 200 structures left standing (page 231).

★ **2. GHOST HUNTING:** Take a guided ghost tour or visit the town's cemetery to explore the lore behind Bodie's spectral residents (page 232 and page 233).

★ **3. CATCHING GOLD FEVER AT THE STANDARD MINE:** Take a guided tour of the Standard Mine's Stamp Mill, where the precious metals from the town's richest mine were extracted (page 233).

PLANNING YOUR TIME

Plan to spend a half day exploring Bodie, including drive times from Lee Vining or Bridgeport.

Nearby state parks include Mono Lake Tufa State Natural Reserve (23 mi/37 km).

ENTRANCE AND FEES

At the end of Bodie Road is the **one entrance** to the state park; visitors park in a parking area with restrooms. An entrance kiosk is usually staffed, but if unstaffed, visitors can leave cash or checks in a self-pay kiosk in the parking lot ($8).

VISITOR CENTER

Bodie State Historic Park Visitor Center

Miners' Union Hall; 9:30am-5:30pm daily late May-Sept.

A visitor center housing a small museum and bookstore is located in the **Miners' Union Hall,** circa 1878, where Bodie's most important social events were held throughout the year. The museum is only open in summer.

EVENTS

Bodie Living History Day

One day in summer only, the Bodie Foundation presents Bodie Living History Day. See wagons travel the streets, meet people from the town's past, and enjoy music, special tours, and children's activity booths at this annual family-friendly event ($8).

Free History Talks

These are offered most days late May through September. The 10am talks take place at the Methodist Church, and the 2pm talks are at the museum boardwalk. Check with the entrance station or museum.

WEATHER

Bodie is open all year; however, summer is the best time to visit because it has the most predictable weather with temperatures in the mid 70s (around 24°C). Due to the town's high elevation (8,375 ft/2,553 m), winter can bring winds, subzero temperatures, and white-out conditions. **Access roads close in winter.** Bodie is accessible only by skis, snowshoes, or snowmobiles during winter months.

SIGHTS

TOURS

★ Self-Guided Tours

When checking in at the entrance kiosk, you can opt to purchase an informational booklet ($3) that takes you on a self-guided walking tour along the historic streets. Proceeds go to stabilizing Bodie's historic buildings. Buildings are numbered corresponding with the booklet and map, guiding visitors to the name, history, and use of each building. Allow 2-3 hours to explore the center of town and visit a site or two on the outer edges.

Methodist Church (top); ruins of a residence (middle); Shell sign (bottom)

Stamp Mill Tours

Seasonal tours of the stamp mill are offered most days late May through September for a small fee ($6). Tours are 45-60 minutes and explore the area closed to the public where ores were processed and extracted. Inquire about and buy tickets for the tour at the museum when you arrive.

★ Ghost Walks

A place with this much history and drama has its ghosts. The Bodie Foundation offers a limited number of docent-led dusk Ghost Walks ($45/person) in summer. Visitors can tour the town, cemetery, or stamp mill to learn about the town's history and residents, both past as well as those who may have never left. If you can't make the official tour, wander the town's cemetery, visit the morgue, and otherwise consider the cycle of life in this harsh locale.

GREEN STREET

The interpretive tour begins at Green Street, just beyond the parking area. Green Street contains several residences, including the **Miller House,** open to the public. The **Methodist Church** erected in 1882 is also along this route. It is the only church still standing in Bodie.

PARK STREET

A small **sawmill** on Park Street was crucial for milling lumber for houses as well as providing firewood, a necessity with Bodie's harsh winters. There are also residences, the **Tom Miller Stable and Ice House,** and **Bob Bell's Machine Shop** nearby on Prospect Street.

CHINATOWN

Located along King Street, the Chinese quarter was self-contained with general stores, gambling halls, saloons, and a Taoist temple. The main sources of income came from selling vegetables, cutting and selling firewood, operating laundries, and working on the Bodie railway.

BONANZA STREET

Also known as Maiden Lane and Virgin Alley, the brothel zone is where ladies lived and worked out of one-room cabins.

MAIN AND KING STREETS

Main and King Streets give good views of the Bodie Mining District to the east.

★ Standard Mine and Mill

The Standard Mine and Mill were at the heart of the frenzy for gold, which swelled the remote location from a small mining camp in 1861 to a booming town of 10,000 by 1879. The most successful of the 30 mining companies in the district, the Standard Mine and its works sit on a lonely slope on the east end of town. The area is hazardous and closed to the public for self-guided tours, but visitors can take a guided tour (11am, 1pm, and 3pm most days depending on staffing, late May-Sept.; $6) of the Standard Mine's stamp mill, where the last precious ore was crushed in 1938.

MUSEUM AT THE MINERS' UNION HALL

9:30am-5:30pm daily late May-Sept., subject to change based on staffing and weather

A small museum and bookstore are housed on Main Street in the old Miners' Union Hall. In addition to union meetings, the hall was important for Bodie society and was used to hold fundraisers, parties, and elegant balls.

★ CEMETERY

In sagebrush on the outskirts of town, west of the park entrance, are a collection of cemeteries. Ward's Cemetery, the Masonic Cemetery, the Miners' Union Cemetery, and the Chinese Cemetery are all located in this zone. Note the position of the Chinese Cemetery outside the cemetery proper, indicating their status in that society.

FOOD AND LODGING

There are no restaurants or concessions at Bodie.

Nearby **Bridgeport** is a small, charming town located along US-395 with several lodging options including inns, lodges, motels, and cabin rentals. **Lee Vining** is another small, scenic town south of Bodie along US-395 with a few lodges and motels as well as RV sites. There are several restaurant options in both towns, most skewing casual and retro with several good options for takeout.

There is **no lodging or camping** inside the park, but camping options abound in the area with most campgrounds run by the US Forest Service (information www.fs.usda.gov, reservations www.recreation.gov), as well as a few privately run campgrounds for RV and tent camping.

BEST PICNIC SPOT

Bodie Picnic Area

A small picnic area is located on the north end of town where there are also restrooms. Located just beyond Chinatown and Bonanza Street, and the jail, it is a good midway stop if you are taking the self-guided tour.

GETTING THERE

CAR

The park is located northeast of Yosemite, in a remote mountain setting. The closest towns are **Bridgeport** and **Lee Vining,** both located along US-395. From Bridgeport, take US-395 7 mi (11 km) south to the turnoff for CA-270/Bodie Road. Head east 10 mi (16 km) until the pavement ends and continue the final 3 mi (5 km) on an unsurfaced road to the parking area and Bodie townsite. From Lee Vining, head north on US-395 for 18 mi (29 km) to CA-270/Bodie Road. Head east 10 mi (16 km) until the pavement ends and continue the final 3 mi (5 km) on an unsurfaced road to the parking area and Bodie townsite.

Note that Bodie Road closes in winter. Traveling on closed roads in this remote area often results in vehicles getting stuck in mud and snow, even with 4WD and chains. During the winter, the park is open but may only be accessible via snowmobile, skis, or snowshoes.

main road to Bodie

MONO LAKE TUFA STATE NATURAL RESERVE

Mono Lake is pitched in the high desert east of the Sierra Nevada mountain range. It covers nearly 70 mi (113 km) and is known for tufa towers, craggy stone pillars that rise from its lakebed and shores. The rock formations are calcium carbonate formed by freshwater springs mixing with the lake's alkaline water. The lake has no outlet, and evaporating freshwater leaves salts and minerals, creating an inland sea saltier than the ocean.

ADDRESS: 1 Visitor Center Dr., Lee Vining

PHONE: 760/647-6331

WEBSITE: www.monolake.org

DAY USE HOURS: Sunrise-sunset

AREA: 55,300 acres (22,400 ha)

This unique ecosystem supports a massive population of alkali flies and brine shrimp, which feed one of the largest gull colonies in California, part of the 1-2 million birds that use the lake as a migratory stop each year. For thousands of years, the Mono Basin was home to the Kutzadika'a people, a Northern Paiute group whose name is a reference to the brine fly. Visitors can walk among these limestone spires and knobs, admiring the contrast with snowcapped mountain peaks and volcanic landscape. From some vantage points you can see Paoha and Negit, volcanic islands in the middle of the lake.

MONO LAKE TUFA STATE NATURAL RESERVE
To Bridgeport
POLE LINE RD
BLACK POINT RD
Mono City
CEMETERY RD
County Park
County Park
BIRD-WATCHING
Mono Inn
Black Point Fissures Trail
Negit Island
Paoha Island
MONO LAKE
Hoover Wilderness
Mono Lake Tufa State Natural Reserve
Old Marina Tufa View Area
Lake Trail
PICNIC GROUNDS RD
Mono Basin Scenic Area Visitor Center
Lee Vining
Mono Lake Committee Information Center & Bookstore
TIOGA RD
To Yosemite National Park
Ranger Station
Ansel Adams Wilderness
To Mammoth Lakes
TEST STATION RD
VISITING THE SOUTH TUFA
KAYAKING NAVY BEACH
Navy Beach
RUSH CREEK RD
Panum Crater
RIM TRAIL
PLUG TRAIL
MONO MILLS RD
Contour Interval = 40 feet

TOP 3

1. VISITING THE SOUTH TUFA: If you only have time for one stop, visit the iconic South Tufa formations, where a self-guided nature trail leads to a small beach and viewing area (page 239).

2. KAYAKING NAVY BEACH: Launch a kayak at Navy Beach to get out on the water and experience a new perspective on the lake and tufa (page 241).

3. BIRD-WATCHING: Spectacular numbers of birds use the lake's shimmering waters and unique ecosystem as a migratory stop (page 241).

PLANNING YOUR TIME

Visiting Mono Lake can be a quick stop off of US-395 at the Old Marina Tufa Viewing Area or a long half day to do a series of short hikes and swim or kayak the lake.

Nearby state parks include Bodie State Historic Park (23 mi/37 km).

ENTRANCE AND FEES

The **main entrance** to the park is at the Mono Basin Scenic Area Visitor Center. From here you can get information from the visitor center and walk a short interpretive trail to the shore and a collection of tufa at the Old Marina. However, it is possible to visit other areas of the park without stopping at the visitor center first. The **Old Marina Tufa Viewing Area** and **South Tufa Area** require a fee ($3) that can be paid at a self-pay kiosk located in the parking areas.

VISITOR CENTERS

Mono Basin Scenic Area Visitor Center

1 Visitor Center Dr., US-395, Lee Vining; www.fs.usda.gov; 9:30am-5pm Thurs.-Sun.

The Mono Basin Scenic Area Visitor Center is located at the main entrance to Mono Lake just north of Lee Vining, off US-395.

Mono Lake Committee Information Center and Bookstore

51359 US-395, Lee Vining; www.monolake.org/visit/infocenterbookstore; 9am-5pm daily

Mono Lake Committee Information Center and Bookstore is located in downtown Lee Vining, at the corner of US-395 and Third Street.

WEATHER

Located at 6,378 ft (1,944 m) elevation in desert terrain, Mono Lake has a high-altitude climate with four distinct seasons. Winter can be cold and snowy with temperatures hovering around 20°F (-7°C). Spring temperatures are warmer, bringing snowmelt that feeds creeks and wildflowers. Summer has warm days and cool nights with possible thunderstorms, making boating conditions dangerous. Fall temperatures are crisp and cool with stunning fall foliage displays. Summer is the best season to visit for its pleasant temperatures and recreation opportunities.

SIGHTS

OLD MARINA TUFA VIEWING AREA

An easy stop off US-395, the Old Marina has an accessible boardwalk that gives quick access to the water's edge with striking views of Mono Lake's islands, and a chance to take in the tufa up close. The tufa towers here have an eroded look compared with the striking pinnacles at the South Tufa area. They are actually pumice-block tufa (as opposed to limestone) created when the smaller island, Negit, erupted, spewing large pieces of volcanic rock across the lake.

The viewing area is located east

of US-395, 1 mi (1.6 km) north of Lee Vining, with a small parking lot and fee kiosk.

★ SOUTH TUFA

Explore one of the lake's largest tufa groves via an easy interpretive trail from the parking area that leads to the lake's shore. Walk amid the craggy limestone pinnacles burgeoning up from the shoreline and wade into the clear, salty water from a small beach. To learn more about the lake's unique ecosystem, join a free, hour-long naturalist-guided tour (www.monolake.org) offered in summer.

The South Tufa is located on the south end of Mono Lake, off of CA-120 east. From the Mono Basin Visitor Center, drive 6 mi (10 km) south on US-395. Turn left on CA-120 east for 5 mi (8 km), continuing onto Test Station Road for 1 mi (1.6 km). At the junction, take the left fork to the South Tufa area.

MONO LAKE TUFA STATE NATURAL RESERVE AND COUNTY PARK

Cemetery Rd. off US-395, 5 mi (8 km) north of Lee Vining

A quiet spot filled with grasses, wildflowers, and fragile tufa, the northwest end of the lake offers a great introduction to Mono Lake's unique ecosystem. A trail and boardwalk begin in the Mono Lake County Park and meander through the willows and marsh of the Mono Lake Tufa State Natural Reserve to the lakeshore. This is also a popular spot for migratory birds. Naturalist-led birding tours are offered in the summer months (www.monolake.org).

HIKING

The lake is circled by 4WD roads to access its most remote points; however, there are only three developed hiking trails highlighting some of the park's special places.

LAKE TRAIL

DISTANCE: 1.2 mi (1.9 km) round-trip
DURATION: 20-30 minutes
EFFORT: Easy
TRAILHEAD: Mono Basin Visitor Center or Old Marina

A 1.2-mi (1.9-km) round-trip trail links the visitor center with the Old Marina, offering a chance to get out in the salty desert landscape and enjoy views of the lake, volcanic tufa on the southwest end, and the lake's two islands.

trail to the South Tufa grove

TOP HIKE

PANUM CRATER: RIM AND PLUG TRAILS

DISTANCE: 1 mi (1.6 km) round-trip Plug Trail; 1.7 mi (2.7 km) round-trip Rim Trail
DURATION: 30 minutes Plug Trail; 45 minutes Rim Trail
EFFORT: Easy
TRAILHEAD: Dirt road off CA-120 east signed for Panum Crater

Panum Crater is a volcanic cone, part of the Mono-Inyo chain of volcanoes. Volcanic activity played a heavy hand in forming the landscape in the Mono Basin. The most recent eruption occurred around 1850, when the Paoha and Negit Islands in the center of Mono Lake erupted.

Two trails, the **Rim Trail** and **Plug Trail,** explore Panum Crater. The longer Rim Trail is a loop that traverses the rim of the crater, offering views into its depths. The shorter out-and-back Plug Trail climbs to the top of the rhyolitic dome and offers views of the lake and Mono Basin.

Panum Crater is a captivating place to hike at sunrise or sunset when the light brings out the landscape's austere features and reflects off of sublime Mono Lake.

The trailhead is 5 mi (8 km) south of Lee Vining. From US-395, turn onto CA-120 east; drive about 3 mi (5 km) and turn left onto a dirt road signed for Panum Crater.

RECREATION

★ KAYAKING

Navy Beach

While tufa-seekers head to the viewing areas, Navy Beach is the best place to get out into the tempting body of water. A small parking area near the shore makes it easy to access the water, as does the gentle slope of the beach. This is a good place to launch kayaks, canoes, and paddleboards. Local wisdom dictates paddling the lake in the morning due to the possibility of storms in the afternoon, which can make the lake choppy and dangerous. Pay attention to weather reports and clouds before heading out. The nearest kayak rentals are available in Lee Vining. The Mono Lake Committee offers **guided canoe tours** launching from Navy Beach in the summer (www.monolake.org; $35).

It is also possible to swim in the salty water, where the alkaline density makes swimming a buoyant experience. If swimming, bring fresh water to rinse off with after your dip.

Navy Beach is located at the south end of Mono Lake, off of CA-120 east. From the Mono Basin Visitor Center, drive 6 mi (10 km) south on US-395, then turn left on CA-120 for 5 mi (8 km), continuing onto Test Station Road for 1 mi (1.6 km). At the junction, take the right fork for 1 mi (1.6 km) to Navy Beach.

WILDLIFE WATCHING

★ Birds

Mono Lake is a hot spot for migratory birds with more than 80 species visiting each spring, summer, and early fall, including impressive numbers of phalaropes, eared grebes, and California gulls that like to nest on the lake's volcanic islands. On the quiet northwest shore, just below the county park, the **boardwalk** is a prime bird-watching spot. The Mono Lake Committee offers free 1.5-2-hour naturalist-led bird-watching tours (www.monolake.org) each summer.

FOOD AND LODGING

There are **no campgrounds** in the State Natural Reserve. Fortunately, Mono Lake is located in the spectacularly beautiful Eastern Sierra, a camping destination full of forests and alpine lakes, and there are many options for developed camping nearby. The small, charming town of **Lee Vining** is a great jumping-off point for exploring Mono Lake and the Eastern Sierra and serves as a gateway to Yosemite National Park. It is located adjacent to Mono Lake along US-395 at the intersection with CA-120 and offers a few rustic roadside motels, a handful of casual restaurants and a destination-worthy fine-dining restaurant (the Mono Inn), gift shops, a sporting goods shop for supplies, and gas.

BEST NEARBY

YOSEMITE NATIONAL PARK

Iconic Yosemite National Park (www.nps.gov; $35/vehicle) is within reach. Its famous waterfalls, granite peaks, and meadows lie just to the west via the Tioga Pass Road (CA-120). The Tioga Pass Road is one of the highest mountain passes in North America, a scenic drive with breathtaking views of the mountains and lakes below. The drive takes you to the idyllic Tuolumne Meadows area of the park, quieter than the main Yosemite Valley, with a river and views of the surrounding mountains, access to the backcountry via the famous Pacific Crest Trail, and a visitor center.

Tuolumne Meadows

From Mono Lake, the Tuolumne Meadows area of the park is 23 mi (37 km) southwest, or a 45-minute drive. From the town of Lee Vining on US-395, take the Tioga Pass Road (CA-120) west for 21 mi (34 km), about a 30-minute drive. To access Yosemite Valley, the main section of the park, the drive from Lee Vining is 76 mi (122 km) and will take approximately 2 hours. Reservations may be required to drive through Yosemite National Park from mid-April to late October. Check the park's website for the most up-to-date information.

BEST PICNIC SPOT

Mono Lake County Park

Take a break from Mono Lake's desert setting in the oasis-like Mono Lake County Park. Cottonwoods shade picnic tables next to a small stream a short walk from the lake's edge.

GETTING THERE

CAR

Mono Lake is located just east of US-395, 13 mi (21 km) east of Yosemite National Park, near the town of Lee Vining, California.

HALF MOON BAY STATE BEACH

With "beach" in its name, you better believe that Half Moon Bay State Beach is centered around water activities, marine life, and lots of sand. Surfing and fishing are popular here, but the strong riptides and chilly waters urge most people to admire the sea from the almost 4 mi (6 km) of sandy shore. Walking or biking the Coastside Trail is one of the more popular activities, with the chance to see a variety of wildlife from snowy plovers to sea lions.

ADDRESS: 95 Kelly Ave., Half Moon Bay

PHONE: 650/726-8820

WEBSITE: www.coastsidestateparks.org

DAY USE HOURS: 8am-sunset

AREA: 181 acres (73 ha)

Thousands of years before the Europeans arrived, the friendly Ohlone people's smart land management practices attracted large and small game such as deer, elk, squirrels, and rabbits. Everything changed when the Spanish missionaries took over the area in the mid-1770s; by 1810 almost three-fourths of the Ohlone population had either died or been driven out of Half Moon Bay. Throughout the years, the area was renamed Spanishtown, then eventually Half Moon Bay. The 2-mi (3-km) crescent-shaped shoreline within the town came under California State Parks management in 1956.

Cool morning fog tends to drift in and blanket the area, but anytime is a good time to picnic, camp, and spend a day at the beach.

HALF MOON BAY
STATE BEACH
AIRPORT ST
Princeton-by-the-Sea
El Granada
Pillar Point Harbor
Coastside Trail
CABRILLO HWY
Pillar Point
WATCHING THE SURFERS AT MAVERICKS
WHALE WATCHING
Miramar
PICNICKING AT ROOSEVELT BEACH
Roosevelt Beach
Park Entrance
Dunes Beach
Park Entrance
To Downtown Half Moon Bay
Venice Beach
Half Moon Bay State Beach
COASTSIDE TRAIL
Half Moon Bay State Beach
Francis Beach
Park Entrance
Visitor Center
Half Moon Bay
0.5 mi
0.5 km
Contour Interval = 40 feet

TOP 3

★ **1. WATCHING THE SURFERS AT MAVERICKS:** The winter waves beckon professional surfers from all over the world (page 247).

★ **2. WHALE WATCHING:** Gray whales, humpback whales, and orcas pass right through Half Moon Bay in the winter and spring months (page 248).

★ **3. PICNICKING AT ROOSEVELT BEACH:** With picnic tables close to the Coastside Trail and surrounded by sandy dunes, this beach is the perfect spot to have lunch (page 249).

PLANNING YOUR TIME

From south to north, Francis Beach is the first stop, with a campground, parking lots, and visitor center past the **fully staffed entrance station.** Venice Beach is a 2.5-mi (3.5-km) drive north of Francis and has a self-pay kiosk in a parking lot next to the Coastside Trail. Dunes and Roosevelt Beaches are farther up, with a **second entrance station,** parking lots, restrooms, and picnic tables between the paved path and the ocean.

A half day is plenty of time to visit all the beaches.

Nearby state parks include Pigeon Point Light Station State Historic Park (22 mi/35 km).

ENTRANCES AND FEES

There are **four entrances,** one for each beach. The cost is $10 to park a vehicle for the day at either Roosevelt, Dunes, Venice, or Francis Beach. All of the beaches can be accessed from CA-1.

VISITOR CENTER

Half Moon Bay State Beach Visitor Center

95 Kelly Ave.; 650/726-8820; 9am-3pm Sat.-Sun.

The visitor center at Francis Beach is open on the weekends, staff permitting. Restrooms, picnic tables, and the campground are nearby.

WEATHER

Half Moon Bay enjoys dry, arid, and sunny summers, while the winters are wet, chilly, and cloudy. The average temperature is 45-67°F (7-19°C), rarely getting above 76°F (24°C). Since Half Moon Bay is so beach oriented, the warmest time to visit is early July through September, but springtime can be best to see the blooming wildflowers. Usually January/February, when it's blustery and storming in the mountains, is when the waves are the biggest and gnarliest at Mavericks.

Coastside Trail (left); Venice Beach (right)

BEACHES

Half Moon Bay is made up of four beaches all connected by the Coastside Trail. When you're walking along the shoreline, all the beaches blend together, but four entrance stations/parking lots give you access to parts of the ocean. From south to north they are:

FRANCIS BEACH

The most south of Half Moon Bay state beaches is Francis Beach on Kelly Avenue, where there's the main entrance station, campground, parking lots, and visitor center. The entrance station is staffed most of the time because the campground and park staff are serious about collecting the daily fee, even if you just want to check out the visitor center.

VENICE BEACH

Below Dunes Beach is Venice Beach, considered the middle point of Half Moon Bay state beaches. Two parking lots are at the end of Venice Boulevard, and there are restrooms and self-pay kiosks. Most people park here to access the Coastside Trail; there's a faucet to wash off sandy feet and a bike station with tools if you need to do any repairs.

DUNES BEACH

A quarter mile (0.4 km) south of Roosevelt Beach, Dunes Beach is a slightly larger version of Roosevelt with restrooms right next to the Coastside Trail, a smattering of picnic tables, and a bigger parking lot facing the ocean. It's at the end of Young Avenue and has an entrance station that also serves Roosevelt Beach.

ROOSEVELT BEACH

Just 2.5 mi (3.5 km) south of Pillar Point Harbor, Roosevelt Beach, also known as Naples Beach, is a short drive from CA-1 (also called the Cabrillo Highway) to the end of Roosevelt Boulevard. About 20 parking spots, restrooms, and a few picnic tables are next to the mounds of dunes leading to the ocean.

RECREATION

★ SURFING

Mavericks

The bay between Half Moon Bay State Beach and **Pillar Point,** known as Mavericks, conjures up elusive waves known by expert surfers worldwide. The winter storm swells in November-March create watery crests that are up to 60 ft (18 m) tall, waves that only the most experienced, bravest surfers can attempt to ride. There used to be a pro invitational contest at Mavericks in February when waves are the most profound, but surfers will surf whenever Mavericks has waves regardless of the time of year. While **El Granada Beach** is at the heart of Mavericks, you may be able to catch the action from **Roosevelt Beach.**

TOP HIKE
COASTSIDE TRAIL

DISTANCE: 7.5 mi (12 km) one-way
DURATION: 3.5 hours
EFFORT: Moderate
TRAILHEAD: Pillar Point Harbor

Almost 4 mi (6 km) of the 7.5-mi (12-km) Coastside Trail go through Half Moon Bay State Beach from Roosevelt Beach to Francis Beach, although the trail extends all the way up to the Pillar Point Harbor and down to the Half Moon Bay Golf Links. A separate horse trail follows along that same route (horses are not allowed on the beach). Restrooms are next to the parking areas. Along with the oceanside views and beach access, hikers/walkers/bikers can also see a variety of plants including lizardtails, beach primroses, mustard, sand verbena, and California poppies. Many people just do an out-and-back section of the trail depending on where they park, but a popular route is starting at Venice Beach and biking up to Pillar Point.

WILDLIFE WATCHING

★ Marine Mammals

This stretch of the ocean is ripe for whale watching, especially in the winter months of January-April, to see **gray and killer whales.** Up to 20,000 gray whales migrate from Alaska down to the Baja Peninsula via the Pacific Ocean route for birthing season. **Humpback whales** will travel north to Alaska April-November, maybe crossing their paths. Orcas, aka killer whales, migrate through Half Moon Bay mid-January-mid-April. Local whale-watching tours based in the town of Half Moon Bay go out of **Pillar Point Harbor.** Sea lions and harbor seals also hang out near Mavericks.

CAMPING

Half Moon Bay State Beach has **one campground** at its southernmost Francis Beach. Standard campsites are $35/night, sites with electricity are $50/night, and oceanfront premium sites are $65/night. North of Francis Beach, the Sweetwood Group Camp has a big open field between cypress trees that accommodates only tents and has picnic tables, a fire ring, and pit toilets close by, but no running water. Half Moon Bay State Beach is a popular place, which is why reservations are highly recommended. Book your campsites through **Reserve California** (800/444-7275; www.reservecalifornia.com) up to six months before your travel dates.

BEST CAMPGROUND

Half Moon Bay State Beach Campground

Along with having the visitor center, day use area, and outdoor showers, the 52-site campground at Francis Beach can accommodate RVs and trailers up to 40 ft (12 m) long. There are no sewage or water hookups, but there is a dump station—$10 to use—and water refill areas. All sites are tent-compatible, with four sites being strictly for tents. Coin-operated hot showers are available as well.

FOOD AND LODGING

Half Moon Bay is a decent-size coastal city of about 12,000 people. Major grocers and a variety of inns, lodges, and hotels are close to the beach or downtown. Its charming main street stretches several blocks and has many shops, parks, eateries, and historic sites.

BEST PICNIC SPOT

★ Roosevelt Beach

This sandy area at the end of Young Road (off CA-1) is the park system's northernmost beach closest to Mavericks and Pillar Point. Along with having picnic tables and restrooms next to a large parking area, this beach is close to Dunes Beach and the paved Coastside Trail.

GETTING THERE

CAR

Half Moon Bay State Beach is off CA-1, about 30 mi (48 km, 45 minutes) south of San Francisco, 50 mi (80 km, 1 hour) north of Santa Cruz, and 42 mi (68 km, 1 hour) west of San Jose on I-280.

BUS

Half Moon Bay is one of the more accessible California state parks due to its proximity to San Francisco. **SamTrans** (800/660-4287; www.samtrans.com) has a Coastside bus service route that stops in Pacifica and Half Moon Bay. It connects to the San Francisco International Airport as well as the Daly City BART (www.bart.gov) station, and it does a loop around Kelly Avenue and Poplar Street, steps away from the Coastside Trail. Use the SamTrans Trip Planner on the website to help map out your trip.

PIGEON POINT LIGHT STATION STATE HISTORIC PARK

Along the scenic CA-1 just south of San Francisco, a 115-ft-tall (35-m-tall) beacon watching over the Pacific Ocean is a must-visit for lighthouse enthusiasts. Pigeon Point was originally named Whale Point due to the migrating gray whales that came close to the shoreline, but was later renamed after the *Carrier Pigeon* ship crashed into the point's fog-shrouded rocks on her 1853 maiden voyage. When other clippers wrecked near the point, the coastal commission built a lighthouse to warn future mariners of the danger.

ADDRESS: 210 Pigeon Point Rd., Pescadero

PHONE: 650/879-2120

WEBSITE: www.coastsidestateparks.org

DAY USE HOURS: 8am-sunset

AREA: 66 acres (27 ha)

Pigeon Point was no ordinary light station, as this one was built with the largest ever ultrabright Fresnel lens. French physicist Augustin Jean Fresnel crafted the 16-ft-tall, 2-ton (5-m-tall, 1.8-tonne) optical device with 1,008 handcrafted prisms, encased in brass and stacked into vertical panels to throw a beam up to 24 mi (39 km) out into the sea.

Pigeon Point became a California historic park in 1976 when it was added to the National Register of Historic Places. Today it is still one of the tallest lighthouses in the US. In recent years it has been undergoing a series of renovations. While the restoration, a project slated to be finished in 2026, is ongoing, you can still tour the grounds, stay the night at the hostel, and do some whale watching from the back of the Fog Signal Building.

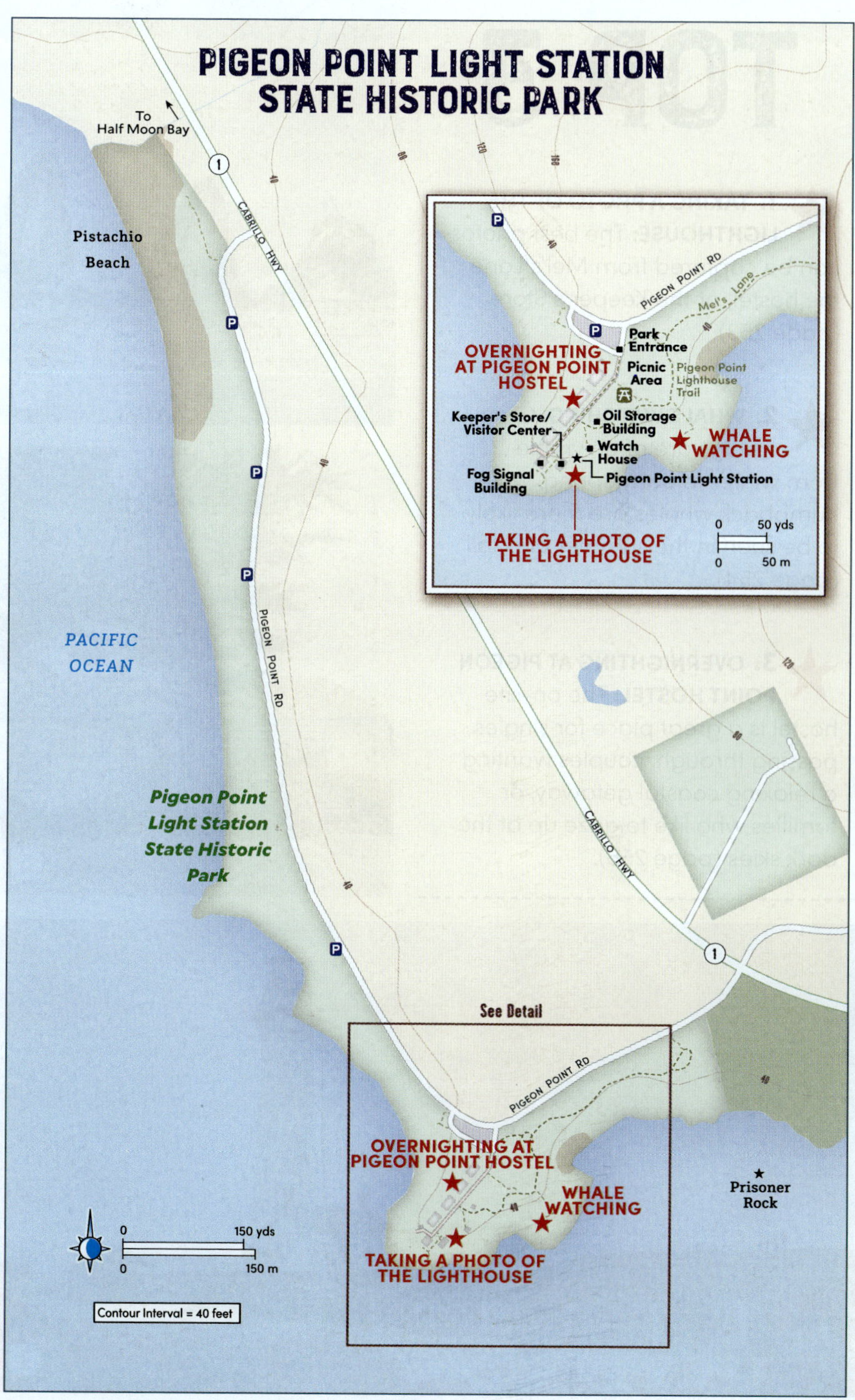

PIGEON POINT LIGHT STATION STATE HISTORIC PARK
To Half Moon Bay
1
CABRILLO HWY
Pistachio Beach
PIGEON POINT RD
PACIFIC OCEAN
Pigeon Point Light Station State Historic Park
See Detail
OVERNIGHTING AT PIGEON POINT HOSTEL
WHALE WATCHING
TAKING A PHOTO OF THE LIGHTHOUSE
Prisoner Rock
0 150 yds
0 150 m
Contour Interval = 40 feet
Park Entrance
Picnic Area
Pigeon Point Lighthouse Trail
Mel's Lane
Keeper's Store/ Visitor Center
Oil Storage Building
Watch House
Fog Signal Building
Pigeon Point Light Station
0 50 yds
0 50 m

TOP 3

★ **1. TAKING A PHOTO OF THE LIGHTHOUSE:** The best photos can be captured from Mel's Lane, the hostel, or the Keeper's Store (page 253).

★ **2. WHALE WATCHING:** Gray whales are often visible from winter to early spring, while humpback whales are more likely to be seen in the summer and fall (page 254).

★ **3. OVERNIGHTING AT PIGEON POINT HOSTEL:** The on-site hostel is a great place for singles passing through, couples wanting a relaxing coastal getaway, or families who like to gaze up at the dark skies (page 255).

2

3

1

PLANNING YOUR TIME

The 66-acre (27-ha) park has a couple of trails and educational buildings, making it easy to explore the grounds in an hour. If you don't feel like driving anywhere for a while, stay the night at the hostel if there's room, and fall asleep to the sound of crashing waves.

Nearby state parks include Half Moon Bay State Beach (22 mi/35 km) and Rancho del Oso—a part of Big Basin Redwoods (10 mi/16 km).

ENTRANCE AND FEES

Admission and parking are free to access the Pigeon Point Day Use Area from its **one entrance** off CA-1 on Pigeon Point Road.

VISITOR CENTER

Visitor Center and Park Store

Carpenter's Shop and Keeper's Store; 650/879-2120; 10am-4pm Fri.-Mon.

Learn more about the lighthouse at the visitor center and park store located inside the **Keeper's Store/historic carpenter's shop.** Here you can buy books, plushies, lighthouse statues, and other souvenirs.

WEATHER

The California coast is known for its cold coastal breezes, no matter what season. It tends to be foggy and rainy in the winter months (November-March), but the fog rolls in early morning even in the summertime. Winds can pick up at any time, so bring warm clothing layers, a beanie, and a waterproof jacket.

SIGHTS

In addition to the sights below, Pigeon Point has gentle sandy (and ADA-accessible) walking paths, a stairway down to the beach, and a few impressive coastal overlooks.

★ PIGEON POINT LIGHT STATION

The 115-ft-tall (35-m-tall) light station jutting out over the Pacific Ocean is still one of the tallest in the US. It became a California historic park in 1976 when it was added to the National Register of Historic Places. Right now, you can view the lighthouse from afar and go inside the Keeper's Store Friday-Monday.

In 2019, the State of California put aside millions of dollars to restore the top of the lighthouse tower, a project slated to be finished in 2026.

FOG SIGNAL BUILDING

Karl the Fog (as it's been nicknamed by residents) doesn't just regularly blast the Bay Area; it fades all the way down the Northern California coastline, upending seafarers for generations. Before the Pigeon Point lighthouse came into play, a steam-train whistle was blasted to warn the ships out at sea. Powered by cordwood and water, the signal needed 45 minutes to build up enough

Pigeon Point Light Station (left); HI Pigeon Point Lighthouse Hostel (right)

pressure for the whistle to blow. The fog signal was in operation until 1909 before it was eventually replaced by a diesel-powered diaphone in 1933 and then rendered obsolete in 1976.

PRISONER ROCK

The easy and flat 0.5-mi (0.8-km) **Mel's Lane** stroll starts at the entrance area and follows the south end of the park parallel to Pigeon Point Road and around the cove in the gray whale migrating path. The single-track dirt trail has the best views of Prisoner Rock, a large, jagged stone in the middle of Whaler's Cove named after the fishermen who were stranded on it when high tides prevented them from reaching the shore. Mel's Lane comes back up through the succulents and ocean scenery to the Council Circle, a nice place to have lunch. Another short path leads down from the Council Circle to a lookout deck, where you can view the vibrant rocky shoreline, and a set of stairs leads down to the beach.

RECREATION

WILDLIFE WATCHING

★ Marine Mammals

Pigeon Point is a great place to catch **gray whales** migrating from the Bering Sea to Baja California in the winter months, then coming back through with their calves in early spring. **Humpback whales** pass by in the summer and fall seasons and tend to be more flamboyant with their tail slaps and acrobatic moves.

FOOD AND LODGING

There are **no campgrounds** or concessionaires on-site, so it's best to stock up on food if you're going to spend the day and/or the night at the hostel. The closest "big" town with grocery stores, gas stations, and other accommodations to Pigeon Point is **Half Moon Bay,** 22 mi (35 km) away north on CA-1. **Pescadero** is inland 8 mi (13 km) north on Pescadero Creek Road from CA-1; it has a tavern, a post office, and a gas station/convenience store/taqueria all wrapped in one location.

★ HI PIGEON POINT LIGHTHOUSE HOSTEL

210 Pigeon Point Rd., Pescadero; 650/879-0633; www.hiusa.org

This historic park is strictly a day use area with a hostel managed by HI USA on its premises. The HI Pigeon Point Lighthouse Hostel turned four light station buildings into bunkrooms that include a mix of female, male, and coed dorms with shared bathrooms, living rooms, and kitchens. Private rooms are available as well. Overnight stays cost around $50 for a bunk bed and shared bathroom, $165 for a private room, or $285 for a family room that sleeps up to six people. It even has a hot tub overlooking the Pacific Ocean behind the Fog Signal Building that can be reserved for an extra fee.

BEST PICNIC SPOT

The Council Circle

A picnic area with a few wooden tables overlooking the ocean is set up near the Oil Storage Building. However, consider having lunch at the Council Circle, a seating area that honors donors who've helped conserve the coastal area. It links to Mel's Lane and the staircase to Whaler's Cove, overlooking Prisoner Rock.

GETTING THERE

CAR

Pigeon Point is 22 mi (35 km) south of Half Moon Bay and 28 mi (45 km) north of Santa Cruz on CA-1. The lighthouse is 55 mi (89 km) west of San Jose, taking CA-280 to the coast.

BIG BASIN REDWOODS STATE PARK

The *Sequoia sempervirens* (aka coast redwoods) have been impressing humans since time immemorial, and fortunately California State Parks, along with conservation groups, have worked tirelessly to keep them around for future generations. This huge swath of forest and chaparral have some trees that are at least 50 ft (15 m) wide and as tall as the Statue of Liberty. Established in 1902, Big Basin Redwoods is California's oldest state park.

ADDRESS: 21600 Big Basin Way, Boulder Creek

PHONE: 831/338-8860

WEBSITE: https://reimaginingbigbasin.org

DAY USE HOURS: 8am-sunset

AREA: 18,000 acres (7,284 ha)

In 2020, the CZU Lightning Complex Fire burned through 97 percent of the park's landscape, destroying all its historic buildings. Despite all the wildfire took out in its path, many of the old-growth redwoods survived, courageously showing off their burn scars. Reimagining Big Basin (https://reimaginingbigbasin.org) is still facilitating the process of rebuilding the park's infrastructure.

The Amah Mutsun Tribal Band (www.amahmutsunlandtrust.org) is still active in the Santa Cruz Mountains, managing a land trust, stewardship, and native plant program, and working with various local agencies to help get the terrain back to its original state using their tried-and-true wildfire suppression and other environmental preservation methods.

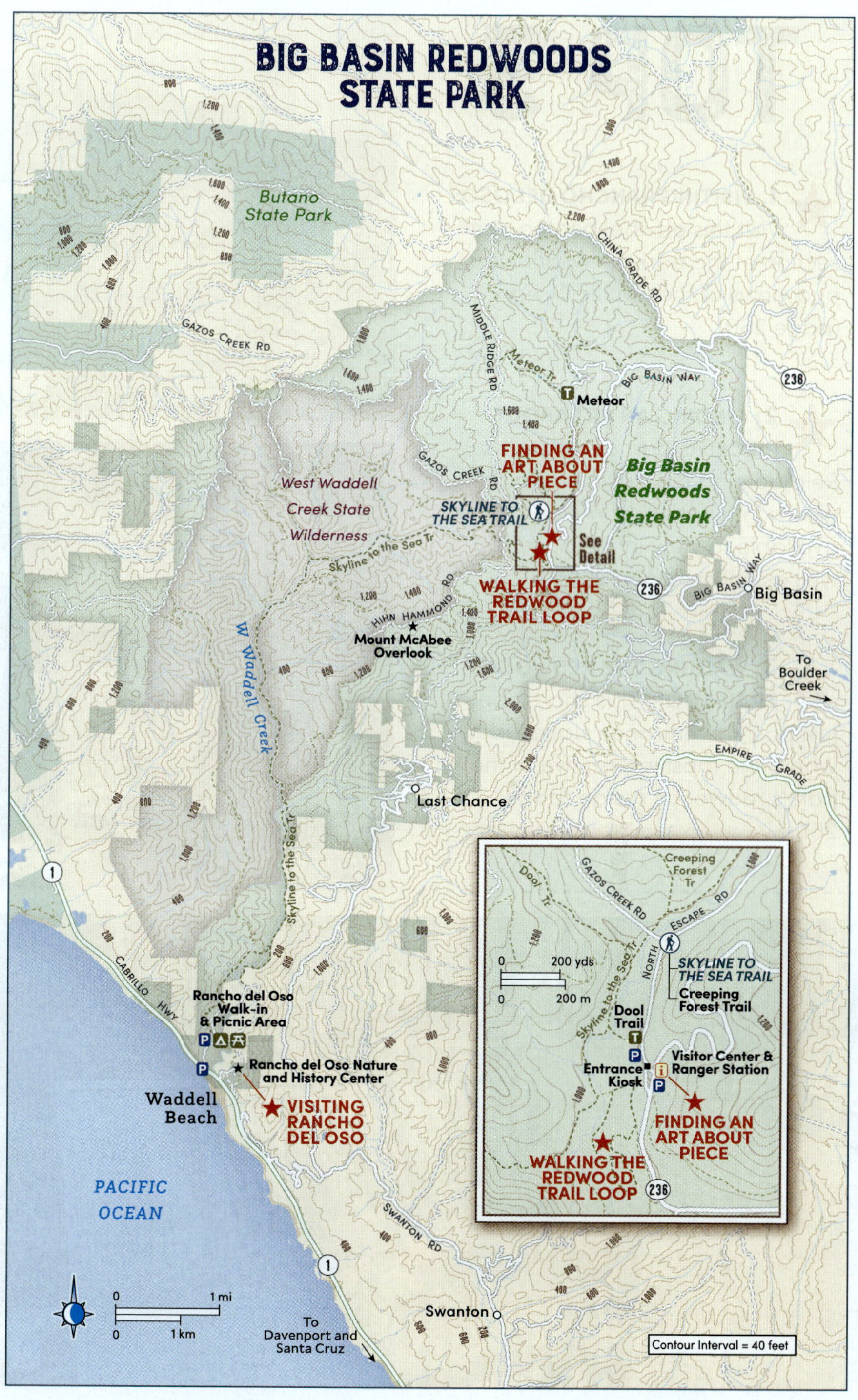
BIG BASIN REDWOODS STATE PARK
Butano State Park
GAZOS CREEK RD
MIDDLE RIDGE RD
CHINA GRADE RD
Meteor Tr
BIG BASIN WAY
236
Meteor
FINDING AN ART ABOUT PIECE
Big Basin Redwoods State Park
West Waddell Creek State Wilderness
GAZOS CREEK RD
SKYLINE TO THE SEA TRAIL
See Detail
Skyline to the Sea Tr
WALKING THE REDWOOD TRAIL LOOP
HIHN HAMMOND RD
Big Basin
Mount McAbee Overlook
W Waddell Creek
To Boulder Creek
EMPIRE GRADE
Last Chance
Skyline to the Sea Tr
CABRILLO HWY
Rancho del Oso Walk-in & Picnic Area
Rancho del Oso Nature and History Center
Waddell Beach
VISITING RANCHO DEL OSO
PACIFIC OCEAN
SWANTON RD
Swanton
To Davenport and Santa Cruz
0 1 mi
0 1 km
Contour Interval = 40 feet
Creeping Forest Tr
Dool Tr
GAZOS CREEK RD
NORTH ESCAPE RD
0 200 yds
0 200 m
SKYLINE TO THE SEA TRAIL
Creeping Forest Trail
Dool Trail
Entrance Kiosk
Visitor Center & Ranger Station
FINDING AN ART ABOUT PIECE
WALKING THE REDWOOD TRAIL LOOP

TOP 3

1. VISITING RANCHO DEL OSO: Visit this off-the-beaten-path section of the park for wildflowers and views of the Pacific Ocean (page 260).

2. FINDING AN ART ABOUT PIECE: As part of the park's Reimagining Big Basin effort, art pieces in a variety of mediums are available to view in the park as well as online (page 260).

3. WALKING THE REDWOOD TRAIL LOOP: This short loop just past the entrance station is where the most impressive of the park's redwoods reside (page 261).

1

3

2

PLANNING YOUR TIME

Big Basin is divided into two portions: the **main park** and the coastal portion, **Rancho del Oso.** It's about an hour's drive to reach Rancho del Oso. Note that at the time of writing, wildfire closures meant there was no way to get from one section to the other within the park.

A half day is enough time to explore the main portion of the park. You'll need a full day to include a visit to Rancho del Oso.

Nearby state parks include Henry Cowell Redwoods State Park (15 mi/24 km). The closest state park to Rancho del Oso is Pigeon Point Light Station State Historic Park (10 mi/16 km).

ENTRANCES AND FEES

There is **one main entrance** to get into Big Basin Day Use Area at 21600 Big Basin Way. CA-236 takes you straight to the park. It costs $10 to park in the Big Basin Day Use Area or $8 if you made a reservation online in advance. There are no entrance fees if you're coming in by bike, by bus, or on your own two feet.

Rancho del Oso is Big Basin Redwoods State Park's coastal segment, located about an hour away from the main park. The entrance is on CA-1, about 17 mi (27 km) north of Santa Cruz. The entrance fee to Big Basin Redwoods is valid here as well.

VISITOR CENTER

Visitor Center

21600 Big Basin Way, Boulder Creek; 831/338-8860; noon-4pm Wed.-Mon.

Step inside the open-air Big Basin Redwoods interim visitor center/information booth to get maps and hiking information and chat with friendly docents.

RESERVATIONS

The park gets extremely busy in the summer and on holidays, so a **parking reservation** (bit.ly/BigBasinParking; $8) is the only way you're guaranteed to get in—and it saves you money. You can make reservations up to the day before your arrival, or the day of before 6am. You don't need a reservation to visit Rancho del Oso, the coastal portion of Big Basin on CA-1.

WEATHER

Central California gets hot in the summer, and even though Big Basin Redwoods can provide some nice shade, there are exposed areas—especially since the fire—and longish hikes that'll make you work up a thirst. Temperatures can climb to over 100°F (38°C) here July-August and hardly ever drop below freezing at any time of the year. It tends to be cloudy, rainy, and cooler in the winter months, with temperatures averaging in the 40-60°F (4-16°C) range; this is the best time to go because it's not crowded. There's no drinking water in the park, so come prepared. The Rancho del Oso coastal subunit of the park is a little cooler and draws in more fog.

SIGHTS

 RANCHO DEL OSO

This area is the coastal region of the park, and though it's not very big, it is home to the Skyline to the Sea Trail, the Rancho del Oso Nature and History Center, Waddell Beach, and a small walk-in campground. Rancho del Oso is about an hour away from the Big Basin Redwoods main entrance.

Rancho del Oso Nature and History Center

3600 CA-1, Davenport; 831/427-2288; https://ranchodeloso.org; noon-4pm Sat.-Sun.

The Rancho del Oso Nature and History Center has interactive exhibits, wall murals, and an expansive deck with a telescope looking out to the Pacific Ocean. Near the parking area are a couple of picnic tables almost consumed by the tall green grasses around them, as well as markers pointing the way to the Hoover and Marsh Trails. At least 376 species of wildflowers grow in this area, including welcoming calla lilies and families of bright orange California poppies.

 BIG BASIN ART ABOUT

For the Big Basin Art About project, 18 local artists were chosen to create a piece of art in their specialized medium focusing on Big Basin post-CZU Lightning Complex Fire. The art pieces were on display in the state park in the summer of 2024 and will eventually have a permanent home in the visitor center. Until all the pieces make it physically into the park, visit the Big Basin Art About website (https://sites.google.com/ports-ca.us/bigbasinartabout/home) to see the short films, digital paintings, cyanotype prints, and other selected works paying homage to the trees and Big Basin's resurgence era.

Big Basin Art About

BEACHES

WADDELL BEACH

On the ocean side of CA-1 across from the turnoff going to the Rancho del Oso Nature and History Center, Waddell Beach is a big open stretch of sand between the sea and a decent-size parking lot. Thanks to its easy access to the ocean, windsurfers and kiteboarders often take advantage of the steady northwest gusts. Swimming here is not advisable since there are no lifeguards on duty and it's not near any emergency services.

HIKING

★ REDWOOD TRAIL LOOP

DISTANCE: 0.6 mi (1 km) round-trip
DURATION: 30 minutes
EFFORT: Easy
TRAILHEAD: Big Basin Day Use Area parking lot

The most extraordinary living legends in the form of infallible coast redwoods stand along the 0.6-mi (1-km) Redwood Loop Trail. Starting right next to the visitor center, the path takes you to the heavily burled **Animal Tree;** next, step inside the hollowed out **Chimney Tree;** and finally, don't strain your neck too much trying to view the top of the 329-ft-tall (100-m-tall) **Mother of the Forest.**

Waddell Beach

CREEPING FOREST LOOP

DISTANCE: 1.7 mi (2.7 km) round-trip
DURATION: 1 hour
EFFORT: Moderate
TRAILHEAD: Skyline to the Sea Trail junction with Dool Trail

To walk this moderately challenging hike clockwise, take the Dool Trail up to Redwood Creek, cross the bridge, and climb toward the **Johnson Family Memorial Grove.** At the Gazos Creek junction, take a right to complete the loop. You may have to navigate through a felled redwood, over a log bridge, and around downed trees, but it just adds to the Indiana Jones-like experience. This trail is also a favorite for banana slugs, so make sure to watch out for them.

CAMPING

Because the park is in a fire recovery era, most campgrounds are currently closed. However, the park's coastal subunit Rancho del Oso has five reservable **walk-in-only campsites** ($23/night) near the nature center. To reserve a site, fill out the form on the Rancho del Oso website or via an iron ranger envelope. This campground has restrooms and drinking water in the parking lot next to the sites. There's also one **bike-in campsite** ($5/night) available in Rancho del Oso on a first-come, first-served basis.

Prior to the fire, Big Basin Redwoods had four campgrounds, two group camps, and cabins. Until the campgrounds reopen, if you are in the main area of Big Basin Redwoods and don't want to drive an hour to the coast to camp, there are a few campgrounds between Boulder Creek (8 mi/13 km south of the main day use area) and Scotts Valley (18 mi/29 km south of the park).

FOOD AND LODGING

The closest place to stock up on food is in the small town of **Boulder Creek,** where there are a few cafés, a gas station, grocery stores, restaurants, and a post office. It's 8 mi (13 km) away on CA-9. **Santa Cruz** is your best bet for finding a bigger variety of accommodations and amenities; to get there from the park take CA-236 to CA-9, turn right, and follow that 14 mi (23 km) to get to the center of town. There are no concessions within the park.

BEST PICNIC SPOT

Big Basin Redwoods Day Use Area

A nicely shaded picnic area courteous of the ancient tall trees is right next to the park's headquarters, parking lot, and visitor center. It's also close to the popular Redwood Trail Loop and the starting/ending points to some of the longer trails.

TOP HIKE

SKYLINE TO THE SEA AND METEOR TRAIL LOOP

DISTANCE: 4.8 mi (7.7 km) round-trip
DURATION: 2.5 hours
EFFORT: Moderate
TRAILHEAD: Big Basin Day Use Area parking lot

From the parking lot, take the Skyline to the Sea Trail and stay right past the Dool and Creeping Forest trailheads. The trail runs parallel to the North Escape fire road, crossing Maddocks Creek. At Rogers Creek, take a left onto the Meteor Trail and follow the creek over to Middle Ridge Road. Take another left on Middle Ridge to make your way back toward the main day use area, passing the 1,689-ft (515-m) **Ocean View Summit.** It surveys the West Waddell Creek State Wilderness area all the way to the Pacific Ocean. Middle Ridge connects to the parking lot via the Dool or Sunset Trail. There's not much difference between the Dool and Sunset Trails, except you'll likely see more banana slugs on the Dool. The sheer amount of trees that survived the Lightning Complex Fire are impressive to see, and have a new distinct character with their whitish bark contrasting with blackened trunks.

GETTING THERE

CAR

Big Basin Redwoods State Park is 60 mi (97 km) south of San Francisco; it takes about 1 hour 15 minutes to get there from downtown San Francisco. There are a couple of ways to get to the park from the Bay Area, either by taking US-101 and cutting over toward the coast on CA-236 or by taking I-280 south and going west on CA-236.

The Rancho del Oso subunit of Big Basin is on CA-1, along the coast about an hour away from the main park's day use area. To get to Rancho del Oso from Big Basin Redwoods, take CA-236 east for 5 mi (8 km), turn right on Jamison Creek Road, and go another 3 mi (5 km) to Empire Grade. Turn left and drive for 6 mi (10 km), then take a sharp right onto Pine Flat Road. In another 3.7 mi (6 km), continue onto Bonny Doon Road. It meets CA-1 in another 3.5 mi (5.5 km); turn right on CA-1 and go 8.5 mi (13.5 km) north to reach Rancho del Oso. It's a windy, two-lane, backwoods route to get there, so take it slow.

BUS

The **Santa Cruz METRO** (www.scmtd.com) bus goes up to Big Basin Redwoods on the weekends in the summer via Route 35B. You can park at the River Front Transit Center in Santa Cruz or Cavallaro Transit Center in Scotts Valley to take the bus into Big Basin. A one-ride pass is $2, or $6 for a day pass. Visit the Big Basin Redwoods website and Santa Cruz METRO page for the most updated maps and schedules.

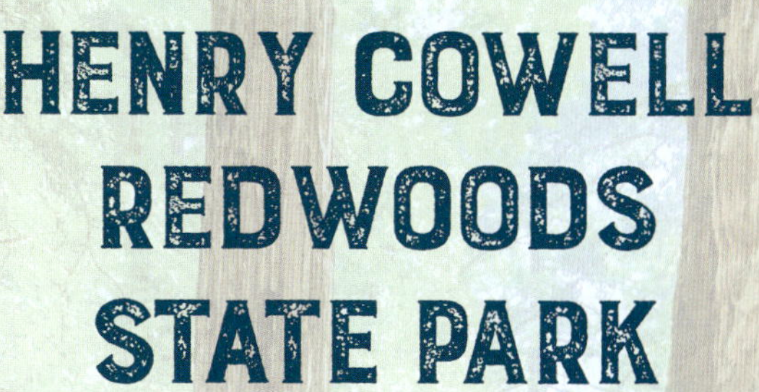

HENRY COWELL REDWOODS STATE PARK

Less than 10 mi (16 km) from the Pacific Ocean, a 40-acre (16-ha) grove of old-growth coast redwoods nestled in the Santa Cruz Mountains is the highlight of Henry Cowell Redwoods State Park. The most impressive tree in the park is The Giant, a 1,500-year-old redwood that stands at 282 ft (86 m) tall.

ADDRESS: 101 Big Trees Park Rd., Felton

PHONE: 831/335-4598

WEBSITE: www.mountainparks.org

DAY USE HOURS: Sunrise-sunset

AREA: 4,650 acres (1,880 ha)

The Sayanta people (a subgroup of the Awaswas) were this NorCal coastal region's original inhabitants before the Spanish seized the area. In 1867, Joseph Warren Welch Sr. bought 350 acres (142 ha) of forest and called it Big Trees Grove. Later, Samuel Cowell donated 1,600 acres (647 ha) of land to California State Parks to be named after his dad, Henry. In 1972, the Cowell Family Foundation deeded the Fall Creek Unit to the park system, and the League to Save the Redwoods pitched in to acquire another 800 acres (324 ha).

In 2020, the CZU Lightning Complex Fire destroyed a lot of the trees in Santa Cruz. While areas of blackened trunks can be seen in the park, the forest has been starting to come back.

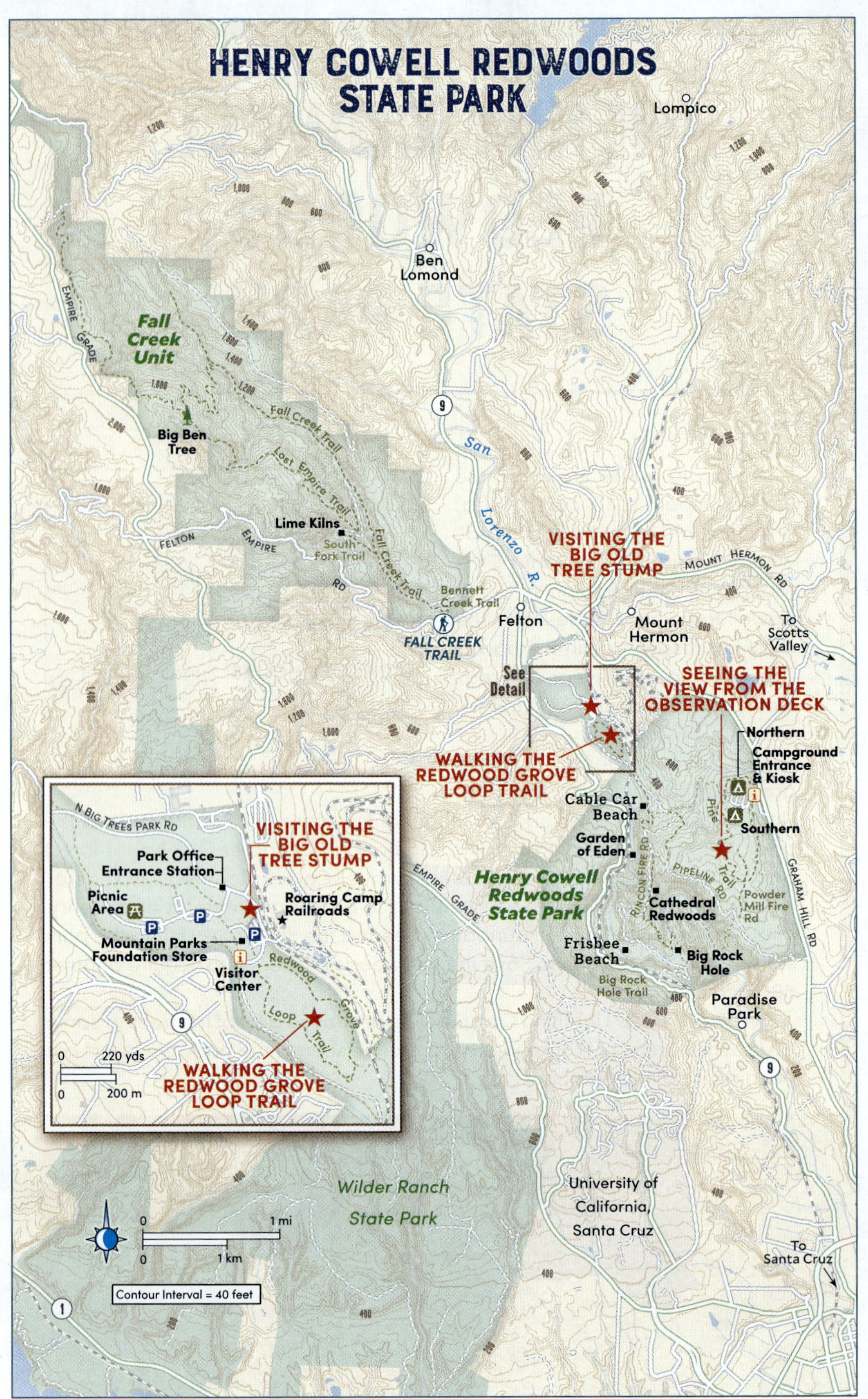
HENRY COWELL REDWOODS STATE PARK
Lompico
Ben Lomond
Fall Creek Unit
Empire Grade
Big Ben Tree
Fall Creek Trail
Lost Empire Trail
Lime Kilns
South Fork Trail
Felton Empire Rd
Bennett Creek Trail
FALL CREEK TRAIL
San Lorenzo R.
Felton
Mount Hermon
Mount Hermon Rd
To Scotts Valley
VISITING THE BIG OLD TREE STUMP
SEEING THE VIEW FROM THE OBSERVATION DECK
See Detail
WALKING THE REDWOOD GROVE LOOP TRAIL
Northern
Campground Entrance & Kiosk
Southern
Cable Car Beach
Garden of Eden
Pine Trail
Pipeline Rd
Rincon Fire Rd
Powder Mill Fire Rd
Graham Hill Rd
Henry Cowell Redwoods State Park
Cathedral Redwoods
Frisbee Beach
Big Rock Hole
Big Rock Hole Trail
Paradise Park
N Big Trees Park Rd
Park Office Entrance Station
Picnic Area
Roaring Camp Railroads
Mountain Parks Foundation Store
Visitor Center
Redwood Grove Loop Trail
220 yds
200 m
Wilder Ranch State Park
University of California, Santa Cruz
To Santa Cruz
1 mi
1 km
Contour Interval = 40 feet

TOP 3

1. **VISITING THE BIG OLD TREE STUMP:** The 2,000-year-old giant tree stump is so big in size that you'll look like a peanut standing in front of it (page 268).

2. **SEEING THE VIEW FROM THE OBSERVATION DECK:** A moderate hike takes you to the tallest point of the park, with panoramic views of the Santa Cruz Mountains and Monterey (page 268).

3. **WALKING THE REDWOOD GROVE LOOP TRAIL:** This short trail accesses the 40-acre (16-ha) grove of coast redwoods, including the park's most impressive tree, The Giant (page 270).

PLANNING YOUR TIME

While you can see the main sights in a day, two are recommended to get the full experience.

Nearby state parks include Big Basin Redwoods State Park (15 mi/24 km) and Pigeon Point Light Station Historic Park (32 mi/51 km).

ENTRANCE AND FEES

Henry Cowell Redwoods State Park's **main entrance** is on the northern end of the park off of CA-9 in Felton. It costs $10 to park for the day. The **Fall Creek Unit** is day use, and parking and trailheads are off of Felton Empire Road.

VISITOR CENTERS

Henry Cowell Redwoods Visitors Center

831/335-0782; 10am-4pm daily

Henry Cowell Redwoods has a lovely spacious and bright visitor center filled with tree exhibits and wildlife displays.

Mountain Parks Foundation Store

831/335-0782; www.mountainparks.org; 10am-5pm daily spring/summer, 10am-4pm daily fall/winter

The Mountain Parks Foundation Store opened in 1973 and was one of the first nonprofits to become a California State Parks cooperating association. It has a ton of books, T-shirts, souvenirs (like banana slug magnets), maps, and delectable Marianne's ice cream treats. It's located next to the day use area parking lot close to the visitor center and Redwood Grove Loop Trail.

WEATHER

The Santa Cruz climate tends to stay pleasantly mild year-round, with highs reaching 82-85°F (28-29°C) in the summer months and dropping to 42-45°F (6-7°C) in the winter months. The redwoods and other plants welcome rainfall in December-April. Keep in mind inclement weather in the winter months can cause the campground to close. The weather is more consistent in the summer, but it's also the busiest time of the year to visit any California state park. If you don't mind a little rain, the springtime is the best time to visit to have the park to yourself.

SIGHTS

BIG OLD TREE STUMP

Across the parking lot from the visitor center is a giant tree stump so big in size that you'll look like a peanut standing in front of it. The rings on this tree show its age, estimated to be well over 2,000 years old. Unfortunately, the tree was cut down in 1934, but the stump was thankfully preserved and remains an educational tool.

OBSERVATION DECK

To get a full panoramic view of what this region has to offer, head to the

ONE DAY IN HENRY COWELL REDWOODS STATE PARK

MORNING

Start your day off with a quick jaunt around the Redwood Grove Loop Trail to access the 40-acre (16-ha) grove, then have brunch at one of the picnic tables by the entrance.

AFTERNOON

Hike up to the Observation Deck—the tallest point in the park—to take in the views of the Santa Cruz Mountains and other tree-packed vistas.

highest point of Henry Cowell Redwoods, the Observation Deck. It's a half-mile (0.8-km) hike away from the campground at an 805-ft (245-m) altitude via the **Pine Trail.** From this elevation, visitors can see Monterey Bay, surrounding mountains, and its unique sandhills.

BIG BEN TREE

Over in the **Fall Creek Unit** on the upper western side of the park, the Big Ben Tree is a medium-size tree in a stand of second-growth redwoods. It's on the side of Ben Lomond Mountain (hence its name) at the intersection of the **Big Ben and Lost Empire Trails.** You can get to it from the short Sunlit Trail parking on Empire Grade, too. With its 6-ft (2-m) width, Big Ben is one of the largest trees in the park.

Observation Deck

THE GIANT

Be sure to stop at The Giant on the **Redwood Grove Loop Trail** as it is the tallest coast redwood in the park. Standing at 282 ft (86 m) tall with a 17-ft-wide (5-m-wide) waistline, The Giant weighs 400 tons (363 tonnes). And to think The Giant grew this big from an oatmeal-flake-size seed.

BEACHES

CABLE CAR BEACH

Just south of the entrance station and Redwood Grove Loop, the paved Pipeline Road leads to the River Trail and Cable Car Beach along the San Lorenzo River. Little kids love this area because it's easy, interesting, and passes under a cool wood-trestle railway bridge.

FRISBEE BEACH

There's a strip of sand along the San Lorenzo River where people like to hang out and possibly cool down in the freshwater bend. The beach is accessible off Big Rock Hole Trail or the Rincon Fire Road, in the southwestern end of the park.

HIKING

Henry Cowell Redwoods State Park in the Santa Cruz Mountains encompasses 2,390 acres (967 ha) of forest and freshwater. The Redwood Grove Loop close to the visitor center is the most popular hike, but the Fall Creek Unit has 20 mi (32 km) of hiking and horseback trails along with some historic sites like the lime kilns.

★ REDWOOD GROVE LOOP

DISTANCE: 0.8 mi (1.3 km) round-trip
DURATION: 20 minutes
EFFORT: Easy
TRAILHEAD: Henry Cowell Redwoods Visitor Center

Just past the Henry Cowell Redwoods entrance station and visitor center, a 0.8-mi (1.3-km) loop trail accesses the 40-acre (16-ha) grove of coast redwoods. See some of the biggest trees in the area via this loop, two that have impressive girth—one has a 17-ft (5-m) diameter—and one that's the tallest in the park. Touch the bark to feel how thick it is; it helps them resist wildfires. Douglas firs, fragrant California bay laurels, and dawn redwoods live in the forest, too. This level, well-marked trail is accessible, suitable for all ages and abilities. A guided audio tour is also available for this walk; download the MP3s on the state park's website. It's the best trail in the park to get your redwood fix in.

PIPELINE ROAD TO BIG ROCK HOLE

DISTANCE: 4.5 mi (7.2 km) round-trip
DURATION: 2 hours
EFFORT: Moderate
TRAILHEAD: Pipeline Rd. at the southern end of the Redwood Grove Loop Trail

There are several ways to get to the Big Rock Hole Trail, either coming in from the Redwood Grove Trail at the north or parking at the lot at the bottom of the Rincon Fire Road and walking up. To take the first option, park at the main lot and walk through the Redwood Grove heading south, taking the Pipeline Road to the River Trail and following that past Cable Car Beach. Take the Rincon Fire Road for a short stint to Big Rock Hole Trail. Follow that for about another mile all the way to the river. To get to Big Rock Hole, you'll probably have to jump across slippery rocks and/or cross through knee-high water, so be sure to bring sturdy water shoes. The easiest way to get back is to cross the San Lorenzo River to join back up with the Rincon Fire Road, then follow the train tracks up to the Garden of Eden where it joins up with Ox Fire Road and leads back to the Redwood Grove.

All these trails intersect and it can be rather confusing, but the Pipeline and Rincon Fire roads are well maintained, and heading north on them will get you back to the main lot. Big Rock Hole is about a mile north of the Rincon Fire Road parking lot off Highway 9.

LOST EMPIRE-FALL CREEK LOOP

DISTANCE: 8.5 mi (13.6 km) round-trip
DURATION: 4.5 hours
EFFORT: Strenuous
TRAILHEAD: Bennett Creek trailhead

Starting at the parking lot/horse camp near the Bennett Creek Trail, this loop covers most of what the Fall Creek Unit has to offer, but it will take a good portion of the day to see it all. To get to the actual loop and historic sites, hike up the **Fall Creek Trail** until you reach the first bridge. From here you can stay on the Fall Creek Trail to access the eastern portion of the loop or take a right on the **South Fork Trail** to go to the lime kilns. The preferred way is to do this loop counterclockwise for a gentler ascent; you'll pass the Barrel Mill remains, climb upward, and loop around to Big Ben Tree. At this point, you'll start your descent on the **Lost Empire Trail.** Lost Camp is on Barrel Mill Creek (across from the Barrel Mill area you passed through before) and ends up down by the **Cape Horn Trail,** connecting to the Fall Creek Trail again.

RECREATION

FISHING

Steelhead trout and coho salmon are available for limited catch-and-release in the **San Lorenzo River.** You must have a valid California fishing license to cast a line here; a one-day license costs around $21 and is sold through the California Department of Fish and Wildlife (https://wildlife.ca.gov).

SWIMMING

Garden of Eden

After hiking through the park all day, it's nice to splash around in the water at the Garden of Eden. The refreshingly cold water is surrounded by rocks and forest, but it is popular and can get crowded—especially on summer weekends. You can get to the Garden of Eden by taking the Ox Fire Road Trail.

TOP HIKE

FALL CREEK TRAIL TO LIME KILNS

DISTANCE: 3.4 mi (5.5 km) round-trip
DURATION: 1.5 hours
EFFORT: Easy
TRAILHEAD: Felton Empire Rd.

The Fall Creek Unit of the state park, added in 1972, has more than 20 mi (32 km) of hiking trails through the once-logged forest. Felton Empire Road (off CA-9) follows the bottom edge of the unit, connecting to trails that lead to the lime kilns, built to turn quarried rock into construction materials and other uses. Since this process required burning tons of redwood logs to keep the kilns blazing, the area was quickly becoming deforested, and the kilns shut down in 1919. Luckily, the surrounding hillsides are filled with greenery again, proving how resilient nature can be. The old kilns are all that remain from that era, available to see on this hike.

To get there, park at the lot by the Bennett Creek trailhead and continue to walk along the Fall Creek Trail. After crossing the bridge, there's a fork in the road—take the South Fork Trail to lead right to the kilns. You'll pass under towering redwoods, along a babbling creek, and through thick greenery to see these moss-covered ovens.

Big Rock Hole

Big Rock Hole is a lovely swimming area with aquamarine waters along the San Lorenzo River. It's accessible via Big Rock Hole Trail.

CAMPING

Henry Cowell State Park has **one campground** with 107 sites on the eastern side of the park often referred to as the Graham Hill Campground, because it's accessible off Graham Hill Road separate from the park's main entrance station. The campground has two big loops within a shady oak and pine forest near the sandhills.

While the campground is open year-round, it may close periodically in the winter months if the weather is too bad. The park fills up quickly in the summertime, so advance reservations are highly recommended and can be booked online through **Reserve California** (800/444-7275; www.reservecalifornia.com; $35/night) six months ahead of your trip.

The sites accommodate trailers up to 31 ft (9 m) long and motor homes up to 35 ft (11 m) long, but there is no sewer, water hookups, or dump station available—the closest one is at New Brighton Beach. All sites have a picnic table, food locker, and fire pit. Coin-operated hot showers, flush toilets, and potable water is close by. Firewood can be purchased from the camp host for $15 a bundle.

BEST CAMPGROUND
Henry Cowell Redwoods State Park Campground

After heading through the campground entrance kiosk off Graham Hill Road, the first 51 campsites are in the southern loops closest to the Observation Deck, Ridge Road, and Powder Mill Fire Road Trails. Head right past the kiosk to access the rest of the sites along the northern loop. The Pine Trail wraps all around the campground. Henry Cowell Redwoods State Park Campground is also unofficially called the Graham Hill Campground.

FOOD AND LODGING

Henry Cowell Redwoods is in the town of **Felton,** where there are a ton of things to do for families aside from seeing the trees and sandhills. There are gas stations and grocery stores, as well as RV parks. There are a few thousand people who live there and a handful of restaurants that mostly serve American food. **Scotts Valley** is a larger town with big-box stores and well-known hotel chains. Scotts Valley is 5 mi (8 km) east of the park on the other side of Mount Hermon.

BEST PICNIC SPOT
Entrance Station Picnic Area

A cluster of picnic tables is in a small stand of old-growth redwoods near the entrance of the park, between the Henry Cowell parking lot and Roaring Camp. To get to them, follow the

trail in Henry Cowell Redwoods State Park

BEST NEARBY

Roaring Camp Railroads

ROARING CAMP RAILROADS

The privately owned Roaring Camp Railroads (5401 Graham Hill Rd., Felton; 831/335-4484; https://roaringcamp.com) is right next to the park. Its locomotives roll through the redwoods as well as over to the Santa Cruz Boardwalk. The 75-minute Redwood Forest Steam Train tour takes passengers through the park's redwood groves, over trestles, and up a sketchy grade to the top of Bear Mountain and back (the train doesn't stop). Tickets cost $45.

gravel trail for a hundred yards, then cross the railroad tracks to reach the shady rest area.

GETTING THERE

CAR

Henry Cowell Redwoods State Park is in the Santa Cruz Mountains, just south of Big Basin Redwoods State Park and hugging the towns of Felton and Scotts Valley. To get to the park from Santa Cruz, take CA-1 to CA-9/River Street heading north and follow it for 6 mi (10 km), then turn right onto Big Trees Park Road. The trip up to the park takes about 15 minutes.

POINT LOBOS STATE NATURAL RESERVE

Called the crown jewel of California State Parks, Point Lobos State Natural Reserve and its emerald, sapphire, and aquamarine waters flushed in its dramatic rock setting does make one wonder if this is what Mother Nature set out to do. Its rich landscape and marine wildlife has garnered the attention of renowned photographers such as Ansel Adams and Edward Weston.

ADDRESS: CA-1, Carmel

PHONE: 831/624-4909

WEBSITE: www.pointlobos.org

DAY USE HOURS: 8am-7pm

AREA: 1,200 acres (486 ha)

Because of its incredible Oz-like environment, Point Lobos is one of the most protected parks in the state. While the reserve is open every day, there's no camping, vehicles over 21 ft (6 m) aren't allowed in the park, and dogs can't enter—even if they stay in the car.

More than 2,000 years before Point Lobos became a state reserve, the Rumsen Ohlone people built seasonal camps in this sacred area they called Ishxenta. They harvested abalone and hunted/gathered around the chaparral plants, Monterey pines, and the now endangered Gowen cypress trees. Point Lobos was acquired by the State of California in 1932 after locals formally organized to preserve the native plants, trees, animals, and seashore wildlife.

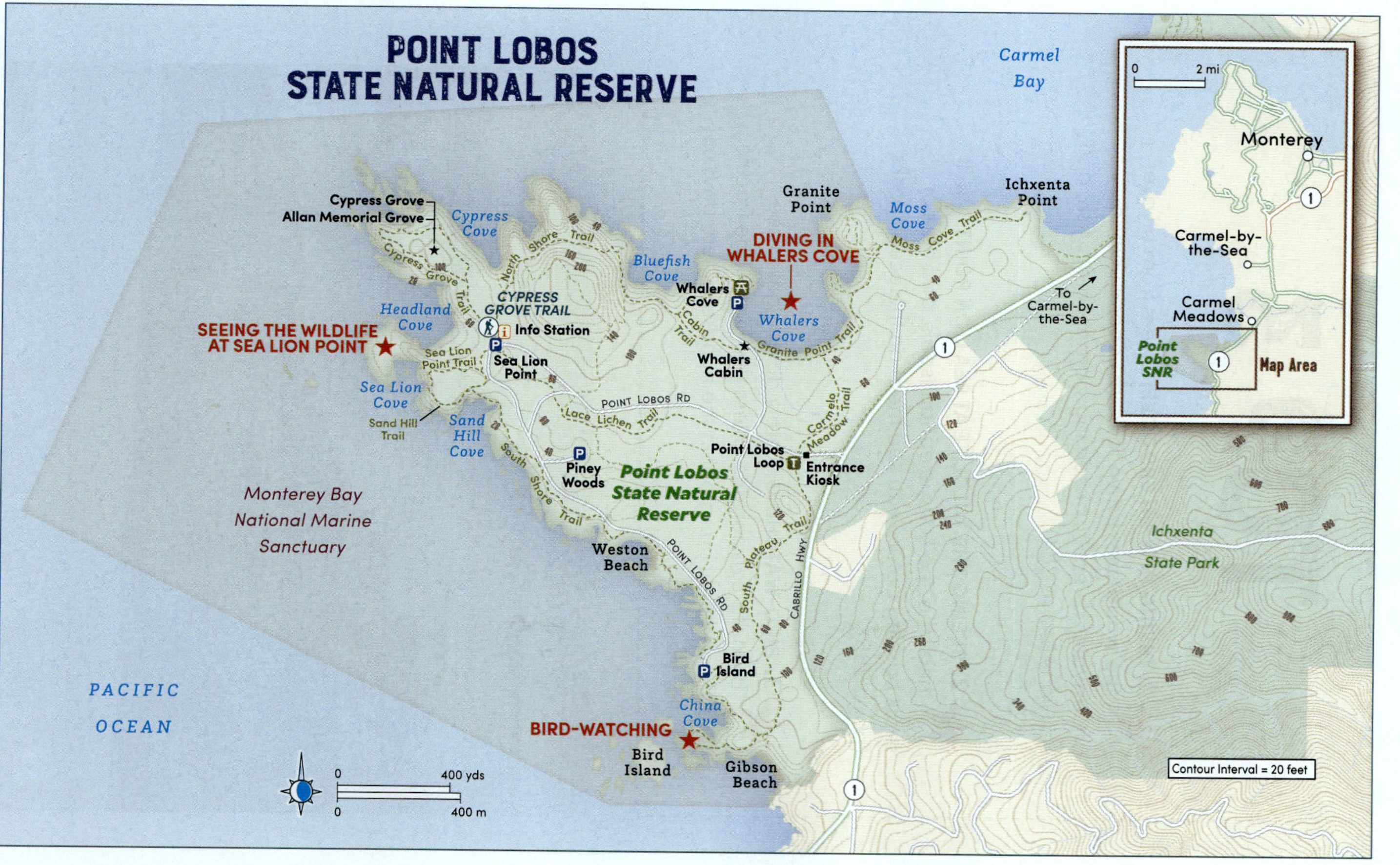

POINT LOBOS
STATE NATURAL RESERVE
Carmel Bay
Cypress Grove
Allan Memorial Grove
Cypress Cove
North Shore Trail
Cypress Grove Trail
Headland Cove
CYPRESS GROVE TRAIL
Info Station
SEEING THE WILDLIFE AT SEA LION POINT
Sea Lion Point Trail
Sea Lion Point
Sea Lion Cove
Sand Hill Trail
Sand Hill Cove
Bluefish Cove
Whalers Cove
Cabin Trail
Whalers Cabin
Granite Point
DIVING IN WHALERS COVE
Whalers Cove
Granite Point Trail
Moss Cove
Moss Cove Trail
Ichxenta Point
To Carmel-by-the-Sea
POINT LOBOS RD
Lace Lichen Trail
Carmelo Meadow Trail
Point Lobos Loop
Entrance Kiosk
Piney Woods
Point Lobos State Natural Reserve
South Shore Trail
Monterey Bay National Marine Sanctuary
Weston Beach
POINT LOBOS RD
South Plateau Trail
CABRILLO HWY
Bird Island
China Cove
BIRD-WATCHING
Bird Island
Gibson Beach
PACIFIC OCEAN
0 400 yds
0 400 m
Ichxenta State Park
Contour Interval = 20 feet
0 2 mi
Monterey
Carmel-by-the-Sea
Carmel Meadows
Point Lobos SNR
Map Area

TOP 3

★ **1. DIVING IN WHALERS COVE:** Divers from all over the world are drawn to Point Lobos's unique underwater diversity, observing vibrant corals, fish, and sea lions (page 284).

★ **2. SEEING THE WILDLIFE AT SEA LION POINT:** You'll hear the sea lions, elephant seals, and harbor seals barking before you see them on the ocean rocks (page 285).

★ **3. BIRD-WATCHING:** Rarely do you get to see Brandt's cormorants unless you live by the Pacific Ocean, and they hang out in the hundreds here on Bird Island (page 285).

PLANNING YOUR TIME

With so much to do, one can easily spend a full day here exploring the reserve. However, keep in mind that it gets crowded, especially on holidays, and the reserve only accommodates 150 cars. While you can park on the main road, don't block CA-1 trying to get into the reserve. You'll have the best chance of getting in if you arrive right at the park's opening at 8am or after 3pm; neither vehicles over 21 ft (8 m) nor dogs are allowed in the park. Note: Day use hours are slightly reduced in winter.

Nearby state parks include Pfeiffer Big Sur State Park (22 mi/35 km).

ENTRANCE AND FEES

Point Lobos State Natural Reserve has **one entrance** into the park off CA-1. It costs $10 per vehicle to go into the park, collected at the entrance station. The **three main parking areas** at Point Lobos (Piney Woods, Whalers Cove, and Bird Island) have picnic tables, restrooms, and water refill stations, and are at the base of major trailheads. The reserve also charges fees to dive or snorkel ($20-30), kayak or SUP ($10), and to hand-launch boats such as canoes, rowing dinghies, or small sailboats ($25). These fees are paid in advance when you make a reservation online through Point Lobos's website.

VISITOR CENTER

Information Station

In front of Sea Lion Point Trail; 831/624-4909; 9am-6:30pm daily summer, 9am-4:30pm daily winter

Point Lobos has an Information Station about 0.75 mi (1.2 km) away from the entrance in front of the Cypress Grove Trail and Sea Lion Point. There you can get maps, brochures, and souvenirs, and it's a meeting point to go on guided hikes in the reserve. Restrooms and water refill stations are also available.

RESERVATIONS

Diving or snorkeling ($30 weekends and holidays, $20 weekdays) must be reserved ahead of time since only around 20 divers (10 teams of 2 people) are allowed in the reserve per day. The coves are strictly controlled, and diving is only allowed in Whalers Cove, Bluefish Cove, and its nearby waters. Divers must show proof of certification from a recognized diving entity when entering the park. Visit the park's website to make online reservations, which can be made for the current month and the month following.

WEATHER

Here at Point Lobos, the fog and cloudy skies come out more in the December-April months. Temperatures average 40-60°F (4-16°C) during that time, ramping up to 55-75°F (13-24°C) July-August. For sightseeing, the best time to visit is in the spring, when the wildflowers are blooming and the marine wildlife such as the harbor seals and seabirds are most active.

the gem-colored water at Point Lobos

SIGHTS

WHALERS CABIN

From the Whalers Cove parking lot, people can take a short walk from the road to the historic Whalers Cabin. The rustic wooden cottage was built in the 1850s by Chinese fishermen and now serves as a cultural history museum, open as staffing permits.

BLUEFISH COVE SCENIC VIEW

Named for the thick schools of blue rockfish that swim here, the vibrant turquoise waters (thanks to the reflection off its sandy bottom) look otherworldly when the sun hits them right. Commanding rocks protect this calm cove from the wind, and this is one of the areas open to divers and snorkelers, too. Vista points over Bluefish Cove are accessible from the East Grove Trail and North Grove Trail.

BEACHES

Since Point Lobos is all about protecting the wildlife, most of the trails here follow the rugged edge overlooking jagged shorelines that harbor seals, birds, and sea lions can access more easily from the ocean. However, there are a few places where people can touch the water.

GIBSON BEACH

At the southernmost part of the reserve past China Cove, a staircase leads to a stretch of the white-sand Gibson Beach off the Bird Island Trail. This beach is great for sunbathing and watching the Brandt's cormorants.

WESTON BEACH

While walking the South Shore Trail, it's common to see families out skipping along the rocks and peering into creature-rich small ocean pools. The rocky edge doesn't make it comfortable to lay out a towel, but it's fun to see what's hidden in the rocks.

WHALERS COVE

On the northern end of the park, a paved roadway leads to a parking lot at Whalers Cove where kayakers and divers can launch via a concrete ramp. The cove is protected, but rocky around the shoreline where you get in. Restrooms and a picnic table are here.

HIKING

Containing 6 mi (10 km) comprising 16 official walking trails, Point Lobos has carved out paths ushering visitors to the best parts of the reserve. Exploration around the reserve is mostly easy, meaning you'll be walking more than doing strenuous hiking. Piney Woods, Whalers Cove, and Bird Island are the three main parking areas with restrooms and water-refill stations at the base of the reserve's main trailheads.

The Point Lobos Foundation (www.pointlobos.org) hosts **guided hikes** throughout the week all year long.

POINT LOBOS LOOP

DISTANCE: 6.4 mi (10.3 km) round-trip
DURATION: 2.5 hours
EFFORT: Moderate
TRAILHEAD: Point Lobos Information Station

See everything Point Lobos has to offer in one fell swoop looping around the entire headlands. This hike passes at least 12 points of interest and different habitats along the Pacific Ocean, ranging from the tropical waters of China Cove to the one-of-a-kind, only-found-here cypress trees on the northern side of the reserve. The best time to do this hike is in the spring or autumn months when it's not as crowded.

To do the entire loop clockwise, start at the South Plateau Trail and follow it to Bird Island Trail for about 0.7 mi (1.1 km). Follow the South Shore Trail around the craggy headlands passing Weston Beach and Sand Hill Cove. Pick up the Sand Hill Trail around to Sea Lion Point Trail, which ends up at the information station. From here you can veer left to do the Cypress Grove Loop or continue straight onto the North Shore Trail. This leads through beautiful endemic shade trees around Bluefish Cove, then follow the Cabin Trail over to the Carmelo Meadow Trail to get back to the entrance.

SOUTH SHORE TRAIL

DISTANCE: 2.2 mi (3.5 km) round-trip
DURATION: 45 minutes
EFFORT: Easy
TRAILHEAD: Bird Island parking area or the south end of the Sand Hill Trail

Thanks to its panoramic views of

China Cove (left); South Shore Trail (right)

TOP HIKE

CYPRESS GROVE TRAIL

DISTANCE: 0.9 mi (1.4 km) round-trip
DURATION: 20 minutes
EFFORT: Easy
TRAILHEAD: Allan Memorial Grove parking lot

This short and easy hike leads visitors to one of the best features of the park: the endemic Monterey cypress trees. These unique oversize-bonsai-looking trees have populated the Monterey and Carmel Bay area for 15,000 years, apparently enjoying the fog-cloaked headlands close to the sea. This trail is also a Point Lobos favorite because it's a relatively flat path that loops around the grove and Pinnacle Point. Bring binoculars to spot birds, whale spouts, seals, and sea otters.

the Pacific Ocean, this hike is popular for whale watchers, birders, and plein air painters. Along with the changing tides, naturalists like to check out the Carmelo Formation—a sedimentary mixture of mudstone, sandstone, and "puddingstone" that makes up its unique shoreline. This trail is mostly flat, running parallel to the main road.

NORTH SHORE TRAIL

DISTANCE: 2.8 mi (4.5 km) round-trip
DURATION: 1 hour
EFFORT: Strenuous
TRAILHEAD: Whalers Cove or Sea Lion Point parking areas

Since this path, though short, requires scrambling over tree roots, rocky ground, and going up and down rough stairs, strong legs are needed to navigate all the obstacles. However, the scenes of granodiorite cliffs, Bluefish Cove marine life, and diverse flora make it well worth the effort.

RECREATION

★ DIVING AND SNORKELING

Monterey Bay National Marine Sanctuary

https://montereybay.noaa.gov

Just north of the reserve's entrance, **Whalers Cove** is a wide inlet with a small cliff-crested shoreline and a small launch ramp. A large rock stands within its shallow cyan-blue waters in this wind-protected harbor, along with kelp beds and access to sea caves and Bluefish Cove in the surrounding area. This entire section of the reserve is part of the Monterey Bay National Marine Sanctuary, and the dive area is limited from Granite Point to Guillemot Island. Pinnacles 60-100 ft (18-30 m) deep in the

harbor seals

ocean out past the coves are abundant with sea stars, torpedo rays, lingcod, sea otters, and interesting rock formations.

WILDLIFE WATCHING

★ Marine Mammals

Spanish settlers originally named this part of the park "Punta de Lobos," short for "lobos marinos," meaning "sea wolves" in Spanish. The best place to see (and hear) the **sea lions, elephant seals,** and **harbor seals,** and maybe catch sea otters or orcas swimming in the distance, is **Sea Lion Point.** See everything from the **Sea Lion Trail loop,** which starts near the Information Station at the end of the road. The 0.6-mi (1-km) loop among cypress trees leads out to the point and connects with the Sand Hill Trail, a wide hardpacked-dirt ADA-compliant path that goes back inland and connects with the South Shore Trail.

During harbor seal birthing season, visit **China Cove** to see moms and their newborn pups basking in the sand. Don't forget to bring your binoculars to really get a good glimpse of these wildlife rituals.

★ Birds

At the southernmost end of the park, the **Bird Island Trail** is the top hike for avian aficionados at Point Lobos, as hundreds of seabirds gather at this area of the reserve every spring and summer to mate, relax, fish, and raise their chicks. The 0.8-mi (1.3-km) trail wrapping around inside the peninsula is accessible from the southernmost parking lot. Once you get to the edge of the cliff, look for the neat granite arch formations and outcrops caused by erosion and the pounding waves. Pretty wildflowers bloom around **Pelican Point,** and this part of the trail also has the best view of **Bird Island,** where hundreds of Brandt's cormorants nest and show off their brilliant blue-black plumage. Western gulls, great blue herons, and black-crowned night herons also fish here.

Brandt's cormorants at Bird Island Overlook

Tide Pools

Weston Beach on the South Shore Trail is great for tide-pooling; just be sure to wear nonslip shoes, watch the ocean, and tread lightly as to not disturb the sea stars, anemones, and other sentient ocean inhabitants.

FOOD AND LODGING

Point Lobos is only open for day use exploration; there is **no camping** to protect the wildlife. **Carmel-by-the-Sea** is the closest town to Point Lobos, just 4 mi (6 km) north of the reserve on CA-1. The picturesque downtown has boutiques, art galleries, quaint inns, and creative restaurants, not to mention the essentials like gas stations and grocery stores, big and small.

BEST PICNIC SPOT

Whalers Cove Picnic Area

Whalers Cove is a great place to put down your blanket and basket because it's within a short walking distance to Whalers Cabin and the Cypress Grove Trail, and at the heart of the scuba-diving area.

GETTING THERE

CAR

Point Lobos State Natural Reserve is on the southern part of Carmel Bay, off CA-1/Cabrillo Highway. It's 7 mi (11 km) south from the heart of Monterey and 121 mi (195 km, 2 hours) south of San Francisco. If driving from San Francisco, try to avoid rush-hour traffic. There's no public transportation system that takes you directly to the reserve.

PFEIFFER BIG SUR STATE PARK

ADDRESS: 47555 CA-1, Big Sur

PHONE: 530/541-3030

DAY USE HOURS: 8am-sunset

AREA: 1,006 acres (407 ha)

In the heart of Big Sur nestled on the edge of the Santa Lucia Mountains, Pfeiffer Big Sur State Park features a rugged and wild landscape full of coast redwoods, ferns, sorrel, and rushing water compliments of the Big Sur River Gorge.

Evidence shows that the Esselen and Rumsien people lived in Big Sur about 8,000 years ago, but only a few archaeological items such as bedrock mortars and arrowheads have been discovered. Interpretive plaques alongside some of the trails highlight their heritage.

After Europeans settled in Big Sur, John Pfeiffer was one of the new immigrants whose family built a cabin in the park in 1884. He sold a good portion of the Big Sur coastal land to California under the provision they preserved its beauty. As the Great Depression took hold of America, the Civilian Conservation Corps built out many of Pfeiffer Big Sur's trails and structures.

Nowadays, Pfeiffer Big Sur's 1,006 acres (407 ha) have 14 moderate and longer trails that go eastward into the Ventana Wilderness. The best ones follow the gorge and coastal bluffs. While there is no access to the Pacific Ocean, Pfeiffer Big Sur has everything else you need for your California inland hiking adventure.

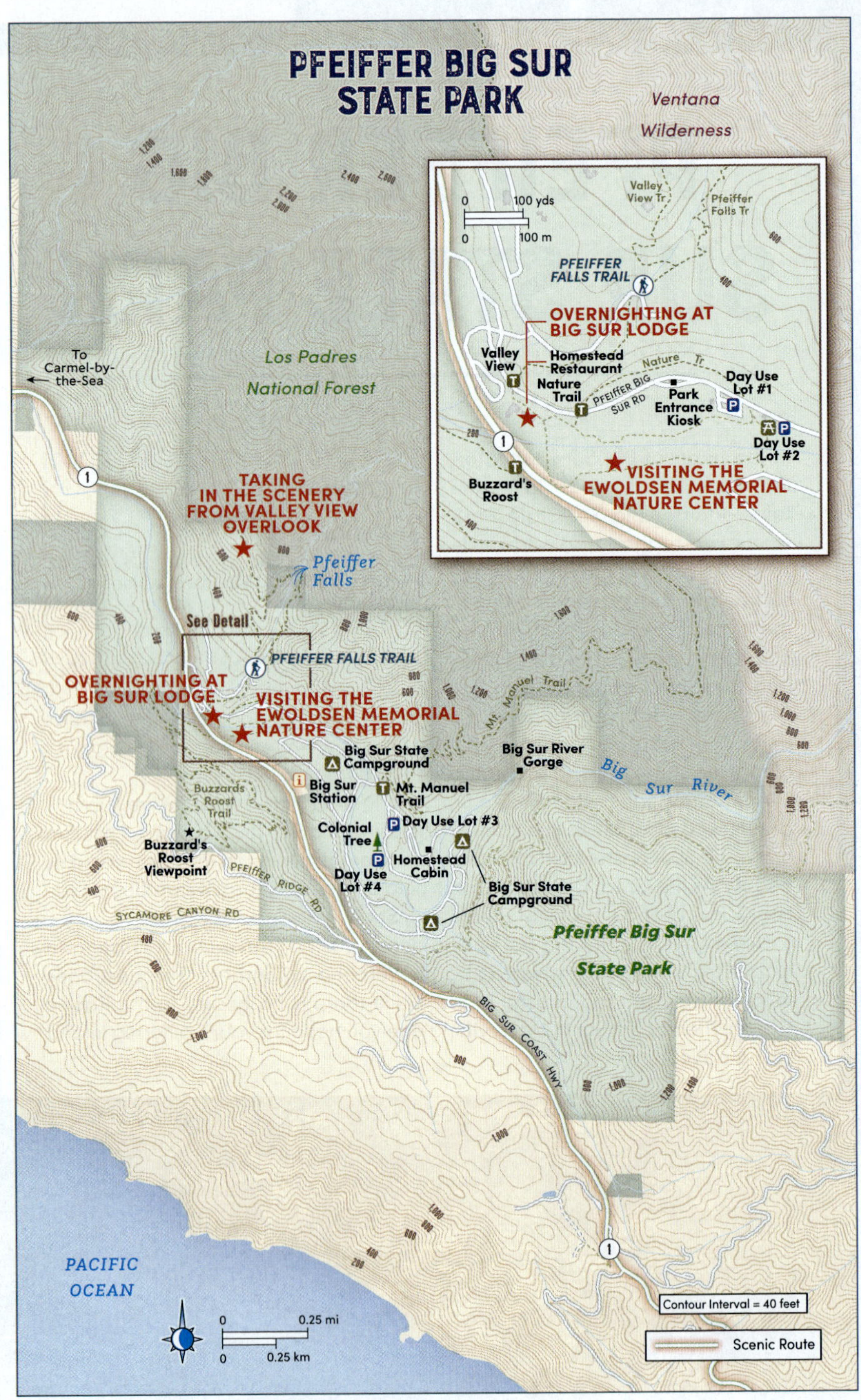

PFEIFFER BIG SUR STATE PARK
Ventana Wilderness
Los Padres National Forest
To Carmel-by-the-Sea
TAKING IN THE SCENERY FROM VALLEY VIEW OVERLOOK
Pfeiffer Falls
See Detail
PFEIFFER FALLS TRAIL
OVERNIGHTING AT BIG SUR LODGE
VISITING THE EWOLDSEN MEMORIAL NATURE CENTER
Mt. Manuel Trail
Big Sur State Campground
Big Sur River Gorge
Big Sur River
Big Sur Station
Mt. Manuel Trail
Buzzards Roost Trail
Buzzard's Roost Viewpoint
Colonial Tree
Day Use Lot #3
Homestead Cabin
Day Use Lot #4
Big Sur State Campground
PFEIFFER RIDGE RD
SYCAMORE CANYON RD
Pfeiffer Big Sur State Park
BIG SUR COAST HWY
PACIFIC OCEAN
0 0.25 mi
0 0.25 km
Contour Interval = 40 feet
Scenic Route
0 100 yds
0 100 m
Valley View Tr
Pfeiffer Falls Tr
PFEIFFER FALLS TRAIL
OVERNIGHTING AT BIG SUR LODGE
Valley View
Homestead Restaurant
Nature Trail
Nature Tr
PFEIFFER BIG SUR RD
Park Entrance Kiosk
Day Use Lot #1
Day Use Lot #2
Buzzard's Roost
VISITING THE EWOLDSEN MEMORIAL NATURE CENTER

TOP 3

1. VISITING THE EWOLDSEN MEMORIAL NATURE CENTER: Along the peaceful Big Sur River Gorge, the stone-lined center stores exhibits and interesting information for people of all ages (page 290).

2. TAKING IN THE SCENERY FROM VALLEY VIEW OVERLOOK: Redwoods and wildflowers line this trail, leading up to the beautiful valley and vistas of the Pacific Ocean (page 292).

3. OVERNIGHTING AT BIG SUR LODGE: A mix of suites and cottages located right next to the park's major trailheads makes this a unique home base (page 294).

PLANNING YOUR TIME

San Simeon is 60 mi (97 km) south, but if the road to Big Sur is washed out then you must go around on US-101 through King City and Monterey. King City is inland, about two hours away from the park, while Monterey is 30 mi (48 km) north of Pfeiffer Big Sur. Portions of CA-1 tend to close more often in the winter depending on the amount of rainfall causing landslides. Check the park's website before you go to see what condition CA-1 is in before jumping in your car.

When people finally get to Big Sur, they tend to stay the night in the park, at the campground, Big Sur Lodge, or somewhere else nearby. If you can, spend at least two days in the park.

Nearby state parks include Point Lobos State Natural Reserve (22 mi/35 km).

ENTRANCE AND FEES

There is **one main entrance** to the park off CA-1. The cost is $10 to enter for the day, which gives you access to all the other state parks within the vicinity (including Point Lobos State Natural Reserve and Julia Pfeiffer Burns State Park, 7.7 mi/12.3 km away) until closing (which varies by park).

VISITOR CENTER

Big Sur Station

47555 CA-1, Big Sur; 831/667-2315; https://lpforest.org/big-sur-station; 9am-4pm daily

Along CA-1 a half mile south of the Pfeiffer Big Sur entrance, Big Sur Station serves as a welcome center for all the Big Sur state parks. Friendly park rangers are available to help visitors with current trail conditions, maps, upcoming events, and backpacking information related to the Los Padres Forest. Souvenirs, gifts, and camp essentials can be purchased here, too.

WEATHER

It's always a good idea to bring layers of clothing because there can be chilling fog, especially in the mornings. In the winter, daytime temperatures are around 50-70°F (10-21°C) and can drop down to 30°F (-1°C) at night. In the summertime, the hottest it gets is 80-85°F (27-29°C), after the morning fog burns off. Rockslides and landslides tend to happen on CA-1 in December/January after heavy rains, but March/April is the best time to visit when the wildflowers are blooming and it's not as busy.

SIGHTS

★ EWOLDSEN MEMORIAL NATURE CENTER

47225 CA-1, Big Sur; 831/667-3130; 10am-noon Sat.-Sun.

The Ewoldsen Memorial Nature Center is right on the Warden's Path along the Big Sur River. It's open on the weekends in the winter for a few hours and may be open longer in the summer. Visitors can learn about

Big Sur's flora and fauna as well as experience the "Fly Like a Condor" interactive exhibit.

HOMESTEAD CABIN

From Day Use Area 3, a mostly paved path leads 0.4 mi (0.6 km) to the river gorge. Halfway there, a steep dirt/rock path leads up to the Homestead Cabin. Built in the late 1800s by John Pfeiffer, its simple wooden exterior still stands today.

HIKING

Pfeiffer Big Sur State Park's main hikes highlight the area's oak woodlands, coast redwoods, and all the other plants and animals that rely on the moist riparian atmosphere to thrive. Nestled between CA-1 and the Los Padres National Forest's 240,026-acre (97,135-ha) Ventana Wilderness, a couple of the trails start in the park and head east through the mountains outside of its boundaries.

MT. MANUEL TRAIL

DISTANCE: 8 mi (13 km) round-trip
DURATION: 6.5 hours
EFFORT: Strenuous
TRAILHEAD: Day Use Area 3

The 8-mi (13-km) Mt. Manuel Trail goes into US Forest Service land after the initial mile, and hikers climb to the 3,379-ft (1,030-m) peak. The exposed mountainside has a decent amount of single-track switchbacks, and the sun tends to get more brutal as the day goes on, so bring water and a hat. The views from the top are worth the long trek on this out-and-back trail.

BUZZARD'S ROOST TRAIL

DISTANCE: 2.8 mi (4.5 km) round-trip
DURATION: 1 hour 45 minutes
EFFORT: Moderate
TRAILHEAD: CA-1 south of Big Sur River at the Redwood Deck

On the coastal side of CA-1 across the street from a parking area, Buzzard's Roost's varied terrain path winds through dramatic blanketed mountains and tall coastal trees along the Big Sur River. Quiet and peaceful with maybe only the banana slugs to keep you company, the highest point on this loop offers views of the Santa Lucia Mountains, Sycamore

Buzzard's Roost Trail (left); Valley View Overlook Trail (right)

Canyon, and the Pacific Ocean on a clear day.

★ VALLEY VIEW OVERLOOK TRAIL

DISTANCE: 1.8 mi (2.9 km) round-trip
DURATION: 1 hour 15 minutes
EFFORT: Moderate
TRAILHEAD: On Pfeiffer Big Sur Rd., south of Pfeiffer-Redwood Creek

From Big Sur Lodge, take the Pfeiffer Falls Trail through the woodlands to the fork in the road, then take the left route to go to the Valley View Overlook instead of to the falls. A moderately challenging 300-ft (91-m) climb will likely get your heart pumping, but you'll be rewarded with incredible views of Point Sur, Andrew Molera State Park, and the Big Sur River Valley at the top.

NATURE TRAIL

DISTANCE: 0.8 mi (1.3 km) round-trip
DURATION: 15 minutes
EFFORT: Easy
TRAILHEAD: Day Use Area Lot 2

This quick and easy self-guided loop focuses on plants such as the laurels, oak trees, and redwoods that help make this ecosystem thrive. Nature guides available at the trailhead give information about what makes the flora here so special.

RECREATION

SWIMMING

Big Sur River Gorge

As the air temperatures creep up as it approaches summer, visitors tend to flock toward Big Sur's waterways to cool off. Be sure to bring your swimsuit to wade around in the clear turquoise-blue waters of the gorge; it's next to the campground and a quarter mile (0.4 km) away from Day Use Area 3. There is a main swimming hole that's unmarked; you might have to do a bit of scrambling to find a good spot to lay out your towel. This place is popular with teenagers over spring break.

CAMPING

Pfeiffer Big Sur State Park maintains **one campground** with 189 sites. The campground is open year-round, including the one hike-in/bike-in site ($5) limited to a two-consecutive-night stay. Pfeiffer Big Sur is very popular, and reservations fill up fast even in the winter months. Sites can be reserved through Reserve California (800/444-7575; www.reservecalifornia.com; $50-60/night) from two days out up to six months in advance. All 189 campsites are on the Reserve California reservation system, and it's usually impossible to find an unreserved site during the peak summer season. Campsites can accommodate two vehicles, but the second car costs $10 to park (a trailer and a vehicle count as one).

All sites include a fire pit, picnic table, and parking for at least one car. Potable water, hot showers, and flush toilets are throughout the campground. There are no hookups available for RVs, but a dump

TOP HIKE
PFEIFFER FALLS TRAIL

DISTANCE: 1.6 mi (2.6 km) round-trip
DURATION: 1 hour
EFFORT: Moderate
TRAILHEAD: On Pfeiffer Big Sur Rd., south of Pfeiffer-Redwood Creek

While this is a moderately challenging hike due to its elevation gain into the Los Padres National Forest, it's well worth it for the view of the 60-ft (18-m) waterfall at the end. The out-and-back trail starts near Big Sur Lodge and heads east, a well-packed dirt path guiding trekkers through redwood forest, up staircases, and over bridges, the Lincoln-log railings lining the path. Breathe in the fresh air as you take in the vistas, plants, and animals along the way.

station is available for free for registered campers. In the far southern side of the park in campsites 1-131, a camp store and laundry machines are open for use in the summertime.

BEST CAMPGROUND

Pfeiffer Big Sur State Park Campground

The campground at this state park is broken down into two areas each containing several loops. Sites 1-130 are closest to parking lots 3 and 4 on the south end of the park and skirting the south end of the Big Sur River. Sites 131-189 are closest to parking lots 1 and 2, the Ewoldsen Nature Center, campfire center, and Big Sur Lodge. A softball field, Colonial Tree (one of the park's more prominent redwoods), restrooms, picnic tables, and lots 3 and 4 are between the two main campsite areas. RVs with onboard flush toilets can stay in these lots for one night only between 5pm-9am for $60.

FOOD AND LODGING

The park should have everything you need to survive in the woods for a few days, but the closest town is **Carmel,** 45 minutes (26 mi/42 km) north on CA-1. It has more grocery stores, gas stations, restaurants, upscale accommodations, and the famous Pebble Beach golf course. Its sister town of **Monterey** is 4 mi (6 km) farther north and has even more amenities like luxury hotels, a legendary aquarium, and famous Cannery Row.

★ BIG SUR LODGE

47225 CA-1, Big Sur; 800/424-4787; https://bigsurlodge.com; $254/night

While there are a few options to stay overnight in the "town" of Big Sur, from Airbnbs to five-star resorts, Big Sur Lodge has suites and cottages that sleep up to four people with kitchenettes, balconies, and/or fireplaces. It is right at the entrance of the park and next to the trailheads for the Valley View Overlook and Pfeiffer Falls. A restaurant, coffee bar, and small grocer are attached.

Day Use Lot 2 (left); camping (right)

BEST NEARBY

DRIVING THE BIG SUR COAST HIGHWAY

Gentle curves, gorgeous wildflowers, succulent-filled bluffs, and dramatic up-close crashing waves make this portion of CA-1 one of the most popular sections and give it its National Scenic Highway designation. Between the 164-mi (264-km) coastal highway stretch between Carmel in the north and San Simeon in the south, many people stop at Bixby Bridge, a historic architectural landmark, to take selfies. Built in 1932, Bixby Bridge is about 11 mi (18 km) north of Pfeiffer Big Sur State Park.

HOMESTEAD RESTAURANT

47225 CA-1, Big Sur; 831/667-3100; https://bigsurlodge.com; 8am-8pm daily; $13-38

Within Big Sur Lodge, the Homestead Restaurant serves delicious dishes for breakfast, lunch, and dinner. Its soups, salads, sandwiches, and burgers are made with locally sourced ingredients. The dinner menu has more upscale options, including vegetarian and gluten-free mains. Or, if you're in a hurry to hit the trails, visit the coffee bar for an espresso and grab-n-go lunch.

BEST PICNIC SPOT

Day Use Lot 2

Pfeiffer Big Sur State Park's tagline should be "the place to picnic" because of its multitude of spots to post up. Many people who spend just the day at Pfeiffer Big Sur and aren't camping or hiking to the gorge stop to rest and refuel at Day Use Lot 2, as it's still next to the river, restrooms, and a variety of easy flat nature trails.

GETTING THERE

CAR

Pfeiffer Big Sur State Park is right in the middle of the Central Coast on CA-1, near mile marker 47.2. Monterey is the closest coastal "city" north of the park, approximately 30 mi (48 km) away. Carmel-by-the-Sea is 4 mi (6 km) south of Monterey.

If there are **landslides on CA-1,** then the road will shut down and you'll be rerouted to US-101 and Monterey to come back down along the coast. It can take about three hours to get to the park from San Simeon if CA-1 is closed between the Esalen Institute and Lucia. From San Simeon going to the park, head south on CA-1 to Cambria for 12 mi (19 km), then get on CA-46 heading east to Paso Robles. From there, follow US-101 north to Monterey and merge onto CA-1 south.

HEARST SAN SIMEON STATE HISTORICAL MONUMENT AND STATE PARK

Hearst San Simeon State Historical Monument and State Park preserves 20 mi (32 km) of dramatic coastline, grasslands, and historic Hearst Castle. Drive this scenic stretch of the Pacific Coast Highway, stopping to explore windswept rocky beaches scattered with driftwood, visit a colony of elephant seals, or stroll one of the boardwalks for breathtaking views. Guided tours of Hearst Castle give access to the elaborate estate built by William Randolph Hearst of newspaper and media fame in the first half of the 20th century. Set on Hearst's original 250,000 acres of ranchland, the property includes a 115-room main house, three guesthouses, two swimming pools, and gardens. The estate also houses a world-renowned 23,000-piece art collection stacked with antiquities from around the world.

Traveling the winding road to Hearst Castle, you will see sweeping views of the Pacific and the hills that make up the former ranchland. During Hearst's time, exotic wild animals including bison and elk roamed the land. Today if you're lucky you can still see wild free-range zebras grazing along CA-1 near the village of San Simeon.

HEARST SAN SIMEON STATE HISTORICAL MONUMENT

ADDRESS: 700 Hearst Castle Rd., San Simeon

PHONE: 800/444-4445

WEBSITE: https://hearstcastle.org

DAY USE HOURS: 9am-last tour

AREA: 209 acres (85 ha)

HEARST SAN SIMEON STATE PARK

ADDRESS: 500 San Simeon Creek Rd., Cambria

PHONE: 805/927-2010

DAY USE HOURS: 8am-sunset

AREA: 2,309 acres (934 ha)

HEARST SAN SIMEON STATE HISTORICAL MONUMENT AND STATE PARK
CATCHING THE MOVIE AT HEARST CASTLE THEATER
San Simeon
Hearst Castle Visitor Center
SAN SIMEON RD
HEARST CASTLE RD
San Simeon
0 200 yds
0 200 m
William Randolph Hearst Memorial Beach
Hearst San Simeon State Park
CABRILLO HWY
TOURING HEARST CASTLE
Hearst San Simeon State Historical Monument
HEARST CASTLE RD
Piedras Blancas Northern Elephant Seal Rookery
Hearst San Simeon State Park
CATCHING THE MOVIE AT HEARST CASTLE THEATER
See "San Simeon" Detail
San Simeon
San Simeon Cove
CABRILLO HWY
PACIFIC OCEAN
Hearst San Simeon State Park
See "Hearst San Simeon State Park" Detail
STROLLING MOONSTONE BEACH BOARDWALK
Moonstone Beach
Cambria
Santa Rosa Creek Preserve
Hearst San Simeon State Park
Park Entrance
Pa-nu Cultural Preserve
San Simeon Creek
Hearst San Simeon State Park
Washburn Day-Use Area
Washburn
San Simeon Natural Preserve
0 200 yds
0 200 m
0 2 mi
0 2 km
Contour Interval = 200 feet

TOP 3

1. TOURING HEARST CASTLE: A number of guided tours allow visitors to see the estate's opulent rooms and elaborate gardens as well as its world-class art collection (page 300).

2. CATCHING THE MOVIE AT HEARST CASTLE THEATER: *Hearst Castle—Building the Dream* tells the story of the castle's construction (page 301).

3. STROLLING MOONSTONE BEACH BOARDWALK: Walk the boardwalk to look for sea otters, whales, and dolphins or take in sunset views over the Pacific (page 301).

PLANNING YOUR TIME

Tours of Hearst Castle are approximately two hours, so plan for a half day to a full day to take one tour and add in a few stops along the coastal stretch of the state park. Book a site at one of the two campgrounds and plan for a long weekend to more fully explore the beaches and quaint towns along this stretch of spectacular coastline.

Nearby state parks include Cayucos State Beach/Estero Bluffs State Park (15 mi/24 km), Morro Bay State Park (25 mi/40 km), and Montaña de Oro State Park (32 mi/51 km).

ENTRANCE AND FEES

There is technically no entry fee for Hearst San Simeon State Historical Monument. You can visit the visitor center for free, but all other access to the park is via guided tour, which requires a reservation and fee. All tours begin at the **Hearst Castle Visitor Center.** Park in the visitor center parking lot, then check in. A series of shuttle buses take visitors up Hearst Castle Road to the castle and grounds at the top of the hill.

There is **no official entrance** and no fee for Hearst San Simeon State Park. Parking is in a series of day use lots along the Pacific Coast Highway.

VISITOR CENTER

Hearst Castle Visitor Center

700 Hearst Castle Rd., San Simeon

The Hearst Castle Visitor Center contains the W.R. Hearst exhibit, a small café, and a gift shop.

RESERVATIONS

The main experience at Hearst San Simeon State Historical Monument is a guided tour. It is strongly recommended to reserve a tour ahead of time online via www.reservecalifornia.com ($35); however, there may be a limited number of tickets available if you show up in person. It is possible to visit the visitor center, tour a small exhibit, and watch a film on the history of Hearst Castle ($6) without a reservation, but there is no access to the castle without a tour.

WEATHER

This section of the Central Coast is moderately cool year-round with temperatures hovering around 62-68°F (17-20°C); September-November are typically the warmest months. A marine layer and wind can bring an additional chill even in summer. Inland, the location of Hearst Castle, temperatures can be much higher, so dress in layers. Summer is the recommended time to visit.

EVENTS

Christmas at Hearst Castle

From the end of November through the end of December, Hearst Castle is festively decorated for the Christmas season. Visitors to the estate at this time will be treated to views of the estate as guests in the 1920s and 1930s would have experienced it with large Christmas trees in the social rooms, and lights, garlands, and wreaths adorning the property.

SIGHTS

While visitors come to tour Hearst Castle to see lifestyles of the rich and famous, what you quickly realize is that the buildings and grounds are filled with historic objects, prominent pieces, and masterpieces from around the world that Hearst purchased to furnish the property. The site is a nationally accredited art museum with a 23,000-piece collection.

★ TOURS

Grand Rooms Tour

$35

The Grand Rooms Tour takes in the social gathering rooms at Casa Grande, the largest house on the estate. Docents lead visitors through rooms where A-listers gathered for cocktail hour, dinner, and after-dinner billiards. The tour also takes in the manicured grounds, the huge outdoor Neptune Pool (which is still used by members of the Hearst family), and the indoor, tiled Roman Pool styled after an ancient Roman bathhouse. This is the park's most popular tour and great for first-time visitors. Accessibly designed tours are available for the Grand Rooms Tour. Accessible transportation is provided from the visitor center, and the tours encompass areas that are wheelchair-accessible.

Upstairs Suites Tour

$35

Take a peek into Hearst's own Gothic Suite as well as other suites, including one in the bell tower level and a duplex suite. Like the Grand Rooms Tour, this guided walk explores Casa Grande, the largest house on the estate, but it goes upstairs via a 322-step winding staircase to see these private chambers. Another highlight is the library with its 150 ancient Greek vases.

Cottages and Kitchen Tour

$35

The word "cottages" here refers to two ornate mansions covering thousands of square feet that housed the Hearst family and guests before Casa Grande was finished. The tour takes in the cottages as well as Casa Grande's kitchen and wine cellar.

Neptune Pool (left); Roman Pool (right)

GARDENS

In addition to its sumptuous main house and guesthouses, the estate has 127 acres (51 ha) of impressively landscaped grounds including gardens, terraces, walkways, and the Neptune and Roman Pools. After their guided tour, visitors are welcome to explore the grounds, gardens, and pools, which, like the buildings, are filled with art and antiquities.

★ HEARST CASTLE THEATER

The Hearst Castle Theater is a five-story-screen theater adjacent to the visitor center. It screens *Hearst Castle—Building the Dream*, a 40-minute movie on the building of Hearst Castle. The movie was produced exclusively for the theater and features original cinematography as well as vintage clips and stills from the 1920s and 1930s. The movie screens every 45 minutes from 9am to 5pm daily. Entrance is included with the tour ticket price.

BEACHES

★ MOONSTONE BEACH AND BOARDWALK

Moonstone Beach Dr., Cambria

The ocean serves as a natural rock tumbler at Moonstone Beach, known for the smooth mineral chalcedony, jade, agate, and jasper stones strewn across the sand. The beach is backed by scenic, rugged bluffs, so most of the access is via the bluff-top Moonstone Boardwalk. Visitors stroll the 1-mi (1.6-km), accessible, wood-plank trail to take in the striking beach and ocean views and look for sea life including gray whales, dolphins, elephant seals, and sea otters. In the evenings, people file onto the walkway to watch the sunset.

Access to the beach is via multiple paths that cut down to the rocky seashore where the sand is made up of tiny polished stones. From shore there are opportunities for swimming, surfing, tide-pooling, and surf fishing. The waves here are powerful, so be cautious when entering the water.

WILLIAM RANDOLPH HEARST MEMORIAL BEACH

750 Hearst Castle Rd.

Located across from Hearst Castle near the village of San Simeon, this sandy beach is popular for swimming, fishing, and picnicking. A day use area has 24 picnic sites and barbecues. There is also a large parking area, water faucets, and restrooms. A recreational pier built in 1958 is a good spot to take in the views or fish. No fishing license is required when fishing off the pier, but limits are enforced. There is also a small Coastal Discovery Center (805/927-6575; https://montereybay.noaa.gov; 11am-5pm Fri.-Sun.; free) with exhibits on the San Simeon Bay's natural and cultural history.

CAMPING

There are **two campgrounds** in Hearst San Simeon State Park. Reservations through Reserve California (800/444-7275; www.reservecalifornia.com; $20-35/night) are required for most sites, and campgrounds fill completely on weekends in high season and on holiday weekends. San Simeon Creek Campground maintains a few first-come, first-served sites for last-minute campers. For RVs, there is a sanitation station and water-fill station located at San Simeon Creek Campground, but no hookups are available.

BEST CAMPGROUNDS

San Simeon Creek Campground

San Simeon Creek Campground offers 134 sites across two separate camping zones. The shaded lower sites are situated near San Simeon Creek, a broad waterway that drains onto the beach. Upper sites are dotted across coastal hills with plenty of space and ocean views. Campsites are walking distance to the beach. Each site has a picnic table and fire pit, and the campground has water spigots, flush toilets, and token-operated showers.

Washburn Campground

Washburn Campground offers 68 campsites 1 mi (1.6 km) inland with views of the Pacific Ocean and the Santa Lucia Mountains. Sites are widely spaced across a grassy plateau dotted with pines, each with a picnic table and fire pit. The campground has chemical toilets. Water and token-operated showers are available at San Simeon Creek Campground.

FOOD AND LODGING

The small village of **San Simeon,** located along CA-1 less than 1 mi (1.6 km) south of the turnoff to the Hearst Castle Visitor Center, has several hotels and restaurants. The town of **Cambria,** 9 mi (14 km) south of Hearst Castle and 2 mi (3 km) south of the state park campgrounds, is a destination known for picturesque Moonstone Beach and a charming Victorian downtown with shops and restaurants. Cambria has a wide choice of lodging, from quaint inns to luxury hotels to vacation rentals. It also has the basics, including groceries and gas.

BEST PICNIC SPOT

Washburn Day Use Area

Located slightly inland, the Washburn Day Use Area offers a good picnic spot because it is not directly subject to the strong coastal breezes while still affording views of the Pacific Ocean. The site has picnic tables, restrooms, and an accessible boardwalk trail that leads through coastal grasses to a small beach area next to San Simeon Creek.

BEST NEARBY

elephant seals

PIEDRAS BLANCAS NORTHERN ELEPHANT SEAL ROOKERY

To make a day or a weekend of it, tour some nearby landmarks. The Piedras Blancas Northern Elephant Seal Rookery (https://elephantseal.org; free) offers a unique chance to see these marine mammals on shore at an elephant seal vista point 4.5 mi (7 km) north of the turnoff to Hearst Castle. Elephant seals may be seen year-round, but the most action happens in January, April, and October. The viewing area is wheelchair-accessible.

GETTING THERE

CAR

Hearst San Simeon State Historical Monument is located along CA-1, 9 mi (14 km) north of the town of Cambria and less than 1 mi (1.6 km) inland from the town of San Simeon. Hearst San Simeon State Park is located along CA-1, 2 mi (3 km) north of the town of Cambria and 5 mi (8 km) south of the town of San Simeon.

CAYUCOS STATE BEACH AND ESTERO BLUFFS STATE PARK

Cayucos State Beach is a lovely crescent of sand framed by low coastal hills on the Central Coast midway between Los Angeles and San Francisco. Its welcome mat is the charming, historic seaside community of Cayucos, where you can eat clam chowder or browse for antiques.

Originally settled by the Chumash, who had a large village to the south at Morro Creek, Cayucos takes its name from a Mexican land grant awarded in 1842 that includes the current footprint of the town.

This stretch along the Pacific is unique for its wide, sandy shore good for swimming and taking long, uninterrupted walks to look for shells and shorebirds. On Cayucos's northern end, the gentle coastline gives way to the low bluffs, coastal terraces, and sea stacks of the Estero Bluffs State Park. A trail along the coast's edge crosses coastal grasslands and is a good place to look for migrating whales or take in a sunset.

CAYUCOS STATE BEACH

ADDRESS: Cayucos State Beach, Cayucos

PHONE: 805/781-5930

DAY USE HOURS: 6am-sunset

AREA: 16 acres (6 ha)

ESTERO BLUFFS STATE PARK

ADDRESS: Hwy. 1, Cayucos

PHONE: 805/772-6101

DAY USE HOURS: 6am-sunset

AREA: 353 acres (143 ha)

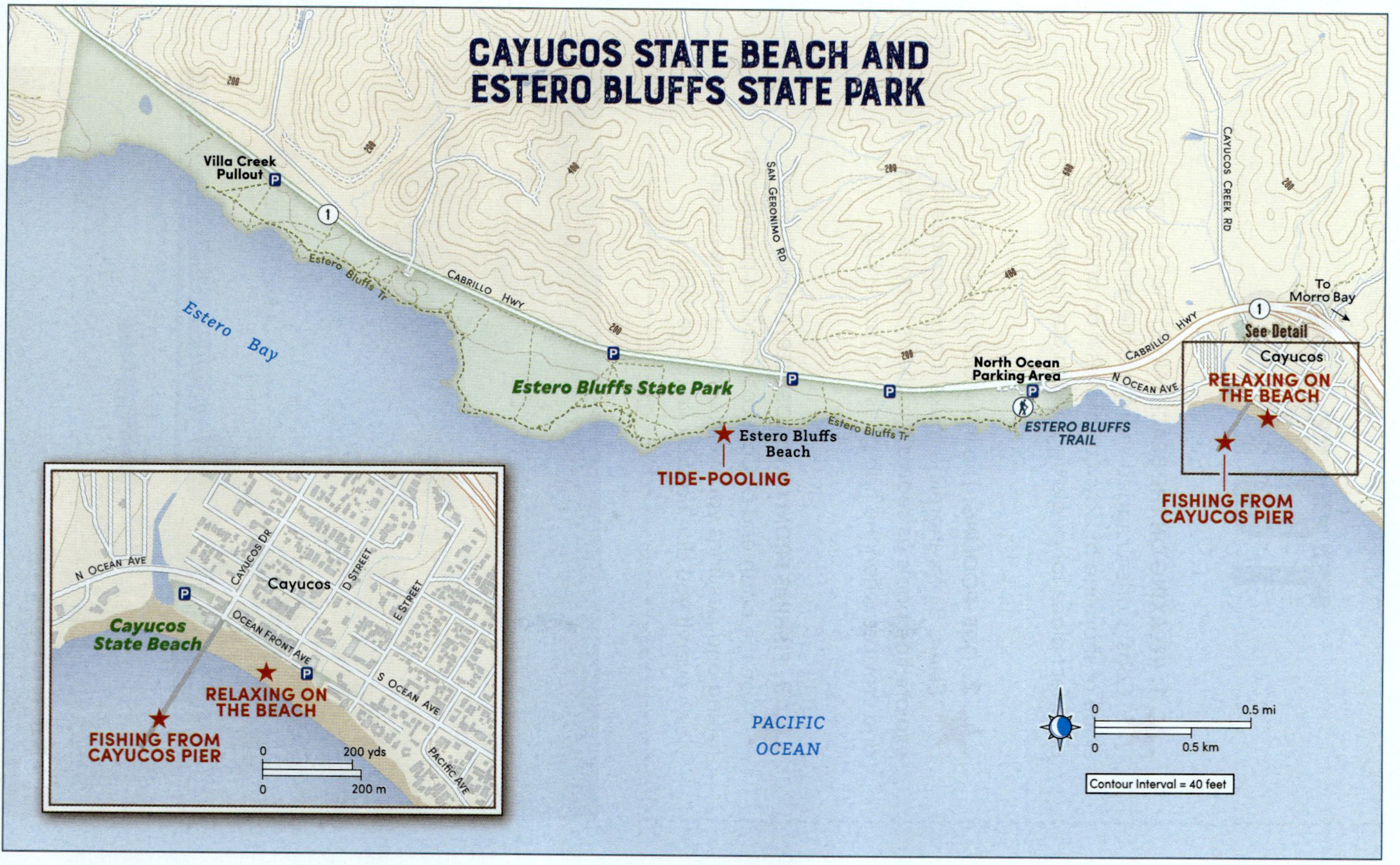

CAYUCOS STATE BEACH AND ESTERO BLUFFS STATE PARK
Villa Creek Pullout
Estero Bluffs Tr
Cabrillo Hwy
San Geronimo Rd
Cayucos Creek Rd
To Morro Bay
See Detail
Cayucos
RELAXING ON THE BEACH
FISHING FROM CAYUCOS PIER
North Ocean Parking Area
N Ocean Ave
Estero Bluffs Trail
Estero Bluffs State Park
Estero Bluffs Beach
TIDE-POOLING
Estero Bay
Pacific Ocean
0.5 mi
0.5 km
Contour Interval = 40 feet
N Ocean Ave
Cayucos Dr
Cayucos
D Street
E Street
Ocean Front Ave
S Ocean Ave
Pacific Ave
Cayucos State Beach
RELAXING ON THE BEACH
FISHING FROM CAYUCOS PIER
200 yds
200 m

TOP 3

★ **1. RELAXING ON THE BEACH:** Along the Central Coast's often rugged shoreline, the gentle, sandy slope of shoreline at Cayucos makes it an anomaly and a perfect place for a relaxing beach day (page 308).

★ **2. TIDE-POOLING:** The intertidal zones of the Estero Bluffs shoreline make it a good place to explore tide pools as seawater collects in holes, cracks, and crevices when the tide goes out (page 310).

★ **3. FISHING FROM CAYUCOS PIER:** A historic pier on the north end of Cayucos Beach is popular for fishing and positions you well for taking in the ocean views even if you don't get a bite (page 310).

PLANNING YOUR TIME

A half day would give you enough time to enjoy the beach, visit the town, and walk a short section of trail at the Estero Bluffs; however, all these activities could easily take up a full day and allow for a longer bluffs hike. A weekend is enough time to get into full vacation mode.

Nearby state parks include Morro Bay State Park (10 mi/16 km), Montaña de Oro State Park (16 mi/26 km), and Hearst San Simeon State Historical Monument (23 mi/37 km).

ENTRANCE AND FEES

There are **no official entrances** and no day use or parking fees for either park.

Main beach access for Cayucos State Beach is near the Cayucos Pier on Pacific Avenue at the intersection of Cayucos Drive and Ocean Front Avenue. There are restrooms and outdoor showers to rinse the sand off. Free parking is available on Ocean Front Avenue, a segmented oceanfront road that has direct beach access. There is also free parking available along the town's main street, Ocean Avenue, and side streets.

Estero Bluffs can be accessed from the south end of the park at the North Ocean Parking Area, on the north end of Cayucos. Access to the north end of the park is via the Villa Creek Pullout off of the Pacific Coast Highway (PCH)/CA-1 north. There are also additional informal turnouts and access points off the PCH/CA-1 north including the intersection of San Geronimo Creek Road and PCH/CA-1 north.

VISITOR CENTER

There are no visitor centers at Cayucos State Beach or Estero Bluffs State Park.

WEATHER

The area has moderate weather, ranging from 45-75°F (7-24°C) year-round with a marine layer that can blanket the area, especially on winter mornings and evenings. It's typically 30 degrees cooler than inland areas in summer. Dress in layers. Surfers generally wear wetsuits. Summer is the best time to visit to enjoy the beach.

Cayucos State Beach (left); Estero Bluffs (right)

THE TOWN OF CAYUCOS

Cayucos (pronounced kai-YOU-kus by locals) is a charming seaside town with a laid-back vibe. It sits adjacent to Cayucos State Beach so that the town and beach are equal parts of the experience. Historic buildings dating to the late 1800s and early 1900s line the downtown. The town caters to tourists, but never feels like it is trying too hard. Deeply patinaed wood and brick storefronts from the town's dairy and shipping past are home to cool boutiques and restaurants.

Downtown runs along Ocean Avenue for 0.5 mi (0.8 km) and is walkable. It is anchored by the Pacific Motel on the south end of town at the intersection of 4th Street and South Ocean Avenue. On the north end of town, Duckie's Chowder House and the Cayucos Pier provide the ballast at the intersection of Cayucos Drive and North Ocean Avenue.

SIGHTS

CAYUCOS PIER

The Cayucos Pier is a picturesque landmark, anchoring the north end of downtown. Construction on the pier began in 1872, and the pier was rebuilt in 2013 following a storm. Measuring nearly 950 ft (290 m), the pier is visible up and down the coast. Visitors and residents walk out on it to fish, look for migrating whales and seals, and take in the ocean breeze or a sunset. A fishing license is not required to fish from the pier, making it a popular spot. The pier is located on Pacific Avenue at the intersection of Ocean Front Avenue and Cayucos Drive. There is free parking as well as bathrooms and outdoor showers for rinsing off sand.

 BEACHES

CAYUCOS STATE BEACH

Stake your umbrella, bring your sandcastle buckets, and tote out the towels. The long arc of sand that makes up Cayucos State Beach makes it perfect for a classic beach day. In addition, free parking, bathrooms, and outdoor showers near the pier make your day easy-breezy in practice but without all the literal wind of some nearby areas. The shape of the coastline here shelters it a bit, making it less windy than places like Morro Bay to the south or Hearst San Simeon to the north. The marine layer can still be tenacious, though, and temps can be cool for swimsuits, somewhere in the mid-60s F (mid-teens C) even in summer, so bring layers for the beach and a wetsuit for the water. Bodyboards

TOP HIKE

ESTERO BLUFFS TRAIL

DISTANCE: 7.2 mi (11.6 km) round-trip
DURATION: 2.5 hours
EFFORT: Easy
TRAILHEAD: South end of trail: North Ocean Parking Area, on north end of Cayucos. North end of trail: Villa Creek Pullout, PCH/CA-1 north.

Estero Bluffs State Park features a trail system that follows coastal bluffs along a section of the Pacific. The bluffs are named after Estero Bay, which indents the coast at Cayucos and for a few miles to the north. The Estero Bluffs Trail snakes through dunes, native grasslands, and coastal sage scrub, and gives views of the rocky coast and bluffs. A few informal trails give beach cove access, especially near Geronimo Creek.

The land was purchased by developers in 1965 for a resort and homes, but the town of Cayucos and other neighboring communities advocated for its preservation. In 2000 the property was purchased by a public land trust, and in 2002 it was deeded to the State of California to protect this wild section of coast.

The wide, flat out-and-back trail with its multiple access points means you can customize your hike. You can spend 20 minutes or a few hours taking in the beautiful viewshed here: wander the few hundred yards from the North Ocean Parking Area to the bluff's edge for sunset or spend a morning hiking the trail's length. Dogs are allowed on the south section of the trail from San Geronimo Creek to the North Ocean Parking Area. Dogs are not allowed on the south section of trail from San Geronimo Creek to Villa Creek. The park has no restrooms or water. Horses and bicycles are not permitted.

and wetsuits are available to rent from **Cayucos Surf Company** (146 N. Ocean Ave.; 805/995-1000; www.surfcompany.com; 10am-5pm daily). There is decent surfing near the pier.

ESTERO BLUFFS BEACH

The shore at Estero Bluffs is made up of a series of narrow coves backed by bluffs and cut off from one another by rocky points along the rugged coastline. Some of these secluded nooks can be accessed with a bit of a scramble. The largest beach can be found near where San Geronimo Creek drains into the Pacific, at the end of a rocky trail.

RECREATION

WILDLIFE WATCHING

★ Tide Pools

With its rocky coastline, Estero Bluffs State Park is a great spot for exploring tide pools. When the tide goes out, pools form in the uneven surfaces, creating a home for mussels and barnacles that cling to the rocks. Keep an eye out also for colorful sea anemones, named for a flowering plant, snails, and hermit crabs. A good spot to explore this natural habitat is the beach near San Geronimo Creek. The best time to go is low tide when the receding waters expose the rocky shore.

Marine Mammals

The trail along the Estero Bluffs is a great vantage point for spotting marine mammals. From December through March you may see **gray whales** migrating south. **Otters** can be spotted year-round, but winter and spring are the best seasons. Look for them toward shore, near coves and kelp forests where they nest and hunt.

From the Cayucos Pier you're positioned well for ocean views that may include otters, seals, dolphins, or whales during migration season.

SURFING AND SWIMMING

The surf scene in Cayucos is laid-back, anchored by the Cayucos Pier with soft rolling waves and a beach break ideal for longboarding. Winter and spring have the wildest waves. Spring is more mellow and suitable for beginners, but keep in mind that you may have an audience watching from the pier. Water temperatures are chilly year-round, so pack your wetsuit.

Cayucos State Beach has a wide stretch of sand, easily accessed from street level, making it the best spot along this section of coast for swimming. The chilly year-round water temperatures mean you may want to consider a wetsuit for getting in the water even if you're not surfing.

FISHING

The **Cayucos Pier** is a favorite fishing spot. Anglers don't need a

tide pools at Estero Bluffs (left); view from Cayucos Beach (right)

fishing license to cast here, but all other regulations apply. Surfperch is a common catch. Other species drawn to the kelp around the pilings include cabezon, lingcod, striped bass, and halibut. Another option is to cast out among the rocks around Estero Bluffs, best fished at low tide.

Unless you're fishing strictly from the pier, make sure you pick up a fishing license. The closest spot to the park is in Morro Bay at Virg's Landing (1169 Market Ave., Morro Bay; 805/772-1222; www.virgslanding.com).

FOOD AND LODGING

Cayucos is a small beach town with hotels, restaurants, gas stations, and basic groceries as well as a walkable downtown with antiques shops and boutiques. The charming town of **Morro Bay,** 6 mi (10 km) south, has waterfront restaurants as well as a downtown with shops and art galleries. It is slightly bigger than Cayucos with grocery stores, gas, and supplies as well as more hotel and restaurant options.

There are **no campgrounds** in Cayucos State Beach or Estero Bluffs State Park. The closest campgrounds for both tent and RV camping are in the nearby state parks.

BEST PICNIC SPOT

Cayucos State Beach

Cayucos State Beach has picnic tables near the Cayucos Pier, where you will also find a small playground for kids, restrooms, and outdoor showers for rinsing off the sand.

GETTING THERE

CAR

The town of Cayucos and adjacent Cayucos State Beach are located along the Pacific Coast Highway/CA-1 north, 6 mi (10 km) north of Morro Bay and 14 mi (23 km) south of Cambria. From either direction, take exit 285 for Cayucos Drive. Follow Cayucos Drive for 0.4 mi (0.6 km) to Ocean Front Avenue, which borders the beach. Estero Bluffs State Park is located 0.8 mi (1.3 km) north of the Cayucos Pier off of North Ocean Avenue.

MORRO BAY STATE PARK

Iconic Morro Rock, an ancient volcanic peak, towers over Morro Bay, sacred to Indigenous Chumash and Salinan tribes, a maritime navigation landmark, and a reserve for the endangered peregrine falcon. Morro Rock is the last in a chain of nine volcanic peaks stretching from San Luis Obispo. While Morro Rock may be the focal point, the land around it draws people for the scenic bay, wetlands, and dunes.

ADDRESS: Morro Bay State Park Rd., Morro Bay

PHONE: 805/772-7434

WEBSITE: www.morrobay.org

DAY USE HOURS: 6am-10pm

AREA: 2,783 acres (1,126 ha)

This is the ancient territory of the Chumash, who had villages based on fishing and gathering. On the south end of the bay, there are middens, huge refuse heaps packed with shells, left by the Chumash people.

Morro Bay is both picturesque and moody as fog weaves among stands of Monterey pine and eucalyptus or rolls over the estuary. In addition to history and scenery, Morro Bay State Park has miles of trails winding through coastal sage scrub and native grasslands, a golf course with views of the Pacific Ocean, a quaint marina, a waterfront café, and a campground a stone's throw from the water.

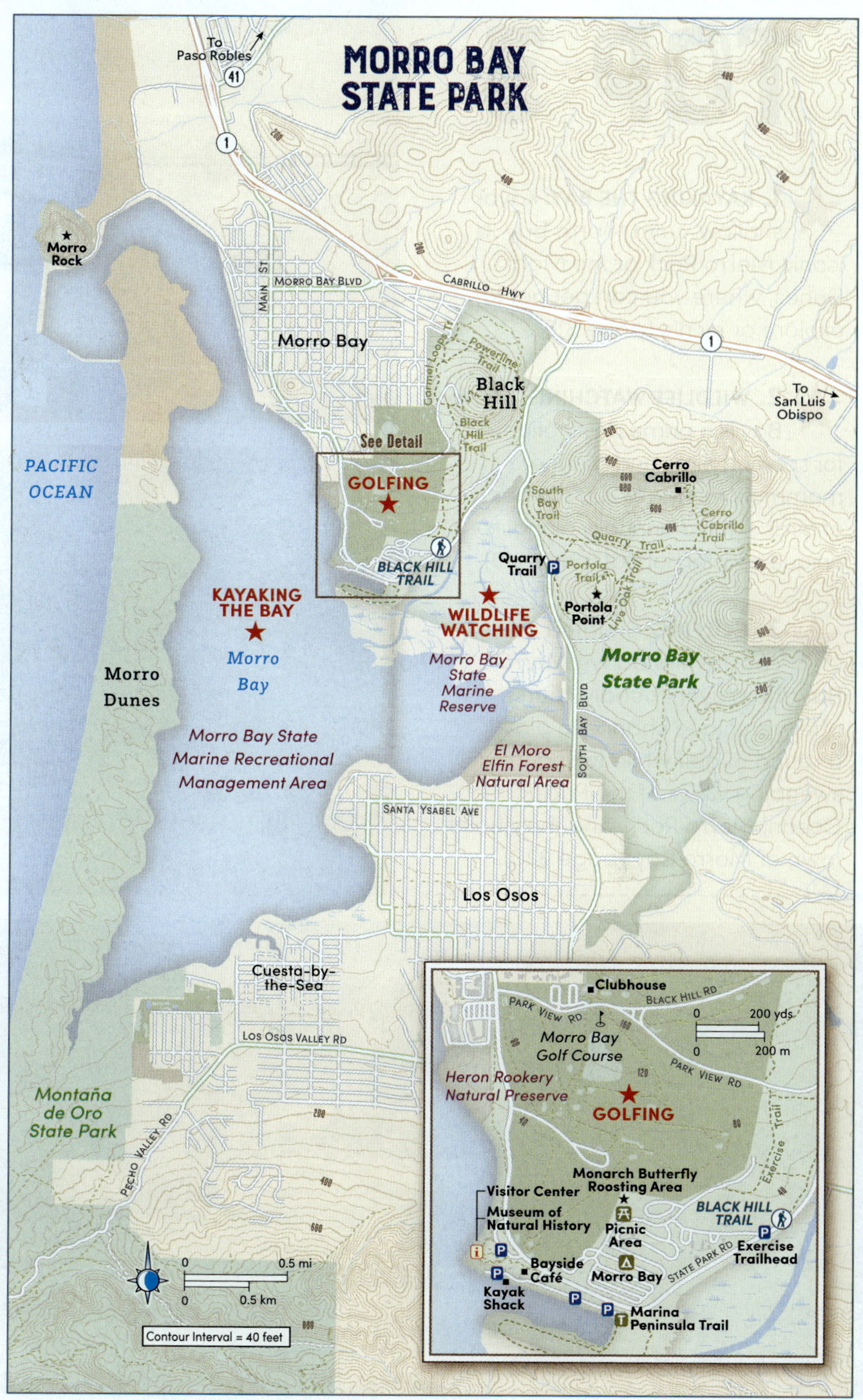
MORRO BAY STATE PARK
To Paso Robles
41
1
Morro Rock
Morro Bay Blvd
Main St
Cabrillo Hwy
Morro Bay
Powerline Trail
Cormel Loops Trail
Black Hill
Black Hill Trail
To San Luis Obispo
See Detail
PACIFIC OCEAN
GOLFING
Cerro Cabrillo
South Bay Trail
Cerro Cabrillo Trail
Quarry Trail
Portola Trail
BLACK HILL TRAIL
Portola Point
Live Oak Trail
KAYAKING THE BAY
WILDLIFE WATCHING
Morro Bay
Morro Bay State Park
Morro Dunes
Morro Bay State Marine Reserve
South Bay Blvd
Morro Bay State Marine Recreational Management Area
El Moro Elfin Forest Natural Area
Santa Ysabel Ave
Los Osos
Cuesta-by-the-Sea
Los Osos Valley Rd
Montaña de Oro State Park
Pecho Valley Rd
0 0.5 mi
0 0.5 km
Contour Interval = 40 feet
Clubhouse
Black Hill Rd
Park View Rd
0 200 yds
0 200 m
Morro Bay Golf Course
Heron Rookery Natural Preserve
GOLFING
Monarch Butterfly Roosting Area
Exercise Trail
Visitor Center
Museum of Natural History
Picnic Area
BLACK HILL TRAIL
Exercise Trailhead
Bayside Café
Morro Bay
State Park Rd
Kayak Shack
Marina Peninsula Trail

TOP 3

★ **1. KAYAKING THE BAY:** Kayak shallow, calm Morro Bay to iconic Morro Rock or the Morro Dunes, where you can get out to explore or picnic (page 318).

★ **2. WILDLIFE WATCHING:** Morro Bay is a prime destination for spotting birds and marine mammals, with over 200 species of birds sighted annually along its unique coastal habitat (page 319).

★ **3. GOLFING:** Situated in the coastal hills above Morro Bay, the player-friendly course offers a unique chance to play a round of golf while taking in sweeping views of the Pacific Ocean, Morro Rock, and the quaint town of Morro Bay (page 320).

1

2

3

PLANNING YOUR TIME

One day is enough time to kayak the bay, do a hike or play a round of golf, and have lunch or dinner at the café. Morro Bay also makes a good base camp for a long weekend exploring the area.

Nearby state parks include Montaña de Oro State Park (9 mi/14 km), Cayucos State Beach/Estero Bluffs State Park (10 mi/16 km), and Hearst San Simeon State Historical Monument/State Park (32 mi/51 km).

ENTRANCE AND FEES

The **main park entrance** is near the marina and campground, but there is no official entrance station and no entrance fees. Day-use visitors can park for free at a parking area next to the marina and campground, which gives easy access to the Kayak Shack kayak rentals, Bayside Café, Museum of Natural History, and Marina Peninsula Trail. There is separate trail parking for Black Hill if you choose to do the shortest version, and for the park's backcountry trails south of South Bay Boulevard in the Cerro Cabrillo area.

There is a separate fee for the natural history museum.

VISITOR CENTER

Morro Bay Museum of Natural History

10am-5pm daily; $3

The Morro Bay Museum of Natural History doubles as a visitor center. A small gift shop is run by knowledgeable staff who can distribute state park maps and brochures and answer questions. Entrance to the natural history museum exhibits requires a fee.

WEATHER

There are microclimates up and down the beaches and towns of the Central Coast. Morro Bay is often blanketed in a marine layer and has moderate-cool temperatures year-round, with daytime highs around 65°F (18°C). In summer, temperatures can be 30 degrees cooler than inland areas. Dress in layers. The ocean water is also cooler than in Southern California, and surfers typically wear wetsuits. Pay attention to weather advisories when swimming, surfing, or boating. Large waves and rip currents can make conditions unsafe.

SIGHTS

MORRO ROCK

You don't have to go out of your way to see Morro Rock. From nearly every angle and elevation along the Morro Bay coast and water, there it is, a 576-ft-tall (176-m-tall) volcanic peak. It is the last in a chain of volcanic peaks referred to as the "nine sisters" that stretch from San Luis Obispo to Morro Bay and range in height from 576 ft (176 m) to 1,559 ft (475 m). Although Morro Rock has the lowest height of the peaks, it is the most dramatic and also most visible, surrounded spectacularly by the waters of Morro Bay. It was used by mariners as a navigational aid for over 300 years. Almost unthinkable

ONE DAY IN MORRO BAY STATE PARK

MORNING

Start at the Museum of Natural History to learn about the estuary and its unique ecosystem. Then hike to the top of Black Hill to get the lay of the land. Have lunch with views of the marina at the Bayside Café.

AFTERNOON

Kayak across the bay to the Morro Dunes if the tide cooperates. If not, paddle the deeper channels and take in views of the open water and coastline. Look for birds and otters.

EVENING

Set up camp and enjoy the cool, coastal weather.

today, the rock was quarried, its sides blasted, and chunks hauled away for other uses including material for Morro Bay's breakwater. The rock became a state landmark in 1968 and later a designated bird sanctuary. The rock's protections mean that no one can climb it (or mine it), but you can get pretty close from two points. The 10-mi (16-km) out-and-back Sand Spit Trail begins in Montaña de Oro State Park to the south and follows the dunes and spit of sand dividing Morro Bay from the Pacific Ocean. It ends at the edge of the sand face-to-face with the monolith. The second option is visiting Morro Rock Beach, a rocky sand beach managed by the city of Morro Bay, 3 mi (5 km) north of Morro Bay State Park. Going out on its shores gets you front row seats to Morro Rock.

MORRO BAY MUSEUM OF NATURAL HISTORY

10am-5pm daily; $3

The Morro Bay Museum of Natural History is situated on a hill overlooking Morro Bay with views of the estuary and Morro Rock. Interpretive exhibits are geared toward all ages, but are great for kids, focusing on the area's unique weather, natural habitat, and cultural history. The museum also offers a small gift shop.

MONARCH BUTTERFLY ROOSTING AREA

Morro Bay's eucalyptus groves provide a haven for overwintering monarch butterflies, and the state park has actively worked to conserve this monarch butterfly habitat, planting trees and nectar plants. Look for the delicate creatures from late October through March as they cluster in branches to roost and rest. They are drawn to the groves in the northern end of the campground and southern end of the golf course, where butterflies drink dew from the turf.

TOP HIKE

BLACK HILL TRAIL

DISTANCE: 2.5 mi (4 km) round-trip
DURATION: 1.5 hours
EFFORT: Moderate
TRAILHEAD: Exercise Trail trailhead intersection with campground boundary road, northeast end of campground

From the top of the 665-ft (203-m) volcanic peak, you will have great views of the estuary, Morro Bay, Morro Rock, and the surrounding volcanic hills. From the campground, take the Exercise Trail. It turns into Black Hill Trail as it crosses Lower State Park Road. The trail winds through dense stands of Monterey pine before beginning final switchbacks through a sage-covered slope with open views to the top.

You can also do this as a short 1-mi (1.6-km) out-and-back hike by starting at the Black Hill Trail parking area at the end of Upper State Park Road. The paved road intersects the Black Hill Trail about halfway up the hillside. For a longer outing, turn the hike into a 4-mi (6-km) loop by adding the Carmel Loops Trail, Powerline Trail, and South Bay Trail.

HIKING

The trail network in Morro Bay State Park is divided into two regions bisected by South Bay Boulevard. The Black Hill area west of the boulevard has a network of trails, including a popular hiking trail to the volcanic peak of Black Hill. This is also where the campground, marina, and golf course are located. The Cerro Cabrillo area east of the boulevard has a network of trails along the base of Cerro Cabrillo, another volcanic peak. Many of the trails are mixed-use hiking and biking trails, except the Marina Peninsula Trail, the Cerro Cabrillo Trail, and an exercise trail that surrounds the campground, which are hiking-only.

MARINA PENINSULA TRAIL

DISTANCE: 0.7 mi (1.1 km) round-trip
DURATION: 20 minutes
EFFORT: Easy
TRAILHEAD: Parking area on east end of marina

This charming walk in the park begins on the east end of the marina and follows a loop around the edge of a small peninsula. The trail winds through coastal scrub with nice views of Morro Rock, the bay, and the marina. Part of the trail follows a boardwalk, and the rest is wide and compacted, but it can get muddy.

CERRO CABRILLO

DISTANCE: 2.5 mi (4 km) round-trip
DURATION: 1.5 hours

EFFORT: Moderate
TRAILHEAD: Quarry Trail parking area on east side of South Bay Blvd.

At 911 ft (278 m), Cerro Cabrillo is the highest point in Morro Bay State Park. It is one of the "nine sisters" chain of volcanic peaks stretching from San Luis Obispo to Morro Bay. An out-and-back trail pays off with a coast and mountain panorama, including Morro Rock to the north and Morro Bay and the mountains of Montaña de Oro State Park to the south.

From the trailhead, take Quarry Trail northeast toward the visible dome of Cerro Cabrillo, an easy walk through coastal sage scrub. At the next intersection past Live Oak Trail, turn left to begin the climb to the peak. The unmaintained trail has washouts and becomes steeper the closer it gets to the peak, and a boulder scramble is required to reach the top.

PORTOLA POINT

DISTANCE: 2 mi (3.2 km) round-trip
DURATION: 1 hour
EFFORT: Moderate
TRAILHEAD: Quarry Trail parking area on east side of South Bay Blvd.

The dome-shaped volcanic rise offers 360-degree views from the top, allowing you to take in the Morro Bay estuary, sandspit, and distant Morro Rock. Hike the trail clockwise, taking a right turn at each junction. Along the way, look out for native coastal plants including hummingbird sage, California buckwheat, and Indian paintbrush. Also, notice the volcanic dome of Cerro Cabrillo to the north, the highest volcanic dome in the park.

Starting from the northeast corner of the parking lot, hike 0.2 mi (0.3 km) to a junction with **Chorro Trail** and angle right to stay on **Quarry Trail.** After 0.5 mi (0.8 km) from the start, turn right at the signed junction onto **Live Oak Trail,** which crosses a grassy meadow. When the trail splits again, turn right to head to the top of Portola Hill and a small loop. After taking in the views and heading back down, turn right onto Live Oak Trail to complete the loop.

RECREATION

 KAYAKING

Kayak the shallow, open waters of Morro Bay to admire Morro Dunes and Morro Rock. The shallow and calm water and short distances make this a fun activity for any age, including kids.

The destination for most people is **Morro Dunes,** a long strip of sand dunes that divide the bay from the Pacific Ocean. Cross the bay, then pull your kayak up and picnic on the sand. From the marina, the most direct route to the dunes is 0.75 mi (1.2 km) and takes about 1 hour round-trip. The other destination is Morro Rock. A wide channel hugs the coastline to the end of the sandspit and Morro Rock. There is no climbing on the rock, but you can get close. From the marina, the outing is 2.5 mi (4 km) and takes approximately 2.5 hours round-trip.

Much of the bay can become mud flats during low tide, so be aware of the tides before heading out (there is a tide schedule on the Kayak Shack website). However, a series of channels crisscross the bay so it can still be navigated, even at low tide.

As you paddle back you will have views of the picturesque town of Morro Bay as well as the marina and volcanic hills beyond.

Kayak Shack

10 State Park Rd.; 805/772-8796; www.morrobaykayakrental.com; 9am-6pm Thurs.-Sun.; $18-34 first hour

Kayak Shack rents kayaks, canoes, and paddleboards from a dock in the state park's marina.

★ WILDLIFE WATCHING

Marine Mammals

Sea otters, sea lions, harbor seals, and **whales** are the mammals to look for in the bay and Pacific Ocean. Keep your eyes trained on the bay near the **marina** for a sight of the adorable sea otters, who like the bay's kelp forest. The **Morro Bay North T-Pier,** a public fishing pier near Morro Rock, is also a dedicated viewing area. Sea lions are the largest and fastest year-round marine mammals in the bay. Look for them basking on harbor docks; there is also a dock to the right of Morro Rock that was specifically built for sea lions. To see harbor seals, look for them on sandy shores where they sometimes relax, or floating in the Pacific Ocean. If you're kayaking the bay, you may catch a glimpse of their big brown eyes popping up out of the water before disappearing again. Year round, there is a chance to see different species of migrating whales.

Birds

The unique landscape of the bay and estuary makes it a hot spot for

Morro Rock (top); the Kayak Shack (middle); sea otter (bottom)

bird-watching. The Audubon Society lists no less than 32 optimal birding spots along the Morro Coast, including prime locations within the park: **Black Hill,** the **Marina Peninsula Trail,** and the **campground.** Trails to Black Hill lead through coastal sage and pine habitat, great for woodpeckers and warblers, while the Marina Peninsula Trail draws grebes, loons, ducks, and black-crowned night-herons. For a high concentration of nesting and roosting herons, egrets, and turkey vultures, visit the **Heron Rookery Natural Preserve** next to the golf course. Nearby, Morro Rock attracts cormorants and pairs of peregrine falcons, among other species. Also nearby, the Elfin Forest attracts too many species to count, except that every year local birders do just that, counting as many species as possible from one spot in a 24-hour period. They once hit the world record with 122 species, and are consistently in the top 10.

For your birding and wildlife journey, start at the **Museum of Natural History.** In addition to information, they have a large glass viewing window where you can scope the estuary and look for birds and water-dwellers. If you are serious about your bird-watching, they have "The Birds of San Luis Obispo" checklist in the museum's bookstore.

★ GOLF

Morro Bay Golf Course

201 State Park Rd.; 805/772-1923; https://golfmorrobay.com; weekdays $30-60, weekends $30-75

Morro Bay State Park offers the unusual option of an 18-hole golf course as one of the things to do in the park. The scenic, player-friendly course is located just north of the campground in the low coastal hills just above the bay, crowned by Black Hill. Originally built in 1923 as part of the Cabrillo Country Club, the golf course was purchased by California State Parks in 1934. Aside from the novelty of a golf course in a state park, the most striking thing about it are its gorgeous views overlooking the Pacific Ocean and picturesque beach town of Morro Bay. To book a tee time at the Morro Bay Golf Course, go online or call.

CAMPING

Morro Bay State Park has **one campground** with 140 sites for tent, RV, and group camping within striking distance of the bay and marina. There are flush toilets, token-operated showers, and water spigots throughout the campground.

Reservations are required through Reserve California (800/444-7275; www.reservecalifornia.com; $35/night), and the campground books fully and well in advance during the summer.

BEST CAMPGROUND

Morro Bay Campground

The campsites at Morro Bay Campground are spread across grassy, coastal landscape dotted with eucalyptus and mixed forest offering some privacy. All sites have a fire ring and picnic table. For RVs, some sites have electrical hookups, and there is also a sanitation station and water-fill station.

Note that this is bay, not beach, camping. Campsites are located near shallow Morro Bay, which is good for kayaking but does not have a beach for relaxing, swimming, or bodysurfing.

FOOD AND LODGING

The charming town of **Morro Bay** is located 1.5 mi (2.5 km) north of the campground and has a handful of inns as well as a waterfront downtown with restaurants, shops, groceries, gas, and supplies.

Less a town and more a village, **Los Osos,** 5 mi (8 km) south of Morro Bay, has an idyllic setting on Morro Bay's quiet southern end, the "back bay" nestled in pine, cypress, and eucalyptus trees. For visitors, there are three inns, a handful of casual restaurants featuring local craft beer and Central Coast wines, and a weekly waterfront farmer's market.

BAYSIDE CAFÉ

805/772-1465; http://baysidecafe.com; 11am-3pm Mon.-Wed., 11am-8pm Thurs.-Sun.; $12-33

As its name suggests, the Bayside Café sits next to the water with bay views. The café is centrally located in the state park between the marina and campground. The food is solid, and the views are delightful from the glassed-in dining room or heated patio. The wide-ranging menu has classic American café fare, seafood, and Mexican specialties. Try the California chowder, a mix of clam chowder and spicy green chile soup. The best news is that you can skip the cooking and stroll over from your campsite.

BEST PICNIC SPOT

Morro Bay Campground

Inland from the marina and parking area, the park offers a picnic area in the campground, scenically pitched in eucalyptus and pine forest.

GETTING THERE

CAR

Morro Bay State Park is located along the Pacific Coast Highway/CA-1, 13 mi (21 km) west of San Luis Obispo. To get to Morro Bay from the south, take US-101 north to exit 203B in San Luis Obispo to merge onto CA-1 north toward Morro Bay/Hearst Castle. Drive CA-1 north for 13 mi (21 km), taking exit 277 toward Los Osos/Baywood Park and following signs for Morro Bay State Park. From the north, take US-101 south to exit 219 in Atascadero for Morro Road/CA-41. Take Morro Road/CA-41 for 18 mi (29 km) to the state park.

MONTAÑA DE ORO STATE PARK

> **ADDRESS:** 3550 Pecho Valley Rd., Los Osos
>
> **PHONE:** 805/772-6101
>
> **DAY USE HOURS:** 6am-10pm
>
> **AREA:** 8,000 acres (3,237 ha)

Take in the smell of coastal sage as you gaze at the Pacific Ocean from one of Montaña de Oro's dramatic promontories. Behind you, wind-sculpted pines dot rocky peaks. Situated along California's Central Coast, the park is characterized by rugged coastline and golden bluffs that crash up against coastal hills.

The Native American history here is tied to the Chumash and Salinan peoples, who inhabited the area for thousands of years before European contact, living in small villages and relying on the ocean for sustenance. In recent history, the land was used for ranching by the Spooner family, who had generations of homesteading in the region of Spooner's Cove. Their home is now a museum and visitor center.

The 7 mi (11 km) of shoreline is perfect for tide-pooling and picnicking, while inland, miles of hiking, biking, and equestrian trails provide coastal perspective and dramatic summits. Sure, you can have a beach day here, but that day will likely be more about exploring the wild scenery and less about staying put on the sand.

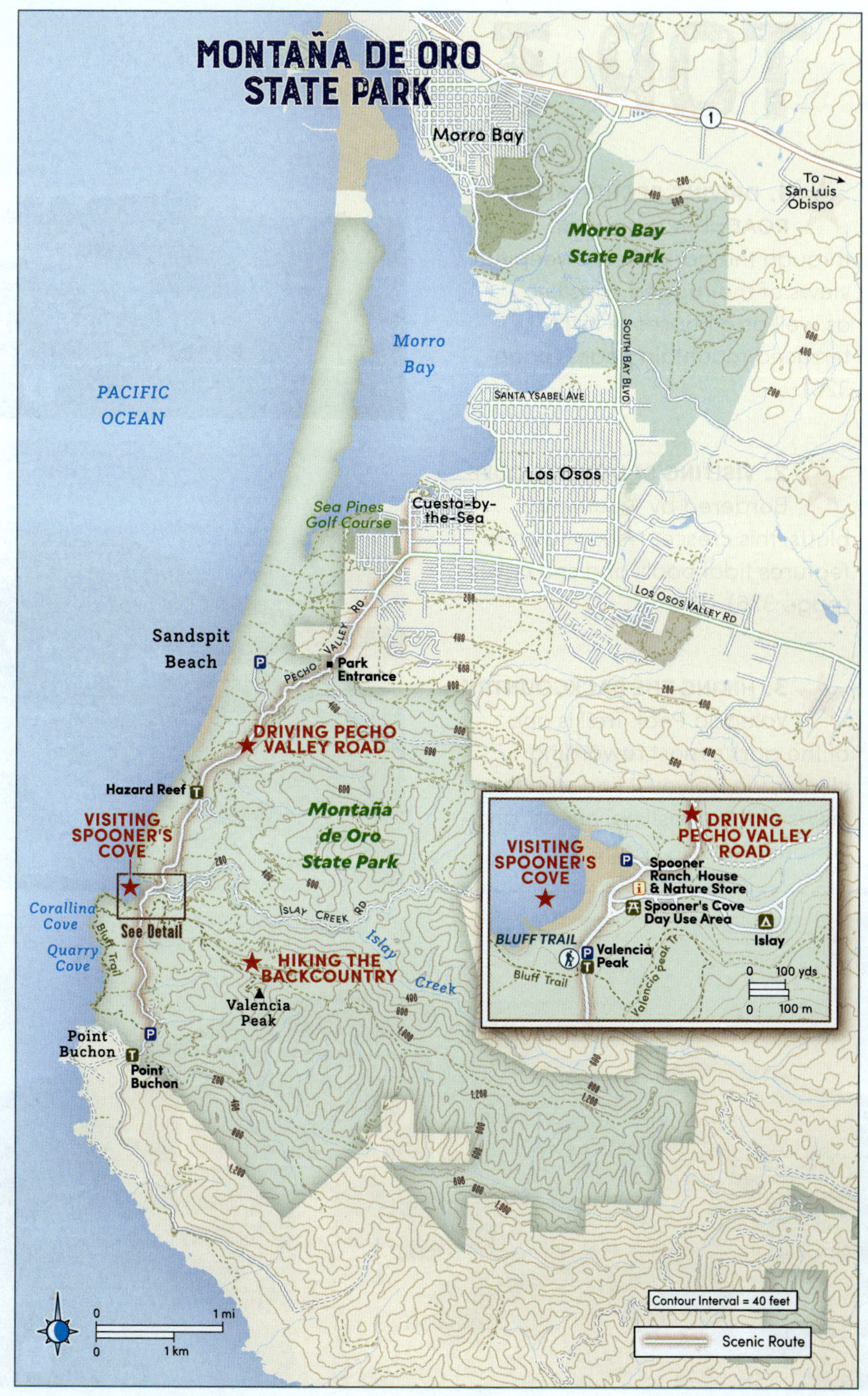
MONTAÑA DE ORO STATE PARK
Morro Bay
1
To San Luis Obispo
Morro Bay State Park
SOUTH BAY BLVD
Morro Bay
PACIFIC OCEAN
SANTA YSABEL AVE
Los Osos
Sea Pines Golf Course
Cuesta-by-the-Sea
LOS OSOS VALLEY RD
PECHO VALLEY RD
Sandspit Beach
Park Entrance
DRIVING PECHO VALLEY ROAD
Hazard Reef
VISITING SPOONER'S COVE
Montaña de Oro State Park
Corallina Cove
See Detail
ISLAY CREEK RD
Quarry Cove
Bluff Trail
Islay Creek
HIKING THE BACKCOUNTRY
Valencia Peak
Point Buchon
Point Buchon
VISITING SPOONER'S COVE
DRIVING PECHO VALLEY ROAD
Spooner Ranch House & Nature Store
Spooner's Cove Day Use Area
Islay
BLUFF TRAIL
Valencia Peak
Bluff Trail
Valencia Peak Tr.
0 100 yds
0 100 m
Contour Interval = 40 feet
Scenic Route
0 1 mi
0 1 km

TOP 3

★ **1. DRIVING PECHO VALLEY ROAD:** The main road through the park offers sweeping views of the rugged coastline as well as glimpses of its rocky, terraced mountain peaks (page 326).

★ **2. VISITING SPOONER'S COVE:** Bordered by weathered bluffs, this crescent-shaped cove features tidal pools and sea caves (page 326).

★ **3. HIKING THE BACKCOUNTRY:** Valencia Peak Trail is one of the park's most rewarding climbs, where you'll find stunning views of the coastline, ocean, and surrounding hills (page 329).

1

2

3

ONE DAY IN MONTAÑA DE ORO STATE PARK

MORNING

Drive the length of the park via Peco Valley Road, taking in the coastal views. Then hike the Bluff Trail.

AFTERNOON

Picnic at Spooner's Cove, then spend the afternoon on the beach, exploring the creek and tide pools.

PLANNING YOUR TIME

A half day is enough time to do a short hike and visit popular Spooner's Cove. A full day allows for a longer hike and more time exploring the park's beaches. If you're planning to camp, note that there are no showers or RV hookups and vault toilets only. You won't run out of things to do if you stay for a weekend, which allows you to explore several of the park's trails and coves.

Nearby state parks include Morro Bay State Park (9 mi/14 km), Cayucos State Beach and Estero Bluffs State Park (17 mi/27 km), and Pismo State Beach (28 mi/45 km).

ENTRANCE AND FEES

The only way to enter the park is via Pecho Valley Road. There is **no entrance station,** and there are no day use or parking fees.

VISITOR CENTER

Spooner Ranch House and Nature Store

Across from Spooner's Cove; 805/539-6857; hours vary by season

You can find trail maps, other information, and a souvenir shop at the visitor center inside Spooner Ranch House, where there are also historical displays about the Spooner family and local history with furnishings from the early 1900s.

WEATHER

The area is characterized by moderate-cool temperatures year-round, with daytime highs around 65°F (18°C). In summer, temperatures can be 30 degrees cooler than inland areas. Dress in layers. Montana de Oro makes a good year-round destination, but summer is recommended for warmer beach temperatures.

SIGHTS

WILDFLOWERS

Translating to "Mountain of Gold," Montaña de Oro earns its name from the vibrant wildflowers that blanket its hills in spring. Flowers include poppies, lupines, wild mustard, and more. The best time to visit to see the golden flowers is **April** and **May.** Hike **Valencia Peak** to walk through these colorful hills.

SCENIC DRIVES

★ PECHO VALLEY ROAD

DISTANCE: 5.5 mi (8.9 km)
DURATION: 15 minutes
START: Sea Pines Golf Resort, Los Osos
END: Point Bouchon trail parking, south end of park

The bluff-top Pecho Valley Road is the main road through the park. Although you have to take it to access any of the park's beaches, hikes, or camps, it is worth noting on its own. Starting in the town of Los Osos, just north of Montaña de Oro, Pecho Valley Road gives access to popular sites like Spooner's Cove, all trailheads including Bluff Trail and Valencia Peak, Islay Campground, and all environmental campsites. It also offers sweeping views of the rugged coastline with its secluded coves, sea stacks, and wave-battered caves as well as glimpses of its rocky, terraced mountain peaks. The drive itself only takes about 15 minutes end-to-end, but in reality, it will take closer to an hour as you stop along the way to explore the mesmerizing sights.

BEACHES

Montaña de Oro is known for dramatic rocky coastline that contributes to powerful waves, rip currents, and undertow. Wading is fine here, but swimming is not recommended. Experienced surfers can contend with some bucket-list surf spots but will want wetsuits, booties, and hoods to combat the chilly water temperatures. There are no lifeguards at Montaña de Oro.

★ SPOONER'S COVE

Nestled along the stunning coastline of Montaña de Oro, Spooner's Cove is a crescent-shaped cove bordered by weathered bluffs. Islay Creek snakes through Montaña de Oro's hills to spill out on the pebbly sand of Spooner's Cove. The beach features a mix of soft sand and smooth pebbles, with tidal pools and sea caves waiting to be explored during low tide. Spooner's Cove is a popular spot for picnics, beachcombing, and simply soaking in the serenity of the Pacific Ocean. It is also a favorite destination for wildlife watchers, offering glimpses of shorebirds, seals, and occasional whales during their migration. Binoculars are helpful for spotting whales.

It is the most easily accessible of the park's rocky coves, requiring only a short walk onto the sand. Ease of access and gorgeous scenery make this the park's most popular spot and a good introduction to the park's raw beauty. Facilities at Spooner's Cove include a convenient parking lot, restrooms, and picnic tables. Spooner's Cove is 2.3 mi (3.7 km) south of the park entrance.

Spooner's Cove

SANDSPIT BEACH

Sandspit Beach is located just inside the northern end of the park. From Pecho Valley Road, turn right onto Sandspit Road toward the Sandspit day use area. There are restrooms and picnic tables in the parking lot. A short, wide trail leads through low dunes to a sandy beach worthy of a beach day. Aside from the gorgeous coast, the real magic here is Sandspit Beach's location on the southern end of the Morro Bay sandspit, the long sand barrier that divides Morro Bay from the Pacific Ocean. It is possible to hike from Sandspit Beach along the length of the sandspit to the northern end of the bay near Morro Rock in 5 mi (8 km). This is less a hike and more a long, Zen walk on the beach with dunes on one side and the lapping waves of the Pacific on the other.

HIKING

The nature of this region, coast colliding with Montaña de Ora's "mountains of gold," means that it has more than its fair share of backcountry hikes. They delve into the park's canyons, peaks, bluffs, and coast. And with over 8,000 acres (3,237 ha) of coastal bluffs, sandy beaches, rolling hills, and rugged peaks, there's a trail for every type of hiker.

HAZARD REEF

DISTANCE: 0.8 mi (1.3 km) round-trip
DURATION: 20 minutes
EFFORT: Easy
TRAILHEAD: Hazard Canyon parking lot, Dune trailhead, Pecho Valley Rd., 1 mi (1.6 km) north of Spooner Ranch House Visitor Center

A narrow trail cuts through coastal-grass-lined hills to an isolated reef area known as Hazard Reef. The trail was named for a prior landowner, not the danger level of the terrain. The submerged rock outcropping here is known for tide pools and is surrounded by a crescent cove and bluffs. A small boardwalk and steps cut down into a short canyon before the sandy trail winds down to the cove. The trail can be muddy and

TOP HIKE

BLUFF TRAIL

DISTANCE: 3 mi (4.8 km) round-trip
DURATION: 1.5 hours
EFFORT: Moderate
TRAILHEAD: North end of Bluff Trail, parking area just south of Spooner's Cove and Spooner Ranch House along Pecho Valley Rd.

The Bluff Trail hugs the coastline, giving spectacular views of the park's sandy coves, natural bridges, and rock islands. From the north end of the trail at Islay Point, the first overlook looks over Spooner's Cove, carved into bluffs where Islay Creek meets the ocean. Continuing south, Corallina Cove is next. A spur trail heads down to the small beach studded with tide pools.

Half a mile (0.8 km) past Corallina Cove, the rocky Quarry Cove has more tide pools. Next, the trail covers more dramatic coastline to Grotto Rock, a tall stone island hollowed with dark caves along its base by the crashing sea around it. The trail continues for 0.25 mi (0.4 km) past Grotto Rock to a final promontory and viewpoint overlooking Coon Creek Beach, and a sinkhole that has created a natural bridge. The trail does continue for another 0.5 mi (0.8 km), making the complete trail a 4-mi (6-km) out-and-back, but it heads inland to intersect with Pecho Valley Road. If you're a Type A hiker, by all means, complete the trail. If the highlights are enough, this is a good spot to turn around. Bluff Trail is hard-packed dirt and gravel, accessible for most wheelchairs and strollers.

wet; wear the shoes for it. The trail is also technically a loop, but the south section can be overgrown, making an out-and-back on the upper trail the most reliable route.

★ VALENCIA PEAK

DISTANCE: 4.4 mi (7 km) round-trip
DURATION: 2.5-3 hours
EFFORT: Moderate
TRAILHEAD: Bluff Trail parking just south of Spooner's Cove and Spooner Ranch House along Pecho Valley Rd.; trail begins from the south parking area on the east side

The climb to Valencia Peak, with 1,150 ft (350 m) of elevation gain, pays off with views up and down the coast. The 1,347-ft (411-m) mountain is the second-highest point in Montaña de Oro, but arguably the most attainable summit with moderate distance and steady grade, making it an option for hikers of all skill levels. A much steeper trail used to go straight up to the summit (you can see this route 0.1 mi/0.2 km in at the Rattlesnake Trail junction), but work on the trail system resulted in a more doable route. The trail cuts inland through wild sage and a series of switchbacks to a junction with Beebe and Badger Trails. Continue on the Valencia Trail for another six switchbacks to a ridgeline of sedimentary rock before climbing the pyramid-shaped summit. The summit is often shrouded in marine layer, limiting views, but if you wait it out, this can change. To the north are Morro Rock, Morro Bay, and the peak of Cerro Cabrillo. To the south, Point Buchon. And of course, the Pacific Ocean to the west. However, the most impressive view may be looking down the spine of the mountain to the ridgeline you just hiked.

POINT BUCHON

DISTANCE: 6.8 mi (10.9 km) round-trip
DURATION: 3 hours
EFFORT: Moderate
TRAILHEAD: Coon Creek trailhead parking

The mostly flat Point Buchon Trail travels grassy bluffs along the rugged shoreline at the south end of Montaña de Oro to take in coastal views and cliff formations. As you walk the wide trail edging the coast, look for headlands jutting out into the sea and vertical sea stacks of wave-eroded rocks. The spectacular point that inspired the trail was named after a Chumash chief. Highlights include Coon Creek Beach, where the creek spills out onto a small cove with sea caves and a sinkhole, a collapsed sea cave where ocean water rushes in via a short tunnel. The trail takes in Point Buchon before connecting with a junction (left) that goes back to the trailhead.

The trail begins in Montaña de Oro and follows the coast south onto land owned and managed by Pacific Gas & Electric (PG&E). Visitors are required to check in at an entrance station (8am-5pm Thurs.-Mon. Apr.-Oct., 8am-4pm Thurs.-Mon. Nov.-Mar.) at the trailhead a few hundred yards west of the parking area.

RECREATION

BIKING

Montaña de Oro is a mountain biking destination with a trail network for a range of skill levels. The terrain offers a scenic backdrop with views of the Pacific, canyons, and eucalyptus groves. Some of the park's trails are mixed-use for hiking and mountain biking or hiking, mountain biking, and equestrian, while others are hiking only. The 12-mi (19-km) intermediate-difficult **Hazard Peak Trail** is a good place to start. There are bike rentals available in Morro Bay.

WILDLIFE WATCHING

The park's unique ecosystem supports shore and migratory birds, marine mammals, and rich tidepool systems. As you walk the trails, look for otters in the ocean, kestrels hovering over the bluff-top grasses, and red-billed oystercatchers on the coast.

Marine Mammals

Wildlife abounds at Montaña de Oro with sightings of **dolphins, sea otters,** and **whales** along its shoreline. **Gray whales** can be seen during their annual migration (Dec.-Apr.), while **humpback whales** can potentially be seen year-round. Try your luck along the Bluff Trail, at the southern end of the park.

Tide Pools

The tide pools along Corallina Cove are home to sea anemones, hermit crabs, and starfish. Just past Corallina Cove, **Quarry Cove** has even more tide pools. Check the tide table before going to make sure you hit low tide.

CAMPING

The park offers **one main primitive campground** and four hike-in campsites. Reservations are required through Reserve California (800/444-7275; www.reservecalifornia.com; $25/night).

The four hike-in environmental camps are primitive and require a hike of approximately 100 yards to half a mile (0.1-0.8 km). They have pit toilets but no potable water. Campfires are not allowed at these sites.

BEST CAMPGROUND

Islay Campground

Islay Campground offers 47 sites tucked in the low hills behind the Spooner Ranch House. The campground is a 5-10-minute walk to popular Spooner's Cove, a sandy beach at the mouth of Islay Creek, and also offers easy access to the Bluff Trail and Valencia Peak Trail. Campsites have fire rings and picnic tables with vault toilets and water spigots available throughout the campground. The campsites are designed for tents and RVs under 27 ft (8 m). There are no showers, RV hookups, or water-fill stations. There is firewood for sale from the camp host with the proceeds benefiting the Central Coast State Parks Association.

view of Spooner's Cove from the Islay Campground

FOOD AND LODGING

The charming town of **Los Osos,** approximately 4 mi (6 km) north via Pecho Valley Road, borders Montaña de Oro State Park. Set on what the locals call the "back bay," the quiet southernmost part of Morro Bay, the town has a handful of family-friendly eateries and breweries and a weekly farmer's market as well as a few small hotels. You can also find the basics including groceries and gas. Approximately 10 mi (16 km) north via Pecho Valley Road and South Bay Boulevard, the bayside town of **Morro Bay** has waterfront dining and a walkable downtown with art galleries and boutiques. It also has a range of hotels and the practical aspects of your vacation covered with groceries, gas, and supplies.

BEST PICNIC SPOT

Spooner's Cove Day Use Area

Popular and scenic Spooner's Cove offers a few picnic tables in its day use area. Enjoy the best of both worlds as you picnic within view of the gorgeous coast without getting sand in your lunch.

GETTING THERE

CAR

Montaña de Oro is located 15 mi (24 km) west of San Luis Obispo off Pecho Valley Road. From downtown San Luis Obispo, take Foothill Boulevard west for 3 mi (5 km). Turn right on Los Osos Valley Road and continue for 8 mi (14 km) until it turns into Pecho Valley Road. Continue on Pecho Valley Road for 3 mi (5 km) to Spooner's Cove.

From the south take US-101 north to exit 200A for Los Osos Valley Road. Turn left onto Los Osos Valley Road and continue for 11 mi (18 km) until it turns into Pecho Valley Road, which leads into the park.

From the north, take CA-1 south to exit 277 toward Los Osos/Baywood Park. Turn right onto South Bay Boulevard and continue for 4 mi (6 km). Turn right onto Los Osos Valley Road and continue for 1.5 mi (2.5 km) until it turns into Pecho Valley Road, which leads into the park.

PISMO STATE BEACH AND OCEANO DUNES STATE VEHICULAR RECREATION AREA

Pismo clams, off-road vehicles, and the Dunites give this particular stretch of the Central Coast its local flavor. Pismo Beach is a classic Southern California beach town that gets more than its fair share of sunny days for the notoriously fogged-in region. Pismo State Beach is wide and sandy, making for good sunbathing, swimming, surfing, and kayaking, drawing more than two million visitors per year. Farther south, the Oceano Dunes State Vehicular Recreation Area, technically its own state park, offers several more miles of sandy beaches as well as a huge dune system that allows off-road vehicles.

PISMO STATE BEACH

ADDRESS: 555 Pier Ave., Oceano

PHONE: 805/473-7220

DAY USE HOURS: 7am-10pm

AREA: 1,412 acres (571 ha)

OCEANO DUNES STATE VEHICULAR RECREATION AREA

ADDRESS: 555 Pier Ave., Oceano

PHONE: 805/773-7170

DAY USE HOURS: 7am-10pm

AREA: 2,675 acres (1,083 ha)

South of the town of Pismo Beach lies the largest, intact coastal dune complex in the world. The Chumash people called the Oceano Dunes home some 10,000 years ago, hunting and fishing the lagoons and coast. Europeans laid claim to the area in 1769, but with the area's harsh terrain, there wasn't a lot of settlement until the 1890s. The next group to call the dunes home were an eccentric group of free thinkers in the 1930s who called themselves "Dunites" and who created a utopian community in the shifting sands. Today, the dunes are best known as the only place in California you are allowed to drive vehicles onto the sand.

PISMO STATE BEACH AND OCEANO DUNES STATE VEHICULAR RECREATION AREA
To Avila Beach
Visitor Center
Pier
Pismo Beach
101
Monarch Butterfly Grove
North Beach
VISITING THE MONARCH BUTTERFLIES
MONARCH BUTTERFLY GROVE AND MEADOW CREEK TRAIL
Oceano Dunes Natural Preserve
Grand Avenue Entrance
WEST GRAND AVE
OAK PARK BLVD
Grover Beach
EAST GRAND AVE
Pismo State Beach
RELAXING ON THE BEACH
Oceano
Pier Avenue Entrance
Oceano Dunes District Visitor Center
S HALCYON RD
LOS BERROS RD
CIENAGA ST
Pismo Dunes Natural Preserve
PACIFIC OCEAN
MESA VIEW DR
Oceano Dunes State Vehicular Recreation Area
WILLOW RD
DRIVING THE DUNES
Oso Flaco Lake
Oso Flaco Lake Trail
OSO FLACO LAKE RD
GUADALUPE RD
0 1 mi
0 1 km
Contour Interval = 40 feet

TOP 3

★ **1. VISITING THE MONARCH BUTTERFLIES:** Go to the Monarch Butterfly Grove from November through February to see thousands of western monarch butterflies (page 337).

★ **2. RELAXING ON THE BEACH:** Pismo Beach's wide, sandy beaches as well as high percentage of sunny days make it a perfect spot (page 337).

★ **3. DRIVING THE DUNES:** Rent or bring your own all-terrain vehicle (ATV) and take a spin through the extensive dune fields at Oceano Dunes SVRA (page 340).

PLANNING YOUR TIME

It is possible to treat Pismo Beach as a one-day destination, spending the good part of your time on the beach, adding in a visit to the Monarch Butterfly Grove and the Pismo Beach Pier. Many visitors choose to turn Pismo Beach into a full vacation destination, spending a weekend or longer camped at one of the resort hotels, enjoying the sand and surf.

Nearby state parks include Montaña de Oro State Park (27 mi/43 km), Morro Bay State Park (27 mi/43 km), Cayucos State Beach (35 mi/56 km), and Estero Bluffs State Park (37 mi/60 km).

ENTRANCES AND FEES

There is **no official entrance station** for Pismo State Beach. For day use, the easiest access is at the Pismo Beach Pier (100 Pomeroy Ave.). Parking for the pier is available adjacent to the pier at the ends of Pomeroy Avenue and Addie Street. Stairs on Main Street lead down to the beach. While there is no fee to enter the beach, the city operates paid parking lots ($3-5/hour). South of the Pismo Beach Pier there are additional access points, including from bluff-top parks overlooking the ocean. The city of Pismo Beach has a good, downloadable map with descriptions of all the beach access points on their website (www.pismobeach.org).

It is also possible to access the state beach via a trail through the **Monarch Butterfly Grove** (400 S. Dolliver St.). Parking is at a small street-parking lot located at the preserve entrance (free). Visitors who are camping in **North Beach Campground** should enter at 399 South Dolliver Street to check in and access the beach from the campground. There is beach access via a short trail from the campground, but there is no day use parking.

For day use (7am-10pm daily) at **Oceano Dunes SRVA,** access the beach near the parking lot for the **Oceano Dunes Natural Preserve/Fin's Bar and Grill** (25 W. Grand Ave.) at the end of Grand Avenue in the community of Grover Beach. To access the beach on foot, there is free parking available in the lot as well as public restrooms and a boardwalk to the beach with no entry fees. To drive your vehicle onto the beach, continue through an entrance kiosk and purchase a day use pass ($5/vehicle). Four-wheel drive is strongly recommended to drive onto the sand with your vehicle.

VISITOR CENTER

There is no official park visitor center for Pismo Beach.

Oceano Dunes District Visitor Center

555 Pier Ave.; noon-4pm daily

The Oceano Dunes District Visitor Center has extensive interpretive displays about the natural and cultural history of the area. Staff and volunteers are also on hand to provide information and answer questions about the park and local area. The visitor center is located at the entrance to the Oceano Campground.

WEATHER

In the land of microclimates that is California's Central Coast, Pismo Beach is known for sunny beach days. Still, temperatures here are cooler than inland, and fog can blanket the coast especially in winter and spring and in the morning and evening year-round. The warmest season is June-October, when temperatures average around 74-76°F (23-24°C).

SIGHTS

★ MONARCH BUTTERFLY GROVE

400 S. Dolliver St.; 805/773-7170; www.parks.ca.gov; free

The Monarch Butterfly Grove is a small preserve within Pismo State Beach. It is situated adjacent to **North Beach Campground** in a eucalyptus and pine grove. It is here that these snowbirds, um, butterflies, escape freezing northern locales and winter in mild Pismo Beach instead. Monarchs come from as far north as Canada, with later summer and fall butterflies heading south to overwintering grounds to escape cold winter temperatures. The season to see the butterflies is late October/November through February/early March. In typical years, the grove receives over 10,000 butterflies, making it one of the five most populated butterfly migration sites in the state. Even if you can't make it during butterfly migration season, you can still visit the preserve, walk the short nature trail, and check out the quaint gift shop located in a travel trailer. Their Pismo State Beach candle smells like butterflies at the beach, or cypress, bayberry, and eucalyptus. Proceeds benefit the Central Coast State Parks Association.

BEACHES

★ PISMO STATE BEACH

Swimming, fishing, kayaking, stand-up paddleboarding, and kiteboarding are all popular pastimes at Pismo Beach. The 6-mi (10-km) stretch of coastline goes from just south of the Pismo Beach Pier to the Oceano Dunes SRVA to the south. To be close to the action, access the beach from the **Pismo Beach Pier** for volleyball courts, a children's playground, public restrooms, and sand showers. To soak in the quieter beauty of the coast with its low dunes and wide, flat beaches,

Pismo Beach Pier

THE TOWN OF PISMO BEACH

Pismo Beach is a classic California beach town drawing surfers and sunbathers to its golden shores. Located on California's beautiful central coast, the area boasts more sunny days—270, to be exact—than many of the surrounding beaches keeping visitors pouring in. From downtown Pismo Beach at the western end of Pomeroy Avenue, check out the area around the Pismo Beach Pier. A trio of airstreams on the pier house a visitor center, bait-and-tackle shop, and food truck. The pier itself was built in 1924 and serves as a landmark, fishing spot, and viewing platform to take in the Pacific Ocean, sunset, and migrating whales. There is no fishing license required to fish from the pier.

The downtown immediately surrounding the pier has a retro vibe with shops and eateries including the essential four S's of beach towns: surf shops, saltwater taffy, seafood, and souvenirs. There is also plenty of other great shopping and dining, including fine dining, in the surrounding blocks from the beach to US-101 three blocks east.

access the beach near **North Beach Campground** via a trail through the **Monarch Butterfly Grove.**

OCEANO DUNES STATE VEHICULAR RECREATION AREA

For a casual picnic or beach day next to your parked vehicle, use the Grand Avenue entrance to access the northern section of Oceano Dunes State Vehicular Recreation Area, which is more mellow since there is no off-highway-vehicle (OHV) action here; it is confined to the dunes to the south.

HIKING

While hiking isn't the main draw for either park, there are a few nice trails to explore the coastal sand dune habitat.

OSO FLACO LAKE

DISTANCE: 2 mi (3.2 km) round-trip
DURATION: 45 minutes
EFFORT: Easy
TRAILHEAD: Oso Flaco Lake parking area, 3098 Oso Flaco Lake Rd., Arroyo Grande

A boardwalk takes you over Oso Flaco Lake lined with willows and other wetland species to a viewing deck with Pacific Ocean vistas. The lake is located on the southern end of Oceano Dunes SRVA (no vehicles allowed in this area), sheltered in coastal dunes that are part of the 22,000-acre (8,900-ha) Guadalupe Nipomo Dunes Complex. Beginning from the west end of the parking area, a paved, then dirt, trail leads to the lake. At the lake's shore, take the boardwalk to cross the lake. There are benches along the boardwalk for fishing or admiring the serene landscape. There are also interpretive panels with information about native

TOP HIKE

MONARCH BUTTERFLY GROVE AND MEADOW CREEK TRAIL

DISTANCE: 1.5 mi (2.4 km) round-trip
DURATION: 30 minutes
EFFORT: Easy
TRAILHEAD: Monarch Butterfly Grove

This trail takes in the small loop through the Monarch Butterfly Grove before continuing on the Meadow Creek Trail through coastal dunes with beautiful ocean views. Begin the trail in the Monarch Butterfly Grove adjacent to North Beach Campground. If you're camping you can simply walk over. If not, there is a street parking area off of CA-1/Dolliver Street. Walk the small loop through the eucalyptus grove favored by monarch butterflies and then pick up the boardwalk at the west end of the preserve, continuing as it eases through low dunes, the beach and ocean just on the other side. At the end of the trail, turn around or head down to explore or relax on Pismo Beach's wide, sandy coast.

plants and animals. The boardwalk ends at a viewpoint overlooking the ocean. You can turn around here or continue to access the beach and Oso Flaco Creek.

The trail surface is paved/packed dirt and boardwalk and likely accessible for visitors using wheelchairs, mobility equipment, or strollers. There are four paved, accessible parking spaces in the parking lot as well as a wheelchair-accessible restroom.

OCEANO DUNES NATURAL PRESERVE TRAIL

DISTANCE: 2 mi (3.2 km) round-trip
DURATION: 1 hour
EFFORT: Easy
TRAILHEAD: Oceano Dunes Natural Preserve day use parking, Grand Ave.

Walk along a sandy trail that follows the contours of the plant-covered dunes in the 570-acre (230-ha) Oceano Dunes Natural Preserve. Find the unmarked trailhead across the street from the Oceano Dunes Natural Preserve day use parking on Grand Avenue. The trail continues for 1 mi (1.6 km) to a Pismo State Beach Road that leads to the Oceano Campground. Turn around and make your way back through the dunes for a 2-mi (3.2-km) round-trip tour.

RECREATION

★ OFF-ROADING

The Oceano Dunes SVRA, south of the Oceano Dunes Natural Preserve area, allows the uncommon experience of driving off-highway vehicles into the dunes. With over 3,500 acres (1,416 ha) of sand, there's plenty of space for visitors to charge and crest the slopes in their ATVs or sand buggies.

off-roading at Oceano Dunes SVRA

If you want to ride the dunes, enter at the southern entrance via Pier Avenue (7am-10pm; $5). There are a number of ATV rentals near the beach entrance along Pier Avenue. Post 2, 1 mi (1.6 km) south of this entrance, marks the beginning of the OHV area. All non-street-legal vehicles need to be transported to this point before they are off-loaded. From here you can ride along the beach or in the long stretch of dunes that ripple south along the coastline. Pay attention to fenced areas and signs that indicate private property or sensitive plant and animal life.

Regulations are in flux here; refer to the park's website for the most updated rules for visiting this zone.

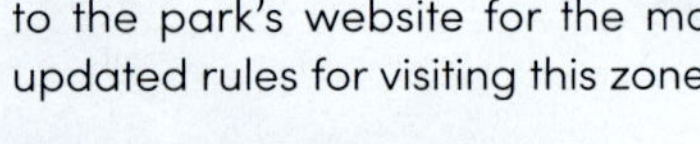

WATER SPORTS

Wide beaches with a sandy ocean

floor make Pismo Beach and Oceano Dunes excellent spots for **swimming, stand-up paddleboarding, surfing,** and **kiteboarding.** Good swim zones are at Pismo State Beach near the Pismo Beach Pier, the North Beach Campground, and Oceano Dunes at the Grand Avenue entrance. The hub for stand-up paddleboarding and surfing is north and south of Pismo Beach Pier. Board and wetsuit rentals are available in Pismo Beach. Drive-up access for kiteboarding is available at the Oceano Dunes Grand Avenue beach ramp entrance.

CAMPING

There are **two developed campgrounds** within Pismo State Beach: North Beach and Oceano Campgrounds. Sites at both campgrounds have picnic tables and fire rings, and campgrounds have restrooms, token-operated hot showers, and firewood for sale. Reservations must be made through Reserve California (800/444-7275; www.reservecalifornia.com; North Beach $25, Oceano $40). There is also dispersed beach and dune camping available in the Oceano Dunes SVRA. These sites can also be reserved (800/444-7275; www.reservecalifornia.com; $10).

BEST CAMPGROUNDS

North Beach Campground

North Beach Campground has 103 sites spaced across an open grassy meadow with direct access to Pismo State Beach and the Monarch Butterfly Grove. The campground is available for tent and RV camping, although there are no hookups available. Beach access is via the short Beach Foot Trail, which leads through low dunes to the beach.

Oceano Campground

Oceano Campground has 35 sites, including hookup sites for both tent camping and RVs located on the Oceano Lagoon. Beach access is via a beach trail that leads through low dunes. This area sits within the Oceano Dunes State Recreational Vehicular Area (SRVA) and is popular for ATV riders.

FOOD AND LODGING

Pismo State Beach fronts three separate towns: **Pismo Beach, Grover Beach, and Oceano.**

Pismo Beach is the largest of the three. It is a full-service town catering to visitors with hotels, restaurants, and a historic pier and promenade as well as gas stations, grocery stores, and supplies. There are also surf shops where you can buy and rent gear, surfboards, and wetsuits. The main hotel zone is located north of North Beach Campground with an additional string of beachfront resort hotels located north of Pismo Pier.

The small town of **Grover Beach** is located just south of the North Beach Campground and Monarch Butterfly Cove. It is primarily a residential community but has grocery stores, gas, and supplies.

The small town of **Oceano** located on the edge of the Oceano Dunes SRVA is also primarily residential but has businesses geared toward tourists concentrated along Pier Avenue, including restaurants, hotels, and ATV rentals.

BEST PICNIC SPOT

Monarch Butterfly Grove

Even if the butterflies are not in season, take advantage of the Monarch Butterfly Grove's picnic tables set under a delightful stand of eucalyptus trees for your al fresco meal.

GETTING THERE

CAR

The town of Pismo Beach is located approximately 15 mi (24 km) south of San Luis Obispo where US-101 and CA-1 intersect.

To reach Pismo Beach from the north, take exit 191-A for CA-1 south/ Dolliver Street, continuing for 0.5 mi (0.8 km) to Pomeroy Avenue. Turn right onto Pomeroy Avenue to the pier's day use parking.

To reach Pismo Beach from the south, take exit 190 for Price Street/ Hinds Avenue/US-101. Continue onto Price Street for 0.2 mi (0.3 km). Turn left onto Pomeroy Avenue for 0.2 mi (0.3 km) to the pier's day use parking.

To reach Oceano Dunes from the north, take US-101 south to exit 191-A for CA-1 south toward Pismo Beach. Continue on CA-1 south/Dolliver Street for 2 mi (3 km) to Grand Avenue. Turn right on Grand Avenue to the park's day use area.

To reach Oceano Dunes from the south, take US-101 north to exit 189 for North 4th Street in Pismo Beach. Continue on North 4th Street for 1.5 mi (2.4 km) to Grand Avenue. Turn right toward the park's day use area.

TRAIN

Pismo Beach can also be reached by train and is one of the stops on Amtrak's Pacific Surfliner (www.pacificsurfliner.com), a passenger train servicing the coast between San Diego and San Luis Obispo. The Grover Beach Station (180 W. Grand Ave.) lets visitors out 0.3 mi (0.5 km) from the park's day use entrance. The station is 1.1 mi (1.8 km) south of North Beach Campground.

BUS

Both Greyhound (www.greyhound.com) and Flixbus (www.flixbus.com) offer bus options to the Grover Beach Amtrak Station (180 W. Grand Ave.).

EL CAPITÁN STATE BEACH

Located along scenic US-101, El Capitán offers a blend of rugged shoreline, sandy beach, and coastal woodland. Just 20 mi (32 km) west of Santa Barbara, it's a favorite spot for camping, surfing, tide-pooling, hiking, and picnicking. El Capitán is located along the lush banks of El Capitán Creek, which is lined with live oaks, sycamores, and willows, while sculpted bluffs preside over a beach that ranges from sandy to rocky, harboring tide pools at low tide. The backcountry gives way to coastal hills and hiking trails with views over the Pacific Ocean and Channel Islands.

ADDRESS: US-101, El Capitán State Beach Rd., Goleta

PHONE: 805/968-1033

DAY USE HOURS: 8am-sunset

AREA: 2,634 acres (1,066 ha)

The area was settled by Chumash Indians along the banks of El Capitán Creek as long as 3,200 years ago, and some of their art is visible at nearby Chumash Painted Cave State Historic Park.

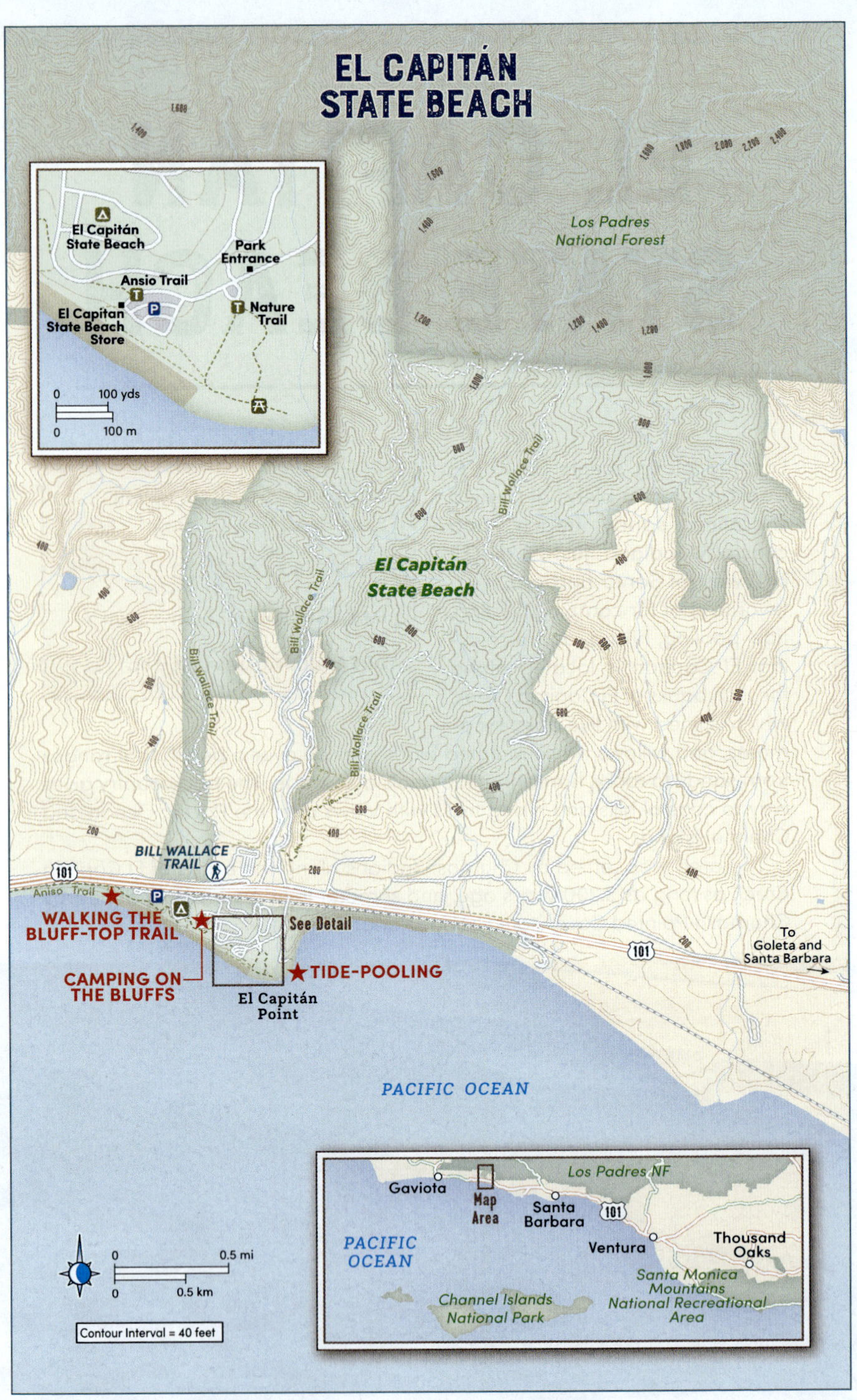

EL CAPITÁN STATE BEACH
El Capitán State Beach
Park Entrance
Ansio Trail
El Capitan State Beach Store
Nature Trail
0 100 yds
0 100 m
Los Padres National Forest
Bill Wallace Trail
El Capitán State Beach
BILL WALLACE TRAIL
101
Aniso Trail
WALKING THE BLUFF-TOP TRAIL
See Detail
CAMPING ON THE BLUFFS
TIDE-POOLING
El Capitán Point
To Goleta and Santa Barbara
PACIFIC OCEAN
Los Padres NF
Gaviota
Map Area
Santa Barbara
Ventura
Thousand Oaks
PACIFIC OCEAN
Channel Islands National Park
Santa Monica Mountains National Recreational Area
0 0.5 mi
0 0.5 km
Contour Interval = 40 feet

TOP 3

★ **1. WALKING THE BLUFF-TOP TRAIL:** Take in sweeping views of the coast and the distant Channel Islands on the trail linking El Capitán with Refugio State Beach to the west (page 347).

★ **2. TIDE-POOLING:** Make your way down to the sand to explore rocky tide pools at low tide (page 348).

★ **3. CAMPING ON THE BLUFFS:** The campground is situated in oak and sycamore woodlands on top of bluffs overlooking the Pacific Ocean (page 348).

1

PLANNING YOUR TIME

It is easy to spend most of a day exploring El Capitán's beach. For a full day, visitors might consider a hike in the morning when it is cool and then spend the afternoon on the beach. Note that in 2025, the park system undertook a construction project to improve the park entrance. While the main road and campground were closed at the time of writing, the park and beach remain open for day use access for pedestrians. Day use restrooms near the beach also remain open. The intended reopening is in 2026.

Nearby state parks include El Presidio de Santa Barbara State Historic Park (20 mi/32 km).

ENTRANCE AND FEES

There is an official park entrance kiosk and ranger station located at the **one park entrance** off of US-101 and the El Capitán State Beach exit. Visitors check in for camping and pay at the kiosk for day use ($10/vehicle).

VISITOR CENTER

El Capitán does not have a visitor center.

WEATHER

El Capitán State Beach has a mild Mediterranean climate with moderate temperatures year-round. Spring and fall bring daytime temperatures around 68-72°F (20-22°C) with cooler nights. Summers are warmer with highs around 75°F (24°C), while winter is cooler with occasional rain. Late spring and early summer bring "June Gloom," a morning coastal fog that usually clears by the afternoon. Spring, summer, and fall are all nice times to visit, with summer bringing the most sunshine and warmest temperatures.

BEACHES

EL CAPITÁN STATE BEACH

El Capitán State Beach covers 2.7 mi (4.3 km) of coastline set against wind- and water-carved bluffs that ranges from sandy beach to rocky tide-pool zone. Access to the beach is via a series of staircases and ramps that lead from the campground and day use parking to the beach. The most popular stretch of shoreline is below the campground and main day use access point, a stretch of sand that lends itself to swimming, relaxing on the beach, and building sandcastles.

TOP HIKE
BILL WALLACE TRAIL

DISTANCE: 4.2 mi (6.8 km) round-trip
DURATION: 2.5-3 hours
EFFORT: Moderate
TRAILHEAD: El Capitán State Beach exit access road parking lot

Named for a local conservationist and environmental champion, this out-and-back hike is a Central Coast classic. It follows an old ranch road through coastal hills carved by El Capitán Creek. In spring the hills may be covered with wildflowers. The entire trail network is actually a 12-mi (19-km) loop, but much of it is washed out and requires bushwhacking. Hiking this initial section will reveal views of the inland mountain ranges of the Los Padres National Forest, the ocean, and the Channel Islands if the day is clear, and gives you a chance to immerse in the landscape.

From US-101 north and the El Capitán State Beach exit, head inland to turn left at the frontage road. Drive past El Capitán Canyon Resort to the signed entrance to Sun Outdoors Santa Barbara (formerly Ocean Mesa Campground). Park immediately in the dirt parking lot on the left and look for the signed trailhead.

HIKING

NATURE TRAIL

DISTANCE: 0.6 mi (0.9 km) round-trip
DURATION: 20 minutes
EFFORT: Easy
LOCATION: Near park entrance station

This accessible out-and-back trail follows the riparian corridor of El Capitán Creek through large sycamore and oak trees, ending at an accessible picnic area with coastal views.

★ BLUFF-TOP TRAIL

DISTANCE: 5.5 mi (8.9 km) round-trip
DURATION: 2.5-3 hours
EFFORT: Easy
LOCATION: El Capitán State Beach day use parking lot

A bluff-top walk/bike trail leads to Refugio State Beach with views of the Pacific Ocean and Channel Islands. The trail is partially closed due to erosion, not allowing full access between the two beaches, but parts of it remain open for walking and biking. Check the park website (www.parks.ca.gov) or inquire at the ranger station for current conditions.

stairs to El Capitán State Beach (left); Nature Trail (right)

RECREATION

SURFING

El Capitán Point is the choicest zone for surfing, although the waves here are fickle and best for advanced surfers. In fall and winter, surfers look for the legendary "El Cap" with a west swell that may bring a clean, hollow wave.

WILDLIFE WATCHING

★ Tide Pools

Farther east along the beach, toward El Capitán Point, the coast gets rockier, and there are opportunities to explore tide pools at low tide. Look for barnacles suctioned to the rocky surfaces, flowery sea anemones, and, occasionally with patience, sea stars and octopus.

Marine Mammals

Winter and spring bring migrating **gray whales,** which can be spied from the Bluff-Top Trail with a little luck.

CAMPING

El Capitán State Park offers **one developed campground** as well as five group campsites that accommodate 40-60 people for tent, RV, and trailer camping. Reservations are required through Reserve California (800/444-7275; www.reservecalifornia.com; $45-55) and are available six months in advance.

BEST CAMPGROUND

★ El Capitán State Beach Campground

El Capitán State Beach Campground offers 135 campsites for tent and RV camping on the bluff-top above El Capitán State Beach with staircase and ramp access to the beach. The campground is in a canopy of sycamores and oaks, and many sites

BEST NEARBY

CHANNEL ISLANDS NATIONAL PARK

The remote Channel Islands National Park (www.nps.gov/chis; free) has isolated beaches, rugged cliffs, sea caves you can kayak through, and miles of uncrowded hiking trails all surrounded by a marine sanctuary in the Pacific Ocean. The five islands are reachable only by boat or plane with transportation leaving from Ventura.

are shaded. Campsites have picnic tables and fire rings. There are no hookups available. There are centrally located bathrooms and token-operated showers.

FOOD AND LODGING

The picturesque, historic town of **Santa Barbara** located 20 mi (32 km) east along the coast is a destination, with a walkable downtown, restaurants, wineries, shopping, and luxury hotels. It also offers the basics including groceries, gas, and supplies. A rustic resort with cabins and a small store and restaurant is located across US-101 from the El Capitán Campground, technically inside the state park lands but operating privately.

EL CAPITÁN STATE BEACH STORE

2 El Capitán State Beach Rd., 10am-5pm daily

The El Capitán State Beach Store, located adjacent to the day use parking area, offers basic supplies including ice, beer, firewood, and camping gear as well as snacks and souvenirs.

BEST PICNIC SPOT

Nature Trail

An accessible picnic area with coastal views is located at the end of the Nature Trail. Find the Nature Trail near the park entrance; the wide trail goes 0.3 mi (0.5 km) through sycamore and oak trees to the picnic spot.

GETTING THERE

CAR

El Capitán State Beach is located 20 mi (32 km) west of Santa Barbara off of US-101.

EL PRESIDIO DE SANTA BARBARA STATE HISTORIC PARK

Explore Santa Barbara's layered past as it melds with its vibrant present. The adobe walls of El Presidio, the Spanish military fortress, are at the heart of the beautiful coastal town that grew up around them, the lively blocks radiating outward now filled with shops, restaurants, and wineries.

ADDRESS: 123 E. Canon Perdido St., Santa Barbara

PHONE: 805/965-0093

WEBSITE: www.sbthp.org

DAY USE HOURS: 10:30am-4:30pm

AREA: 5.8 acres (2.3 ha)

Before the Presidio was built, the Santa Barbara Coast and Channel Islands were occupied for tens of thousands of years by the Chumash, who had villages and trade networks from Morro Bay to Malibu. A 1769 Spanish expedition led to the then Mexican-owned territory being colonized for Spain, which led to the construction of the Presidio in 1782.

Visitors can explore the original and reconstructed buildings that served as a hub for Europeans until 1830. As Santa Barbara grew, other buildings were constructed on the site of the Presidio including the 1920s Santa Barbara School of the Arts and the 1947 Jimmy's Oriental Gardens, a Chinese restaurant complex, all now protected within the historic park. Wander the dynamic neighborhood once settled by Chumash, Mexican, Spanish, Euro-American, Chinese, and Japanese settlers, appreciating the strata of history.

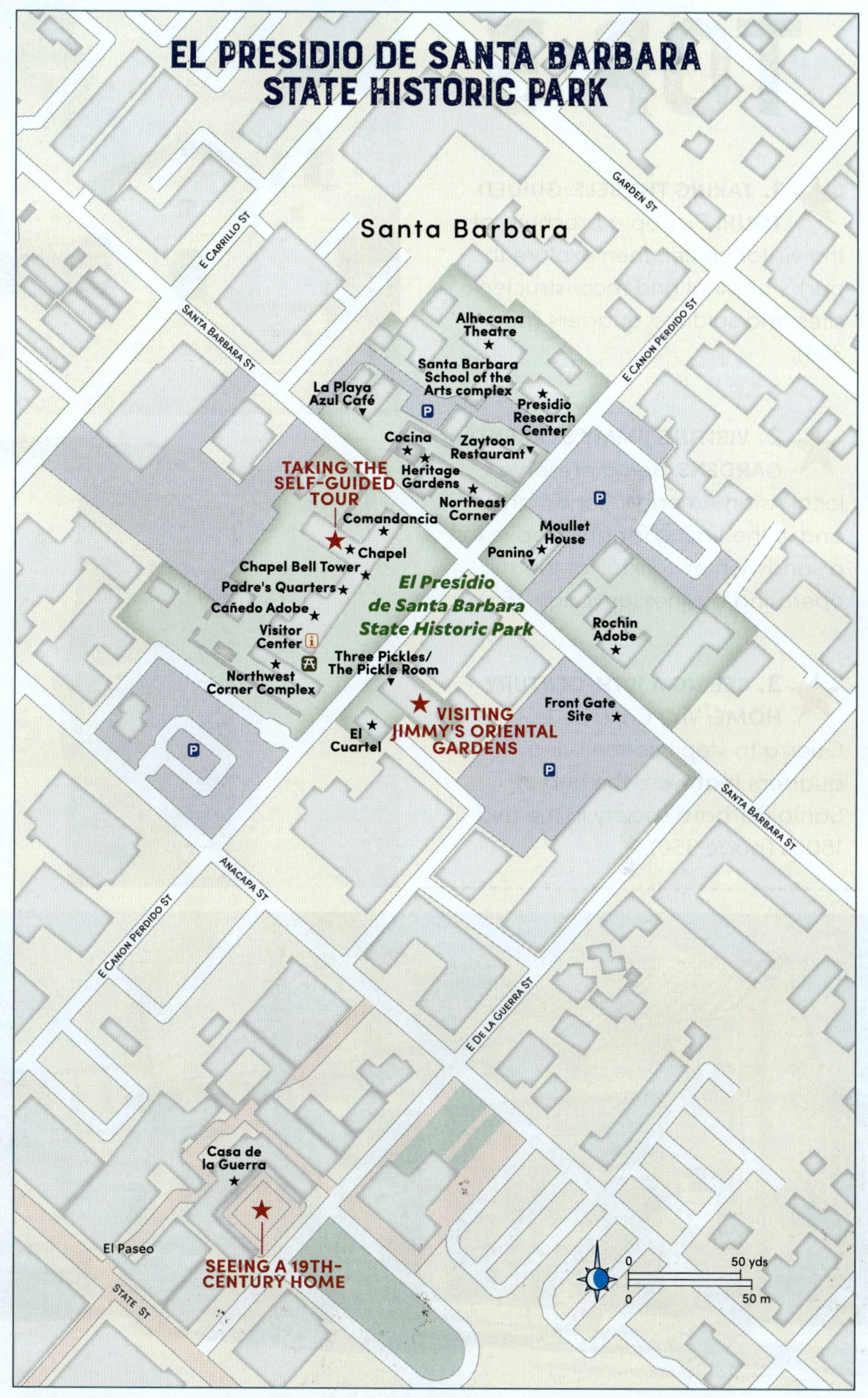

EL PRESIDIO DE SANTA BARBARA STATE HISTORIC PARK
Santa Barbara
GARDEN ST
E CARRILLO ST
SANTA BARBARA ST
E CANON PERDIDO ST
Alhecama Theatre
Santa Barbara School of the Arts complex
La Playa Azul Café
Presidio Research Center
Cocina
Zaytoon Restaurant
Heritage Gardens
TAKING THE SELF-GUIDED TOUR
Northeast Corner
Comandancia
Moullet House
Chapel
Panino
Chapel Bell Tower
Padre's Quarters
El Presidio de Santa Barbara State Historic Park
Cañedo Adobe
Visitor Center
Rochin Adobe
Three Pickles/ The Pickle Room
Northwest Corner Complex
Front Gate Site
El Cuartel
VISITING JIMMY'S ORIENTAL GARDENS
SANTA BARBARA ST
ANACAPA ST
E CANON PERDIDO ST
E DE LA GUERRA ST
Casa de la Guerra
El Paseo
SEEING A 19TH-CENTURY HOME
STATE ST
0
50 yds
0
50 m

TOP 3

★ **1. TAKING THE SELF-GUIDED TOUR:** Pick up a brochure at the visitor center, then explore the park's original and reconstructed sites and soldiers' quarters (page 354).

★ **2. VISITING JIMMY'S ORIENTAL GARDENS:** See a preserved local Asian American landmark, and, if the timing is right, stop in for a sandwich or cocktail at the still operating businesses (page 355).

★ **3. SEEING A 19TH-CENTURY HOME:** Visit Casa de la Guerra to step into the living quarters that were the hub of Santa Barbara society in the mid 1800s (page 356).

PLANNING YOUR TIME

Plan for a few hours to tour the historic buildings and have lunch. Explore the larger Presidio neighborhood for a full day.

The park aligns with the original footprint of the Presidio, which was divided into quadrants expanding out from the center at the intersection of Canon Perdido Street and Santa Barbara Street. The **Northwest Corner** is home to the visitor center, chapel, and padre's quarters and is a good place to start your tour. The **Northeast Corner** houses reconstructed quarters, a cocina, and Heritage Gardens as well as the 1920s Santa Barbara School of the Arts complex. The **Southwest Corner** features El Cuartel, soldiers' quarters circa 1788, and Jimmy's Oriental Gardens restaurant dating from 1947. The quiet **Southeast Corner** features a historic adobe not open to the public and an Italianate home that houses a restaurant.

Casa de la Guerra is a short walk (0.2 mi/0.3 km) south of the visitor center off of East De la Guerra Street.

Nearby state parks include El Capitán State Beach (20 mi/32 km).

ENTRANCE AND FEES

Enter through the visitor center in the **Cañedo Adobe** and pay an entrance fee ($5). Entrance includes admission to **Casa de la Guerra.**

Hourly public parking is available in a parking lot adjacent to the park (115 E. Canon Perdido St.).

VISITOR CENTER

Cañedo Adobe

123 E. Canon Perdido St.; 10:30am-4:30pm daily

The visitor center is located in the Cañedo Adobe, one of the original buildings named after the soldier to whom the building was deeded when the Presidio ceased operations.

WEATHER

Santa Barbara has a mild Mediterranean climate with plenty of sunshine year-round. Daytime temperatures typically range from 65-75°F (18-24°C), making it an excellent year-round destination.

EVENTS

El Presidio de Santa Barbara hosts rotating events on its historic grounds throughout the year including open-air artisan markets, interactive history events, and wine tastings. To find a list of events go to the Santa Barbara Trust for Historic Preservation's website (www.sbthp.org) or the city's tourism website (www.santabarbaraca.com).

SIGHTS

TOURS

★ Self-Guided Tour

A park brochure with a numbered map corresponds to structures and sites, giving visitors a chance to take a self-guided tour. Pick up the brochure in the visitor center and pay the entrance fee. The fee is required to gain entry to the Northwest Corner complex, padre's quarters, chapel, and Casa de la Guerra. To visit these sites as well as the Northeast, Southwest, and Southeast Corners takes approximately two hours.

NORTHWEST CORNER

Cañedo Adobe

The Northwest Corner has the highest concentration of original and reconstructed buildings, including the Cañedo Adobe, which houses the visitor center. The adobe is one of the fort's two original buildings (the other is El Cuartel). Dating to 1788, it was constructed as officers' quarters. The property passed through many hands, most notably preservationist Elmer Whittaker, who bought the building in 1920 and restored it in the 1940s, planting the citrus trees you can see behind the adobe.

Northwest Corner Complex

This area includes the Northwest Corner complex, residences for soldiers and their families, the reconstructed **padre's quarters** with period furnishings, and a hand-painted chapel. By contrast with the padre's austere religious quarters, the more sumptuous **Comandancia** shows what housing was like the for the military officers.

inside the walls of the Northwest Corner complex

NORTHEAST CORNER

Northeast Corner Complex

The Northeast Corner refers to a reconstructed complex including a two-story observation tower and reconstructed officers' and soldiers' quarters.

Cocina

The area also includes a cocina, the officers' kitchen, stocked with cookware as well as a sampling of spices and food items.

Heritage Gardens

The interpretive Heritage Gardens extend the length of the narrow passageway between the cocina and living quarters and outer wall and highlight plant varieties that were grown by the Spanish settlers including grapevines for wine, peppers, herbs, bananas, prickly pear cactus, and Sonora wheat for flour.

Santa Barbara School of the Arts Complex

The 1920s Santa Barbara School of the Arts complex, including the **Alhecama Theatre,** occupies much of the northeastern corner. Visitors can see the buildings' exteriors and dine in two restaurants housed in the historic complex. The restored Alhecama Theatre also occasionally hosts screenings and events (www.sbthp.org/calendar).

SOUTHWEST CORNER

El Cuartel

El Cuartel, an adobe built in 1788, is the oldest building in the state park system and the anchor of the original Presidio here. This was the residence of Presidio soldier Jesus Valenzuela for more than three generations.

★ Jimmy's Oriental Gardens

126 E. Canon Perdido St.

Jimmy's Oriental Gardens preserves a local landmark and reminder

El Cuartel

of Santa Barbara's Asian American heritage. The Chinese-owned restaurant and bar operated on Canon Perdido Street from 1947 to 2006. An interpretive exhibit from the neighborhood's vibrant Asian heritage, including Japanese Americans, is located next to the visitor center.

SOUTHEAST CORNER

Stroll quiet Santa Barbara Street to see historic buildings built on the site of the original Presidio.

Rochin Adobe

The 1856 Rochin Adobe was built from adobe blocks from the Presidio ruins and later covered in siding.

Moullet House

The 1896 Moullet House was a private residence constructed of bricks in the Italianate style.

★ CASA DE LA GUERRA

15 E. De la Guerra St.; noon-4pm Thurs.-Sun.

To see how the other half lived, visit the prestigious Casa de la Guerra, now a restored period museum. The casa was constructed for José de la Guerra, the fifth comandante of the Presidio, and his children and grandchildren lived here until 1943. Step into the dark, cool depths of the adobe residence featuring a furnished living room, bedroom, and office restored to their appearance from 1828 to 1858, when the adobe was a cultural, political, and social center of Santa Barbara.

Casa de la Guerra also offers rotating exhibits on the rich history of the Central Coast.

FOOD AND LODGING

Santa Barbara is a destination town with all the services. El Presidio de Santa Barbara State Historic Park is at the heart of the larger historic Presidio neighborhood with restaurants, hotels, wine tasting, and shopping. There is **no camping** at the state historic park.

Adjacent to Casa de la Guerra, **El Paseo** is a charming 1920s-built adobe complex of shops surrounding interior courtyards listed on the National Register of Historic Places. Notable are the many local wineries and tasting rooms, some family friendly, with courtyard seating. **State Street,** two blocks west of El Presidio, and the main walking route between the train station and the historic district, is lined with restaurants, bars, and shops.

Within the historic park, several of the protected buildings house restaurants and bars.

ZAYTOON RESTAURANT

209 E. Canon Perdido St.; 805/963-1293; www.zaytoon.com; 5pm-9pm Tues.-Thurs and Sun., 5pm-10pm Fri.-Sat.; $26-37

The Santa Barbara School of the Arts complex in the northeast quarter is home to the upscale Zaytoon Restaurant, featuring Lebanese fare and handcrafted cocktails in an outdoor patio setting.

LA PLAYA AZUL CAFÉ

914 Santa Barbara St.; 805/966-2860; https://laplayaazulcafe.com;

11am-8pm Tues.-Thurs. and Sun., 11am-9pm Fri.-Sat.; $19-27
Visitors can dine on the deep covered porch, bougainvillea-edged patio, or quaint indoor space that make up La Playa Azul Café, enjoying margaritas and traditional Mexican specialties.

PANINO

834 Santa Barbara St.; 805/963-3700; www.eatpanino.com; 10am-4pm Mon.-Sat., 10am-3pm Sun.; $14-17
Panino, located at the Moullet House, features gourmet, Italian-inspired sandwiches and salads with lots of vegetarian options.

THREE PICKLES/ THE PICKLE ROOM

126 E. Canon Perdido St.
The historic **Jimmy's Oriental Gardens** (www.sbthp.org/jimmys; 10:30am-3pm Mon.-Sat.; $9-15) has sandwich shop **Three Pickles** (https://threepickles.com) and cocktail bar **The Pickle Room** (https://threepickles.com; 4:30pm-close; $10-16), honoring the local favorite Chinese-owned restaurant and bar that resided in the space for decades.

Pacific Surfliner

BEST PICNIC SPOT
Northwest Corner

Once a communal space for soldiers and their families, the Northwest Corner between the Cañedo Adobe (visitor center) and the defense wall offers picnic tables in a quiet grassy space under citrus trees.

GETTING THERE

CAR

El Presidio de Santa Barbara State Historic Park is located in the town of Santa Barbara in the Central Coast along US-101.

TRAIN

Santa Barbara is a stop on the Amtrak train line, the Pacific Surfliner (www.pacificsurfliner.com). The train lets out at the Amtrak Station (Santa Barbara, 209 State St.), 1 mi (1.6 km) south of the historic park, approximately a 20-minute walk, mostly along popular State Street lined with restaurants, bars, and shops.

Providence Mountains State Recreation Area

SOUTHERN CALIFORNIA

Southern California is known for its endless sunshine and gleaming sandy shoreline, doing its part to support the official state nickname, the "Golden State."

Unlike the fishing piers of Central California, the piers here host amusement parks and surf competitions. Paved beach trails entice visitors to bike along miles of sand and waves, and the vibe is carefree. The coast has a wilder side as well. Find wind-twisted Torrey pines, eroded bluffs, and secluded coves punctuated with rocky tide pools.

There are pockets of history along the coast, preserved in dreamy beach cottages from the 1930s and historic adobes from the early 1800s before California was a state, with cultural sites representing Southern California's Kumeyaay, Spanish, Mexican, and early American heritage.

Going inland, the landscape gets wilder still: Granite snow-capped peaks and forested wilderness push up against stark deserts with hidden oases, rugged canyons, volcanic turrets, and badlands. In spring, the desert comes alive with wildflowers and the state's signature California poppy, aka golden poppy or California sunlight, more California gold.

For all of Southern California that is developed, there is much that is preserved and even remote.

BEST SOUTHERN CALIFORNIA STATE PARKS

PARK NAME	LANDSCAPE	DAY-USE ENTRANCE FEE
Red Rock Canyon State Park	Desert	$6
Antelope Valley California Poppy Reserve	Desert	$10
Saddleback Butte State Park	Desert	$6
Providence Mountains State Recreation Area	Desert	$10
Point Mugu State Point	Coast	$12
Leo Carrillo State Park	Coast	$12
Santa Monica State Beach	Coast	free
Huntington State Beach	Coast	$15/$20
Crystal Cove State Park	Coast	$15/$20
San Clemente State Beach	Coast	$10
South Carlsbad State Beach	Coast	free
Torrey Pines State Beach and Natural Reserve	Coast	$12–25
Old Town San Diego State Historic Park	Historic site	free
Mount San Jacinto State Park	Mountain	free
Cuyamaca Rancho State Park	Forest	$10
Anza-Borrego Desert State Park	Desert	$10
Picacho State Recreation Area	Desert	$10

CAMPING OPTIONS	SUGGESTED VISIT LENGTH	PAGE
1 campground	half day	page 368
none	half day	page 378
1 campground	half day	page 385
1 campground	half day	page 393
2 campgrounds	1 day	page 403
1 campground	1 day	page 412
none	1 day	page 420
none	1 day	page 428
1 campground	1 day	page 436
1 campground	1 day	page 447
1 campground	1 day	page 455
none	half day	page 462
none	half day	page 470
2 campgrounds, 4 wilderness campgrounds	1 day	page 479
3 campgrounds	1 day	page 490
12 campgrounds, dispersed sites	2–3 days	page 500
2 campgrounds, backcountry campgrounds, boat-in camps	2–3 days	page 514

BEST SOUTHERN CALIFORNIA STATE PARKS
Red Rock Canyon SP
Bakersfield
Mojave
Antelope Valley California Poppy Reserve (SNR)
Mojave National Preserve
Providence Mountains SRA
Barstow
Needles
Saddleback Butte SP
Victorville
Santa Barbara
Ventura
Point Mugu SP
Oxnard
Malibu
Los Angeles
San Bernardino
Mount San Jacinto SP
Joshua Tree National Park
Leo Carrillo SP
Channel Islands National Park
Santa Monica SB
Huntington Beach
Palm Springs
Blythe
Irvine
Huntington SB
San Clemente SB
PACIFIC OCEAN
Crystal Cove SP
Borrego Springs
Salton Sea
ARIZONA
Oceanside
South Carlsbad SB
Escondido
Anza-Borrego Desert SP
Picacho SRA
Carlsbad
Encinitas
Solana Beach
Ramona
Torrey Pines SB and SNR
El Centro
San Diego
Cuyamaca Rancho SP
Calexico
Old Town San Diego SHP
Chula Vista
MEXICO
0
30 mi
0
30 km

SOUTHERN CALIFORNIA STATE PARKS 3 WAYS

TRAIN-HOPPING ALONG THE COAST

Skip Southern California's notorious traffic to hop onboard Amtrak's **Pacific Surfliner,** which hugs California's coastline. Explore a series of dynamic coastal towns, take in California history, and enjoy some beach time in this three-day adventure that spans 217 mi (349 km) and highlights several gems in the state park system.

Day 1

Begin your journey in Santa Barbara to visit **El Presidio de Santa Barbara State Historic Park's** former Spanish military fortress set in the vibrant Presidio neighborhood with shops, restaurants, and wineries. Explore the historic structures and have lunch at one of the state park's preserved venues. Santa Barbara is technically located in the Central Coast, but the train easily connects these coastal destinations. Your next stop will be **San Clemente State Beach** (5 hours 15 minutes), where you will arrive in time to check into your fully equipped vintage trailer and enjoy a bluff-top sunset over the Pacific.

Day 2

Today is a beach day. Spend the day relaxing on the sand beneath San Clemente Beach's scenic bluffs. Walk the San Clemente Beach Trail, which connects a series of beaches and offers views of the Pacific the whole way. Take advantage of your trailer's amenities, which include boogie boards for the beach, outdoor games, and a central fire pit.

Day 3

Back on the train, continue south to **Old Town San Diego State Historic Park** (1.5 hours). Take in the core of restored and original buildings around Plaza de las Almas, shop at the Fiesta de Reyes marketplace, and enjoy delicious dining at one of the Mexican restaurants.

SOUTHERN CALIFORNIA DESERT ESCAPE

Travel from forest to desert to appreciate California's wildly diverse landscape. Along a 229-mi (369-km) road trip, travelers can camp and hike in a series of state parks with natural features ranging from granite peaks to Joshua trees to red rock cliffs.

Day 1

Your desert journey begins with the forested mountains of **Mount San Jacinto State Park.** From the desert floor on the edge of Palm Springs, the Palm Springs Aerial Tramway provides a literal desert escape as it lifts visitors nearly 6,000 ft (1,829 m) from the desert floor to the forested slopes of the San Jacinto Mountains. Enjoy the cool air and pine forest with a hike to Round Valley, or opt for the shorter Desert View Trail to look out over the stark landscape below. Finish with lunch and views at Mountain Station. Lodging tonight is in the town of Idyllwild, just over a one-hour drive south (49 mi/78 km) via CA-243. Check into your inn or cabin or set up your tent at the Idyllwild Campground. Dinner is in the charming town center, walking distance from the campground and lodging.

Day 2

Your travels today will take you into the ancient landscape of the Mojave Desert. Head two hours (113 mi/182 km) north via I-10 and CA-138 to **Saddleback Butte State Park.** Enjoy the Joshua trees and tackle the hike to the park's signature formation via the Saddleback Butte Peak Trail. After lunch in the park's picnic area, drive one hour to **Red Rock Canyon State Park** (68 mi/109 km), your destination for the next two nights. If the spring wildflowers are blooming, consider a detour to the **Antelope Valley California Poppy Reserve** (38 mi/61 km, 45 minutes) to wander the trails and enjoy the colorful hills.

At Red Rock Canyon's Ricardo Campground, set up camp under the red cliffs.

Day 3

Spend the day exploring Red Rock Canyon State Park through a series of short hikes and a 4WD. The Hagen Canyon Nature Trail is a must-do for the spectacular cliffs and hidden formations of Hagen Canyon. Your next short hike, the Red Cliffs Trail, gives a perspective on the soaring Red Cliffs and a peek into Iron Canyon, the location of your off-roading adventure. The highlight of this mostly mellow drive is the Scenic Cliffs, striated and turreted folds located in the quiet corner of the canyon. When you return to camp, if you're still up for more, cap off your day with a hike along the Desert View Nature Trail. Enjoy the sunset as it sweeps across the desert, ending the last night of your desert escape.

Day 1

Day 2

Day 3

EXPLORING SAN DIEGO'S BACKCOUNTRY

Take in the wild, green spaces in San Diego's backyard. The region boasts a dramatic coastline, rare pine forest, oak and conifer woodland, meadows, desert canyons, hidden oases, and craggy mountains. Explore three state parks, including California's largest, in this 122-mi (196-km) adventure.

Day 1

Torrey Pines State Natural Reserve protects spectacular carved sandstone cliffs dotted with cacti and coastal sage scrub, as well as the rare Torrey pine. Delve into this landscape with a hike along the Broken Hill Trail, which also gives you a hiking route to the beach below. From here, get ready for a geographic shift as you head toward **Anza-Borrego Desert State Park** (78 mi/125 km, 1 hour 45 minutes). There are a few routes into the park, but entering via the Montezuma Valley Road gives spectacular views over the Borrego Valley. Set up camp at Borrego Palm Canyon Campground just north of Borrego Springs or stay in one of the town's lovely lodging options. End the day with sunset over Fonts Point, admiring the light over the Borrego Badlands.

Day 2

As the largest state park in California, Anza-Borrego deserves a full day, and you have lots of options for adventure. Begin the day with a hike to nearby Borrego Palm Canyon, exploring deep pools and a hidden oasis in a 3-mi (5-km) out-and-back hike. From here, pack a picnic lunch and head south along County Roads S-3 and S-2 to take in any number of hikes and sites; options include a stop at the Cactus Loop Trail, Carrizo Badlands Overlook, and a short hike to explore the ancient Kumeyaay village site at Little Blair Valley. If you have time, add in a soak at the Agua Caliente Hot Springs. Spend the evening stargazing in this International Dark Sky Park.

Day 3

Drive a little over one hour to **Cuyamaca Rancho State Park** (44 mi/71 km) and get the lay of the land with a hike to Stonewall Peak. The granite peak gives a bird's-eye view of the forest, meadow, and low hills quilting the landscape, as well as Lake Cuyamaca to the north. Trailhead parking is located at Paso Picacho Campground, so you're positioned to check into your campsite or nature cabin. After setting up, take an outing to Green Valley Falls before a peaceful evening under the campground's pine and oak canopy. The next morning, it's a 45-minute (43-mi/69-km) drive back to San Diego.

Borrego Palm Canyon

RED ROCK CANYON STATE PARK

ADDRESS: 37749 Abbot Dr., Cantil

PHONE: 661/946-6092

DAY USE HOURS: Sunrise-sunset

AREA: 25,325 acres (10,249 ha)

Red Rock Canyon features dramatic sandstone cliffs, an unexpected crop of rock formations that pops up along the creosote-filled expanse of the northern Mojave Desert. The formations create a scenic drive through the area, and indeed many people breeze through on their way to skiing, camping, and fishing in the Eastern Sierra region to the north. But a stop reveals a place that is a destination in its own right with a campground set against cliffs, a series of nature trails, and miles of backcountry drives.

Just as the park's colorful formations serve as a landmark for vacationing families, they were a marker on the Native American trade route for thousands of years, a beacon for Death Valley expeditions in the 1850s, and a welcome stop for 20-mule-team freight wagons in the 1870s.

This area is situated between the southernmost tip of the Sierra Nevada and the El Paso Mountains and was once home to the Kawaiisu people. There are petroglyphs and pictographs in the El Paso and neighboring mountains.

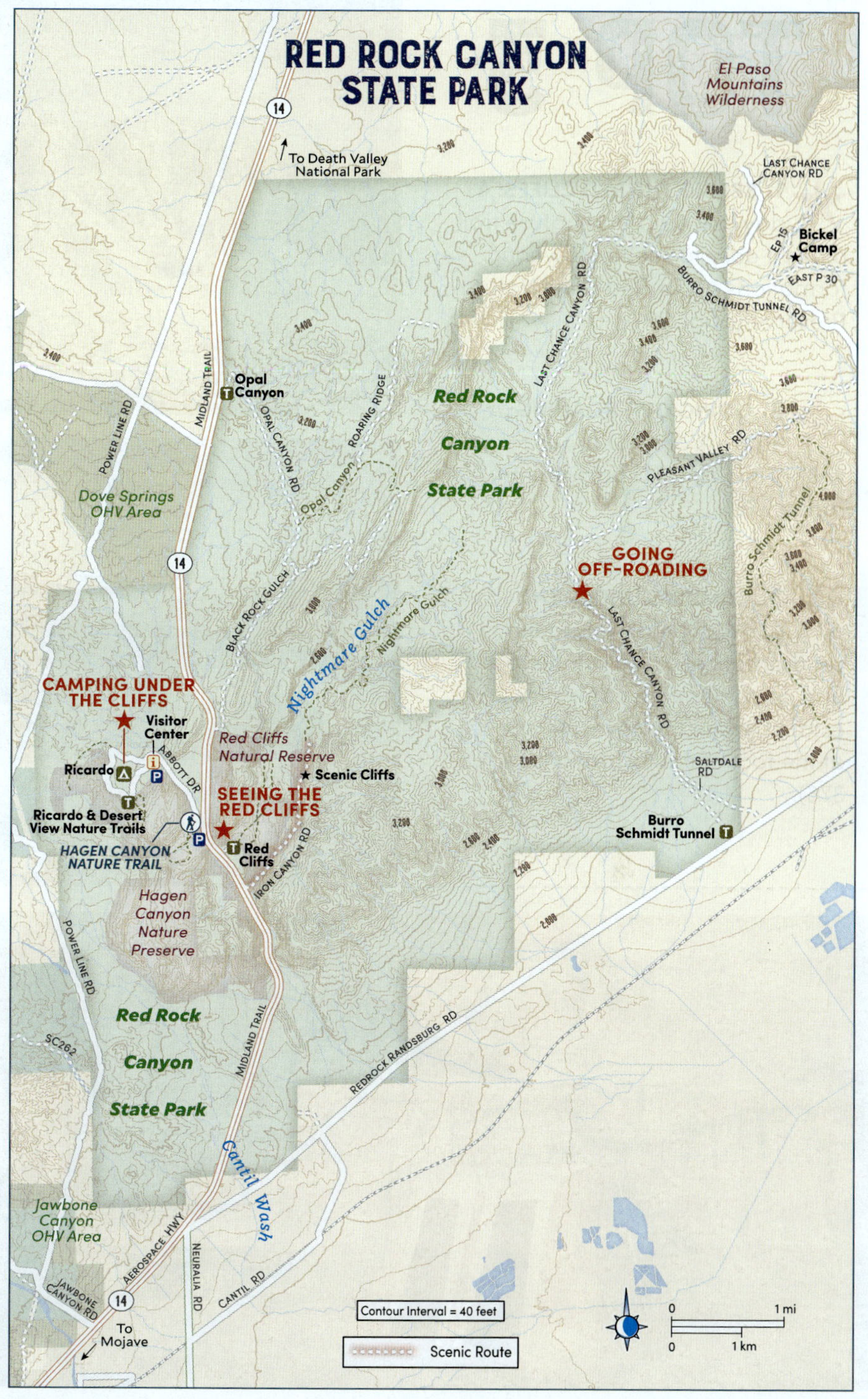
RED ROCK CANYON STATE PARK
El Paso Mountains Wilderness
To Death Valley National Park
LAST CHANCE CANYON RD
Bickel Camp
EP 15
EAST P 30
BURRO SCHMIDT TUNNEL RD
LAST CHANCE CANYON RD
Red Rock Canyon State Park
Opal Canyon
MIDLAND TRAIL
OPAL CANYON RD
ROARING RIDGE
Opal Canyon
POWER LINE RD
Dove Springs OHV Area
PLEASANT VALLEY RD
Burro Schmidt Tunnel
GOING OFF-ROADING
BLACK ROCK GULCH
Nightmare Gulch
Nightmare Gulch
CAMPING UNDER THE CLIFFS
Visitor Center
ABBOTT DR
Red Cliffs Natural Reserve
Scenic Cliffs
Ricardo
SEEING THE RED CLIFFS
Ricardo & Desert View Nature Trails
HAGEN CANYON NATURE TRAIL
Red Cliffs
IRON CANYON RD
SALTDALE RD
Burro Schmidt Tunnel
Hagen Canyon Nature Preserve
POWER LINE RD
Red Rock Canyon State Park
SC262
MIDLAND TRAIL
REDROCK RANDSBURG RD
Cantil Wash
Jawbone Canyon OHV Area
AEROSPACE HWY
NEURALIA RD
CANTIL RD
JAWBONE CANYON RD
To Mojave
Contour Interval = 40 feet
Scenic Route
0 1 mi
0 1 km

TOP 3

★ **1. SEEING THE RED CLIFFS:** A day use area and nature trail make it easy to see the towering formations of the Red Cliffs Natural Preserve (page 371).

★ **2. GOING OFF-ROADING:** A network of 4WD roads takes visitors into rugged backcountry (page 375).

★ **3. CAMPING UNDER THE CLIFFS:** The campground is set dramatically against the red and gold cliffs with campsites established in the cove-like spaces at the foot of the formations (page 376).

1

2

3

PLANNING YOUR TIME

Spend half a day to see the rock formations and hike one or two nature trails. The park also makes a good destination for a weekend of camping when you can add in a backcountry drive.

Nearby state parks include Antelope Valley California Poppy Reserve (61 mi/98 km) and Saddleback Butte State Park (72 mi/116 km).

ENTRANCE AND FEES

The Red Rock Canyon Visitor Center serves as the **official park entrance** where you can pay day use and camping fees. It is located off the Abbot Road turnoff from CA-14 near the Ricardo Campground. If the visitor center is closed, self-registration is at a kiosk at the entrance to the visitor center and day use parking. There is also a self-pay kiosk at the Red Cliffs day use parking lot. Day use is $6 per vehicle per day and is good from sunrise to sunset.

VISITOR CENTER

Red Rock Canyon Visitor Center

37749 Abbot Dr., Cantil; 9:30am-4:30pm Thurs., 9am-5pm Fri.-Sun.

The Red Rock Canyon Visitor Center offers exhibits on the natural and cultural history of the area, and a small gift shop with firewood, books, and maps.

WEATHER

The park is situated in the northern Mojave Desert at an elevation of 2,600 ft (792 m). The best months to visit are October-April for moderate temperatures with daytime highs around 75-85°F (24-29°C) and the possibility of spring wildflowers. Summer can bring extreme heat with highs approaching 100°F (38°C), and winter can bring cold and rain with daytime highs around 55-65°F (13-18°C). Prepare for temperature shifts of 30-40 degrees between day and night.

SIGHTS

★ RED CLIFFS NATURAL PRESERVE

CA-14 across from turnoff to visitor center and Ricardo Campground

It may seem that most of the cliffs in the park are red, but the pointedly named Red Cliffs refers to a specific set of hued cliffs in the Red Cliffs Natural Preserve. The sandstone formations are located just off CA-14. From a day use area, visitors can admire the cliffs, picnic, and also take a 1-mi (1.6-km) nature trail loop.

HAGEN CANYON NATURE PRESERVE

CA-14 and entrance road to visitor center and Ricardo Campground

Hagen Canyon marked the beginning of Red Rock Canyon State Park as a tourism destination, and the elaborate stands of ochre sandstone are still a draw. The preserve

ONE DAY IN RED ROCK CANYON

Spend a day basking in Red Rock Canyon's gorgeous scenery through a series of sights and short hikes.

MORNING

Start the day by checking in at the **Red Rock Canyon Visitor Center,** then hike **Hagen Canyon.**

AFTERNOON

Picnic at the base of the spectacular **Red Cliffs,** then walk the **Red Cliffs Trail.**

EVENING

Set up camp, then settle in for dinner and stargazing from your campsite at **Ricardo Campground.**

is located directly along CA-14 at the entrance road to the visitor center and campground. Park at the day use area to admire the rocks or delve into them along a 1.2-mi (1.9-km) nature trail.

SCENIC CLIFFS

Red Cliffs Trail or Iron Canyon Rd. northern entrance

Located just east of the Red Cliffs is yet another spectacular stand of colorful, sandstone formations, the pragmatically named Scenic Cliffs. The cliffs can be appreciated as a sight, hike, or drive. They can be viewed from the ridgeline of the Red Cliffs Trail and can be reached via a sandy hiking track that spurs off of the Red Cliffs Trail. To reach them by driving, take the unmarked turnoff to Iron Canyon Road on the east side of CA-14, 0.9 mi (1.4 km) north of Red Cliffs. Continue for approximately 1 mi (1.6 km) for views of the cliffs. This road has a very steep grade and 4WD is recommended. You can also park at the turnout and walk to the cliffs from here.

HIKING

With its scenic rock formations, washes, buttes, and acres of backcountry, there are plenty of possibilities for exploring the park on foot for adventurous hikers. However, there are only four developed trails in the park, short nature trails that highlight the unique landscape. Wear sturdy shoes, and always bring water even for hiking short distances.

RICARDO TRAIL

DISTANCE: 0.6 mi (0.9 km) round-trip
DURATION: 20 minutes
EFFORT: Easy
TRAILHEAD: Visitor center parking lot

This short 0.6-mi (0.9-km) loop hike is a good introduction to the desert landscape. It begins at the visitor center, makes a gentle loop, and

TOP HIKE

HAGEN CANYON NATURE TRAIL

DISTANCE: 1.2 mi (1.9 km) round-trip
DURATION: 1.5 hours
EFFORT: Moderate
TRAILHEAD: Parking area located at turnoff to Ricardo Campground and visitor center

Get up close to the spectacular eroded cliffs of Hagen Canyon via a short loop through the Hagen Canyon Nature Preserve. Beginning at the small parking area, a trail strikes into a wide canyon, revealing more strikingly sculpted sandstone formations. The canyon was named after Rudolph Hagen, who acquired the land by buying mining claims but actually made a living by operating the area as his own private park. He created maps, named some of the formations, and built a diner with a bar, lodging, and a post office where the visitor center is today.

rock formation in Hagen Canyon Nature Preserve (left); Red Cliffs Trail (right)

then returns. In spring you may see wildflowers along the desert floor; at other times, the Mojave Desert's signature creosote.

DESERT VIEW NATURE TRAIL

DISTANCE: 1 mi (1.6 km) round-trip
DURATION: 30 minutes
EFFORT: Easy
TRAILHEAD: Ricardo Campground, site 50

A short, steep climb follows a ridgeline on this 1-mi (1.6-km) out-and-back trail. From the trail's end at a viewpoint, you will have a bird's-eye view of the campground and its stunning cliffs to the north. To the south, the greater Mojave Desert unfolds with the San Gabriel Mountains in the distance.

RED CLIFFS TRAIL

DISTANCE: 0.9 mi (1.4 km) round-trip
DURATION: 30 minutes
EFFORT: Easy
TRAILHEAD: Red Cliffs Natural Preserve, across from turnoff to Ricardo Campground and visitor center

While it is possible to admire the soaring cliffs from the day use area, a 0.9-mi (1.4-km) loop hike adds different views of the spectacular wall of sandstone. From the parking area, a sandy trail climbs a ridge where you can take in the Red Cliffs from a bench at the top. The trail continues down the back of the ridge, where you can see other enticing formations in the distance. You can visit these formations, the equally practically named Scenic Cliffs, by continuing on an obvious track, adding 1.8 mi (2.9 km) to the hike for a total of 2.7 mi (4.3 km).

RECREATION

★ OFF-ROADING

A network of 4WD dirt roads crisscrosses the state park on the east side of CA-14. Sections of the roads are easy with packed dirt, but there are also patches with steep grades, sandy washes, and narrow spots. A stock SUV with all-terrain tires and high clearance will work on some roads and sections, but other roads and sections require 4x4 and experience. The official state park maps available at the visitor center or downloadable online include the road network with mileages. For a detailed description of 4WD roads in the area, Charles A. Wells and Matt Peterson's *Guide to California Backroads & 4-Wheel-Drive Trails* has detailed maps, descriptions, and mileage logs to a few of the trails in and around the state park.

Iron Canyon

DISTANCE: 6.4 mi (10.3 km) round-trip
DURATION: 1 hour
START AND END: CA-14 north 0.9 mi (1.4 km) north of Red Cliffs, unsigned turnout on east side of road

Iron Canyon is an easygoing dirt road that travels past the Scenic Cliffs, gorgeous sandstone formations hidden from the highway in the Red Cliffs area of the park. The road has a few points where 4WD is recommended, including a steep grade close to the start of the trail. The road is technically a loop intersecting with CA-14 at its northern and southern points; however, a washout blocked out its southern access to CA-14, making it an out-and-back until the road is repaired.

Opal Canyon

DISTANCE: 5.7 mi (9.2 km) one-way
DURATION: 1.5-2 hours
START: CA-14 north mile marker 4'4 across from entrance to Dove Springs OHV Area
END: Cudahy Camp

Opal Canyon begins off of CA-14 about 3.5 mi (5.6 km) north of the entrance to Red Rock Canyon's Ricardo Campground. It starts as a relatively easy desert route with some sand in the washes. At the 4-mi (6-km) point, the trail crests a hill and descends 600 ft (183 m) past multicolored bluffs to the bottom of Last Chance Canyon, where there are the scant remains of Cudahy Camp, an old mining camp that served opal mines in the area.

Last Chance Canyon

DISTANCE: 19.3 mi (31 km) round-trip
DURATION: 4 hours
START: Redrock-Randsburg Road 6 mi (10 km) northeast of intersection with CA-14
END: Redrock-Randsburg Road approximately 3 mi (5 km) east of starting point

This pavement-to-pavement loop starts at the southern boundary of the park to follow Last Chance Canyon, a scenic route with a few challenges including a narrow V-slot, steep grades, and rocky sections. Highlights include the colorful rock formations near Cudahy Camp and historic sites that lie to the east of Last Chance Canyon just across the park boundary on BLM land. **Bickel Camp** is a 1930s-era mining camp with the original cabins and lots of artifacts. The **Burro Schmidt Tunnel** is a tunnel to nowhere dug through the side of a mountain by one man over the course of 30 years.

For an easier route, both sites can be reached via EP15, north of the park. The route travels BLM land, dipping only briefly into the park. The road surface is easier, but it is easy to get lost. Carry a map and directions.

CAMPING

The park has **one developed campground** with first-come, first-served sites. There is no dispersed camping in the state park. Campers should register at the visitor center when it is open. When it is closed, campers can self-register at a kiosk at the entrance to the visitor center and parking area. Self-registration is payable by cash or check only. Sites are typically easy to come by, but they can fill by Thursday night or Friday morning in spring and fall or on holiday weekends.

BEST CAMPGROUND

★ Ricardo Campground

Abbott Dr., CA-14; $25/night with one vehicle, $6 additional vehicle

Campsites at Ricardo Campground are tucked under soaring sandstone cliffs, creating a dramatic backdrop for your tent or RV. Kids will love exploring the mini slot canyons and hollows around the base of the cliffs. There are 50 sites available for tent or RV camping. There are no hookups. Each campsite has a fire ring and picnic table. The campground has potable water and pit toilets.

Ricardo Campground RV site

BEST NEARBY

DEATH VALLEY NATIONAL PARK

Death Valley National Park (www.nps.gov/deva; $30/vehicle) offers a dramatic desert landscape 100 mi (161 km) north. Some of the highlights include the expansive salt flats of Badwater Basin, the lowest point in the Western Hemisphere at 282 ft (86 m) below sea level; the Racetrack, a remote dry lakebed where rocks skate across the surface leaving trails; and the Eureka Dunes, the tallest dunes in California. From Red Rock Canyon, head north on CA-14 north, then take US-395 for 70 mi (113 km) to the town of Olancha. Turn right onto CA-190 east and continue for 33 mi (53 km) to the western park boundary. Panamint Springs, another 13 mi (21 km) on CA-190 east, has the closest services.

FOOD AND LODGING

There are no services within the park. The closest services are located 27 mi (43 km) south along CA-14 in the small town of **Mojave,** about a 25-minute drive. The town functions as a basic highway stop and has gas, firewood, fast food, a grocery store, and a few budget motels.

BEST PICNIC SPOT

Red Cliffs Day Use Area

Tables positioned in the day use area give great views of the formations, making it a scenic spot for a picnic and also a convenient stop off the highway if you're just passing through.

GETTING THERE

CAR

Red Rock Canyon is located in the northern Mojave Desert off of CA-14, 27 mi (43 km) north of the small town of Mojave and 26 mi (42 km) south of the intersection with US-395, the major highway along the eastern side of the Sierra Nevada. It is located 80 mi (129 km) east of Bakersfield via CA-58 east and CA-14 north.

ANTELOPE VALLEY CALIFORNIA POPPY RESERVE

ADDRESS: 150th St. W. and Lancaster Rd.

PHONE: 661/724-1180

DAY USE HOURS: Sunrise-sunset

AREA: 1,781 acres (721 ha)

Nearly every spring the arid hills of the western Mojave Desert come alive with orange California poppies, the state flower. These gentle rolling hills of the Antelope Valley harbor some of the most consistent blooms in the state. The Mojave Desert grassland habitat is typically austere; golden brown hills undulate across windswept desert, giving way to a series of buttes and the Tehachapi Mountains. It is a good place to hike and take in the quiet pulse of the desert. Burrows shelter mice, kangaroo rats, gophers, and lizards, while hawks circle the wide sky. When conditions are right, the flowers burst upward and people flock to the area for a glimpse of the wondrous sight. Poppies are mixed with other wildflowers, and the landscape becomes a mosaic of shifting color. It is impossible to predict peak wildflower density—only in retrospect is it detected, when there are fewer flowers than the week before. The hills fade, and we wait for another bloom, made all the more special by its fleeting nature.

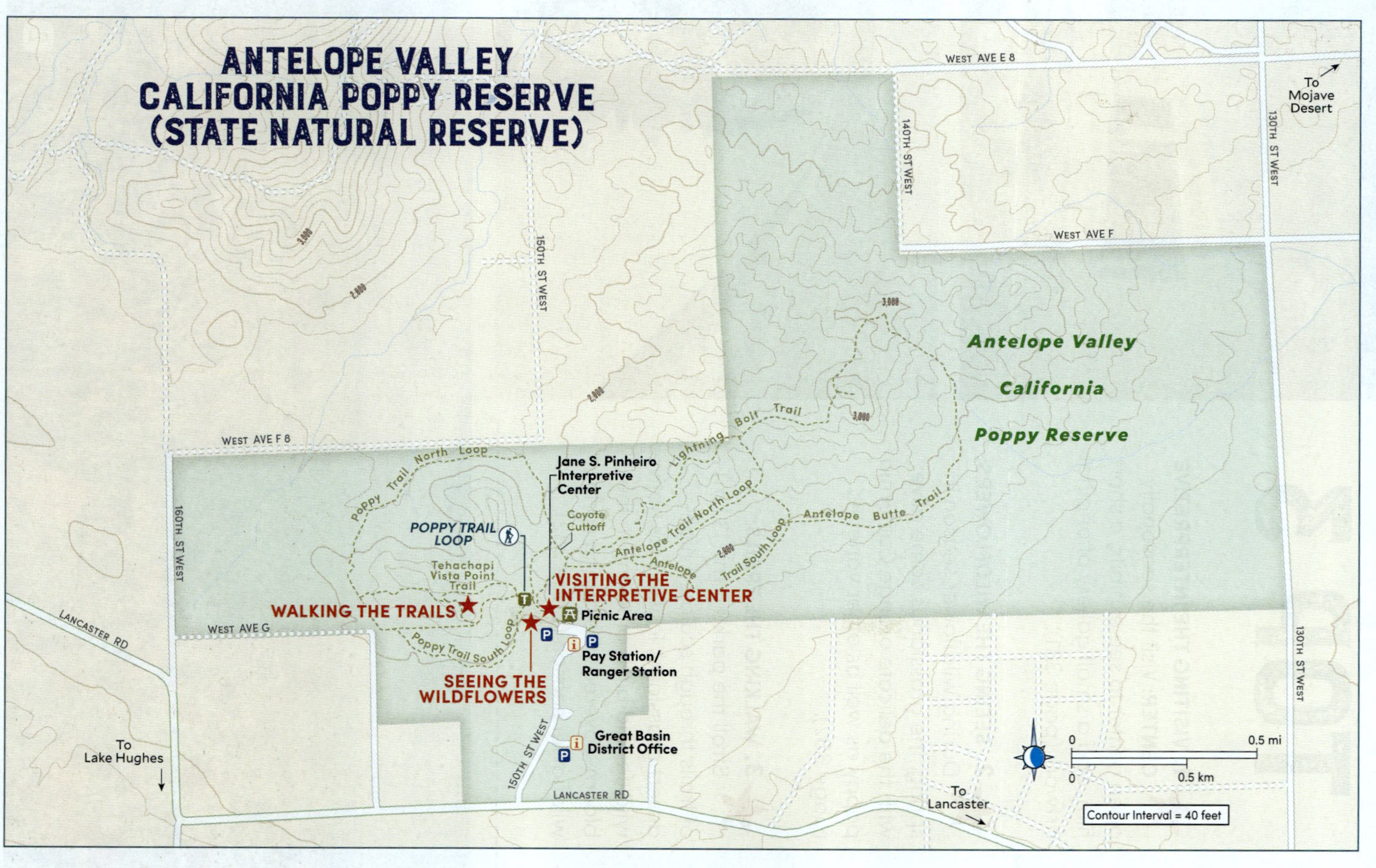
ANTELOPE VALLEY
CALIFORNIA POPPY RESERVE
(STATE NATURAL RESERVE)
Antelope Valley
California
Poppy Reserve
West Ave E 8
West Ave F
West Ave F 8
West Ave G
130th St West
140th St West
150th St West
160th St West
Lancaster Rd
To Mojave Desert
To Lake Hughes
To Lancaster
Lightning Bolt Trail
Antelope Butte Trail
Antelope Trail North Loop
Antelope Trail South Loop
Poppy Trail North Loop
Poppy Trail South Loop
Coyote Cuttoff
Tehachapi Vista Point Trail
POPPY TRAIL LOOP
Jane S. Pinheiro Interpretive Center
VISITING THE INTERPRETIVE CENTER
WALKING THE TRAILS
SEEING THE WILDFLOWERS
Picnic Area
Pay Station/ Ranger Station
Great Basin District Office
3,000
2,800
0
0.5 mi
0.5 km
Contour Interval = 40 feet

TOP 3

★ **1. VISITING THE INTERPRETIVE CENTER:** Visit the seasonally open center to see exhibits, a short film, and a small gallery of original artwork (page 381).

★ **2. SEEING THE WILDFLOWERS:** During wildflower season in spring, the grasslands come alive with the delicate orange California poppy as well as other varieties (page 382).

★ **3. WALKING THE TRAILS:** Stroll the park's 8 mi (13 km) of trails through sculpted high-desert grassland, looking for native wildlife and birds or taking in the bloom-covered hills during spring wildflower season (page 382).

PLANNING YOUR TIME

The poppy reserve takes just a few hours to visit including a hike and stopping by the visitor center. The window for wildflower blooms is spring from **mid-February to May,** with peak blooms typically occurring in late March or early April. For safety, park along the road and walk in via the entrance gate, or park in the official parking lot. Do not stop in the middle of the road. To preserve the landscape, stay on official trails. Do not trample or pick flowers.

Nearby state parks include Saddleback Butte State Park (36 mi/58 km) and Red Rock Canyon State Park (61 mi/98 km).

ENTRANCE AND FEES

Enter the park on 150th Street West off of Lancaster Avenue through the **official entrance kiosk** and pay station ($10/vehicle). If it is closed, there is an electronic pay station in the parking lot. It is also possible to park along Lancaster Road and enter along a footpath that parallels the entrance road.

Fee usage is rigorously patrolled in this area; make sure you pay fees and have the proper pass displayed. Fees are only required for parking and are not required if you walk in.

VISITOR CENTER

★ Jane S. Pinheiro Interpretive Center

10am-4pm Mon.-Fri., 9am-5pm Sat.-Sun. Mar. 1-Mother's Day

The Jane S. Pinheiro Interpretive Center serves as the park's visitor center and offers interpretive exhibits, a junior ranger program, and a gift shop. It is located 0.5 mi (0.8 km) north of the intersection of 150th Street West and Lancaster Road, a short, paved walk from the main parking area. The park is open all year, but the interpretive center is only open during wildflower season.

The Jane S. Pinheiro Interpretive Center is named after the self-taught artist and botanist who worked to conserve natural spaces in the Antelope Valley. It features a small gallery of her original artwork featuring high desert plants and flowers, interpretive exhibits for the reserve, and a gift shop. Jane S. Pinheiro moved to the rural Antelope Valley desert north of Los Angeles in 1940 and became passionate about preserving its landscape. Her efforts resulted in the poppy reserve being established in 1976. She also worked to establish nearby Saddleback Butte State Park in order to protect Joshua trees.

WEATHER

Staff at the interpretive center don't say the "W" word, as they jokingly call the wind, afraid that they will stir up the airy gusts. While temperatures may be moderate (around 62-82°F/17-28°C), spring can bring on fierce winds across the exposed landscape. Check weather conditions and wear layers for unexpected weather changes. Also note that cold and wind can cause poppies to curl up.

SIGHTS

★ WILDFLOWERS

The park is open year-round but is a must-see during wildflower season when the state's signature orange flowers lace the hillsides. Combined with other wildflowers, including white cream cups, purple lupine, and yellow goldfields, the hills come alive with color and fragrance. A good wildflower year depends on well-spaced rainfall throughout the year as well as a decent dose of sunlight. Without these factors, the bloom might not happen, and the hills stay quiet.

In wildflower years, the bloom begins as early as mid-February and can last through May, with the **peak bloom** in **late March or early April.** To keep tabs on the scene and plan your visit, check out the park's live **PoppyCam** (www.parks.ca.gov/PoppyReserve) or call the Poppy Reserve Wildflower hotline at 661/724-1180.

HIKING

The park has 8 mi (13 km) of hiking trails, which carve elegant loops through its 1,781 acres (721 ha) of rolling hills. During wildflower blooms, hiking can be an ethereal (if crowded) experience, as you stroll through carpets of orange. During non-bloom years and other times of the year, the hiking experience can be more meditative as you walk the quiet grasslands in the company of lizards and birds.

Pick up a trail map in the visitor center or download one from the park website and choose a specific loop or just start wandering the hills. All trails connect and lead back to a central hub near the visitor center.

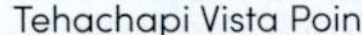

Tehachapi Vista Point

TEHACHAPI VISTA POINT TRAIL

DISTANCE: 0.6 mi (1 km) round-trip
DURATION: 20 minutes
EFFORT: Easy
TRAILHEAD: Visitor center

A 0.6-mi (1-km) accessible trail leads to the Tehachapi Vista Point in 0.3 mi (0.5 km) before bending back. There is a bench at the top for admiring views of the Tehachapi Mountains. The trail is concrete and boardwalk with a maximum 7 percent slope.

ANTELOPE TRAIL LOOP

DISTANCE: 1.5 mi (2.4 km) round-trip
DURATION: 30 minutes

TOP HIKE
POPPY TRAIL LOOP

DISTANCE: 2.2 mi (3.5 km) round-trip
DURATION: 30-45 minutes
EFFORT: Easy
TRAILHEAD: Visitor center

This 2.2-mi (3.5-km) loop begins at the visitor center to follow the **Poppy Trail North Loop** and **Poppy Trail South Loop** clockwise in an easy-to-access circuit that allows hikers to experience the natural character of the park. The loop coils through two of the park's rolling hills, offering views to the Tehachapi Mountains to the north. Observing the immediate landscape, look for lizards and birds including horned larks, white-crowned sparrows, and hawks. During a wildflower bloom, the poppies will of course be the star of the show.

EFFORT: Easy
TRAILHEAD: Visitor center

A 1.5-mi (2.4-km) loop combines the Antelope Trail North Loop and Antelope Trail South Loop to explore the hills northeast of the visitor center. The hike offers a pleasant walk through rolling hills and desert grasslands tinged with orange poppies during spring bloom.

ANTELOPE BUTTE TRAIL

DISTANCE: 3.6 mi (5.8 km) round-trip
DURATION: 1.5 hours
EFFORT: Moderate
TRAILHEAD: Visitor center

The Antelope Butte Trail adds a little more challenge and elevation gain than other trails in the reserve. This 3.6-mi (5.8-km) loop gains nearly 450 ft (137 m) of elevation, reaching a vista point that takes in scenic Antelope Butte to the north. The trail continues back to the visitor center via the Lightning Bolt Trail.

FOOD AND LODGING

The sprawling city of **Lancaster** in northern Los Angeles County is located 15 mi (24 km) east of the park. The city is best visited for utilitarian purposes and has chain hotels, a wide variety of restaurants, groceries, gas, and all of the main box stores for supplies. There is **no camping** at the Antelope Valley California Poppy Reserve.

The small mountain community of **Lake Hughes** is located 10 mi (16 km) south of the reserve, with one historic restaurant and a country store.

BEST PICNIC SPOT

Jane S. Pinheiro Interpretive Center

To picnic at the reserve, there are shaded picnic tables located near the visitor center with a view across the valley to the San Gabriel Mountains.

GETTING THERE

CAR

The Antelope Valley California Poppy Reserve is located 90 mi (145 km) north of downtown Los Angeles in the Antelope Valley of the western Mojave Desert in Southern California. The closest town is Lancaster, located 15 mi (24 km) to the east.

From CA-14, take the Avenue I exit and head west 15 mi (24 km) until Avenue I becomes Lancaster Road. From I-5, take CA-138 east and turn right on 170th Street West. When the road ends after 2.5 mi (3.5 km), make a left onto Lancaster Road and continue for 2 mi (3 km) to the park entrance.

SADDLEBACK BUTTE STATE PARK

Saddleback Butte rises over low-lying alluvial desert while spiky Joshua trees and creosote bushes wave dark green leaves in the breeze that is almost always present. The small park was created to protect the butte and native Joshua tree woodlands that were prevalent here. In fact, the park was originally called Joshua Trees State Park, but the name was changed due to confusion with the popular national park 120 mi (193 km) to the southeast.

ADDRESS: 17102 E. Ave. J, Lancaster

PHONE: 661/946-6092

DAY USE HOURS: 9am-5pm

AREA: 2,954 acres (1,195 ha)

Over the past 2,000 years the Antelope Valley was home to various native groups, including the Kawaiisu in the immediate vicinity, the Kitanemuks and Serranos of the Antelope Valley to the west, and the Tataviam people of the Santa Clarita and southern Antelope Valleys. Several flowing springs and easy access from all directions made the region a major prehistoric trading crossroads.

Today the park feels under the radar, tucked into a collection of rural neighborhoods in the farthest northern reaches of Los Angeles County. It's a good place to experience the quiet beauty of this far-flung corner of the Mojave Desert.

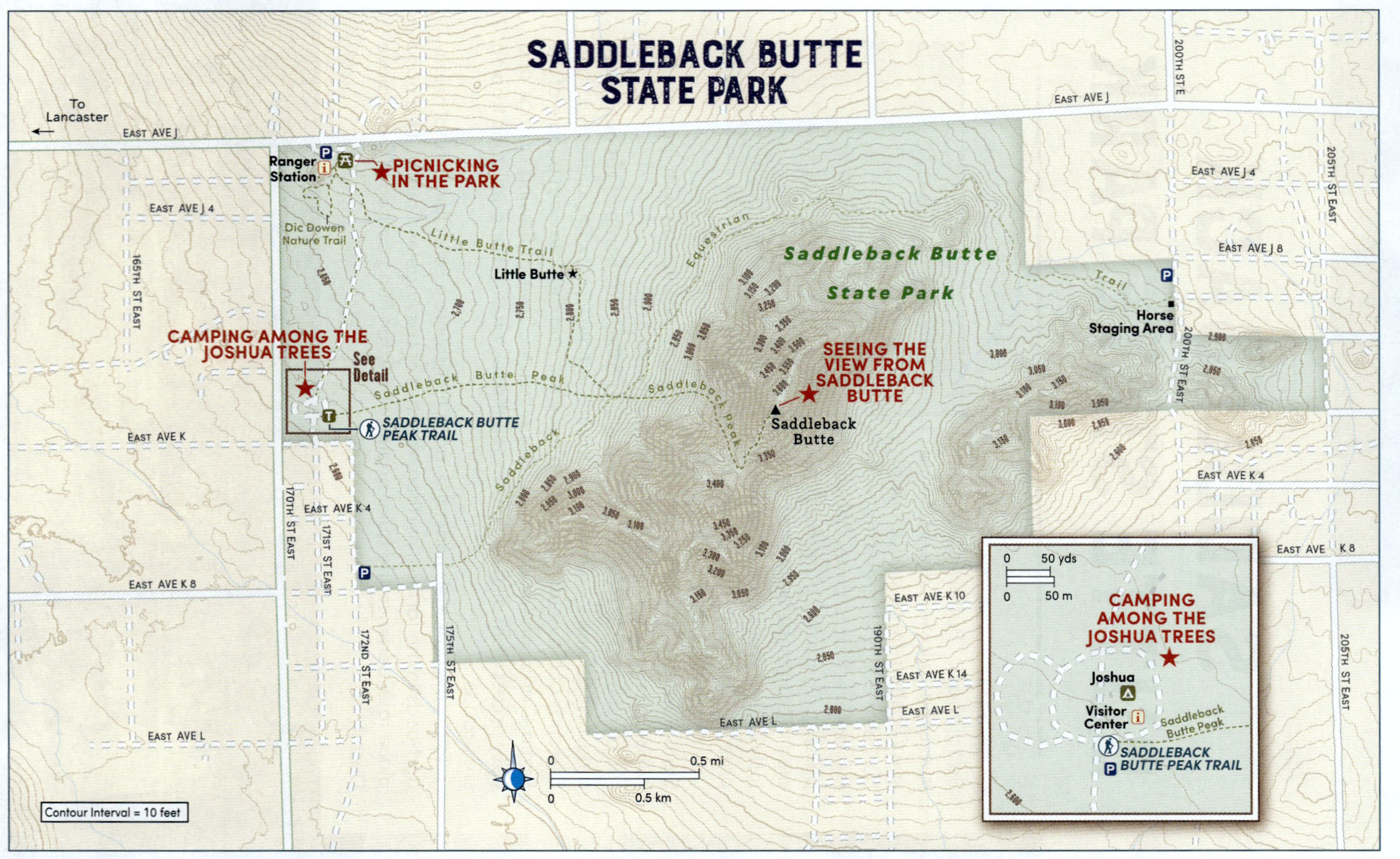
SADDLEBACK BUTTE STATE PARK
To Lancaster
Ranger Station
PICNICKING IN THE PARK
Dic Dowen Nature Trail
Little Butte Trail
Little Butte
Equestrian
Saddleback Butte State Park
Trail
Horse Staging Area
CAMPING AMONG THE JOSHUA TREES
See Detail
Saddleback Butte Peak
Saddleback Peak
Saddleback
SADDLEBACK BUTTE PEAK TRAIL
SEEING THE VIEW FROM SADDLEBACK BUTTE
Saddleback Butte
EAST AVE J
EAST AVE J 4
EAST AVE J 8
EAST AVE K
EAST AVE K 4
EAST AVE K 8
EAST AVE K 10
EAST AVE K 14
EAST AVE L
165TH ST EAST
170TH ST EAST
171ST ST EAST
172ND ST EAST
175TH ST EAST
190TH ST EAST
200TH ST E
200TH ST EAST
205TH ST EAST
0 0.5 mi
0 0.5 km
Contour Interval = 10 feet
0 50 yds
0 50 m
CAMPING AMONG THE JOSHUA TREES
Joshua
Visitor Center
Saddleback Butte Peak
SADDLEBACK BUTTE PEAK TRAIL

TOP 3

★ **1. SEEING THE VIEW FROM SADDLEBACK BUTTE:** Take in the 360-degree views of the Antelope Valley and Mojave Desert (page 388).

★ **2. CAMPING AMONG THE JOSHUA TREES:** Campsites are situated in open desert with spiky Joshua trees interspersed across the landscape (page 391).

★ **3. PICNICKING IN THE PARK:** Saddleback Butte takes its picnicking seriously, dedicating 27 picnic sites with tables, barbecue grills, and shade ramadas with views of Saddleback Butte (page 392).

PLANNING YOUR TIME

Set aside a half day to hike Saddleback Butte. Or spend a night camping at Saddleback Butte among the Joshua trees.

Nearby state parks include Antelope Valley California Poppy Reserve (36 mi/58 km) and Red Rock Canyon State Park (68 mi/109 km).

ENTRANCES AND FEES

There are **two entrances** to the park, 1 mi (1.6 km) apart off of East Avenue J. Day use visitors can access the day use area off of East Avenue J and 170th Street East. There is a self-pay kiosk ($6/vehicle) to use the picnic area and hiking trails.

For campers, there is a self-registration kiosk at the entrance to the campground (off East Avenue K and 170th Street East, Lancaster) where visitors can register and pay for campsites.

VISITOR CENTER

Saddleback Butte Visitor Center

E. Ave. J and 170th St. E.; 11am-5pm Sat.-Sun.

A visitor center in the day use area houses exhibits on the natural and cultural history of the area.

WEATHER

The best time to visit is spring, February through May, for the wildflower displays and mild temperatures with daytime highs around 68-82°F (20-28°C). Fall temperatures are similarly mild, making it a nice time to visit as well. Winter can bring frost and below-freezing temperatures. In summer, temperatures can soar to over 100°F (38°C). Nighttime lows can drop by as much as 30 degrees. For all seasons, prepare for drastic temperature swings and wind.

SIGHTS

★ SADDLEBACK BUTTE

Saddleback Butte, the namesake of the park, rises 3,651 ft (1,113 m), a dramatic feature in the low-lying alluvial desert of the Antelope Valley. A trail leads to the highest point on the ridge, offering panoramic views over the Antelope Valley to the west and Mojave Desert to the north and east. The mountains to the south are the San Gabriel Mountains, part of the Angeles National Forest. The green patch to the south is the small community of Lake Los Angeles.

JOSHUA TREES

Saddleback Butte State Park is notable for its high concentration of Joshua trees, which thrive in the southwestern US but are primarily found in the Mojave Desert between 1,300 and 5,900 ft (396 and 1,798 m) in elevation. The park was created in 1960 to protect this landscape in an area where the trees once proliferated but have dwindled due to development and environmental factors. Look for their distinctive white blooms between February and April.

WILDFLOWERS

From February to April, flowering species from the iconic California orange poppy to the purple lupine, as well as flowering cacti and Joshua trees, can fill the Joshua tree and creosote woodland. In drier years the bloom may be more modest or nearly nonexistent. To check on wildflower status, follow the park's social media or check weekly regional reports from the Theodore Payne Foundation's wildflower hotline (818/768-1802 ext. 7; https://theodorepayne.org).

HIKING

All the hikes in the parks are exposed with no shade. Wear layers and carry more water than you think you will need.

DIC DOWEN NATURE TRAIL

DISTANCE: 0.5 mi (0.8 km) round-trip
DURATION: 15 minutes
EFFORT: Easy
TRAILHEAD: Saddleback Butte Visitor Center

An accessible nature trail loops through high desert terrain, bringing visitors up close to creosote bushes, Joshua trees, and animal life, all surviving in this often harsh desert habitat. Pick up an interpretive brochure in the visitor center before starting.

LITTLE BUTTE TRAIL

DISTANCE: 5 mi (8 km) round-trip
DURATION: 2.5 hours
EFFORT: Moderate
TRAILHEAD: Saddleback Butte Visitor Center, day use area

This out-and-back trail leaves from the day use area below the visitor

Dic Dowen Nature Trail

TOP HIKE

SADDLEBACK BUTTE PEAK TRAIL

DISTANCE: 4 mi (6.4 km) round-trip
DURATION: 2 hours
EFFORT: Moderate
TRAILHEAD: Trailhead parking in campground

This trail follows a wide, sandy track through Joshua tree and creosote habitat to the base of the butte with the granite formation in sight the entire time. The grade steepens and becomes rocky as it navigates the butte, especially in the last stretch of the hike. From the peak the effort pays off with spectacular 360-degree views over the Antelope Valley and across the Mojave Desert.

center and follows a well-maintained path through open Joshua tree and creosote habitat to reach the base of the butte. It then joins the Saddleback Butte Peak Trail to ascend to the highest point along the ridge, Saddleback Butte Peak.

SADDLEBACK BUTTE LOOP

DISTANCE: 3 mi (4.8 km) round-trip
DURATION: 1.5 hours
EFFORT: Easy
TRAILHEAD: Saddleback Butte Visitor Center, day use area

To immerse in the quiet landscape in a hike that is longer than the nature trail but less rigorous than the peak hike, combine the **Little Butte Trail** and **Saddleback Butte Peak Trail** into a 3-mi (4.8-km) loop connected by the campground road.

CAMPING

The park has **one developed campground** with sites that are first-come, first-served. There is no dispersed camping available in the park. The campground is lightly used with spots typically easily available. Spring has the highest use.

BEST CAMPGROUND

★ Saddleback Butte State Park Campground

Saddleback Butte offers 37 sites ($20/night, includes one vehicle and one towed trailer, $5 additional vehicle) in open desert at the broad base of the granite butte. Sites on the eastern side of the campground loop are recommended because of more unobstructed desert views and their location farther from the main road. The campground can become a destination during wildflower blooms, but otherwise it is used as an easy getaway from surrounding metro areas or a nice enough stop on a larger trip.

Most sites have a wood ramada with a roof and one wall to protect from sun and wind. All sites have a picnic table, barbecue grill, and fire ring. The campground offers full restrooms with flush toilets and sinks but no showers. There is potable water throughout the campground. There are no hookups for RVs, but slots are angled for ease of backing and can accommodate up to 30 ft (9 m) or longer, depending on the campsite. There is a fee-based dump station on-site ($10, credit card only). Firewood is available from the camp host ($6/bundle).

campsite

FOOD AND LODGING

The sprawling city of **Lancaster** in northern Los Angeles County is located 17 mi (27 km) west of the park via Avenue J, about a 20-minute drive. The city has a suburban feel with plenty of options for chain hotels, restaurants, and box stores interspersed with independently owned businesses.

BEST PICNIC SPOT

★ Saddleback Butte Day Use Area

The park has a dedicated day use area with 27 picnic sites with tables, barbecue grills, and shade ramadas near the visitor center, nature trail, and Little Butte trailhead.

GETTING THERE

CAR

Saddleback Butte State Park is located 90 mi (145 km) north of downtown Los Angeles in the Antelope Valley of the western Mojave Desert in Southern California. The closest town is Lancaster, located 17 mi (27 km) to the west.

The park entrance is located on 170th Street East, between East Avenue J and East Avenue K. From CA-14, which runs north-south to the west of the park, take exit 30 to CA-138 (Pearblossom Hwy.). Continue for 27 mi (43 km) to 170th Street East and turn left. The campground entrance is on the right, and the day use entrance is 1 mi (1.6 km) farther.

From I-15 to the east of the park, exit CA-138 west toward Palmdale/Silverwood Lake, and travel 26 mi (42 km). Turn right on 165th Street East. Continue as it becomes 170th Street to East Avenue K and J.

PROVIDENCE MOUNTAINS STATE RECREATION AREA

ADDRESS: 38200 Essex Rd., Essex

PHONE: 760/928-2586

DAY USE HOURS: 8am-5pm Fri.-Sun. and holiday Mon. Sept.-June

AREA: 5,890 acres (2,380 ha)

Mitchell Caverns, a set of deep limestone caves studded with an impressive array of stalagmites and stalactites, are the reason this state-protected area exists. The state park is pitched on the eastern slope of the rugged Providence Mountains, ensconced inside the spectacular 1.6-million-acre (647,500-ha) Mojave National Preserve. To reach the park, Essex Road climbs from the desert floor, making a beeline to the timberline where pinyon pines cling to the steep stone towers of the gray limestone mountains, topped with red volcanic rhyolite.

The park is tucked in the shadow of these rugged peaks on the site of what was once a native Chemehuevi seasonal camp and, later, the homestead of Jack and Ida Mitchell, who offered lodging and gave guided tours of the caves until 1954. They hand-built their home, now the picturesque visitor center, out of native rock, also constructing the three other buildings that stand in the park today and which were used for guest lodging. They made their living by charging $1 per person for cave tours. In addition to the caverns, the area is a standout for its sawtooth mountain crest, natural cactus and yucca gardens, and stellar views.

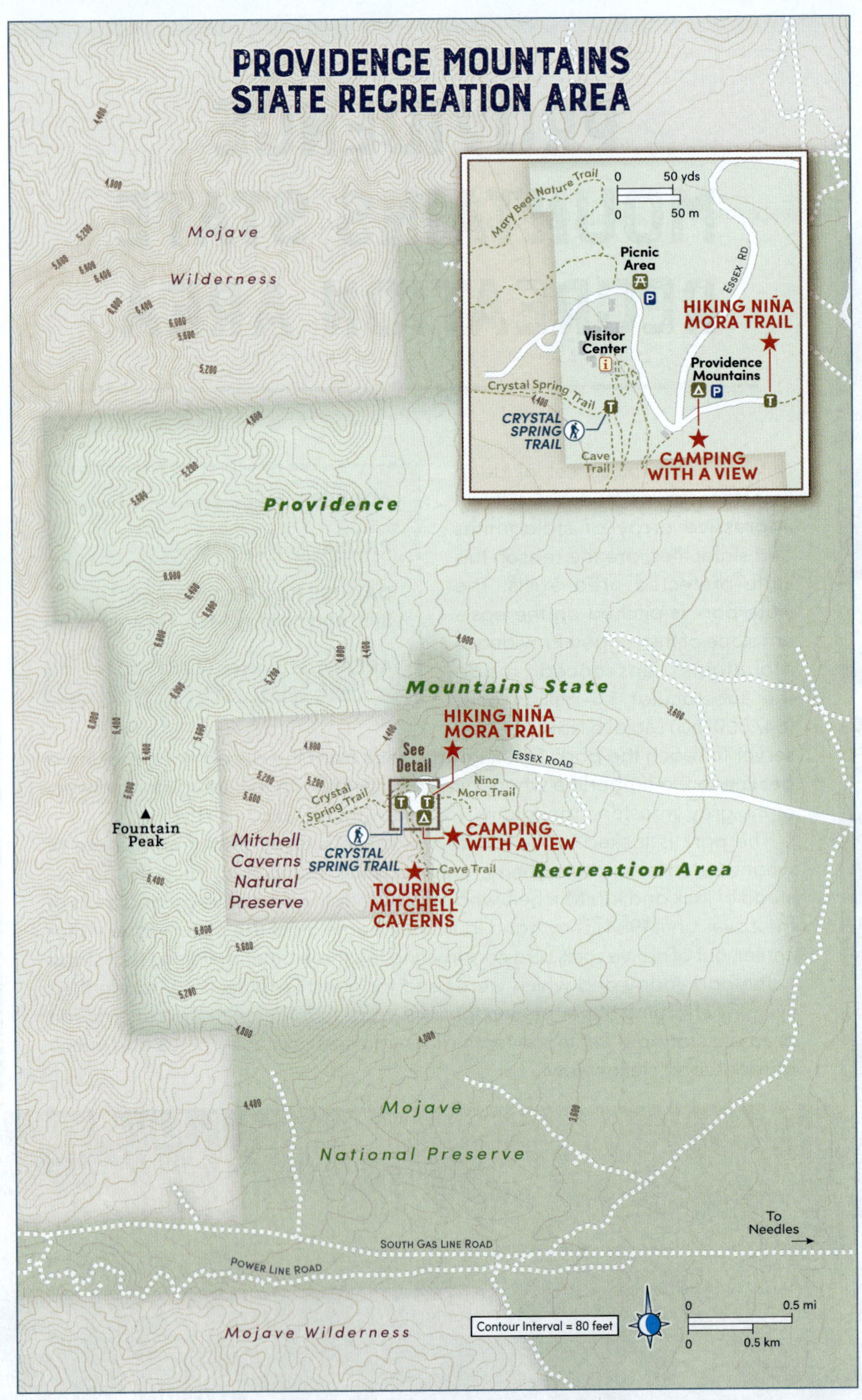

PROVIDENCE MOUNTAINS STATE RECREATION AREA
Mojave Wilderness
Providence Mountains State Recreation Area
Mary Beal Nature Trail
0 50 yds
0 50 m
Picnic Area
ESSEX RD
HIKING NIÑA MORA TRAIL
Visitor Center
Providence Mountains
Crystal Spring Trail
CRYSTAL SPRING TRAIL
Cave Trail
CAMPING WITH A VIEW
See Detail
Essex Road
Nina Mora Trail
Fountain Peak
Mitchell Caverns Natural Preserve
TOURING MITCHELL CAVERNS
Mojave National Preserve
To Needles
South Gas Line Road
Power Line Road
Contour Interval = 80 feet
0 0.5 mi
0 0.5 km

TOP 3

1. TOURING MITCHELL CAVERNS: Guided tours take visitors into the side of the Providence Mountains where a cathedral-like limestone cave is draped with stalactites and stalagmites (page 397).

2. HIKING NIÑA MORA TRAIL: A walk along the ridgeline takes in wide views of the desert valley to the east (page 398).

3. CAMPING WITH A VIEW: The campground is situated on an isolated ridge with sweeping views of the wide desert valleys, jagged mountain ranges, and volcanic mesas below (page 401).

PLANNING YOUR TIME

One day in the Providence Mountains State Recreation Area gives you enough time to tour Mitchell Caverns and do a few of the nature hikes. However, the park is remote with the closest lodging 1-2.5 hours away in the towns of Needles, Barstow, and Las Vegas. If you want to limit your drive time, take in the spectacular desert scenery, or check out more of the Mojave National Preserve, add a night or two camping on one or both ends of your caverns tour.

While the park is well-signed and easy to reach from Essex Road, the park website warns not to rely on navigational aids, particularly Google Maps. There is little to no cell service after I-40, and it is best to navigate this area with a paper map or carry directions.

Note: The park is closed for the months of July and August.

ENTRANCE AND FEES

Access to the park is via gated Essex Road. The gate is locked outside of open hours with no park access.

The visitor center serves as the **entrance station,** but you can also pay fees by scanning a barcode posted on signs near the restrooms. Day use is $10 per vehicle, and guided cavern tours including day use are $20 per person.

VISITOR CENTER

Providence Mountains Visitor Center

760/928-2586; 8am-5pm Fri.-Sun. and holiday Mon. Sept.-June

A small visitor center is housed in the rock house Jack and Ida Mitchell built by hand for their own residence. It is staffed by park rangers and has a selection of books as well as a small display of archaeological finds from the nearby caves. Visitor center hours coincide with the park's operating hours.

RESERVATIONS

Access to the caverns is only available through a **guided tour.** Make a reservation through Reserve California (800/444-7275; www.reservecalifornia.com). Tours book up quickly so it's essential to reserve ahead at least two weeks, longer for holiday weekends. If you happen to be driving in the direction of Mitchell Caverns and do not have a reservation, it's possible to check at the visitor center for last-minute availability.

WEATHER

The park is located midway up the Providence Mountains at an elevation of 4,300 ft (1,311 m). This is a desert sweet spot, offering moderately tolerable temperatures year-round compared with the blazing inferno of the valley floor. However, temperatures can be unpredictable and drop by as much as 40 degrees at night. Daytime temperatures can average 35-65°F (2-18°C) in winter and 45-85°F (7-29°C) in spring and fall. Bring layers. It can also get intensely windy—prepare to anchor your gear if camping. The park is fully **closed for the months of July and August due to heat.** October through May is the best time to visit.

ONE DAY IN PROVIDENCE MOUNTAINS STATE RECREATION AREA

To explore Providence Mountains State Recreation Area, make the tour of Mitchell Caverns your focus, adding on nature hikes and a picnic near the visitor center.

MORNING

Start your visit at the visitor center to get oriented. Then hike the Mary Beal Nature Trail to take in a concentration of native plants or the Crystal Spring Trail to see the forested spring behind the visitor center. If you have time, these short hikes are both easily doable.

AFTERNOON

Picnic at one of the three picnic tables next to the visitor center and take in outstanding views of the desert valley and distant mountain ranges. Afternoon is spent on the Mitchell Caverns tour in the cool recesses of the mountain, marveling over the delicate limestone formations. (Note that the afternoon tour is offered October-May, with morning tours only in September and June.)

EVENING

After your tour, walk past the campground to the short stroll along the Niña Mora Trail, which ends at a viewpoint where you can get even more of an eyeful. Depending on the time of year, admire the late afternoon golden light or take in a stunning sunset before heading to camp or making the long drive to your lodging.

SIGHTS

★ MITCHELL CAVERNS

A short walk along a trail chiseled into the mountainside leads to two gaping holes framed by rocks that looks like a giant's face. This is the cave entrance, the "eyes of the mountain" so named by the Chemehuevi tribe who used these caves. Stepping through the right "eye," a short entrance tunnel leads to a cathedral-like room adorned with forests of stalactites hanging from the ceiling and stalagmites protruding from the floor. Occasionally they connect in impressive columns or hang in fan-like draperies. The caves are pitch black, and the artificial lighting is sparse, revealing the formations in flashes at a time, some of them unusual, like shields and cave mushrooms. The rooms get smaller the deeper in you go, eventually opening to a second cave. Here the room is not ornate, but what it lacks in dripstones it makes up for in

entrance to Mitchell Caverns (left); Cave Trail (right)

archaeological significance. Pottery, food storage vessels, and the fossil of a ground sloth dating to 11,600 years ago were all found here.

Access to the caverns is only available through a **guided tour** ($20 pp), which is offered on Fridays, Saturdays, Sundays, and holiday Mondays from September to June. From October to May tours are offered twice a day at 11am and 2pm. In June and September, tours are offered once at 10am only. **There are no tours in July and August.**

Tours are limited to 15 people and fill up quickly, especially on holiday weekends, so it's essential to reserve ahead. Check-in for the tours is 30 minutes ahead of time. Tours take approximately 90 minutes and include an easy 0.5-mi (0.8-km) trail to reach the caves. There are restrooms and a water-refill station near the visitor center at the start of the tour.

HIKING

From pinyon forest to volcanic views, a small collection of nature trails offer a great way to experience a cross section of the park's unique landscape. The Mary Beal Nature Trail explores a twisting drainage with an unusually high concentration of cholla and yucca, creating a desert garden. A hike to Crystal Spring strikes partway into a rugged canyon with pinyon pines and boulder outcroppings against the rock amphitheater of Fountain Peak, following the path the Mitchells used to bring water to the homestead.

★ NIÑA MORA TRAIL

DISTANCE: 0.5 mi (0.8 km) round-trip
DURATION: 30 minutes
EFFORT: Easy
TRAILHEAD: East end of campground at site 5

Vegetation is less dense on this trail than in the canyons and drainages close to the visitor center, making this an easy walk with big views. Near the trailhead is a grave marker for Benita Mora, for whom this trail is named. She died in 1911 when she was only eight days old. Her parents worked at the nearby Mexican Mine. The trail

DISTANCE: 1.4 mi (2.3 km) round-trip
DURATION: 45 minutes
EFFORT: Easy
TRAILHEAD: Behind the visitor center

Dramatic rock formations, dense cactus gardens, and the spring the Mitchells used to supply water to the homestead are highlights of this hike. The trail starts on a ridge behind the visitor center before partially entering a canyon at the foot of the mountains. Towering over the canyon is Fountain Peak at 6,988 ft (2,130 m), possible to summit for experienced hikers with gear and route-finding skills. The trail cuts through dense cactus gardens spiked with blue yucca and prickly pear, following switchbacks and short, constructed rock stairways. Random boulder outcroppings add to the scenery. The trail reaches Crystal Spring at 0.7 mi (1.1 km) in a narrow canyon wash choked with willows and evergreen shrubs.

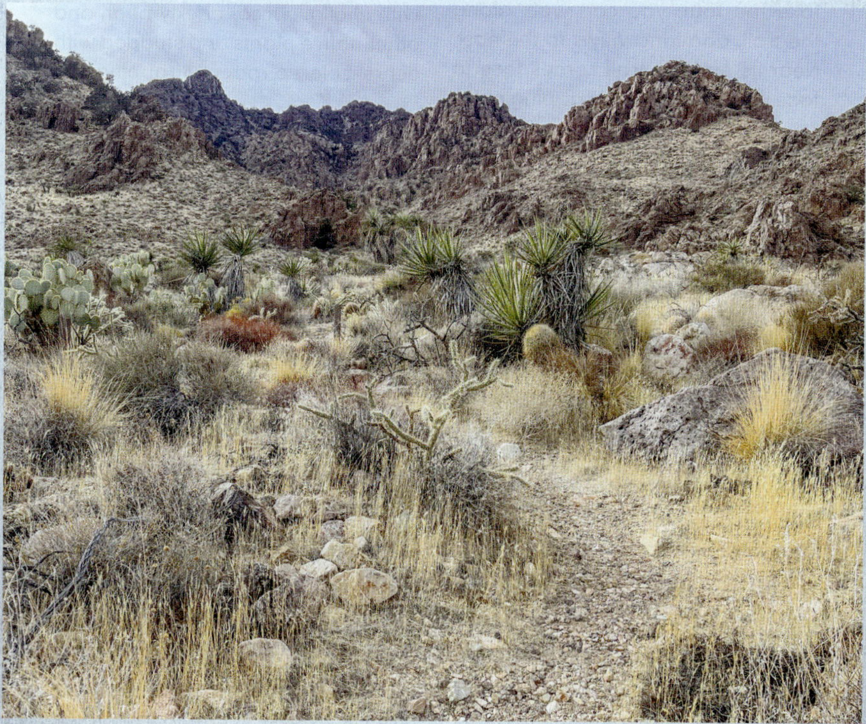

heads easts over open terrain to a rocky prominence and viewpoint. From here there are commanding views of the Clipper Valley to the east. To the southeast, the craggy Clipper Mountains and Piute Mountains form rugged layers. To the northeast you'll see the stark lines of Wild Horse Mesa. On the way back, the jagged wall of the Providence Mountains takes center stage.

CAVE TRAIL

DISTANCE: 1 mi (1.6 km) round-trip
DURATION: 20-30 minutes
EFFORT: Easy
TRAILHEAD: Below the visitor center

A hard-packed path is carved into the side of the mountain leading from the visitor center to the Mitchell Caverns entrance. This walk is part of the tour, but even if you do not take the tour, you can walk along the trail, admiring views to the east. Near its end the trail comes face to face with the two large gaping holes in the mountainside that lead into the caverns, the "eyes of the mountain."

MARY BEAL NATURE TRAIL

DISTANCE: 0.4 mi (0.8 km) round-trip
DURATION: 15-30 minutes
EFFORT: Easy
TRAILHEAD: North end of the visitor center parking area

Mary Beal must have been one hardy soul. A botany expert and friend of the Mitchells, she spent 50 years exploring the Mojave Desert and studying its flora. The trail named for her, jokingly dubbed the "Trail of Terror" by my family for the high number of spiky plants edging into the path of the innocent-sounding nature trail, drops into a hilly basin and makes a loop. For all its potential pitfalls, the trail is beautiful, clustered with cholla, yucca, prickly pear, and other native plants and studded with ochre-colored rock outcroppings.

CAMPING

The park offers **one small developed campground** with five campsites. Sites need to be reserved ahead of time through Reserve California (800/44407275; www.reserveca-lifornia.com; $20/night, $10 extra vehicle). The campground is only open when the park is open. Campsites are available to reserve Fridays, Saturdays, and Sundays with holiday Mondays September through June.

Providence Mountains State Recreation Area Campground

BEST CAMPGROUND

★ Providence Mountains State Recreation Area Campground

The small campground is perched at 4,300 ft (1,311 m), with spectacular views making camping here feel like lodging in a remote, windswept castle. Sunsets are particularly dramatic. As the sun sinks, the landscape below glows pink and orange in the shifting light.

There are five sites, three for tent camping and two for RVs or trailers, with no hookups. Sites include a fire pit and picnic table. There are bathrooms with flush toilets and handwashing sinks at the end of the day use parking lot. There is very limited water at the campground; bring your own for drinking, washing, and cooking. There is no firewood available; bring your own. The campground can get extremely windy; secure all belongings and tents.

FOOD AND LODGING

Bring everything you need to visit the Providence Mountains, including food and extra water, and make sure you have enough gas. There are no services inside the Providence Mountains State Recreation Area or the larger Mojave National Preserve. The closest services are in the town of **Needles,** a one-hour drive (56 mi/90 km) to the east along I-40. Needles is a small, desert town located along the Colorado River and historic Route 66 with river access for boating and swimming, RV camping, chain hotels, and a few casual restaurants, some of them waterfront. The town also offers gas and basic supplies.

Camping is the only option in the state park and national preserve. Needles has the closest lodging, and there are other nearby developed campgrounds located along Black Canyon Road.

BEST PICNIC SPOT

Mitchell Homestead

Plenty of visitors drive the potholed byway that is Essex Road up the mountain just to stop in at the picturesque visitor center and picnic on the grounds of the former Mitchell homestead. Three picnic tables are optimally positioned next to the stone cabin turned visitor center at the base of the jutting limestone Providence Mountains and take in sweeping views to the east.

GETTING THERE

CAR

The Providence Mountains State Recreation Area is a state-protected area within the Mojave National Preserve. It lies at the northern end of Essex Road. Interstate access is via I-15 to the northwest, I-40 to the south, and Nevada US-95 to the east. The park lies between Joshua Tree National Park, 105 mi (169 km) to the

BEST NEARBY

MOJAVE NATIONAL PRESERVE

The Mojave National Preserve (www.nps.gov/moja; free) literally surrounds the Providence Mountains State Recreation Area. The spectacular 1.6-million-acre (647,500-ha) park protects cultural sites as well a bounty of natural destinations including the Kelso Dunes, volcanic cinder cones, one of the largest Joshua tree forests in the world, craggy mountain ranges, and miles of hikes and scenic drives. Paved Kelbaker Road gives access to some of its scenic wonders including the Kelso Dunes and Cinder Cone Lava Beds.

Mojave National Preserve

south, and Las Vegas, Nevada, 140 mi (225 km) north.

From the south, access is from the town of Twentynine Palms on the northeastern edge of Joshua Tree National Park. From the Twentynine Palms area, take Amboy Road north to the mostly ghost town of Amboy. From Amboy, continue east for 7 mi (11 km) on historic Route 66 (National Trails Highway), to the signed Kelbaker Road. Turn left to head north for 11 mi (18 km) to I-40. At the I-40 junction, head east toward Needles for 21 mi (34 km). Take the Essex Road exit. Drive 14 mi (23 km) north, entering the Mojave National Preserve, and follow signs for Providence Mountains State Recreation Area. From Twentynine Palms, the drive is about 1 hour 45 minutes.

The town of Needles is the eastern gateway to the Mojave National Preserve. From Needles, follow I-40 west 41 mi (66 km) to exit 100 for Essex Road. Take Essex Road north for 14 mi (23 km) to the signed Providence Mountains State Recreation Area. From Needles the drive is approximately one hour.

To access the park from the north, the jumping-off point is the town of Baker located just off I-15. Kelbaker Road is the main, continuous route through the Mojave National Preserve connecting Baker to I-40. From Baker head south on Kelbaker Road for 57 mi (92 km). At I-40 head east toward Needles for 21 mi (34 km). Take exit 100 north at Essex Road for 14 mi (23 km) to the signed Providence Mountains State Recreation Area. From Baker the drive is about 1.5 hours.

POINT MUGU STATE PARK

Point Mugu State Park follows the curving coastline north of Malibu for 5 mi (8 km) as the wind-sculpted hills of the Santa Monica Mountains come down nearly to the coast's edge, adding a striking contrast to the blue sparkle of the Pacific. The beaches range from wide sandy coves to narrow stretches of rocks and sand. Point Mugu has another whole world in its backcountry, where canyons crossed by seasonal creeks lead to grassy valleys dotted with sycamores and oaks. From inland peaks the Channel Islands are visible, adding a mystique to the horizon.

ADDRESS: 9000 Pacific Coast Hwy., Malibu

PHONE: 310/457-8144

DAY USE HOURS: 8am-sunset

AREA: 13,947 acres (5,644 ha)

Mugu is named after the Chumash village of Muwu once located near Mugu Peak. For thousands of years the Santa Monica Mountains sustained the Chumash and Tongva/Gabrielino people. Sycamore Canyon, where the now-popular campground is located, was part of a trade route. In spring there are bluffs where you can watch migrating gray whales and see wildflowers that blanket the hills in wet years. The warmer temperatures of summer and fall make the beaches good for swimming, bodysurfing, and fishing.

POINT MUGU STATE PARK
Round Mountain
La Jolla Peak
La Jolla Valley National Park
Laguna Peak
Mugu Peak
Mugu Rock
Mugu Beach
Point Mugu Beach
VISITING MUGU ROCK
Thornhill Broome
Thornhill Broome Beach
Ray Miller Backbone Trail
Sand Dune
See Detail
HIKING ALONG THE PACIFIC
PICNICKING AT SYCAMORE COVE BEACH
Point Mugu State Park
Big Dome
Tri Peaks
Boney Peak
Exchange Peak
Boney Mountain
Clarks Peak
Leo Carrillo State Park
PACIFIC OCEAN
To Oxnard
To Malibu
Sycamore Canyon
Serrano Canyon
Sycamore Nature Center
Scenic Trail
Contour Interval = 20 feet
Contour Interval = 100 feet

TOP 3

1. VISITING MUGU ROCK: The distinctive landmark was created when the Pacific Coast Highway was cut through the sheer mountain (page 406).

2. HIKING ALONG THE PACIFIC: A network of trails in the backcountry offer sweeping views over the Pacific, including the aptly named Scenic Trail (page 408).

3. PICNICKING AT SYCAMORE COVE BEACH: A mix of pines and palm trees line the scenic beach cove backed by Sycamore Canyon (page 411).

PLANNING YOUR TIME

The park spans nearly 14,000 acres (5,666 ha) with 5 mi (8 km) of coast and over 70 mi (113 km) of hiking trails. One day is sufficient for a beach day or a hiking day, or a day split between the two. With camping, hiking, and beach options, there is enough recreation to fill a weekend.

Nearby state parks include Leo Carrillo State Park (5 mi/8 km).

ENTRANCE AND FEES

The park stretches along the Pacific Coast Highway (PCH) with many stopping points and **no official entrance.** The **main park day use area** is located at Sycamore Cove Beach (9000 Pacific Coast Hwy., Malibu; $12/day or $3/hour). Additional day use fee areas include Thornhill Broome Beach, 2 mi (3 km) north of Sycamore Cove, and Mugu Beach, 4 mi (6 km) north of Sycamore Cove. There are also opportunities for free parking on the PCH the length of the state beach.

VISITOR CENTER

Sycamore Nature Center

9000 Pacific Coast Hwy., Malibu; 310/457-8144; noon-3pm Sat.

Sycamore Nature Center is located near the entrance to Sycamore Canyon Campground. The small nature center hosts exhibits of local wildlife.

WEATHER

Point Mugu has mild coastal weather year-round with cool ocean breezes and temperatures ranging from 55-85°F (13-29°C). Winter can be cool and wet. Expect morning coastal fog, especially in spring and early summer. Fall can bring hot and dry Santa Ana winds. Visit in summer for the sunniest beach weather.

SIGHTS

 MUGU ROCK

Mugu Rock is a distinctive triangle rock formation formed in 1937 when the Pacific Coast Highway was redirected and a passage was blasted through the mountain. Prior to this the road went around the rock, dangerously close to the waves. The rock can be seen from vantage points along the coast, but it presides over Mugu Beach.

SAND DUNE

A giant sand dune next to the PCH unexpectedly spills out of the steep coastal hills just north of Sycamore Cove Beach. It is located on the opposite side of the PCH from the beach, tempting visitors to stop along the highway to take photos or climb its slippery incline.

BEACHES

Point Mugu's 5 mi (8 km) of coastline offer an easing from the crowds to the south and several beaches to pick your perfect spot. Consider the deep sandy crescent of Sycamore Cove; the wild, windswept stretch of Thornhill Broome; or the triangle of rock-flanked sand at Mugu Beach.

SYCAMORE COVE BEACH

9000 Pacific Coast Hwy., Malibu

Point Mugu's most popular beach, Sycamore Cove, is an excellent deep cove of sand flanked by palm trees and signature sycamore trees. A developed picnic area and proximity to the campground and network of hiking trails add to the draw.

THORNHILL BROOME BEACH

Windswept Thornhill Broome Beach, 2 mi (3 km) north of Sycamore Cove Beach, offers a long sliver of sandy coastline running up against the PCH. Just on the other side of the coast road, arid golden hills make a stark contrast. Amenities are minimal here, and the sound of cars can compete with the sound of the waves, but ease of access combined with the austere beauty of the spot make it worth visiting.

MUGU BEACH

Mugu Beach is a triangle of sand just north of the distinct landmark that is Mugu Rock, created by blasting through the hills to build the PCH. The beach is located 4 mi (6 km) north of Sycamore Cove Beach, across from the trailhead to the Chumash Trail and a network of trails in the northern Santa Monica Mountains.

Mugu Rock

HIKING

There are more than 70 mi (113 km) of hiking trails in Point Mugu State Park traversing two major river canyons and the Boney Mountains State Wilderness Area. The popular Backbone Trail also begins here and is the gateway into the Boney Mountain State Wilderness Area. Terrain ranges from wooded canyons and grassy valleys to coastal ridges offering striking views of the Pacific Ocean and the Santa Monica Mountains.

All of the hikes included here begin in the south along the PCH and coast side of the park. It is also possible to access the trail network from the north and the Rancho Sierra Vista/ Satwiwa (4121 Potrero Rd., Newbury Park), a hiking area and Native American Culture Center located in Newbury Park.

★ SYCAMORE CANYON FIRE ROAD AND SCENIC TRAILS LOOP

DISTANCE: 2.7 mi (4.3 km) round-trip
DURATION: 1-1.5 hours
EFFORT: Easy
TRAILHEAD: Sycamore Canyon Campground parking

Get a taste of the sculpted coastal hills of the backcountry with this easy 2.7-mi (4.3-km) loop that offers sweeping views of the Pacific. The trail begins along the **Sycamore Canyon Fire Road,** then joins the **Overlook Fire Road** that switchbacks over to the **Scenic Trail.** The route loops back to camp along the Scenic Trail.

SERRANO CANYON TRAIL

DISTANCE: 9 mi (14 km) round-trip
DURATION: 4 hours
EFFORT: Moderate
TRAILHEAD: Sycamore Canyon Campground parking

The trail begins along the Sycamore Canyon Fire Road before hitting the heart of the walk, lovely wooded Serrano Canyon, crisscrossed by a seasonal stream. Beyond Serrano Canyon, the gentle rolling grasslands of Serrano Valley emerge, framed by the steep backdrop of the Boney Mountains. This is the site of the Serrano Homesite and where the trail intersects with the Boney Trail, a good place to turn around.

RAY MILLER BACKBONE TRAIL

DISTANCE: 5.4 mi (8.7 km) round-trip
DURATION: 2.5-3 hours
EFFORT: Moderate
TRAILHEAD: Parking area 1.6 mi (2.6 km) west of Sycamore Canyon Campground along PCH

The Ray Miller trail zigzags in a steady incline over sculpted coastal ridgelines overlooking the Pacific. The trail is beautiful in spring when there may be wildflowers garnishing the hills. Otherwise, enjoy the dramatic views of the chaparral-covered promontories juxtaposed with the gleaming ocean below.

TOP HIKE
MUGU PEAK

DISTANCE: 2.8 mi (4.5 km) round-trip
DURATION: 2 hours
EFFORT: Strenuous
TRAILHEAD: Chumash Trail parking north of Point Mugu Beach/Mugu Rock

Hike Mugu Peak for spectacular ocean views of the Channel Islands, Anacapa and the larger Santa Cruz, as well as the distinct line of Boney Mountain with the highest peaks in the Santa Monica Mountains. The Chumash Trail follows an ancient route used for over 7,000 years by the Chumash, who hunted and fished along the coast and then returned to villages in the valleys behind Mugu Peak. The route gains over 1,200 ft (366 m) in the first mile as its single track snakes over the spine of a hill through coastal scrub and cactus.

RECREATION

WILDLIFE WATCHING

Marine Mammals

From December through April, there is a possibility of seeing migrating **gray whales** as they make the epic journey from the Arctic to Baja California, Mexico, and back again. Look for their distant spouts or a dark hump from shore or from a higher vantage point like the Scenic Trail.

SWIMMING

Swimming and bodysurfing are popular along Point Mugu's beaches, especially at **Sycamore Cove** with its curve of sandy beach making for mellow waves. Thornhill Broome is more rugged and is known for occasional rip currents. There are lifeguard towers at each of the main day use beaches, and lifeguards patrol them in summer from Memorial Day to Labor Day. In between these zones, there are stretches of coast without lifeguard towers that are more lightly patrolled.

FISHING

Surf fishing is popular along Point Mugu's beaches where anglers try for sculpin, bass, perch, rockfish, and lingcod. A valid California fishing license is required.

CAMPING

The park has **two developed campgrounds** with reservations available through Reserve California (800/444-7275; www.reservecalifornia.com) up to six months in advance. Reservations are required, and campgrounds book fully in summer and most weekends year-round.

BEST CAMPGROUNDS

Sycamore Canyon Campground

Sycamore Canyon Campground has 50 campsites ($45/night) for tent and RV camping across the PCH in a canyon with sycamores and oaks. Campsites have picnic tables and fire pits, and the campground has flush toilets and token-operated showers.

Thornhill Broome Campground

Thornhill Broome Campground has 34 campsites ($35/night) for tents or trailers located oceanfront along the PCH. Campsites have picnic tables and fire pits. Tents are allowed, but trailers are recommended because of wind and traffic sounds from the PCH. Trailers cannot be longer than 31 ft (9 m). This campground is 2 mi (3 km) north of Sycamore Canyon Campground.

FOOD AND LODGING

The city of **Oxnard** is located 15 mi (24 km) north of Point Mugu. The city has numerous sandy beaches and beach parks, the Channel Islands Harbor with a marina and restaurants, a beachfront resort hotel and other chain hotels, and a downtown with lots of restaurant options including taquerias and breweries.

The city of **Ventura** is located 25 mi (40 km) north of Point Mugu. It is known for its beaches like San Buenaventura State Beach and destination surf spots. It has the Ventura Pier, a historic downtown, and resort hotels.

BEST PICNIC SPOT

★ Sycamore Cove

Sycamore Cove Beach has a great day use area with picnic tables and barbecues in a grassy area shaded by sycamores and pines, all within view of the beach.

GETTING THERE

CAR

The park is 15 mi (24 km) south of Oxnard on the Pacific Coast Highway/CA-1. The main beach is Sycamore Cove (9000 W. Pacific Coast Hwy., Malibu), located 4 mi (6 km) west of the Ventura County line and the first beach within the Point Mugu State Park boundaries heading north. The park extends 3.5 mi (5.5 km) north to Mugu Beach and can be accessed from several day use, beach parking, and trailhead parking areas along the PCH.

Sycamore Cove

LEO CARRILLO STATE PARK

Located along the scenic Pacific Coast Highway north of Malibu, Leo Carrillo State Park spans over 1.5 mi (2.5 km) of shoreline renowned for its coastal bluffs, tide pools, sea caves, sandy beaches, and rocky coves. There are also miles of rugged backcountry, from rolling hills to sycamore-filled canyons. From the tide pools at Sequit Point to the grassy meadows of Nicholas Flat, the park is a draw for its natural beauty.

ADDRESS: 35000 Pacific Coast Hwy., Malibu

PHONE: 310/457-8144

DAY USE HOURS: 8am-10pm

AREA: 2,513 acres (1,017 ha)

The park is named after actor and conservationist Leo Carrillo, who was instrumental in preserving the land that is now the state park. The land also serves as a reminder of the Chumash people who inhabited the area nearly 8,000 years ago. They built plank boats to access the Channel Islands, visible from the park's hills, to trade and fish. There are over 1,000 documented archaeological sites in the Santa Monica Mountains.

Along this distinct coastline, swimming, surfing, beachcombing, hiking, and camping are all possibilities. If you happen to be at the park in spring, stand on the bluffs and look for migrating gray whales.

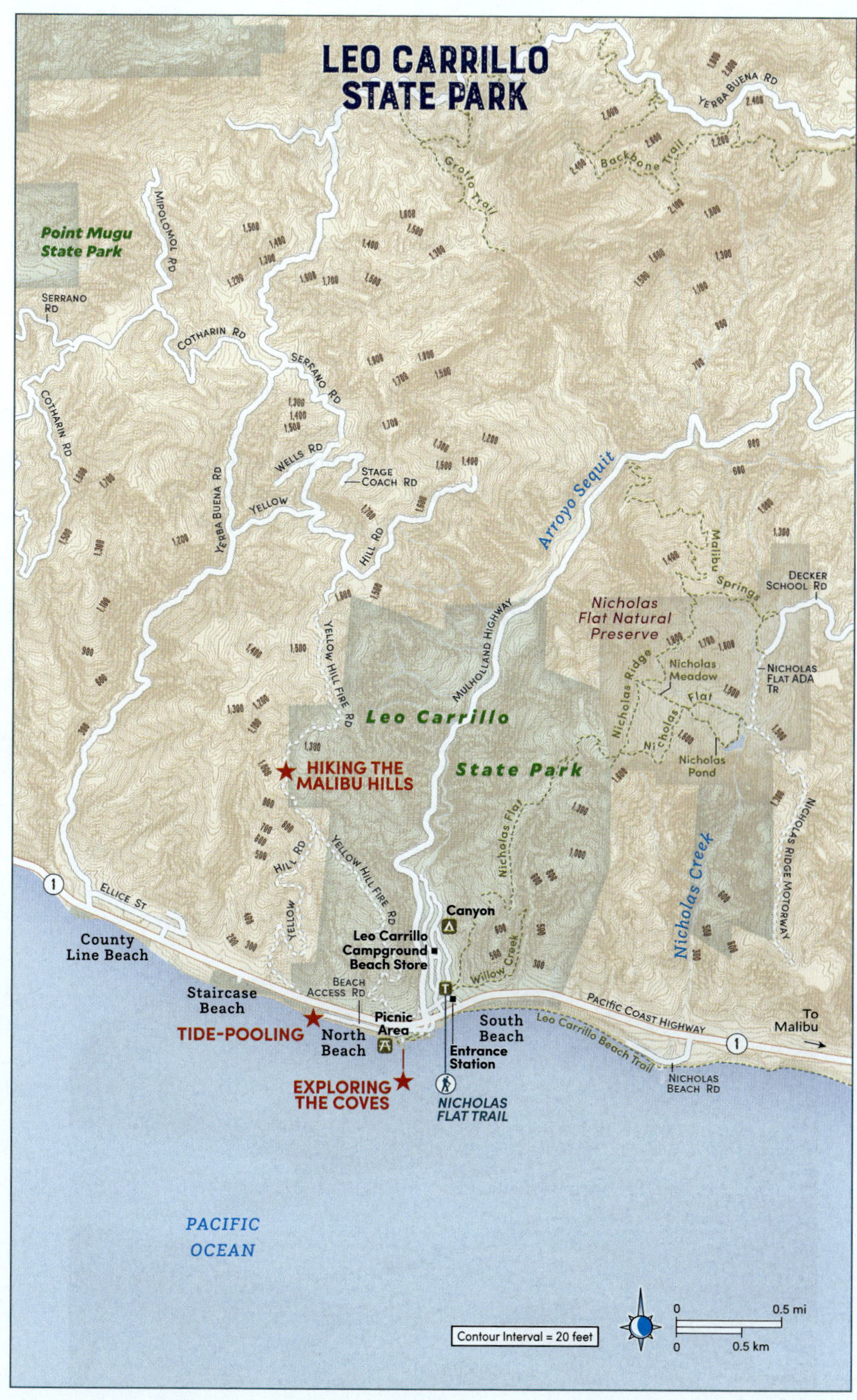
LEO CARRILLO
STATE PARK
Point Mugu
State Park
Serrano
Rd
Mipolomol Rd
Cotharin Rd
Cotharin Rd
Serrano Rd
Wells Rd
Stage
Coach Rd
Yellow
Yerba Buena Rd
Hill Rd
Grotto Trail
Backbone Trail
Yerba Buena Rd
Arroyo Sequit
Malibu
Springs
Decker
School Rd
Nicholas
Flat Natural
Preserve
Nicholas Ridge
Nicholas
Meadow
Nicholas Flat
Nicholas
Pond
Nicholas
Flat ADA
Tr
Yellow Hill Fire Rd
Mulholland Highway
Leo Carrillo
State Park
HIKING THE
MALIBU HILLS
Nicholas Flat
Nicholas Creek
Nicholas Ridge Motorway
Hill Rd
Yellow
Yellow Hill Fire Rd
Canyon
Leo Carrillo
Campground
Beach Store
Willow Creek
1
Ellice St
County
Line Beach
Staircase
Beach
Beach
Access Rd
TIDE-POOLING
North
Beach
Picnic
Area
South
Beach
Entrance
Station
Pacific Coast Highway
Leo Carrillo Beach Trail
To
Malibu
1
Nicholas
Beach Rd
EXPLORING
THE COVES
NICHOLAS
FLAT TRAIL
PACIFIC
OCEAN
Contour Interval = 20 feet
0
0.5 mi
0
0.5 km

TOP 3

★ **1. EXPLORING THE COVES:** A series of small, sandy coves tucked into the bluffs just west of Sequit Cove can be explored at low tide (page 415).

★ **2. HIKING THE MALIBU HILLS:** Leo Carrillo's backcountry offers a chance to hike the hills above Leo Carrillo State Beach, including the Yellow Hill Fire Trail, where an exposed climb pays off with sweeping views over the Pacific Ocean (page 416).

★ **3. TIDE-POOLING:** At low tide, check out the rocky pools near Sequit Point to observe a rich ecosystem of marine life, including sea stars and crabs (page 417).

PLANNING YOUR TIME

It's easy to spend most of a day exploring Leo Carrillo's beaches and tide pools. For a full day, visitors might consider hiking in the morning when it's cool and spending the afternoon on the beach.

Nearby state parks include Point Mugu State Park (5 mi/8 km).

ENTRANCE AND FEES

The **official park entrance** is located at the turnoff for the Leo Carrillo State Beach and Canyon Campground (35000 Pacific Coast Hwy.). There is an entrance station, day use parking lot ($12/day or $3/hour), and restrooms.

VISITOR CENTER

The park does not have a visitor center.

WEATHER

The climate is mild year-round with warm, dry summers and average temperatures around 75-85°F (24-29°C). Winters are cooler and wetter, with temperatures usually around 64-67°F (18-20°C). Fog can blanket the coast in the mornings, particularly in late spring and early summer, but it usually burns off by afternoon. Spring, summer, and fall are all nice times to visit, with summer being the most popular.

SIGHTS

★ COVES

Leo Carrillo has a series of scenic coves. Backed by sculpted bluffs, divided by surf-blasted rocks, and secluded from the main beaches, they can be explored at low tide. From the pedestrian walkway at the main parking area, follow the coastline west. The coves are located between **North Beach** and **Sequit Point.**

BEACHES

SOUTH BEACH

The highlight at crescent-shaped South Beach is picturesque Sequit Point. Waves break around this point and have carved out sea caves and tunnels in the rock walls. During low tide, there are tide pools to explore. The break at the point also makes it a choice spot for surfing.

South Beach is located across the Pacific Coast Highway (PCH) from the main day use parking lot. The beach is accessed via a pedestrian tunnel under the PCH.

NORTH BEACH

North Beach is a wide, dog-friendly beach just north of South Beach. With a wider stretch of sand than South Beach, it's a good spot for sunbathing. You can also explore Sequit Point and its tide pools, sea caves,

Leo Carrillo State Beach

and rock arches on the south end of the beach.

Enter through the main park entrance and continue to a day use parking lot adjacent to the beach ($3/hour, max $12/day). There may also be parking directly along the PCH.

STAIRCASE BEACH

4000 Pacific Coast Hwy.

The beach is secluded and rocky at this spot that is popular with surfers. Ironically, there is no staircase; instead, a trail switchbacks down a bluff face from the parking lot. There are no facilities. Access is via a day use parking area adjacent to state park-owned residences ($3/hour, max $12/day), and the beach can also be accessed by walking from North Beach. There may also be free parking along the PCH.

COUNTY LINE BEACH

42398 E. Pacific Coast Hwy.

County Line Beach is located north of Leo Carrillo's other beaches in a separate section just over the Ventura County line. With its easy beach access, the small, sandy stretch is good for surfing, fishing, scuba diving, swimming, and sunbathing.

The beach is 2 mi (3 km) north of the main entrance to Leo Carrillo State Beach and across from Neptune's Net seafood restaurant at the intersection of Yerba Buena Road. Parking is in a small dirt parking lot (free) or along the PCH.

HIKING

Leo Carrillo State Park's backcountry offers a chance to explore scenic former ranchlands in the hills above Malibu.

LEO CARRILLO BEACH TRAIL

DISTANCE: 5 mi (8 km) round-trip
DURATION: 1.5-2 hours
EFFORT: Moderate
TRAILHEAD: South Beach just below main day use parking area

It is technically possible to walk along the beach for 2.5 mi (4 km) one-way beginning at Leo Carrillo's South Beach down coast to El Pescador, part of the Robert H. Meyer Memorial State Beach. The sandy "trail" gives dramatic views of the rocky coastline and ocean. Go at low tide for the most continuous access. Depending on the tides, a few rocky scrambles may be necessary, including midway at Nicholas Canyon County Beach.

★ YELLOW HILL FIRE TRAIL

DISTANCE: 6 mi (9.7 km) round-trip
DURATION: 3 hours
EFFORT: Difficult

TOP HIKE
NICHOLAS FLAT TRAIL

DISTANCE: 6.4 mi (10.3 km) round-trip
DURATION: 3.5-4 hours
EFFORT: Strenuous
TRAILHEAD: Signed for Camp 13 just east of main park entrance station

The out-and-back Nicholas Flat Trail connects the Pacific Coast with the hilly backcountry above Malibu as it climbs nearly 1,700 ft (518 m) to the Flat, a wide meadow that's part of an old ranch where there is sometimes a seasonal pond. On the way it passes through various plant communities and species including wildflowers, purple sage, and California sagebrush. The backbone of the trail is a long, steep ridgeline that reveals interior views of the Santa Monica Mountains and the distinct line of Boney Mountain. At 2.5 mi (4 km), continue heading east on the Nicholas Flat Trail as the trail gives way to large swaths of grassland. On your return, look for views of the Pacific on the last stretch of the hike.

TRAILHEAD: Main park entrance, northwest side of day use parking area

This out-and-back hike follows a fire road over exposed hillside, following Sequit Ridge. The payoff for this steady climb is sweeping views over the Pacific Ocean, where on a clear day you can see the Channel Islands. Down the coast, look for the promontory of Point Dume and the Palos Verdes Peninsula. On clear days you may be able to see some of the higher peaks in the Santa Monica Mountains from the top of the trail.

RECREATION

WILDLIFE WATCHING

★ Tide Pools

The best tide-pooling is located at **Sequit Point,** a scenic promontory that divides South Beach and North Beach and can be accessed from either side. At low tide, the water recedes, revealing hidden pools rich with marine life. Look for barnacles, crabs, mussels, sea anemones, sea urchins, and sea stars in the frothy pools.

Marine Mammals

Look for **gray whales** in April and May as mothers (cows) and babies (calves) migrate north. They can be seen from the beach or from vantage points on the hiking trails above the beach. Keep an eye out for dolphins, harbor seals, and sea lions as well, which may swim close to shore.

SURFING AND SWIMMING

The small swells and mostly sandy shores at **North and South Beaches** make them good spots for swimming and bodysurfing. There are also lifeguards on duty year-round.

Staircase Beach and **County Line** are recommended for surfing. Tucked-away Staircase Beach has a beach break over a sand bottom with something for beginners and advanced surfers. The fast, powerful waves at County Line Beach make a good surf spot for intermediate to advanced surfers, but these same wave types can also turn dangerous.

CAMPING

The state park has **one very popular campground.** Reservations are necessary and can be booked through Reserve California (800/444-7275; www.reservecalifornia.com; $45/night) on a rolling basis six months ahead of the check-in date. The campground books fully well in advance during summer, holidays, and weekends the rest of the year.

BEST CAMPGROUND

Canyon Campground

35000 Pacific Coast Hwy.

Canyon Campground is located on the inland side of the PCH in a canyon shaded by sycamores. The campground has 135 sites for tents and RVs including hookup sites. Campsites have picnic tables and fire pits, and the campground offers flush toilets and token-operated showers. The campground is located just before Mulholland Highway (CA-23) within walking distance of the beach. Beach access is via a pedestrian tunnel that runs under the PCH.

rocks along the shoreline (left); kids tide-pooling (right)

FOOD AND LODGING

The town of **Malibu** is located 10 mi (16 km) east (down coast) of Leo Carrillo along the PCH. The town is known as a stylish destination for its homes and hotels, and for its beautiful mountain and coast setting and surrounding beaches. Many businesses are located along the PCH, including hotels, restaurants, groceries, and gas stations.

LEO CARRILLO CAMPGROUND BEACH STORE

35000 Pacific Coast Hwy.; 8am-8pm daily

The campground has a small camp store, Leo Carrillo Campground Beach Store, with snacks, beer, ice, and sundries.

BEST PICNIC SPOT

Park Entrance Picnic Area

Look for a picnic area just west of the main park entrance, near popular Sequit Point.

GETTING THERE

CAR

Leo Carrillo State Park is located along the Pacific Coast Highway (CA-1) 10 mi (16 km) west (up coast) of Malibu. From US-101, exit at Kanan Road and head south for 6 mi (10 km). Turn right onto Mulholland Highway for 1 mi (1.6 km). Turn left on Encinal Canyon Road for 9 mi (14 km). Turn right onto CA-1 north (Pacific Coast Highway) and continue for 2 mi (3 km) to the park entrance on your right.

SANTA MONICA STATE BEACH

Santa Monica State Beach is a vibrant stretch of California coastline that blends natural beauty with classic seaside fun. Its 3 mi (5 km) of wide, sandy shores are set against a backdrop of palm trees and the Santa Monica Mountains. On the beach's northern end, Santa Monica Pier's iconic Ferris wheel is silhouetted against the scene. At the heart of the beach the Santa Monica Pier is a historic landmark dating to 1909 and host to Pacific Park amusement park, arcade games, restaurants, and the Santa Monica Aquarium. The beach is also an ideal spot for a Sunday Funday (or any other day of the week) of sunbathing, swimming, beach volleyball, or strolling or biking along the Marvin Braude Bike Trail. Another unique offering is the park's Annenberg Community Beach House, a historic beachfront complex with a swimming pool, splash pad, playground, and cultural events.

ADDRESS: 200 Santa Monica Pier, Santa Monica

PHONE: 310/458-8300

WEBSITE: www.santamonicapier.org

DAY USE HOURS: 6am-10pm

AREA: 48 acres (19 ha)

SANTA MONICA STATE BEACH
Topanga State Park
Will Rogers State Historic Park
Rustic Creek
Kenter Creek
Will Rogers State Beach
Annenberg Community Beach House
North Beach Playground
Main Visitor Information Center
SANTA MONICA
Santa Monica State Beach
See Detail
VISITING THE ICONIC SANTA MONICA PIER
RELAXING ON THE SAND
Dorothy Green Park
Santa Monica Beach
BIKING THE BEACH PATH
PACIFIC OCEAN
Venice Beach
Ballona Wetlands Ecological Reserve
Ballona Lagoon
Ballona Creek
Dockweiler State Beach
Del Rey Lagoon
Marvin Braude Bike Trail
Santa Monica Pier Shop & Visitor Center
MariaSol Sunset Cantina
Heal the Bay Aquarium
Perry's Café
Pacific Park on the Pier
The Albright
Looff Hippodrome
Big Dean's Oceanfront Café
Original Muscle Beach
Contour Interval = 100 feet

TOP 3

1. VISITING THE ICONIC SANTA MONICA PIER: The landmark pier was built in 1909 and continues to amuse with arcade games, rides, and carnival treats (page 423).

2. RELAXING ON THE SAND: Santa Monica's signature wide, sandy beaches have plenty of space to enjoy a relaxing beach day (page 424).

3. BIKING THE BEACH PATH: Bring your bike or rent one along the bike path and cycle a section of the 22-mi (35-km) Marvin Braude Bike Trail (page 425).

1

2

3

PLANNING YOUR TIME

Plan for a full day at Santa Monica Beach to enjoy the pier and spend time on the beach. Santa Monica is also a destination for visitors who come for a few days and stay in one of the city's high-end hotels.

Nearby state parks include Leo Carrillo State Park (52 mi/84 km) and Point Mugu State Park (58 mi/93 km).

ENTRANCE AND FEES

Santa Monica Beach stretches for 3 mi (5 km) north and south of the pier from the **Annenberg Community Beach** House to the north to Venice Beach at Rose Avenue to the south. While there is **no official entrance,** and no fees to enter the beach, there are day use parking lots that charge fees ($6-15/day) lining the beach. There is also paid street parking within walking distance of the beach.

VISITOR CENTER

There are no visitor centers dedicated to the state beach, but there are places to get tourist information in the area.

Santa Monica Pier Shop and Visitor Center

200 Santa Monica Pier; 310/804-7457; 9am-5pm Wed.-Mon.

Santa Monica Pier Shop and Visitor Center is a kiosk in the Looff Hippodrome, the historic building housing Santa Monica Pier's carousel. It offers a small selection of merch, books, and maps.

Main Visitor Information Center

2427 Main St.; www.santamonica.com; 9am-5:30pm Mon.-Fri., 9am-5pm Sat.-Sun.

Main Visitor Information Center is located 1.3 mi (2 km) south of the pier and is staffed by people who can provide information and recommendations. It also offers visitor maps and guides and a selection of souvenirs.

WEATHER

Santa Monica Beach is moderate year-round with winter temperatures around 60-65°F (15-18°C) and summer temperatures around 68-72°F (20-22°C). Expect fog in the mornings.

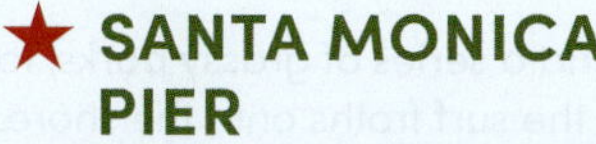

SIGHTS

★ SANTA MONICA PIER

The Santa Monica Pier is an iconic Southern California landmark blending seaside fun and scenic views. The pier was built in 1916 as the Looff Pleasure Pier after the company that constructed its carousel and continues its tradition of entertainment. The pier is home to **Pacific Park,** an amusement park with a solar-powered Ferris wheel and classic carnival rides. Other attractions include a hand-carved carousel, an aquarium, shops, and restaurants. The pier is also the historic end of Route 66, making it a must-see for fans of Americana.

Looff Hippodrome

1624 Ocean Front Walk, adjacent to the Santa Monica Pier; free entry, $3 carousel

The Moorish-influenced Looff Hippodrome building was constructed in 1916 adjacent to the pier to house a carousel built by the Looff company. Today the unique architecture is on the National Register of Historic Places and houses a carousel, visitor kiosk, and ice cream stand. The carousel is not the original from 1916, but it has been dated to 1954 and is notable for its hand-carved wooden horses, whimsically painted upper rim, and 1,100 electric lights.

Pacific Park on the Pier

Santa Monica Pier; https://pacpark.com

Pacific Park is an amusement park on Santa Monica Pier featuring a dozen rides and midway games. It is known for its iconic Ferris wheel, which gives riders stunning views of the coastline and is also noteworthy as the first solar-powered Ferris wheel. Admission to the park is free, but rides require single-ride tickets or an unlimited-ride wristband (single ride $8-17, unlimited rides $30-50).

Heal the Bay Aquarium

1600 Ocean Front Walk at the Santa Monica Pier; https://healthebay.org; noon-4pm Wed.-Sun.; $12

Run by the nonprofit that focuses on protecting the coastal waters of Southern California, the aquarium features over 100 local species as well as hands-on activities and educational programs.

ANNENBERG COMMUNITY BEACH HOUSE

415 Pacific Coast Hwy.; 310/458-4904; www.santamonica.gov

No membership is required to access the historic property, once the location of the Marion Davies Estate, on the northern end of Santa Monica State Beach. The beachfront property has coastal views, a splash pad, a playground, an art gallery, the Marion Davies Guest House, and volleyball courts, as well as a café. A beautiful on-site swimming pool is one of the remaining elements of the historic estate featuring a marble deck and hand-restored tiles. The pool is open to the public from Memorial Day weekend through Labor Day weekend and is the only area that requires an admission fee ($10).

BEACHES

★ SANTA MONICA BEACH

Along California's famously rugged coastline, Santa Monica is known for its wide, sandy beach. It stretches out, level and golden, from the top of the sand, where there is a bike path and a series of grassy parks, to where the surf froths onto the shore. With so much sand, it can actually be a trek to get to the water's edge. All this sand means there's room for volleyball courts and still plenty of space to spread out your beach blanket.

RECREATION

SWIMMING AND SURFING

The surf at **Santa Monica Beach** is mild, making it a popular place for families to enjoy swimming, body-surfing, and boogie-boarding the waves. The beach is patrolled by lifeguards year-round, with a particularly high presence in the busy summer months.

These same mellow waves mean that surfing here is mostly good for beginners. The best spots are near the **Santa Monica Pier,** where the wave types vary, and **Bay Street,** two blocks south of the Santa Monica Pier. During the summer surfing is limited to these two zones. It is best to check with a lifeguard before surfing. There are also surf lessons and surf camps available in Santa Monica.

★ BIKING

Marvin Braude Bike Trail

https://pacpark.com/marvin-braude-bike-trail

A paved path runs along Santa Monica Beach, connecting Venice Beach to the south and the Santa Monica Pier. It is great for biking and in-line skating, all with views of the sea and sand. The Marvin Braude Bike Trail is a 22-mi (35-km) paved bike path that connects a series of beachside cities from Will Rogers State Beach a few miles north of Santa Monica to end at Torrance County Beach to the south.

Perry's Café

320 Santa Monica Pier; 310/393-9778; https://perryscafe.com

Bring your own bike or rent one at Perry's Café, which has several locations along the bike trail in Santa

biking the Marvin Braude Bike Trail

Monica and Venice, including on the Santa Monica Pier.

BEACH VOLLEYBALL

Beach volleyball is a popular sport along Santa Monica Beach. There are six different areas with courts, including the **Santa Monica Pier Courts** (1560 Appian Way), which has four courts with lights available for nighttime play, and the **Annenberg Community Beach House** (415 Pacific Coast Hwy.), which has six courts. These courts are available by **reservation** (www.santamonica.gov; $15/hour). Nets are provided, but you will need to bring your own volleyball. There are also eight courts available on a first-come, first-served basis at the **Ocean Park North Player's Courts** (100 Hollister Ave.).

One-hour group beach volleyball **classes** are available for all levels (213/446-3771; https://santamonicabeachvolleyball.com; $34 single class, packages available).

FOOD AND LODGING

Santa Monica has a few beachfront hotels as well as upscale hotels and restaurants within walking distance of the beach, particularly along Ocean Avenue. East of the pier, the **Third Street Promenade** (1351 3rd St. Promenade) and downtown Santa Monica (www.santamonica.com) offer an open-air car-free haven for shopping and dining as well as one of the best farmer's markets in the city.

There are **no camping** or lodging options at Santa Monica State Beach, but there are lots of food choices on the Santa Monica Pier, from amusement park snacks, burgers, and tamales to sit-down seafood and Mexican.

THE ALBRIGHT

258 Santa Monica Pier; 310/394-9683; www.thealbright.com; 11:30am-8pm Mon.-Fri., 11am-8pm Sat.-Sun.; $16-25

The Albright serves great seafood in a location that's been tried and true for over 40 years.

MARIASOL SUNSET CANTINA

401 Santa Monica Pier; 310/917-5050; www.mariasol.com; $18-35

MariaSol Sunset Cantina is notable for its location on the end of the Santa Monica Pier. It's a great place to have a margarita and watch the sunset.

BIG DEAN'S OCEANFRONT CAFÉ

1615 Ocean Front Walk; 310/393-2666; https://bigdeansoceanfrontcafe.com; $6-16

Big Dean's Oceanfront Café boasts its status as the oldest bar in Los Angeles. Founded in 1902, the now kitschy sports bar offers pub grub and rotating taps. Kids are welcome.

PERRY'S CAFÉ

320 Santa Monica Pier; 310/393-9778; https://perryscafe.com; $8-24

Perry's is ubiquitous along the bike path connecting Santa Monica and Venice for its bikes and burgers, offering 10 locations. All locations rent bicycles, and four of the locations also offer a café with breakfast, burgers, pizzas, a kids' menu, and beer and wine. Two of the locations with food are north of the pier (1200 Pacific Coast Hwy. and 930 Pacific Coast Hwy.) and two are south of the pier (26000 Ocean Front Walk and 2400 Ocean Front Walk).

BEST PICNIC SPOT

Dorothy Green Park

There are several beachfront parks adjacent to the state beach with grassy areas, palm trees, and picnic tables. In addition to these picnic basics, Dorothy Green Park (2600 Barnard Way), south of the pier between Pacific Street and Ocean Park Boulevard, has a playground, paved plaza, art sculptures, and restrooms.

GETTING THERE

CAR

Santa Monica State Beach is located in Santa Monica along the Pacific Coast Highway, 17 mi (27 km) west of downtown Los Angeles.

PUBLIC TRANSPORTATION

The LA Metro system has an aboveground light-rail station (Line E) that connects from various points in the city to end at the downtown Santa Monica Station metro station (402 Colorado Ave., Santa Monica) 0.4 mi (0.6 km) east of the Santa Monica Pier.

HUNTINGTON STATE BEACH

Huntington State Beach is a stunning stretch of coastline between Los Angeles and San Diego known for its golden beaches, excellent surf, and vibrant beach culture. Located in the town of Huntington Beach, also known as Surf City USA, the beach is a destination for sun-seekers, water enthusiasts, and surfers. Surfing got its start here in 1910 when city founder Henry Huntington hired George Freeth, the Hawaiian-born "father of modern surfing," to demonstrate the ancient Polynesian art of wave-riding using a long wooden board. Surfing pioneers like Duke Kahanamoku helped popularize the sport in the early 20th century, and today the city remains a global surf mecca, hosting the annual US Open of Surfing. Visitors can enjoy a classic California beach day here for swimming and sunbathing as well as biking and skating along a scenic beachside path.

ADDRESS: CA-1 and Magnolia St., Huntington Beach

PHONE: 714/536-1454

DAY USE HOURS: 6am-10pm

AREA: 121 acres (49 ha)

HUNTINGTON STATE BEACH
Yorktown Ave
Goldenwest St
Beach Blvd
Magnolia St
Huntington Beach
West Adams Ave
Adams Ave
Main St
Lake St
Huntington St
Delaware St
Palm Ave
Orange Ave
Talbert Channel
Indianapolis Ave
Huntington Beach Channel
International Surfing Museum
6th St
2nd St
1st St
Atlanta Ave
Huntington City Beach
Lifeguard Headquarters
Huntington Beach Visitor Center kiosk
Newland St
Hamilton Ave
WATCHING THE SURFERS
BIKING THE BEACH TRAIL
The Huntington Beach House
Bushard St
Ocean Strand Tr
Pacific Coast Highway
Huntington Beach Wetlands
Banning Ave
Shade Ramadas
Huntington State Beach
Park Entrance
Sahara Sandbar and Pizza
Brookhurst St
BUILDING A BONFIRE
Bonzai Surf School
Shade Ramadas
Santa Ana River
PACIFIC OCEAN
0 0.5 mi
0 0.5 km
Contour Interval = 5 feet

TOP 3

★ **1. WATCHING THE SURFERS:** Huntington Beach is a premier surf spot with a deep-rooted surf culture, including the world's largest surf competition (page 431).

★ **2. BUILDING A BONFIRE:** Bring the firewood and s'mores and nab one of Huntington Beach's first-come, first-served fire pits for a beach bonfire at sunset (page 434).

★ **3. BIKING THE BEACH TRAIL:** A paved, multiuse trail extends from the southern end of Huntington State Beach to Bolsa Chica State Beach in the north, where you can bike and take in views of Huntington Beach and the Pacific Ocean (page 434).

★ SURF CITY USA

The world's largest surf competition, the **US Open of Surfing** (www.surfcityusa.com), is held every summer at the Huntington Beach Pier featuring professional surfing. It takes place over one week in late July and is free and open to the public. Visitors can follow the surf schedule for competition times and attend skateboarding and BMX events, product and art demos, signings, and live music, as well as exclusive ticketed events. If you can't make the event, there are a couple of surfing sights where you can learn more. The **International Surfing Museum** (411 Olive Ave.; 714-960-3483; www.huntingtonbeachsurfingmuseum.org; 11am-5pm Fri.-Sun.) has exhibits on the history of surfing, surfing-related art, and a collection of surfboards. They also sponsor **Surfin' Sundays** on the pier featuring surf rock and vendors (9am-6pm Sun. Apr.-Oct.). Or pay homage at the **Surfing Walk of Fame** (300 Pacific Coast Hwy., corner of PCH and Main St. in front of Huntington Surf & Sport; https://surfingwalkoffame.com).

PLANNING YOUR TIME

It's easy to spend a full day enjoying the beach. To make a weekend of it, camp at one of the nearby state parks or book a hotel at one of Huntington Beach's resort hotels.

Nearby state parks include Crystal Cove State Park (10 mi/16 km).

ENTRANCE AND FEES

The **official entrance** is located off of the Pacific Coast Highway (PCH) at Magnolia Street. Visitors enter here and park in one of the giant parking lots to the north and south adjacent to the beach ($15/vehicle, $20/vehicle weekends May-Sept.).

VISITOR CENTER

There is no official visitor center for Huntington State Beach. The city operates a Huntington Beach Visitor Center kiosk at the base of the Huntington Beach Pier.

WEATHER

Huntington Beach has a lot of great beach days with average summer temperatures around 75-80°F (24-27°C). Winter is cooler with temperatures typically around 65°F (18°C). A morning marine layer when fog blankets the coast is common.

Huntington State Beach

BEACHES

★ HUNTINGTON STATE BEACH

Huntington State Beach stretches over 2 mi (3 km) along the Pacific Coast Highway, a destination for beachgoers seeking sun, surf, and other recreation. Swimming is allowed at the beach, which is staffed by lifeguards year-round; however, the area is prone to rip currents, especially during spring and summer, so it is advisable to swim near lifeguard towers and stay close to shore. Beach volleyball and basketball courts offer other opportunities for recreation in the sand. In the evening, cozy up at one of the beach's 200 large fire rings available on a first-come, first-served basis until 9:30pm for a classic **beach bonfire** experience.

RECREATION

SURFING

Take a surf lesson or simply watch surfing from Huntington State Beach, a premier surf spot where the waves break steep and hollow, making it a great spot for experienced surfers.

Banzai Surf School

22355 Pacific Coast Hwy., intersection of PCH and Brookhurst St.; https://banzaisurfschool.com; $99 group, $100-169 pp private

Banzai Surf School, a California State Parks partner, offers seasonal 90-minute group lessons for 2-6 people and year-round 2-hour private lessons on the south end of Huntington State Beach. Lessons include a surfboard, wetsuit, ocean safety instruction, and surfing skill instruction. Lessons are geared from novice to advanced and tailored to individuals. Book ahead at least a day in advance.

★ BIKING

Beach Trail

Take in Huntington Beach's broad, sandy beaches and views of the Pacific from a multiuse trail that parallels the coastline. Also known as the Ocean Strand Trail, the paved path extends for 8.5 mi (13.7 km) from the southern end of Huntington State Beach at the Santa Ana River to Bolsa Chica State Beach in the north with Huntington City Beach in between. The trail passes the Huntington Beach Pier and downtown area, where there are shops and restaurants. There are bicycle concessionaires along the path for bicycle rentals by the day or hour. The trail is mostly flat and multiuse, great for walking, jogging, biking, or in-line skating.

FOOD AND LODGING

With plenty of sun, sand, and surf, the city of **Huntington Beach** is a destination for beachgoers and vacationers. The Huntington Beach Pier anchors the tourist district with oceanfront resort hotels south of the pier, and plenty of restaurant options on the pier and stretching inland to Main Street. Huntington Beach also has surf shops and all the basics including groceries, gas, and supplies. Huntington State Beach is day use only with **no camping.**

There are beachfront food and drinks available at Huntington State Beach through California State Parks' partnerships with several concessionaires.

THE HUNTINGTON BEACH HOUSE

21601 Pacific Coast Hwy.; www.thehbhouse.com; 11am-sunset Mon.-Fri., 9am-9pm Sat.-Sun.; $13-17

The Huntington Beach House is an all-ages open-air restaurant and music venue with a spring break party vibe located at Beach Boulevard and the PCH. The menu features California-style comfort food including ramen, tamales, and burgers.

SAHARA SANDBAR AND PIZZA

21601 Pacific Coast Hwy.; https://saharasandbar.com; noon-sunset daily summer, 11am-sunset Fri.-Sun. off-season; $12-20

Sahara Sandbar and Pizza is an all-ages beachfront pizza spot and bar; the closest cross-streets are Magnolia and the PCH.

BEST PICNIC SPOT

Shade Ramadas

The park offers a series of shade ramadas with picnic tables and fire pits at the Brookhurst Boulevard entrance and the Newland Boulevard entrance. These ramadas are available for events with advance reservation. Ramadas that are not reserved are available on a first-come, first-served basis.

GETTING THERE

CAR

Huntington State Beach is located in the town of Huntington Beach along the Pacific Coast Highway (CA-1) in Orange County. Huntington Beach is 38 mi (61 km) south of downtown Los Angeles and 94 mi (151 km) north of San Diego via I-5.

CRYSTAL COVE STATE PARK

Amid Southern California's miles of spectacular coastline, Crystal Cove's 3.2-mi (5.1-km) stretch is a standout. Coast-carved cliffs, rocky tide pools, sandy coves, coastal points, and inland canyons make it a destination.

Even with all the natural beauty, the biggest draw may be Crystal Cove Historic District, a collection of picturesque vacation cottages dating from the 1920s and 1930s. These beachfront cottages were falling into disrepair when they were purchased by the California State Parks and National Register in 1979. The cottages have been restored and put into circulation so that visitors can vacation like it's 1939. The bungalows are tucked into the low cliffs edging Crystal Cove's beaches and feature decks and large glass windows to take in views of the Pacific.

Crystal Cove's human history extends way back before the vacationers of 100 years ago. The Gabrielino (Tongva) and Juaneño (Acjachemen) have lived in the area that is now Crystal Cove State Park for at least 9,000 years. They established villages near water sources like Trancas Creek where the historic seaside colony is nestled.

ADDRESS: 8471 N. Coast Hwy., Laguna Beach

PHONE: 949/494-3539

WEBSITES: www.crystalcovestatepark.org, https://crystalcove.org

DAY USE HOURS: Park 6am-sunset, historic district 6am-10pm

AREA: 3,936 acres (1,593 ha)

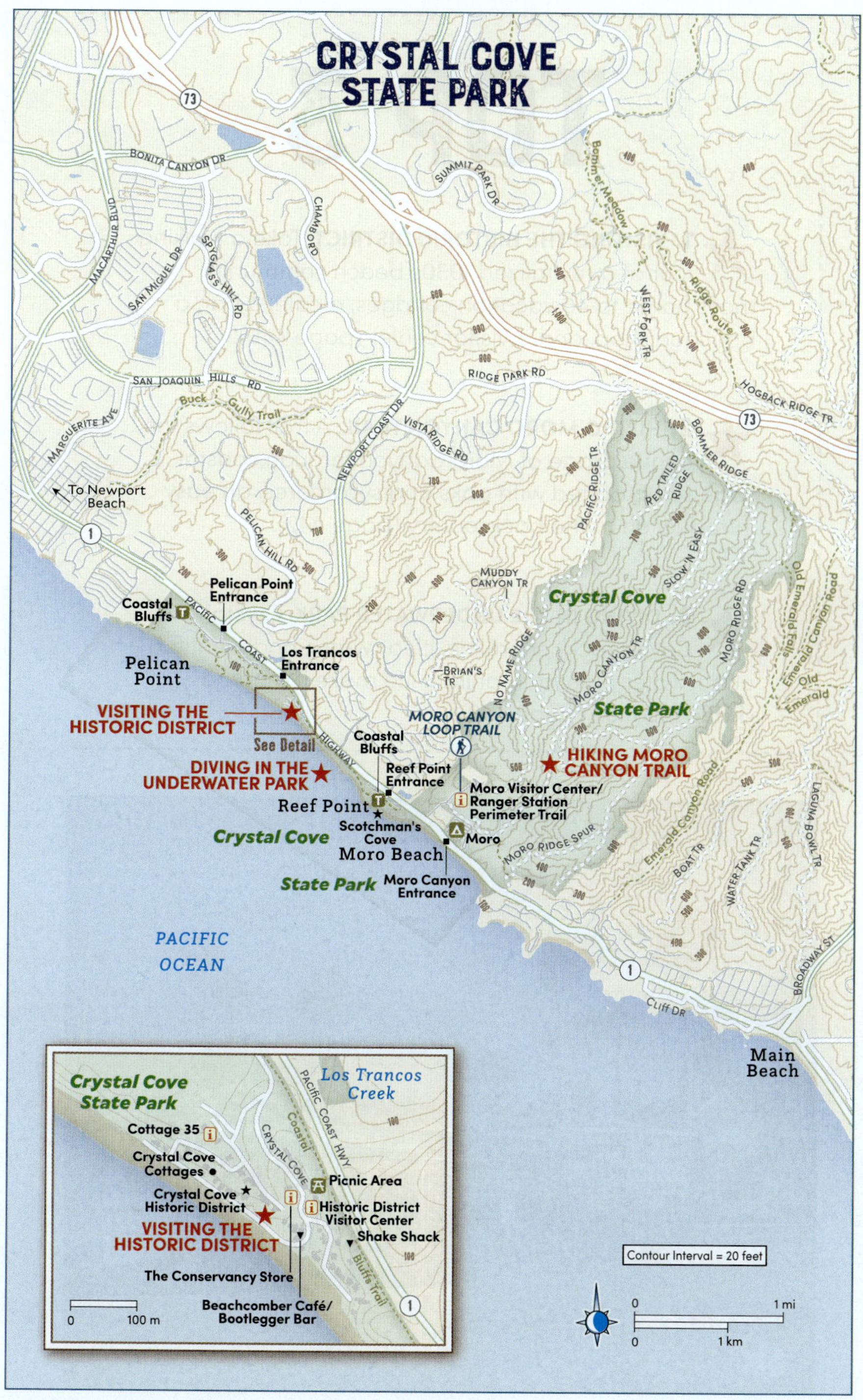

CRYSTAL COVE STATE PARK
BONITA CANYON DR
SUMMIT PARK DR
CHAMBORD
MACARTHUR BLVD
SAN MIGUEL DR
SPYGLASS HILL RD
Bommer Meadow
Ridge Route
WEST FORK TR
SAN JOAQUIN HILLS RD
RIDGE PARK RD
HOGBACK RIDGE TR
Buck Gully Trail
MARGUERITE AVE
NEWPORT COAST DR
VISTA RIDGE RD
BOMMER RIDGE
PACIFIC RIDGE TR
RED TAILED RIDGE
To Newport Beach
PELICAN HILL RD
SLOW 'N EASY
MUDDY CANYON TR
Crystal Cove
MORO RIDGE RD
Old Emerald Falls
Old Emerald Canyon Road
Pelican Point Entrance
Coastal Bluffs
PACIFIC COAST HIGHWAY
Pelican Point
Los Trancos Entrance
BRIAN'S TR
NO NAME RIDGE
MORO CANYON TR
Old Emerald
VISITING THE HISTORIC DISTRICT
See Detail
MORO CANYON LOOP TRAIL
State Park
HIKING MORO CANYON TRAIL
DIVING IN THE UNDERWATER PARK
Coastal Bluffs
Reef Point Entrance
Moro Visitor Center/ Ranger Station
Perimeter Trail
Reef Point
Scotchman's Cove
Crystal Cove
Moro
Moro Beach
MORO RIDGE SPUR
Emerald Canyon Road
BOAT TR
WATER TANK TR
LAGUNA BOWL TR
State Park
Moro Canyon Entrance
PACIFIC OCEAN
BROADWAY ST
CLIFF DR
Main Beach
Crystal Cove State Park
Los Trancos Creek
PACIFIC COAST HWY
Cottage 35
Coastal
CRYSTAL COVE
Crystal Cove Cottages
Picnic Area
Crystal Cove Historic District
Historic District Visitor Center
VISITING THE HISTORIC DISTRICT
Shake Shack
Bluffs Trail
The Conservancy Store
Beachcomber Café/ Bootlegger Bar
0 100 m
Contour Interval = 20 feet
0 1 mi
0 1 km

TOP 3

★ **1. VISITING THE HISTORIC DISTRICT:** Take a walking tour of a revitalized 1930s beach community that's home to 46 vacation cottages, a café, a bar, a boutique shop, and a visitor center (page 440).

★ **2. HIKING MORO CANYON TRAIL:** A trail follows the gentle grade of Moro Canyon through coastal sage scrub dotted with oaks and sycamores, an easy introduction to the backcountry (page 442).

★ **3. DIVING IN THE UNDERWATER PARK:** Crystal Cove's rocky shoreline, clear water, and plentiful underwater plant and animal life make it a prime diving location (page 442).

PLANNING YOUR TIME

The park is an excellent day use destination, but the unique offering of the historic cottages plus camping options makes it an enticing multiday stay.

Nearby state parks include Huntington Beach State Park (10 mi/16 km) and San Clemente State Beach (20 mi/32 km).

ENTRANCES AND FEES

Day use is $15 per vehicle and $20 on summer weekends and holidays. Fees must be paid when parking at any of the **four entrance stations.** Day use parking fees are required even if you are staying at the cottages. For campers at Moro Campground, parking is included with your camping fee starting at your check-in time. If you arrive early, plan to pay a day use fee.

The **Pelican Point Entrance** provides four bluff-top parking lots, each with beach access. Restrooms and outdoor showers are available.

The **Los Trancos Entrance** is used to access the historic district and cottages as well as the historic district's beach. It is located on the other side of the Pacific Coast Highway, with a tunnel that runs under the PCH. Alternately, there is a pedestrian crosswalk at the Los Trancos signal light. It is approximately a 5-10-minute walk to reach the historic district from the parking area. A shuttle also connects the areas and runs continuously.

The **Reef Point Entrance** has two parking areas linking to three beach access points. To the north, a quarter-mile (0.4-km) multiuse trail descends to 3.5 Cove. A stairway accesses the beach at Scotchman's Cove. To the south, a ramp leads to the Muddy Creek section of the beach.

The **Moro Canyon Entrance** is located just below Moro Campground. A short tunnel under the PCH provides access to Moro Beach. The day use lot also provides access to backcountry hiking trails.

VISITOR CENTERS

Historic District Visitor Center

Crystal Cove Historic District; 949/494-3539; 9am-6pm daily depending on staffing

The Historic District Visitor Center is housed in a single-story light yellow cottage dating from 1928. It is located on the left as you enter the district from the walking trail or shuttle drop-off. It contains historic artifacts and interpretive exhibits about the history of the Crystal Cove cottages.

Moro Visitor Center

8471 N. Coast Hwy.; 949/494-9143; 9am-5pm daily

The Moro Visitor Center and ranger station is located near Moro Campground and backcountry trail parking, offering information and backcountry trail maps.

WEATHER

The weather stays temperate year-round, with daytime temperatures hovering between 65-75°F (18-24°C). Mornings are typically foggy, but the fog burns off to bring sunny afternoons followed by cool evenings. With its moderate temperatures, Crystal Cove is a year-round destination.

ONE DAY IN CRYSTAL COVE STATE PARK

MORNING

Hike the backcountry in the cool of the morning while the marine layer is still blanketing the hills and beaches.

AFTERNOON

Have lunch at the Beachcomber Café, then explore the historic district. Spend the rest of the afternoon on the beach.

EVENING

Enjoy sunset from your cottage or campsite, or take a stroll along the coastal bluff-top trail.

SIGHTS

★ HISTORIC DISTRICT

Tucked against scenic bluffs, the 12.3-acre (5-ha) Crystal Cove Historic District is home to a preserved 1930s beach community. The seaside colony originally started as a tent camping destination where families came to summer. The tent sites got more and more elaborate, eventually turning into a collection of 46 rustic **coastal cottages** dating from the 1920s-1940s. The cottages were built by employees and friends of the landowners, James Irvine II and James Irvine III, as early as 1917. Of the remaining cottages, the oldest dates to 1921. Residents created their own homespun, regional style using scavenged materials and even hauled pieces of older houses to the cove for their vacation homes. As the cottages got more elaborate and the stays got longer, the property owners gave residents a choice: Move their cottages or lease them from the Irvine Company. The short-term leases ended up preserving the community because residents were not allowed to change the footprint. In 1979 the State of California purchased the land to become a state park.

Today you can walk the restored historic district; dine in Cottage 15 circa 1938, aka the Beachcomber Café; and even rent a cottage for the weekend.

To explore the historic district, take a **self-guided walking tour** of the area. The seemingly haphazard numbering system on the cottages indicates the order a gas line was installed. Information is available from a staffed visitor center that also has interpretive displays.

BEACHES

Crystal Cove State Park features 3.2 mi (5.1 km) of beach, one of the largest areas of natural seashore in Orange County. The park has four distinct beach and cove areas. The park's wide sandy coves and typically calm swells make it a good place for swimming. Due to these same calm swells, Crystal Cove is one of the lesser-surfed spots in the area; however, a few reef breaks offer opportunities, with Scotchman's Cove at Reef Point being the most popular. Crystal Cove's beaches are seasonally staffed with lifeguards.

PELICAN POINT

This northernmost beach is great for diving, surfing, and tide-pooling. The best tide pool spots are at Pelican Point itself and the north end of Treasure Cove.

HISTORIC DISTRICT

This beach is located directly in front of the historic district's scenic cottages. It's a great choice if you're planning on a meal at the Beachcomber Café. It's also a good beach for swimming and body surfing.

REEF POINT

From the bluff-top parking, a stairway takes you to **Scotchman's Cove,** a popular surf spot. For swimming and bodysurfing, a ramp leads down to the Muddy Creek section of the beach, a great spot for both.

MORO BEACH

The closest beach to the campground and easily accessed, this beach stretches from Muddy Creek to Abalone Point, the southern end of the park. It is popular for swimming, body boarding, fishing, paddleboarding, and kayaking.

Historic District Visitor Center (left); shoreline at Crystal Cove (right)

HIKING

Tucked between beaches and pricey housing developments, Crystal Cove State Park protects 2,400 acres (971 ha) of native wilderness and open space in its backcountry. There are 18 mi (29 km) of established trails winding through native vegetation including coastal sage scrub, allowing hikers to create their own loop hike. The lower trails follow seasonal Moro Creek through riparian woodland with oak and sycamore trees, while higher trails offer views over the backcountry and the Pacific Ocean. The Crystal Cove website (www.crystalcovestatepark.org) has a good hiking map with trails color-coded by difficulty.

★ MORO CANYON TRAIL

DISTANCE: 3 mi (5 km) round-trip
DURATION: 1 hour
EFFORT: Easy
TRAILHEAD: Lower Moro parking lot past ranger station

Walk the gentle grade of Moro Canyon, which connects the coast with the coastal backcountry. A wide trail winds through coastal sage scrub with wildflowers in spring, until you reach the junction with Poles and West Cut Across Trails. Turn around and retrace your steps.

PERIMETER TRAIL

DISTANCE: 9 mi (14 km) round-trip
DURATION: 4.5 hours
EFFORT: Strenuous
TRAILHEAD: Ranger station

This trail follows the perimeter of the backcountry in a clockwise loop along the backcountry's ridgelines, passing through the state park's three environmental campgrounds and offering sweeping views of the Pacific Ocean. To find the trailhead, from the ranger station walk uphill to a dirt road. The trail begins on the other side of a gate. The elevation gain and lack of shade make the hike challenging.

COASTAL BLUFFS TRAIL

DISTANCE: 3 mi (5 km) one-way
DURATION: 1.5 hours
EFFORT: Easy
TRAILHEAD: Pelican Point or Reef Point parking areas

This paved multiuse trail follows the Crystal Cove's bluffs for the entire length of the park, offering sweeping views of the ocean and coastline. There are also access points down to the beach.

RECREATION

 DIVING

Stretching adjacent to Crystal Cove State Park, the **Crystal Cove State Marine Conservation Area** protects more than 3 sq mi (8 sq km) of marine habitat extending from the sandy beaches to depths of almost 250 ft (76 m). The waters protect marine habitat that supports rocky reefs, kelp forests, a variety of fishes, invertebrates, dolphins, and sea lions. **Pelican Point, Rocky Bight,**

TOP HIKE

MORO CANYON LOOP TRAIL

DISTANCE: 5 mi (8 km) round-trip
DURATION: 2 hours
EFFORT: Moderate
TRAILHEAD: Lower Moro parking lot past ranger station

This trail follows the gentle grade of lovely Moro Canyon through coastal sage scrub and then continues in a loop with Moro Ridge for some elevation gain and views. From the ridge you can see the Pacific Ocean, the cliff-carved coastline of Crystal Cove, and the jutting Balboa Peninsula and community of Newport Beach.

and **Reef Point** have some of the best dive spots in the park.

WILDLIFE WATCHING

Tide Pools

With its distinct rocky outcroppings, Crystal Cove is known for thriving tide pools. There are four tide pool viewing areas near the shoreline's rocky points: Reef Point, Rocky Bight at the south end of the Historic District Beach, Pelican Point, and Treasure Cove on the northern end of Pelican Point Beach. Visit tide pools at low tide when the water recedes and the trapped water creates a temporary home for marine life including barnacles, mussels, sea anemones, and hermit crabs.

Marine Mammals

Look for migrating whales year-round with prime viewing in winter and spring. Gray whales can be seen traveling between Alaska and Baja California, Mexico, from December to May. There is a chance of spotting migrating blue and humpback whales from March to May, and fin and minke whales as they feed off the coast in summer. You may also spot dolphins year-round just beyond the waves.

CAMPING

Crystal Cove State Park offers two types of camping: **one developed campground** and primitive backcountry camping. For energetic backpackers, there are three environmental campgrounds, one in a canyon and two at the higher elevations.

Camping is open year-round, and sites can be booked online from two days up to six months of arrival through Reserve California (800/444-7575; www.reservecalifornia.com; $55/night developed, $25/night primitive). Reservations are required, and are highly competitive for Moro Campground, booking six months out from when they open.

BEST CAMPGROUND

Moro Campground

Moro Campground offers developed, coastal bluff-top camping on the other side of the Pacific Coast Highway. Beach access is via a tunnel under the PCH. The campground is located where Tyron's Camp offered a café and camping in the 1920s; the area was redeveloped as a campground for the public in 2005. The campground offers 58 campsites with 28 designated for RVs and trailers. They have picnic tables, restrooms, and showers. No wood or charcoal fires are allowed.

SHOPPING

THE CONSERVANCY STORE

Crystal Cove Historic District; 949/376-6200; https://crystalcove.org; 9am-5pm daily

The Crystal Cove Conservancy is a partner of Crystal Cove State Park and responsible for historic restoration, cottage rentals, and the park's restaurants. They operate a little store next to the visitor center with unexpectedly excellent curated offerings. The shop features locally made jewelry, clothing, wares for the retro-stylish house or camp, beach toys, and gear and souvenirs. Each supports the Crystal Cove Conservancy, which is reinvested into the park's preservation.

FOOD AND LODGING

The upscale coastal town of **Newport Beach,** located 3 mi (5 km) to the north, is known for its luxury resorts and waterfront dining. It also offers the basics, including grocery stores and gas stations. There are also a number of options within the park itself.

BEACHCOMBER CAFÉ

15 Crystal Cove; 949/376-6900; https://thebeachcombercafe.com; 7am-9:30pm daily; $18-65

Second only to the marvel that is the rentable cottages is the Beachcomber Café. Housed in a restored beachfront cottage, the café serves breakfast, lunch, and dinner with ocean views. The menu features California favorites and seafood, with avocado toast, chilaquiles, and lemon ricotta pancakes for breakfast giving way to clam chowder, poke bowls, and burgers for lunch. Dinner brings well-executed pasta, seafood, and steaks.

BOOTLEGGER BAR

15 Crystal Cove; 949/376-6900; https://thebeachcombercafe.com;

Moro Campground (left); tables at the Beachcomber Café (right)

11am-9:30pm Mon.-Fri., 10am-9:30pm Sat.-Sun.

On an adjacent deck, the tropical, thatch-roofed Bootlegger Bar serves up an extensive cocktail menu, wine, beer, mocktails, and small bites. Barstools are lined up facing the center of "town," the sandy arroyo that comprises the central path through the historic district. The combination of retro backdrop, beach views, people on vacation, and their menu of The Big Jars cocktails make this a festive spot.

SHAKE SHACK

7703 East Coast Hwy.; 949/464-0100; www.crystalcoveshakeshack.com; 7am-8pm daily

For a casual option, Shake Shack serves breakfast, tacos, burgers, and seafood baskets in a roadside shack next to the Pacific Coast Highway. Dining is on an outside deck with ocean views, a great place to catch the sunset.

CRYSTAL COVE COTTAGES

www.reservecalifornia.com; $228-320/night

The historic cottages can be rented for stays through the state park system's reservation system. The Crystal Cove Conservancy partnered with the state park to restore and preserve the cottages and offer this unique, time-machine beach getaway. The cottages are rustic with period-appropriate furniture (and beds, meaning smaller and less comfortable than today). They have electricity, running water, bathrooms, and refrigerators with kitchens but no way to cook. Perched beachside, they have sweeping views of the Pacific and are steps from the sand. The fact that they have the views and beach access of a luxury resort but with way more charm and affordability makes them highly competitive to reserve. Cottages book six months out to the second. However, there are sometimes cancellations through the system. Also, hot tip from the overnight check-in desk (Cottage 35): It is possible to get a same-day cottage reservation if there is a cancellation or no-show.

BEST PICNIC SPOT

Historic District

The obvious choice is to picnic anywhere on one of the stunning beaches. If you prefer a picnic table, there is one table beachfront in the historic district located scenically under the pergola of a cottage that now houses rotating art and history exhibits.

GETTING THERE

CAR

Crystal Cove is located in Orange County in between the coastal towns of Newport Beach to the north and Laguna Beach to the south. The park is located directly off CA-1, the Pacific Coast Highway, and can be accessed from the north or south via the PCH. From the east, I-405, a bypass of I-5, connects with CA-133 and heads along the park's southern border to intersect with the PCH just south of the park's several entrance points.

SAN CLEMENTE STATE BEACH

Located halfway between Los Angeles and San Diego, San Clemente has some of the most popular beaches in the state. It's wide sandy beaches, ocean swells, and balmy climate make it a year-round haven. Here Spanish-style architecture meets laid-back surf culture. Trestles, T-Street, and San Onofre, other San Clemente beaches, have some of the best and most consistent waves in California. Tourism descriptions of the town reference "Endless Summer," a nod to the classic 1966 surf documentary as well as its many days of sunshine.

ADDRESS: 225 W. Avenida Calafia, San Clemente

PHONE: 949/492-3156

DAY USE HOURS: 6am–10pm

AREA: 117 acres (47 ha)

San Clemente State Beach is a particularly scenic stretch of coastline, backed by eroded sandstone bluffs, striped in hues of red and gold, topped with wild coastal grasses. Designated a state beach in 1937, San Clemente is a classic beach experience, too low-key to be called a destination, although it is. It is more like your best buddy's best recommendation.

SAN CLEMENTE STATE BEACH
San Clemente
Lobos Marinos Creek
San Clemente Municipal Golf Course
S EL CAMINO REAL
AV DEL PRESIDENTE
San Clemente Beach Tr
Montalvo Creek
Park Entrance Kiosk
SAN CLEMENTE BEACH TRAIL
AV CALAFIA
San Clemente State Beach
AV SAN LUIS REY
Visitor Center
Day-Use Picnic Area
BEACHING IT BENEATH THE BLUFFS
STAYING IN A VINTAGE HOLIDAY TRAILER
San Clemente State Beach
Group #2
San Clemente Beach
SWIMMING IN THE SURF
Lifeguard Headquarters/ First Aid
Group #1
PACIFIC OCEAN
200 yds
200 m
Contour Interval = 20 feet

2

3

TOP 3

★ **1. BEACHING IT BENEATH THE BLUFFS:** Spend a beach day relaxing on the sand backed by scenic eroded bluffs (page 450).

★ **2. SWIMMING IN THE SURF:** San Clemente's wide beach and gradual slope make it a prime spot for swimming, surfing, and snorkeling (page 451).

★ **3. STAYING IN A VINTAGE HOLIDAY TRAILER:** Book one of the park's colorful vintage trailers for a retro glamping experience (page 453).

1

PLANNING YOUR TIME

San Clemente is a hugely popular day use destination for visitors who come to swim, sunbathe, and picnic on the beach. It is also a great place to spend a few days, camping and getting into vacation mode.

Nearby state parks include Crystal Cove State Park (20 mi/32 km) and South Carlsbad (27 mi/43 km).

ENTRANCE AND FEES

Campers and day use visitors enter through an **official entrance kiosk** (225 Avenida Calafia; $10/vehicle day use, $20/vehicle holiday) to pay a day use fee, check in for camping, or present your camping pass, which is good for day use. The entrance gate is locked and closed daily 10pm-6am.

VISITOR CENTER

San Clemente State Beach Visitor Center

225 Avenida Calafia; 10am-4pm daily

The San Clemente State Beach Visitor Center is housed in a historic 1934 ranger's cottage and features exhibits on the natural and cultural history of the area as well as a gift shop. It is located next to the day use parking area.

SAFETY

There is a Lifeguard Headquarters/First Aid Station located in the campground near sites 80-99.

WEATHER

The adjacent town of San Clemente proclaims itself home of the "world's best climate," referring to the moderate year-round temperatures that draw visitors to the coast. For most of the year San Clemente daytime temperatures hover around 68-75°F (20-24°C) with summer getting up to 80-85°F (27-29°C). Evening temperatures can dip to 45-55°F (7-13°C). Spring can experience a coastal fog that typically burns off in the afternoons. Winter temperatures are the coolest, but rarely cold, with daytime highs tending to hover around 65°F (18°C). Summer is the most popular season to visit, but early fall (Sept.-Oct.) is a great time to go when temperatures are still warm, skies are generally clear of marine layer, and beaches are less crowded.

BEACHES

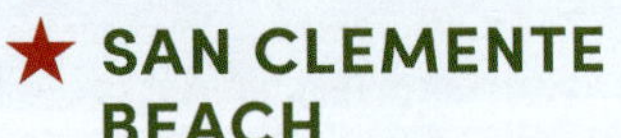

★ SAN CLEMENTE BEACH

San Clemente is known for its mild year-round climate, drawing visitors to escape the heat or the cold on its beautiful stretch of sand. From the San Clemente State Beach day use area and campground, two trails cut between crags of eroded sandstone, making for a striking entrance to the sandy beach below. The mile-long (1.6-km-long) beach stretches between frothing ocean surf and weathered escarpment, sand and scenery in every direction.

THE TOWN OF SAN CLEMENTE

San Clemente, nicknamed the "Spanish Village by the Sea," is known for the white stucco walls, red tile roofs, and soft arches of its Spanish Colonial Revival architecture. The town is nestled in the hills above the Pacific, adorned with palm trees. A historic wooden pier in the center of town is a popular spot for surfing, sunsets, and dining at the pier's landmark restaurant. A charming, walkable downtown extends from the pier along Avenida del Mar lined with boutiques, breweries, wineries, and restaurants. San Clemente has a small-town vibe and is also known for its rich surfing culture with destination breaks and a healthy concentration of surf shops.

RECREATION

★ SWIMMING AND SURFING

San Clemente is a destination surf zone most known for Lower Trestles, famous for its reliably peaked waves. Slightly north at San Clemente State Beach, conditions are more mellow, offering a beach break with consistent waves that's appropriate for a range of skill levels. The same waves that make this a good spot for surfing are also fun for swimming, boogie-boarding, and bodysurfing. There are lifeguard towers, and the beach is patrolled by lifeguards year-round.

CAMPING

The state park offers **one developed campground** as well as two group campsites, one geared toward RVs and another that is tent-only. Reservations are required and can be made through Reserve California (800/444-7275; www.reservecalifornia.com; $45/night); like all beach campgrounds in Southern California, they are highly competitive to book, especially in summer when the campground fills completely and weekends year-round. Sites are available to book six months out and fill as soon as they open.

BEST CAMPGROUND

San Clemente State Beach Campground

San Clemente's large family campground has 160 sites spread across grassy open space on bluff tops above the ocean. The campsites do not have ocean views, but there is direct access to the beach from the campground via a hard-packed sandy path that cuts through the bluffs. Of the 160 sites, 72 are RV sites with electric and water hookups. All sites have fire rings and picnic tables. Throughout the campground there are water spigots, bathrooms, and token-operated showers.

TOP HIKE

SAN CLEMENTE BEACH TRAIL

DISTANCE: 2.3 mi (3.7 km) one-way
DURATION: 30 minutes-1 hour
EFFORT: Easy
TRAILHEAD: San Clemente State Beach day use parking

The popular 2.3-mi-long (3.7-km-long) multiuse trail hugs the boundary between San Clemente's beaches and town with sparkling views of the Pacific along the entire stretch. The trail begins at the San Clemente State Beach day use parking area and follows the beach north, passing popular T-Street Beach just south of the San Clemente Pier and then the pier itself before ending at North Beach/North Beach Train Station. You can also do shorter sections of the trail. The easiest places to pick it up are San Clemente State Beach, the San Clemente Pier, and North Beach. The trail is wide and flat, making it hugely popular with joggers, walkers, cyclists, and dog-walkers. No e-bikes are allowed, and dogs must be leashed and are not allowed on the beach.

FOOD AND LODGING

The state beach and campground are located in the charming town of San Clemente. The beach town caters to visitors and has a collection of boutique lodging ranging from hotels to condos to cottage-style inns. There are also plenty of restaurant options ranging from seafood with a view to tacos, as well as wineries and breweries. The proximity of all these great dining options means that you can go out to dinner or even order pizza to your campsite and skip the camp cooking.

★ VINTAGE TRAILERS

833/268-8956; www.theholidayscamping.com; $228 Mar.-Oct., $206 Nov.-Feb.

Enjoy a retro camping experience by renting one of the state park's four vintage trailers. The Drifter, Roadrunner, Wrangler, and Muir are colorful aluminum trailers sometimes referred to as "canned hams" because of their boxy shape. They are arranged in their own section of the campground around a central fire pit. Not only are the vintage trailers charming, they make for an easy glamping weekend without having to pack up all the gear.

Each site has its own individual fire pit, grill, and picnic table with shade pergolas. The trailers are solar-powered and have the amenities you might expect from a cabin, including a small cookstove, refrigerator, and electricity. They also come with bedding, bath and beach towels, coffee, and a percolator. Bathrooms are in the campground's communal facilities. Trailers comfortably fit 2-4 people, but reservations allow for up to eight, and campers are allowed to bring a tent to set up next to the trailer.

vintage trailer

BEST PICNIC SPOT

Day Use Picnic Area

Picnic on the bluff tops 150 ft (46 m) above the beach with sweeping views of the Pacific. A designated picnic area is located next to day use parking and the visitor center.

GETTING THERE

CAR

San Clemente State Beach is located off of I-5 halfway between Los Angeles and San Diego. From I-5 south, exit Avenida Calafia and proceed straight for 0.25 mi (0.4 km). The state beach entrance will be on your left. From I-5 north, exit Cristianitos Road. Turn left and continue over the freeway. Turn right onto Avenida del Presidente. Turn right onto Avenida Calafia and continue straight for 0.25 mi (0.4 km). The state beach entrance will be on your left.

TRAIN

San Clemente is also a stop on the **Pacific Surfliner** (www.pacificsurfliner.com), a scenic train route that hugs the coast with stops in communities from San Diego to San Luis Obispo. The train station is located at the San Clemente Pier (615 Avenida Victoria, San Clemente), 2.5 mi (4 km) north of the state beach and campground.

TROLLEY

www.san-clemente.org; noon-10pm Mon.-Fri., 10am-10pm Sat., 10am-8pm Sun. end of May-Sept., limited service weekends Oct.-May

The city of San Clemente offers a free trolley service that runs from the north end of town at Camino de Estrella to access the downtown Del Mar shopping district and the San Clemente Pier. It continues south with several stops for the state beach, including Avenida Calafia and the state park day use area and Avenida del Presidente and the state beach campground.

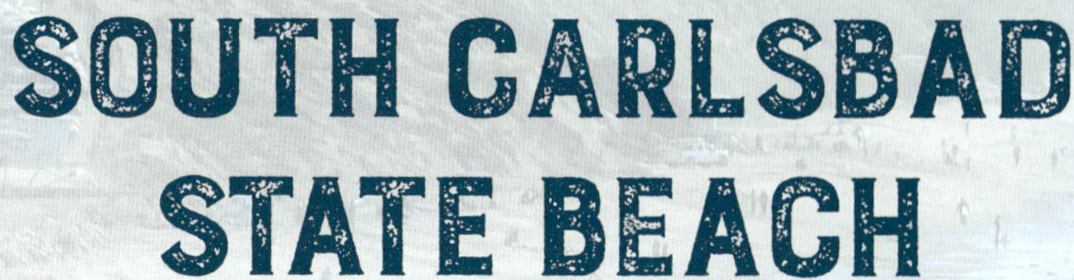

SOUTH CARLSBAD STATE BEACH

ADDRESS: 7201 Carlsbad Blvd., Carlsbad

PHONE: 760/438-3143

DAY USE HOURS: Sunrise-sunset

AREA: 118 acres (48 ha)

South Carlsbad's beaches are covered with miles of soft sand, classic Southern California shoreline. Sometimes winter swells strip the sand, revealing a natural seawall of smooth cobblestones and changing the shore's character. Beaches along this stretch of San Diego's Coast District live up to a reputation for both highly scenic natural coast and the fun-in-the-sun strips of sand where we surf and swim.

South Carlsbad has three distinct sections: the northern, with its narrow strip of wave-bashed sand lining the base of eroded hills; the central, with wide, sandy beaches backed by steep, rugged bluffs; and the southern end, where the cliffs give way and so does the development. The Pacific Coast Highway hugs the wide coastline here lined with dunes and wetlands. At the end of a beach day, families grill up dinner at camp or have pizza at the Camp Store while kids ride bikes. There is a moment of pause at sunset, the last streaks of light over the Pacific. Everyone prepares for another beach day tomorrow.

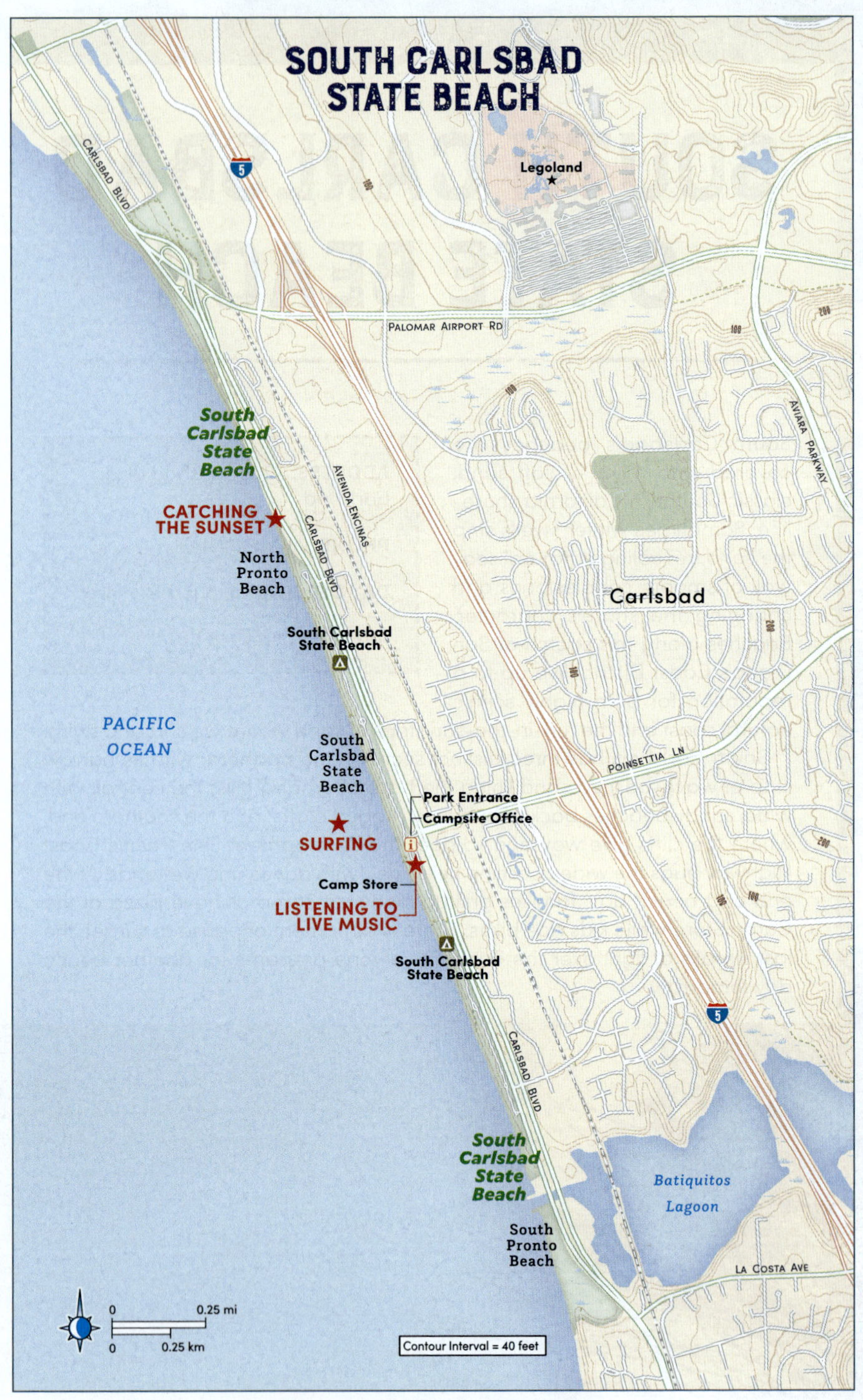
SOUTH CARLSBAD
STATE BEACH
Legoland
CARLSBAD BLVD
5
PALOMAR AIRPORT RD
South
Carlsbad
State
Beach
CATCHING
THE SUNSET
North
Pronto
Beach
AVENIDA ENCINAS
CARLSBAD BLVD
AVIARA PARKWAY
Carlsbad
South Carlsbad
State Beach
PACIFIC
OCEAN
South
Carlsbad
State
Beach
POINSETTIA LN
Park Entrance
Campsite Office
SURFING
Camp Store
LISTENING TO
LIVE MUSIC
South Carlsbad
State Beach
5
CARLSBAD BLVD
South
Carlsbad
State
Beach
Batiquitos
Lagoon
South
Pronto
Beach
LA COSTA AVE
0
0.25 mi
0
0.25 km
Contour Interval = 40 feet

TOP 3

1. CATCHING THE SUNSET: Every evening as the sun dips toward the horizon, locals and visitors angle to watch the colorful event, setting up camp chairs at South Ponto to wait for the sun to go down (page 459).

2. SURFING: Consistent waves and optimal surfing conditions in summer make South Carlsbad a popular spot for surfers of all levels (page 460).

3. LISTENING TO LIVE MUSIC: The Camp Store at the state beach campground hosts live music from its bluff-top stage with views over the Pacific (page 461).

PLANNING YOUR TIME

Many visitors come to South Carlsbad State Beach to spend the day. The best places to do this are North Ponto, on the northern end of the state beach, and South Ponto, on the southern end. The main beach, in the center, is easiest to access if you are camping at the campground, via a series of stairways. The campground is strict about its 2pm check-in time. If you arrive early, head to one of the day use beach areas.

Nearby state parks include Torrey Pines State Beach and Natural Reserve (13 mi/21 km) and Old Town San Diego State Historic Park (26 mi/42 km).

ENTRANCES AND FEES

There are **two day use areas.** North Ponto, on the north end of the campground, has no entrance kiosk and relies on a free parking lot along Carlsbad Boulevard. South Ponto, on the south end of the campground, has some free parking along the street and a paid parking lot ($15/vehicle in peak season).

The official entrance for the campground is on Carlsbad Boulevard (7201 Carlsbad Blvd., Carlsbad). Campers with reservations must check in here beginning at the 2pm check-in time and then park at their campsite. There is no day use parking here.

VISITOR CENTER

There is no visitor center for South Carlsbad State Beach. The campground check-in is staffed by rangers who can answer questions.

WEATHER

The coastal weather keeps temperatures moderate year-round, with daytime temps hovering around 62-75°F (17-24°C) for most of the year. The warmest months are July-October, when average temperatures are closer to 80°F (27°C). Winter brings the coolest temperatures and also the possibility of rain and large ocean swells. Cool water temperatures mean wetsuits are recommended for surfers and swimmers most of the year, but water temperatures can be significantly warmer than along more northern beaches during the warmest times of the year.

BEACHES

A nearly 5-mi (8-km) stretch of coastline makes up South Carlsbad State Beach from North Ponto Beach on the northern end to South Ponto Beach on the southern end. Visitors flock to the beach for camping, swimming, skin-diving, picnicking, and surfing.

NORTH PONTO BEACH

North Ponto Beach is the northernmost stretch of South Carlsbad State Beach and its northern day use beach access point. It is a narrow beach edged with low bluffs popular with surfers, but it is also a good spot for swimming and sunbathing when the tides are low. It's a great spot to spend a few hours, especially if you are looking for an easy spot to have a beach day before checking into the campground. The North Ponto parking lot is located along Carlsbad Boulevard at the north end of South Carlsbad Campground.

SOUTH CARLSBAD STATE BEACH

Nice sand and rugged bluffs make up the central section of South Carlsbad State Beach, which lies adjacent to the campground. Access is via several sets of stairs that lead from the bluff-top campground. There is no dedicated day use parking for this section of beach, so it is mostly filled with campers. If you're not camping, you can walk from either North Ponto or South Ponto.

★ SOUTH PONTO BEACH

The cliffs disappear south of the campground, giving way to wide, sandy South Ponto Beach. Located along a rare stretch of undeveloped land, the beach comprises a large sand spit that shelters Batiquitos Lagoon, a protected coastal wetland, game sanctuary, and bird estuary.

The PCH hugs the shoreline here at beach level with coastal views, making it an ideal place to watch the sunset. There are free parking spaces along the southbound lanes of the highway. During peak season, a pay lot is available at Carlsbad Boulevard north of La Costa Avenue with demand pricing. The beach is popular for swimming, sunbathing, and surfing. There are public restrooms, showers, and volleyball courts.

South Carlsbad State Beach (left); watching surfers (right)

RECREATION

★ SWIMMING AND SURFING

The stretch of coast that makes up **South Carlsbad State Beach** shifts in topography from the narrow beach to the north, the sandy bluff-backed section in the middle, and the wide shores on the south end. What they all have in common are mellow breaks and gentle swells, making this a great destination for swimming, boogie-boarding, bodysurfing, and skin-diving. It also draws surfers, particularly at **South Ponto Beach** where a pair of jetties create consistent waves year-round. Lifeguard towers are staffed in summer. There is limited staffing in spring and fall and no staffing in winter.

BEACH VOLLEYBALL

South Ponto Beach has a beach volleyball court that is open on a first-come, first-served basis. You will have to bring your own ball and net.

CAMPING

South Carlsbad State Beach has **one developed campground.** Reservations are required through Reserve California (800/444-7275; www.reservecalifornia.com; $50-70) and can be booked six months ahead of time. Campsites are typically snapped up minutes after the dates open, and the campground books fully in spring, summer, and fall. If you don't get your dates, check back for cancellations.

Check-in begins strictly at 2pm. Lines can be long with everyone trying to check in at once, so get there ahead of time to line up.

The Camp Store

BEST CAMPGROUND

South Carlsbad State Beach Campground

The 220-site campground occupies prime real estate along a bluff overlooking Carlsbad State Beach and the gleaming Pacific Ocean. There are two rows of decently spaced campsites divided by a campground road. The camping spots closest to the bluff's edge with unobstructed ocean views are considered "premium" and cost more, while campsites on the other side of the road are considered standard sites. Despite the utilitarian layout, they have more privacy than you may expect because of coastal shrubbery dividing many of the sites.

All campsites have a firepit and picnic table, and there is potable water throughout the campground. There are token-operated showers and laundry facilities on-site. For RVs, there are hookup sites and an RV sanitation station.

FOOD AND LODGING

The state beach is located in the city of Carlsbad, and there are plenty of restaurants, hotels, groceries, gas stations, and supplies nearby. Carlsbad Village (www.carlsbad-village.com), 3 mi (5 km) north of the campground, has a walkable concentration of restaurants and shopping with easy access to city beaches.

★ THE CAMP STORE

7201 Carlsbad Blvd.; 714/478-2487; https://thecampstore.com; 3:30pm-7pm Wed.-Thurs., noon-7pm Fri.-Sun.; $5-19

Located near the campground entrance on a bluff overlooking the ocean, The Camp Store offers fresh pizza, salad, and a kids' menu alongside local beer and wine. The store also has live music on its stage 4pm-6pm Wednesday-Sunday year-round with the music schedule posted on its website. The combination of music, scenery, pizza, and libations inspires a family-friendly party every evening as campers, day-trippers, and locals gather. If you want to get serious about this scene, the store offers two-hour bluff-top table rentals for up to six people ($15/hour) and a firepit rental for up to eight people ($45/hour).

BEST PICNIC SPOT

South Ponto Beach

The fact that South Ponto Beach is level with the PCH along a coastline otherwise stacked with dramatic bluffs makes it a good spot to tote out your beach blanket and set up a picnic with views of the Pacific.

GETTING THERE

CAR

South Carlsbad State Beach is located 30 mi (48 km) north of San Diego off I-5 on the Pacific Coast Highway (Carlsbad Blvd.). From the south, exit Poinsettia Lane and continue to Carlsbad Boulevard. From the north, exit at Palomar Airport Road in the city of Carlsbad and head south along Carlsbad Boulevard.

TORREY PINES STATE BEACH AND NATURAL RESERVE

ADDRESS: 12600 N. Torrey Pines Rd., La Jolla

PHONE: 858/755-2063

WEBSITE: https://torreypine.org

DAY USE HOURS: 7:15am-sunset

AREA: Natural Reserve 1,461 acres (591 ha), State Beach 61 acres (25 ha)

Torrey Pines is named for our nation's rarest pine tree, *pinus torreyana*. Also rare is the green space along Southern California's developed coast. The Torrey Pines State Natural Reserve protects both of these rarities within the nearly 1,500-acre (607-ha) reserve. The landscape it preserves is dramatic, featuring steep broken sandstone cliffs, eroded into wrinkled folds and deep ravines on headlands overlooking the Pacific. Framed by these towering bluffs, Torrey Pines State Beach below is a place where the juxtaposition of rugged cliffs and serene Pacific Ocean continues the captivating tone of the setting. Along these bluff tops are the stands of wind-lashed pines for which the park is named, but also cacti, coastal sage scrub, and wildflowers.

This place is the historic land of the Kumeyaay, whose lands extended south to Ensenada, Mexico, east to the Colorado River's sand dunes, and north to what is now Oceanside, linked together in vast trading networks.

The way to explore this fragile place now is through a series of hikes that traverse the craggy cliffs dotted with the endangered native trees all set against the backdrop of the Pacific Ocean. Or venture down to the beach where you can swim, surf, or stroll along the sand.

TORREY PINES STATE BEACH AND NATURAL RESERVE
Torrey Pines State Natural Reserve
Del Mar Heights
North Beach
North Beach Entrance
Torrey Pines State Beach
N TORREY PINES RD
CARMEL VALLEY RD
South Beach
Torrey Pines State Natural Reserve
STROLLING THE BEACH
CHECKING OUT THE LODGE
Guy Fleming
Torrey Pines Visitor Center
High Point Overlook
South Beach Entrance
Beach
West Overlook
HIKING THE BLUFFS
North Fork
South Fork
North Fork Tr
South Fork Trail
Broken Hill Tr
Beach Tr
Flat Rock
BROKEN HILL TRAIL
Torrey Pines Golf Course
PACIFIC OCEAN
Torrey Pines State Beach
Torrey Pines
0 0.5 mi
0 0.5 km
Contour Interval = 20 feet

TOP 3

★ **1. CHECKING OUT THE LODGE:** Stop by the picturesque Torrey Pines Visitor Center, built in 1923 as the Torrey Pines Lodge, a restaurant that served visitors to the area (page 466).

★ **2. STROLLING THE BEACH:** At low tide, stroll along the beach's sandy coastline, backed by strikingly sculpted cliffs (page 466).

★ **3. HIKING THE BLUFFS:** A series of trails explore the reserve's dramatic landscape, including the 1-mi (1.6-km) Razor Point Trail that leads to an overview of badlands and wind-sculpted trees (page 467).

1

3

2

PLANNING YOUR TIME

Plan for a half a day to stop by the visitor center and hike some of the reserve's trails. Plan for an additional half day to spend time on the beach.

In addition to the main reserve, there is an extension to the north, not connected to the main reserve. It has several hiking trails but no direct beach access. The only available parking is street parking.

Nearby state parks include Old Town San Diego State Historic Park (15 mi/24 km) and South Carlsbad State Beach (13 mi/21 km).

ENTRANCES AND FEES

For both Torrey Pines State Natural Reserve and Torrey Pines State Beach, visitors should enter and pay fees at an **entrance kiosk** in the **South Beach Parking Lot** (12600 N. Torrey Pines Rd.; $12-25), which gives access to the Torrey Pines State Beach upper lots in the State Natural Reserve located next to the visitor center and to the trailheads. When the reserve's upper lots are full the road closes, and visitors to the reserve will need to walk the paved, 1-mi (1.6-km) Park Road from the South Beach Parking Lot. Fees at the South Beach entrance are valid for both the state beach and reserve.

If the South Beach Parking Lot is full, entrance is via a kiosk in the **North Beach Parking Lot** (1800 McGonigle Rd.; $12-25), 0.5 mi (0.8 km) to the north.

Both the South Beach Parking Lot and the North Beach Parking Lot give direct access to the beach. The beach can also be reached by a 0.75-mi (1.2-km) hiking trail from the reserve.

VISITOR CENTER

Torrey Pines Visitor Center

12600 N. Torrey Pines Rd., La Jolla; 9am-5pm daily

The visitor center is housed in the building that opened in 1923 as the Torrey Pines Lodge. Today it serves as a ranger station, offers exhibits on natural and cultural history, and also has a small gift shop.

WEATHER

The area has moderate temperatures year-round, rarely dipping below 60°F (16°C), even in winter. Summer brings great beach weather with temperatures typically around 85°F (29°C) June-October. There can be a marine layer cooling the air, especially in the mornings, and wind and temperatures can change quickly. Torrey Pines State Beach and Natural Reserve are year-round destinations.

SIGHTS

HIGH POINT OVERLOOK

North of visitor center off Torrey Pines State Park Rd., access via steep stairs

A 100-yard (90-m) series of stairs leads to the highest point in the park with panoramic views of the reserve, the Pacific Ocean, and inland toward the Los Penasquitos Lagoon and wetlands.

WEST OVERLOOK

Visitor center, wheelchair accessible

An accessible alternative to the High Point Overlook, West Overlook offers scenic views of the reserve, ocean, and lagoon, without the stairs.

★ TORREY PINES VISITOR CENTER

Oh, to see the Torrey Pines Visitor Center when it opened to the public in 1923. Originally opened as the Torrey Pines Lodge, it was, as described on the Torrey Pines Conservancy's website, "a restaurant with stumpy tables, chintz curtains, lampshades made of Torrey pine needles, and a jukebox." Visitors in Model T's would chug up the steep road, sometimes stalling out and having to make the ascent in reverse because of the placement of the gas tank on those early cars. The description continues, "By the time you got to the top, your car needed water and you needed a beer." Although the function is different today, the adobe building that houses the visitor center is still picturesque and worth a stop. It was designed by architects Richard Requa and Herbert Lewis Jackson and styled after Hopi Indian houses in Arizona. It is surrounded by native gardens. Unlike early visitors, you will likely be able to make the drive without having to back up the hill.

BEACHES

★ TORREY PINES STATE BEACH

Explore a different perspective on the strikingly corroded sandstone cliffs that form the backbone of the reserve by spending time on the beaches below. Torrey Pines State Beach runs for 4.5 mi (7.2 km) of coastline extending from Del Mar to the north of the reserve to the cliffs of Torrey Pines Mesa south of the reserve. The section adjacent to the reserve is accessible via the 0.75-mi (1.2-km) Beach Trail. For safety, always make sure you stay at least 10 ft (3 m) from the base of the cliffs due to the threat of rockslides and cliff collapses. Time your visit for low tide to ensure there will be enough sand so that you can keep this 10-ft safety buffer.

TOP HIKE

BROKEN HILL TRAIL

DISTANCE: 2.7 mi (4.3 km) round-trip
DURATION: 1-1.5 hours
EFFORT: Moderate
TRAILHEAD: Torrey Pines State Park Rd. south of visitor center

The Broken Hill Trail, named for the park's signature eroded sandstone, gives up-close views of the wrinkled hills, particularly from **Broken Hill Overlook.** It is the park's longest trail at 1.3 mi (2 km) (one-way) via the **North Fork Trail** or 1.4 mi (2.3 km) (one-way) via **South Fork Trail.** It passes through California sage and chaparral, also known more whimsically by naturalists as "elfin forest." It is also possible to access the beach from this trail where it connects with **Beach Trail** at its western end.

HIKING

By definition, state natural reserves have outstanding natural scenic value, and Torrey Pines more than meets this criterion. Layers of wildly eroded sandstone make up the coastal terrace that edges right up to the crashing Pacific in a series of steep broken cliffs and ravines. The bluff tops are home to diverse plant life, from wind-sculpted pines to cacti. Lucky for us, a series of short hiking trails allow us to explore this special protected place.

BEACH TRAIL

DISTANCE: 1.5 mi (2.4 km) round-trip
DURATION: 30 minutes
EFFORT: Easy, but steep steps to beach
TRAILHEAD: Visitor center

A 0.75-mi (1.2-km) trail leads from the visitor center through the reserve to the beach at Flat Rock. Although this is the way to the beach, the trail also treats hikers to the park's striking terrain, cutting through native coastal sage with views of the desiccated bluffs. The trail then dramatically descends via staircase through a pocked sandstone terrace. For a longer hike, turn this into a loop that includes a walk along the beach (2.3 mi/3.7 km total). Check the tides before you start; the loop can only be walked at low tide. To begin the loop, park at South Beach Parking Lot and walk Torrey Pines State Park Road south through the park to intersect with the Beach Trail. Follow the Beach Trail to the beach and finish the loop by walking along the back to the parking lot.

GUY FLEMING TRAIL

DISTANCE: 0.7 mi (1.1 km) round-trip
DURATION: 20 minutes
EFFORT: Easy
TRAILHEAD: Torrey Pines State Park Rd. trailhead pullout south of South Beach Parking Lot

view from Broken Hill Trail

This easy loop trail offers spectacular ocean views via two scenic overlooks. The trail is also a standout for its plant diversity. Along this short loop, hikers will pass through pine forest, stands of cacti, ferns, and wildflowers.

FOOD AND LODGING

There is **no camping** in the Torrey Pines State Natural Reserve or Torrey Pines State Beach.

The parks are an island in a sea of development and surrounded by food and lodging options in the coastal neighborhood of La Jolla in northern San Diego. A concentration of hotels and restaurants can be found near La Jolla Cove Beach, 9 mi (14 km) south along Torrey Pines Road. The upscale coastal town of **Del Mar** 2 mi (3 km) to the north via Carmel Valley Road and South Camino del Mar has a high concentration of restaurants and hotels (www.visitdelmarvillage.com).

BEST PICNIC SPOT

Torrey Pines State Beach

There is a picnic area with shaded tables at the southern end of the South Beach Parking Lot, a convenient spot whether you are visiting the beach or the natural reserve.

Alternately, picnic on the shores of Torrey Pines State Beach. Note: There are no food or drinks except water allowed in the reserve.

GETTING THERE

CAR

Torrey Pines State Natural Reserve and Torrey Pines State Beach are located along the Pacific Coast Highway in the coastal community of La Jolla within the San Diego city limits, 18 mi (29 km) north of downtown San Diego. I-5 passes within a few miles of the park. From the I-5, exit Carmel Valley Road west continuing onto Torrey Pines Road south (PCH).

The main parking and access point for both Torrey Pines State Natural Reserve and Torrey Pines State Beach is in the South Beach Parking Lot (12600 N. Torrey Pines Rd.). If that lot is full it will close; staff will indicate the closure with a blinking light that can be seem from the road before pulling in. There is alternate parking available in the North Beach Parking Lot (1800 McGonigle Rd.), 0.5 mi (0.8 km) north.

OLD TOWN SAN DIEGO STATE HISTORIC PARK

ADDRESS: San Diego Ave. and Twiggs St., San Diego

PHONE: 619/220-5422

WEBSITE: www.oldtownsandiego.org

DAY USE HOURS: 10am-5pm

AREA: 29 acres (12 ha)

Old Town San Diego is a dynamic mix of living history museum and bustling marketplace celebrating the early days of the city from 1821 to 1872. San Diego's cultural history spans thousands of years, beginning with the Kumeyaay people, who thrived in the region before Spanish explorers arrived.

In 1769, Spanish settlers established the first European settlement, profoundly impacting the Indigenous population. After Mexican independence from Spain in 1821, San Diego became part of Mexico, and Old Town flourished as a civilian pueblo with ranchos and adobe homes.

Following the US takeover in 1848, San Diego became part of the US and California, and by the late 1800s, the district faded to a relic of the past, preserving its unique blend of Kumeyaay, Spanish, Mexican, and early American heritage. It began a new era in 1968 when Old Town San Diego became a state historic park.

The Old Town district showcases restored and reconstructed 19th-century adobe and wood-frame buildings that visitors can explore. Old Town is also a hub for authentic Mexican cuisine, with restaurants serving handmade tortillas and traditional dishes; artisan boutiques; craft shops; and markets offering pottery, souvenirs, and handmade goods.

OLD TOWN SAN DIEGO
STATE HISTORIC PARK
0
100 yds
0
100 m
Contour Interval = 20 feet
TAYLOR ST.
JUAN ST.
Kumeyaay Interpretive Area
WALLACE ST.
Casa de Reyes
SHOPPING
FIESTA DE REYES
Barra Barra Saloon & Mexican Restaurant
EATING
MEXICAN FOOD
Amtrak Old Town Station
McCoy House
Ghost Tours
CALHOUN ST.
GARDEN ST.
EXPLORING
OLD TOWN SAN DIEGO'S
HISTORIC BUILDINGS
Robinson Rose Visitor Center
Plaza de las Almas
Cosmopolitan Hotel
Seeley Stable
OLD BEACH RD.
Old Town San Diego State Historic Park
MASON ST.
La Casa de Estudillo
TWIGGS ST.
The Schoolhouse
Wallach & Goldman Square
SAN DIEGO AVE
Casa de Maria Restaurant
Whaley House Museum
PACIFIC HIGHWAY
PACIFIC HIGHWAY
CONGRESS ST.
To El Campo Santo Cemetery
OLD TOWN
Map Area
WASHINGTON ST.
PASEO DE MISSION HILLS
NORTH PARK
San Diego International Airport
San Diego Zoo
Balboa Park
SOUTH PARK
0
1 mi
0
1 km
San Diego Bay
DOWNTOWN
EAST VILLAGE
GOLDEN HILL

TOP 3

1. EXPLORING OLD TOWN SAN DIEGO'S HISTORIC BUILDINGS: Visitors can explore restored original historic buildings that bring early San Diego to life (page 474).

2. SHOPPING FIESTA DE REYES: The adobe marketplace features locally owned specialty shops offering a range of handcrafted and imported goods (page 477).

3. EATING MEXICAN FOOD: Within the historic park and surrounding blocks, there are dozens of options for enjoying authentic Mexican food (page 477).

1

2

3

PLANNING YOUR TIME

Plan to spend half a day taking in the park's historic buildings and museums and enjoying the park's restaurants and shopping.

Nearby state parks include Torrey Pines State Beach and Natural Reserve (15 mi/24 km) and South Carlsbad State Beach (28 mi/45 km).

ENTRANCE AND FEES

There is **no official entrance** to the park, and visitors are free to walk in and out of the historic zone. However, one main entrance is at the corner of Twiggs Street and Juan Street, where there is a large public parking lot and an entrance sign. Park admission is free, and there are free public parking lots surrounding the historic zone.

VISITOR CENTER

Robinson Rose Visitor Center

4098 Mason St.; 619/220-5422; 10am-5pm daily

The Robinson Rose Visitor Center is housed in the reconstructed Robinson Rose house, originally built in 1853 as a residence and law office. The visitor center offers maps and information as well as a small bookstore. A historic diorama of the San Diego of 1872 is a surprising draw as you take in the scope of the small outpost compared with today.

WEATHER

San Diego has a mild, Mediterranean climate with warm, dry summers and cool, wet winters. Temperatures are generally comfortable year-round, averaging around 70°F (21°C). Rain is scarce, mostly falling between November and March, and the city enjoys plenty of sunshine. Moderate weather makes Old Town San Diego a year-round destination.

EVENTS

Old Town San Diego hosts a range of events throughout the year, from cultural festivals to casual live music performances to street markets, celebrating the region's rich history as well as holidays including the Fourth of July and Cinco de Mayo. For a full listing check the Old Town San Diego website's event page (www.oldtownsandiego.org).

Dia de los Muertos

Dia de los Muertos, traditionally celebrated on November 1 and 2, kicks off each year over the course of a weekend to honor the Mexican tradition that pays tribute to loved ones who have passed away. In Old Town San Diego, the event is a huge deal with more than 40 elaborate ofrendas (altars) honoring loved ones, historic figures, and celebrities as well as free music, culture, and food. Live mariachi and ballet folklorico grace a central stage, and there are family-friendly activities including face-painting and sugar skull-making. The festival concludes with a procession down San Diego Avenue. Fiesta de Reyes is ground zero for the celebration.

Mormon Battalion Parade

The Mormon Battalion Parade is a military reenactment and community event commemorating a battalion of the US Army in the mid-1800s during the Mexican American War. The event is held at the end of January, featuring a historical reenactment,

ONE DAY IN OLD TOWN SAN DIEGO

Spend a day enjoying the history and culture of Old Town San Diego and its extended historic walking district.

MORNING

Explore the historic buildings of Old Town San Diego State Historic Park, including its living history museums.

AFTERNOON

Have lunch at one of the Mexican restaurants, then browse the shops at Fiesta de Reyes.

EVENING

Choose another restaurant for dinner, then end the evening with a ghost-hunting tour.

family-friendly games and activities, and a Dutch-oven cook-off.

Taste of Old Town

Taste of Old Town features Old Town restaurants that create signature dishes and food and drink samples for visitors to enjoy on a three-hour self-guided tour each September.

SIGHTS

The core of restored and original historic buildings surround **Plaza de las Almas/Washington Square** located in the center of the historic park. A blacksmith shop, a one-room schoolhouse, and a two-story hotel, among other buildings, provide a backdrop for interpreting life in San Diego from 1821 to 1872. There are five original adobe structures interspersed with reconstructed buildings designed in the same style. Styles range from red-roofed adobe homes and businesses to Greek Revival residences built by San Diego's wealthier residents. Many of these are open as museums, filled with period furniture and wares and staffed by docents in period clothing who can provide interpretive information. Other historic buildings offer concessions ranging from candy to leather goods.

TOURS

Self-Guided Tours

To add structure to your exploration of Old Town, stop by the Robinson Rose Visitor Center for a map and a self-guided tour booklet of the park, available for a small fee. The park website also offers itineraries for visitors looking to spend between one hour and a full day.

Walking Tours

Stop by the Robinson Rose Visitor Center to inquire about free public walking tours available on a first-come, first-served basis. They are provided at 11am and 2pm daily as staffing permits and last approximately 45 minutes.

Ghost Tours

2754 Calhoun St.; 619/972-3900; www.oldtownsmosthaunted.com; from $25/pp

Old Town's Most Haunted Ghost Tours is the only authorized ghost tour concessionaire in the park. Ghost hunter Michael Brown offers ghost tours seven nights a week. Reservations are required; call or text to get one.

WHALEY HOUSE MUSEUM

476 San Diego Ave., Old Town Historic Walking District; 619/273-5824; www.whaleyhousesandiego.com; 10am-4:30pm daily; from $13

The Whaley House draws a steady stream of visitors because of its claim as "America's most haunted house." While this may be up for debate, the house is still worth touring as a period piece. Thomas Whaley began construction on the home in 1856, and today the two-story Greek Revival home, which also housed a commercial theater, the county courthouse, and a general store, stands as an iconic attraction in Old Town. In addition to standard tours, the Whaley House offers after-hours paranormal investigation tours; ghost-hunting equipment is provided.

THE SEELEY STABLE

2648 Calhoun St.

Once a barn used to stable horses and stagecoaches, the reproduction Seeley Stable now houses an impressive exhibit of rare overland

Whaley House Museum (top); the schoolhouse (middle); La Casa de Estudillo (bottom)

transportation vehicles and gear. Among the collection are a carreta (ox-drawn cart); a mud wagon used to transport people, mail, and freight along potentially wet dirt roads; and a two-wagon freighter, which required a team of horses to pull.

The back of the property includes the **Blackhawk Livery Stable** with more transportation artifacts and a living history display staffed by docents who work forging and shaping iron and chatting with visitors.

KUMEYAAY INTERPRETIVE AREA

North end of Old Town at Taylor St. between Juan and Wallace St.

The Iipay-Tipai Kumeyaay Mut Niihepok (Land of the First People) interpretive area features trilingual displays (Kumeyaay, Spanish, and English) that tell the story of the first people in this area. The displays are interspersed with benches, boulders, ceramic sculpture, and river stones in an open-air gathering space.

MCCOY HOUSE

4002 Wallace St.; 10am-5pm Thurs.-Sun.

The McCoy House was originally constructed in 1869 by James McCoy, a well-to-do Irish immigrant who served as sheriff then state senator for San Diego. The Greek Revival home was built for his wife Winnifred and featured a white picket fence and green shutters. In 1995 state park archaeologists excavated the site of the residence and gained enough information to reconstruct it. The current McCoy House features one period domestic room, the parlor. Other rooms are devoted to interpretive displays of the area through different cultural points in history.

THE SCHOOLHOUSE

3966 Mason St.

Kids will enjoy visiting the one-room schoolhouse, the small structure filled with rigid rows of desks where children learned in the late 1800s. The schoolhouse was built in 1865 and served children in grades K-8 until 1873. It was heated by a pot-bellied stove and had no running water, only a water bucket and dipper.

LA CASA DE ESTUDILLO

4000 Mason St.

Built during 1827-1829, La Casa de Estudillo was home to one of San Diego's most prominent families, the Estudillo family, during the Mexican and early American periods. The 12-room adobe block townhouse included bedrooms, a living room, and a dining room enclosing a courtyard. It also had a turreted balcony where the family could watch fiestas, bull fights, and horse races on the plaza. The house operated as a tourist attraction from 1906 to the 1960s and became part of the state park system in 1968. The courtyard gardens are available to walk through, as well as some of the adobe's rooms. La Casa de Estudillo is one of the five original 19th-century adobes and the only individual site in the park listed on the National Register of Historic Places.

SHOPPING

★ FIESTA DE REYES

Amid a tangle of pencil cactus and adobe, Fiesta de Reyes features 19 locally owned specialty shops offering everything from silver jewelry to hot sauce. They are tucked along red-tiled pathways that circle the lush courtyard that is home to the Casa de Reyes open-air restaurant. Shops stay true to the region's history, with Mexican handcrafted goods, local San Diego products, and imports from Peru and Ecuador celebrating San Diego's early trading partners.

There are the touristy items you might expect to find, like old-timey portrait photography and souvenirs, but a majority of the markets feature artisanal goods. There is hand-pressed olive oil from nearby Temecula, chocolate from a local San Diego chocolatier, and a tasting room for local wines and microbrews. Handcrafted Mexican goods include copperware, tiles, and silver jewelry from Mexico's Taxo region. Also look for garden supplies, kitchenware, Dia de los Muertos merchandise, clothing, toys, roasted nuts, baked goods, and beef jerky. It's easy to spend a few hours browsing.

★ FOOD AND LODGING

Just in case you thought you were going to be wandering around a bunch of old buildings with no sustenance, I'm pleased to report that one of the main pastimes in the park is eating delicious Mexican food. Ladies in traditional Mexican dresses embroidered with flowers hand-make tortillas, the smell of enchiladas wafts through the air, and tables full of diners sip goblet-size margaritas while mariachi bands strike up. Restaurants can be found in the **Wallach & Goldman Square** and **Fiesta de Reyes courtyard.** Adjacent to the park, there is also a concentration of restaurants along San Diego Avenue in Old Town San Diego's Historic Walking District ranging from an unassuming adobe with street tacos to a sleek mezcal bar.

There are plenty of nearby hotel options outside the park and one within the park boundaries. There is **no camping** at the park.

CASA DE MARIA RESTAURANT

2611 San Diego Ave.; 619/310-6188; https://casademariarestaurant.com; 11am-8:30pm Sun.-Thurs., 11am-9:30pm Fri.-Sat.; $19-27

Casa de Maria Restaurant has a large patio with a Western ranch aesthetic in a corner of historic Wallach & Goldman Square. They serve tried-and-true Mexican dishes and cocktails accompanied by live acoustic music on weekends.

BARRA BARRA SALOON & MEXICAN RESTAURANT

4016 Wallace St.; 619/291-3200; https://barrabarrasaloon.com; 11am-9pm daily; $18-23

Barra Barra Saloon & Mexican Restaurant is housed in a low-slung adobe with a full bar indoors and a cheerful bougainvillea- and cactus-adorned patio for dining. Their menu features house specialty platters including carnitas, Baja shrimp, and vegetarian options.

CASA DE REYES

2754 Calhoun St.; 619/220-5040; https://casadereyesrestaurant.com; 11am-9pm Mon.-Thurs., 11am-10pm Fri., 10am-10pm Sat., 10am-9pm Sun.; $16-27

Casa de Reyes is the life of the party with a giant outdoor patio in the center of **Fiesta de Reyes,** where the margaritas flow and mariachi takes center stage on weekends. You come here for the ambience and location, but the food is pretty decent as well, featuring Mexican standards like burritos, tacos, enchiladas, and fajitas.

COSMOPOLITAN HOTEL

2660 Calhoun St.; 619/297-1874; www.oldtowncosmopolitan.com; $269-299

The Cosmopolitan Hotel offers historic lodging within the park. The 1827 adobe was built as a home and also served as a hotel, restaurant, stagecoach office, and olive cannery before being restored to its 1870s glory. The hotel's 10 rooms are furnished with period furniture, and there is an on-site bar and restaurant with limited hours (10am-2pm Sat. brunch, 4pm-6:30pm Wed.-Sat. happy hour).

BEST PICNIC SPOT

Plaza de Armas

Never mind the large cannon, and instead enjoy the picnic tables in the town square, the green space around which all of Old Town's historic homes and businesses were built, listed as Plaza de Armas or Washington Square on maps.

GETTING THERE

CAR

The historic park is located in San Diego just off I-5 at San Diego Avenue and Twiggs Street.

PUBLIC TRANSPORTATION

Old Town San Diego is one of the few state parks in Southern California you can visit without a vehicle. There is an Amtrak Old Town station (4005 Taylor St.) located a short 0.3-mi (0.5-km) walk into Old Town, making it possible to take the train from many destinations in Southern California, including downtown Los Angeles. Flixbus (www.flixbus.com), a point-to-point bus service with stops in many popular destination cities, also has a stop adjacent to Old Town at 2728 Congress Street.

For getting around San Diego, the Old Town Transit Center, with Coaster, Trolley, and MTS Bus, is conveniently located at the park entrance at San Diego Avenue and Twiggs Street.

MOUNT SAN JACINTO STATE PARK

ADDRESS: 25905 CA-24, Idyllwild

PHONE: 951/659-2607

DAY USE HOURS: Open 24 hours

AREA: 13,718 acres (5,551 ha)

Subalpine forests, granite peaks, and mountain meadows quilt the Mount San Jacinto State Park and Wilderness in the heart of the San Jacinto Mountains. Craggy San Jacinto Peak, the highest peak in the park and the second highest in the San Jacinto Range (after Mount San Gorgonio), reaches nearly 11,000 ft (3,350 m) and is snowcapped for much of the year. The steep mountain escarpments of the San Jacinto Range plunge 9,000 ft (2,740 m) in less than 4 mi (6 km) to the stark desert floor. Hiking trails offer sweeping views toward Palm Springs and over 100 mi (160 km) to the southeast and the desert Salton Sea.

Originally the summer home of the Cahuilla people migrating from the desert valleys below, the area began to be settled by homesteaders in the 1890s. At the same time, local and national conservation efforts began in the area. Mount San Jacinto officially became a state park in 1937.

Mount San Jacinto State Park is now a year-round destination for its beauty and recreation. In summer visitors escape the extreme heat below to hike forested trails or picnic in the shade. In winter, the park is popular for visitors seeking snow.

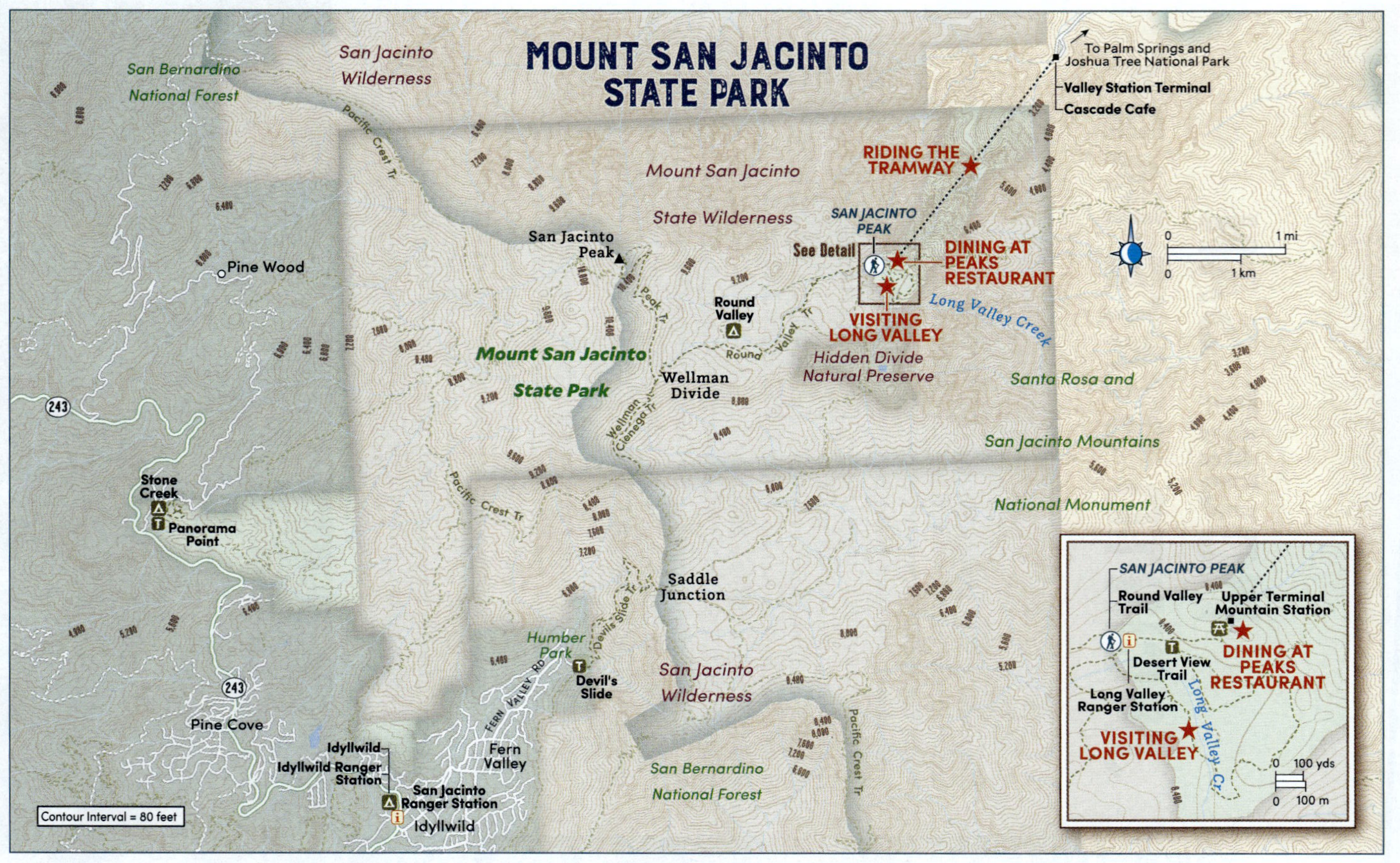
MOUNT SAN JACINTO STATE PARK
San Bernardino National Forest
San Jacinto Wilderness
Pacific Crest Tr
To Palm Springs and Joshua Tree National Park
Valley Station Terminal
Cascade Cafe
RIDING THE TRAMWAY
Mount San Jacinto State Wilderness
SAN JACINTO PEAK
See Detail
DINING AT PEAKS RESTAURANT
VISITING LONG VALLEY
Long Valley Creek
Hidden Divide Natural Preserve
San Jacinto Peak
Peak Tr
Round Valley
Round Valley Tr
Pine Wood
243
Mount San Jacinto State Park
Wellman Divide
Wellman Cienega Tr
Santa Rosa and San Jacinto Mountains National Monument
Stone Creek
Panorama Point
Pacific Crest Tr
Saddle Junction
Humber Park
Devils Slide Tr
Devil's Slide
San Jacinto Wilderness
Fern Valley Rd
Fern Valley
Pine Cove
Idyllwild
Idyllwild Ranger Station
San Jacinto Ranger Station
Idyllwild
San Bernardino National Forest
Pacific Crest Tr
Contour Interval = 80 feet
0 1 mi
0 1 km
SAN JACINTO PEAK
Round Valley Trail
Upper Terminal Mountain Station
Desert View Trail
Long Valley Ranger Station
DINING AT PEAKS RESTAURANT
VISITING LONG VALLEY
Long Valley Cr
0 100 yds
0 100 m

TOP 3

★ **1. RIDING THE TRAMWAY:** Suspended cable cars zip visitors from Valley Station on the desert floor to Mountain Station in the San Jacinto Mountains (page 484).

★ **2. VISITING LONG VALLEY:** Long Valley features an idyllic meadow and pine forest edged by the Desert View Trail (page 484).

★ **3. DINING AT PEAKS RESTAURANT:** Enjoy fine dining with a view from the top of Mountain Station where the restaurant's glass walls offer dramatic desert views (page 488).

PLANNING YOUR TIME

The two jumping-off points for hiking and camping in the state park are the **Palm Springs Aerial Tramway** and the town of **Idyllwild.** The most direct park access is via the Palm Springs Aerial Tramway, which leaves from **Valley Station** (1 Tram Way) in Palm Springs to travel to **Mountain Station** in the heart of Mount San Jacinto State Park. From there, visitors can spend from a few hours to a day, taking in the views from Mountain Station's observation decks, eating in the restaurants, picnicking, or hiking the trails from Long Valley. There are also longer overnight hikes from here.

Near the town of Idyllwild on the southwest edge of the park, there are two developed campgrounds maintained by the park. Other access to the park from Idyllwild is via hiking trail. Visitors to Idyllwild usually spend a day to a long weekend to hike the surrounding trails and explore the mountain town.

ENTRANCES AND FEES

From Palm Springs, access to the park is via the **Palm Springs Aerial Tramway** (1 Tram Way; 888/515-8726; www.pstramway.com; $34.95 round-trip). Free day use hiking permits are available from the Long Valley Ranger Station at the top of the tramway.

From Idyllwild, there is **no official park entrance.** A **Forest Adventure Pass** ($5 daily, $30 annual) is required to park at trailheads and day use areas. Adventure Passes are available at the **San Jacinto Ranger Station** (54270 Pine Crest Ave., Idyllwild) or at **Nomad Ventures** (54415 N. Circle Dr.; 951/659-4853; www.nomadventures.com; 9am-5pm daily) as well as at other ranger stations and retailers throughout the San Bernardino, Angeles, and Los Padres National Forests. They can also be purchased online (www.myscenicdrives.com). Rules regarding where Adventure Passes are required are somewhat in flux. Pay attention to signage; the default is that Adventure Passes are required.

VISITOR CENTER

There are no park visitor centers.

Idyllwild Ranger Station

25905 CA-24, Idyllwild; 951/659-2607; 8am-4pm daily

The Idyllwild Ranger Station, which serves as the park headquarters, is located at the entrance to the Idyllwild Campground.

San Jacinto Ranger Station

54270 Pine Crest Ave., Idyllwild; 909/382-2921; 8am-4pm Thurs.-Mon.

The San Jacinto Ranger Station manages the surrounding national forest and also has Adventure Passes and permits.

Long Valley Ranger Station

Long Valley; 760/327-0222; open daily, hours vary

The Long Valley Ranger Station is located at the top of the Palm Springs Aerial Tramway after descending the ramp from Mountain Station.

WEATHER

Mount San Jacinto State Park has four distinct seasons with often snowy winters and peaks so high they can create their own weather, including snow, wind, and fog. Summers are

THE MOUNTAIN VILLAGE OF IDYLLWILD

Idyllwild

Idyllwild is a charming mountain town, a forest island situated 1 mi (1.6 km) high in the San Jacinto Mountains and surrounded by the outlying desert. The artsy, rustic community is nestled amid pines, cedars, manzanitas, and scenic rock outcroppings. Picturesque cabins with A-frame roofs hint at snow. Seasonal streams and hiking trails crisscross the hills. Inns with chainsaw-carved wildlife sculptures and fireplaces welcome visitors escaping the heat and traffic of the urban areas below. In the 1960s and 1970s an influx of hippies to the area changed the cultural fabric in Idyllwild. Browse the boutique shops in the town center now and you'll find cowboy hats as well as healing crystals. The aesthetic here is rustic, and hotel accommodations range from boutique mountain lodges with elaborate amenities to frayed cabin motels with charming exteriors and interiors that have seen better days. A concentration of restaurants includes coffee shops, breakfast diners for pre-hike fuel-ups, a brewery, a pizza joint, and full-service dinners with fairy lighting among the pines.

mild with average temperatures around 72-76°F (22-24°C), lovely for hiking. The park is a year-round destination, with summer the optimal season for hiking. If taking the tramway, expect drastic changes in weather from the valley floor to the mountains with temperatures dropping a minimum of 30 degrees. Trails and roads within the park can close due to heavy snow and ice. Check the park website or call the ranger stations for conditions. The Palm Springs Aerial Tramway can close due to wind or other inclement weather.

SIGHTS

★ PALM SPRINGS AERIAL TRAMWAY

1 Tram Way; 888/515-8726; www.pstramway.com; summer 10am-8pm Mon.-Thurs., 10am-9pm Fri., 8am-9pm Sat., 8am-8pm Sun., winter 10am-8pm Mon.-Fri., 8am-8pm Sat.-Sun.; $34.95 round-trip

The tramway leaves from Valley Station on the desert floor (elevation 2,643 ft/806 m) and lifts visitors on a dizzying ride via suspended cable cars to traverse the length of rugged Chino Canyon, alighting in a crisp alpine climate at Mountain Station (elevation 8,516 ft/2,596 m) in Mount San Jacinto State Park over the course of 10 minutes. From Mountain Station, a network of trails totaling 54 mi (87 km) within the 14,000-acre (5,670-ha) wilderness leads to pine forests, meadows, and striking views.

MOUNTAIN STATION

summer 10am-9:30pm Mon.-Thurs., 10am-10:30pm Fri., 8am-10:30pm Sat., 8am-9:30pm Sun., winter 10am-9:30pm Mon.-Fri., 8am-9:30pm Sat.-Sun.

At the top of the Palm Springs Aerial Tramway, Mountain Station offers a series of observations decks as well as a casual cafeteria, a fine-dining restaurant, a bar, a gift shop, two documentary theaters, and a natural history museum. The gift shop sells sleds during snowy weather for sliding down the easy slopes just outside the station door.

★ LONG VALLEY

Long Valley sits at the top of the Palm Springs Aerial Tramway at an elevation of 8,400 ft (2,560 m), featuring an idyllic meadow and pine forest. Once the park's backcountry, Long Valley is now an accessible mountain oasis thanks to the tramway, offering a relaxing place to enjoy the fresh mountain air. Two short nature trails, the Long Valley Discovery Trail and the Desert View Trail, circle the valley.

HIKING

Hikes begin in either Long Valley, accessed via the Palm Springs Aerial Tramway, or the town of Idyllwild. The trail system is shared between Mount San Jacinto State Park and San Bernardino National Forest. Day use wilderness permits issued by either agency are honored by both agencies.

For day use hiking from Idyllwild, visitors fill out a free **wilderness permit** at the **Idyllwild Ranger Station** (park headquarters) at the entrance to Idyllwild Campground (25905 CA-243) or the display board near day use parking at **Stone Creek Campground** (21181 CA-243).

From the Palm Springs Aerial Tramway, to hike any trails beyond the nature trails, Discovery Nature Trail, and Desert View Trail, you must stop at the **Long Valley Ranger Station** to fill out a free **day use permit.**

TOP HIKE

SAN JACINTO PEAK

DISTANCE: 11.6 mi (18.7 km) round-trip
DURATION: 6-8 hours
EFFORT: Strenuous
TRAILHEAD: Long Valley Ranger Station

San Jacinto Peak dominates the landscape. At 10,834 ft (3,302 m), it is the highest peak in the San Jacinto mountain range. You are confronted with it as you lounge poolside in Palm Springs or from the I-10 freeway as you slog into or out of the desert towns: snowcapped, formidable, sheer, beautiful. Although some superhumans hike the peak from the desert floor along the Cactus to Clouds Trail, a grueling point-to-point 21-mi (34-km) hike with 10,800 ft (3,290 m) of elevation, a more manageable approach is from the top of the Palm Springs Aerial Tramway, where a climb through Round Valley leads you to Wellman Divide and its spectacular views. From there, continue the trek north to the snowcapped peak with its stunning panorama.

Desert View Trail (left); views from the trail (right)

LONG VALLEY

Desert View Trail

DISTANCE: 1.5 miles (2.4 km)
DURATION: 30 minutes
EFFORT: Easy
TRAILHEAD: Long Valley

One of the paradoxes of California's dramatic geography is that at times, stark desert and green alpine push up against each other as strange neighbors, separated only by a few thousand feet of rocky elevation. Appreciate this contrast by walking the 1.5-mi (2.4-km) Desert View Trail in Long Valley and stopping at each of its five lookout points giving way to sweeping views of the Coachella Valley below.

Round Valley Loop Trail

DISTANCE: 4 mi (6 km) round-trip
DURATION: 3 hours
EFFORT: Moderate
TRAILHEAD: Long Valley Ranger Station

A loop trail from the Long Valley Ranger Station leads through pine forest with views of picturesque Round Valley. The trail can be hiked either direction. From the upper trail, Round Valley Trail, climb southeast through pine forest toward Round Valley. In early summer you may be crossing or traveling alongside bubbling seasonal snowmelt streams. At 1.8 mi (2.9 km), the trail splits. Return by taking the right loop and lower trail (named High Trail then Willow Trail on the park map), which gives views of Mountain Station as you descend the last 1 mi (1.6 km) to the ranger station.

IDYLLWILD

Panorama Point Trail

DISTANCE: 0.75 mi (1.2 km) round-trip
DURATION: 20-30 minutes
EFFORT: Easy
TRAILHEAD: Stone Creek Campground near site 14

Follow a loop through a forest of pines, cedar, firs, and manzanita with a short spur to a panoramic viewpoint. Panels along the trail offer interpretive information about the landscape. The trail is hard-packed aggregate sand and rock with a 4-ft (1-m) width and is accessible for wheelchairs.

Devil's Slide

DISTANCE: 5 mi (8 km) round-trip
DURATION: 2-3 hours
EFFORT: Moderate
TRAILHEAD: Humber Park, upper level of parking area

The Devil's Slide Trail offers a scenic climb through idyllic forest and is a key connector trail that leads to the Pacific Crest Trail as well as routes to San Jacinto Peak and Tahquitz Peak.

The trail begins in the upper parking level of **Humber Park.** A short climb quickly gives way to stunning views of Tahquitz Rock, a local landmark, then views of Idyllwild and Strawberry Valley to the southwest before reaching **Saddle Junction.** From Saddle Junction, return the way you came or continue on to Tahquitz Peak (8.6 mi/13.8 km round-trip), Wellman Divide (10.6 mi/17 km round-trip), San Jacinto Peak (16 mi/26 km round-trip), or an array of other backpacking or day-hiking destinations.

CAMPING

The park offers **two developed campgrounds** located near the town of Idyllwild; sites can be reserved through Reserve California (800/444-7275; www.reservecalifornia.com) up to six months ahead. Campsites at Idyllwild Campground near the town of Idyllwild book fully on weekends in summer a few months out. Stone Creek Campground, 5 mi (8 km) north of town, typically has availability with only a little advance planning. There are also four backcountry camps located along the trail system in the San Jacinto Wilderness with the Palm Springs Aerial Tramway as the nearest access point.

Camps are remote and require everything to be packed in and out, including water. Permits are required for overnight camping ($5 pp) and are available at the Idyllwild Ranger Station, the Long Valley Ranger Station, or by printing and mailing an application permit in advance (www.parks.ca.gov).

BEST CAMPGROUNDS

Round Valley

www.parks.ca.gov; $5 advance permit required

Round Valley is the closest campground to Long Valley, offering the most sites and amenities. Located 2 mi (3 km) from Long Valley, it is a great first stop for a longer trek. It has 28 sites, primitive vault toilets, and water (must be purified and can run dry). The campground is pitched at 9,100 ft (2,774 m) in elevation in pine forest studded with granite boulders.

Idyllwild Campground

25905 CA-243; 951/659-2607; www.parks.ca.gov; $25/night tent, $35/night electric, $45/night full hookup

Idyllwild Campground is located in pine forest in the town of Idyllwild, walking distance to the town center and restaurants and shops. It has full hookups as well as electric hookup sites, flush toilets, and coin-operated showers.

Stone Creek Campground

21181 CA-243; www.parks.ca.gov; May-Oct.; $25/night

Stone Creek Campground, located 5 mi (8 km) north of Idyllwild on CA-243, offers 50 sites tucked into manzanita and pine forest. The campground is more rustic than Idyllwild Campground, offering vault toilets and no showers. There are five electric hookup sites, but no full hookups.

FOOD AND LODGING

The charming mountain town of **Idyllwild** has lodging including motels and cabins, restaurants, shopping, an outfitter, and a small grocery. There is no gas in town. Most business are concentrated near the Village Center with a few located on North Circle Drive near Humber Park. The destination desert resort town of **Palm Springs** has oodles of hotels, restaurants, and shopping as well as groceries, gas, and supplies.

When taking the Palm Springs Aerial Tramway, both the Valley Station and Mountain Station offer food and drinks.

★ PEAKS RESTAURANT

Mountain Station; 760/325-4537; https://pstramway.com; 11am-4pm and 5pm-8pm daily; $18-62

The fine dining Peaks Restaurant is situated in a glass-walled dining room in Mountain Station at the top of the tramway offering steaks and seafood with a side of spectacular desert views. The small, curated menu features a well-balanced mix of items from filet mignon and pan-seared salmon to a vegetable curry and artichoke ravioli.

PINES CAFÉ

Mountain Station; https://pstramway.com; 10am-8pm Mon.-Fri., 8am-8:30pm Sat.-Sun.

Pines Café is a cafeteria-style restaurant with grab-and-go sandwiches, salads, soups, pizza, beverages, beer, and wine. An open dining room with glass walls affording views of the pines and desert below offers first-come, first-served seating.

LOOKOUT LOUNGE

Mountain Station; https://pstramway.com; 11am-8:30pm daily

The Lookout Lounge is a full cocktail bar adjacent to the restaurants with an L-shaped bar and cocktail tables positioned to take in the views with your beverage. They also offer a light appetizer menu.

CASCADE CAFÉ

Valley Station; https://pstramway.com; hours vary

Cascade is a snack bar with sandwiches, pizza, chips, cookies, coffee, soft drinks, and beer and wine at the Valley Station. The humble offerings are given a delightful patio for dining with views of the ascending tram cars and a small waterfall.

BEST PICNIC SPOT

Mountain Station Patio

At the top of the tramway, seek out the Mountain Station patio with sweeping views looking past the pines toward the desert below.

GETTING THERE

CAR

The state park extends from the Palm Springs Aerial Tramway's Valley Station in Palm Springs southwest to the town of Idyllwild, adjoining the San Jacinto Wilderness on its

BEST NEARBY

Joshua Tree National Park

JOSHUA TREE NATIONAL PARK

Joshua Tree National Park (www.nps.gov; $30/vehicle) draws visitors from all over the world to its striking desert landscape filled with iconic Joshua trees and signature cracked boulders for hiking, rock climbing, and outdoor adventure. From Idyllwild, it is 73 mi (117 km) to Joshua Tree. Take CA-243 north for 24 mi (39 km) to Banning. From Banning pick up I-10 east toward Indio for 15 mi (24 km). Take exit 117 for CA-62 east toward Yucca Valley/29 Palms and continue for 27 mi (43 km) to the town of Joshua Tree. Turn onto Park Boulevard and continue 5 mi (8 km) to the park's west entrance.

southern boundary. The two main jumping-off points for hiking and camping in the state park and wilderness are the town of Idyllwild and the Palm Springs Aerial Tramway.

The Palm Springs Aerial Tramway is located on the north end of Palm Springs. From the Palm Springs Visitor Center (2901 N. Palm Canyon Dr.), follow Tramway Road for 3.7 mi (6 km) to the parking area for the tramway's Valley Station.

The town of Idyllwild, approximately a one-hour drive from the tramway, is located off of CA-243 in the San Jacinto Mountains. From the north and the town of Banning on I-10, take CA-243 for 24 mi (39 km) to the town of Idyllwild. The road is a curvy, mountain road with switchbacks. From the south, access is via CA-74.

CUYAMACA RANCHO STATE PARK

PHONE: 760/765-3020

DAY USE HOURS: 6am-8pm

AREA: 24,693 acres (9,993 ha)

Oaks and conifers blanket the rolling hills and mountains east of San Diego, a patchwork of woodland and meadow laced with small creeks, quiet pools, and gentle cascades. Rocky granite outcroppings and the deep red bark of manzanita add texture. The backcountry is home to wild turkey and deer, and the occasional mountain lion. Stonewall Peak, at 5,730 ft (1,747 m) is a landmark, capped with a smooth dome of white granite.

The Kumeyaay Indians had village sites throughout the area including the grasslands of the East Mesa (Cuish Cuish Cultural Preserve), where you can see morteros (grinding stones).

The story of Cuyamaca Rancho necessarily includes the Cedar Fire. On October 25, 2003, a lost hunter lit a signal fire, hoping to be rescued, and the fire quickly burned out of control, becoming the worst wildfire in California's recorded history. Included in the devastation were 90 percent of the state park's acres. In the decades since, grasses, shrubs, and some conifers have begun a process of natural regeneration, and combined with reforestation, the land is springing back.

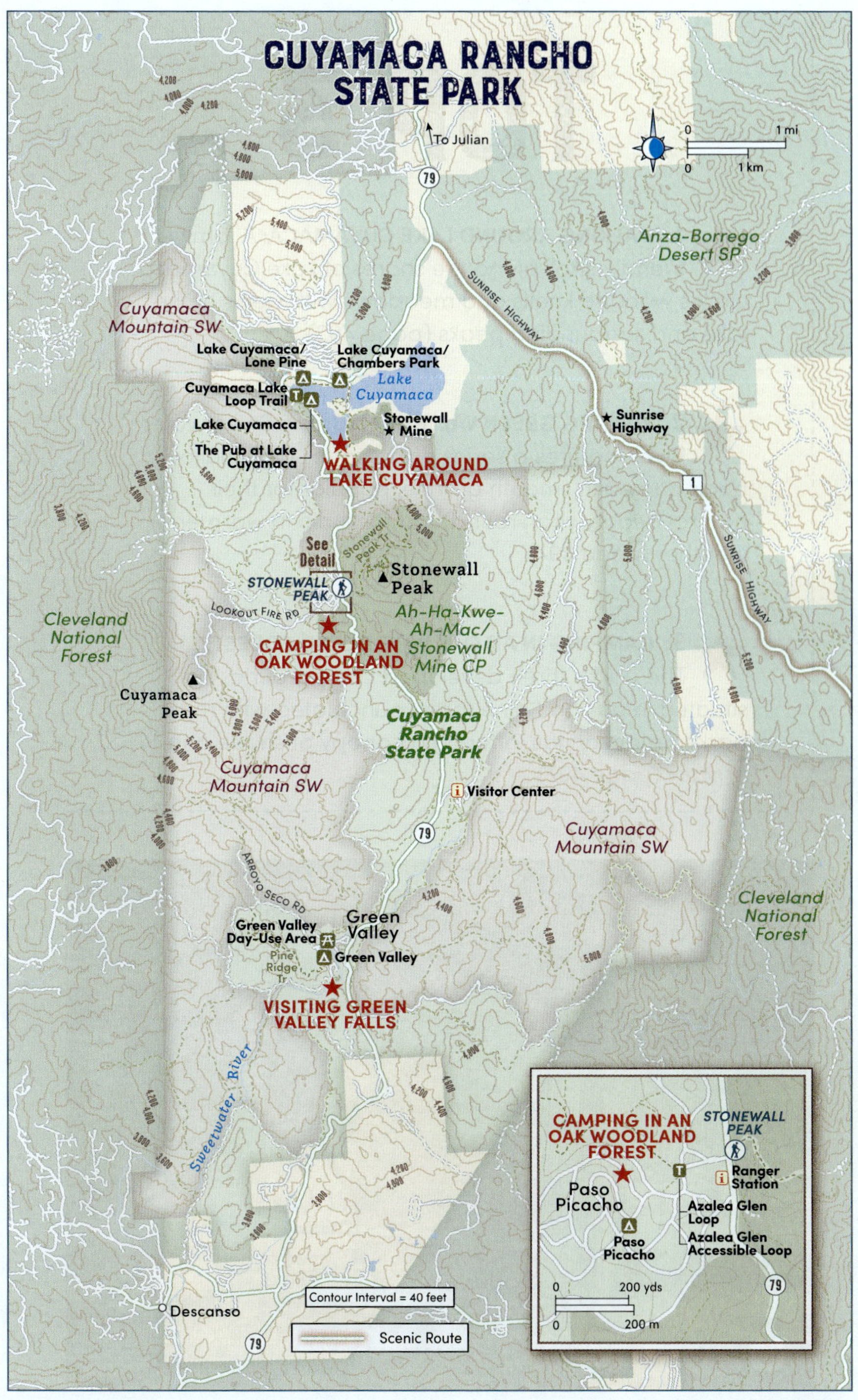

CUYAMACA RANCHO STATE PARK
To Julian
79
0
1 mi
0
1 km
Anza-Borrego Desert SP
Sunrise Highway
Cuyamaca Mountain SW
Lake Cuyamaca/ Lone Pine
Lake Cuyamaca/ Chambers Park
Lake Cuyamaca
Cuyamaca Lake Loop Trail
Lake Cuyamaca
The Pub at Lake Cuyamaca
Stonewall Mine
Sunrise Highway
1
WALKING AROUND LAKE CUYAMACA
See Detail
Stonewall Peak Tr
Stonewall Peak
STONEWALL PEAK
Lookout Fire Rd
Cleveland National Forest
CAMPING IN AN OAK WOODLAND FOREST
Ah-Ha-Kwe-Ah-Mac/ Stonewall Mine CP
Cuyamaca Peak
Cuyamaca Rancho State Park
Cuyamaca Mountain SW
Visitor Center
79
Cuyamaca Mountain SW
Arroyo Seco Rd
Cleveland National Forest
Green Valley Day-Use Area
Green Valley
Green Valley
Pine Ridge Tr
VISITING GREEN VALLEY FALLS
Sweetwater River
CAMPING IN AN OAK WOODLAND FOREST
STONEWALL PEAK
Ranger Station
Paso Picacho
Azalea Glen Loop
Paso Picacho
Azalea Glen Accessible Loop
0
200 yds
79
0
200 m
Contour Interval = 40 feet
Descanso
Scenic Route
79

TOP 3

★ **1. WALKING AROUND LAKE CUYAMACA:** A family-friendly stroll along the shores of Lake Cuyamaca circles wooded knolls and meadows with views of the lake and surrounding peaks (page 493).

★ **2. VISITING GREEN VALLEY FALLS:** The Sweetwater River features a series of cascades and shallow pools carved in smooth granite, popular for their natural beauty year-round and for a dip in warmer weather (page 494).

★ **3. CAMPING IN AN OAK WOODLAND FOREST:** The park's three developed campgrounds are situated in oak and pine forest punctuated with red-barked manzanitas, offering a canopy of shade and privacy (page 497).

PLANNING YOUR TIME

With the park being so close to San Diego, many visitors come for the day to hike and picnic at the many day use areas. The park's campgrounds and extensive trail system make it worthy of an overnight or a long weekend. Lake Cuyamaca in the northern part of the park offers opportunities for boating, fishing, camping, and hiking. The Paso Picacho Campground and day use area is the starting point for some of the park's most popular hiking trails, including Stonewall Peak and Cuyamaca Peak. The Sweetwater River cuts through the Green Valley Campground and day use area, making it a popular spot for hiking and splashing in summer.

Nearby state parks include Anza-Borrego State Park (42 mi/68 km).

ENTRANCE AND FEES

There is **no official entrance** for the park. The park is bisected by CA-79, and all of the campgrounds and day use areas are accessed via this road. A day use fee ($10/vehicle) is required at the park's most popular day use areas including Paso Picacho, Dyar, Sweetwater, Green Valley Falls, Stonewall Mine, and Merrigan. Have exact change and pay using the fee collection kiosk. There are also staffed entrance kiosks and automated machines at Paso Picacho and Green Valley.

VISITOR CENTER

Cuyamaca Rancho State Park Visitor Center

CA-79; 10am-4pm most Sat. and Sun.

Cuyamaca Rancho State Park Visitor Center is located off of CA-79 halfway between the Green Valley Campground and Paso Picacho Campground and features natural and cultural history exhibits.

WEATHER

The park sits at an elevation of 4,000-5,000 ft (1,219-1,524 m), making it a year-round destination. Temperatures are lovely in spring and fall. Wet winters can bring snow, closing roads and trailheads. Summers can be hot, making the swimming holes near the Green Valley Campground popular. Summer is a popular time to visit for hiking, boating, and swimming.

SIGHTS

★ LAKE CUYAMACA

15027 CA-79, Julian, northern end of the state park between CA-79 and S-1 Sunrise Hwy., 2 mi/3 km north of Paso Picacho Campground; www.lakecuyamaca.net

Lake Cuyamaca sits in the low mountains east of San Diego at the northern end of the state park. Technically a reservoir operated by the local water district, it offers camping, boating, fishing, cabins, a restaurant, a general store, and a bait and tackle shop. There are also two picnic areas with tables and grills for day use. Beginning at the marina, you can stroll the 3-mi (5-km) circumference of the lake in

landscape at Cuyamaca Rancho (left); Lake Cuyamaca (right)

about an hour, going through the wooded knolls of the southern shoreline and open meadows to the east with good views of the surrounding peaks.

★ GREEN VALLEY FALLS

A short loop trail (0.4 mi/0.6 km) leads to the upper and lower Green Valley Falls, a series of lovely cascades that flow into carved stone pools. It is a destination for a scenic stroll, and in warm weather, a dip into the cool waters. The short loop begins in the Green Valley Picnic Area to follow Falls Fire Road before paralleling the Sweetwater River.

STONEWALL MINE

southern end of Lake Cuyamaca, Stonewall Mine Picnic Area

Gold was discovered at the Stonewall Mine site in 1870, sparking the most productive mine in California's brief gold rush. The remains of the mine and its small workers' community are located at the northern end of Cuyamaca Rancho State Park along the wooded shores of Lake Cuyamaca. You can see the remains of scattered equipment behind a fenced area. There is also a restored miner's cabin that now houses an interpretive exhibit with photos and the history of the mine. You can access the site by driving, and there is a small parking area and picnic area, but the Lake Cuyamaca loop hike also passes through the mine site. A 0.6-mi (1-km) accessible trail circles the site.

WILDFLOWERS

Cuyamaca Rancho has a long wildflower season lasting from early spring through fall with the peak typically from April through July. Wildflowers can be found in its meadows, rocky slopes, and riparian areas. Across the park look for the tiny petals of the golden yarrow, vivid orange flowers of paintbrush, grape-soda lupine, and many others.

The park website has a helpful field guide for identifying flowers organized by color, where they grow best, and suggested trails. The **Azalea Glen Loop** has meadow, shade, and riparian zones, making it a good first choice to look for wildflowers along the trail.

SCENIC DRIVES

SUNRISE HIGHWAY

DISTANCE: 24 mi (39 km) one-way
DURATION: 30 minutes
START: Laguna Summit, I-8 exit 47
END: Sunrise Hwy. and CA-79 junction north of Lake Cuyamaca

The scenic byway (www.fs.usda.gov) winds 24 mi (39 km) through the Laguna Mountains rising from 4,000 ft (1,219 m) in elevation to just over 6,000 ft (1,829 m). Along the way it passes through pine, spruce, and fir forest with vista points taking in mountains, meadows, and, most strikingly, the Anza Borrego Desert abruptly jutting up against the forested slopes. A good spot to see this transition is from the popular Desert View Picnic Area located in the village of Mt. Laguna, where you will have a bird's-eye view of the desert 6,000 ft (1,829 m) below. Other highlights include the Pacific Crest Trail, the 2,627-mi (4,228-km) trail stretching from Mexico to Canada, which can be accessed at four points along the scenic byway. The byway runs through the Cleveland National Forest adjacent to the east side of Cuyamaca Rancho State Park. There is no gas along the route, but the village of **Mt. Laguna** has cabins, a general store, and two rustic restaurants. On the north end of the drive, Lake Cuyamaca has a restaurant and store.

HIKING

The park has more than 100 mi (161 km) of hiking trails; some are also open for mountain biking and horseback riding.

AZALEA GLEN LOOP

DISTANCE: 4 mi (6 km) round-trip
DURATION: 1.5 hours
EFFORT: Moderate
TRAILHEAD: Paso Picacho day use area

A 4-mi (6-km) loop via the Azalea Glen Trail and Azalea Glen Fire Road bring you up close to recovering forest, a small brook, and water-loving plants including ferns and western azalea. From the western end of the day use picnic area, follow the Azalea Glen Trail west through pine and oak forest for 0.5 mi (0.8 km) to a fork in the trail. Take the right split to hike the trail counterclockwise. Reforestation efforts aided by a relative abundance of water in the area are bringing back the coniferous forest that used to thrive here. At the halfway point, Azalea Spring, a grassy area with a cistern that was undamaged by the fires, is a popular resting and water stop. The return follows the Azalea Glen Fire Road as the trail skirts the campground and returns to the day use area.

CUYAMACA PEAK

DISTANCE: 5.6 mi (9 km) round-trip
DURATION: 3.5 hours
EFFORT: Moderately strenuous
TRAILHEAD: Southern end of Paso Picacho Campground near sites 7-10 and 68-70

Stunning views are the payoff on the trail to San Diego County's second highest summit at 6,512 ft

DISTANCE: 4.5 mi (7.2 km) round-trip
DURATION: 2.5 hours
EFFORT: Moderate
TRAILHEAD: Across the street from the Paso Picacho Campground entrance

Stonewall Peak's white granite summit is a prominent monument throughout the park. From the Paso Picacho Campground, it appears as dauntingly sheer, but the trail is gentler than it looks and has enough scenery to keep your attention. The out-and-back trail starts out with a steep climb before settling into a series of manageable switchbacks. The warm ochre color of the trail is lined with the striking red of manzanita and juxtaposed with white boulder outcroppings, making the trail scenic even before the views begin. About halfway up, views to the north and east reveal Cuyamaca Reservoir, its level varying with season and precipitation. The ascent to the peak is dramatic. Rough-hewn steps are carved into the exposed cap, and a guardrail lines the final section to the peak. Small children will need supervision here, and the peak can be icy after winter storms. Take in the park's topography from this vantage point, its meadows and nearby peaks, and keep an eye out for ravens, hawks, and even eagles cruising by.

(1,985 m). The trail itself is a relentless climb along Lookout Fire Road to the antennae-cluttered peak. The structures are left over from a fire lookout that was removed. Park and pay the day use fee for the Paso Picacho day use area, then make your way to the southern end of the campground to pick up the fire road. The hike begins in the pine and oak forest of Paso Picacho Campground but becomes exposed as it enters the forest recovery area. As you climb, you will begin to see the Cuyamaca Reservoir and the ranges of the Anza Borrego Desert to the northeast. The last stretch of the climb has a patch of forest that survived the fire, including sugar pines. From the top during the best clear-air conditions, the views extend for up to 40 mi (64 km), taking in the peaks and mountain ranges of the Anza Borrego Desert, Santa Rosa Mountains, and Vallecito Mountains to the northeast; Tecate Peak and Otay Mountain straddling the Mexico border; and the Pacific Ocean and coastal peaks.

RECREATION

BOATING AND FISHING

Lake Cuyamaca is a popular local spot for fishing and boating. Visitors can bring their own boat or rent one from the small marina ($15-225), which offers motorboats, rowboats, pedal boats, kayaks, and pontoons. Fishing is allowed with a valid CA state fishing license from one hour before sunrise until one hour after sunset. The lake is stocked with trout year-round except for July and August. There are two bait shops on the lake, one on the west side next to the marina and The Pub at Lake Cuyamaca, and the other in Chambers Park on the north side of the lake.

★ CAMPING

The park offers **two campgrounds,** Green Valley and Paso Picacho, reservable through Reserve California (800/444-7275; www.reservecalifornia.com; $40/night) up to six months in advance. Reservations are necessary weekends April-October when campgrounds fill.

BEST CAMPGROUNDS

Green Valley Campground

Green Valley Campground is a popular summer campground because of its location next to the Sweetwater River and the Green Valley Falls, which create a series of shallow swimming holes. With 81 sites, it is open seasonally from April through October for tent, trailer, RV, and equestrian camping. Campsites are mostly shaded and have picnic tables and fire rings. Throughout the campground there are bathrooms with flush toilets and running water, token-operated showers, and potable water. It is located along CA-79, 17 mi (27 km) south of Julian and 6 mi (10 km) north of the hamlet of Descanso.

Paso Picacho Campground

Paso Picacho Campground is situated at 5,000 ft (1,524 m) in pine and oak forest with immediate access to some of the park's most popular hiking trails, including Stonewall Peak. It is open year-round with a small section of the campground maintained for first-come, first-served sites in the off-season, November-March. Sites are reservable April-October. In wet winters, the campground can close for snow. Check the park website for current conditions. Throughout the campground there are bathrooms with flush toilets and running water, token-operated showers, and potable water. It is located along CA-79, 11 mi (18 km) south of Julian and 10 mi (16 km) north of the hamlet of Descanso.

The campground also offers five nature **cabins** (www.reservecalifornia.com; $80-100) that can accommodate up to eight people. The cabins are like glorified tents with outdoor fire pits and picnic tables, but no kitchens or bathrooms. They have double bunk-bed platforms for sleeping, but you will need to bring your own bedding. The three standard cabins have woodstoves. A premium cabin has a fireplace, minimal furniture, and minimal electricity. One accessible cabin requires a disabled placard or license plate to reserve and does not have a woodstove.

Lake Cuyamaca Campground

15027 CA-79, Julian; www.lakecuyamaca.net; $40 tent, $50 RV, $95-275 cabin

Lake Cuyamaca Campground, operated separately by the Lake Cuyamaca Recreation and Park District, offers three campgrounds on its shores for year-round tent and RV camping. The campgrounds are situated in oak and pine forest with nice views of the small lake and easy access to the restaurant, fishing, and boating; however, sites are small with little to no privacy. The lake is popular for RV camping because it has hookups. There are no wood fires allowed in the campgrounds. Cabins are also available to rent and range from rustic sleeping cabins to lakeview cabins with full amenities.

FOOD AND LODGING

The historic gold mining town of **Julian** 15 mi (24 km) north is a tourist destination known for its apple pie with a few historic inns, cafés, bakeries, cideries, and breweries along Main Street and the surrounding blocks, making it a walkable town. There are cabin rentals available in the surrounding wooded hillsides. The town also has the basics, including gas and a small market for groceries.

THE PUB AT LAKE CUYAMACA

15027 CA-79; 760/765-0077; https://thepubatlakecuyamaca.com; 11am-6pm Mon.-Thurs., 11am-7pm Fri., 9am-7pm Sat.-Sun.; $12-23

The Pub at Lake Cuyamaca has a restaurant and bar popular with weekenders and day-trippers overlooking the small lake. The menu features pub fare, including burgers and fish-and-chips, with vegetarian options and the tater tots of your post-hike dreams. Adjacent to the pub is a small general store (10am-5pm Mon.-Fri., 9am-5pm Sat.-Sun.) with camping supplies, locally branded merch, and beer and wine.

BEST PICNIC SPOT

Green Valley Day Use Area

A day use area next to the Green Valley Campground has picnic tables, restrooms, and barbecues a short walk from the carved granite pools and cascades of Green Valley Falls.

GETTING THERE

CAR

The park is located approximately 50 mi (80 km) east of San Diego on CA-79 and 15 mi (24 km) south of the historic town of Julian. The closest major interstate is I-8 to the south, with access to the park via the CA-79/Japatul Valley Road exit.

accessible campsite at Paso Picacho Campground

ANZA-BORREGO DESERT STATE PARK

Anza-Borrego Desert State Park is the largest state park in California, second largest in the lower 48 states. Its stats: 500 mi (805 km) of dirt roads, 12 wilderness areas, 110 mi (177 km) of hiking trails, 12 campgrounds, endless possibilities for open camping. The vast rugged beauty of the Sonoran Desert is on full display across the park's nearly 1,000 sq mi (2,420 sq km), with its eroded badlands and remote valleys. There is plenty of space to seek solitude in rocky canyons, explore a fan palm oasis, visit ancient Kumeyaay village sites, and stand on land that feels hallowed with thousands of years of human experience. At times the terrain can be otherworldly—sculpted sandstone caves high on a remote ridge—and at other times charming—vibrant wildflowers carpeting the desert most springs. The landscape shifts with the season and light; there's always another place to explore, so you can come back again and again.

ADDRESS: 200 Palm Canyon Dr., Borrego Springs

PHONE: 760/767-4205

WEBSITE: https://theabf.org

DAY USE HOURS: Sunrise-sunset

AREA: 600,000 acres (242,811 ha)

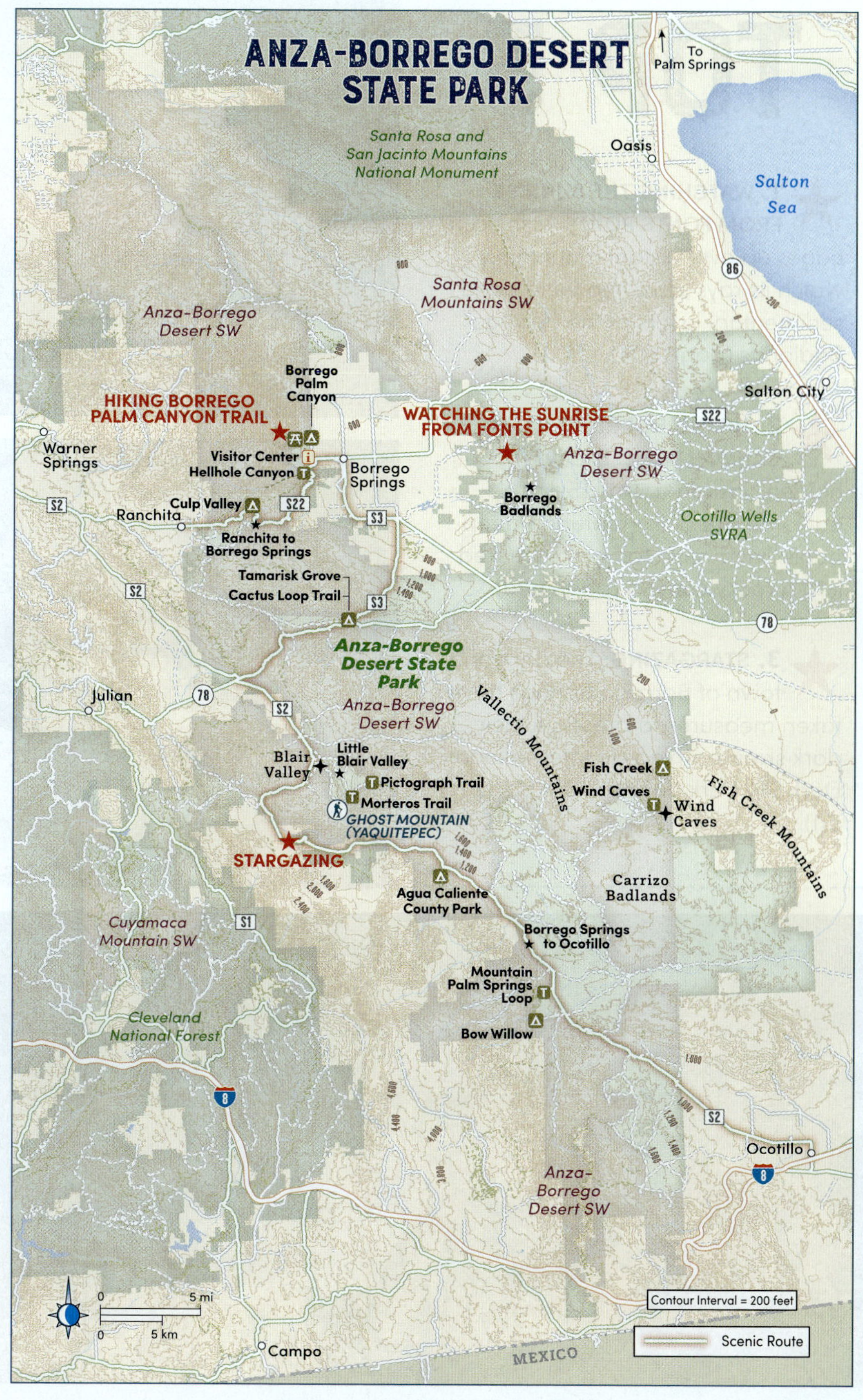

ANZA-BORREGO DESERT STATE PARK
To Palm Springs
Santa Rosa and San Jacinto Mountains National Monument
Oasis
Salton Sea
86
Santa Rosa Mountains SW
Anza-Borrego Desert SW
Borrego Palm Canyon
HIKING BORREGO PALM CANYON TRAIL
WATCHING THE SUNRISE FROM FONTS POINT
Salton City
S22
Warner Springs
Visitor Center
Hellhole Canyon
Borrego Springs
Anza-Borrego Desert SW
Borrego Badlands
S2
Ranchita
Culp Valley
S22
S3
Ocotillo Wells SVRA
Ranchita to Borrego Springs
Tamarisk Grove
Cactus Loop Trail
S2
S3
78
Anza-Borrego Desert State Park
Julian
78
S2
Anza-Borrego Desert SW
Vallectio Mountains
Blair Valley
Little Blair Valley
Pictograph Trail
Morteros Trail
GHOST MOUNTAIN (YAQUITEPEC)
Fish Creek
Wind Caves
Wind Caves
Fish Creek Mountains
STARGAZING
Agua Caliente County Park
Carrizo Badlands
Cuyamaca Mountain SW
S1
Borrego Springs to Ocotillo
Mountain Palm Springs Loop
Bow Willow
Cleveland National Forest
8
S2
Ocotillo
8
Anza-Borrego Desert SW
0
5 mi
0
5 km
Campo
MEXICO
Contour Interval = 200 feet
Scenic Route

TOP 3

★ **1. WATCHING THE SUNRISE FROM FONTS POINT:** As the sun edges up over distant mountains, watch its rays strike into the eroded sedimentary layers of the Borrego Badlands (page 504).

★ **2. HIKING BORREGO PALM CANYON TRAIL:** Explore a hidden oasis in a 3-mi (5-km) out-and-back hike featuring deep pools and native fan palms tucked into a rocky canyon (page 509).

★ **3. STARGAZING:** The park and town of Borrego Springs have taken measures to preserve their dark skies, earning an International Dark Sky Park designation (page 511).

1

2

3

PLANNING YOUR TIME

It is possible to do a scenic drive through the park in one day, but the area is best visited as a two- to three-night destination. **Borrego Springs** is a good place to start your trip and makes a great base camp. The visitor center in Borrego Springs provides information and maps, and the town has lodging, restaurants, supplies, and reservable campsites. The popular Borrego Palm Canyon Trail and Fonts Point badlands viewpoint are also located in this region. South of Borrego Springs along County S-2, the **Blair Valley and Vallecito Mountain region** is home to secluded campgrounds, hot springs, cultural sites, scenic drives, and hikes. The **Fish Creek Mountains area** to the east is home to one primitive campground and the spectacular wind caves. The drive is long but worth it to visit this natural and cultural site. If you have time, add on a special trip east from Borrego Springs using CA-78 and Split Mountain Road. The **Jacumba Mountains** region in the southern end of the park along County S-2 is home to the Carrizo Badlands, a series of fan palm oases, and two primitive campgrounds.

Nearby state parks include Cuyamaca Rancho State Park (42 mi/68 km).

ENTRANCE AND FEES

There is **no official entry point.** Visitors can enter the park from any direction via a series of paved state and county highways. The park's visitor center is in the town of Borrego Springs, a good starting point for first-time visitors.

There are no official park entry fees; however, day use fees ($10) may be charged at high visitation areas and trailheads including the visitor center parking area, Borrego Palm Canyon trailhead, Horse Camp, Tamarisk Grove Campground, Hellhole Canyon trailhead parking, Sheep Canyon trailhead parking, Mountain Palm Springs Primitive Camp, and Bow Willow Primitive Camp. Check the park website (www.parks.ca.gov) or stop in at the visitor center for the most current information on fee areas.

VISITOR CENTER

Anza-Borrego Desert Vistor Center

200 Palm Canyon Dr., Borrego Springs; 9am-5pm daily Oct.-May, 9am-5pm Sat.-Sun. and holidays June-Sept.

The park's visitor center is located within the park boundaries in the town of Borrego Springs. The visitor center is staffed by park rangers and offers maps, a book and gift shop, exhibits, and a desert garden providing a look at some of the vegetation spanning the park's 600,000 acres (242,811 ha). Parking is available at the visitor center 7am-7pm daily.

WEATHER

In this desert climate, the weather can be extreme. Expect excessive heat in the summer (May-Sept.) with temperatures over 100°F (38°C). Winter is cooler, with daytime temperatures in the 50-70°F (10-21°C) range. Temperatures drop by 30-40 degrees at night. Winter can bring snow. Spring can bring rain.

The best time to visit is in spring when wildflower displays carpet the

ONE DAY IN ANZA-BORREGO DESERT STATE PARK

For an introduction to Southern California's Sonoran Desert, spend the day experiencing short hikes, sights, and drives.

MORNING

Start at the visitor center in the town of Borrego Springs. Then explore a desert oasis on a quintessential 3-mi (5-km) nature hike at **Borrego Palm Canyon** featuring a soaring rocky canyon, a small creek, and native fan palms.

AFTERNOON

Drive south, taking in the scenery, and consider a walk through the **Cactus Loop,** or explore an ancient Kumeyaay village site at **Little Blair Valley.**

EVENING

For the grand finale, admire the sunset over the Borrego Badlands from **Fonts Point.**

landscape and spring up in rocky canyons. Fall brings fewer crowds and gorgeous weather. Summer is the low season due to extreme heat.

SIGHTS

BORREGO SPRINGS

★ Fonts Point

The 4-mi (6-km) Fonts Wash dirt road signed for Fonts Point strikes into the corrugated mud hills of the Borrego Badlands. From the road's end at Fonts Point, you can look out over the sunken mesas and arid geography. Sunrise and sunset bring out the palette of colors in the twisted sedimentary layers, making these the best times for a breath-taking view.

From the visitor center head east on Palm Canyon Drive for 5.5 mi (8.9 km). Turn left and continue north for 2.7 mi (4.3 km) as the road turns into Pegleg Road; then turn right onto the Borrego Salton Seaway (S-22) and head east for 3.4 mi (5.5 km). The unnamed road to Fonts Point is signed on the right. It cuts through Fonts Point Wash and areas of wash-board and soft sand. High clearance is necessary, and 4WD may be required. The road reaches Fonts Point and a small parking area after 4 mi (6 km).

The Borrego Badlands can also be glimpsed from County Road S-22. Other 4WD access roads into the badlands from County Road S-22 include Inspiration Point Wash and Thimble Trail.

Blair Valley Primitive Campground (left); wildflowers (right)

BLAIR VALLEY AND THE VALLECITO MOUNTAINS

Little Blair Valley

This remote desert valley has been used by humans since prehistoric times, and signs of human habitation are layered in the washes and mountains. A designated cultural site, the region contains scattered evidence of a native Kumeyaay village. The **Morteros Trail** (0.5 mi/0.8 km round-trip, 30 minutes, easy) follows a wide, sandy path up an easy rise to a granite mortar rock worn smooth by Kumeyaay Indians over a thousand years.

The **Pictograph Trail** (2.5 mi/4 km round-trip, 1-2 hours, easy) leads through scenic rock formations to a pictograph panel. The pictograph panel is located approximately 1 mi (1.6 km) into the hike. Turn around or continue on to look for more evidence of native habitation and a natural turnaround point at an overlook of Smuggler's Canyon.

Access Little Blair Valley from Route S-2 and the signed turnoff to Blair Valley. From the turnoff, a dirt road continues for 4 mi (6 km) to the signed parking area for the Morteros Trail. For the Pictograph Trail, turn left before the parking area and continue for 1 mi (1.6 km) to the signed Pictograph Trail parking.

JACUMBA MOUNTAINS

Carrizo Badlands

Admire views of the wildly eroded hills from the Carrizo Badlands Overlook. The Carrizo Badlands are in the southern end of the park, extending from Sweeney Pass south of Bow Willow Campground, east to the Coyote Mountains. The Carrizo Badlands Overlook south of Bow Willow Campground is a popular place to view these geologic wonders. A well-traveled Jeep trail through Canyon Sin Nombre puts you in the midst of the desiccated hills. In the distance are the Fish Creek Mountains.

DESERT WILDFLOWERS

In wet years the park's desert landscape transforms with vibrant displays of wildflowers, which typically bloom from February to April. Hundreds of flowering species, from the iconic California orange poppy to the purple desert sand verbena,

sunset at Fonts Point

as well as flowering cacti and Joshua trees, blanket the fields and fill the canyons. In these dramatic years you don't have to go out of your way to see the riot of color; however, the Anza-Borrego Foundation offers an **interactive map** (https://theabf.org/experience-anza-borrego/wildflowers) with crowd-sourced, real-time updates for where to see the best blooms. In drier years the bloom may be more modest or nearly nonexistent. Leave the display for everyone to enjoy, and make sure not to pick or trample the flowers.

SCENIC DRIVES

RANCHITA TO BORREGO SPRINGS

DISTANCE: 14 mi (23 km)
DURATION: 30 minutes
START: Ranchita
END: Borrego Springs

Enter the park via the scenic Montezuma Valley Road. Starting from the mountain hamlet of Ranchita, drive County Road S-22 east as it winds through the San Ysidro Mountains before spilling out onto the Borrego Valley desert floor. Over the course of 14 mi (23 km), the elevation drops 3,403 ft (1,037 m), the climate going from cool green mountain to warm earthy desert. Along the way, grassy fields give way to rocky hills dotted with ocotillos, the road hugging the curves of the hills as it makes its final descent down to the valley floor. Scenic overlooks offer views across the Borrego Valley with Borrego Springs in the distance.

BORREGO SPRINGS TO OCOTILLO

DISTANCE: 66 mi (106 km)
DURATION: 1.5 hours
START: Borrego Springs
END: Ocotillo

Traverse the main route through the Anza-Borrego via County Routes S-3 and S-2. Travel south from Borrego Springs to the town of Ocotillo for scenic overlooks, nature trails, hiking, and camping access. The drive gently follows the lines of the Borrego, Blair, and Carrizo Valleys flanked by the Vallecito Mountains to the east and Laguna Mountains to the west. Stroll the Cactus Loop Trail near Tamarisk Grove Campground. Admire the Carrizo Badlands from the Carrizo Badlands Overlook south of Mountain Palm Springs Campground. If you have time, add in a soak at the developed Agua Caliente Hot Springs or explore the ancient Kumeyaay village site at Little Blair Valley.

HIKING

BORREGO SPRINGS

★ Borrego Palm Canyon Trail

DISTANCE: 3 mi (5 km) round-trip
DURATION: 2 hours
EFFORT: Moderate
TRAILHEAD: Northwest side of Borrego Palm Canyon Campground

The Borrego Palm Canyon Trail treats visitors to a well-watered oasis set against a soaring rocky desert gorge. A 3-mi (5-km) out-and-back hike leads to the well-watered oasis, tucked away in a soaring, V-shaped canyon. The hike has changed since 2004 when an isolated rainstorm flooded the canyon and uprooted hundreds of native fan palms. They are once again taking root, returning the spot to its lush riparian state. The trail begins in open desert dotted with ocotillos cut through with a lively stream. As the canyon narrows, young fan palms cluster around deep pools until the trail's end at a lush oasis. The popular trail is short on solitude but heavy on scenery as the austerity of the rocky canyon walls juxtapose with the riparian corridor. If you're lucky you may see a bighorn sheep. This is also a great kid-friendly trail.

Hellhole Canyon

DISTANCE: 4.8 mi (7.7 km) round-trip
DURATION: 3 hours
EFFORT: Moderate
TRAILHEAD: 3 mi (5 km) west of Borrego Springs at the bottom of the Montezuma Grade, mile marker 16.5 on Montezuma-Borrego Hwy.

Although the name of the trail makes it sound like you are descending into the fiery depths, the out-and-back hike actually leads to a sparkling waterfall surrounded by mosses, ferns, and palms. To reach Maidenhair Falls, follow the well-established path from the parking area across Hellhole Canyon's alluvial fan. After 1.2 mi (1.9 km), the canyon walls begin to narrow with the route, generally avoiding the dense vegetation on the canyon bottom. The last section requires a scramble over or around large boulders and trees. About 600 ft (183 m) past the densest cluster of palms where the canyon narrows tightly, look for the hidden grotto containing the falls.

FISH CREEK MOUNTAINS

Wind Caves

DISTANCE: 1.4 mi (2.3 km) round-trip
DURATION: 1.5 hours
EFFORT: Moderate
TRAILHEAD: Near Fish Creek Primitive Camp

A rocky, well-defined trail climbs from a wash to the wind-sculpted sandstone formations known as the **Wind Caves.** Located on a high ridge above Split Mountain wash, the caves were used as shelters by early Native Americans. This knowledge adds an extra layer of awe to the already ethereal site. You can enter the caves to fully immerse in the history and landscape. For more awe, take in the sweeping views of the Carrizo Badlands below.

To reach the trailhead, from Ocotillo Wells head south on Split Mountain Road for 8 mi (13 km) to the Fish Creek/Split Mountain Road turnoff on the right. Drive 4 mi (6 km) up Fish Creek Wash and park near

TOP HIKE

GHOST MOUNTAIN (YAQUITEPEC)

DISTANCE: 2 mi (3.2 km) round-trip
DURATION: 1.5 hours
EFFORT: Moderate
TRAILHEAD: Little Blair Valley

A rugged trail switchbacks up the face of remote **Ghost Mountain** to the remains of the **Marshal South homesite**. In the 1930s, poet Marshal South fled civilization with his family and established a primitive home on top of the mountain Native Americans called Yaquitepec. Explore the weathered stone and adobe ruins and take in the spectacular 360-degree views of Little Blair Valley, the Vallecito Mountains, and the distant Salton Sea on clear days.

To reach the trailhead, from Scissors Crossing, head south on S-2 for 6 mi (10 km) to the Blair Valley turnoff on the left just before milepost 23. Follow the dirt road east past campsites for 3 mi (5 km) to a signed junction. Turn right (southwest) on a spur road signed for the Marshall South Home that leads to a small parking area and the trailhead.

the information panel just past the signed Wind Caves trailhead.

JACUMBA MOUNTAINS

Mountain Palm Springs Loop Trail

DISTANCE: 2.5 mi (4 km) round-trip
DURATION: 1.5 hours
EFFORT: Moderate
TRAILHEAD: Mountain Palm Springs Campground

The Mountain Palm Springs Loop Trail winds past a series of charming fan palm oases tucked into washes and ravines, some with shallow, standing pools. The trail starts at the westernmost canyon from the Mountain Palm Springs Campground and parking area, then follows a series of established trails and washes through Pygmy Grove, Southwest Grove, Surprise Canyon Grove, and Palm Bowl before turning back to camp.

RECREATION

★ STARGAZING

Designated an International Dark Sky Park, Anza-Borrego Desert State Park is dedicated to preserving its spectacular night skies. Look up from your campsite, find a viewpoint, or wander outside from your Borrego Springs lodging to take in the dazzling constellations and unkempt halo of the Milky Way. Anywhere in the park is good for stargazing, including the town of Borrego Springs, which protects the night sky. Additionally, Blair Valley and Little Blair Valley are popular with stargazers due to the valley's wide geography, unobstructed views, and remote location 25 mi (40 km) south of the town of Borrego Springs.

HOT SPRINGS

Agua Caliente County Park

39555 Great Southern Overland Stage Route of 1849; 760/765-1188; www.sdparks.org; 9:30am-5pm daily, 6pm-9pm Fri.-Sat. Labor Day-Memorial Day; $5 non-campers, free campers

Natural hot springs feed a series of developed swimming and soaking pools at the Agua Caliente County Park, located within the state park boundaries. The park is located 43 mi (69 km; 1 hour) south of Borrego Springs off of County Road S-2. A popular campground surrounding the springs offers 120 fully developed sites for tent, RV, and cabin camping. For RVs there are full and partial hookups available. Potable water, showers, and flush toilets can be accessed throughout the campground. Reservations are available by calling County of San Diego Parks and Recreation (858/565-3600 or 877/565-3600).

CAMPING

The **10 state park campgrounds** in Anza-Borrego range from developed with showers to primitive with dirt road access and plenty of solitude. Reservations through Reserve California (800/444-7275; www.reservecalifornia.com; $35) are required October-May for two campgrounds in the park: Borrego Palm Canyon and Tamarisk Grove. Sites are available to book six months ahead of time; however, usually only a few weeks to a few months are necessary. The campgrounds can book fully and well in advance during spring wildflower season. All the others are first-come, first-served. Primitive campgrounds have chemical pit toilets but no picnic tables, fire rings, or water. Blair Valley Primitive Campground offers some of the best dispersed camping in the park with plenty of space and opportunities for stargazing, wildflower viewing, and hiking. There are also two county campgrounds with reservable sites located within the park boundaries.

BEST CAMPGROUNDS

Borrego Palm Canyon Campground

Borrego Palm Canyon Campground is a large, developed campground near the park headquarters in Borrego Springs with 120 sites for tent and RV camping (including hookups). Showers are available, and it's a quick drive into town for dinner. The popular Borrego Palm Canyon Trail is accessed from the campground.

Tamarisk Grove

Tamarisk Grove is a small, developed, seasonal campground, located 12 mi (19 km) south of Borrego Springs at the intersection of S-3 and CA-78. The shaded campground offers 27 sites for tent, RV, and cabin camping. Eight rustic cabins ($70) offer outdoor fire pits and shaded picnic tables, but no electricity or running water.

FOOD AND LODGING

Borrego Springs is a charming, full-service town with hotels, restaurants, gas stations, and grocery stores as well as art galleries and shops located inside the park boundaries. The next closest full-service town with lodging, dining, and supply options is **Palm Springs,** 1.5 hours (88 mi/142 km) north via CA-86 and CA-111.

BEST PICNIC SPOT

Borrego Palm Canyon Trailhead

Shaded picnic tables at the Borrego Palm Canyon trailhead, 2 mi (3 km) north of the visitor center, make a good spot for a snack before or after exploring the lush fan palm oasis and canyon.

BEST NEARBY

Cleveland National Forest

Cleveland National Forest (www.fs.usda.gov/Cleveland; Adventure Pass for fee and day use areas $5/day), the southernmost national forest in California, spans 460,000 acres (186,155 ha) of rugged mountains, oak woodlands, and chaparral-covered hills for hiking and camping. The famed Pacific Crest Trail has a 110-mi (177-km) scenic stretch here. Other highlights include Palomar Mountain and Observatory, popular Cedar Creek Falls, and the historic gold mining turned tourist town of Julian. From Borrego Springs, the town of Julian is a 45-minute drive (30 mi/48 km) southwest via CA-78.

GETTING THERE

CAR

The park can be accessed from any direction via state and county highways. Two state highways intersect the park: CA-79 runs north-south along the western edge of the park from Temecula in the north to I-8 at the southern end of the park. CA-78 runs east-west from the mountain town of Julian in the west to intersect with CA-111 in the east near the Salton Sea. To reach the park headquarters in Borrego Springs from the north, most visitors take CA-79 southeast to Warner Springs and head east via San Felipe Road/County Road S-2 and Montezuma Borrego Road/County Road S-22. Eastern access is via north-south CA-86 from Indio and then County Road S-22 or CA-78. From the south, County Road S-2 trends north from its intersection with US-8, which originates in San Diego.

PICACHO STATE RECREATION AREA

In a remote southeastern corner of California, in the arid Colorado Desert, the powerful Colorado River flows through Picacho State Recreation Area. The glassy jade of the river is juxtaposed against rugged desert, striking rock formations, and vistas that stretch into Arizona.

ADDRESS: Interpark Rd. at Picacho Rd., Winterhaven

PHONE: 760/996-2963

DAY USE HOURS: Open 24 hours

AREA: 6,759 acres (2,735 ha)

Nearly 9 mi (14 km) of river wind through palo verde, cottonwoods, and willows, fanning out into backwater lakes, a natural haven to boat, fish, and swim. The geology showcases ancient rocks and canyons to explore on foot or by 4WD. A drive traverses the length of the park, giving access to washes, bluffs, and river views.

Gold was discovered in 1862, and by the 1890s, Picacho was a thriving mining town. Imagine paddlewheel boats traversing the river, delivering supplies and passengers. For the Quechan (Yuma) who lived along this part of the Colorado for thousands of years, logs, rafts, and clay vessels were used for travel. The federally recognized Quechan is one of California's largest inland native groups.

Hard to get to, far from everything, with an inhospitable climate, the desert guards its treasures well.

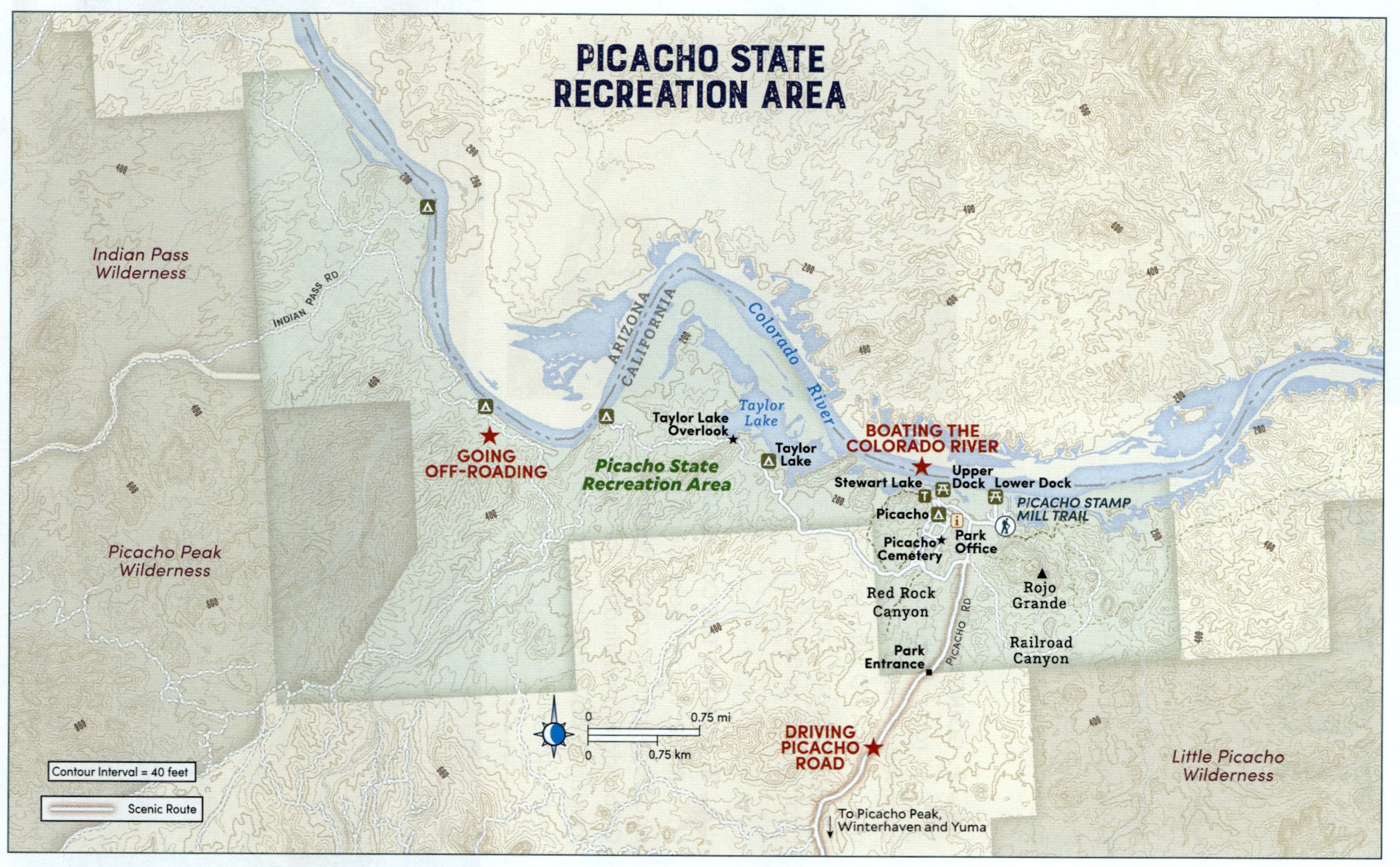
PICACHO STATE RECREATION AREA
Indian Pass Wilderness
INDIAN PASS RD
ARIZONA
CALIFORNIA
Colorado River
Taylor Lake
Taylor Lake Overlook
Taylor Lake
GOING OFF-ROADING
Picacho State Recreation Area
BOATING THE COLORADO RIVER
Stewart Lake
Upper Dock
Lower Dock
PICACHO STAMP MILL TRAIL
Picacho
Picacho Cemetery
Park Office
Picacho Peak Wilderness
Red Rock Canyon
Rojo Grande
PICACHO RD
Park Entrance
Railroad Canyon
0 0.75 mi
0 0.75 km
DRIVING PICACHO ROAD
Little Picacho Wilderness
Contour Interval = 40 feet
Scenic Route
To Picacho Peak, Winterhaven and Yuma

TOP 3

★ **1. DRIVING PICACHO ROAD:** The adventure begins with the drive into the park along the 24-mi (39-km) unpaved Picacho Road as the landscape gets wilder and the rocks more tortured (page 519).

★ **2. GOING OFF-ROADING:** All roads in the park are unpaved, making the park a mecca for 4WD vehicles to access remote canyons, camps, and beaches (page 520).

★ **3. BOATING THE COLORADO RIVER:** With its boat launches and boat-in river camps, the Lower Colorado is a destination for those looking to navigate the tempting water (page 522).

1

2

3

PLANNING YOUR TIME

The area is so remote and difficult to reach that it is best spent as a long weekend, camping at one of the campgrounds in the park. If you somehow find yourself in the vicinity of Yuma, Arizona, it is possible to do a day trip to include a drive along Picacho Road, a picnic or fishing on the river, and possibly adding in a hike to the stamp mill or a drive to Taylor Lake before returning.

Nearby state parks include Anza Borrego Desert State Park (151 mi/243 km) and Cuyamaca Rancho State Park (156 mi/251 km).

ENTRANCES AND FEES

The park is accessed via Picacho Road beginning in the tiny town of Winterhaven, California. Picacho Road is paved for the first 6 mi (10 km), then graded dirt for the remaining 18 mi (29 km). High-clearance vehicles are recommended, but 4WD is usually not necessary, and the road is accessible for vehicles towing trailers or boats. There may be washouts and areas of sand. The road can become temporarily impassable after storms in any vehicle.

At the park boundary, visitors pay fees and self-register at a **basic kiosk** that includes registration envelopes and a metal drop box ($10 day use, $5 boat launch, $20 main campground with one vehicle, $30 main campground with two vehicles, $25 4-S and Outpost riverfront camping with one vehicle, $35 4-S and Outpost riverfront camping with two vehicles). Bring cash and exact change. The kiosk does not take credit cards or electronic payments.

Rugged, 4WD access is also possible via Indian Pass Road. The road includes a steep, rocky mountain pass as well as areas of sand. Four-wheel drive and experience are required. This road is not recommended to access the park.

VISITOR CENTER

Park Office

760/996-2963; hours vary

A small park office near the main campground serves as a low-key information hub. Staff are available to answer questions about camping, hiking, fishing, and boating in the area. The park office also provides park brochures with overall park maps and basic handouts with information about hiking and fishing.

WEATHER

In this desert climate, the weather can be extreme. Summer temperatures (May-Sept.) can top out at 120°F (49°C). Summer and winter can bring seasonal rains. The best times to visit are mid-October through mid-April.

ONE DAY IN PICACHO STATE RECREATION AREA

To immerse in Southern California's Colorado Desert, start the day with a scenic drive into the area followed by river recreation and marveling at the unique landscape.

MORNING

Check in at the small visitor center on the edge of the campground to get the lay of the land, then hike the Stamp Mill Trail for views of the Colorado River and an intro to the region's gold-mining history. For lunch, picnic riverside at picnic tables at the Lower or Upper Dock along the banks of the blue-green Colorado River.

AFTERNOON

Afternoon is spent exploring the river and its backwaters. Make the short drive to Taylor Lake, where you can admire views of the quiet, reed-lined lake. Alternately, canoe or kayak a section of the river. No craft? No problem. You can walk down one of the boat ramps to wade in the cool waters.

EVENING

Admire the spectacular reds and golds of golden hour reflecting off the surrounding rock formations on the drive out, or from your campsite.

SIGHTS

PICACHO PEAK

The 1,097-ft (334-m) volcanic dome of Picacho Peak is central to the park's geography and history. Gold was discovered here in 1862, and the peak featured in Quechan myth and legend. Picacho Peak is a challenge for mountaineers and technical rock climbers, with few people attempting the peak due to its difficulty and remoteness. The vertical feet near the peak involve dubious ladders and sheer drop-offs, and require rock-climbing gear. Fortunately, you don't have to hike it to admire this jagged sentinel that rises sharply from the desert floor. This peak, along with other exposed cliffs and hills, is made up of sedimentary rocks that have been shaped by volcanic activity, erosion, and weathering, leaving behind sharp ridgelines and stunning outcrops, some of which are much easier to explore on foot or via a series of dirt roads and 4WD.

TAYLOR LAKE OVERLOOK

This 9-mi (14-km) stretch of the lower Colorado River overspills its banks into numerous backwater lakes. One of these, Taylor Lake, is its own calm oasis surrounded by marsh tule, native to freshwater marshes, and carrizo cane, a giant reed. Just past the entrance station, turn left on a dirt road signed for Taylor Lake. A graded dirt road usually suitable for any vehicle reaches Taylor Lake in 2 mi (3 km). The site is primarily used for camping, with four sites overlooking the lake, but it is also a good spot to take in the views. There is a small parking area, restrooms, and a short spur trail to the overlook. You can also walk to the water's edge to stand in the reeds or launch a small non-motorized boat.

PICACHO CEMETERY

The historic Picacho Cemetery is located on the road ringing the main campground before the park office. Residents of old Picacho, which swelled to its highest population during its gold-mining days in the 1890s, are buried here. The cemetery was originally east of this site, by the river and the now gone Picacho town jail. It was moved to its present location in 1936 when river waters began to rise behind the then newly completed Imperial Dam. Eighteen of the residents are named, but many remain unidentified.

SCENIC DRIVES

Roads in the region are all unpaved with much of the road network requiring 4WD. Entry into the park via Picacho Road is passable to most vehicles, and Inter-Park Road is passable for most vehicles to Taylor Lake. Beyond this, all roads require 4WD. Vehicles must be street-legal for California. Check road conditions before you go; storms can make roads temporarily impassable with any vehicle. Bring plenty of water and know that cell service is spotty to nonexistent. If your vehicle breaks down, stay with it. It is easier to find a large vehicle that reflects sunlight than a wandering person.

★ PICACHO ROAD

DISTANCE: 24 mi (39 km) one-way
DURATION: 45 minutes
START: Winterhaven
END: Entrance Station/Picacho Campground

Picacho Road, the main road into the park, begins in the tiny town of Winterhaven, California, and strikes north toward the banks of the Colorado River as rock formations increasingly contort and stretch skyward. For the first 6 mi (10 km) the road is paved, covering flat desert tamed by agriculture and irrigation canals. Then the pavement stops, signaling that the scenery and fun are about to begin.

For the next 18 mi (29 km), the road winds through expanses of creosote and ocotillo, past named and unnamed washes, with changing views of whipped hills and volcanic rock formations in the distance punctuated by towering monoliths. The road is mostly graded and passable with a 2WD with some clearance in good weather, including vehicles towing small trailers or boats. In bad weather and storms there can be washouts, making the road impassable. Drive the road at sunrise or sunset for the most bang, watching the interplay of light as it sweeps the rocky points and hollows, intensifying the golds and reds. The road ends at the entrance station with the main campground just beyond.

★ OFF-ROADING

Inter-Park Road

DISTANCE: 9 mi (14.5 km) one-way
DURATION: 1 hour
START: Picacho Campground
END: The Outpost boat-in campground

Head west on Inter-Park Road from Picacho Campground to experience the park's volcanic geology and access primitive riverfront campgrounds and beaches. Beginning at Picacho Campground, the road heads northwest to end at the Outpost campground along the park's northwestern boundary. The 2 mi (3 km) from Picacho Campground to Taylor Lake Campground are graded dirt accessible by most vehicles. Stop at Taylor Lake for the views before continuing on. Beyond Taylor Lake, for the next 7 mi (11 km) to the road's end, the road is steep and rocky; 4WD is necessary. The road generally stays within striking distance of the river, diverging at times as it follows the region's twisting canyons and washes. The road dips to the river with opportunities for camping, fishing, boating, and swimming at 4-S Beach Campground and its end at the Outpost campground.

Inter-Park Road

Indian Pass Road

DISTANCE: 25 mi (40 km) one-way; 50 mi (80 km) out-and-back; or 56-mi (90-km) loop with Inter-Park Rd. and Picacho Rd.
DURATION: 1 hour; 2-2.5 hours; or 2.5-3 hours
START: Ogilby ghost town, 3.8 mi (6 km) north of I-8 on Ogilby Rd.
END: Colorado River, 4-S Beach Campground

A dusty 4WD trail through open desert and carved volcanic hills pays off in beautiful views of the Colorado River. The road begins on BLM land at the site of Ogilby ghost town (no remains). For 9.4 mi (15 km) along Ogilby Road, the track crosses open desert, passing a few historic gold-mining sites lost to time and the elements. A right turn onto Indian Pass Road takes you through the twisting canyons of Indian Pass Wilderness in the Chocolate Mountains. The area is home to bighorn sheep as well as wild horses and burros. Indian Pass Road goes through a mountain corridor between the Picacho Peak Wilderness and Indian Pass Wilderness before descending a sandy wash draining toward the river. It ends with gorgeous views of the Colorado River at 4-S Beach Campground. Pack a lunch; it's a perfect spot to picnic before heading back out. To return, go the way you came in or make a partial loop by taking the 4WD Inter-Park Road southeast for 7 mi (11 km) to its intersection with Picacho Road near the park entrance. The way back to civilization is via the 24-mi (39-km) Picacho Road ending in Winterhaven, California.

TOP HIKE

PICACHO STAMP MILL TRAIL

DISTANCE: 2 mi (3.2 km) round-trip
DURATION: 1 hour
EFFORT: Moderate
TRAILHEAD: Between park office and Lower Dock

This trail crosses barren volcanic hills to reach the ruins of two stamp mills in operation during Picacho's gold-mining era. Along the way, the trail affords wide views of the Colorado River and backwater lakes. Bring binoculars for wildlife viewing. Across the river over the Arizona border, the Imperial National Wildlife Refuge edges the river's banks.

HIKING

STEWART LAKE TRAIL

DISTANCE: 2.5 mi (4 km) round-trip
DURATION: 1 hour
EFFORT: Easy
TRAILHEAD: Picacho Campground site 18

An easy loop winds through desert fauna and volcanic scenery around this usually dry lake. The trail is named for Clyde Stewart, an old-time Picacho prospector who lived in a small house here. Look for the palm tree on the low-lying ridge at the beginning of the trail.

RED ROCK CANYON

DISTANCE: 1.5 mi (2.4 km) round-trip
DURATION: 1 hour
EFFORT: Easy
TRAILHEAD: Picacho Campground T intersection past site 54 at southern end of campground

Walk a sandy wash to see the effects of water on the stark desert landscape. The wash ends at a dry waterfall, its vivid volcanic rock carved into a chute by flash flood waters. Hike out the way you came in or climb out of the wash and return on the high terraces lined with desert pavement, a packed surface layer embedded with pebbles.

RAILROAD CANYON

DISTANCE: 4 mi (6 km) round-trip
DURATION: 1.5-2 hours
EFFORT: Moderate
TRAILHEAD: Just past the park entrance station on Picacho Rd.

This 4WD Jeep trail on the park's eastern side taps into the region's geology and mining history. It can be driven or hiked. The trail leaves Picacho Road on the right (eastern) side of Picacho Road and follows a U-shape through Railroad Canyon. It eventually links up with the historic narrow-gauge railroad bed developed for the region's gold-mining efforts. The trail ends with views over the river where a train trestle once spanned the canyon. The trail's end viewpoint is also good for wildlife viewing.

RECREATION

★ BOATING AND FISHING

We ask so much of the **Colorado River.** It provides water for huge cities and water for agriculture, and is siphoned off as it runs its course over 1,450 mi (2,333 km) from the Rocky Mountains through seven southwestern states and the Grand Canyon, then through two Mexican states to the sea in Mexico. Yet when we see it at Picacho just before it crosses the Mexico border, it still looks grand and beautiful flowing its 9 mi (14 km) through the park's lower Colorado River Basin landscape.

Sunrises and sunsets are spectacular from the Lower Dock, Upper Dock, Taylor Lake Overlook, or one of the small, primitive campgrounds upriver. October through April are optimal for a float in a **kayak or canoe.** Visitors come year-round for the fishing along the river or its backwater lakes. People brave the extreme temperatures of late spring and early fall for water-skiing and swimming.

The **Upper Dock and Lower Dock** are good spots for shore **fishing.** The Upper Dock is good for channel catfish and also has a fish-cleaning station. The Lower Dock has been known for blue and flathead catfish catches. Boat fishing on the backwater lakes is best for catching bass. Stop in at the park office for a handout and intel on the best fishing in the area. Anyone 16 years or older needs a valid California fishing license to fish. An Arizona fishing license is also valid for Arizona residents. Fishing licenses are for sale in El Centro, Brawley, or online.

Boat ramps are available at the Upper Dock and Lower Dock for shallow draft powerboat launches as well as kayaks and canoes.

WILDLIFE WATCHING

Birds

Picacho is a hot spot for birding year-round. The lake setting attracts eagles, egrets, herons, and Gila woodpeckers, while migratory birds including ducks, geese, and cormorants swoop through in spring and fall. Muskrats and beavers are also active near the river. The steady chirping of Gambel's quail is your soundtrack. Bring binoculars.

CAMPING

The park has **one main, developed campground** for tent and RV camping as well as five small boat-in campsites upriver along Inter-Park Road. Three of these are also available for car camping. There is limited dispersed camping available on BLM land adjoining the park with several sites along Picacho Road before the park entrance. All sites, including the developed campground, are first-come, first-served. Seniors (62 and over) receive $2 off per site per night. Register and pay for sites at the self-serve entrance kiosk and pay with cash (exact change) or check.

canoes on the Colorado River

BEST CAMPGROUNDS

Picacho Campground

$20/night, $10 extra vehicle

The beautifully developed main campground offers amenities in a remote setting with easy river access and stargazing. The main campground has 54 widely spaced sites set amid rock formations. They are available for tent and RV camping with concrete picnic tables, shade pergolas, and fire rings. Restrooms and solar showers are available.

Taylor Lake

$20/night, $10 extra vehicle

Taylor Lake offers four family campsites on the bluffs overlooking Taylor Lake. To get there, take a left on the signed road after the entrance station. The campground offers incredible views, a boat ramp, and the basic amenities including fire pits and restrooms. There is no potable water. The road to Taylor Lake is graded, similar to Picacho Road and suitable for most vehicles. It gets rougher and requires 4WD beyond. The site is accessible by car and for boat-in camping. The sites are first-come, first-served, so be prepared with a plan B.

FOOD AND LODGING

Yuma, Arizona, is the closest full-service town, located 25 mi (40 km) south of Picacho State Recreation Area via Picacho Road. It has hotels, restaurants, gas stations, and grocery stores as well as a small historic downtown.

BEST PICNIC SPOT

Lower Dock and Upper Dock

Once you take Picacho Road in, pass the park entrance and park office to a fork in the road. The right fork leads to the Lower Dock, and the left fork leads to the Upper Dock. Both are excellent spots to picnic and take in the views with riverfront picnic tables, parking, and restrooms.

Picacho Campground at night (left); campsite at Taylor Lake (right)

GETTING THERE

CAR

Picacho State Recreation Area is located in the remote southeastern corner of California on the California-Arizona-Mexico border. The closest major interstate is I-8, which runs east-west and extends from San Diego into Arizona. The park is accessed from the south in the town of Winterhaven, California, located along I-8. From Winterhaven, Picacho Road heads north for 24 mi (39 km) to the park entrance. Only the first 6 mi (10 km) are paved. Winterhaven is 170 mi (274 km) east of San Diego.

a galis dungal bark house in Ed Z'berg Sugar Pine Point State Park

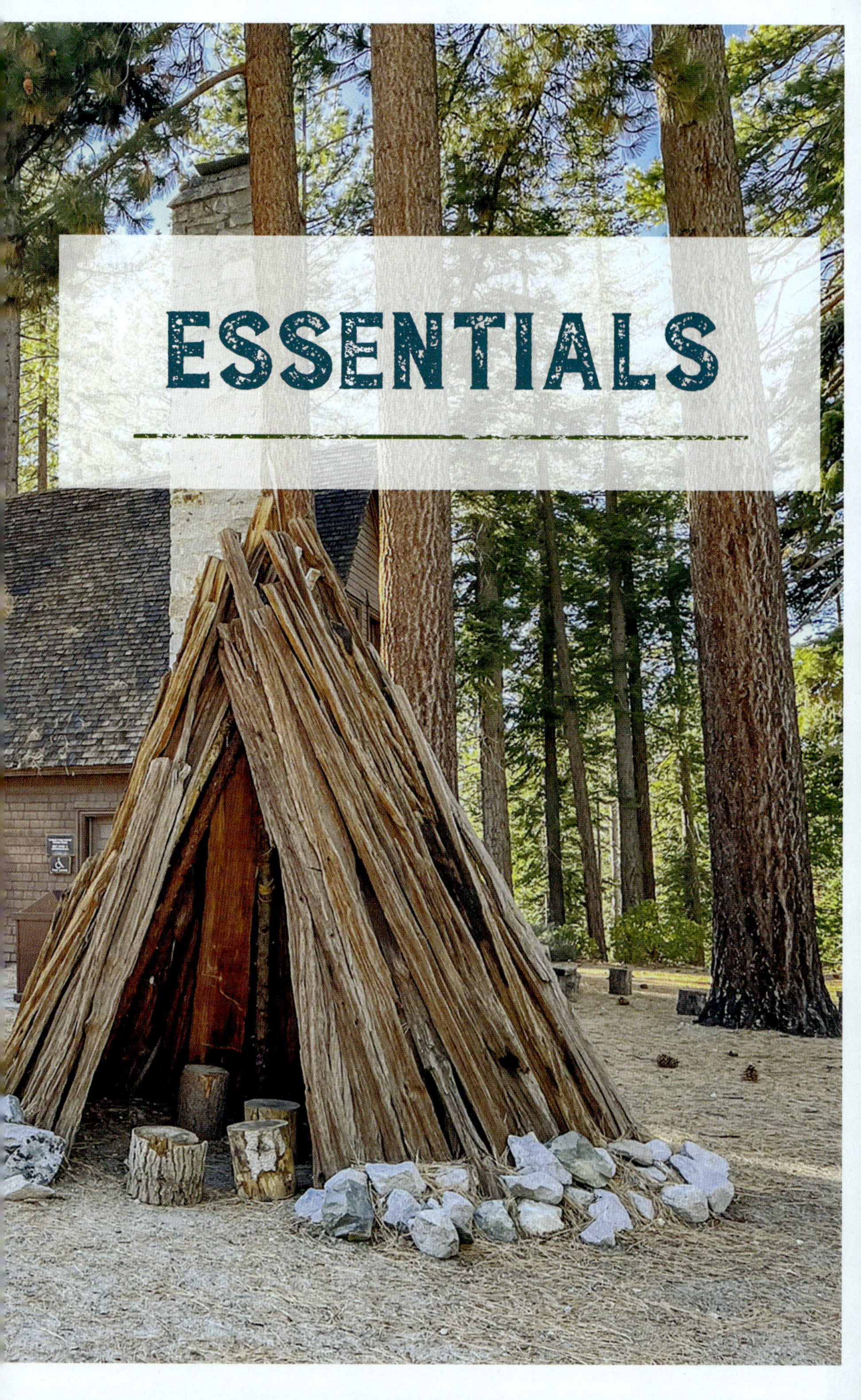

ESSENTIALS

THE HISTORY OF THE STATE PARKS

INDIGENOUS PEOPLES

Long before European settlers infiltrated the state in the mid-1700s in search of gold and other valuable materials, more than 300,000 people were already living in California. Native people such as the Yurok, Miwok, Tolowa, and at least 100 other federally recognized groups hunted elk, deer, and small animals; gathered acorns, medicinal herbs, and plants; made intricate baskets out of willows and red bud; and traded seashells and beads with other groups. In eastern deserts, Kumeyaay, Kawaiisu, and Chemehuevi had vast trading networks linking to the coast and to the Colorado River. Along the coast, the Chumash fished, traded, and built plank boats to access the distant Channel Islands.

Parks such as Fort Humboldt State Historic Park, Indian Grinding Rock State Historic Park, McArthur-Burney Falls Memorial State Park, and Sue-meg State Park recognize and celebrate Indigenous culture by preserving, rebuilding, and showcasing traditional structures and gardens. Examples of this include conserving the 1,185 granite bedrock mortars at Indian Grinding Rock, rebuilding galis dungal bark houses available to view at D.L. Bliss and Ed Z'berg Sugar Pine Point State Parks in Lake Tahoe, and cultivating a native plant garden at Sue-meg State Park. The park system also designates cultural preserves to protect culturally and historically significant areas. In Anza-Borrego Desert State Park and Cuyamaca Rancho State Park, for example, cultural preserves protect grinding sites, pictographs, and village sites. Many California schoolchildren are exposed to this history through field trips to California State Parks, seeing firsthand the materials, traditions, and culture that complemented the ancient generations' way of life.

In 2020, the California State Parks system launched its **Reexamining Our Past Initiative,** taking stock of contested names of monuments, historic sites, and interpretations of the past. One of the biggest examples of this is the renaming of Patrick's Point to Sue-meg State Park. Long before Irishman Patrick Beegan claimed the northwestern piece of the headlands and built a homestead, the Yurok people called that area up by Trinidad "Sue-meg." When the State of California bought the land in 1930, they kept its most widely used name even though the Yurok still referred to it as Sue-meg. In 1990, the state parks system worked with the tribe to re-create a village within the park, which they called "Sumêg," and in January 2021, the entire park adopted it. Along with renaming the park, more than 50 land acknowledgement signs have been installed throughout the North Coast redwoods parks, and interpretive signage now exists in a few founders' redwoods groves. In 2022, Old Town San Diego State Historic Park opened the Kumeyaay Interpretive Area to more fully tell the history of the region's converging cultures. An interpretive area tells the story of the first people through interpretive signs in three languages (Kumeyaay, Spanish, and English) amid native gardens and sculpture.

FOUNDING OF THE PARK SYSTEM

California's oldest state park is Big Basin Redwoods, established in 1902. Two years before, at the mark of the new millennia, a group of citizen activists formed the Sempervirens Fund to save the coast redwoods from destructive logging. The Sempervirens Fund was the state's first land trust, soon partnering with the California State Parks system to protect 6 sq mi (16 sq km) of the ancient arbors.

The California State Parks system was originally formed in 1864, though. As new settlers infiltrated California to develop its lands into cities and exploit its natural resources, California Senator John Conness wanted to set aside some land near Yosemite for preservation and

SUSTAINABILITY TIPS

As California State Parks are becoming more popular, treading lightly, minimizing our carbon footprint, and practicing responsible/eco-conscious tourism is more important than ever. Consider visiting the parks during off-peak times to help reduce overcrowding, use reef-safe sunblock when getting in the ocean, and limit your waste by bringing a reusable water bottle. Be mindful of those around you and help those in need.

Remember, if you pack it in, pack it out; take pictures and not anything else; and follow these seven **Leave No Trace** principles:

- Principle 1: Plan Ahead & Prepare
- Principle 2: Travel & Camp on Durable Surfaces
- Principle 3: Dispose of Waste Properly
- Principle 4: Leave What You Find
- Principle 5: Minimize Campfire Impacts
- Principle 6: Respect Wildlife
- Principle 7: Be Considerate of Others

Families can also make a big difference by joining the California State Parks' **Litter Getter program.**

public recreation. He introduced a bill to the Senate that quickly got passed and signed by President Abraham Lincoln in June 1864. "Yo-Semite Valley" and the Mariposa Big Tree Grove came under California's care. The land was returned to the federal government in 1906, folded into the existing Yosemite National Park that was established in 1890. After many heated public meetings and discussions, California Governor Henry Gage signed a bill in March 1901 to acquire the first 2,500 of its 18,000 acres (1,000 of 7,280 ha) at Big Basin.

Thanks to California's lawmakers and citizens working together at the turn of the century to preserve its land, up to 280 parks, natural reserves, beaches, and recreation areas are now in the California State Parks system. Fortunately for California, lands did not have to prove their economic unviability for them to be become a CSP; however, since much of California is on federal land already, any new parks are mostly purchased from private landowners. California's newest state park is the 1,600-acre (650-ha) Dos Rios in Modesto, which opened to the public in June 2024.

TRANSPORTATION

AIR

While by no means a comprehensive list, the following are the major airports throughout California.

Northern California

SAN FRANCISCO INTERNATIONAL AIRPORT

SFO; Airport Access Rd., San Francisco; 650/821-8211; www.flysfo.com

The biggest international hub serving the Northern California area is the San Francisco International Airport, about 13 mi (21 km) south of downtown. Fifty-five airlines based all over the world fly in and out daily, so it's best to get to the airport three hours before your flight to have enough time to get through the security lines.

OAKLAND INTERNATIONAL AIRPORT

OAK; 1 Airport Dr., Oakland; 510/563-3300; www.oaklandairport.com

To avoid the hustle and bustle of SFO, consider booking a flight into the Oakland International Airport. It's on the other side of the bay, 20 mi (32 km) away from downtown San Francisco, but you can still take the BART (Bay Area Regional Transit) train to get all around the Bay Area. Close to 30 major airlines fly in and out of OAK daily.

SACRAMENTO INTERNATIONAL AIRPORT

SMF; 6900 Airport Blvd., Sacramento; 916/929-5411; https://sacramento.aero/smf

The Sacramento International Airport, 10 mi (16 km) north of the state capital, is serviced by 12 major and regional airlines, including American Airlines, Delta, United, Southwest, and Alaska.

Central California

SAN JOSÉ MINETA INTERNATIONAL AIRPORT

SJC; 2077 Airport Blvd., San Jose; 408/392-3600; www.flysanjose.com

San José Mineta International Airport is 45 mi (72 km) south of San Francisco. Its airlines fly to and from 40 nonstop destinations domestically and internationally to Mexico and Asia.

SLO COUNTY AIRPORT

SBP; 975 Airport Dr., San Luis Obispo; 805/781-5205; https://sloairport.com

The San Luis Obispo (SLO) County Airport is roughly 3 mi (5 km) south of San Luis Obispo and has three major carriers.

SANTA BARBARA AIRPORT

SBA; 500 James Fowler Rd., Santa Barbara; https://flysba.santabarbaraca.gov

About 15 mi (24 km) outside the city, Santa Barbara Airport has five major carriers with 23 nonstop flights to 12 major hubs.

Southern California

LOS ANGELES INTERNATIONAL AIRPORT

LAX; 1 World Way, Los Angeles; 424/646-5252; www.flylax.com

Los Angeles International Airport is a major international airport with many carriers and flight options, as well as car rentals. Airport shuttles, hotel shuttles, long-distance vans, ride-share vans, and taxis can all be accessed at the lower arrivals level outside of the baggage claim area; median waiting platforms are marked by overhead signs.

SAN DIEGO INTERNATIONAL AIRPORT

SAN; 3225 N. Harbor Dr., San Diego; 619/400-2404; www.san.org

The San Diego International Airport is located in the city of San Diego. Major airline carriers include Southwest, American, United, Alaska, and Delta, and there is a consolidated rental car center on-site.

JOHN WAYNE AIRPORT

SNA; 18601 Airport Way, Santa Ana; www.ocair.com

Just south of Los Angeles, John Wayne Airport is the biggest airport for Orange County, with 12 airlines including American Airlines, Delta, Alaska, United, and Southwest.

PUBLIC TRANSPORTATION

Amtrak trains travel to more than 500 destinations throughout the US (and even a few in Canada), but in Northern California its routes generally stick to the inland regions, running parallel to major roadways like I-5 and I-80. This makes it difficult to find a train going directly to a state park, but sometimes regional transit services have buses that you can pick up at the train station to take you closer to your destination. For instance, Calaveras Connect goes by Calaveras Big Trees, and the Mendocino Transit Authority stops near the Mendocino Headlands.

In Southern California, travelers are lucky to have the **Pacific Surfliner** line of Amtrak. It traverses a 351-mi (564-km) route from the city of San Luis Obispo on the Central Coast to San Diego on the Southern coast, stopping at destinations along the way and giving access to major metropolitan areas including Los Angeles. It also hugs the coast for a portion of its route for spectacular views and direct access to several state parks, including Pismo State Beach, El Presidio de Santa Barbara State Historic Park, San Clemente State Beach, and Old Town San Diego State Historic Park.

Amtrak

800/872-7245; www.amtrak.com

Amtrak trains go to more than 150 destinations in California, from Los Angeles up to the Oregon border, and all the way east to Truckee, stopping at national parks, beaches, wineries, and major cities. It has partnered with **Greyhound** (www.greyhound.com) to provide buses to places where railroad track isn't laid. Its main California-only trains include the Capitol Corridor, Pacific Surfliner, and San Joaquins, but the California Zephyr and Coast Starlight are popular options that lead outside of the state as well.

CAR

CA-1 and **US-101** are the state's major coastal routes, with many of California's Southern coast, Central Coast, and Northern California state parks right off CA-1. Also known as Highway 1 or the Pacific Coast Highway, it stretches 656 mi (1,056 km) from Mendocino County to Orange County.

CA-89 travels north-south through California's mountain communities and grazes the Sierra Nevada and Cascade ranges. It meanders along the West Shore of Lake Tahoe up to McArthur-Burney Falls Memorial State Park.

Amtrak train coming into San Clemente Station

I-80 stretches west to east from the San Francisco Bay Area across to Lake Tahoe, climbing the 7,056 ft (2,151 m) over Donner Pass before dropping down into Reno, Nevada. At that elevation, I-80 is subject to snow in the winter months, which can shut down the highway. Chains or 4WD may be required; check the Caltrans website (www.dot.ca.gov) for current road conditions.

CA-14 cuts northeast from Los Angeles to access the northern Mojave Desert and state parks including Saddleback Butte State Park and Red Rock Canyon State Park.

CA-395 originates in the Mojave Desert at its nexus with CA-14 and continues north, threading the region between the Sierra Nevada to the west and Death Valley National Park to the east. The highway gives access to Mono Lake State Tufa Natural Reserve and Bodie State Historic Park before continuing north to the Oregon border. Sections of the road near Mono Lake and farther north can close in winter. Check the Caltrans website (www.dot.ca.gov) for current road conditions.

I-8 is a major highway that runs east-west from San Diego to Arizona near the Mexico border with access to several parks including Cuyamaca Rancho State Park, Anza-Borrego Desert State Park, and Picacho State Recreation Area.

I-5 is a major highway that runs north-south through inland California from the Oregon border to Mexico.

Car Rentals

Most car rental companies are located at the major California airports. To reserve a car in advance, contact **Budget Rent A Car** (US 800/218-7992, outside US 800/472-3325; www.budget.com), **Dollar Rent A Car** (800/800-5252; www.dollar.com), **Enterprise** (855/266-9289; www.enterprise.com), or **Hertz** (US and Canada 800/654-3131, international 800/654-3001; www.hertz.com).

To rent a car in California, drivers must be at least 21 years of age and have a valid US-issued driver's license. It can cost a little more to rent a car if you're under 25. California law also requires that all vehicles carry liability insurance, which can also ratchet up the daily rate, so check your car insurance policy first to see if rental car coverage is included.

The **average cost** of a rental car is $80 per day or $410 per week; however, rates vary greatly based on the time of year and distance traveled. Weekend and summer rentals can cost a lot more and are subject to sell out during those busy times when people are traveling more.

Another option is to rent an **RV.** You won't have to worry about stopping to find a place to go to the bathroom, and many state parks accommodate RVs. However, RVs are more difficult to maneuver than a standard car and can be stressful to drive in highly trafficked metropolitan areas or single-lane off-the-beaten-path state park roads. They can also be gas-guzzlers and expensive to rent, and you still have to pay standard camping fees to park it for the night (it is illegal to park a camper van or RV on the side of CA-1 overnight and subject to a hefty fine). Rates during the summer average $1,400-2,200 per week or $230-370 per night. **Cruise America** (800/671-8042; www.cruiseamerica.com) and **El Monte RV** (888/337-2214; www.elmonterv.com) are good options.

Road Conditions

In the summer parts of CA-1 along the coast can shut down due to flooding or landslides. I-5 through the Central Valley can close or be subject to hazardous driving conditions resulting from tule fog inversion, which can reduce visibility to only a few feet.

In addition, road closures are common in winter when traveling in higher elevations subject to snow. For instance, I-80 getting to Lake Tahoe can shut down over Donner Pass, and CA-89 going around Emerald Bay closes if there's avalanche danger.

When traveling in the winter, always carry chains or drive a 4WD vehicle since the weather can turn on a dime.

Traffic jams, accidents, mudslides, fires, and snow can affect California highways at any time. Before heading out on your adventure, consider checking road conditions online with the state highway department, **Caltrans** (www.dot.ca.gov).

Gas and Charging

Gas stations are close to many of the California state parks, usually no more than 45 minutes or so away. Electric vehicle charging stations are quite prevalent all throughout California, too—there are hundreds of them. Some charging stations are right in the state parks, including Folsom Lake State Recreation Area, Van Damme State Park, and Russian Gulch State Park. Visit the PlugShare website (www.plugshare.com/directory/us/california) to see where all the EV charging stations are located close to where you're going.

Maps and GPS Navigation

Using your smartphone or vehicle's GPS navigation system is pretty reliable getting to and around the parks, but it's still good to check road conditions and have a general sense of where you're going in case you lose cell service somewhere. Cell service tends to be spottier up in the North Coast redwoods and in Big Sur. Cell service is spotty to nonexistent in several desert parks, including Providence Mountains State Recreation Area, Anza-Borrego Desert State Park, and Picacho State Recreation Area.

PARK INFORMATION

TYPES OF PARKS

The California State Parks system distinguishes the units it manages based on their purpose, programming, and geography. For instance, California State Parks are focused on providing public access while protecting the area's natural resources, while a **state historic park** preserves a certain era. A **state recreation area** allows for more human impact, while a **state natural reserve** is more stringent on protecting its plants and animals as they tend to have ecological resources endemic to the area (like the Monterey cypress trees in Point Lobos State Natural Reserve). Fewer amenities are available at state reserves because the parks system tries to leave the area as undisturbed as possible.

PARK PROGRAMS

Pretty much all the California State Parks support the **Junior Ranger Program,** encouraging kids to pick up an activity book that can be worked on at the park or at home. Most parks have docents that host **guided walks** along its most interesting trails, talking about the flora and fauna in that area. Parks along CA-1 such as Pigeon Point and those in Big Sur also have whale-watching walks in the spring months when the migrating marine mammals are most active. State parks with campgrounds usually have outdoor amphitheaters where they host **campfire talks** in the summer months that are engaging for families. Volunteers are also vital to California State Parks, and opportunities to be park hosts, rangers, and help maintain the parks are always welcome. Check with your local park on how to get involved.

CAMPING

One way to experience all that a California State Park has to offer is to stay the night and camp. Many of the state's campgrounds are wildly popular and fill up fast; the demand during the **high season** (Memorial Day-Labor Day) and holiday weekends can far exceed supply. That's why most campsites at state parks during the high season must be reserved in advance through **Reserve California** (800/444-7575; www.reservecalifornia.com) from two days up to six months out of your vacation. Outside of the high season, many campgrounds that are open year-round take campers on a first-come, first-served basis.

Campfires are usually allowed in provided fire rings, but fire restrictions or bans may be in effect during peak wildfire season (summer–early fall). Check the webpage for the campground you're staying at for the most updated conditions. Buy **firewood** near where you're planning to burn it, since invasive forest insects and diseases can be transported on the wood.

CELL SERVICE

Cell phone reception is good in most major cities. However, there are many places in Northern California and remote inland areas of Central and Southern California where cell service is less reliable or nonexistent—cell service is spotty to nonexistent in most of Southern California's desert parks. Map out your route and take care of any important business in metropolitan areas before heading to the more remote state parks.

TRAVEL TIPS

ACCESSIBILITY

Many California State Parks are accessible for **travelers with disabilities** with ADA-accessible campsites, restrooms, and visitor center entrances. Certain hiking trails are also accessible to wheelchair users, retrofitted with wooden ramps. A few of the most popular state parks (like Calaveras Big Trees) have a wooden ramp and other sensory features such as signage in braille. State parks with beach access also tend to have at least one or two rentable beach wheelchairs, which can be reserved in advance by calling their entrance station. The State of California also provides a free telephone TDD-to-voice relay service; just dial 711.

If you are traveling with a disability, there are many resources to help you plan your trip. **Access California** (https://accessnca.org) is a nonprofit organization that offers general travel tips, including recommendations on accommodations, parks and trails, transportation, and travel equipment.

Wheelchair Traveling (www.wheelchairtraveling.com) provides lots of guides and tips for how to best get around California State Parks' trails. It shares path widths, where the accessible ramps are, trail grades, and obstacles. Some parks give discounts on day use fees to those with disabilities (and their friends) to encourage equity for all.

TRAVELERS OF COLOR

Although California has come a long way in welcoming diversity and equal access to its state parks, its history of violence against people of color may still make some feel uneasy when in outdoor public spaces. It's one of the most visited states in the nation, attracting domestic as well as international tourists, and although demographics and political stances vary widely between areas, that just reflects how big of a state California is.

The 2020 Census shows that out of California's 39.4 million people, approximately 39 percent are Hispanic/Latino; 38 percent are white; 17 percent are Asian; 6.4 percent are African American; and 1.3 percent are Native American or other. Understanding that California State Parks were originally built on the land of Indigenous peoples who were forced out of their homes in the mid-1800s, the California State Parks Foundation (www.calparks.org) has made a JEID (Justice, Equity, Inclusion, Diversity) commitment to bring those marginalized groups back. The park system also celebrates the state's diversity with cultural heritage days and places, like San Diego State Historic Park recognizing Black History Month with all kinds of special events.

The **American Hiking Society** has a list of resources (https://americanhiking.org/hiking-resources/racism-in-the-outdoors) for BIPOC and other marginalized groups interested in the outdoors, including community organizations and affinity groups.

LGBTQ+ TRAVELERS

The Golden State is a golden place for gay travel. However, the farther you venture into rural regions, the less likely you are to experience liberal attitudes and acceptance. The **Pride Outside** (https://parkscalifornia.org) initiative provides ways to support LGBTQ+ inclusion in outdoor spaces, so everyone can feel safe in the outdoors. **Great Outdoors California** (https://greatoutdoors.org) is a nonprofit social hub constantly hosting camping trips, hikes, mountain bike rides, fishing trips, and more. San Francisco, Sacramento, Palm Springs, and San Diego are a few of the top gay-friendly cities in America.

SOLO TRAVELERS

California State Parks have become hot spots for single travelers as places like Big Sur, San Diego, the Redwoods, Lake Tahoe, and San Francisco regularly top out the lists. A solo California State Parks trip is perfect for those who want to go at their own pace and see it all. However, if you plan to solo camp and crash in your vehicle after a long day of hiking, still bring a tent—many spots around CA-1, Santa Cruz, and Mount Tamalpais won't let you sleep in your car even if you pay the overnight parking fee.

SENIOR TRAVELERS

People ages 62 and older can get $1 off a vehicle daily use fee or $2 off overnight camping fees at the majority of California State Parks. Just show a state-issued photo ID at the entrance stations. The **Senior Golden Bear Pass** is only $20 and gets a person 62 or older plus their spouse into the park, but is not valid during high season, Memorial Day Weekend-Labor Day Weekend. Visit the California State Parks website to apply.

TRAVELING WITH CHILDREN

The California State Parks system is welcoming to kids, with certain programs in place to help them foster their curiosity and instill responsible tourism in them at a young age. The **Adventure Pass** gives fourth-graders and their families free entry into 54 of California's 280 state parks, and many California libraries allow you to check out a California State Parks pass. Kids can hunt for hidden treasure at six North Coast redwoods parks by taking a Redwood EdVenture Quest, or download the augmented reality Agents of Discovery app—let's face it, these activities are fun for adults, too.

Sonoma Coast State Park, Half Moon Bay State Beach, and Cayucos State Beach are perfect for building sand castles. Teenagers hang out at the River Gorge at Pfeiffer Big Sur during spring break. Catch little ones in sturdy shoes picnicking or having a snack while tide-pooling at Point Lobos State Natural Reserve, Sonoma Coast's Shell Beach, or up at Sue-meg State Park. On the Southern coast there are plenty of tide-pooling opportunities at Montaña de Oro State Park, Crystal Cove State Park, and Leo Carrillo State Park. Take the kids to Calaveras Big Trees to dance on the Discovery Stump or find banana slugs at Henry Cowell Redwoods or Big Basin. Look for butterflies at Pismo State Beach's Monarch Butterfly Grove. Kids will love climbing the rocks and exploring the miniature slot canyons at Red Rock Canyon State Park or splashing in the creeks of Cuyamaca Rancho State Park. The sense of wonder is limitless at California State Parks; visit https://kids.parks.ca.gov to learn more.

The **Junior Ranger Program** is designed for children ages 5-13 and offers a structured way for kids to learn about the park and enjoy a sense of stewardship. Pick up a copy of the Junior Ranger adventure activity guide at a visitor center, have the kids complete age-appropriate activities, do a park project, and attend a ranger program.

TRAVELING WITH PETS

Those traveling with canine companions may note that **leashed, well-behaved dogs** are allowed at some state park campgrounds, though rules and regulations vary (and pets may not be allowed in other parts of the parks, such as on trails, even if allowed in campgrounds). Helpful resources for visiting parks with pets can be found on the California State Parks website (www.parks.ca.gov/dogs), but it's best to check online for the specific campgrounds you're planning to visit for details; use the "Park Info" tab on California State Parks webpages (www.parks.ca.gov). **Service animals** are allowed on all public lands, but keep in mind that misrepresenting your dog as a service animal without the proper paperwork is a misdemeanor under state law.

HEALTH AND SAFETY

HOSPITALS AND EMERGENCIES

For an emergency, **dial 911.** Full-service hospitals are in the major cities closest to the park you're visiting, and park rangers are the best ones to find first in case something happens.

WILDERNESS SAFETY

Being out in the elements can present its own set of challenges. Despite California's relatively mild climate, **heat exhaustion** and **heatstroke** can affect anyone during the hot summer months, particularly during a long, strenuous hike in the sun or at higher mountain elevations. Common symptoms include nausea, lightheadedness, headache, or muscle cramps. **Dehydration** and loss of electrolytes are the common causes of heat exhaustion. If you or anyone in your group develops any of these symptoms, get out of the sun immediately, stop all physical activity, and drink plenty of water. Heat exhaustion can be severe, and if untreated can lead to heatstroke, in which the body's core temperature reaches 105°F (40°C). Fainting, seizures, confusion, and rapid heartbeat and breathing can indicate the situation has moved beyond heat exhaustion. If you suspect this, call 911 immediately.

Similar precautions hold true for **hypothermia,** which is caused by prolonged exposure to cold water or weather. For many in California, this can happen on a hike or backpacking trip without sufficient rain gear, or by staying too long in the ocean or another cold body of water without a wetsuit. Symptoms include shivering, weak pulse, drowsiness, confusion, slurred speech, or stumbling. To treat hypothermia, immediately remove wet clothing, cover the person with blankets, and feed him or her hot liquids. If symptoms don't improve, call 911.

Ticks live in many of the forests and grasslands throughout California, except at higher elevations. Tick season generally runs late fall-early summer. If you are hiking through brushy areas, wear pants and long-sleeve shirts. Ticks like to crawl to warm, moist places (armpits are a favorite) on their host. If a tick is engorged, it can be difficult to remove. There are two main types of ticks found in California: dog ticks and deer ticks. Dog ticks are larger, brown, and have a gold spot on their backs, while deer ticks are small, tear-shaped, and black. Deer ticks are known to carry Lyme disease. While Lyme disease is relatively rare in California, it is very serious. If you get bitten by a deer tick and the bite leaves a red ring, seek medical attention. Lyme disease can be successfully treated with early rounds of antibiotics.

There is only one major variety of plant in California that can cause an adverse reaction in humans if you touch the leaves or stems: **poison oak,** a common shrub that inhabits forests throughout the state. Poison oak has a characteristic three-leaf configuration, with scalloped leaves that are shiny green in the spring and then turn yellow, orange, and red in late summer-fall. In fall, the leaves drop, leaving a cluster of innocuous-looking branches. The oil in poison oak is present year-round in both the leaves and branches. Your best protection is to wear long sleeves and long pants when hiking, no matter how hot it is. A product called Tecnu is available at

10 ESSENTIALS

When heading out into the wilderness or spending a day hiking California State Parks trails, it's always a good idea to have some basic items with you in case of an injury, sudden weather change, or some other unplanned event. Here are 10 essential items to always have in your pack:

- Navigation (compass, map, and/or GPS tracking)
- Sun protection (sunglasses, hat, sunscreen)
- Illumination (flashlight, headlamp, solar-powered lantern)
- Insulation (waterproof jacket, gloves, thermal socks and undergarments)
- First-aid kit (Band-Aids, medical tape, Neosporin)
- Fire (matches, a lighter, fire-starters)
- Tools (scissors, screwdriver, and multitool) and duct tape
- Nutrition (trail mix, nuts, granola bars)
- Hydration (water and water filter)
- Emergency shelter (space blanket, tent, a tarp)

most California drugstores; slather it on before you go hiking to protect yourself from poison oak. If your skin comes into contact with poison oak, expect a nasty rash known for its itchiness and irritation. Poison oak is also extremely transferable, so avoid touching your eyes, face, or other parts of your body to prevent spreading the rash. Calamine lotion can help, and in extreme cases a doctor can administer cortisone to help decrease the inflammation. Remember, "leaves of three, let them be."

WILDLIFE

Many places are still wild in California, making it important to use precautions with regard to wildlife. While California no longer has any grizzly bears, **black bears** thrive and are often seen in the mountains foraging for food in the spring, summer, and fall. Black bears certainly don't have the size or reputation of grizzlies, but there is good reason to exercise caution. Never get between a bear and her cub, and if a bear sees you, identify yourself as human by waving your hands above your head, speaking in a calm voice, and backing away slowly. If a bear charges, do not run. If a bear is in a building, do not block its escape route. One of the best precautions against an unwanted bear encounter is to keep a clean camp; store all food in airtight, bearproof containers, and strictly follow any guidelines given by the park or rangers.

Even more common than bears are **mountain lions,** which can be found in the Coast Range as well as in grasslands and forests. Because of their solitary nature, it is unlikely you will see one, even on long trips in the backcountry. Still, there are a couple things to remember. If you come across a kill, probably a large partly eaten deer, leave immediately. If you see a mountain lion and it sees you, identify yourself as human, making your body appear as big as possible, just as with a bear. And most importantly: Never run. As with any cat, large or small, running triggers its hunting instincts. If a mountain lion should attack, fight back; cats don't like to get hurt. Mountain lion attacks are rare but do occur if they are starving.

The other slightly dangerous creature to watch out for at California State Parks is the **rattlesnake.** They can be found in summer in generally hot and dry areas from the coast to the Sierra Nevada. When hiking in this type of terrain (many parks will indicate if rattlesnakes are a problem in the area), keep your eyes on the ground and an ear out for the telltale rattle. Snakes like to warn you to keep away. The only time this is not the case is with baby rattlesnakes that have not yet developed their rattles and don't know how to control their venom. Rattlesnakes are becoming more prominent in places like Lake Tahoe, Folsom Lake State Recreation Area, and even the Armstrong Redwoods, so it's important to always stay alert and on the trails. The good news is rarely do rattlesnakes lash out unless they are messed with. Should a rattlesnake get you, go to the emergency room immediately.

WILDFIRES

As the environment continues to change, wildfires are becoming more devastating in California, especially in its state parks. Parks such as Big Basin Redwoods are still trying to recover from recent wildfires. Wildfires tend to be most prevalent in the June–September months, but earthquakes, floods, and power outages can affect state park operations as well. Before you visit, check out the California State Parks Significant Incidents Updates page to make sure the park(s) you want to go to aren't affected by a natural disaster.

OCEAN AND WATER SAFETY

Not all California coastline beaches are safe to swim in, so be sure to look for signs about riptides and heed caution when entering the water. For instance, at North Coast parks (like Prairie Creek Redwoods and Sue-meg State Park) the water is extremely cold, and jagged corals can be lurking below the surface. Rogue and sleeper waves can also catch you off-guard when out tide-pooling, which is why you should never turn your back on the ocean. Some other safety items to keep in mind:

- Don't swim alone.
- If caught in a current, don't try to fight it. Swim parallel to the shoreline, and once out of the current try to swim toward shore.
- Yell for help and wave your arms if you have to.
- If you see someone in trouble out in the water, call 911.

DESERT SAFETY

Vast spaces, remote roads, and weather extremes can create potentially risky situations, but traveling in a desert is not any more dangerous than in other parks if you are prepared for the unique environment. Know what weather to expect and where you're going, and be prepared for the unexpected.

- **Tell Someone Where You're Going:** Whether you're hiking, driving, or a combination, make sure you tell someone where you are going and when to expect your return. Deserts can cover a huge area, and in the event that you are stranded, the search effort can be pinpointed.
- **Bring Supplies:** Temperatures can fluctuate 40 degrees between day and night. Bring a sleeping bag or emergency blanket even if you do not plan to be out overnight. Pack appropriate clothing for a range of temperatures, and be prepared for cold temperatures at night. Always bring extra water and extra nonperishable food that does not have to be

cooked. Have a paper map or an electronic offline map and a charger (cell phones may not work in some areas). Be prepared to survive until help arrives if you are stranded.

- **Vehicle Breakdowns:** Sharp rocks, long bumpy roads, and heat can cause your vehicle to break down on backcountry roads. Always drive with a full-size spare tire. A fix-a-flat tire kit may also be helpful. If you are stranded, stay with your car until help arrives. It is much easier to spot a big metal car that flashes in the sunlight than a person walking. Also, it is dangerous to overexert yourself in the heat of the desert, so hiking out to safety is not generally the best option. Be prepared with extra supplies, including food, water, and warm clothes.

RESOURCES

California State Parks
www.parks.ca.gov
The official website lists hours, accessibility, activities, camping areas, fees, and more information for all parks in the state system.

Caltrans (California Department of Transportation)
www.dot.ca.gov
Check Caltrans for state map and highway information before planning a coastal road trip.

ReserveCalifornia
www.reservecalifornia.com
Most camping and lodging accommodations located within California State Parks must be reserved from two days up to six months in advance through this website.

lifeguard towers at Huntington Beach

INDEX

E

F

G

H

I

J

KL

QR

S

T

UV

WY

LIST OF MAPS

PHOTO CREDITS

Title page photo: California State Parks, Brian Baer Photographer,090-P103269; page 2 © Spvvkr | Dreamstime.com; Kayla Anderson; Kayla Anderson; page 3 © California State Parks, Brian Baer Photographer, 090-P112701; California State Parks, Brian Baer Photographer, 090-79832; Davidmschrader | Dreamstime.com; page 5 © California State Parks, Brian Baer Photographer, 090-P118456; page 7 © Maislam | Dreamstime.com; page 8 © Annefrigon | Dreamstime.com; page 10 © Sheldon573 | Dreamstime.com; Asterixvs | Dreamstime.com; page 11 © Jenna Blough; page 12 © Chrislabasco | Dreamstime.com; Jenna Blough; page 13 © Rolf52 | Dreamstime.com; Kayla Anderson; page 14 © Snehitdesign | Dreamstime.com; page 18 © California State Parks, Brian Baer Photographer, 090-68174; page 23 © California State Parks, Brian Baer Photographer, 090-P108691; page 24 © Andreistanescu | Dreamstime.com; page 25 © Jenna Blough; Jenna Blough; Kayla Anderson; page 26 © Idealphotograph | Dreamstime.com; page 27 © Andreistanescu | Dreamstime.com; Franky | Dreamstime.com; California State Parks, Brian Baer Photographer, 090-P97168; page 28 © Hartemink | Dreamstime.com; page 30 © Kat Bennett; page 31 © Jenna Blough; Kayla Anderson; page 32 © California State Parks, Brian Baer Photographer, 090-73132; page 33 © Jenna Blough; page 34 © California State Parks, Brian Baer Photographer, 090-P112681; Ajà Miller; page 35 © Rinusbaak | Dreamstime.com; page 36 © Jenna Blough; page 37 © Jenna Blough; page 39 © California State Parks, Brian Baer Photographer,090-P83363; page 45 © California State Parks, Brian Baer Photographer, 090-P93041; Kayla Anderson; California State Parks, Brian Baer Photographer, 090-P120426; page 46 © California State Parks, Brian Baer Photographer, 090-71937; California State Parks, Brian Baer Photographer, 090-P71580; page 47 © Kayla Anderson; page 48 © Grace Fujimoto; page 50 © Kayla Anderson; Kayla Anderson; Tristanbnz | Dreamstime.com; page 53 © Kayla Anderson; page 54 © California State Parks, Brian Baer Photographer, 090-P89424; page 55 © California State Parks, Brian Baer Photographer, 090-P89430; page 56 © Kayla Anderson; Grace Fujimoto; page 58 © California State Parks, Brian Baer Photographer, 090-P111313; page 60 © ; Chrisjbabcock88 | Dreamstime.com Kayla Anderson; Kayla Anderson; page 64 © Kayla Anderson; page 66 © Andreistanescu | Dreamstime.com; Blac16 | Dreamstime.com; page 68 © Kayla Anderson; page 69 © California State Parks, Brian Baer Photographer, 090-P109660; page 71 © Kayla Anderson; page 74 © Kayla Anderson; California State Parks, Brian Baer Photographer, 090-P109649; page 75 © Kayla Anderson; page 78 © Kayla Anderson; page 80 © California State Parks, Brian Baer Photographer, 090-78151; page 82 © Kayla Anderson; Kayla Anderson; Kayla Anderson; page 84 © Kayla Anderson; California State Parks, Brian Baer Photographer, 090-78171; page 86 © Moehlestephen | Dreamstime.com; page 88 © California State Parks, Brian Baer Photographer, 090-68115; Martinabirnbaum | Dreamstime.com; Svecpetr | Dreamstime.com; page 91 © California State Parks, Brian Baer Photographer,090-68137; page 92 © Tristanbnz | Dreamstime.com; page 96 © California State Parks, Brian Baer Photographer, 090-64326; page 98 © Kayla Anderson; California State Parks, Brian Baer Photographer, 090-64363; Jerry Hamblen | iStock.com; page 100 © California State Parks, Brian Baer Photographer, 090-64334; page 102 © Alessandrarc1 | Dreamstime.com; page 105 © Picchupro | Dreamstime.com; page 107 © Mkojot | Dreamstime.com; Grace Fujimoto; Fernley | Dreamstime.com; page 109 © California State Parks, Brian Baer

Photographer, 090-P101479; page 111 © Grace Fujimoto; page 112 © Fernley | Dreamstime.com; page 114 © California State Parks, Brian Baer Photographer, 090-P101463; page 116 © Kayla Anderson; California State Parks, Brian Baer Photographer, 090-76918; Mikefusaro | Dreamstime.com; page 118 © Snyfer | Dreamstime.com; California State Parks, Brian Baer Photographer, 090-77241; page 120 © California State Parks, Brian Baer Photographer, 090-P101434; page 123 © California State Parks, Brian Baer Photographer, 090-77216; page 126 © California State Parks, Brian Baer Photographer, 090-P88248; page 128 © Kayla Anderson; Stevehymon | Dreamstime.com; Kayla Anderson; page 130 © Kayla Anderson; Kayla Anderson; page 131 © Kayla Anderson; page 133 © Alessandrarc1 | Dreamstime.com; page 135 © Weriset | Dreamstime.com; page 136 © Mkojot | Dreamstime.com; Kayla Anderson; page 138 © Kayla Anderson; page 140 © Kayla Anderson; Kayla Anderson; page 142 © Kayla Anderson; page 144 © Yhelfman | Dreamstime.com; page 146 © Kayla Anderson; Sherrrrrye | Dreamstime.com; page 149 © Devon Lee; page 151 © Kapu | Dreamstime.com; page 153 © California State Parks, Brian Baer Photographer, 090-P70483; page 155 © Lizziemaher | Dreamstime.com; page 157 © Devon Lee; California State Parks, Brian Baer Photographer, 090-P120425; page 158 © Devon Lee; Devon Lee; page 160 © Devon Lee; Devon Lee; page 163 © California State Parks, Brian Baer Photographer, 090-P109898; page 165 © California State Parks, Brian Baer Photographer, 090-80942; page 168 © Kayla Anderson; Kayla Anderson; page 173 © Edb316 | Dreamstime.com; page 175 © Kayla Anderson; California State Parks, Brian Baer Photographer, 090-71952; Kayla Anderson; page 179 © California State Parks, Brian Baer Photographer, 090-P104459; page 180 © Spvvkr | Dreamstime.com; California State Parks, Brian Baer Photographer, 090-P102305; page 183 © Dcarter112 | Dreamstime.com; page 185 © Poggensee | Dreamstime.com; page 187 © Bavdekar | Dreamstime.com; Kayla Anderson; page 188 © Kayla Anderson; page 191 © Kayla Anderson; page 193 © Wirestock | Dreamstime.com; page 195 © Kitleong | Dreamstime.com; page 196 © Ericfehrenbacher | Dreamstime.com; Kayla Anderson; page 197 © Kayla Anderson; page 199 © Cristina Glebova | Unsplash.com; page 201 © California State Parks, Brian Baer Photographer, 090-73138; page 203 © Kayla Anderson; Kayla Anderson; Kayla Anderson; page 204 © Kayla Anderson; Kayla Anderson; page 208 © California State Parks, Brian Baer Photographer, 090-P68768; page 210 © California State Parks, Brian Baer Photographer, 090-P113763; page 212 © Kayla Anderson; Kayla Anderson; page 213 © John Michnowicz | Shutterstock.com; page 215 © Kayla Anderson; page 217 © arah_Robson | Dreamstime.com; page 219 © Kinolebid | Dreamstime.com; page 225 © California State Parks, Brian Baer Photographer,090-P72929; California State Parks, Brian Baer Photographer, 090-P111725; page 226 © California State Parks, Brian Baer Photographer,090-P72682; Jenna Blough; page 227 © California State Parks, Brian Baer Photographer, 090-79684; page 228 © California State Parks, Brian Baer Photographer, 090-81112; page 230 © Jenna Blough; Karenfoleyphotography | Dreamstime.com; Raagoon | Dreamstime.com; page 232 © Jenna Blough; Kat Bennett; California State Parks, Brian Baer Photographer, 090-P81314; page 234 © Jenna Blough; page 235 © California State Parks, Brian Baer Photographer, 090-P81566; page 237 © Jenna Blough; Jimpanzer | Dreamstime.com; Celsodiniz | Dreamstime.com; page 239 © Jenna Blough; page 240 © Luciavegaphotography | Dreamstime.com; page 242 © Carrieanne | Dreamstime.com; page 243 © California State Parks, Brian Baer Photographer, 090-P116876; page 245 © Nalukai | Dreamstime.com; California State Parks, Brian Baer Photographer, 090-P118453; Chasedekker | Dreamstime.com; page 246 © Kayla Anderson; Kayla Anderson; page 250 © California State Parks, Brian Baer Photographer, 090-P92785; page 252 © svetlanasf |

Dreamstime.com; Kayla Anderson; Chasedekker | Dreamstime.com; page 254 © Kayla Anderson; Grace Fujimoto; page 256 © Palms | Dreamstime.com; page 258 © Kayla Anderson; Kayla Anderson; Kayla Anderson; page 260 © Kayla Anderson; page 261 © California State Parks, Brian Baer Photographer, 090-P92762; page 263 © Kayla Anderson; page 265 © California State Parks, Brian Baer Photographer, 090-67926; page 267 © Kayla Anderson; page 269 © Kayla Anderson; page 272 © Kayla Anderson; page 274 © California State Parks, Brian Baer Photographer, 090-67924; page 275 © Yhelfman | Dreamstime.com; page 276 © Kayla Anderson; page 278 © Ravina Schneider; page 280 © Courtney Packard; page 282 © Kayla Anderson; Courtney Packard; page 283 © Kayla Anderson; page 284 © Ravina Schneider; page 285 © Kwiktor | Dreamstime.com; page 287 © HandmadePictures | Dreamstime.com; page 289 © Kayla Anderson; Kayla Anderson; Kayla Anderson; page 291 © Kayla Anderson; Kayla Anderson; page 293 © Kayla Anderson; page 294 © California State Parks, Brian Baer Photographer, 090-P98957; Kayla Anderson; page 298 © Tovelynn | Dreamstime.com; Jenna Blough; page 303 © Hannator92 | Dreamstime.com; page 304 © California State Parks, Brian Baer Photographer,090-79730; page 306 © California State Parks, Brian Baer Photographer,090-P94594; page 307 © Biolifepics | Dreamstime.com; Hannator92 | Dreamstime.com; page 310 © California State Parks, Brian Baer Photographer,090-P94607; California State Parks, Brian Baer Photographer, 090-79729; page 312 © California State Parks, Brian Baer Photographer, 090-P108381; page 314 © Jenna Blough; Nflane | Dreamstime.com; Jenna Blough; page 319 © Jenna Blough; Kat Bennett; Jenna Blough; page 322 © California State Parks, Brian Baer Photographer, 090-P111745; page 324 © Jenna Blough; Andreistanescu | Dreamstime.com; Beverett | Dreamstime.com; page 327 © Jenna Blough; page 328 © Jenna Blough; page 331 © Jhaw20 | Dreamstime.com; page 333 © California State Parks, Brian Baer Photographer, 090-P91467; page 335 © Ajà Miller; Rinusbaak | Dreamstime.com; Ajà Miller; page 337 © Rusper | Dreamstime.com; page 339 © Jenna Blough; page 340 © Ajà Miller; page 343 © Astranger9 | Dreamstime.com; page 345 © Astranger9 | Dreamstime.com; page 348 © California State Parks, Brian Baer Photographer,090-P121341; Christinahswanson | Dreamstime.com; page 350 © California State Parks, Brian Baer Photographer, 090-79832; page 352 © California State Parks, Brian Baer Photographer, 090-P121370; Jenna Blough; Jenna Blough; page 354 © Jenna Blough; page 355 © Jenna Blough; page 357 © Jenna Blough; page 359 © California State Parks, Brian Baer Photographer, 090-P97579; page 365 © Jenna Blough; Jenna Blough; Jenna Blough; page 367 © California State Parks, Brian Baer Photographer, 090-P112414; page 368 © California State Parks, Brian Baer Photographer, 090-P112701; page 370 © Jenna Blough; Jenna Blough; Jenna Blough; page 373 © Jenna Blough; page 374 © Jenna Blough; Jenna Blough; page 376 © California State Parks, Brian Baer Photographer, 090-P88634; page 378 © California State Parks, Brian Baer Photographer, 090-P102818; page 380 © Jenna Blough; California State Parks, Brian Baer Photographer, 090-P102800; Jenna Blough; page 382 © Jenna Blough; page 383 © Wollertz | Dreamstime.com; page 385 © California State Parks, Brian Baer Photographer, 090-75799; page 387 © California State Parks, Brian Baer Photographer, 090-75764; page 389 © California State Parks, Brian Baer Photographer, 090-75786; page 390 © Jenna Blough; page 391 © Jenna Blough; page 393 © California State Parks, Brian Baer Photographer, 090-P91908; page 395 © Jenna Blough; Jenna Blough; Jenna Blough; page 398 © Jenna Blough; Jenna Blough; page 399 © Jenna Blough; page 400 © Jenna Blough; page 402 © Jenna Blough; page 403 © California State Parks, Brian Baer Photographer, 090-85488; page 405 © Pixelthat | Dreamstime.com; Guobeihua |

Dreamstime.com; Stevehymon | Dreamstime.com; page 407 © California State Parks, Brian Baer Photographer, 090-85487; page 409 © trekandshoot | Dreamstime.com; page 411 © Guobeihua | Dreamstime.com; page 412 © Davidmschrader | Dreamstime.com; page 414 © Jenna Blough; page 416 © Tupungato | Dreamstime.com; page 418 © Jenna Blough; Jenna Blough; page 420 © Luckyphotographer | Dreamstime.com; page 422 © Katiechizhevskaya | Dreamstime.com; California State Parks, Brian Baer Photographer, 090-P94519; Mortenelm | Dreamstime.com; page 425 © Rolf52 | Dreamstime.com; page 428 © California State Parks, Brian Baer Photographer, 090-P107346; page 430 © Mbrittain01 | Dreamstime.com; page 432 © Evgeniyaphotography | Dreamstime.com; page 436 © California State Parks, Brian Baer Photographer, 090-P101622; page 438 © JenningsSayre | Dreamstime.com; page 441 © Jimfeliciano | Dreamstime.com; Jenna Blough; page 443 © trekandshoot | Dreamstime.com; page 445 © Jenna Blough; California State Parks, Brian Baer Photographer, 090-P75273; page 447 © Appalachianviews | Dreamstime.com; page 449 © California State Parks, Brian Baer Photographer, 090-82868; California State Parks, Brian Baer Photographer, 090-P115672; Jenna Blough; page 452 © Jenna Blough; page 453 © Jenna Blough; page 455 © California State Parks, Brian Baer Photographer, 090-82090; page 457 © Xcorps | Dreamstime.com; Sherryvsmith | Dreamstime.com; Bree Madden; page 459 © California State Parks, Brian Baer Photographer, 090-82098; Jenna Blough; page 460 © Bree Madden; page 462 © California State Parks, Brian Baer Photographer, 090-P102869; page 464 © trekandshoot | Dreamstime.com; Hsandler | Dreamstime.com; SailingstoneTravel | Dreamstime.com; page 468 © SailingstoneTravel | Dreamstime.com; page 470 © California State Parks, Brian Baer Photographer, 090-76487; page 472 © Jenna Blough; Jenna Blough; Jenna Blough; page 475 © Jenna Blough; California State Parks, Brian Baer Photographer, 090-P103832; Jenna Blough; page 479 © California State Parks, Brian Baer Photographer, 090-78889; page 481 © California State Parks, Brian Baer Photographer, 090-78976; California State Parks, Brian Baer Photographer, 090-78969; Jenna Blough; page 483 © bildradar | Dreamstime.com; page 485 © Danielschreurs | Dreamstime.com; page 486 © California State Parks, Brian Baer Photographer, 090-78967; Jenna Blough; page 489 © Agap13 | Dreamstime.com; page 490 © California State Parks, Brian Baer Photographer, 090-P93934; page 492 © Jenna Blough; page 494 © California State Parks, Brian Baer Photographer, 090-P93984; California State Parks, Brian Baer Photographer, 090-P93960; page 496 © Jenna Blough; page 499 © Jenna Blough; page 500 © California State Parks, Brian Baer Photographer, 090-P102677; page 502 © Jenna Blough; Kevinkey4 | Dreamstime.com; Jenna Blough; page 505 © California State Parks, Brian Baer Photographer, 090-P102591; Jenna Blough; page 506 © California State Parks, Brian Baer Photographer, 090-P109564; page 510 © Htbphotos | Dreamstime.com; page 514 © California State Parks, Brian Baer Photographer, 090-75611; page 516 © Jenna Blough; California State Parks, Brian Baer Photographer, 090-75613; Jenna Blough; page 520 © Jenna Blough; page 523 © California State Parks, Brian Baer Photographer, 090-75616; page 524 © California State Parks, Brian Baer Photographer, 090-75606; Jenna Blough; page 527 © Kayla Anderson; page 531 © Festypsx | Dreamstime.com; page 539 © Appalachianviews | Dreamstime.com

National Parks Travel Guides from Moon

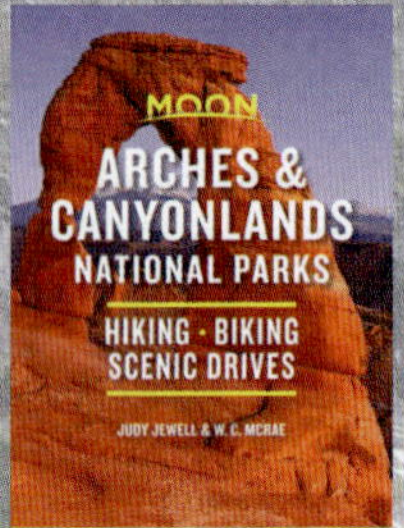

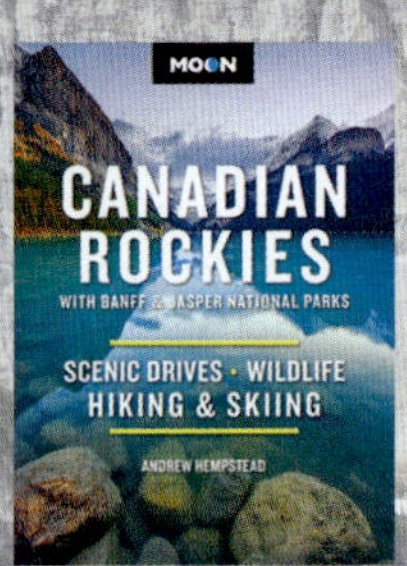

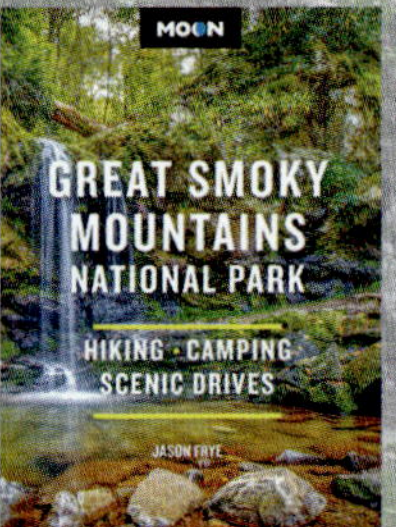

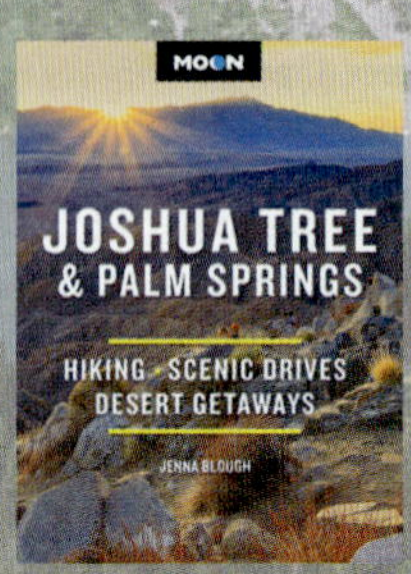

More Great Guides from Moon

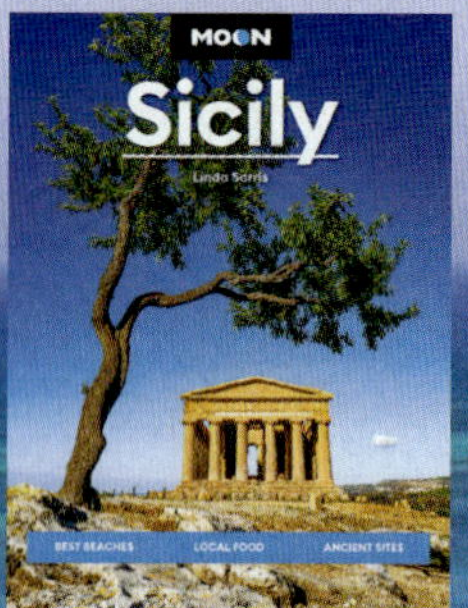

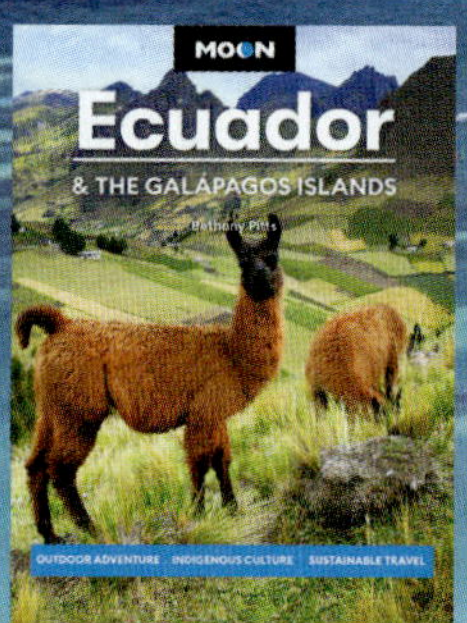

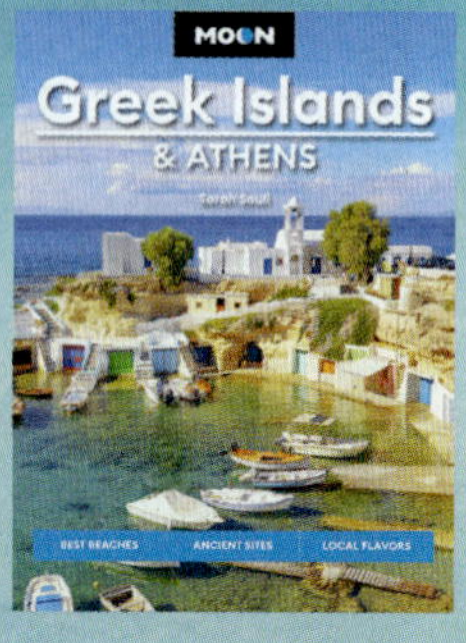

MOON
Oaxaca

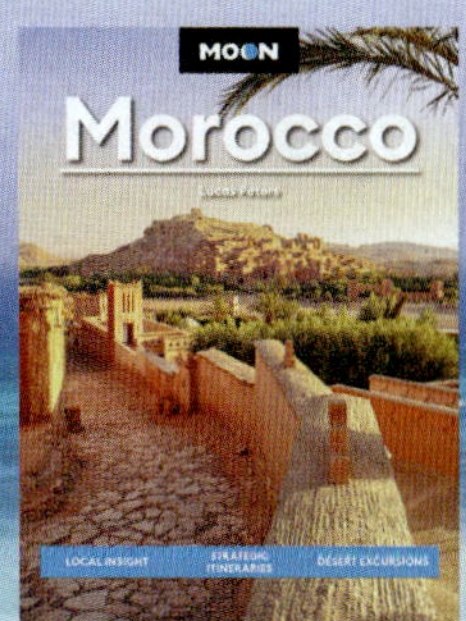
MOON
Morocco

MOON
New Zealand

MOON
San Miguel de Allende
WITH GUANAJUATO & QUERÉTARO

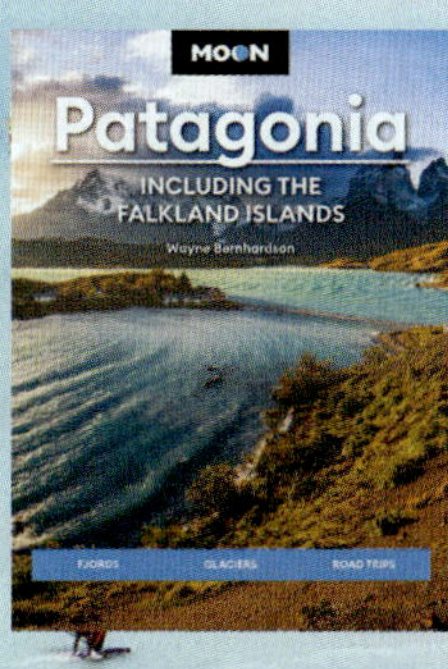
MOON
Patagonia
INCLUDING THE FALKLAND ISLANDS
Wayne Bernhardson

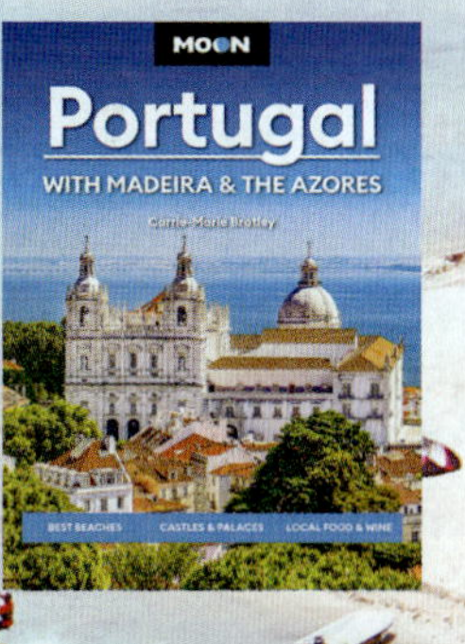
MOON
Portugal
WITH MADEIRA & THE AZORES

MOON
Prague, Vienna & Budapest

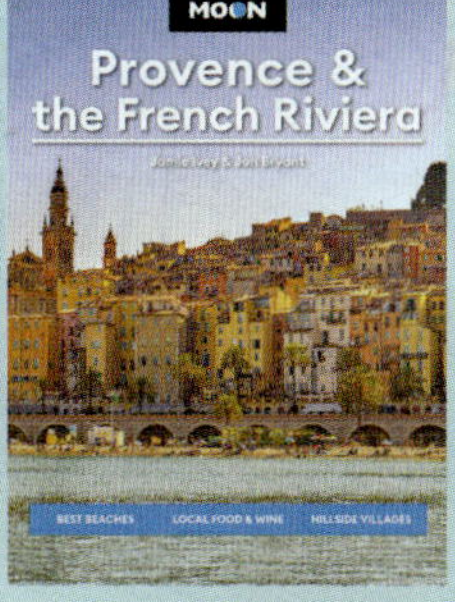
MOON
Provence & the French Riviera

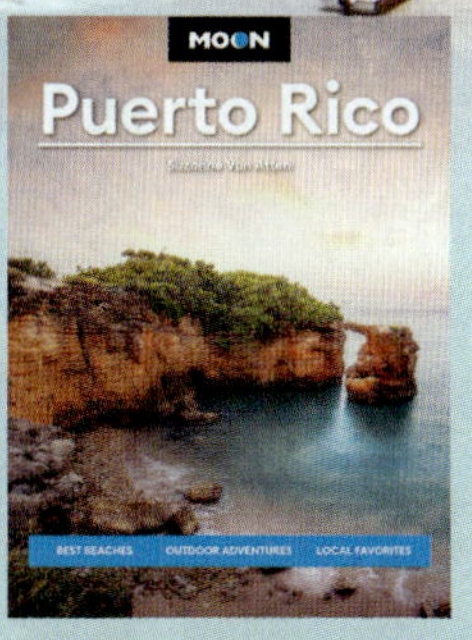
MOON
Puerto Rico

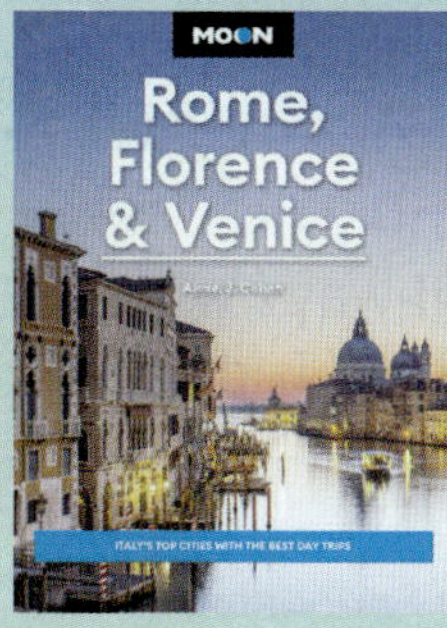
MOON
Rome, Florence & Venice

MOON
Scotland

MOON
Southern Italy
WITH SICILY, PUGLIA, NAPLES & THE AMALFI COAST

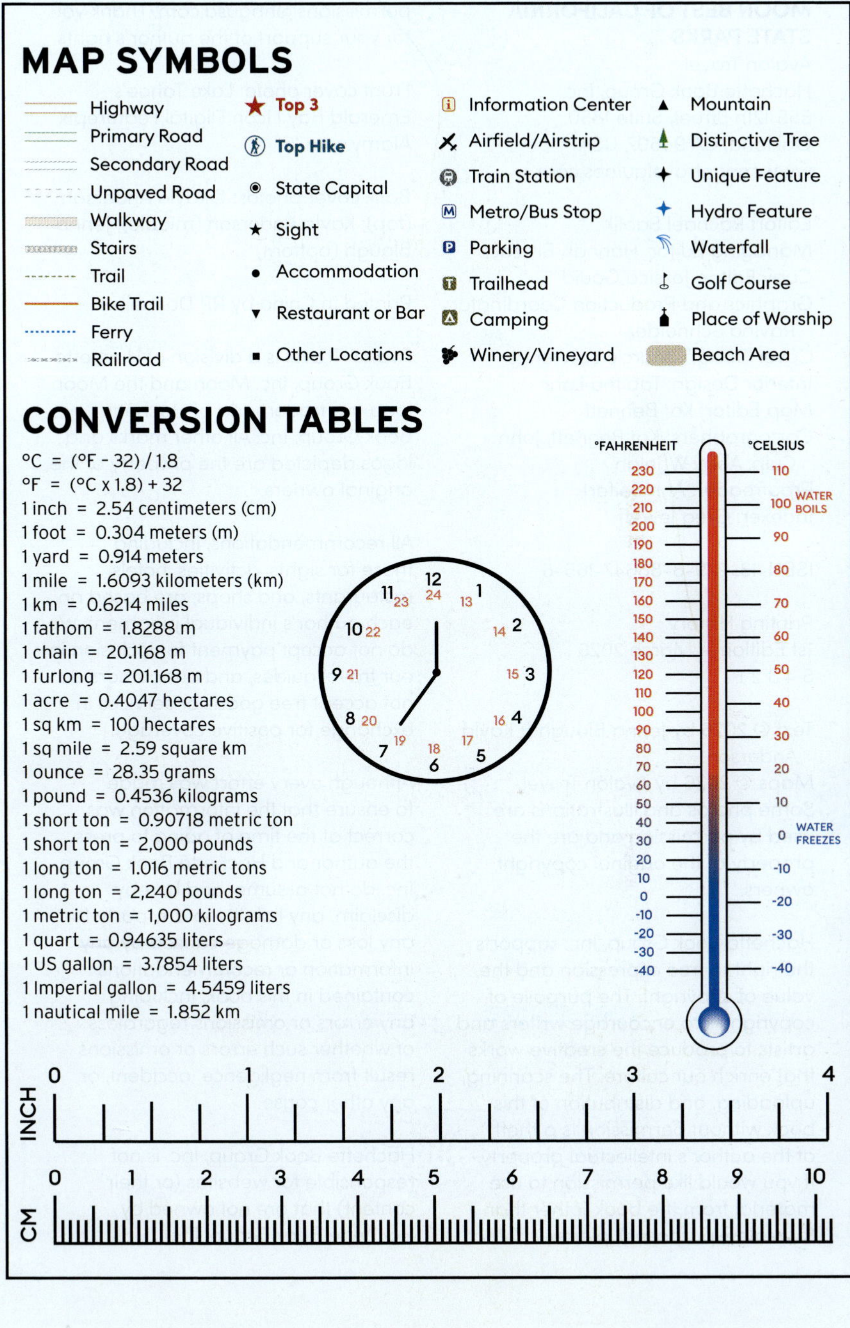

MAP SYMBOLS

CONVERSION TABLES

°C = (°F - 32) / 1.8
°F = (°C x 1.8) + 32
1 inch = 2.54 centimeters (cm)
1 foot = 0.304 meters (m)
1 yard = 0.914 meters
1 mile = 1.6093 kilometers (km)
1 km = 0.6214 miles
1 fathom = 1.8288 m
1 chain = 20.1168 m
1 furlong = 201.168 m
1 acre = 0.4047 hectares
1 sq km = 100 hectares
1 sq mile = 2.59 square km
1 ounce = 28.35 grams
1 pound = 0.4536 kilograms
1 short ton = 0.90718 metric ton
1 short ton = 2,000 pounds
1 long ton = 1.016 metric tons
1 long ton = 2,240 pounds
1 metric ton = 1,000 kilograms
1 quart = 0.94635 liters
1 US gallon = 3.7854 liters
1 Imperial gallon = 4.5459 liters
1 nautical mile = 1.852 km

MOON BEST OF CALIFORNIA STATE PARKS
Avalon Travel
Hachette Book Group, Inc.
555 12th Street, Suite 1850
Oakland, CA 94607, USA
www.moontravelguides.com

Editor: Rachael Sablik
Managing Editor: Hannah Brezack
Copy Editor: Jessica Gould
Graphics and Production Coordinator: Ravina Schneider
Cover Design: Marcie Lawrence
Interior Design: Tabitha Lahr
Map Editor: Kat Bennett
Cartographers: Kat Bennett, John Culp, Abby Whelan
Proofreader: Ann Seifert
Indexer: Greg Jewett

ISBN-13: 979-8-88647-165-6

Printing History
1st Edition — March 2026
5 4 3 2 1

Front cover photo: Lake Tahoe's Emerald Bay | Icon Digital Featurepix Alamy.com

Back cover photos: ©Kayla Anderson (top); Kayla Anderson (middle); Jenna Blough (bottom)

Printed in China by RR Donnelley